OXFORD STUDIES IN LANGUAGE CONTACT

Series editor: Suzanne Romaine, Merton College, Oxford

Mobilian Jargon

OXFORD STUDIES IN LANGUAGE CONTACT

Most of the world's speech communities are multilingual, making contact between languages an important force in the everyday lives of most people. Studies of language contact should therefore form an integral part of work in theoretical, social, and historical linguistics. As yet, however, there are insufficient studies to permit typological generalizations.

Oxford Studies in Language Contact aims to fill this gap by making available a collection of research monographs presenting case studies of language contact around the world. The series addresses language contact and its consequences in a broad interdisciplinary context, which includes not only linguistics, but also social, historical, cultural, and psychological perspectives. Topics falling within the scope of the series include: bilingualism, multilingualism, language mixing, codeswitching, diglossia, pidgins and creoles, problems of cross-cultural communication, and language shift and death.

Mobilian Jargon

*Linguistic and Sociohistorical Aspects
of a Native American Pidgin*

EMANUEL J. DRECHSEL

CLARENDON PRESS · OXFORD
1997

Oxford University Press, Walton Street, Oxford OX2 6DP

Oxford New York
Athens Auckland Bangkok Bogota Bombay
Buenos Aires Calcutta Cape Town Dar es Salaam
Delhi Florence Hong Kong Istanbul Karachi
Kuala Lumpur Madras Madrid Melbourne
Mexico City Nairobi Paris Singapore
Taipei Tokyo Toronto
and associated companies in
Berlin Ibadan

Oxford is a trade mark of Oxford University Press

Published in the United States
by Oxford University Press Inc., New York

British Library Cataloguing in Publication Data
Data available

Library of Congress Cataloging in Publication Data
Mobilian jargon: linguistic and sociohistorical aspects of a
Native American pidgin/Emanuel J. Drechsel.
(Oxford studies in language contact)
Includes bibliographical references and index.
1. Mobilian trade language—History. 2. Mobilian trade language—
Social aspects. 3. Mobilian trade language—Grammar. I. Title.
II. Series.
PM1855.D74 1996   497′.3—dc20   96-20837
ISBN 0-19-824033-3

1 3 5 7 9 10 8 6 4 2

Typeset by Best-set Typesetter Ltd., Hong Kong
Printed in Great Britain on acid-free paper by
Bookcraft (Bath) Ltd., Midsomer Norton

To my parents

and in memory of

the last speakers of Mobilian Jargon

especially the late Lessie B. Simon

as well as of

James M. Crawford (1925–1989)

and Claude Medford (1940–1989)

Preface and Acknowledgments

Like many Europeans, I grew up with a romantic fascination for the native peoples of North America, which eventually led me to the study of ethnology at the Universität Basel, Switzerland. Before long, my education exposed me to issues of culture contact and acculturation between native peoples and immigrants, and introduced me to linguistics, including questions of language in culture and society. An opportunity to continue my studies at the University of Wisconsin in 1972 permitted me to combine these areas of interest into one—Native American language contact in its sociocultural context.

This focus gained inspiration in part from a visit to the Winnebago Indians near Black River Falls, Wisconsin, with their distinct form of English. Many of these people had maintained their native Siouan language, and spoke English with a characteristic "accent" of their own. Noticeably, they also were quite perceptive about my English, and pinpointed my provenance on the basis of my speech. In the years to come, I was to encounter similar reactions among Indians of the South. Recognition of my German accent in English induced some Native American veterans of World War II to share their service experiences in Europe, where they had apparently developed an "ear" for accents of German-speaking people, as had some older rural African Americans.

My observations would hardly be extraordinary, were it not for the fact that Americans of European ancestry have been less discerning about my Swiss German linguistic background. In guessing my origin on the basis of my English speech, most European Americans have claimed to hear Briticisms rather than a remnant German accent in my English, which led them to identify my native home as either England or some former British colony. Other Americans have guessed my home country to be specifically Australia; I used to assume that they had simply confused it with (German-speaking) Austria, but references to "down under" left little doubt about their intended meanings. Those who recognized my German accent, among them also a few white Southerners, still remained less perceptive than their Native American or African American neighbors, and identified me with a community of German or Swiss immigrants in the United States. Such an American identity would prove quite convenient on occasions when I did not need to provide a long explanation of my ancestry.

These experiences led me to pay attention to the English of Native Americans with distinct dialectal differences, evident even in the speech of those who had never acquired a Native American language, but had grown up with English as their first and perhaps only language. Although informal, my observations among the Winnebago suggested a distinct dialect characteristic of the speech community at large and extending beyond a few phonological features of "accent" to morphosyntactic and semantic peculiarities. Closer examination by William L. Leap and others has since lent support to the idea of not only a distinct American Indian English, but several varieties of it (see Leap 1993).

The notion of Native American English raised questions of origin analogous to those of Black English as a form of creolized or, rather, decreolized English; accordingly, Black English related via decreolization to English-based creoles of the Caribbean, which had developed from a West African pidgin. My visit to the Winnebago made me wonder whether their English speech had a similar history of pidginization-creolization-de-creolization, although it presumably draws on Native American rather than African roots. In other words, is American Indian English an Anglicized Native American creole, which—with an expanded lexicon and grammar, and by establishing itself as the primary language of a multilingual community—originated from a pidgin or a semantactically limited contact medium?

This question directed my attention to the application of theoretical concepts derived from pidgin and creole studies to Americanist linguistics and to the role of Native American languages in other instances of pidginization and creolization in North America, such as Black English (Drechsel 1976a). I received further inspiration from a survey essay on Native American contact media, "Recent Language Contact" prepared by Michael Silverstein (1973 MS) for the *Handbook of North American Indians*, and from a study of the Chickasaw-Choctaw trade language or Mobilian Jargon by James M. Crawford (1978). When Crawford invited me to continue this research, a unique opportunity arose for me to examine ideas of pidgin and creole studies in a specific Native American setting. Over the years, research on Mobilian Jargon has led me to new questions, a wider perspective beyond linguistics and ethnology to include findings from archaeology, and the present book.

En route, I have drawn on the assistance of many individuals and several institutions.

I have long been indebted to my parents Rita and Stanley Hubbard; they have provided generous financial, intellectual, and moral support with a congenial environment in their home where I wrote portions of this book.

Recognition also goes to my sister Cornelia Drechsel for her unfaltering backing as well as to my wife T. Haunani Makuakāne-Drechsel for her patience and numerous insights.

I further recognize Meinhard Schuster and the late Alfred Bühler, professors of ethnology at the Universität Basel, Switzerland, who first encouraged me to pursue my interest in Native Americans in the United States. By building on my doctoral dissertation (Drechsel 1979), this book has benefited substantially from the encouragement, support, and wisdom of my mentor, William W. Elmendorf, and reflects the influence of my other teachers at the University of Wisconsin-Madison, especially Frederic G. Cassidy, Catharine McClellan, and Louisa Stark. Moreover, I owe much to the late James Crawford, who freely shared his recordings and observations of Mobilian Jargon with me.

Acknowledgment is foremost due to those who helped me in my field studies from September 1976 through July 1977 and on my follow-up visits through 1989. I express appreciation for their welcome to the Coushatta Indians of Louisiana and their neighbors in the greater vicinity of Elton (Louisiana), the Tunica-Biloxi in Marksville (Louisiana), the Jena Band of Choctaw (Louisiana), the Alabama-Coushatta near Livingston (Texas), the Five Civilized Tribes in Oklahoma, and all other communities, including their officials, whom I visited in my search for surviving speakers of Mobilian Jargon. Special recognition goes to the late Claude Medford, Ernest Sickey, and Hiram F. ("Pete") Gregory for their generous hospitality and assistance. Just as Medford, a distinguished basketmaker of part-Choctaw ancestry, had originally brought the existence of surviving Mobilian Jargon speakers to the attention of Mary Haas and Crawford, he tirelessly offered new clues about the contact medium to me, and raised many stimulating questions. Sickey, Chairman of the Coushatta Indians of Louisiana at the time, likewise took a personal interest in the project, made invaluable suggestions, and assisted me in the transcription and reconstitution of an early vocabulary of Mobilian Jargon (Anonymous 1862 MS). Gregory generously helped by locating additional speakers of the pidgin and by discussing sociohistorical aspects of Louisiana Indians and Mobilian Jargon's origin. My thanks also extend to Rose Marie Pierite-Gallardo and her family of the Tunica-Biloxi as well as to Jesse Lewis and Clyde Jackson of the Jena Band of Choctaw for their hospitality.

Most importantly, I wish to express my gratitude to those individuals who patiently taught me Mobilian Jargon or about it: the late Bel Abbey, Chief Martin Abbey, the late Carrie Barbry, the late Nathan Barbry, the late Clementine Broussard, Dennis Cole, Dazary Fuselier, John Gidlow, the late Elsie John, Deo Langley, Boston Obe, and especially the late Lessie B. Simon, one of the last fluent speakers of Mobilian Jargon. Recognition is further due to the late Arzelie Langley[1] and Leonard Lavan, neither of whom I had the privilege to meet, but whose voices have carried on in Crawford's recordings and notes.

For assistance in my archival research over the years, I am grateful to the staffs of several libraries, in particular the Memorial Library of the University of Wisconsin-Madison, the Library of the Wisconsin State Historical Society (Madison), the Newberry Library (Chicago), the Special Collections of the Tulane University Library (New Orleans), the Interlibrary Loan Office of the University of Oklahoma Library (Norman), the Interlibrary Loan Office of the University of Hawai'i at Mānoa, and the Library of Congress (Washington). Special acknowledgments are due to John Aubrey of the Newberry Library and Sally H. Drake of the University of Hawai'i Interlibrary Office for their generous help.

Throughout the years, I have gained insights from discussions with Derek Bickerton, Joe L. Dillard, the late Mary R. Haas, Ian F. Hancock, Charles Hudson, Geoffrey D. Kimball, Pamela Munro, and the late John E. Reinecke with his encouragement of research of non-European contact languages. In addition, my book has benefitted from valuable comments by several people reviewing related writings of mine, portions of this study, or a pre-publication version: David J. Costa, Willem de Reuse, Hiram F. Gregory, George Huttar, Dell Hymes, Geoffrey Kimball, Konrad Koerner, John E. Koontz, William L. Leap, Nancy McKee, Pamela Munro, Thurston Dale Nicklas, Robert L. Rankin, William J. Samarin, Sarah G. Thomason, and anonymous reviewers of related manuscripts. I have also enjoyed the support of Byron W. Bender, Chair of the Linguistics Department, and Peter Manicas, Director of the Liberal Studies Program, both at the University of Hawai'i at Mānoa, throughout the past years. The present text further reflects the painstaking editorial assistance by Stanley Hubbard and Pat Matsueda of the journal *Mānoa* as well as valuable suggestions by Frances Morphy and Suzanne Romaine at Oxford University Press.

Funding for various stages of this research has come from the following institutions: the Werenfels-Fonds der Freiwilligen Akademischen Gesellschaft der Stadt Basel (Switzerland), the University of Wisconsin-Madison, the Newberry Library in Chicago, the National Institute of Mental Health (National Research Service Award 5 F31 MH05926-01/02), the University of Georgia, the Phillips Fund of the American Philosophical Society in Philadelphia (two grants), the University of Oklahoma, and the University of Hawai'i at Mānoa.

I have received permission to quote linguistic data or selected passages from the following manuscripts: "Essai sur quelques usages et sur l'idiôme

---

[1] I follow Crawford's spelling of her first name, which variably appears as "Arzalie" (Kniffen, Gregory, and Stokes 1987; 8, 268), "Arzilie," and even "Azalea" (Kimball, personal communication).

des Indiens de la Basse Louisiane" by an anonymous author, courtesy of the Special Collections of the Howard-Tilton Memorial Library, Tulane University, New Orleans; an English translation of this manuscript entitled "An Essay on the language on the Indians of Lower Louisiana" [*sic*], courtesy of the Gilcrease Museum, Tulsa, Oklahoma; "Miami-Illinois Dictionary" by David J. Costa; untitled notes on Choctaw and Mobilian Jargon by Caroline Dormon, courtesy of the Caroline Dormon Collection, Cammie G. Henry Research Center, Watson Memorial Library, Northwestern State University of Louisiana, Natchitoches; "Journal d'un voyage fait avec M. d'Iberville de la rade des Billochis dans le haut du Mississipi avec un detail de tout ce qui s'est fait depuis ce temps jusqu'au depart du vaisseau . . ." by Paul du Ru, courtesy of the Edward E. Ayer Collection, Newberry Library, Chicago; "Memoire De Lxx Dxx Officier Ingenieur, Contenant les Evenemens qui se sont passés à la Louisiane depuis 1715 jusqu'à présent ainsi que ses remarques sur les moeurs, usages et forces des diverses nations de l'Amerique Septentrionale et de ses productions" by Jean Benjamin François Dumont de Montigny, courtesy of the Edward E. Ayer Collection, Newberry Library, Chicago; letter from Opelousas to William Dunbar by Martin Duralde, courtesy of the Library, American Philosophical Society, Philadelphia; "Ata'kapa Language" and "Words and Sentences of the Biloxi Language, Siouan Family" by Albert S. Gatschet, courtesy of the National Anthropological Archives, Smithsonian Institution, National Museum of Natural History, Washington, DC; "Ndjuká-Trio Pidgin" by George L. Huttar and Frank J. Velantie; "Muskogean Cognate Sets" by Pamela Munro; "Letters to L. C. Draper" and "A Historical Narration of the Genealogy Traditions and Downfall of the Ispocoga or Creek Tribe of Indians, Written by One of the Tribe" by George Stiggins, courtesy of the State Historical Society of Wisconsin, Madison; and "Itineraries VI" by Ezra Stiles, courtesy of the Beinecke Rare Book and Manuscript Library, Yale University, New Haven.

This book also includes some extended quotes from the following copyrighted works with permission of their publishers: *Travels in the Interior of North America, 1751–1762* by Jean-Bernard Bossu, translated and edited by Seymour Feiler, copyright © 1962 by the University of Oklahoma Press, Norman; *The Mobilian Trade Language* by James M. Crawford, copyright © 1978 by the University of Tennessee Press, Knoxville; and "Comments on the Late Prehistoric Societies of the Southeast" by James B. Griffin, in *Towns and Temples Along the Mississippi*, edited by David H. Dye and Cheryl Anne Cox, copyright © 1990 by the University of Alabama Press, Tuscaloosa.

To all of the above, I express my sincere gratitude. Any shortcomings of the present research remain solely my responsibility.

Readers might wish to know that with this book will appear a Mobilian

Jargon vocabulary of some 1,250 entries, including reconstituted words, early attestations, comparative evidence in source languages, and an English–Mobilian Jargon index. This vocabulary was originally to be included as an appendix in the present book, but is now published separately because of considerations of size (see Drechsel, 1996).

E.J.D.
Honolulu
Spring 1995

Contents

List of Figures and Tables

Figures

Tables

Abbreviations and Symbols

Adj	adjective	Rel	relative pronoun
Adv	adverb or adverbial	S	noun subject
AIPE	American Indian Pidgin English	s	pronoun subject
		sg	singular
comp.	comparative	V	verb
Dem	demonstrative pronoun	X	sentence segment other than the subject, the verb, or the direct object, such as a second, indirect object, adverbs, or adverbial phrases
INSTR	instrumental marker		
MOD	modality marker		
N	noun		
NEG	negative marker		
NP	noun phrase		
O_1	direct object		
O_2	indirect object	†	reconstituted sample with historical documentation (see Ch. 3 n. 3)
PAST	past-tense marker		
Pers	personal pronoun		
pl	plural		
Poss	possessive pronoun	*	historical reconstruction without independent evidence
Pred	predicate		
Ques	interrogative pronoun		

Examples of Mobilian Jargon appear in bold print, which represents a broadly phonetic quasi-phonemic transcription sufficiently consistent and integrated to show grammatical regularities, but adequate enough to account for a substantial range of interlingual variation (for further discussion, see Sect. 4.5).

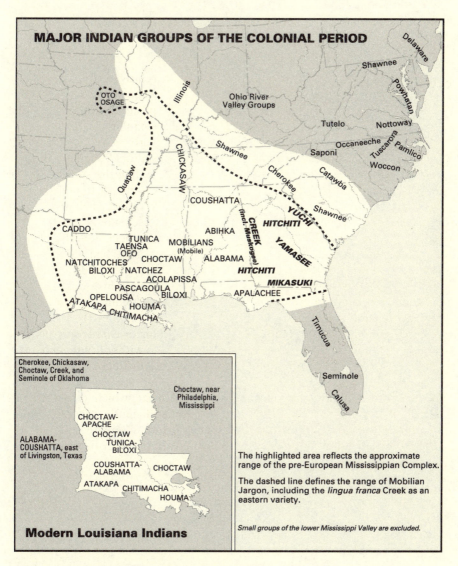

MAJOR INDIAN GROUPS OF THE COLONIAL PERIOD

Delaware

Shawnee

Powhatan

OTO
OSAGE

Illinois

Ohio River
Valley Groups

Tutelo

Nottoway

Occaneeche

Tuscarora

Pamlico

Saponi

Woccon

CHICKASAW

Shawnee

Cherokee

Catawba

Shawnee

Quapaw

COUSHATTA

YUCHI

CADDO

ABIHKA

CREEK
(incl. Muskogee)

HITCHITI

TUNICA
TAENSA
OFO

MOBILIANS
(Mobile)

YAMASEE

NATCHITOCHES
BILOXI

CHOCTAW

ALABAMA

NATCHEZ

ACOLAPISSA

HITCHITI

PASCAGOULA

MIKASUKI

OPELOUSA

BILOXI

APALACHEE

ATAKAPA

HOUMA

CHITIMACHA

Timucua

Seminole

Calusa

Cherokee, Chickasaw,
Choctaw, Creek, and
Seminole of Oklahoma

Choctaw, near
Philadelphia,
Mississippi

CHOCTAW-
APACHE

ALABAMA-
COUSHATTA, east
of Livingston, Texas

CHOCTAW
TUNICA-
BILOXI

COUSHATTA-
ALABAMA

CHOCTAW

ATAKAPA

CHITIMACHA

HOUMA

The highlighted area reflects the approximate
range of the pre-European Mississippian Complex.

The dashed line defines the range of Mobilian
Jargon, including the *lingua franca* Creek as an
eastern variety.

Modern Louisiana Indians

Small groups of the lower Mississippi Valley are excluded.

Capital letters identify speakers of Mobilian Jargon, and bold italics identify those
of the lingua franca Creek as an eastern variety

PART I

The Study of Mobilian Jargon: Perspective, Theory, and Methodology

1

Introduction

1.1. Native Americans in Louisiana and Elsewhere in the US South

Louisiana brings to mind pictures of a unique place—bayous, or marshy and usually sluggish tributaries to a river or lake, associated with images of a slower, more relaxed lifestyle. This part of North America also demonstrates passion in *lagniappe*, Mardi Gras, spicy Creole cuisine, jazz, and New Orleans with its long and unique history. All these impressions evoke memories of a good time, epitomized by *Laissez les bons temps rouler!*

As a stronghold of French language in North America, Louisiana has maintained a distinct French colonial heritage. A closer examination of its history further shows significant Spanish and African influences. Place names such as *Lac des allemands* or *Bayou des allemands* remind one even of German settlers, who accompanied the first French colonizers to the Mississippi delta area in the early eighteenth century. Yet conspicuously absent from Louisiana's history, as presented conventionally, has been her Native American population. The *Guide to the History of Louisiana* (Cummins and Jeansonne 1982) covers various periods and specific communities such as African Americans, urban New Orleans, and women, without including any systematic discussion of American Indians. In this regard, the *Guide*'s editors have not been unusual, for historians of the South have regularly overlooked Native Americans in the area. A common but unsupported justification for this neglect draws on arguments as to the historical insignificance of native peoples, based on the erroneous supposition that they either have perished (such as the frequently cited Natchez) or else have been removed to "the Indian Territory" in the Plains (like the Five Civilized Tribes of Oklahoma). Other scholars (e.g. Perdue 1988) have interpreted Native Americans of the South primarily in terms of its racist plantation history, and apparently do not recognize indigenous traditions still alive today.

While genocide, enslavement, and displacement of Native Americans, especially Southeastern Indians, by Europeans and their American descendants remain facts of history to be remembered, there are several native groups who successfully resisted repeated attempts at their enslavement, extinction, or removal and have survived in the South until today. The naturalist Caroline Dormon, who in the 1930s became quite intimately acquainted with various Indians of central Louisiana, called them "the invisible people" (Kniffen, Gregory, and Stokes 1987: 1). Native Americans have indeed resided right "in the backyards" of non-Indian communities, who remain unaware of their Indian neighbors or refuse to acknowledge them other than as "colored."

The undifferentiated view of non-white peoples by many Americans of European ancestry not only explains their surprise at "discovering" Native American neighbors, but has also reflected much ignorance and prejudice on their part. Misconceptions about Louisiana Indians have prevailed in spite of a considerable amount of linguistic, ethnographic, and ethnohistorical research conducted by prominent scholars such as Frances Densmore, Mary R. Haas, Frank G. Speck, Morris Swadesh, and John R. Swanton among others. Unfortunately, their findings have had less than ample impact, even among fellow Americanists, for the scholarly community outside a small circle of social scientists interested in Southern Indians has not revealed much more understanding of Louisiana's history. At a conference at the University of Michigan several years ago, a senior anthropological linguist and specialist in the study of indigenous languages of eastern North America responded in disbelief when he learned about the survival of Native Americans and their languages in Louisiana. Similarly, some anthropologists who have worked with Native American communities in Oklahoma indicated little awareness of their relatives in Louisiana, let alone traditions of the latter. An Americanist ethnologist with claims of expertise in the study of Southeastern Indian societies even derided those of Louisiana as "Government Indians," although he could not draw on any firsthand observations. In his opinion, these people did not show any evidence of native traditions, but just claimed Indian identity and ancestry in an attempt to gain recognition from the federal government as Native Americans and, with it, special benefits and reparations.

Only during the past few years have Louisiana and other Southern Indians begun receiving some long overdue, well-deserved recognition (see e.g. Kniffen, Gregory, and Stokes 1987; Usner 1992). Reflecting this development, the recent *Encyclopedia of Southern Culture* has made changes to amend the previous neglect, even mentioning Mobilian Jargon in a short article entitled "Indian Trade Languages" (Barnhill and Reinecke 1989). Among the more prominent Native American groups have been the Houma and the Chitimacha in the lower delta area of the Mississippi and Atchafalaya Rivers, the Coushatta in southwestern Louisiana, and the Tunica-Biloxi near Marksville. There are several other communities with legitimate claims to Indian ancestry, such as the Choctaw in the greater vicinity of Alexandria. Still others, while no longer living within the modern boundaries of Louisiana or even within the actual South, have found a way to continue their existence and lifestyle elsewhere—like today's descendants of the very Natchez long thought extinct, but surviving in Oklahoma until recently (see Drechsel 1987*c*).

Throughout history, Native Americans have sufficiently influenced life and culture in Louisiana to make a considerable, if not always obvious difference. For an example, take *filé*, the Native American spice consisting of pounded sassafras leaves, that is indispensable to gumbo and numerous other dishes of the local cuisine. Related to the tongue is another aspect of Louisiana culture and history on which Native Americans have exerted influence—the domain of language. The very word 'bayou,' identified so much with Louisiana, is not French in origin as we might presume from its French-influenced spelling. Like other terms and many place names in and around the state, 'bayou' is derived from Choctaw, specifically from **bayuk** 'river, creek' (Read 1963 [1931]: 82), but has a rather complex history. The word entered European languages only indirectly, via a Native American lingua franca known as the Chickasaw-Choctaw trade language or Mobilian Jargon.

Until a few decades ago, this "international" language was the major medium between Native Americans and descendants of European or African immigrants in Louisiana and neighboring states. As "the Indian language," Mobilian Jargon confirmed the presence of Native Americans all these years, and has reflected a central role played by them in the area's history. This contact medium also helped Native Americans to maintain their native identity, and even served them as a source of linguistic and cultural resilience in a racist environment, which simply lumped Indians, African Americans, and other non-European ethnic groups into a single sweeping category of "colored" (Perdue 1988). What follows is an examination of the structure, functions, and history of Mobilian Jargon in full complexity.

1.2. Outline of Current Study

The next chapters offer as comprehensive a description and analysis of now defunct Mobilian Jargon as is still possible, and examine its linguistic structure, functions, and history from a broad sociolinguistic-diachronic perspective.

Chapter 2 begins with an examination of the sociolinguistic diversity of southeastern North America as a context for the study of Mobilian Jargon, and proceeds with a historical review of research on language contact and especially of pidginization and creolization in Americanist linguistics. Among major issues are the role of language-contact studies in historical-linguistic models, the nature and extent of Native American contact media, and questions relating to their origin. Discussion then reviews previous research on Mobilian Jargon, a genuine pidgin.

With a comprehensive description and analysis in mind, Chapter 3 turns attention to the question of how to pursue the study of Mobilian Jargon by making use of a wide variety of resources and drawing on fieldword as well as archival research. Of major concern here is the nature of field research with people who spoke this pidgin some thirty to forty years ago and have remembered only traces of what was not even their mother tongue, but merely a functionally limited second language. Another methodological issue is the validity of historical documentation and comparative materials for the reconstruction of linguistic and extralinguistic aspects of Mobilian Jargon. In particular, the discussion examines the reliability of documentary attestations for the reconstitution of early linguistic forms, and explores for this purpose the use of philological reconstructions based on lexical resemblances in the pidgin's source languages. The limitations of both field and archival research make necessary a comprehensive historical-sociolinguistic approach, best defined in terms of an ethno*history* of speaking (in contrast to the predominantly synchronic ethnography of speaking). Such an approach provides for the reconstruction of Mobilian Jargon within a broader sociohistorical context, and even prompts some inferences about its origin. By necessity, methodological limitations keep separate the description and analysis of the pidgin's linguistic characteristics on the one hand and its sociocultural aspects on the other, which is also the reason for their presentation in separate sections below.

Part II offers a grammar of Mobilian Jargon with attention to all linguistic aspects: phonology, lexicon, syntax, semantics, and beyond (Chapters 4 to 7). Most of the discussion is complementary to that in James M. Crawford's *The Mobilian Trade Language* (1978). While the present study expands on such intriguing and recurrent questions as that of Algonquian loan-words in Mobilian Jargon (see Sect. 5.4), it also addresses new issues as they relate, for example, to the pidgin's unusual word order (see Sect. 6.5 in particular). To the extent that the historical and modern data permit, Chapter 8 explores patterns and the range of variation in Mobilian Jargon. A broader diachronic perspective taking into account historical-sociolinguistic evidence allows the examination of the pidgin's relationship to two other Muskogean-based contact media, namely the lingua francas Apalachee and Creek, and argues for these to have been Eastern Muskogean varieties of Mobilian Jargon, frequently misconceived as an exclusively Western Muskogean-based pidgin.

Part III deals with extralinguistic, sociohistorical aspects of Mobilian Jargon. Chapter 9 focuses on the pidgin's social history, including names and other extralinguistic clues of identification, and reviews attestations for both eastern and western varieties. Historical documents present a geographic range for Mobilian Jargon beyond Louisiana, in fact across much of central southeastern North America, for more than two centuries. A section also documents how the pidgin survived in several Louisiana Indian communities well into the first half of the twentieth century before declining altogether.

Chapter 10 turns to the role of Mobilian Jargon in traditional Southeastern Indian societies and to specific sociocultural aspects: its geographic and social distribution as well as its communicative and meta-communicative functions. Both historical and ethnographic data show the pidgin as an indigenous institution that was very much part of the Native Americans' daily life from at least the beginning of French colonial times until the mid-twentieth century. Of special interest here is the role of Mobilian Jargon as a linguistic and sociocultural buffer against uninvited influences from non-Indian immigrants, beginning at the latest in the nineteenth century with growing pressures from American settlers and their government.

More speculative in nature, Chapter 11 examines Mobilian Jargon's early history, pre-dating any available historical attestations, and specifically raises the question of aboriginal, pre-European origin and development by retrospection from both linguistic and sociohistorical evidence of the preceding chapters. The discussion presents a case in favor of Mobilian Jargon's existence in pre-European times, and argues that it served as an "international" language of the so-called Mississippian Complex, a pre-European network of linguistically diverse but socioculturally similar paramount chiefdoms primarily known for their massive earthen mounds in the valleys of the Mississippi River and its tributaries.

What emerges is a picture of an American Indian pidgin quite distinct in many ways from that of other contact media. In terms of its structure as well as its functions and history, Mobilian Jargon not only differed substantially from better-known pidgins, most of them European-based, but contrasted also with another Native American pidgin, namely Chinook Jargon, as presented by Michael Silverstein (1972) in a highly variable, "macaronic" model.

Attention to description and analysis is not to suggest a lack of interest in methodology or theory. Both have in fact provided a strong motivation for this research in the first place, and receive closer attention in Part IV, addressing wider implications that arise from the study of American Indian pidgins.

Chapter 12 examines the linguistic relationships of Mobilian Jargon to the native languages of southeastern North America under the heading of linguistic convergence in diversity. A contrast with its Muskogean source languages contributes a better understanding of the nature and extent of pidginization in Mobilian Jargon. A comparison of the pidgin with other Southeastern Indian languages with attention to selected shared features and common loan-words, however fragmentary, also brings forth a sense of the linguistic area that ties together speakers of very different languages, and sheds light on the nature and extent of Mobilian Jargon's function as a medium of linguistic diffusion and maintenance among Southeastern Indians. The chapter closes with a survey of other, less well-known American Indian lingua francas of greater southeastern North America.

This comparative angle provides the dimension necessary for examining long-neglected methodological and theoretical concerns in greater detail (Chapter 13). Prime concerns are: Mobilian Jargon's typological similarities with other Native American pidgins, especially with Chinook Jargon; the role of linguistic convergence in the history of American Indian languages, as illustrated by Mobilian Jargon's unusual word order; and the significance of Native American cases in the comparative study of pidgins and creoles. Discussion moreover addresses sociohistorical implications of Mobilian Jargon's perseverance for Americanist anthropology and history. The final section explores the philology and the ethnohistory of speaking of non-European contact languages as part of a broadly conceived historical methodology—with eyes on an alternate theory of language change that integrates differential linguistic processes including language contact and that accounts for external "interference," i.e. the sociocultural context.

This book should be of special interest to students of Native American languages as well as of pidgins and creoles. Americanist linguists traditionally favoring models of language diversification find here a major Native American case of linguistic convergence and especially pidginization, equivalent to only a few others such as Chinook Jargon. Creolists relying primarily on data from pidgins and creoles based on European languages gain access to a major non-European example, which—although well within the language and culture area of the Caribbean and circum-Caribbean—differed in important ways from other pidgins-creoles of the region. The description and analysis of Mobilian Jargon thus provides a major instance for a broader range of comparison for linguists with interest in both Native American languages and contact languages, and serves as a basis for typological research in historical sociolinguistics. Yet Mobilian Jargon need not remain a sociolinguistic curiosity of American history to non-Americanists; as an interlingual medium, it brings to light general historical-sociolinguistic aspects of language function, bilingualism and multilingualism, language survival, and related issues that are of relevance to linguists outside the study of Native American languages or pidgins and creoles.

In the end, the present study is not solely linguistic in nature. A major portion consists of extralinguistic, ethnographic and historical findings, and constitutes a study of acculturation with focus on language that also addresses Americanist ethnologists, historians, and archaeologists, especially those with focus on the South. This book offers answers to some long neglected issues in the area's extended history: the discrepancy between the linguistic diversity and cultural uniformity of Southeastern Indians, the successful survival of Southeastern Indian traditions in the "backyards" of Louisiana and elsewhere in the South, and the Native Americans' role in the recent past. The following pages, I hope, also provide members of the former Mobilian Jargon-speaking communities with a few new insights into their unique and rich past.

2

Language Contact and Contact Languages in Native North America

2.1. Sociolinguistic Diversity in Southeastern North America as Context

The study of Mobilian Jargon and its sociolinguistic context first depends on an understanding of the diversity of *first* languages in southeastern North America—on the premiss that language contact logically presupposes linguistic differences.

As a distinctive culture area of native North America, the Southeast extended from the Atlantic Coast into the Prairies (including the lower Mississippi River valley) and from the Potomac and Ohio Rivers to the Gulf Coast (including Florida), and was distinguished by a linguistic diversity surpassed only by the Northwest Coast and native California (see Crawford 1975a: 74 and Haas 1971: 44; 1973: 1,210). For this area, linguistic research has documented five separate language families plus several language isolates, both unrelated and distantly related:

- Algonquian: Pamlico, Powhatan, and Shawnee
- Iroquoian: Cherokee, Nottoway, and Tuscarora
- Siouan and distant relatives: Biloxi, Catawba, Ofo, Quapaw, Tutelo, and Woccon
- Caddoan: Adai and Caddo
- Muskogean, divided into two major branches:[1]
    - (i) an eastern division consisting of three subgroups: Alabama, Koasati (Coushatta), and Apalachee; Hitchiti and Mikasuki; and Muskogee (Creek/Seminole)
    - (ii) a western division of Choctaw and Chickasaw

---

[1] This division of Muskogean languages follows Mary Haas's traditional classification (Haas 1941a, 1949), which Pamela Munro (1987a) and others have recently challenged with a mirror version by aligning Western Muskogean with Alabama and Koasati into Southwestern Muskogean and these two subbranches with Hitchiti and Mikasuki into Southern Muskogean against a fourth division of Northern Muskogeans consisting of Creek and Seminole. At this time, there still exists considerable disagreement about the internal division of Muskogean languages, which reflects some of the sociolinguistic complexities of southeastern North America as well as the difficulty of sorting out genetic from areal features (see Hardy and Scancarelli 1993 and Nicklas 1994). The specifics of Muskogean classification do not significantly affect the following discussion. This book uses the categories of Eastern and Western Muskogean as broad geographic divisions rather than specific historical-linguistic lineages, with the aim of recognizing linguistic differences that were both "genetic" and areal in nature.

- Language isolates:
    (i) Atakapa, Chitimacha, Natchez, and Tunica (related distantly to Proto-Muskogean and classified by Mary Haas as Gulf); and
    (ii) Yuchi and Timucua (mutually unrelated and of uncertain origins).

Of the attested languages and linguistic families, only Muskogean, distantly related Gulf isolates, and possibly Yuchi had roots in southeastern North America; the other language families and possibly Timucua represent Southeastern members of native language groupings with representatives and likely ancestry in adjacent areas. Yet there are indications for the existence of additional native languages of the same linguistic families in the area: various Algonquian, Iroquoian, and Siouan languages along the Atlantic Coast, its hinterland, and in the greater Ohio valley; Caddoan languages in the Red River valley; and Muskogean languages plus isolates and numerous unidentified languages across much of southeastern North America (for recent surveys of Southeastern Indian languages, see Crawford 1975a and Haas 1979).

A closer examination of relevant historical documents reveals several compounding factors, which suggest an even greater native linguistic diversity and—with it—a greater sociolinguistic complexity than recognized until recently:

(*a*) Southeastern Indians have had a longer history of direct contact with Europeans than most other areas of native North America. European colonialism and its encroachments, including the introduction of new diseases with epidemic effects on the native population, as well as the enslavement and deportation of natives to Caribbean islands, resulted in early and extensive language death with a rapid concurrent population decline and widespread sociocultural disintegration. The destructive effects probably were greater in the Southeast than in other, less densely populated areas of North America (see Haas 1973: 1,210).

(*b*) In comparison with the colonists in New England and French Jesuits in northeastern North America, the first European explorers and settlers to the Southeast—primarily Spaniards in search of treasures such as gold and the French expanding their American colonies in pursuit of furs and hides—showed relatively little interest in the area's native languages, and committed but limited resources to proselytizing. Systematic linguistic research on Southeastern Indian languages (such as translations of the Bible) remained largely absent until the nineteenth century (see Crawford 1975a: 2, 7). Americanist linguists and anthropologists, familiar with the already established research tradition in northeastern North America, may inadvertently have projected its lesser linguistic diversity with principally two language families, namely Algonquian and Iroquoian, onto the Southeast as part of the larger area east of the Mississippi River.

(*c*) Those Europeans who paid some attention to the languages of Southeastern Indians (even if they offered but few descriptive details) made frequent references to a great linguistic diversity among native peoples and the presence of mutually unintelligible languages within the range of just a few miles (see e.g. Adair 1968 [1775]: 267; Beverley 1855 [1722]: 148; Dumont de Montigny 1753: i. 181–2; Lawson 1967 [1709]: 35, 233, 239; Le Jau 1956 [1706–17]: 19; Strachey 1849 [1612]: 41).

(*d*) Repeatedly, observers of the colonial Southeast recognized "mother tongues" or "national languages" that served as contact media among several native communities speaking mutually unintelligible languages, as was in fact the very case with Mobilian Jargon and other indigenous lingua francas (see Chapter 9 and Sect. 12.4). These observers were usually unaware of, or simply ignored, the first languages spoken by the different communities, and failed to provide further information about the native sociolinguistic complexities.

(*e*) Muskogean-derived ethnonyms and place names, suggesting at first sight that their bearers spoke some Muskogean language, have proved to be deceptive clues about the communities' linguistic identities. Southeastern Indians often adopted names from politically or culturally dominant neighbors in another language, which does not disclose their own languages (see Booker, Hudson, and Rankin 1992). This situation applied to numerous peoples who had accepted names from Muskogeans (such as the Muskogee or Choctaw), but spoke diverse unrelated and possibly even undocumented languages, as already surmised by Albert S. Gatschet (1887: 412). Linguistic identifications by ethnonyms and place names are especially suspect when there exists evidence for a widespread intertribal medium that could have served as the names' immediate source, as was the case with Mobilian Jargon in the central Southeast.[2]

(*f*) Similarly, single Muskogee- and Choctaw-related words or even entire vocabularies have served as an unreliable basis for linguistic identifications of Southeastern Indians; for lexical information without supplementary grammatical data, specifically clues from morphology or syntax, could represent a lexically related contact medium (such as the lingua franca Creek or Mobilian Jargon) instead of Muskogee or Choctaw proper.

---

[2] For a prime example, note the Atakapa (< Western Muskogean/Mobilian Jargon **hat(t)ak** 'person, people' + **apa** 'to eat; food'). By ethnonymic reasoning, they were not only cannibals—an unsupported presumption; they would also have spoken Choctaw or some closely related dialect, whereas in fact their native language was an isolate, at best distantly related to Proto-Muskogean. Similar ethnonymic complications applied to several other Southeastern Indians with characteristic Muskogean names for whose native languages there exist few or no recordings to determine their linguistic affiliations: the Acolapissa, the Bayogoula, the Chakchiuma, the Mobile, the Okelousa, the Opelousa, the Pascagoula, the Pensacola, the Quinipissa, and the Tuskegee among probably others (for Muskogean-derived ethnonyms, see Swanton 1946: 216–19, and Sect. 12.3).

The linguistic evidence thus identifies only a second language, and leaves open what these so-called Muskogeans spoke for their first languages.

(*g*) Significantly, the relative sociocultural homogeneity and the sociopolitical integration of Southeastern Indians in complex or paramount chiefdoms such as pre-European Mississippian alliances, the Creek Confederacy, and even the Five Civilized Tribes have long misled students of Southeastern Indians into presuming a corresponding linguistic uniformity. However, consideration of the available evidence from both the ethnography and the archaeology of Southeastern Indians in comparison with that of linguistics proves such a simplified language–culture identification to be invalid.

Once Europeans and their American descendants began paying closer and systematic attention to the native languages of southeastern North America in the nineteenth century, only a small number survived. For many, there remained but a name; still other languages and perhaps some entire linguistic families had become extinct without even leaving that much of a trace (Crawford 1975*a*: 2). Moreover, the historical relationships between many of the attested languages and families, be they due to common ancestry or contact, still awaits clarification, as observed by Regna Darnell and Joel Sherzer (1971: 27):

The nature of the connection between the stable grammatical kernel of a language and superficial changes which occur through borrowing still remains an issue in Amerindian linguistics. For example, Sapir's grouping of many southeastern languages with Hokan, Siouan, and Iroquoian languages defies consistent classification. The southeastern languages share with neighboring Siouan languages many grammatical traits, although they exhibit regular sound correspondences with the Algonkian languages. The relative role of genetic and areal factors in explanation still remains unclear.

This point holds true today as much as when it first appeared in print (see Bright 1984).

Thus, early historical-linguistic surveys not only offered over-simplified classifications of Southeastern Indian languages with poorly documented and unjustifiable "genetic" relationships, but also reinforced perceptions of Southeastern Indian languages as being less diverse than they really were (Haas 1971: 45–7; Haas 1973: 1,229–34). By all indications, the loss of indigenous linguistic diversity was far greater than Europeans could ever make up in colonial times by introducing various European languages (Spanish, French, English, German, and others), Spanish-, French-, and English-based pidgins-creoles, and possibly a few African languages.

In no way does the recognition of linguistic diversity among Southeastern Indians and the complexity of their historical relationships contradict widespread sociocultural uniformity and intertribal alliances among alloglossic speakers. The answer to this apparent paradox is language

contact in the form of bilingualism and multilingualism as well as areal
contact languages such as Mobilian Jargon.

2.2. A Historical Review of Language-Contact Studies in Twentieth-Century Americanist Linguistics

Academic questions take on greater clarity when examined from a histori-
ographic perspective of science and relevant disciplines rather than from
presentistic angles.[3] A historical review of research on language contact in
Americanist linguistics, albeit by necessity limited for the present purpose,
paves the way to the issues related to the study of Mobilian Jargon, and
best begins with the period around the turn of the century when modern
anthropological linguistics and the study of Native American languages
became established as academic pursuits.

Traditionally, linguists have favored the study of Indo-European languages in their standard representations, as is still evident from the technical nomenclature for languages other than Indo-European or standard ones
in principally negative terms. By comparison, little attention has gone to
either non-Indo-European languages or non-standard linguistic phenomena (including contact languages). Although the significance of non-
European languages was already evident to founding scholars of linguistics
such as Wilhelm von Humboldt (1767–1835), it took another century before
Franz Boas (1858–1942) and Edward Sapir (1885–1939) established their
study as a systematic scientific endeavor in America. Rather diffuse in its
subject matter, research on non-standard languages (such as contact media
and other phenomena ignored by mainstream linguistics) has had an even
more twisted history, and struck its first roots only with pioneers like the
creolist Hugo Schuchardt (1842–1927).

Modern Americanist and anthropological linguistics developed from a
stage set by nineteenth-century linguists, most of whom delved in the comparative method as developed on the basis of Indo-European languages.
Linguistics of that period was very much identical with historical linguistics, preoccupied with the Neogrammarian subject of regularity in sound
change. While espousing the traditional *Stammbaum* ('tree model') of language brachiation or diversification, most nineteenth-century linguists projected evolutionary stages into their reconstructions, which admitted little
room for language contact or other processes of linguistic interference.

---

[3] In anthropology, this truism has been evident at latest since A. Irving Hallowell (1965)
and George A. Stocking (1968) called for a meta-anthropological and historicist examination
of its past, and also extends to the study of American Indian languages and closely related
anthropological linguistics (for selected surveys, see Campbell and Mithun 1979*b*; Haas 1976,
1977*a*; Hoijer 1973; Hymes 1983; Lounsbury 1968; Murray 1983; Stocking 1974).

Major exceptions to this standard model of the time were only the *Wellen-theorie* ('wave theory') of linguistic diffusion by Johannes Schmidt (1872) and the *Kreolische Studien* ('creole studies') by Schuchardt (1979, 1980), who with his concept of *Mischsprache* ('mixed language') was not only one of the harshest critics of contemporary historical linguistics, but also the principal founder of pidgin and creole studies.

Shaped by nineteenth-century scholarship, early Americanist linguistics took a turn with Boas, pioneer of modern American anthropology. As a self-trained anthropologist and linguist, Boas brought along comparatively few preconceptions about the nature of language change to the study of Native American languages (Stocking 1974: 455–6). He came to regret not having attended lectures by Heyman Steinthal, a major inheritor of Wilhelm von Humboldt's legacy and a comparativist. Boas had met him while still a student in Berlin, but never adopted a dogmatic belief in the model of language diversification. Admiring Schuchardt, Boas was quite familiar with the arguments for mixed languages (Landar 1965: 136, 139). In his opinion, the comparativists' ideas were attenuated by language diffusion and mixture, as Boas found them in his extensive field studies with Native Americans, especially with Indians of the Northwest Coast. Such evidence led him to adopt a diffusionist perspective, which together with his philosophy of cultural relativism formed the basis for his rejection of evolutionary schemes, explicit or implicit in nineteenth-century models of language and culture change.

Boas probably developed his views on language change from his experiences on expeditions to the Northwest Coast under Horatio E. Hale (1817–1896), who had done research on Chinook Jargon (Hale 1848, 1890) among various linguistic and ethnographic contributions. At the time, the literature on Chinook Jargon was already quite extensive, but much still suffered from poor quality (see Reinecke *et al.* 1975: 712–26). Only as a result of Boas's interest, dedication, and influence did Chinook Jargon come to be the best documented Native American pidgin (see Boas 1888, 1892, 1933), and his knowledge of it provided a strong reinforcement, if not the basis, for his ideas on language change (see Boas 1933: 209). His research of Chinook Jargon stimulated in turn Melville Jacobs (1932, 1936), the latter's student William W. Elmendorf (1939 MS), and probably other linguists to continue doing research on this pidgin. Boas's direct or indirect influence also shines through in short descriptions of Eskimo Jargon of Herschel Island by Vilhjálmur Stefánsson (1909) and Delaware Jargon of New Jersey by J. Dyneley Prince (1912). However, neither study produced as much information as research on Chinook Jargon; even less was then known about any other Native American contact media such as Mobilian Jargon.

As the early eminent scholar of a contact language in Native American linguistics, Boas passed on an interest in language contact to other students.

Alfred L. Kroeber, Roland Dixon, and Edward Sapir conducted studies on areal-typological questions in the early decades of this century (see Darnell and Sherzer 1971: 23–5). With accumulating comparative data on Native American languages of California, Kroeber in particular helped to define areal-typological research by developing the principle of areal linguistic relationships, which predated the writings on *Sprachbünde* ('language areas') by members of the Prague school and apparently Boas's own statements on the subject (Hymes 1961: 8–9, 23). With his concern for centers of adaptation and integration as well as for their historical implications, Kroeber moreover went a step beyond the atomistic Boasian approach of primarily listing traits and trait complexes, and addressed the question of historical interpretation of areal traits (Silverstein 1978: 738–39).

In the second decade of the century, Americanist linguists shifted their focus in historical research from an areal-typological perspective to a predominantly "genetic" view, with the aim of reducing the widely accepted classification by John Wesley Powell and his collaborators into fewer and larger stocks (Darnell 1971*a, b*; see also Darnell and Hymes 1986). The most influential person in this trend was Sapir. On the basis of his earlier studies in Germanic philology, he had learned to place much more confidence in the comparative method and the tree model of language diversification than Boas, and—together with Leonard Bloomfield—applied them successfully to the study of Native American languages. Sapir had also inherited from his philological studies a Humboldtian organic view of language as an integrated system (Drechsel 1988); accordingly, the configurational pressure in language change as manifested in linguistic drift (see Malkiel 1981) admitted little disruption in the inner form or the basic structure of a language by external sources such as contact with neighboring languages. With extensive training and expertise in comparative linguistics, Sapir came to disagree with his former mentor Boas in their well-known controversy regarding "archaic residue" and "diffusional cumulation" in language change (Swadesh 1951; Darnell and Sherzer 1971: 25–7).

Contrary to widespread presumption and as pointed out by Morris Swadesh (1951: 5), Boas did not deny the fact of common origin for "genetically" related languages; nor did Sapir lack awareness of, or an interest in, linguistic diffusion, as illustrated by his discussion of the topic in his classic monograph *Time Perspective in Aboriginal American Culture: A Study in Method* (Sapir 1949 [1916]: 444–9). Similar misconceptions have applied to Kroeber's role in the Boas–Sapir dispute. Sometimes presumed suspicious of Boas's arguments and allegedly persuaded by Sapir's, Kroeber actually took an intermediate stance, and in his later years came to sympathize more with Boas's position (Hymes 1961: 23). These scholars' disagreement regarding language change, then, concerned primarily the relative weight and importance of diffusion and common origin in historical explanations.

In what proved an offshoot Neogrammarian debate by Americanists, Boas and Kroeber apparently lost the argument to Sapir by virtue of the latter's linguistic ingenuity and success in applying the comparative method, including the inspection technique, to Native American languages. Sapir, together with Bloomfield, convinced subsequent generations of Americanist and anthropological linguists of the diversificationist position's validity. Their confidence in the tree model led them to "genetic" relationships of greater and greater time depth. Consequently, the study of language contact, identified with more recent language history and viewed as obscuring reconstructions, received little attention (see Sherzer and Bauman 1972: 131).

During the Bloomfieldian era and for some time thereafter, most Americanist linguists continued to shun any systematic discussion of linguistic diffusion in their preoccupation with linguistic diversification. Among the few taking into consideration language contact were Melville Jacobs, who—like Boas and Kroeber—did fieldwork among Indians on the West Coast, displaying many conspicuous areal features (Darnell and Sherzer 1971: 27–8). Another scholar concerned with linguistic diffusion was Sapir's student Morris Swadesh, usually associated with glottochronology and the related study of language origin and diversification in great time depth. He not only expressed awareness of language contact as manifested in loan-words, areal influences, interlanguage, lingua francas, pidgins, and creoles, but also made specific contributions to its study. In his article "The Mesh Principle in Comparative Linguistics," Swadesh suggested the representation of language change as a chain, mesh, or net rather than in a tree model, and credited the concept of dialect intergradation to Johannes Schmidt and Hugo Schuchardt (Swadesh 1959: 7; see also Swadesh 1971: 17–18, 26–34, 46, 74, 119, 215–18).

Swadesh's mesh principle received scant recognition among fellow students of American Indian languages, and apparently had no direct impact on their thinking. As one among the few continuing the discussion, Charles F. Voegelin (1945, 1961) reviewed the issue of language area in Americanist linguistics, and addressed the question of linguistic homogeneity and diversity within culture areas of North America. Yet he paid no closer attention to other phenomena of language contact. Apart from Chinook Jargon, Voegelin (1961: 169, 176–7) made only an incidental reference to Ojibwa as a contact language and a medium of cultural diffusion, which he considered the only widespread American Indian lingua franca in eastern North America.

In the 1960s, the study of language contact in Americanist linguistics experienced a new breath of life. In a doctoral dissertation, Oswald Werner (1963) offered a description of broken varieties of Navajo as spoken by non-Indian traders with their Navajo customers and commonly known as Trader Navaho. In another instance, Mary Haas's book *The Prehistory of Languages*, with its focus on the remote past of Native American languages, devoted an entire chapter to problems of lexical borrowing and structural diffusion (Haas 1969: 78–97). As part of this trend, areal studies, building on earlier statements such as those by Voegelin (1945, 1961), received new attention (Darnell and Sherzer 1971: 28), and have even gained recognition with Joel Sherzer's comprehensive typological study (1976), related surveys (Bright and Sherzer 1976; Sherzer and Bauman 1972), and research of specific areas (e.g. Silverstein 1974; Campbell, Kaufman, and Smith-Stark 1986). Similarly, the revitalized discussion of language contact in Americanist linguistics has inspired, and benefited from, related case studies such as the ethnography of speaking of multilingual Fort Chipewyan in Alberta by Ronald and Suzanne B. K. Scollon (1979).

Still fairly representative of the discipline's state of art on the subject matter is the volume on Native American languages in the four-part *Linguistics in North America* (Sebeok 1973). In a separate essay on language contact, William Bright (1973) made repeated references to dialect continua, areal classifications, linguistic acculturation, and convergence in American Indian languages in contrast to the traditional tree model of language diversification. None the less, the study of Native American language history did not develop a systematic discussion of language-contact phenomena or an alternative framework.

If one were to take a later and widely cited historical-linguistic survey of American Indian languages, *The Languages of Native America: Historical and Comparative Assessment* (Campbell and Mithun 1979a), as standard, language contact and other forms of language convergence would not be part of a model of language change. Although the editors recognize areal relationships and borrowing as a source of negative evidence for linguistic relatedness (Campbell and Mithun 1979b: 22, 37, 55, 56), they do not take language contact and linguistic convergence into serious consideration; the topic appears to concern most contributors to this collection of historical-linguistic reviews even less. By defining comparative-historical linguistics in narrow, purely "genetic" terms, Americanist linguists have principally focused on questions of classification. Preoccupied with either "splitting" or "lumping" native languages into smaller or larger classificatory units, many Americanist linguists have forgotten language contact in their models of language change (Bright 1984). Even a scholar as sympathetic towards the study of language contact and contact languages as Bright has not attributed much theoretical significance to pidgins, because presumably "such languages have, in general, not survived over long periods" (Bright 1984: 21). Perhaps the worst outgrowth of a continuing diversificationist fallacy in American Indian linguistics is Joseph Greenberg's *Language in the Americas* (1987). His book has extended the tree model into the earliest "prehistory" without really addressing the methodological problem of distinguishing "genetic" from areal-typological relationships; much less does it give recognition to language convergence including language contact as a significant linguistic process (see also Matisoff 1990 for an outsider's critical assessment on these very points).

Recent surveys of Americanist linguistics have willy-nilly reintroduced questions of language contact. Marianne Mithun (1990*b*) addresses the topic primarily as an issue of contact with Europeans and language obsolescence, but has omitted to mention any indigenous contact language, and—perhaps symptomatically—does not make language contact part of the subsequent discussion on linguistic diachrony (see Mithun 1990*b*: 319–25). Assessing research on change in Native American languages, Lyle Campbell and Ives Goddard (1991: 25–6) similarly cite areal features, language death, and dialect mixture as instances of language contact, yet ignore more dramatic examples such as pidginization and related processes of linguistic convergence.

2.3. Pidginization and Creolization of Native American Languages

Through much of its modern history, Americanist linguistics has paid even less attention to contact languages than to the topic of language contact. Over a century ago, Schuchardt addressed the question of American Indian English as part of his *Kreolische Studien* (Schuchardt 1889; 1980: 30–7); but he had no impact on most students of American Indian languages. In the early twentieth century, Boas apparently was the only major Americanist linguist aware of Schuchardt's ideas and sympathetic to the notion of *Mischsprache*, and little research came forth on this topic beyond that undertaken or inspired by Boas. Among Americanist linguists of subsequent generations, Swadesh remained one among few to acknowledge the creolist's contributions.

At the time, most of those interested in contact languages of the Americas focused their attention on pidgins and creoles with a European lexical base, and assigned a greater role to the Europeans in their communications with Native American peoples in early colonial periods than is evident from historical records. Creolists came to be preoccupied with African influences as major non-European elements, and left little room for American Indian contributions beyond single, often stereotypical loan-words in interethnic communication. The only one to accord some attention to Native

American pidgins was John E. Reinecke. He had studied "race relations" at Yale University (with Sapir among others), was interested in the sociology of language, and included reviews of Chinook Jargon, Mobilian Jargon, and Eskimo Jargon as part of his doctoral dissertation, a world-wide survey of marginal languages (Reinecke 1937: 635–76).

An interest in questions of pidginization and creolization involving Native Americans re-emerged only in the 1950s and again primarily among scholars outside Americanist linguistics. Following in Schuchardt's steps, Douglas Leechman and Robert A. Hall (1955) as well as Mary R. Miller (1967) examined the English spoken by Native Americans, whose different varieties came to be known as American Indian Pidgin English (AIPE). Pidginized English by Native Americans also attracted the attention of J. L. Dillard (1972: 139–85; 1975; 99–111; 1976: 6–20; 1985: p. x, 16–29, 44–9, 61, 67–8, 125–8, 149–63; 1992: 10–21, 30–1, 144–7), whose study of Black English and related Gullah (Geechee) of the southern Atlantic Coast led to an interest in the communication between Seminole Indians and their African associates in Florida. Lilith M. Haynes (1977) and Ian F. Hancock (1980*a*, *b*, 1986) have extended Dillard's research to a creolized variety of this Seminole pidgin, interpreted as a variety of Gullah known as Afro-Seminole Creole and probably related to the English of other so-called "tri-racial" communities such as that of Brandywine in southern Maryland (see Gilbert 1986).

Expansion of pidgin and creole studies in the late 1960s (see Hymes 1971) led to a growing interest in Native American contact media as well. In an essay prepared for the *Handbook of North American Indians*, Michael Silverstein (1973 MS) drew attention to a great variety of indigenous lingua francas, both pidginized and others. Research addressing questions of pidginization and creolization in the history of American Indian languages has since produced new descriptive-analytical and sociohistorical studies of varying detail for the better known instances:

(*a*) Eskimo Jargon (Schuhmacher 1977; de Reuse 1988: 492–507);
(*b*) Chinook Jargon (Hancock 1972; Harris 1985; Hymes 1980: 405–18; Hymes 1990; Hymes and Hymes 1972; Hymes and Zenk 1987; Johnson 1978; Kaufman 1971; Powell 1990; Samarin 1986; Silverstein 1972; Thomason 1981, 1983; Zenk 1984, 1988) plus apparently a Nootka variety (Samarin 1988);
(*c*) Delaware Jargon (Thomason 1980); and
(*d*) Mobilian Jargon (Crawford 1978; Drechsel 1979, 1983*b*, 1984, 1985, 1986, 1987*a*, *b*, 1993, 1994*a*, *b*; Haas 1975; Munro 1984; York 1982).

In addition, there has come forth a growing body of information for a variety of other Native American *Mischsprachen*: Mednyj Aleut (Golovko and Vakhtin 1990; Gray 1994), Métis, Mitchif, or Métif (e.g. Crawford 1983; Douaud 1985; Papen 1984; Rhodes 1977, 1986), central Algonquian trade languages (Rhodes 1982), an Algonquian medium with some Basque words on the coast of northeastern North America (Bakker 1988, 1989, 1991), various media between the Dutch and Indians of New Netherland in the seventeenth century (Feister 1973), the lingua franca Occaneeche (= Saponey?) or Tidewater Pidgin of Virginia (Alexander 1971, Miller 1986 MS), and the lingua franca Creek (Drechsel 1983a; for further discussion, see also Sects. 8.5 and 9.2) among others. At the same time, continual attention has gone to AIPE as illustrated in historical and literary representations (Flanigan 1981) and in instances from southwestern North America (Brandt and MacCrate 1982). Drawing an analogy to Mobilian Jargon, Julian Granberry (1987: 20–1, 26–55) has described the Timucua language of Florida as a pidgin-creole that blended elements from Macro-Chibchan, Arawakan, Muskogean, and other languages. These studies leave little doubt that pidginization—that is a linguistic process leading to a compromise contact medium among several linguistically diverse peoples—and related processes of language convergence occurred more frequently in the history of American Indian languages than either creolists or Americanist linguists have suspected (see Drechsel 1976a, 1977; Silverstein 1973 MS; Taylor 1981).

Much research on such Native American lingua francas was preoccupied with questions of origin. A few creolists have interpreted the development of AIPE and even Chinook Jargon, a contact medium clearly based on native languages of northwestern North America, in terms of the monogenetic hypothesis of pidgin-creole origin. This model suggests that the world's pidgins and creoles developed from the lingua franca Sabir of the Mediterranean via the process of repeated relexifications, as if it served as an original pidgin similar to an ancestral proto-language of "genetically" related languages. Accordingly, AIPE presumably grew out of an English-based pidgin or creole spoken by African Americans (see Dillard 1972: 14–15, 20–1), whereas Chinook Jargon supposedly arose from the relexification of either AIPE or some Pacific pidgin-creole with native languages of the Northwest Coast (see Johnson 1975 MS: 1, 12, 18).

If this scenario caught the attention of Americanist linguists at all, most needed first to be convinced of the applicability of the pidginization-creolization model to their subject matter. Modern research has since demonstrated not only the validity of studying Native American contact languages, but also a great variety in their structures and functions, which strongly speaks against the monogenetic hypothesis of pidgin-creole origin. The idea of a world-circling proto-pidgin-creole as the ancestral form of modern contact languages conveys far-reaching historical and theoretical

implications that few creolists and even fewer Americanist linguists are prepared to accept today (Drechsel 1976*a*: 66–70).[4]

An alternative and preferable interpretation espouses the idea of polygenetic origins, which assumes multiple and independent developments for
Native American and other pidgins. This model recognizes a greater historical role for indigenous peoples than the monogenetic hypothesis has
admitted, without logically precluding long-distance historical ties among
various contact languages, as they existed throughout North America and
beyond. A prime example for the latter consists of Hawaiian loan-words in
Chinook Jargon and Eskimo Jargon, which came about as a result of colonial trade and whaling in the northeastern Pacific in the nineteenth century,
but do not lend support to a Pacific or monogenetic origin for Chinook
Jargon or Eskimo Jargon (Drechsel and Makuakāne 1982*a*).

Recent studies have begun probing questions of pre-European origins
for various Native American pidgins, as already suggested by anthropologists and philologists of the nineteenth century, and have presented new
evidence and fresh arguments with respect to Chinook Jargon (Hymes 1980;
Samarin 1986, 1988; Thomason 1981, 1983), Delaware Jargon (Thomason
1980), and Mobilian Jargon (Drechsel 1984, 1986, 1994*a*). The hypothesis of
pre-European origin for these American Indian pidgins has since expanded
discussion to the sign language of Plains Indians. Following Allan R. Taylor
(1975: 329–53) and others, William J. Samarin (1987) has interpreted it as
the result of contact with Europeans and, by analogy, as a challenge to scenarios of pre-Columbian origin for Native American contact languages. In
response, Susan Wurtzburg and Lyle Campbell (1995) have offered historical documentation in favor of the aboriginal use of a gestural code or a
fully developed sign language on the western Gulf Coast.

The application of concepts derived from pidgin and creole studies to
Americanist linguistics has spurred broader, theoretical concerns. Part of
this development is an interest in a sociolinguistic typology as developed
for four different Native American pidgins, namely Eskimo, Chinook,
Delaware, and Mobilian Jargons (Drechsel 1981). Chinook Jargon, Métis,
and Mednyj Aleut furnish three major examples in a recent synthesis of
contact-induced language change, *Language Contact, Creolization, and
Genetic Linguistics* by Sarah Grey Thomason and Terrence Kaufman (1988:
228–38, 256–63). In the mean time, major Native American pidgins, creoles,
and related phenomena—Afro-Seminole Creole, Native American English,

---

[4] In his recent writings, Dillard (e.g. 1985: 9, 44–8, 124–5, 130–4, 146–63, 178–9; 1992: 10–21,
30–1, 144–7) has apparently softened his position regarding the origin of AIPE. He has
retracted the existence of a "world-encompassing" pidgin, and has acknowledged relexifications from Native American languages to English (rather than vice versa). Dillard has generally given greater recognition to native influences and to indigenous pidgins, especially
Chinook Jargon and Mobilian Jargon, and has left open the question of direction in the transmission of Pidgin English by considering various possibilities.

Chinook Jargon, Delaware Jargon, Eskimo Jargon, and Mobilian Jargon—
have also attracted the attention of creolists in general, if sketches in the
reference survey of pidgins and creoles by John Holm (1989; ii. 494–8,
506–10, 595–606) are an indication. When Americanist linguists and creolists can conclude with little or no doubt that pidginization and possibly
creolization occurred before the arrival of European explorers and
colonists, discussion can no longer exclude these processes of linguistic convergence from the pre-Columbian history of America, but would have to
incorporate them in our models of long-term language change.

The recognition of a diversity of Native American pidgins and other contact
languages with polygenetic and possibly even pre-European origins has
raised serious questions about the nature and historical sources of AIPE,
which seemingly characterized the speech of Native Americans within the
domain of the English-speaking colonies of North America and dissemi-
nated with their expansion across much of the continent.

If one presumed literary and other sources as reliable historical linguistic docments, there remains the issue of whether AIPE was a genuine
pidgin, arising in a multilingual environment from so-called *tertiary* linguistic hybridization (see Whinnom 1971), or rather was a phenomenon of
second-language acquisition and bilingualism comparable to modern
American Indian English. Conceivably, AIPE was associated with thoroughly acculturated American Indians such as the "Praying Indians" of
early historic New England (see Salisbury 1974), students and graduates of
boarding schools such as the Carlisle School in Pennsylvania and the
Haskell Institute in Kansas specifically commissioned to teach Native
Americans how to speak, read, and write English (Schuchardt 1889 and
Malancon and Malancon 1977), and perhaps other Europeanized native
groups. Yet AIPE could hardly have represented the speech of interior
groups who maintained their traditional languages with a greater independence than acculturated native communities. Indians of the hinterland regularly addressed Europeans, other immigrants, and their American
descendants in their own diverse languages, and relied on bilingual interpreters or indigenous contact media, rather than some European tongue,
well into the twentieth century. These native groups came to switch to European languages as their major lingua francas in one form or another only
later, when their native languages and contact media were in decline, and
then learned them like any other second language without intermediate
pidginization.

Closer examination of AIPE actually raises fundamental doubts about
the historical accuracy and interpretation of its documentation, and suggests an interpretation in terms of a *literary* medium with considerable
poetic license, as evident from a telling instance of "Pidgin English" in place

of a Native American language of southeastern North America: "We have endeavoured to put into the Indian-English, as more suitable to the subject, and more accessible to the reader, that dialogue which was spoken in the most musical Catawba" (Simms 1856: 391). The language to which the author of this quote, W. Gilmore Simms, referred was Catawba (classified frequently as Siouan or rather as an isolate distantly related to Proto-Siouan) or possibly a Catwaba-based contact medium (see Sect. 12.4). In another instance, Simms (1856: 197–9, 205–6) similarly made a Choctaw of Mississippi in the early nineteenth century speak "Indian English" rather than Choctaw or Mobilian Jargon, as indicated by historical documentation. AIPE appears as a literary relexification of several other indigenous contact languages such as Delaware Jargon (see Thomason 1980: 182–6), native contact media of Virginia (Miller 1986 MS: 4–5, 19–20), and the lingua franca Creek, the latter via Seminole Pidgin (Drechsel 1976*b*, 1979; 47–50; see also Sects. 8.5, 8.6, and 9.2).

Inquiries about a distinct form of Native American (Pidgin-Creole?) English proved no more productive for the nineteenth-century creolist Hugo Schuchardt (1889: 470):

Als ich vor jahren mich mit den kreolischen mundarten zu beschäftigen begann, lenkte ich meine aufmerksamkeit auch auf das Englische der Indianer. Allein ich konnte nicht in erfahrung bringen, dass ein solches irgendwo in fester ausprägung wie das Negerenglisch auftrete, und selbst über die sprachfehler der einzelnen, worin sich natürlich zum theil die eigenthümlichkeiten der sehr verschiedenen muttersprachen wiederspiegeln, erlangte ich keine bestimmte auskunft. Wohl aber kamen mir, besonders durch die güte des herrn Albert S. Gatschet, nummern von Indianerschulzeitungen in die hand, welche zahlreiche proben von dem Englischen der rothen zöglinge enthalten. Man sollte zwar meinen, dass es dabei mehr auf gute zeugnisse für lernende und lehrende, als auf merkwürdige von sprachmischung ankomme. [Lower cases in nouns are original to the German version.][5]

Schuchardt's research on the Indians' English speech could only raise the problem of hypercorrections in its attestations.

A review entitled *American Indian English in History and Literature: The Evolution of a Pidgin from Reality to Stereotype* by Beverly Olson Flanigan (1981) has since documented AIPE as little else than fiction consisting of literary replacements of native languages by English, stereotypical rep-

---

[5] 'Some years ago, when I first became interested in the creole dialects, I also directed my attention to the English of the American Indians. However, I could not determine whether it manifests itself as a distinct variety, as does Negro English. I could not even get definite information on the linguistic errors of individuals, in whom, to some extent, the peculiarities of the very different mother tongues are clearly reflected. Thanks to the kindness of Mr Albert S. Gatschet I did succeed in obtaining copies of Indian school newspapers which contain numerous samples of the English of the Indian pupils. To be sure, it is to be expected that these newspapers would show the best efforts of the pupils and teachers, rather than the peculiarities of language mixture' (Schuchardt 1980: 31–2).

resentations, and hypercorrections towards some real or imagined standard. Still, these limitations have not substantially undermined the author's confidence in the accuracy of AIPE's documentation. In simply accepting historical-literary attestations as prima-facie evidence, research on AIPE has so far not adequately questioned the historical validity of its sources (see Flanigan 1981), or has even ignored such concerns altogether (see Brandt and MacCrate 1982). Similarly, a recent study explicitly committed to "deconstructing" representations of Native American speech in European-American texts in the spirit of postmodernistic critique (Murray 1991) neglects to address the question of AIPE or related issues of historical documentation.

My negative findings have not met the approval of Elizabeth Brandt and Christopher MacCrate (1982: 214–16), who have taken me to task with erroneous assumptions about AIPE and have neglected to define what constitutes typical pidgin features in their historical attestations. In the process, Brandt and MacCrate omitted to address questions and issues raised earlier (see Drechsel 1976*a*, 1977), which leaves several points of contention. For one, the authors pay little attention to the fact that many of the attestations of AIPE appear in standard English orthography, which should have made them cautious not only with respect to its pronunciation and phonology, but in regards to aspects of syntax and the lexicon as well. The very absence of Native American features in AIPE, recognized by the authors themselves, should have raised doubts in their minds about the nature and the accuracy of their historical data. Brandt and MacCrate (1982: 215) have attempted to resolve this issue by assuming that "the tremendous diversity of Indian languages and intertribal enmity would also have worked against significant influence from specific languages." Yet such reasoning has little basis in fact, when one considers other comparable contact situations. The native peoples of the southwestern North America would have left their linguistic mark on AIPE, just as they did in Trader Navaho, and would have done so even with an alloglossic immigrant population, consisting of Europeans, Chinese, and Africans. With no less linguistic diversity and intertribal enmity, Indians of the Northwest Coast and eastern North America still imposed their own contact languages, Chinook Jargon, Mobilian Jargon, and Delaware Jargon, onto linguistically diverse immigrant communities. If there indeed was no comparable Native American medium in the Southwest, the question is why, an issue that Brandt and MacCrate have not explored further. The authors also underestimate the problem of mutual intelligibility or, rather, its lack in pidginization. With different first-language backgrounds and much linguistic variation, pidgin speakers did not always communicate, and must often have misunderstood each other. Aside from serving as functional media, pidgins have served purposes other than that of mutual communication between people of different linguistic backgrounds. Brandt and Mac-

Crate (1982: 210) have cited a case of their own in which a woman of half-Paiute ancestry, competent in English, used alleged AIPE to confuse whites rather than to communicate with them. Another case of linguistic buffer is Mobilian Jargon (Drechsel 1987*b*; see Sect. 10.3). Finally, Brandt and Mac-Crate (1982: 215) make two curious claims. In one, the two authors allege that my distinctions between Native American contact media and AIPE (Drechsel 1976*a*) built on a misinterpretation of an essay by Charles A. Ferguson and Charles E. DeBose (1977), not available to me at the time of writing. Brandt and Christopher MacCrate also reproach me for "trying to reimpose static models and rigid criteria on a dynamic process"—apparently unaware of my suggestions for multilectal continua enmeshing indigenous contact languages with any interrelated Europeanized varieties (see Drechsel 1976*a*: 73–4). Logically, the recognition of such interrelations between the two ends of such proposed speech continua does not preclude typological differences between the basilect and acrolect or between a Native American pidgin and AIPE. Ignoring such only leads to an over-simplified model of complex sociolinguistic situations such as Brandt and MacCrate unfortunately present for the US Southwest.

What some linguists have called a pidgin was an amalgam of various literary embellishments that Europeans and European Americans superimposed with considerable liberties of fiction and little basis in fact. AIPE tells us more about English speakers' *perception* of the Indians' speech than about their actual ways of speaking with immigrants or their descendants. Early observers usually were less impartial in describing American Indians' attempts at speaking English or some other European language than in their accounts of indigenous languages. Native Americans presumably spoke "primitive tongues," but—worse—used "bad, broken, or corrupted" versions of European languages.

To the extent that AIPE was not just a product of imagination by European colonists, it could have been a kind of European "foreigner talk" with the native population, which exhibited some of the very same result of incomplete foreign-language learning as pidginization. Quite possibly, European and American colonists even drew on widely attested forms of non-Indian Pidgin English for models. Any similarities to Black English could easily have come about from the European Americans' erroneous projection of their experiences with African Americans onto Native Americans, reinforced by their racist perception of mixed Native American and African communities (see Forbes 1988; Foster 1935; Porter 1971; Willis 1971). In this case, Native Americans supposedly spoke like members of the large, undifferentiated category of "colored" people that European Americans naïvely applied to non-European peoples from early colonial times. However, these observations do not support the conclusion that Native Americans spoke AIPE as well; it could have existed without Native

American speakers, just as Trader Navaho remained a one-sided affair by non-Indian traders in their interactions with Navajo.

As a "broken" English put into the Indians' mouth, AIPE has a modern analogy in Western novels, comic strips, and movies, which have regularly distorted Native American speech for the purpose of rendering it intelligible to their audience and presenting American Indians from a certain, usually stereotypical, perspective. In particular, the study of AIPE faces problems of derivation and analysis analogous to those of the interpretation of *kemosabe*, by which the Indian guide Tonto addressed the Masked Man in the radio and television show *The Lone Ranger*. Traditionally derived from a "corrupted" form of Spanish *quien no sabe* or *el que lo sabe* or even Portuguese *quem o sabe*, this name has been the subject of alternative etymologies in various, mostly unrelated Native American languages: Western Apache, Potawatomi, Tewa, Yavapai, Cree, Southern Paiute, Osage, Tunica, Navajo, Iroquois (without any further specification), and Apache (Golla 1992, Kendall 1977). Recently, Algonquianists have insisted on an Algonquian derivation for *kemosabe* (Valentine and Cowan 1993).

This parallel leads to the issue of whether records of AIPE permit any substantive historical research beyond the study of linguistic stereotypes. At this time, there appears little promise—not only because of major methodological and theoretical handicaps as already stated, but also because of the problem of alternate and even multiple interpretations in terms of different Native American languages analogous to that of *kemosabe* and attested for many pidgins. For this reason, further research on AIPE and other presumably European-based lingua francas should first call for a careful study of their broader historical-sociolinguistic contexts in an attempt to reduce the number of diverse possible origins and subsequently for an examination of remaining alternatives in terms of Native American languages. This endeavor need not be an impossible problem, but hardly promises support for any grand schemes of origin.

Serious doubts about AIPE as an accurate representation of Native American speech also raise questions about the historical relationships of American Indian pidgins to American creoles and perhaps even the latter's nature, as in the case of Seminole Pidgin (English?) and Afro-Seminole Creole. Haynes (1977: 283–6, 292–4) already doubted the accuracy of historical attestations for Afro-Seminole Creole, and criticized its interpretation as a creole or American Indian English. Significantly, by presuming any preceding American Indian pidgin to have been a form of Pidgin English, creolists have given little or no recognition to native peoples in its history. As a result, they have presented Afro-Seminole Creole (Hancock 1986, Holm 1989: 494–8) and related speech forms in other so-called "tri-racial" communities such as Brandywine of southern Maryland (Gilbert 1986) as varieties of Gullah—that is a Creole English of the southeastern United

States related to Caribbean creoles with possible African roots. Yet, conceivably, the Anglification of Seminole Pidgin came about only shortly before or with its creolization or as part of its subsequent decreolization, reflecting the growing influence of the English-speaking population in the nineteenth century. This alternative scenario gives more recognition to Native Americans in the history of American creoles, even if influences from Native American languages are difficult to trace today and their precise, full role may be indeterminable now.

When considered in a wider perspective, the currently available evidence for AIPE does not support an interpretation in terms of a full pidgin-creole cycle, much less a three-phase model of pidginization-creolization-decreolization (see Drechsel 1976*a*: 70–4, Goddard 1977: 38, 1978, and Silverstein 1973 MS: 82–7).

The study of Native American contact languages ultimately raises the issue of the nature and extent of creolization in Native American pidgins. At present, there are no systematic or substantial data available on the creolization of any American Indian pidgin, much less on its subsequent decreolization. Métis, a *Mischsprache* that incorporated French noun phrases in a Cree-based syntax, has served as a community's first language (Rhodes 1977); but it is doubtful that its ancestral form was a true pidgin. Similarly, Chinook Jargon underwent creolization in the late nineteenth and early twentieth centuries, and apparently has served as a first language to new intertribal and multilingual communities (Hymes and Hymes 1972; Zenk 1984, 1988). Still, nativized Chinook Jargon requires further documentation, including clarification of its competition with English or any other European language (such as French or Russian) that already served as the new intertribal and interethnic lingua franca of the Northwest Coast. Another creolized Native American pidgin was Afro-Seminole Creole, which developed from a Seminole or Creek pidgin in rather intimate associations between Seminole Indians of Florida and African runaway slaves, only to merge with Gullah (Geechee) and Black English, and eventually to decreolize (Drechsel 1976*b*; Hancock 1980*a*, *b*, 1986; see also Sect. 8.6).

Except for single instances such as Chinook Jargon and the pidgin ancestor of Afro-Seminole Creole, Native American pidgins did not assume communicative functions beyond those of interlingual media. Many native groups of North America maintained considerable political and economic independence during colonial times, and did not experience a subordination equivalent to that of Africans by Europeans in slavery and plantation labor; those who did (as Southeastern Indians in early colonial times) were often deported to Caribbean islands with few opportunities to escape because of environmental restrictions. If indentured later, American Indians usually submerged among poor European settlers or in the general population of "colored folks," and sometimes lost their traditional identities. In these cases, Native Americans, Europeans, and Africans blended their traditions, including ways of speaking, into a new creole culture, as was the case among speakers of Afro-Seminole Creole and other people of "mixed" ancestry in eastern North America.

By all indications, contact between Native Americans and newcomers was not intimate enough for the creolization of Native American pidgins to have occurred on a large and regular scale. Few indigenous groups ever attained a position of so much power or prestige in relation to European, African, or other non-native peoples for these to adopt indigenous pidgins as their *first* languages. Before long, American Indian contact media, except for major ones such as Mobilian Jargon and Chinook Jargon, came into disuse, and possibly survived only in relexified and restructured form, as apparently happened with Seminole Pidgin. With the immigrants' push westward across North America and their growing control of the entire continent, native and immigrant groups met their needs to communicate with each other via native interpreters competent in one of the European tongues and, increasingly, by native communities adopting Spanish, French, or English as second or even first languages. Former multilingual contact situations turned bilingual or even monolingual, while some indigenous communities apparently experienced a process similar to creolization—that is the expansion and nativization of some incompletely acquired second-language forms, as apparently in the cases of Hopi (Voegelin 1959) and Métis. Still, the lack of intervening pidginization (including tertiary as opposed to secondary hybridization) would not justify calling these speech forms creole languages by conventional definition (see Drechsel 1976*a*: 74–5).

Interest in Black English has led to research on its Native American counterpart—that is, American Indian English—as initiated by William L. Leap (1977, 1982) and pursued by others (see e.g. Bartelt, Penfield-Jasper, and Hoffer 1982). In analogy to creole histories of Black English, Beth Craig (1991) has interpreted the origin of American Indian English as the result of creolization and decreolization of AIPE, which supposedly occurred in Indian mission and boarding schools in the Indian Territory (now Kansas and Oklahoma) after 1830 and subsequently spread to other tribes. This scenario however does not explain how American Indian (Creole) English diffused; nor can it account for the great variety in dialects of American Indian English nationwide. In spite of some structural similarities to English-based creoles, modern American Indian English (except for single instances such as Afro-Seminole Creole) rather developed from situations of plain bilingualism with a wide range of variation characteristic of second-language acquisition and due to substrata influences from many diverse Native American languages as the speakers' first or former first languages. In most instances, American Indian English grew directly out of the Indians' assimilation of English as a second language rather than a full cycle of pidginization-creolization-decreolization (for recent surveys, see Bartelt 1991 and Leap 1993).

Few answers and more questions leave us painfully aware of how limited and tentative our understanding of language contact and contact languages is in Americanist linguistics. There remains a great need for a broader perspective and an alternative theoretical framework of language change that systematically incorporates linguistic convergence in the study of Native American languages. Such in turn call for additional and better substantive evidence including descriptive-analytical case studies beyond that of better known Chinook Jargon. A prime instance is Mobilian Jargon.

2.4. Previous Research on Mobilian Jargon

Until recently, the interest paid by Americanist linguists, anthropologists, and historians to Mobilian Jargon amounted to little more than a few incidental inferences, quoted repeatedly throughout the literature on Southeastern Indians (for details, see Crawford 1978: 30–60; also Preliminaries to Part II and Chapter 9). Scholars could draw on little substantive information that they recognized as Mobilian Jargon.

There had already existed a sizable description in manuscript form entitled *Essai sur quelques usages et sur l'idiôme des Indiens de la Basse Louisiane* (Anonymous 1862 MS) and an English translation (Anonymous n.d. MS) for over a century. This study contains a vocabulary of some 750 entries, which the author organized according to major semantic categories or fields (such as body parts, animals, colors, clothing, navigation, etc.) and supplemented with lexicographical explanations as well as other, incidental descriptive and grammatical notes. The second part of the manuscript consists of French–Mobilian Jargon and Mobilian Jargon–French indexes plus a few additional entries and some modifications, apparently based on Choctaw or some other Western Muskogean language. The indexes show a distinct handwriting, which suggests a second author and closely resembles that of linguistic notes by Albert S. Gatschet (1885 MS; 1886 MS), containing a few words of Mobilian Jargon with other linguistic and ethnographic observations on Louisiana Indians in the late nineteenth century. Unfortunately, William A. Read (1940: 546), who brought the anonymous manuscript to public attention, mistook the language for "virtually pure Choctaw," as did apparently Mary Haas (1941*b*: 129; 1973: 1212).

The first person to identify "the Indian language of lower Louisiana" as Mobilian Jargon was Claude Medford (Hiram F. Gregory, personal communication), who eventually convinced James M. Crawford (1978: 57–8) of the same conclusion. There are several considerations that support such an interpretation. First, the grammatical data and also the lexical entries provided by the anonymous author (1862 MS) reveal little morphological complexity in contrast to Choctaw, and conform in surprisingly close ways with recent recordings of Mobilian Jargon (see Preliminaries to Part II). Second, in referring to the Indians of southern Louisiana and their language in the introductory passages of his first chapter, the author (Anonymous 1862 MS: 2–8) listed the Biloxi (Siouans), the Choctaw (Muskogeans), the Opelousa (unidentified), the Atakapa (speakers of a Gulf isolate), the Alabama (Muskogeans), the Natchitoches (Caddoans), and still other groups. These communities spoke different languages, some distantly related or unrelated among each other and thus mutually unintelligible with Choctaw. The only medium that these communities shared with each other was in fact Mobilian Jargon. Third, the anonymous author's principal linguistic informant was a Creole (Anonymous 1862 MS: 1), that is a person of European and perhaps African ancestry born in America, who as a non-Indian was unlikely to have learned Choctaw or some other closely related Western Muskogean language of the area at that time (see Sect. 10.3).

The first professional anthropological-linguistic recordings of Mobilian Jargon likewise carried the heading of Choctaw. Whether the suspected co-author of the anonymous *Essai* or not, Gatschet (1885 MS: 24–5; 1886 MS: 11) took down a few words of "Mobilian (= Choctaw)" among Atakapa Indians and two words of so-called "Chá'hta" among Biloxi. Around the turn of the century, he may have done some research on the pidgin with full awareness of its true nature, but apparently did not publish his findings (Taylor 1981: 184); nor are these known to have survived in manuscript form. Similarly, John R. Swanton (1911: 32) recorded a few Choctaw-like utterances among two brothers of Biloxi-Pascagoula descent, yet recognized Mobilian Jargon as their probable explanation. References to Mobilian Jargon and Choctaw also appear throughout William A. Read's discussion of "Indian Words" in Louisiana French (Read 1963 [1931]: 76–110). Moreover, Americanist scholars of the period—among them James Mooney, Gatschet, and especially Swanton—mentioned Mobilian Jargon in passing in their publications (see Crawford 1978: 58–9). At the time, focus on the lexicon and a lack of comparative morphosyntactic evidence in Muskogean languages made it difficult to recognize the unique grammatical structure of Mobilian Jargon by contrasting it with a related standard language.

Before long, social scientists supposed Mobilian Jargon to have become extinct, and made no further inquiries about it. Referring to relevant passages from James Mooney's *Myths of the Cherokee* (1900: 187–8), John E. Reinecke (1937: 666) observed in his comprehensive survey of the world's marginal languages that "Evidently it [Mobilian Jargon] died out, unrecorded, when the southeastern Indians learned English early in the nineteenth century." At the time, Mary R. Haas, dean of the study of Gulf languages, still learned of the pidgin from a Tunica consultant, but did not pursue any leads for its recent survival:

When I worked on the Tunica language in the 1930's, Sesostrie Youchigant, my Tunica informat, also knew of the jargon, which he referred to by its French name, Mobilienne, and he was able to remember two or three words which appeared to be Choctaw or Chickasaw. I unfortunately did not make any inquiries about the jargon among the Koasati in western Louisiana or the Alabama in east Texas. (Haas 1975: 258)

Elsewhere in an essay on Biloxi, Haas (1968: 81 n. 14) confirmed that "the existence of this trade language was well known" in 1934, when she and Morris Swadesh did a survey of Native American languages in southern Louisiana, eastern Texas, and eastern Oklahoma—only to bemoan that "no one seems to have taken the trouble to write it down."

It was only in the 1970s that Mobilian Jargon received closer attention from Haas (1975) and Crawford (1978). The source of inspiration was Medford, a Native American craftsman of part-Choctaw ancestry famous for his artistry in weaving split-cane baskets and for his rich knowledge of other native traditions. In the late 1960s, he had already alerted Crawford and Haas to surviving speakers of Mobilian Jargon in Louisiana (Crawford 1978: 115 n. 155; Haas 1975: 258). In 1970 and 1971, Crawford recorded numerous words and several phrases on two visits to the Coushatta Indians in southwestern Louisiana, which spurred him on to conduct an extensive search for historical documentation on Mobilian Jargon (Crawford 1978: p. v, 60–2). His studies subsequently furnished most of the background data for Silverstein's discussion of this pidgin (1973 MS: 29–39) and a brief paper by Haas (1975), and resulted in his book *The Mobilian Trade Language*, winner of the second James Mooney Award of the Southern Anthropological Society in 1977. Crawford's research in turn served as a basis for a review essay by the Mississippi Choctaw Kenneth H. York (1982) and for much of the lexicographical analysis by Pamela Munro (1984).

Crawford and the other authors focused their attention on the origin, spread, and decline of Mobilian Jargon as well as its vocabulary, with special attention to Algonquian loan-words, and made no claims for an exhaustive study. As a result, little information was available about the pidgin's overall grammatical pattern and variation, its linguistic and extralinguistic functions, or its relationships to source languages and even other contact languages of the area. These and related questions have been concerns of subsequent research. Mobilian Jargon's survival in and around Indian communities of Louisiana in the late 1940s and into the 1950s provided a situation favorable in comparison with that of other Native American contact languages, for it still admitted memory fieldwork with its last speakers together with philological and ethnohistorical inquiries.

A comprehensive description and analysis of the pidgin including a social history first became available in my doctoral dissertation, "Mobilian Jargon: Linguistic, Sociocultural, and Historical Aspects of an American Indian *lingua franca*" (Drechsel 1979). Discussions of selected structural-functional and sociohistorical aspects have since appeared in various publications of mine (see References). While drawing on this earlier research, the present book offers a description and analysis of Mobilian Jargon in fully integrated fashion, and relies on a revised and expanded vocabulary (see Drechsel, 1996). Follow-up visits in the field, additional ethnohistorical research, and reconstructions of early linguistic attestations made possible with modern comparative data (see Munro, forthcoming) also lend support to new findings.

3

Perspective and Research Methods in Studying Mobilian Jargon

3.1. A Comprehensive Approach

The long-standing bias towards Indo-European languages in their standard forms bequeathes the study of non-European languages and non-standard linguistic phenomena, including contact media, with major methodological limitations—poor historical records with little philological tradition and frequently restricted or lost opportunities for field research. Many non-Indo-European languages and certain registers such as classic pidgins have passed away with their last speakers before anybody had an opportunity to record them in detail. For those lingua francas that have survived and are not only linguistically but also socially marginal, fieldwork has required linguists to overcome a greater social distance to their consultants, adding to the difficulty of gathering essential data.

Problems in the study of non-Indo-European and that of non-standard languages appear to become compounded, in some instances perhaps even amplified, in research on non-European contact media such as Mobilian Jargon. One could expect field research with speakers of a non-Indo-European marginal language to be even more difficult than with speakers of its standard relative. Similarly, historical documentation of a non-standard non-European language should be harder to find than that of either a European marginal language or a non-European "standard" language. These methodological complications would presumably be due to speakers' reticence towards outsiders.

Notwithstanding such methodological handicaps, the research situation in the study of non-Indo-European marginal languages need not be discouraging, because there are unexpected benefits stemming precisely from what makes these language structurally and socioculturally distinct. The little information that Europeans and their American descendants cared to record about Native American contact media has proved remarkably reliable in quality, surprisingly consistent with other historical information as well as modern documentation, and sometimes quite enlightened, even if it hardly meets the descriptive standards of modern sociolinguistics. There are several reasons for this finding.

Apart from reporting a form of relexified American Indian Pidgin English (AIPE), early observers usually had no reason to misrepresent will-fully what they heard Indians say in contact situations; they recorded their observations as accurately as they could under the circumstances, although they lacked experience in transcribing strange new sounds and recognizing unusual grammatical categories. Frequently, early observers also were unaware of the special social functions of indigenous contact media; like most non-Indian speakers of such languages, they referred in their descrip-tions to "the national language" or "the mother tongue" in thinking that what they had learned was the Indians' principal or ancestral language rather than some related contact medium. In their ignorance of the true sociolinguistic complexities, Europeans and their American descendants offered descriptions that did not suffer from as many prejudices as compa-rable portraits of European-based "marginal" languages.

Even when early observers eventually did become aware of the special sociolinguistic role of an indigenous lingua franca or come to recognize it as a "corrupted" version of some related standard, they rarely acquired access to the target language as model; nor did they have any obvious reasons for hypercorrecting data on the native contact medium towards the related standard, understood by an even smaller readership than the first. Conversely, if colonial observers Europeanized their examples of some American Indian lingua franca, they probably followed the rules employed by European speakers. In this case, their documentation would provide some historical information on how Europeans or their American descen-dants acquired and spoke the indigenous contact language, as perhaps occurred in some instances of AIPE (see Sect. 2.3). Were some chroniclers to misrepresent what they heard spoken or even to invent data, they could hardly do so consistently without allowing their misconceptions about lan-guage to shine through or without losing credibility when more, compara-tive evidence came to light, as illustrated by the Taënsa language hoax (see Auroux 1984).

Although perhaps non-standard in linguistic terms, a non-Indo-European contact medium need not have been socially marginal or objectionable in the minds of its own speakers. Such a secondary language may even have been the only appropriate medium to use in contact with strangers, espe-cially foreigners from a great distance. Wide acceptance and spontaneous use of the contact medium would then have provided outsiders with easier access to it than the community's first language, thus facilitating historical research as well as fieldwork.

These very sociolinguistic circumstances applied to Mobilian Jargon. Chroniclers could hardly hypercorrect their recordings towards Choctaw, Chickasaw, or related Muskogean languages, mostly inaccessible to them in early colonial times. Nor does early documentation on this contact medium harbor the major pitfalls associated with historical research on predominantly European-based lingua francas, among them literary relexifications, comic-book-style stereotyping, hypercorrections, and other embellishments characteristic of AIPE (see Sect. 2.3). Significantly, Mobilian Jargon was a well-established and socially acceptable contact medium, which Native Americans used as an identity marker and a convenient sociolinguistic buffer against undesirable influences from non-Indian outsiders, beginning at the latest in the early nineteenth century (see Chapter 10).

Such qualitative advantages of research on non-European contact languages make up for some of its limitations, and warrant a substantial commitment to their study. The remaining shortcomings such as sparse attestations call for a comprehensive perspective and approach defined in the broadest conceivable sociolinguistic and historical terms. Our understanding of indigenous lingua francas can reap substantial gains only by drawing on all suitable resources of data, methods, and concepts. The importance of this point is evident in the case of a letter written in Chinook Jargon over one hundred years ago; a careful analysis of this document requires an examination of the extralinguistic context including geographic, social, and historical information to resolve lexical and grammatical ambiguities (see Harris 1985).

The present study takes a broadly conceived historical-sociolinguistic approach in the spirit of Uriel Weinreich's original book *Languages in Contact* (1953) by recognizing that language contact does not take place in a social vacuum, but reveals much about its extralinguistic context. Linguistic features usually pair with sociocultural data in ways that are not always predictable or one-to-one; instead, they often demonstrate significant correlation only over an extended period, and do so more obviously in language contact than in other forms of language change. Thus, evidence for the prevalence of certain elements in a language and particular kinds of linguistic data (such as the morphosyntactic patterns of single loanwords) yield hints about the historical role, social status, and other cultural traits of the speakers of these languages. Conversely, attestations of intimate, mutually dependent but unequal social relationships suggest that the dominant group has had a greater linguistic impact on the subordinate one than vice versa.

Consequently, research on Native American contact media should build on a comprehensive methodology and theory integrating linguistic and extralinguistic data in a systematic fashion, with multilectal grammars as its aim. A possible model might serve a broad variationist analysis (see e.g. Bailey 1973; Bickerton 1975) enriched by an ethnography of speaking (see e.g. Hymes 1974; Saville-Troike 1982). Alternatively, a narrowly conceived sociolinguistics could hardly account for a wide range of linguistic variation or a great diversity of sociocultural factors expected in a contact language; nor would focusing on a few single case histories including a description of the speakers' idiolects prove promising or interesting, as exemplified by Oswald Werner (1963) for Trader Navaho.

Ideally, this comprehensive approach requires statistically relevant and demographically representative samples of speech and extensive ethnographic observations for the implicational scaling of variable linguistic data and their methodical correlation with sociohistorical information. Such is obviously out of reach for moribund Mobilian Jargon. The linguistic, ethnographic, and historical data available on the pidgin are too sparse and disparate in quality and quantity to permit more than casual correlations among linguistic variables or with extralinguistic factors. This restriction applies to a variationist analysis as much as to an integrated sociolinguistic methodology. By necessity, linguistic variation and extralinguistic aspects of Mobilian Jargon remain domains of description and analysis separate from its basic grammar.

None the less, the fact of limited data need not relegate variationist analysis or ethnography to the backburner in salvage research. Although deficient by themselves in the study of Mobilian Jargon, these methodologies allow research to focus on "natural" speech, wide linguistic variation beyond the range of dialects, and sociocultural factors other than obvious social variables (such as age, gender, and ethnicity) as useful guidelines in eliciting and interpreting historical-sociolinguistic data of various kinds in an encompassing model of language change. A broadly conceived historical sociolinguistics further recognizes fieldwork and archival research as mutually complementary by drawing on both to the fullest possible extent. Despite many restrictions, evidence from historical attestations can do more than embellish modern field data, and may actually provide valuable clues to their analysis and interpretation in addition to answers to historical questions.

If modern sociolinguists ever saw much theoretical significance in the Saussurean distinction between synchrony and diachrony, they have long adopted a model of language incorporating the dimension of time along with extralinguistic factors, as persuasively presented by Uriel Weinreich, William Labov, and Marvin I. Herzog (1968). In the best of anthropological traditions, the ethnography of speaking and communication has paid considerable attention to language change (see e.g. Gumperz and Hymes 1972: part III; Blount and Sanches 1977), producing some case studies with an explicitly diachronic perspective (see e.g. Scollon and Scollon 1979).

The methodological-theoretical reaffirmation of diachrony would hardly appear necessary were it not for the fact that philological reconstructions have been peripheral to most Americanist linguists and creolists, foremost committed to fieldwork (see Goddard 1973; Hancock 1977). Their paramount objective has been to record as many of the rapidly vanishing Native American languages or pidgins and creoles as possible. Likewise, most ethnographers of speaking, including those committed to studying language change, have betrayed little time depth in their projects, limited usually to the life and memory spans of their consultants. Until today, ethnographic descriptions with a few notable exceptions (such as Bauman 1974; Hymes 1966) have barely incorporated historical documentation as a major source of information, although previous sociolinguistic histories made regular use of early records (see e.g. Cassidy 1961; Reinecke 1969).

On the other hand, sociolinguistic issues have been of no more interest to ethnohistorians, although they have regularly encountered these in their research and have made free, often uncritical use of philological data and methods. The largely absent role of linguistics in the field was already of concern to Karl Schwerin (1976: 329–30), former editor of *Ethnohistory*. A close examination of contributions to this representative journal leads one to several essays on linguistic topics, but only a few that are truly sociolinguistic in nature and that do not have notable flaws. In one article, Lois M. Feister (1973) examined the various means of communication (including lingua francas) between the Dutch and American Indians in New Netherland during the seventeenth century, while passing over new studies on pidgins and creoles emerging at the time (especially Hymes 1971) and other relevant literature (such as Leechman and Hall 1955; Miller 1967; Prince 1912 in particular). In another essay, Elizabeth Brandt and Christopher MacCrate (1982) surveyed the use of so-called American Indian Pidgin English (AIPE) in the US Southwest during the second half of the nineteenth century, but omitted a critical evaluation of their documentation (see Sect. 2.3). In a third instance, Nancy L. Hagedorn (1988) looked at the role of interpreters between Iroquois Indians and European colonists as vehicles of interethnic contact, without making references to sociolinguistic aspects beyond "rudimentary bilingualism" and "Indian multilingualism" (Hagedorn 1988: 75 n. 9). When the author observed (Hagedorn 1988: 77 n. 18) that "Delawares seem to have served as interpreters much more frequently than the Iroquois," she did not explore whether Delaware Jargon served as the medium of interpretation or even what languages Delaware interpreters employed. In a more recent article. James L. Axtell (1990) discussed interethnic humor shared by American Indians and European colonists, and even made reference to pidgins, specifically Europeanized varieties (Axtell 1990: 111, 112). Yet his examples of humor appeared in translation without further sociolinguistic explication. If judged by their journal, ethnohistorians have generally shown little appreciation for sociocultural variations in language use, by assuming identical functions for different languages and their varieties in oversight of modern sociolinguistic findings.

Ethnohistorians and sociolinguists (including the ethnographers of speaking and communication) still have to find a common middle ground on which to participate in co-operative interdisciplinary research. The incorporation of a greater time depth and an ethnohistorical approach benefits especially the study of non-European non-standard linguistic phenomena, by extending its range to earlier periods of history. Not only can an expanded time frame provide the basis for an in-depth understanding of the interactions between linguistic and extralinguistic factors in language and culture change; to some degree, it can also compensate for the inability of researchers to study, under laboratory-like field conditions, speech forms, behaviors, and communities that are extinct today. A prime example is the pidginization of Native American languages, a matter of history now. The availability of attestations solely in older documentation would constitute a poor excuse for neglecting this topic.

Skeptics might question the feasibility of incorporating diachronic data in an ethnography of speaking for any great time depth by making several arguments. For one, the ethnography of speaking as a product of the 1960s, thus of a fairly recent vintage, has studied particular speech behaviors and communities only over short periods. For another, concentration on field research for the purpose of recording unique speech behaviors, common to the study of Native American languages or pidgins and creoles, has left little room for historical research in spite of its acknowledged relevance. Yet, and perhaps most importantly, ethnographers tacitly assume that historical documentation could never meet their standards of description, that—in other words—it is not sufficiently detailed and comprehensive to be of any relevance or interest to them. This reasoning would hold true especially in cases of secondary dialects and languages including contact media, which presumably only few early observers considered worth recording in any detail.

After careful examination, the first two arguments do not appear irrefutable, and the third is clearly subject to verification. Although we cannot realistically expect historical sources to yield as much descriptive information or detail as those produced in modern sociolinguistic field research, especially at the micro-sociolinguistic level, the quality and quantity of historical-sociolinguistic data differ from case to case so that early documents need first to be assessed as to their value as evidence.

For Mobilian Jargon, some fairly detailed historical-sociolinguistic information is available, for instance, in the *Histoire de la Louisiane* by Antoine Simon Le Page du Pratz (1758), a Dutch-born settler to Louisiana, who was probably the first to leave us any systematic ethnographic details about the pidgin. Singularly perceptive as compared to observers of his time and later, Le Page du Pratz (1695?–1775) sketched two scenes of conversations in Mobilian Jargon with special emphasis on greetings, while commenting on the speech behavior and manners of Louisiana Indians in the early eighteenth century. Although selective, his observations are sufficiently detailed to surpass the more common, macro-sociolinguistic historical documentation, such as which community spoke what language. His descriptions include details on particular speech settings, scenes, and events, and offer explicit information on who said what to whom, where, when, in what manner, and under what circumstances (see Sect. 9.3). Le Page du Pratz's sketches also prove reliable in light of other historical information and modern evidence, and suggest the feasibility of an ethnohistorical approach to the study of the structure and function of language, even those of a non-European marginal medium, notwithstanding other methodological shortcomings and large gaps in information.

Thus, there remains a need for a truly comprehensive historical sociolinguistics that, if hardly novel in conception, follows anthropological tradition by drawing on a broad range of resources for data, methods, and theories. Such a historical sociolinguistics even merits wider recognition with a designation of its own: ethno*history* of speaking analogous to the holistic, but predominantly synchronic ethnography of speaking (Drechsel 1983*b*). An ethnohistory of language contact specifically examines the history of interactions between speakers of two or more languages (or dialects). The result usually is some compromise form of speech, emerging from "the transference of a linguistic form or rule from one person to another—more specifically, from one linguistic system to another" (Weinreich, Labov, and Herzog 1968: 155). Often, such linguistic acculturation is not a one-way process as this definition implies; rather it operates in each direction, and takes on multiple dimensions with several alloglossic parties interacting with each other. In process, language contact can manifest itself in a variety of phenomena, described in seemingly disparate terms: loan-words or lexical borrowings; linguistic interference; areal features; forms of "foreigner talk" and lingua francas; pidginization, creolization, and decreolization; diglossia and bi- or multilingualism; and language replacement, obsolescence, and extinction.

The terminological variety of language-contact processes and their results deceptively suggests a catalogue of typologically dissimilar, mutually exclusive linguistic phenomena, whereas in reality these terms simply reflect different angles of a single process—language contact. At the same time, the diversity of these aspects indicates that language contact is more complex than recognized by many linguists, social scientists, and historians. Consideration of the full range of language contact invites the examination of these phenomena in their sociohistorical context, with the result that researchers pay closer attention to relationships between various, otherwise ignored aspects of the same phenomenon, as they occur for instance between a lingua franca, its source languages, and areal-typological features shared by the communities in contact.

3.2. Field Research

As one among a few Native American contact media to persist through the first half of the twentieth century, Mobilian Jargon has lived on only in the memories of a handful of elderly individuals. Fortunately, it did not pass into oblivion before Claude Medford alerted Haas and Crawford to the feasibility of fieldwork (Crawford 1978: 115 n. 155; Haas 1975: 258).

Building on Crawford's initial inquiries, I continued the search for former speakers of Mobilian Jargon in various Indian communities during an eleven-month period from September 1976 through July 1977, with obtaining salvage recordings as the paramount objective. I first spent five months among the Coushatta and their non-Indian neighbors, both African and European Americans, in the greater area of Elton in southwestern Louisiana, where Crawford (1978: 60–2) had previously recorded most of his pidgin samples and where Mobilian Jargon had endured the longest (see Sect. 9.4). I also paid visits of several weeks to the following communities: the Alabama-Coushatta near Livingston in eastern Texas; the Tunica-Biloxi and the Jena Band of Choctaw, both in central Louisiana; the Five Civilized Tribes of eastern Oklahoma, including Cherokee, Chickasaw, Choctaw, Creek, and Seminole; and non-Indian neighbors of these groups. I then made excursions to other Native American or part-Indian communities in the Gulf region: the Atmore Creek and a community known as "Cajuns" in southwestern Alabama; the Choctaw near Philadelphia in central Mississippi; the Houma and Chitimacha in southeastern Louisiana; people of mixed Native American, African, and European ancestry at Spanish Lake, Clifton, and Ebarb in the greater vicinity of Alexandria and Natchitoches in west-central Louisiana; African Americans of part-Creek descent on the Penwau Slough and Kickapoo Creek west of Livingston in eastern Texas; and the Afro-Seminole community of Brackettville in southwestern Texas. On occasions, I consulted individuals whom relatives, friends, or acquaintances thought to remember some Mobilian Jargon, but who lived away from their home communities in various towns and cities of Louisiana, eastern Texas, southeastern Arkansas, and eastern Oklahoma. Finally, I paid follow-up visits to major Indian communities of Louisiana, most notably during the academic year of 1980–1 and in the summer of 1989.

By then, Mobilian Jargon had already been out of practical use as long as forty years or so (see Sect. 9.4). From my first contacts, it looked as if Crawford (1978: 60–2) had recorded the last two truly fluent speakers, both of whom had died before either he or I had had an opportunity to resume field research. Still, my goal was to find and record any remaining speakers, however knowledgeable, in an attempt to learn as much as possible from them. Eventually, I succeeded in not only substantiating most of Crawford's findings, but also adding a significant amount of new linguistic and ethnographic data. The following description incorporates single utterances recorded by Crawford, Hiram F. Gregory, and Geoffrey D. Kimball (personal communications) that I could not confirm independently and I duly identify so, but most of the field data in this book consist of recordings and new evidence that I collected.

As Crawford (1978: 117 n. 167) had suspected, Mobilian Jargon survived in the memories of several senior people, most of them over 60 years old and members of the Coushatta community near Elton or their neighbors. There were a few elderly individuals among other Louisiana Indians, the Alabama-Coushatta in Texas, and the Oklahoma Choctaw of Louisiana provenance who remembered some words of the pidgin or bits of sociohistorical information, but most of whom could no longer speak it.

With the aim of making the best use of limited resources, I pursued fieldwork through informal and open-ended interviews, which allowed each consultant full control over the format and topic of conversation and thus encouraged spontaneity and productive reminiscences without external constraints. My initial attempts proved rather disappointing, and I elicited little information beyond short word lists. The former speakers whom I consulted did not appear to remember more than individual lexical items or short phrases. When they had ceased to use Mobilian Jargon some forty years previously, they apparently had begun forgetting it as quickly and easily as they had once acquired it; as a second language, the pidgin had not become "imprinted" in the memories of these speakers as deeply as their mother tongues (see Sect. 9.4).

Informal and open-ended interviews proved insufficient by themselves in my salvage fieldwork on Mobilian Jargon. Citing examples gathered from other speakers and historical attestations occasionally helped in stirring the recollections of consultants. Yet to overcome major shortcomings of memory linguistics and ethnography (i.e. the description of what former speakers remembered about the structure and use of the language rather than firsthand recordings and observations) and to render the study of a moribund auxiliary language like Mobilian Jargon more productive, required a special technique of field research—"reduced awareness" elicitation (Bickerton and Odo 1976: 29–34). It promotes recording settings as natural and casual as possible so as to limit speakers' attention to the formality of interviews and other factors related to a researcher's visits. My subsequent field research proved quite successful in comparison with what one might have gained solely through methods of formal elicitation, in rather unexpected ways. Later, I was to meet speakers who imparted valuable new information to me, among them a Choctaw woman by the name of Lessie Simon, who lived near Oakdale north of Elton and still demonstrated considerable fluency in the pidgin.

Mobilian Jargon's advanced state of decline no longer permitted bringing together two or more former speakers with *different* first-language backgrounds in order to have them converse in the interlingual medium and to record their dialogue. For such an undertaking, Mobilian Jargon had not survived in sufficient strength in various alloglossic communities of Louisiana or elsewhere. The most fluent speakers were Choctaw or Coushatta of part-Choctaw descent, all fluent in Choctaw. The enactment of an exchange in Mobilian Jargon would have been rather awkward for them, as they would have found it more natural to resort to Choctaw, possibly Koasati, or even both. Much less was it possible to recreate or simulate in any natural fashion the historical and sociocultural conditions under which Mobilian Jargon had been spoken a few decades earlier (see Chapters 9 and 10).

There remained only one option that would come close to reproducing a social situation in which Mobilian Jargon had been used—to learn and use this American Indian pidgin myself as well as I could. In doing so, I improved my fieldwork in other ways, as I quickly learned to my pleasant surprise. Obtaining a firsthand, even if limited, knowledge of Mobilian Jargon not only helped me in understanding its structure better, but also familiarized me directly with learning an interlingual medium. My acquisition and use of Mobilian Jargon was by no means an anomalous process, for many non-Indians, including individuals with a German-language background like me, had once learned and spoken the pidgin in Louisiana and neighboring areas such as eastern Texas (see e.g. Dresel 1920–1: 371, 407). One might maintain with some reservations that my use of Mobilian Jargon provided an opportunity for participant observation of a situation in which a speaker of German had learned the pidgin, although such was not the objective of my research. This study was not to depend any more on a single idiolect than on my own intuitions or competence; rather, my description and analysis of Mobilian Jargon have principally relied on data recorded as naturally as possible from persons who had once spoken it fluently.

What I acquired of Mobilian Jargon amounted to little else than a repertoire of small talk, allowing me to conduct short conversations on such topics as the weather and daily activities. This limited knowledge was, however, sufficient to create an environment of participant observation and to make my fieldwork considerably more productive and successful in several ways.

First, my knowledge and use of the pidgin was of great advantage in expediting the laborious process of identifying former speakers, which involved not only repeated visits to numerous individuals in several communities, but also time-consuming efforts to find out who had once learned and still knew any Mobilian Jargon. For good historical reasons, Louisiana Indians have remained skeptical towards outsiders (see Sect. 10.3). Some were willing to share information only after they had become acquainted with me, which usually required more than one or two visits on my part.[1] Once I had established some minimal rapport with a consultant, I still faced the problem of reducing misunderstandings about the subject matter. Asking a consultant about Mobilian Jargon by the names of which I was aware or describing it in non-technical terms (such as "broken" Choctaw) was useless if he or she knew it by another name or in different terms, as many indeed did (see Sect. 9.1). In this situation, the use of a few sentences in Mobilian Jargon was of great advantage in identifying former speakers by simply observing their linguistic and extralinguistic reactions to my attempts at speaking the pidgin. Just a phrase or two often helped to break the ice in making the acquaintance of a person who still remembered some Mobilian Jargon. Several individuals who might first deny any such knowledge, be it due to their initial suspicion about me or because of their confusion about what I was requesting, could rarely hide reactions of surprise when I addressed them in the pidgin: **yama ešno tana**? 'Do you know Mobilian Jargon?' (literally 'Mobilian Jargon you know?' with rising intonation towards the end of the question) or **yoka anõpa eno tana banna. ešno anõpole**? 'I want to know Mobilian Jargon. Do you speak (it)?' (literally 'Mobilian Jargon I know want. You speak [it]?', again with rising intonation towards the end of the question). That a young non-Indian with a strange accent made an effort to use "Indian" instead of French or English apparently had not occurred for decades, and most people who knew Mobilian

---

[1] At first, I inadvertently complicated my fieldwork by driving a small yellow Japanese car with Wisconsin license plates. I had selected my car because of its energy efficiency, and the color of its body for the purpose of deflecting the sun's heat and for safety. Yet small Japanese cars of my type and of such a glowing color, not to mention my "Yankee" license plates, were unusual in the countryside South at the time, even during the afteryears of the energy crisis, and I initially raised distrust from afar and solely by appearance. Not surprisingly, a local person once suspected me of being a federal-government agent from out of state, checking on people's due taxes and land deeds. With the sheriff's assistance, another concerned citizen once ordered me at gunpoint to leave his parish. His Choctaw mother, one of my consultants, had already taken to me, and did not feel threatened or bothered by me; but her attempts to convince her suspicious son and the sheriff of my harmless intentions were in vain. Fortunately, she had by then shared with me everything that she remembered about Mobilian Jargon. As my visit was social in nature, I did not need to take any unnecessary risks in facing her son or the sheriff again; I am only sorry not to have seen her again before she passed away a few years later. Apart from these few incidents, my fieldwork proved a fully successful project, in which most people whom I visited received me with much hospitality. My then unusual car eventually turned into a trademark and even an asset, which aroused considerable curiosity among Indians and non-Indians alike and served as a convenient topic of conversation breaking the ice.

Jargon or something about it then became curious about where I had acquired my knowledge.

There were other benefits that resulted from this approach. Once acquainted with me, most people who could remember some Mobilian Jargon took pleasure in teaching it to somebody who was still interested; in this way, they themselves created a favorable environment for my fieldwork. As "nobody's language" shared by many communities, the pidgin was comparatively value-neutral, and was not socially stigmatized, except by a few younger Indians who had no real knowledge of it. Moreover, my interest in Mobilian Jargon limited our conversations to largely trivial matters of "the public domain," thus avoiding possibly sensitive issues of descent, religion, or property rights, although the pidgin was once structurally and lexically complex enough to permit discussion of any topic. With all my inquisitiveness about Mobilian Jargon, I hardly invaded anybody's private spheres; if I had been studying a Native American language proper such as Choctaw, Koasati, or Alabama, I would inadvertently have asked potentially prying questions about private matters for a full understanding of the language's larger sociocultural setting. In attempting to speak the pidgin, however, I fitted into a traditional role because it was the appropriate medium of communication between Indians and non-Indians in the past. As it turned out, Mobilian Jargon functioned in my encounters with former speakers precisely as it had in contact between Indians and non-Indians for over a century, which proved a benefit more important than I had realized at first (see Sects. 10.3 and 10.4).

Most importantly, talking with former speakers of Mobilian Jargon in the pidgin, if only about some trivial topic, helped to revive their memories and to generate more natural speech than I could ever have elicited in formal interviews. They often came to remember entire phrases and sentences, and with them additional words in a kind of "snowballing" effect. The resulting evidence proved indispensable for the study of the pidgin's syntactic and semantic pattern.[2]

When granted permission and whenever possible, I made tape recordings of my interviews and our conversations, and at the same time took down essential words and sentences in phonetic transcription so as to improve the accuracy of my recordings. Agility in phonetic transcription came in handy, because several consultants preferred not to be recorded onto tape. In these instances, I relied entirely on my written transcriptions, as I eschewed use of any surreptitious or other illicit recording techniques. Yet once we had begun an interview or a conversation, I avoided unnecessarily drawing the attention of my consultant to my recording equipment, an

---

[2] For a similar discussion of the benefits that studying natural speech has for the description and analysis of obsolescent languages, see Mithun (1990*a*).

unobtrusive but high-quality cassette recorder of regular size and a lavalier microphone.

With all efforts concentrated on obtaining socially representative speech samples of Mobilian Jargon, the salvage-research situation no longer allowed me to record the full historic range of variation—for the same reasons that I could not bring together more or less fluent pidgin speakers with different first-language backgrounds to converse with each other. Those who remembered any substantial amount of Mobilian Jargon lived in the greater vicinity of Elton, and were Choctaw or Coushatta of part-Choctaw descent with similar first-language backgrounds, including Choctaw. The remaining consultants, a few other Louisiana Indians and their neighbors of African–American or European–American ancestry with a French-language background, could no longer recall enough of the Indian medium to converse in it.

The speech samples that Crawford (1978) and I documented thus gravitate towards varieties influenced by Louisiana Choctaw, Koasati, and—to a lesser extent—perhaps French in its variant Acadian ("Cajun") and Creole forms. These languages were the various speakers' different "mother tongues," which served as their prime sources of ethnic identity. When compared to attestations from historical records, the modern evidence available until recently does not reflect the full range of multilectal variation in the pidgin. Evidence of such variation exists in an old song that I recorded among the Tunica-Biloxi Indians in Marksville and in various historical sources, especially the *Essai sur quelques usages et sur l'idiôme des Indiens de la Basse Louisiane* (Anonymous 1862 MS) with its sizable vocabulary of some 750 entries (see Chapter 8).

Because Mobilian Jargon had survived not in a natural setting but in the memories of a few older individuals, I could elicit information on its sociocultural aspects only via conventional ethnographic methods—that is by writing down what my consultants still remembered ("memory ethnography") and by supplementing their recollections with my own observations of how they used the pidgin in our conversations. Former speakers could still pass on a substantial amount of information about its use and broader sociocultural setting, at times more detailed than their linguistic recollections. My own supplementary observations of their speech in Mobilian Jargon, while less comprehensive due to the limited nature of our conversations, yielded some useful clues as well. A prime example is the increased use of facial expressions, hand signs, and other body language with Mobilian Jargon, as also attested in historical records (see Sect. 8.6).

In striving to gather as much linguistic and extralinguistic information on Mobilian Jargon as was possible under the circumstances, I attempted to record all the remaining speakers. Still, I may have missed a few persons with some knowledge of the pidgin. According to other community members, they had once learned Mobilian Jargon and still remembered some, but did not wish to share their knowledge.

3.3. *Archival Research*

As opportunities for field research have become fewer for many non-European languages now obsolete and for some earlier registers (such as classic pidgins and creoles), archival research has gained significance as a tool for their study, thus making historical documentation a major source of information for Mobilian Jargon and other native contact languages of southeastern North America (see Drechsel 1983*b*; 1994*b*).

Archival research of Mobilian Jargon has involved a laborious and painstaking search through piles of primary sources for what are often tiny bits of information. Relevant data have come from a variety of documents: diaries, journals, and correspondence by explorers, travellers, traders, and settlers; reports by officials of various colonial governments, especially those concerned with so-called Indian affairs, and by missionaries of different denominations; and writings by early naturalists, geographers, historians, anthropologists, linguists, and other scholarly observers. Several of these records are rare publications or original manuscripts that are accessible only at special archives; they have included: the University of Wisconsin Memorial Library; the archives of the Wisconsin Historical Society (with an extraordinarily rich collection of materials on Louisiana); the Newberry Library in Chicago; the libraries of Tulane University, Louisiana State University, and Northwestern State University of Louisiana; and the Library of Congress in Washington, DC. Defining my documentary search in comprehensive terms and extending it across some fifteen years, I have attempted to examine all important historical sources of information on Mobilian Jargon, but would not make any claim to exhaustiveness. More documentation possibly exists in archives of documents from the early colonial governments of southeastern North America in Cuba, Canada, Spain, France, and England. Additional relevant sources may be found in holdings of the Vatican and other religious bodies that committed missionaries to eastern North America.

Publication of the present materials will make easier the identification of other relevant documents. A prime concern of historical research has been how to identify Mobilian Jargon in documents. The best evidence obviously consists of linguistic and specifically morphosyntactic characteristics of the kind presented in Part II; isolated lexical entries without any accompanying morphological, other grammatical, or extralinguistic information leave doubt as to whether they represent some native, most likely Muskogean language or a pidginized variety of it. In the absence of morphosyntactic traces, the next best evidence by which to interpret historical and ethnographic documentation has been sociocultural clues. Focus on information on who spoke what when, where, and under what circumstances has directed attention to the sociolinguistic features of Mobilian Jargon that distinguish it from its Muskogean source languages (see Chapters 9 and 10).

As already suggested, much of the available information has proved quite incidental and limited in scope, if surprisingly accurate in quality. Mobilian Jargon and other American Indian contact languages were of only minor interest to observers of colonial and recent southeastern North America. Most of them had little more than a utilitarian concern for Mobilian Jargon, even if it was mistaken as "the national language" or "the mother tongue" in the modern sense of principal or ancestral language rather than some related contact medium. While accepting the pidgin as the prime medium in interactions with Indians, colonists still relied on translators (often using Mobilian Jargon in their interpretations), and expected it to decline shortly in favor of a European language without paying much further attention to it (see Chapter 9). Few early observers developed sufficient awareness of the native sociolinguistic complexities to make further inquiries. The immigrants' lack of interest in Mobilian Jargon thus related not so much to its "non-standard" status as to their indifference towards, if not prejudice against, anything Native American.

The linguistic evidence found in historical documents consists variously of single words, compounds, short phrases, and occasional longer utterances. These recordings do not meet the standards of modern, phonetic transcriptions because of limits in descriptive resources at the time. In recording strange sounds, early observers barely knew better than to use the orthography of their own languages—Spanish, French, English, or even German. If they ventured to record phrases and sentence-long utterances, their incidental grammatical observations could likewise reflect interference from their European mother tongues or—at times—some other language. Thus, the orthography of the author of *Essai* (Anonymous 1862 MS) was "typically French,—so much so that some of his transcriptions might perplex even one thoroughly familiar with Choctaw," according to William A. Read (1940: 546–7). Bewildering differences from Choctaw are actually due to the fact that the manuscript does not describe Choctaw proper, but rather its lexically related pidgin, which differs grammatically. A knowledge of the early chroniclers' first and other languages has helped resolve many puzzles of historical records; proper interpretation in fact has been impossible without a solid understanding of the orthography, phonology, and grammar of the authors' mother tongues. In light of French conventions of spelling and grammar, early attestations of Mobilian Jargon by French observers as well as the anonymous author have turned out to be remarkably accurate in comparison with modern recordings.

Residual questions in the interpretation of historical attestations can sometimes be resolved by a comparison with modern data or by additional fieldwork. Just as former speakers occasionally remembered a word, phrase, or some other feature of the contact medium if given a clue from some earlier recording, so they could assist in interpreting a historical document. When consultants had exhausted their memories and data gathered earlier provided no remedy, information on the languages of origin or even related ones could be useful. In examining the *Essai* in particular, I was fortunate to draw on the assistance of quadrilingual Ernest Sickey, at the time Chairman of the Coushatta Indian Tribe of Louisiana. He had grown up speaking Koasati, Choctaw, French, and English; he still remembered hearing his maternal grandmother, Arzelie Langley, converse in Mobilian Jargon in his childhood, and had even learned some of the language from her. His multilingual competence served as an excellent basis for comparing the anonymous author's vocabulary of Mobilian Jargon with resemblances in Choctaw, Koasati, and other languages and for retranscribing many of the historical attestations in the manuscript. Of the doubtful attestations that remained in other documents, some could eventually be reconstituted by contrasting them with comparable materials for different Southeastern Indian languages.

This approach to the study of historical documents follows well-established procedures of philology, as applied in those areas of Americanist linguistics that can draw on a substantial body of early documents, such as the study of Algonquian languages. The basic method consists of comparing different documentary sources, modern related evidence, and other relevant linguistic data known as phonetic triangulation (Goddard 1973: 731), with the aim of reconstructing or reconstituting early attestations in terms of modern linguistic transcription.

Counter to expectation, reconstitutions need not be limited to standard languages, but can be successfully extended to marginal linguistic phenomena such as contact media, including pidgins (see Hancock 1977). Nor is the variable nature of lingua francas an insurmountable obstacle, for they have exhibited fairly regular patterns upon closer examination and in comparison with modern data. Yet in order to present a convincing case, the reconstitution of marginal linguistic phenomena—perhaps more than orthodox philological problems—must rely on all available resources: internal orthographic evidence such as conventions, idiosyncrasies, and inconsistencies in spelling that resulted from the recorders' reliance on their first languages; other, comparable recordings; pertinent evidence gathered from persons who still remembered the contact medium; and equivalent resemblances in their sources or even closely related languages (for further details on the reconstitution of Mobilian Jargon words and a comprehensive vocabulary, see Drechsel, 1996: 9–11).

As in conventional philological research, these reconstitutions— identified by a dagger (†)[3]—are not mere transliterations, but historical reconstructions, whose use requires proper caution. At best, reconstitutions approximate the pronunciation and other aspects of early recordings, so they cannot recover all details, even under ideal conditions. For this reason, early examples of Mobilian Jargon appear throughout this book in both their reconstituted forms and original attestations, which allow readers to evaluate the evidence on their own. Remarkably, these reconstitutions represent instances of linguistic convergence rather than language diversification, which is based on the tree model of language change (as predicated in conventional philology).

Archival research should not be limited solely to the examination of linguistic data, but extends to extralinguistic sociocultural and historical aspects of Mobilian Jargon as well. Ethnographic and sociohistorical information can actually enrich linguistic description and analysis in more than just an anecdotal manner. This point gains support from a telling example of erroneous interpretation in the study of Mobilian Jargon. When Read (1940: 546) identified the anonymous author's *Essai* as a description of "virtually pure Choctaw, very few words being drawn from other Indian sources," he oddly cited single examples of Chickasaw and Mobilian Jargon for contrast. Closer attention to the anonymous author's extralinguistic information (such as who spoke the language and under what circumstances), as well as to linguistic indicators, could have alerted Read to an alternative interpretation of the document—that it described the pidgin rather than Choctaw, already comparatively well-attested at the time—and this unique source might not have escaped the attention of Americanist linguists for so long.

Ethnohistorical research of Mobilian Jargon can specifically benefit from a broadly conceived ethnography of speaking by drawing attention to any relevant sociohistorical information on who spoke or did not speak what, to whom, where, when, and under what circumstances. Although no known historical documentation covers all these aspects, select information from diverse documents provides the outlines of a broader picture, an ethnohis-

---

[3] In adopting the dagger to identify reconstituted forms, I follow the suggestion of an anonymous reviewer of my doctoral dissertation who recommended a careful distinction of philological reconstructions or so-called *reconstitutions* from reconstructions of the comparative method of historical linguistics, identified by an asterisk. Whereas the former are based on early written records, the latter usually draw on modern linguistic recordings—a distinction that does not necessarily preclude an overlap in methodology or ignore similarities in principles of reconstruction. To this date, I have not been able to determine who deserves credit for first introducing the dagger as a symbol of reconstitutions.

tory of Mobilian Jargon. What often appears as a search for a needle in a haystack has occasionally uncovered true nuggets of historical information, as was the case with the anonymous author's *Essai*, a manuscript that describes Mobilian Jargon in seventy-four pages (Anonymous 1862 MS).[4]

3.4. *Towards a Grammar and an Ethnohistory of Mobilian Jargon*

In an effort to draw a comprehensive sociolinguistic portrait of Mobilian Jargon, this book integrates disparate sources of information, and thus cannot entirely escape the perils of a catalogue-style inventory characteristic of salvage research. The heterogeneous nature of the linguistic, ethnographic, and documentary data does not permit their presentation in a synthesized fashion that correlates linguistic aspects with extralinguistic ones in the point-for-point fashion expected in modern sociolinguistics. Accordingly, the subsequent description and analysis follow a more traditional format covering grammar, linguistic variation, and extralinguistic aspects in separate sections. What this conventional presentation misses without the formularism of some recent sociolinguistic analyses, it gains by greater accessibility to a broader audience, including readers with little exposure to linguistics.

My description and analysis of Mobilian Jargon proceed within the broad theoretical framework of pidgin and creole studies (for recent surveys, see

---

[4] The original handwritten version is located in the Special Collections of the Howard-Tilton Memorial Library at Tulane University in New Orleans, and a type-written transcript (including several blank spaces and handwritten comments by William A. Read in the margins) is in the Louisiana Room of the Louisiana State University Library in Baton Rouge. An English translation of this document in a different handwriting (Anonymous n.d. MS) also exists at the library of the Gilcrease Museum in Tulsa, Oklahoma. The characteristic French orthography used in the English version indicates that "the author wrote the essay in French and translated it, or had it translated, into English" (Crawford 1978: 114 n. 138).

Apparently neither Crawford nor Read (1940: 546), who first brought this most valuable document to public attention, had access to the original manuscript in French, but made use of the type-written copy. Especially noteworthy about the original manuscript is the fundamentally different style of handwriting in the second part, which consists of alphabetical French–Mobilian Jargon and Mobilian Jargon–French indexes, a list of compounds, and place names and which suggests a second author. Closer inspection reveals several discrepancies between the two parts. Some are minor, such as incorrect alphabetical orders and spelling differences; others are more significant, such as missing entries, modifications (apparently based on Choctaw or some other Western Muskogean language), and a few unaccountable, but perfectly consistent additions, which reveal some independent expertise in Mobilian Jargon.

The question of authorship for either the first or the second part remains unresolved. At this time, there exists no suggestion whatsoever of who wrote the first, major part. However, the person who compiled the second part could have been Albert S. Gatschet, whose handwriting as evident from manuscripts of his (see Gatschet 1885 MS and 1886 MS) is strikingly similar to that used in the manuscript's second part and who did some research on Mobilian Jargon at the end of the nineteenth century, without publishing his findings (Taylor 1981: 184). All investigations so far have produced no further clues.

Holm 1988; Mühlhäusler 1986; Romaine 1988). This area of specialization within linguistics need not prejudice one into *a priori* thinking of a contact medium as a pidgin, although Mobilian Jargon proves to be such by meeting all the definitional requirements (see Sect. 13.3). Pidgin and creole studies provide the necessary theoretical emancipation for understanding marginal languages as linguistic systems in their own right rather than in terms of their related target languages. Just as it would be misleading for one to describe Chinook Jargon as a corrupted form of Chinook, Mobilian Jargon cannot be understood as a "run-down" form of Chickasaw, Choctaw, or some other Muskogean language. However closely related Mobilian Jargon proves to be to any of these languages (see Sect. 12.1), it is only on the basis of an analysis in the pidgin's own terms that we can compare it with its source and other, contributing languages. This approach follows the same relativistic philosophical principles as those of the modern study of non-Indo-European languages, including emic analysis as first applied in phonology and successfully extended to other aspects of grammar.

This reasoning bears directly on the definition and usage of *Mobilian Jargon*, the most common and widely recognized label in the linguistic and ethnological literature, although its speakers and observers throughout history knew it by various other names (see Sect. 9.1). My book follows convention, most importantly to avoid confusion with *Mobilian proper*, as inadvertently suggested by the use of the short form by Crawford (1975*a*: 45–8; 1978) and others (e.g. Haas 1975; Munro 1984; York 1982). The terminological distinction between Mobilian and Mobilian Jargon is justifiable, even imperative, on the reasonable assumption that the Mobilian Indians spoke some language other than Mobilian Jargon as their mother tongue, although there is little substantive evidence available about it or its historical affiliation. The attested fact that they used Mobilian Jargon as a second language has no direct bearing on their linguistic identity. Conceptual lucidity would be necessary even if the Mobilians had spoken a creolized variety of Mobilian Jargon, a supposition for which there is no evidence; the contact medium would still have exhibited fundamental sociolinguistic differences from the alleged creole to justify this terminological distinction, as is evident from the study of other pidgins and related creoles.

In the context of language-contact research, the term *Jargon* in Mobilian Jargon requires further explanation. As employed here, this term does not carry any pejorative implications in terms of some everyday usage or refer to a form of technical speech full of special terms; nor does it suggest any of the specifications related to a highly variable pre-pidgin stage with differing deep structures, depending on mother-tongue influences but converging at the surface-structure level, as Michael Silverstein (1972) has proposed for Chinook Jargon in particular. While Mobilian Jargon was a *Mischsprache* or 'mixed language' in typological terms, *Jargon* need not even presuppose a hybrid speech form, as Allan R. Taylor (1981: 175) has maintained in his survey of North American Indian contact languages. Instead, *Mobilian Jargon* merely parallels the names of comparable and typologically similar Native American contact languages such as Chinook Jargon and Delaware Jargon, and happens to apply to an established pidgin (see Sects. 13.1–13.3).

PART II

Linguistic Aspects of Mobilian Jargon

Preliminaries

Until recently, little published information was available on the linguistic pattern of Mobilian Jargon. The earliest observers rarely offered descriptive details beyond incidental, vague references about the pidgin's structure.

Perhaps the first to record any details about Mobilian Jargon was the French Jesuit priest Paul du Ru, who—while serving on one of the first major French explorations of the lower Mississippi River valley in 1700—left the following inkling:

Joubliois de dire que je vay a l'ecole dun vieux [?] sauvage depuis 2 jours pour aprendre le bayagoula [actually Mobilian Jargon], jay desja cinquante mots des plus necessaires, je croy cette langue assez pauvre [;] elle accomoderoit assez les gens qui gracient car elle bannit entierement tous les R. les D. [;] je crois aussy ny sont guere connus et les bayagoulas ne peuvent venir a bout de prononcer ceux qui se rencontrent dans nos mots.   [*sic*]   (du Ru 1700 MS: 9–10)[1]

Fellow missionaries such as François Jolliet de Montigny and Henri Roulleaux de la Vente (in Gosselin 1906: 38, 39) simply compared Mobilian Jargon to Western Muskogean languages in vague terms difficult to interpret. Only several decades later did the Dutch-born French settler Antoine Simon Le Page du Pratz (1758: ii. 218–19, 242) offer new information by characterizing Mobilian Jargon as "la Langue Tchicacha, quoiqu'un peu corrompue" ('the Chickasaw language, although a bit corrupted') or "la Langue vulgaire" ('the common language'). But he did not care to provide a grammar, for he thought that "elle s'apprend mieux par l'usage que par

---

[1] In interpreting barely legible portions of du Ru's manuscript for their correct interpretation, I acknowledge the assistance of Samantha Kahn Herrick of the Newberry Library. The corresponding passage in English translation reads as follows: 'I forgot to say that for two days I have been going to school to the old Savage to learn to speak the Bayogoula language [actually Mobilian Jargon]. I have already fifty of the most necessary words. I believe this language is rather meagre. It would well suit people who stammer for it makes absolutely no use of R and D. I think these sounds are unknown to it for the Bayogoulas cannot succeed in pronouncing them when they occur in our words' (du Ru 1934: 8–9). Du Ru's reference to "Bayogoula" as one of the most widespread languages of Louisiana spoken by eight or ten tribes (du Ru 1700 MS: 31; 1934 [1700]: 23), presumably with different first languages, suggests an interpretation in terms of Mobilian Jargon instead of Bayogoula proper or some widespread, apparently non-pidginized Western Muskogean language in early historic Louisiana, as surmised by Crawford (1978: 28–32). This conclusion is born out by du Ru's linguistic evidence, which clearly is Mobilian Jargon and leaves Bayogoula proper unidentified (for further discussion of du Ru's evidence, see Sects. 8.4 and 9.3).

principes; d'ailleurs cette Langue n'est plus si nécessaire que dans le temps que je demeurois dans cette Province, parce l'on n'est plus si voisins ni en si grande relation avec les Naturels" (Le Page du Pratz 1758: ii. 323).[2] Contemporaries of Le Page du Pratz did not trouble to leave any further descriptive details of Mobilian Jargon. Probably inspired by his reference to it as "la Langue du Pays" (Le Page du Pratz 1758: iii. 89) or 'the language of the country,' later observers—among them Jean Benjamin François Dumont de Montigny (1747 MS: 430; 1753: i. 181–2), Bernard Romans (1962 [1775]: 59), and a French settler by the last name of Berquin-Duvallon (1803: 191)—simply referred to Mobilian Jargon as a 'mother language,' and perhaps supplemented their vague observations by a short comparative reference to Choctaw or Chickasaw.

Whereas du Ru, Le Page du Pratz, and others had already interspersed their observations with samples of single words or even occasional phrases, the first few vocabularies, small in size, did not appear until the end of the eighteenth century: one compiled by Nicolas Louis Bourgeois (1788: 296–7) for Indians of the Mississippi River and another collected by a surveyor named Selden among Osage or Oto Indians on the Missouri River some five hundred miles upstream from its confluence with the Mississippi (Stiles 1980 [1794]: 51; cf. Sherwood 1983: 440–1). It took still another visitor to Louisiana, Louis Narcisse Baudry des Lozières (1802: 266), to notice the pidgin's "mixed" nature when he made reference to "les différens patois dont elle [Mobilian Jargon] est mêlée" ('the different languages of which it is mixed'). Eventually in 1858, an American trader and settler in Louisiana, Thomas S. Woodward (1939 [1859]: 79), portrayed Mobilian Jargon specifically as "mixture of Creek, Choctaw, Chickasaw, Netches [Natchez] and Apelash [Apalachee]."

Beginning with the nineteenth century, most observers only repeated what must by then have become standard wisdom about Mobilian Jargon: its (lexical) similarity to Muskogean languages, especially Chickasaw and Choctaw, with some admixtures from others; its "meager," "reduced," or "corrupted" structure and thus its easy acquisition; its role as the Indians' "national language" or "mother tongue," at times misinterpreted as their ancestral language; and its functions as the common or "international" medium of greater Louisiana (see e.g. Baudry des Lozières 1802: 266–7; Berquin-Duvallon 1803: 191; Robin 1807: 54–5; Schermerhorn 1814: 27–8). Others such as Albert Gallatin (1973 [1836]: 100–1, 117) and Henry R. Schoolcraft (1852: 344) confused Mobilian Jargon with Choctaw and Chickasaw, and paid no further attention to the pidgin.

The first descriptive details about the linguistic structure of Mobilian

---

[2] 'it is easier to learn by practice than by rules; besides, this language is no longer as necessary as it was during the time when I lived in that country, because one is no longer as close to or in as much intercourse with the natives' (see Le Page du Pratz in Crawford 1978: 44).

Jargon emerged only with the "Essai sur quelques usages et sur l'idiôme des Indiens de la Basse Louisiane" in 1862, in which its perceptive author (Anonymous 1862 MS: 8–9) outlined several grammatical rules:

1° Les verbes qui sont en petit nombre et qui, presque tous ne designent que les operations les plus indispensables de la vie animale et naturelle, ne se presentent que sous un seul mot que l'on peut considérer comme leur infinitif. Quelquefois pour completer l'idée, ils sont accompagnés d'un substantif qui sert alors à en determiner la signification, par example: *Souba-bénilé* mot à *Souba* cheval bénilé s'asseoir; s'asseoir sur un cheval, ou pour mieux dire: chevaucher, monter à cheval.

La forme negatif se fait en ajoutant *ekcho* non pas, qui est la negatijon qui gouverne tous les mots de la langue.

La forme du passé se fait en ajoutant: *taha*, qui veut dire partie fini, c'est-à-dire passé.

La forme du future se fait en désignant l'époque où l'on accomplira la chose et en continuant à se servir du měme mot employé pour le verbe.

Quant aux verbes: être et avoir, ils se rendent par l'emploi du pronom en le faisant suivre du mot qui exprime la façon d'être ou l'objet qui est possédé.

2° Les noms n'ont pas de genre, même pour les animaux. Les mots femelle et mâle ajoutés au nom de l'espèce, indiquent le sexe de l'individu. On en trouvera un exemple detaillé à la tête du chapitre où est traité des animaux.

3° Les adjectifs et en general tous les mots qui servent à determiner la nature, la qualification et l'état d'un animal ou d'une chose, n'ont que la forme affirmative, c'est-à-dire que Bon, par exemple qui se dit: *tchoucouma* n'a pas pour contre-partie le mot special: mauvais, il faut dire *tchoucouma ekcho*, c'est-à-dire pas bon. Il en est de même dans tous les cas semblables. [*sic*][3]

---

[3] '1° The verbs are few in number and which for the most part designate only the most indispensable operations of animal and material life, present themselves in the form of a single word which may be considered as their infinitive mood. Sometimes, that the idea may be complete, they [are] accompanied by a noun serving to complete the signification, for example: *souba-bénilé* word for word: *souba*, horse; *bénilé*, to sit; to sit on a horse, or rather to ride on horseback.

The negative form is obtained by adding *ekcho*, no, which is the negative governing all the words of the language.

The form of the past is obtained by adding *taha* which means gone, finished.

The form of the future, by designating the time when the thing will be accomplished and continuing to use the same word.

As to the verbs to be and to have they are rendered by the use of the pronoun followed by the word expressing the State of being or the object possessed.

2° Nouns have no genders, not even for animals. The words male and female added to the name of the species indicates the sex. An example fully explained will be found at the beginning of the chapter which treats of animals.

3° Adjectives and in general all words which serve to determine the nature, qualification and state or condition of an animal or thing, have but the affirmative form, that is to say *good*, for example, in indian *tchoucouma*, has not for counterpart the special word *bad*. You must say: *tchoucouma-ekcho*, that is to say: *not good*. The same holds good in all similar cases' [*sic*] (Anonymous n.d. MS: 8–9).

The anonymous author used a vocabulary of some 750 entries to provide additional, mostly incidental observations about the structure of Mobilian Jargon throughout the *Essai*, and then concluded boldly:

Il est facile de voir, que bien que dépourvu des éléments qui constituent les langages modernes, le langage dont nous avons essayé de donner un aperçu, ne manque pas d'un certain ordre et d'une certaine liaison dans la formation de ses locutions, ainsi qu'on peut le voir par les remarques, dont nous avons fait suivre chaque chapitre.

La langue dont nous avons reproduit les mots que nous avons pu receuillir devait nécessairement être relativement moins parfaite en son état primitif: c'est-à-dire avant l'arrivée des Europeens. Des objects inconnus d'abord et des besoins nouveaux, crées par un changement de vie et des relations nouvelles, ont du augmenter et améliorer leur vocabulaire en apportant plus de rectitude et de *co-ordonnation* dans leur idées; si l'on peut s'exprimer ainsi. [*sic*]   (Anonymous 1862 MS: 71–2)[4]

As much insight as the author showed into the structure of Mobilian Jargon, as little was the understanding eventually displayed of its overall nature, sociolinguistic functions, or relationship to other American Indian languages. The co-author who, in a handwriting characteristic of Albert S. Gatschet, added French–Mobilian Jargon and Mobilian Jargon–French indexes plus some modifications (based on Choctaw or some other Western Muskogean language) and a few entries of his own revealed some independent expertise; but he did not challenge the primary author's conclusions.

Whether or not the co-author of the *Essai*, Gaschet (1885 MS: 14–5; 1886 MS: 11) made the first professional anthropological-linguistic recordings of Mobilian Jargon among Atakapa and Biloxi Indians in Louisiana by compiling short word lists with a few phrases, which he erroneously identified as Choctaw. Subsequently, John R. Swanton made occasional references to Mobilian Jargon throughout his ethnographic writings, yet took down only a few words and phrases of Mobilian Jargon from one of two brothers of Biloxi-Pascagoula descent, whom he suspected of speaking the pidgin (Swanton 1911: 32). The Louisiana naturalist Caroline Dormon (n.d. MS) similarly collected single words of Mobilian Jargon along with Choctaw, but provided only few morphosyntactic or other clues that now permit one to

---

[4] 'It is easy to see that, although wanting elements that make up modern languages, the language of which we have tried to give a general survey does not lack a certain order or a certain cohesion in the formation of its phrases, as one can see from the remarks that we have added to each chapter.

The language of which we have reproduced the words that we have been able to collect necessarily had to be comparatively less perfect in its primitive condition; that is before the arrival of the Europeans. Objects first unknown and new wants, created by a change in life and new relations, have had to increase and improve their vocabulary by bringing more straightness and *coordination* in their views, if one can express it in this manner' (author's translation; this passage does not occur in Anonymous (n.d. MS)).

sort out the two kinds of data. The lack of contrastive grammatical information for Muskogean languages, especially at the level of morphosyntactic analysis, left Mary R. Haas (1953: 195) to recognize the difficulty of
determining the source of Western Muskogean loan-words in Tunica as
either Choctaw or Mobilian Jargon, but this did not stop her from describing the pidgin as "based to a large extent on Chickasaw, a Muskogean
language mutually intelligible with Choctaw."

It took two more decades until modern linguists came to pay closer attention to Mobilian Jargon and its structure. From her analysis of data gathered by Crawford, Haas (1975: 258) in a short paper revised her description
of the pidgin to "a mixture of Choctaw and Alabama." Apart from listing
selected words in these languages and Mobilian Jargon for comparison, she
gave special attention to its reduced morphology, as illustrated by personal-
pronoun and negative constructions in contrast to corresponding forms in
Choctaw, Alabama and closely related Koasati, and introduced a vowel-
deletion rule (Haas 1975: 259–60). In his book *The Mobilian Trade Language*, consisting of a historical study and vocabulary of some 150 entries,
Crawford devoted a short chapter each to Algonquian loan-words and the
pidgin's linguistic features. While principally concerned with the issue of
Mobilian Jargon's lexical resemblances to its various source languages, the
author addressed aspects of articulation, phonological processes, and morphology; in particular, he focused his description on his two principal consultants' rendering of s, š, and ł, the negative marker, and personal pronouns
in comparison with related forms in the possible languages of origin (Crawford 1978: 76–80). Similarly, the two other scholars concerned with Mobilian Jargon (Munro 1984; York 1982) have concentrated their attention on
its vocabulary, just as some of my own research (Drechsel 1979: 64–81,
101–10, 199–347; 1985; 1987*a*; 1996) has dealt with various aspects of the
lexicon.

In their focus on vocabulary, these studies have followed a long-standing
tradition of Americanist linguists concentrating on morphology along with
phonology—with a resultant neglect of other aspects of grammar such as
syntax. Only in recent years has there emerged an interest in Mobilian
Jargon's sentence patterns and related aspects of linguistic structure such
as the nature and extent of its grammatical variation (Drechsel 1979:
81–110; 1984; 1993), in tandem with explicitly syntactic studies of other
Native American pidgins (Silverstein 1972 and Thomason 1983 on Chinook
Jargon; Thomason 1980 on Delaware Jargon).

The following chapters fill earlier descriptive-analytical gaps with a comprehensive grammar of Mobilian Jargon including selected illustrations.

4

Phonology

4.1. Inventory of Basic Sounds

Among basic or major sounds, speakers of Mobilian Jargon distingished the following consonants:

(a) the voiceless stops **p**, **t**, and **k** plus the asymmetrical voiced bilabial stop **b**, the latter of which also occurred as a voiced allophonic counterpart of **p**, just as [g] did for the velar stop **k**;

(b) the voiceless palatal affricate **č**, which had variable apical-alveolar and even alveolar realization as [č̣] and [c] respectively;

(c) the voiceless fricatives **f**, **ł**, **s**, **š**, and **h**, of which **s** and **š** often appear as mere variants of each other, with the intermediate alveolar and apical-alveolar realizations of [ṣ] and [ṣ̌] (see Crawford 1978: 77–8);

(d) the nasals **m** and **n**; and

(e) the non-nasal continuants **w**, **l**, and **y** plus a rare **r**-like sound, apparently limited to a few words of non-Muskogean origin such as **rehkən** (?) 'hole' (< Tunica **ríhkuníri** 'hole in a tree' [Haas 1953: 250]) and **segaret** 'cigarette' (< French or English); **w** and **y** functioned mostly as semiconsonants in Mobilian Jargon rather than as mostly semivowels, as judged on the basis of their distribution at the syllable level.

This inventory of Mobilian Jargon consonants may be summarized in (1) (with the swung dash standing for "variable with" and the parentheses around a sound or the swung dash indicating limited occurrence of that particular sound or variation). With **r** as an infrequent exception, this inventory of consonants confirms du Ru's observation of a missing voiced alveolar stop and **r**-like sound (see quotation from du Ru above).

In addition, Mobilian Jargon exhibited three basic vowels: **e**, **a**, and **o**, which varied considerably in their phonetic realizations:

(a) **e** could change in height from [ɪ] to [ɛ], even extending to [i] and occasionally to [æ], and exhibited a greater range in its height than the corresponding front vowel in Muskogean languages, due to interference from the speakers' first languages. As a median representation of the variation in the pronunciation of the front vowel, this grammar uses the vowel symbol **e** instead of **i** as customarily used by Muskogeanists.

(1)

	Bilabial	Labio-dental	Dental/alveolar	Palatal	Velar	Glottal (faucal)
Stops and affricates						
vl.	**p**		**t; (c~)**	**č**	**k**	
	(~)				**~**	
vd.	**b**				**(g)**	
Fricatives		**f**	**ɬ; s (~) š**			**h**
Nasals	**m**		**n**			
Liquids			**l; (r)**			
Glides	**w**			**y**		

(*b*) Similarly, speakers of Mobilian Jargon pronounced **a** variably as [a], [a], [ʌ], or—on rare occasions—as [ɒ]. According to Geoffrey Kimball (personal communication), one speaker often pronounced **a** even as [ɔ].[1]

(*c*) **o** could also take the shape of [ʊ], at times [u] or [ɔ].

In a few instances, I moreover recorded [ə] as a variant of all three basic vowels in unstressed position. Such schwa variations were comparatively rare and probably exceptions rather than the rule, for the simple reason that they obliterated already minimal vowel contrasts. On the other hand, Mobilian Jargon speakers whose first language was English frequently added diphthongization in their articulation of **e**, **a**, and **o**, which remained phonemically insignificant, but immediately gave away their identity.

The basic vowels in Mobilian Jargon appear in (2). These vowels and their variants could also occur allophonically with nasalization, represented with a tilde on top. Nasalized vowels were quite widespread in Mobilian Jargon, as evident from both modern and historical recordings (for historical attestations, see Drechsel, 1996). In view of this evidence, Pamela Munro (1984: 441) erred when she suggested in her recent contrast of the pidgin with Chickasaw that "nasalized vowels are exceedingly rare in the Mobilian [Jargon] corpus." She possibly based this conclusion on a perfunctory review of Crawford's short vocabulary (1978: 81–97), and apparently did not take into consideration the evidence available in my doctoral dissertation (Drechsel 1979: 55). Yet even a closer examination of Crawford's data alone documents vowel nasalization: **tã:šwa**, a variant form for 'corn' **kaŋkã puškuš/kaŋkõ poškoš** small chicken, 'egg,' **čukmã/čukmõ** 'good,' **hatak**

---

[1] For the printer's convenience, the letter a represents the basic vowel of low central quality and its variable phonetic realizations as [a], [a], [ʌ], and even [ɒ] rather than the low front vowel known as the Boston "a."

(2)	Front	Central	Back
Mid	e ~	ə	~ o
		~	
Low		a	

hommõ 'Indian,' and **yamã** /yamõ/yo:mĩ 'yes, Mobilian Jargon;' secondary regressive nasalization of vowels also occurred in such words as **(a)kaŋka** 'chicken,' **tanči** 'corn,' **inkɛ** 'father,' **čampulɛ** 'sugar,' and **anompa/anompole** 'talk' (Crawford 1978: 82–97).[2] Further analysis of vowel nasalization in Mobilian Jargon reveals that this feature was not limited to any particular group such as French speakers with their wide use of nasalized vowels (as perhaps suggested by Crawford's data), but occurred throughout the contact speech community, including speakers of Muskogean languages and probably Southern English. Historical evidence furthermore indicates that vowel nasalization in the pidgin existed in the earliest recordings even if it was not original to Mobilian Jargon. Thus, the anonymous author of the *Essai* (Anonymous 1862 MS) already rendered nasalized vowels throughout the manuscript in characteristic French transcription as, for example, in "Kankan" or **(a)kãkã** 'chicken,' "Hinki" or **ẽke** 'father,' "Mangoula" or †**mõgola** 'friend,' and "Sapantak" or **sapõtak** 'mosquito.' Earlier, Le Page du Pratz (1758: iii. 6), writing in French, had similarly recorded the word for 'friends' as "mongoula," which he translated as '*my* friend,' probably by drawing on the French possessive pronoun "mon" or [mɔ̃] for 'my' instead of its Muskogean etymology. While speakers whose first language was French or a nasalized variety of Southern English probably reinforced this articulatory feature in Mobilian Jargon, it is most unlikely that they introduced or superimposed vowel nasalization in their transcriptions of Mobilian Jargon where there had been none. Speakers of French have clearly distinguished oral from nasal vowels in both pronunciation and spelling, and would simply have represented a non-nasalized vowel followed by a nasal consconant as double "n" or "m" plus a mute "e." More importantly, Muskogean languages have traditionally exhibited quite widespread nasalization of vowels (see Munro, forthcoming), and were probably the primary source of vowel nasalization in Mobilian Jargon.

---

[2] A reviewer of an early draft for this book suggested that Munro was still correct if she intended her observation to apply to nasalized vowel *phonemes*; but I find no such indication in her discussion, focused on Western Muskogean sources for **ela** and **ẽla** 'different, other, else, strange' rather than the phonemic status of nasalized vowels in Mobilian Jargon. The nasalized variant did not occur in the data set by Crawford (1978: 83–4), upon which Munro based her remark (for further discussion, see Sect. 5.3).

(3)   Examples

pl-	**plata** 'silver, silver money,' **pleša** 'to work'
bl-	**blaka** 'to lay down, to lie down'
kš	**kšo** 'no, not'
sp-	†**spane** 'Spaniard'
st-	†**stellepayka** 'shoe,' **stomak trabəl** 'stomach ache'
sk-	†**skale** 'bit,' †**skefoše** 'hatchet, club,' †**skona** 'intestine, bowels'
sl-	**slašo** 'fish'
šk-	**škefa** 'axe'
šn-	**šno** 'you, your'
šl-	**šla** 'Here you are! Hello! Howdy! Welcome!' **šlašo** 'fish,' †**šlokata** 'whip' (n.), †**šloko** 'horse'

4.2. *Distribution of Basic Sounds*

A word in Mobilian Jargon could begin with any consonant followed by a vowel. Initial clusters of two consonants did occur, but were not common. Attested are the initial consonant clusters shown in (3). Aside from a few combinations of bilabial stops and **l**, most consonant clusters consisted of **s** or **š** plus a voiceless stop or **l**. A word-initial affricate and a second consonant, again **l**, possibly occurred in the Muskogee-derived reconstituted word for 'horse:' †**ečo ɬako** ~ †**č(ə)loko**/†**š(ə)loko**. However, as this example illustrates, most of the initial consonant clusters in Mobilian Jargon resulted from the deletion of a preceding, unstressed vowel **e** present in the non-deleted, variant forms of **ekšo** 'no, not,' †**eskona** 'intestine, bowels,' **eškefa** 'axe,' **ešno** 'you, your,' and **ešla** 'Here you are! Hello! Howdy! Welcome!' French-derived **skale** 'bit' (< French *escalin* < Dutch *schelling* [a coin worth 12$\frac{1}{2}$ cents]) and related compounds also followed this pattern, but the variable form with initial **e** has not survived in this instance. Whereas Mobilian Jargon adopted **plata** 'silver' from Spanish as such, vowel deletion was similarly responsible for the initial consonant clusters **pl-** in **pleša** 'to work' and **bl-** in **blaka** 'to lie down, to lay down,' but in these cases applied to the vowels in the first syllable with an initial consonant; **pleša** was a variation of **pelesa** 'to work; busy,' and **blaka** derived etymologically from Alabama **bala:ka** 'to lie' and Koasati **balla:ka** 'to lie' (Munro, forthcoming).[3] Of special interest are the initial consonant clusters **sl-** and **šl-** as in **slašo** ~

---

[3] The recognition of this regularity, suggesting an unattested variable form **balaka** in Mobilian Jargon, helped to determine the source of **blaka**, unidentified in my doctoral dissertation (Drechsel 1979: 288, 289).

šlašo 'fish' and †**šlokata** 'whip' (n.) respectively, in which **sl-** or **šl-** was not the product of some initial vowel deletion, but the closest rendering of the Mobilian Jargon voiceless lateral fricative [ɫ], uncommon in the sound repertoire of non-Indian speakers. Koasati and other Muskogean Indians pronounced the same words as ɫaɫo 'fish' and †ɫokata 'whip' (see Crawford 1978: 78).

All of the known Mobilian Jargon consonants could occur singly in inter-vocalic position. Intervocalic consonants could undergo gemination re-corded for all except bilabial stops, affricates, ɫ, **h**, and **w**. Double consonants were not always easy to distinguish from the single ones of the same place and manner of articulation. Geminates and their singular counterparts usually varied with each other without any effect on meaning, and thus carried no distinctive functional value, as we would expect in a language-contact situation with different rules regarding gemination. If there were any true minimal pairs in which single consonants contrasted with their related geminate forms, such were few, as possibly in the instances of (4). What makes the status of these examples as true minimal pairs question-able is the fact that half of the four examples for geminate consonants are reconstituted and there are few independent, modern data to support them.

However, clusters with two different consonants within a word ($-C_1C_2-$) were common in Mobilian Jargon, and regularly occurred in the combina-tions shown in (5) and possibly in others. Although about a quarter of these consonant clusters are reconstituted, they were all well within the realm of

---

(4) Single consonants	Geminate forms
†**ala** 'to arrive'	†**alla** 'child, baby'
bes(s)a 'to see'	†**bessa** 'blackberry'
ese 'to get, to take, to receive'	**esse** 'deer'
hanale 'leg'	**han(n)ale** 'six'[4]

---

[4] My doctoral dissertation (Drechsel 1979: 57) also listed the pair of **sok(k)o** 'muscadine' and †**sok(k)o** 'thick', which—in light of additional considerations—appears a questionable example of a minimal pair for the demonstration of phonemic geminates in Mobilian Jargon. Not only would the phonemic contrast between these two words have been minimal, if exis-tent at all, due to the occurrence of the single consonant **k** and its geminate variant in both; but there also exists a close semantic relationship between the two words, as the Mobilian Jargon word for 'muscadine,' a grape of the southern United States with a skin thicker than regular grapes, probably derived from the word for 'thick' (Hiram F. Gregory, personal com-munication). More significant is the revised if still uncertain reconstitution of the latter word as †**sotko** (?).

(5)

		p	t	c	č	k	b	f	ł	s	š	h	m	n	l	w	y
	p														pl		
	t					tk						†th			tl		
	č														†ǯ		
	k	kp	kt	kc	kč		kb	kf	kł	ks	kš	kh	km	kn	kl	†kw	†ky
	b														bl		
	ł	†łp	łt		łč	łk											
C_1	s		st			sk								†sn	sl		
	š	šp	št			šk								šn	šl	šw	
	h	hp	ht		hč	hk	hb						†hm	hn	†hl	†hw	†hy
	m	mp					mb										
	n		nt		nč	nk						nh			†nl		
	l	†lp	†lt		lč	lk	lb	†lf				†lh				†lw	
	y	yp				†yk	yb								yl		

possibility. In contrast, clusters consisting of three consonants were exceptional, and appear only in single reconstituted instances of **-mph-** and **-lhp-** as in †**amphata** 'plate' and †**alhpetta(?)** 'to ram a gun.' Their absence in modern recordings of Mobilian Jargon as well as their overall rarity suggest an interpretation in terms of simple consonant clusters plus insignificant nasalization or secondary aspiration rather than a continuous sequence of three distinct consonants.

Consonant clusters usually did not occur in final position with the exception of the particle-like instrumental †**ešt**, which—significantly—did not appear by itself in any attestations other than in compounds and apparently assumed almost the form and function of a prefix (see Sects. 5.5 and 5.6). However, Mobilian Jargon words could end in a single consonant as attested for **p, t, k, f, s, š, n**, and **l**. Their occurrence was rather sporadic, as most words ended in a vowel.

Any of the three basic vowels could occur at the beginning, in the middle, or at the end of a Mobilian Jargon word. Geminate vowels did not exist *per se*, and vowel lengthening appeared simply to be the result of stress (see Sect. 4.4). Yet clusters consisting of two different vowels were possible, as attested for **ea, ae**, and **oa**. These vowel combinations were infrequent, occurred predominantly in reconstituted forms, and exhibited a limited distribution as to position within a word; see (6). The available examples suggest that **ea** appeared only in mid and final position, **ae** solely in mid position, and **oa** exclusively at the end of a word. Some modern attestations of **ea** and **ae** were also variants of forms with the epenthetic glide **y**. The limited number of attestations should, however, caution one against extrapolating these patterns to Mobilian Jargon in general.

(6)   Examples

ea	**bea** 'beer;' †**čeašwa** (?) 'nerve;' †**es(s)e nea pešeleče** 'woodcock'; **kane(y)a** 'gone, lost; to go away, to leave;' †**peakemena** 'persimmon;' **te(y)ak** 'pine'
ae	†**okhaeyãle** 'squint-eyed;' **ta(y)ek** 'female; woman, lady, wife, girl, Indian woman'
oa	†**ak(k)oa** 'to descend;' †**balaykestafoa** (?) 'circle;' †**ešt pãšpõa** 'broom;' †**haše tabokoa** 'noon, midday'

(7)   V   CV
       VC   CVC

4.3. Syllabic Structure

Mobilian Jargon syllables exhibited the combinations of consonants and vowels shown in (7). These syllables reveal an overall pattern of (C)V(C), with C standing for any consonant and V for any vowel, oral or nasal. There is only one, at that questionable instance that does not fit this pattern: the single consonant †**š** as a variable form of †**eš** 'you' (sg., pl.).

Mobilian Jargon exhibited few obvious constraints in the combination of these syllables except with respect to their number. While including single-syllable words, much of the recently recorded vocabulary consisted of entries with two or three syllables, and some with four syllables. Except for compounds including antonym constructions (see Sect. 5.5), there occurred only a few single words with more than four syllables: †**anõpesače** 'to aim,' †**balaykestafoa** 'circle' (n.), †**hapõnak(o)lo** 'to listen,' †**nakbatepole** 'rainbow,' †**okhaeyãle** 'squint-eyed,' the second part of the compound †**pala ayõ(he)keya** 'candlestick,' and †**peakemena** 'persimmon.' All these examples are reconstituted, and suggest that multiple-syllable words thrived only during Mobilian Jargon's better days and that their etymologies may derive from compounds, albeit currently not analyzable as such.

The linguistic data additionally reveal a tendency for speakers of Mobilian Jargon to have favored an overall syllable structure alternating between a consonant and a vowel. As already noted in the preceding section, clusters of three consonants were rare, and possibly were merely nasalized or aspirated variations of double consonants. Mobilian Jargon speakers even broke up clusters of two consonants or vowels by inserting a vowel or consonant respectively. Vowel epenthesis was evident in variant forms for the widely used word **(a)čokma** 'good; well' in both modern and historical attestations: **čokəma** or "shoke me" (Dresel 1920–2: 407), †**čokoma** or "tchoucouma" (Anonymous 1862 MS: 45), †**čokomã** or "tchoukouman" (Tixier 1940: 56), **cokəma**, **čekama** or "chikke-mau" (Stiles 1794: 92; cf. Sherwood 1983: 441), "chicamaw" (Flores 1972: 72), and "tchikamá" (Gatschet 1886 MS: 11). On the other hand, the epenthesis of consonants such as **y** appeared variably in vowel clusters as in the case of a few examples in (6). A historical instance of consonant epenthesis is available in an account by Antoine Simon Le Page du Pratz (1758: iii. 7) with "*Apas-Ich*, manges" ('Eat!') or †**apas eš**, literally 'Eat you!' with an apparently epenthetic **s**. This example illustrates his own restructuring of a standard Mobilian Jargon phrase such as **ešno apa** 'You eat!' following French grammar. In this case, Le Page du Pratz reversed the order of pronoun and verb following French reflexive constructions, and inserted what appears to be the French verbal suffix -*s* for the second person singular, thus breaking up the sequence of two vowels between the verb and the subsequent pronoun (for further informaton, see Sect. 9.3).

An alternating consonant–vowel pattern could also come about as a result of various phonological processes, including the coalescence of two contiguous vowels and perhaps consonants as well as aphaeresis among other possible alternations (see Sect. 8.2).

4.4. Stress and Vowel Length

Historical and modern recordings of Mobilian Jargon give no indications for any significant suprasegmental features except for rising intonation in questions. The pidgin exhibited only one other easily identifiable suprasegmental stress at the word level, which, however, had a fairly regular pattern and had no distinctive grammatical function. In bisyllabic words, stress occurred most frequently on the final syllable, and in trisyllabic words on the penultimate one. Words consisting of four syllables exhibited stress on either of the medial syllables. Antonymous compounds constructed with the negative marker **-(e)kšo** usually followed a highly regular pattern of stress, occurring on the final syllable of the entire negative construction irrespective of whether it consisted of three or four syllables (see Sect. 5.5).

Yet stress was not fully predictable, and could in fact vary, occasionally even in the pronunciation of the same word. I recorded the same speaker switching patterns of prominence in the time-span of seconds, as, for example, in the frequently used word **čokma** for 'good; well,' pronounced as [čúkma] [čukmá], or [čukma], the latter without any primary stress. Some variations could be the result of formal elicitation, in which the speaker changed stress in repetitions to articulate a previously unstressed syllable more distinctly. Other variations in prominence were undoubtedly due to different stress patterns in the speakers' various first languages. Since systematic variable data have no longer been available for this contact language, it has been difficult to deduce any further regularities of stress or to determine their underlying rules. The existing evidence offers no indications for the conditioning of prominence by the immediate linguistic environment or as a result of some grammatical function.

Stress concurred with two other phonological processes in Mobilian Jargon. On the one hand, prominence in the Indians' speech apparently kept the front and back vowels in unstressed syllable(s) quite high, as, for example, in **noksõpa** [nʊksõmpa] 'afraid, frightened, scared' and **benele** [bɪnélɪ] 'to sit (down), to say, to live.' On the other hand, stress resulted in some lengthening of prominent vowels, as expected. Such vowel lengthening remained secondary, extended to less than the double length of an unstressed vowel in modern recordings, and—like stress—had no distinctive effect on meaning. The only exception was the emphatic or intensifying adverb **fe(h)na** 'very, especially, really; intimate,' which could exhibit an extra long vowel in the first syllable, lending phonetic support in proportion to the intended intensity. In this case, some speakers might draw out **e** more than twice the length of a regular vowel for extra emphasis.

4.5. Basic Sound and Orthography

What systematic phonological data were still available from field recordings reveals considerable variation. This finding is hardly surprising in view of the fact that Mobilian Jargon as an interlingual medium and a second language reflected substantial interference from its speakers' diverse first languages.

In its variant forms, Mobilian Jargon incorporated elements of the phonemic systems of several different, mutually unintelligible, even unrelated languages. Their phonologies overlapped in part, neutralized some sound distinctions, and interfered or conflicted in other domains. For example, Choctaw speakers of Mobilian Jargon recognized [s] and [š] as functionally distinct sounds or separate phonemes, whereas speakers of Koasati, another Muskogean language, considered these sounds merely as non-distinctive or allophonic variants. A similar relationship applied to French and certain dialects of Southern English that merged distinctions between these two sibilants. Mobilian Jargon speakers with a native Muskogean-language background were also inclined to perceive fewer distinctions in vowel height than French, Spanish, or English speakers. Conversely, most Europeans, unfamiliar with the lateral fricative, had great difficulty identifying or producing [ɬ] as such, and usually rendered it as [sl], [šl], or [š] (see Sect. 8.2).

By reflecting phonological distinctions of several languages, Mobilian Jargon exhibited a polysystemic phonology, which raises questions about its phonemic representation and underlying principles of organization. A first-sight solution might be to adopt the sound system of the source language with the largest number of phonemic contrasts; it would account for corresponding ones in the pidgin, but could handle neither sound distinctions introduced by speakers of another language, nor phonological neutralizations, nor any new developments. For the same reasons, the monosystemic concept of *phoneme* is inadequate, if not inappropriate, to refer to sound distinctions in what really were conflicting phonologies of the speakers' first languages.

Such a polysystemic sound system reflecting interference from different languages recalls the description and analysis by Michael Silverstein (1972: 382–5) for Chinook Jargon, which exhibited even more phonological variations—the result of a larger diversity in the speakers' native languages and a greater complexity in their sound systems. To describe the convergence of phonemic contrasts of different languages in a pidgin, Silverstein (1972: 383) has introduced the concept of *interlingual archiphonemes*—that is phonological neutralizations resulting from language interference in contact situations.

Similarly, this book avoids the monosystemic concept of *phoneme* for Mobilian Jargon, and employs *basic sound* instead to refer to any phonemic contrasts that some, but not necessarily all speakers recognized for the pidgin. The concept of basic sound permits for the necessary flexibility in the description and analysis of major phonological distinctions in Mobilian Jargon, and best appears in a broadly phonetic, quasi-phonemic transcription as indicated by bold print rather than in phonemic slashes.

An orthography based on basic sounds can account for all the expected phonological variation in Mobilian Jargon, and is sufficiently integrated and consistent to prove useful in the description of other grammatical aspects, to serve as a general orthography, and to permit easy retrieval of lexical entries in a vocabulary (see Drechsel, 1996). This orthography continues making use of the symbols in the consonant and vowel charts in (1) and (2), and reverts to variant symbols in parentheses (such as **c** and ə), and phonetic transcriptions, as there arises a need for them. Such might be the case in describing the initial alveolar affricate in **cokfe** 'rabbit' when pronounced by a Koasati Indian, who would rely on his or her native [cokfi] rather than the Choctaw or Chickasaw cognate [čokfi] as the word's source. On the other hand, schwa (ə) is necessary to indicate an unstressed, neutralized vowel of mid-central quality, as it occurred in instances of epenthesis such as **cokəma** 'good; well' in contrast to **čokma**. In this case, the underlying quality of the epenthetic vowel is difficult, if not impossible, to determine, and could reflect the influence of either the initial or the final vowel (i.e. a partial progressive or regressive assimilation) or perhaps a combination of both. Occasionally, there also arises a need to specify additional articulatory details such as nasalization, aspiration, stress, and vowel length, easily supplemented in a phonetic transcription.

5

Lexicon

5.1. General Aspects

The recorded vocabulary of Mobilian Jargon consists of some 1,250 entries. More than 500 words make up modern recordings from recent speakers of the pidgin, while about 750 entries are reconstitutions of historical attestations, based on phonetic triangulation (see Sect. 3.3). The size of the attested lexicon discourages its inclusion here, and warrants a separate study, including a Mobilian Jargon–English section (with early attestations and comparative evidence in source languages) and an English–Mobilian Jargon index (see Drechsel, 1996). The lexicon has still exhibited several traits of a general nature that bear on the pidgin's grammar, use, and history and that deserve closer attention here.

First, words in Mobilian Jargon were fundamentally invariable in form, and lacked morphological markings in the form of inflections or affixations that distinguished one kind of words from another, except in the case of the negative marker **-(e)kšo** and possibly the instrumental **ešt** (see Sect. 5.5). Accordingly, there was no inflectional morphology or accompanying morphophonological variation. Without formal distinctions at the level of morphology, speakers determined the syntactic function of a word solely by its relation to others—that is by its position within a phrase or sentence, and its larger sociolinguistic context (see Chapter 6).

The analytic nature of Mobilian Jargon did not keep its users from recognizing several lexical categories relevant for syntax: verbs, nouns, pronouns, adverbs, adjectives; the negative, a past-tense marker, an instrumental nominalizer, and other words of grammatical function such as postpositions and interrogatives; plus exclamations, interjections, and words of approval and acknowledgment. Although fundamentally invariable in form, many Mobilian Jargon parts of speech operated in more than one grammatical function. A prominent example is polysemous **lašpa**, which could variably mean 'hot,' 'to be hot,' 'heat,' 'summer,' or even 'year,' depending on its grammatical and pragmatic context.

Previously estimated to range in number of words from a few hundred to a few thousand, the lexicon of Mobilian Jargon was probably larger than 1,250 entries, but still remained limited in size, even during its heyday. To make up for any shortages in their vocabulary, speakers borrowed from their native tongues or other languages, and did so quite freely, as illustrated

by subsequent examples. This fact leads to the question of the etymological composition of Mobilian Jargon, by nature a *Mischsprache* or a mixed
language, as evident from its lexicon (see Sect. 5.2). Of special interest are
words from two sources—Chickasaw on the one hand, Algonquian and
perhaps other native languages of northeastern North America on the other
(see Sects. 5.3 and 5.4 respectively). For an alternative means of lexical
expansion, speakers of Mobilian Jargon employed compounding, that is the
creation of two- or multi-word phrases with meanings of their own (see
Sects. 5.5 and 5.6), whose discussion conveniently leads to an examination
of the pidgin's syntax in Chapter 6.

5.2. Etymological Composition

The principal names of Mobilian Jargon or the Chickasaw-Choctaw trade
language, sometimes known simply as "Choctaw," "Chickasaw," or varieties
thereof (see Sect. 9.1), have left the erroneous impression that its lexicon,
no less than its grammar, was the same as that of the native languages
spoken by the Native Americans of these names. On other occasions, the
intertribal medium has been identified as the first language of the Mobilian Indians, who lent their name to the pidgin; by virtue of this association,
they presumably spoke a Western Muskogean language as their "mother
tongue," although there exists no record.

Once European colonists discovered that Mobilian Jargon was not the
only indigenous language of Louisiana, but a lingua franca in use between
linguistically diverse native peoples, they came to recognize contributions
from different indigenous languages in its etymological composition. After
Thomas S. Woodward (1939 [1859]: 79; see also Preliminaries to Part II)
described Mobilian Jargon as a hybrid of Creek or Muskogee, Choctaw,
Chickasaw, Natchez, and Apalachee, Mary R. Haas (1975: 258) analyzed the
lexicon of one speaker recorded by Crawford as "a mixture of Choctaw and
Alabama" in the first modern study of Mobilian Jargon. With additional
data, Crawford (1978: 76) observed the following about the pidgin's lexical
make-up:

An examination of the more than one hundred and fifty words and phrases in the
vocabulary shows that the greatest portion of them are Western Muskogean and
closely resemble Choctaw and Chickasaw. Some of them, about twenty items, resemble Alabama and Koasati as closely as they resemble Choctaw and Chickasaw.
About fourteen items are closer to Alabama and Koasati than to Choctaw and
Chickasaw. Two words which resemble Choctaw are ultimately from Spanish. One
word which resembles Choctaw and Alabama is ultimately from French. Three
words, one by way of Alabama, came in from English. One word apparently entered
directly from French and another directly from Algonquian.

Crawford (1978: 76–80) documented his analysis by listing the glosses of his Mobilian Jargon vocabulary according to origin or resemblances in its source languages, supplemented by comments on their similarities and divergences.

A comparable analysis of the Mobilian Jargon vocabulary now attested (Drechsel, 1996) would produce similar proportions: a majority of resemblances in Choctaw and in Western Muskogean at large, smaller portions of apparent Eastern Muskogean and common Muskogean elements, and incidental occurrences of Algonquian and European origin next to a few words of mixed, uncertain, or unidentified sources. A careful examination yields a slightly higher percentage of Eastern Muskogean elements in my recordings as compared with Crawford's, although both sets of data originate from the greater vicinity of Elton in southwestern Louisiana and within the time span of just a few years. Moreover, a comparison of the modern vocabulary with that by the anonymous author (Anonymous 1862 MS) reveals a substantially larger Choctaw and Western Muskogean element in the etymological composition of the latter (for details, including figures and percentages, see Sect. 8.3).

These digressing proportions in the etymological composition of Mobilian Jargon can be explained by several considerations. For one, Crawford's vocabulary of some 150 entries is small in comparison with the latest set of data (more than three times larger) or with the lexicon at large, including historic data (more than eight times as many listings). In a small sample, any increase in the number of entries can significantly alter the proportions of the resemblances in one language in relation to those of another for purely statistical reasons. Yet the proportions of etymologies have also changed with the availability of new and better comparative data for Muskogean languages (see Munro, forthcoming), which—while insignificant in single instances—have accumulated in numbers. Most importantly, some of the changing proportions are the result of including historical data, which introduce the factors of time and space. The entire recorded vocabulary reveals numerous synonyms with double, triple, or even some multiple entries with resemblances in different languages, which reflect alternating influences by speakers of diverse first-language backgrounds. This fact points to variations and shifts in the etymological make-up of Mobilian Jargon's lexicon from community to community and over periods.

Changes in the proportions of resemblances indicate that spatial and temporal variations played a more significant role in the lexicon of Mobilian Jargon than is first evident from modern data. A closer examination of the latter reveals a distinct bias towards Choctaw. All of the last fluent speakers of Mobilian Jargon were Choctaw Indians or people of part-Choctaw descent, who had acquired Choctaw as their first language, often together with another such as Alabama or Koasati. Those who remembered some pidgin, but were members of other native communities or non-Indians had learned it primarily in association with Choctaw-speaking people. The predominant Choctaw and Western Muskogean influence in the anonymous author's vocabulary (Anonymous 1862 MS) similarly indicates Choctaw from whom the source, a Creole, had learned Mobilian Jargon. Historical documentation indeed confirms a community of Choctaw in the greater area of Opelousas at the time (see Drechsel and Makuakāne 1982*b*: 21–3). The Choctaw language thus was as a major source for the pidgin's persistence and survival (see Sect. 9.4).

Speakers of Mobilian Jargon in other communities and over time could and did substantially change the composition of its vocabulary via lexical replacement. Both modern and historical documents indicate that, in different locations and at various periods, there existed varieties of Mobilian Jargon that exhibited greater proportions of other languages than Choctaw in their lexica (see Sect. 8.3). This conclusion raises the question of relevance for determining the etymological composition of Mobilian Jargon.

If the etymological composition of modern Mobilian Jargon were to serve as a measurement of the input by different languages throughout its entire history, there exists a great risk of drawing conclusions on the basis of limited evidence and ignoring the full sociolinguistic complexity of the pidgin, in particular its role as a second language with varying vocabularies over space and time. The modern lexical composition of Mobilian Jargon permits no more than a few conclusions about its extended past, and hardly constitutes conclusive evidence about its origin. For this reason, Crawford was fully justified in his reluctance to name a single and exclusive source for Mobilian Jargon's vocabulary and to draw from it conclusions about the pidgin's roots—contrary to the expectations of apparently simple answers evinced by one reviewer of his book *The Mobilian Trade Language* (Dumas 1981: 264). Yet the study of Mobilian Jargon's lexical composition, keeping in mind its variation, can provide some limited indications of the diversity of contributions and perhaps the speakers' first-language backgrounds. The nature and extent of influences by one or the other language in Mobilian Jargon, determined on the basis of a shared lexicon, may also offer some historical insights of a short time-depth, as illustrated in the cases of Chickasaw and Algonquian languages.

5.3. Nature and Extent of Chickasaw Influences

That the modern etymological composition of a pidgin reveals little about its long-term past would hardly need emphasis were it not for the fact that conclusions of precisely such a nature have repeatedly appeared with respect to the influence of Chickasaw or, rather, its absence in Mobilian Jargon. Whereas Haas (1953: 195) had once described the pidgin as "based to a large extent on Chickasaw," other scholars have underestimated or rejected Chickasaw elements in Mobilian Jargon, an equally erroneous portrayal in need of revision.

In a study of Louisiana French, William A. Read (1963 [1931]: 77) described Mobilian Jargon and its lexicon in terms of their similarity to Choctaw, apparently at the exclusion of influences from Chickasaw and other Muskogean languages:

To British traders it [Mobilian Jargon] became known as the Chickasaw trade jargon, because of the close resemblance between the Chickasaw and the Choctaw or Mobilian [Jargon] vocabulary. Now the Mobilian [Jargon] is based chiefly on Choctaw, and contains indeed so much of the Choctaw vocabulary that this circumstance proved to be decisive in rendering the influence of Choctaw greater on the French language than that of any other Indian dialect.

While there is no doubt about a dominant influence of Choctaw in Mobilian Jargon and its impact on French, Read offered no support for his conclusion. When he made this observation in the early 1930s and even some thirty years later with the publication of a second edition, there existed little comparative evidence for Western Muskogean languages to permit such sweeping conclusions. Quite possibly, Read based his conclusion on the anonymous *Essai* of 1862, which he interpreted as "virtually pure Choctaw" (Read 1940: 546) rather than as Mobilian Jargon.

Several years ago, Kennith H. York (1982) raised the issue of the principal source language in a summary essay largely based on Haas's analysis and Crawford's book. Disputing the role of Chickasaw or some closely related dialect, he argued: "A look at the entire vocabulary recorded in Mobilian [Jargon] by Crawford, however, indicates that the trade language is much closer to Choctaw than he wishes to credit" (York 1982: 144). Like Read, York provided neither comparative data nor any other justification in support of his conclusion.

Pamela Munro (1984) then addressed the question of the role of Chickasaw in the lexicon of Mobilian Jargon in her essay "On the Western Muskogean Source for Mobilian." In a comparison of the Mobilian Jargon vocabulary collected by Crawford (1978: 81–97) with Chickasaw data of her own, Munro (1984: 439–45) examined words of Western Muskogean origin in order to determine the pidgin's closer affinity to either Chickasaw or Choctaw. These included pronominal forms for 'I,' 'you,' and 'we' as well as words for the following English entries: 'big,' 'cornmeal,' 'different,' 'everything,' 'father,' 'frightened,' 'give,' 'good,' 'green,' 'head,' 'laugh,' 'marriage,' 'name,' 'night,' 'old,' 'rice,' 'run,' 'sharp,' 'short,' 'sick,' 'tall,' 'this,' 'tobacco,' 'town,' 'turkey,' 'white,' 'woman,' 'work,' and 'yesterday.' Munro classified these words into four categories as regards their similarity to Chickasaw: (1) lack of related Chickasaw forms or else presence of substantial segmental differences between the comparable Mobilian Jargon and Chickasaw words, applying to eighteen to twenty of the above twenty-nine items; (2) presence of five Chickasaw forms exhibiting fewer phonetic, semantic, or pragmatic similarities than the comparable Choctaw variants; (3) greater similarity to Chickasaw, Alabama, or even Koasati than to Choctaw, as in the cases of 'name' and 'sharp;' and (4) no greater similarity to either Chickasaw, Choctaw, or Alabama in four instances, including 'different.' On the basis of this evidence, Munro (1984: 447) suggested a conspicuous dissimilarity between Mobilian Jargon and corresponding Chickasaw forms:

Many of the proposed Western Muskogean sources for Mobilian words are simply not used in Chickasaw, while others occur in markedly different form. Significantly, there seem to be no lexical items (other than the independent personal pronouns, which show as much similarity to Alabama as to Chickasaw) which show a clear phonological similarity to Chickasaw rather than Choctaw, and no items at all where there is a potential Chickasaw source but no corresponding Choctaw form exists.

Munro did not find any distinctive Chickasaw influences among the lexical items of Western Muskogean origin, and concluded that Chickasaw could hardly have served as a major lexical source for Mobilian Jargon. She called into question any fundamental role that the Chickasaw language might have played in the origin and history of the pidgin partially named after it.[1]

Yet in drawing this conclusion, apparently neither Munro nor York had considered all the evidence for Mobilian Jargon already available. There was a variant form for at least one word that, on the basis of Munro's reasoning, reflected the influence of Chickasaw or some closely related dialect rather than Choctaw and that she had evidently overlooked. For 'run' in Mobilian Jargon, Munro cited only Choctaw-derived **balili**, which she contrasted with the Chickasaw cognate **malili** and included in her first category (Munro 1984: 444). But precisely such a variant appears in a sample of Mobilian Jargon by a person of Biloxi and Pascagoula descent as attested by John R. Swanton (1911: 32) and recognized by Crawford (1978: 91): **maleli̇**' or [maleli] 'to run (like a horse or other animal).' This sample is identifiable as Mobilian Jargon rather than Chickasaw or some closely related dialect by reference to sociolinguistic clues as well as a distinctive

---

[1] The following draws on an earlier essay (Drechsel 1987*a*) in response to Munro's, but includes some revisions based on new and better comparative data as well as valuable suggestions by Munro.

pattern of negative constructions in the accompanying data (see (86) in Sect. 9.3). This instance thus does not hold up Munro's conclusion of missing Chickasaw resemblances in Crawford's vocabulary of Mobilian Jargon.

Furthermore, for a number of lexical items in Munro's list, there existed synonymous variable forms that resemble common Western Muskogean equivalents. They belong to the category of those items for which a decision between either Chickasaw or Choctaw as prime source would be difficult to reach. For 'different,' there existed not only **i:la** corresponding to Choctaw **ila** (see Crawford 1978: 83; Munro 1984: 441), but also a variant nasalized form **ẽla**, which related as much to Chickasaw **ĩla** as to the corresponding Choctaw form.[2] For 'sharp,' there was—in addition to Eastern Muskogean-derived **(h)alokpa** and its possible resemblance in Chickasaw— the common Western Muskogean form †**halopa** as in "Alloupa Choukoulitché" (Anonymous 1862 MS: 15) or †**halopa šoɬeče** 'to sharpen' (literally: 'sharp' + 'to grind'). For 'white,' speakers of Mobilian Jargon used not only **hat(t)a**, but also **toh(o)be**, which—without the second, epenthetic vowel— corresponds to the standard term **tohbi** 'white' in both Chickasaw and Choctaw (Munro 1984: 444). Likewise, 'work' in Mobilian Jargon was not limited to one word, **pelesa**, which Munro (1984: 445) derived from Choctaw; I also recorded **toksale**, which she would probably consider as a good example for a form deriving from either Choctaw or Chickasaw. These instances thus complicate matters further.[3]

Munro (1984: 447) asserted not to have found any distinctive Chickasaw influences in my extended Mobilian Jargon lexicon either. In many

---

[2] In my original response to Munro's article, I erroneously argued that Mobilian Jargon **ẽla** reflected the influence of exclusively Chickasaw rather than common Western Muskogean, and incorrectly classified it with 'run' (Drechsel 1987a: 22). Nasalization of vowels was a nondistinctive variable of pronunciation in Mobilian Jargon (see Sect. 4.1), and may at best have had some sociolinguistic significance, possibly by identifying the speaker's first language or dialect and thus helping to reveal his or her ethnic identity.

[3] For 'name,' Munro (1984: 443) contrasted Mobilian Jargon **olčifo** with Chickasaw **hoɬčifo** 'to be named' and Alabama **holčifa**, and considered this Mobilian Jargon word to exhibit at best a questionable resemblance to Chickasaw and a closer relationship to Alabama. In a footnote, Munro (1984: 446 n. 10) further argued following Haas and Crawford that the **l** in **olčifo** was a noun-forming infix, suggesting another tie to Alabama and an additional difference from Western Muskogean languages, in which historically related /l/ (assimilated to [ɬ] if followed by a voiceless consonant) is not a true nominalizer but a "passive" infix. While I would agree with Munro that Mobilian Jargon **olčifo** shows a greater resemblance to the equivalent form in Alabama or even Koasati **holcifo** 'name' rather than Chickasaw, her case for syntactic functions in the identification of resemblances does not apply here because grammatical categories such as the infix **-l-** were insignificant in Mobilian Jargon. Its speakers adopted words with particles without consideration of their syntactic functions, and used them interchangeably as nouns, verbs, adjectives, and so on, lacking morphological alterations. Likewise, there was little, if any, restriction with respect to permissible combinations of particular types of words except word order (see Chapter 6). For example, unlike the Chickasaw quantifier **lawa**, which apparently modifies nouns only (Munro 1984: 446 n. 10), its corresponding form in Mobilian Jargon qualified different kinds of words, among them nouns, verbs, and adjectives, and functioned also as an intensifier, as in **lašpa lawa** 'very hot' in (35) in Sect. 6.2.

instances, she dismissed it as less reliable than Crawford's, because it included data from speakers who were no longer fully fluent in the pidgin, a point that applies equally to Crawford's data (see Crawford 1978: 60–2). However, all the recordings by the less fluent speakers have received a careful review in light of the data provided by the more knowledgeable consultants, Crawford's recordings, and historical documentation, and conform closely with all three. The vocabulary that I have compiled has incorporated systematic comparisons with resemblances in likely source languages, which provide further support.

A closer examination by York and Munro of my extended Mobilian Jargon vocabulary and its resemblances in various possible source languages, already available at the time of their research (Drechsel 1979: 240–347), would have demonstrated several distinctive Chickasaw influences in addition to 'run.' Similarly, my revised vocabulary (see Drechsel, 1996) not only reveals some 500 entries or about 40 per cent of the entire vocabulary with resemblances in Western Muskogean—that is both Choctaw and Chickasaw; it also includes several instances that—at least on the basis of the comparative data currently available—reflect the influence of Chickasaw or some closely related dialect rather than Choctaw or some other Muskogean language (for comparative data, see Munro, forthcoming):

(8) 'arm', 'hand' (plus related compounds such as 'finger,' 'finger nail,' 'finger ring,' 'fist,' and 'thumb') †**elbak** ("elback" (Anonymous 1862 MS: 39)) < Chickasaw **ilbak** 'hand' in contrast to Choctaw **ibbak** 'hand.'

'aunt': **eškose** (?) < Chickasaw **iško?si** 'maternal aunt' versus Koasati **isko:si** and apparently without any corresponding form in Choctaw

'axe': †**oskefa** ("osquifa" [Anonymous 1862 MS: 54]) < Chickasaw **oksīfa** (including a metathesis of the first two consonants) in contrast to Choctaw **iskīfa** 'bird' (plus related compounds such as 'feather'): †**foše** ("fouchi" (Anonymous 1862 MS: 30)) < Chickasaw **foši** in contrast to Choctaw **hoši** or Alabama/Koasati **fo:si**

'eye': †**ešken** ("esquen" (Bourgeois 1788: 297)) < Chickasaw **iškin** in contrast to Choctaw **niškin**[4]

'flat' ††**empa** (?; "liampa" [Bourgeois 1788: 269]) < Chickasaw **łimpa** 'lying on one's stomach' in contrast to Choctaw **łi:pa** 'turned over'

'name': **hołčefo** < Chickasaw **hołcifo** in contrast to Choctaw **hohcifo**

---

[4] The Chickasaw and Choctaw words for 'eye' may ultimately have an Algonquian origin (see Sect. 5.4).

'run': **malele** ("malilé" (Anonymous 1862 MS: 16); "mạlelî' " (Swanton 1911:32)) < Chickasaw **malili** in contrast to Choctaw **balili**

'star': †**foček** ("foutchick" (Anonymous 1862 MS: 33)) < Chickasaw **focik** in contrast to Choctaw **ficik**

'string', 'cord': †**polona** ("poulona" (Anonymous 1862 MS: 54)) < Chickasaw **polona** 'thread' in contrast to Choctaw **pono:la** 'cotton'

'throat', 'neck': †**nonka** ("nonqua" (Bourgeois 1788: 297)) < Chickasaw **inonka?** 'voice, throat' in contrast to the Choctaw prefix **nok-** 'neck, throat' or **ikõlla** 'neck'

'we', 'us': **pošno** < Chickasaw **pošno** 'we' in contrast to Choctaw **pišno** 'we' or Alabama **posno** 'we'

Over the years, the original list of Mobilian Jargon words resembling Chickasaw rather than any other language (Drechsel 1987*a*: 23–4) has undergone some revision with a few subtractions and additions. Similarly, one or the other of the above comparisons may require amendment with better comparative data for Muskogean languages, possibly reducing the number of Chickasaw resemblances in Mobilian Jargon. Alternatively, there is an equally good chance that additional historical documentation of the pidgin yet to be uncovered will reveal still other Chickasaw resemblances.

Significantly, two-thirds of the above entries—all other than those for 'aunt,' 'name,' 'run,' and 'we'/'us'—are items reconstituted on the basis of historical information rather than recently recorded data. This fact might at first render one suspicious about the accuracy of these early attestations; but such fears are without justification in this case. The major source is the anonymous *Essai*. Although collected more than a century ago and lacking phonetic transcription, this vocabulary, with its sizable number of entries, provides consistent information and sufficient phonetic detail to permit precise reconstitutions in all of the above instances and to leave little doubt about their pronunciation. Some of the anonymous author's attestations also find independent confirmation in other historical and modern recordings, as in the case of 'run.'

A closer examination of both modern and historical lexical evidence for Mobilian Jargon hence demonstrates a greater amount of Chickasaw influence in its lexicon than is evident solely from recent recordings. This conclusion receives support from non-linguistic historical references, which confirm that Chickasaw Indians played a notable role in the pidgin's early recorded history. The first reference to what was clearly Mobilian Jargon, dated 1699 and provided by the French explorer Pierre Le Moyne, Sieur d'Iberville, already listed the Chickasaw among its speakers (Margry 1876–86: iv. 412). A contemporary, François Jolliet de Montigny, called the pidgin simply "la langue des Chicachas" (Gosselin 1906: 38). More importantly, the singularly perceptive observer of colonial life in Louisiana of the early eighteenth century, Antoine Le Page du Pratz (1758: ii. 218–19, 242) alluded to Mobilian Jargon as "la Langue Tchicacha corrompue" ('the corrupted Chickasaw language') as one among its many names. He also suggested that the Chickasaw were one of the major centers in the larger speech community of Mobilian Jargon when he recognized "toutes les Nations qui sont dans les environs des Tchicachas" ('all the peoples that are in the vicinity of the Chickasaw') among its speakers. Le Page du Pratz (1758: iii. 89) further cited a Yazoo Indian by the name of "Moncacht-apé," a neighbor and friend of the Chickasaw, from whom "vient la Langue du Pays, (la Langue vulgaire;)" ('came the country's language (the common language)')—that is Mobilian Jargon. He observed that even the Choctaw Indians, traditionally hostile towards the Chickasaw, "entremêlent quelques mots de la Langue Tchicacha" ('intersperse some words of the Chickasaw language') in their Mobilian Jargon speech (Le Page du Pratz 1758: ii. 219). Authors of historical documents from other periods (such as Louis Narcisse Baudry des Lozières and Thomas S. Woodward) similarly suggest Chickasaw elements in Mobilian Jargon, although without further details (see Sect. 8.3).

In the nineteenth century, the influence of Chickasaw on Mobilian Jargon began waning as the pidgin's speech community declined in size. With the exception of a few Mobilian Jargon examples recorded among the Alabama-Coushatta in eastern Texas, all the modern linguistic data on the pidgin originated within the boundaries of modern Louisiana (see Crawford 1978: 60–2 and Sect. 9.4). Similarly, most of its historical attestations, including the comprehensive historical vocabulary in the anonymous *Essai* (Anonymous 1862 MS), came from Louisiana (see Crawford 1978: 30–60, and Sect. 9.3). Yet, to the best of our knowledge, Chickasaw had not been spoken in the area for over a century—unlike Choctaw, which survived in several Louisiana Indian communities until recently. Some Chickasaw Indians, whose home was in southwestern Tennessee and northern Mississippi during the age of European colonization, visited Louisiana in the early nineteenth century; but, unlike so many other groups of Southeastern Indians, they apparently did not settle there or join local Native American communities. Instead, they left again, probably in order to move to the Indian Territory (see Drechsel and Makuakāne 1982*b*: 23). In what is Oklahoma today, neither the Chickasaw nor—for that matter—any other native group has left any indication for the use of Mobilian Jargon in recent history.

Chickasaw thus had no known impact on Mobilian Jargon during its recent history of the past 150 years or so. That we have not found more evidence of Chickasaw influences in the pidgin should not then be a surprise. Knowing the variable nature of pidgins, one should rather be astonished at the persistence of so many resemblances to Chickasaw or some closely related dialect as could still be found in Mobilian Jargon. These probably derive from varieties of Mobilian Jargon spoken outside Louisiana and during a period before Removal to the Indian Territory in the 1830s, and assume the special status of survivals in this case.

5.4. *The Special Case of Algonquian Loan-Words*

If elements of Chickasaw, once spoken in Tennessee and even Kentucky, are already strange in Mobilian Jargon, all the more exotic must then appear words of a still farther northern origin—Algonquian loans. They have intrigued Americanist anthropologists ever since Mobilian Jargon first attracted their attention by raising the question of how elements of languages principally associated with the Great Lakes area and northeastern North America had found their way into a pidgin of the lower Mississippi area. Because Algonquian Indians were not among the known speakers of Mobilian Jargon at least in recent history (see Sect. 10.1), the following discussion retains the term loan-word in reference to its Algonquian-derived vocabulary.[5]

The first to recognize Algonquian loans in Mobilian Jargon was Albert S. Gatschet. Relying partly on early French documentation, he listed four words: "píshu" 'lynx;' "piakímina" 'persimmon;' "shishikushi" 'gourd-rattle, drum;' and "sacacuya" 'war-whoop' (Gatschet 1969 [1884]: 96). But Gatschet offered an Algonquian resemblance only for the first item, **pishīu** in Ojibwa. Probably drawing on Gatschet's word list as a major source, James Mooney (1900: 187 n. 2) then sketched the following larger picture, without adding any linguistic details or other supporting evidence:

This trade jargon, based upon Choctaw, but borrowing also from all the neighboring dialects and even from the more northern Algonquian languages, was spoken and understood among all the tribes of the Gulf states, probably as far west as Matagorda bay and northward along both banks of the Mississippi to the Algonquian frontier about the entrance of the Ohio.

The Louisiana French scholar William A. Read (1963 [1931]: 76–7) similarly thought that Mobilian Jargon by extending "its influence as far north even as the mouth of the Ohio" had been "enriched by loans from the dialects of Algonquian tribes who inhabited the region lying to the north of the Southern Indian territory." Like Gatschet, Read (1963 [1931]: 99–106), using a slightly different, francophone transcription, listed "pichou" 'bob-tailed

[5] This section is based in part on an earlier essay on the same topic (Drechsel 1986), but provides an expanded discussion and more comparative information. It has benefited a great deal from insights by David J. Costa, based on his knowledge of Miami-Illinois.

wild cat, bobcat, Bay Lynx' and "plaquemine" 'persimmon fruit' among the Algonquian loans with equivalent forms in Mobilian Jargon, and added "pacane" 'pecan nut' and "sacamité" 'hominy,' all of which Louisiana French had accordingly borrowed from northern Algonquian languages via Mobilian Jargon. Among other Algonquian loans in Louisiana French, Read listed "sacacoua" or "sasacoua" 'hubbub, racket, uproar, confused cries, shouts,' but—unlike Gatschet—did not mention the occurrence of any corresponding form in Mobilian Jargon; this latter word apparently found its way to Louisiana with the French of Canada rather than through the intertribal medium (Read 1963 [1931]: 104). Almost a decade later, Read (1940: 548) added to this list "mitasses," the French gloss for 'leggings' in the anonymous *Essai* (Anonymous 1862 MS: 57), which had supposedly entered Louisiana French via Mobilian Jargon like other Algonquian loans.

While one can argue for an Algonquian origin for all these words, supporting historical or modern evidence for their occurrence in Mobilian Jargon is poor, even missing in most instances. Gatschet did not indicate whether he relied principally on historical sources—as he apparently did in one case, that of "shishikushi" with a reference to the journal of 1699 by the French explorer Pierre Le Moyne, Sieur d'Iberville (Margry 1876–1886: iv. 175)—or whether he had recorded any of the Algonquian loans in fieldwork of his own (see Taylor 1981: 184). More meticulous, Read cited early attestations plus resemblances in various Algonquian languages for all Algonquian loans in Louisiana French; but he, too, neglected to give an explanation of how he had determined corresponding forms in Mobilian Jargon.

Recognizing the need for a closer examination of alleged Algonquian loan-words in Mobilian Jargon as well as their historical implications, Crawford (1978: 63–75) devoted an entire chapter of his book on Mobilian Jargon to this question. In scrutinizing early attestations for 'gourd-rattle'/'rattle'/'drum,' 'persimmon,' 'uproar'/'racket'/'hubbub'/'war-whoop,' and 'bobcat,' he found no evidence for their presence in Mobilian Jargon, but listed corresponding forms in various Algonquian languages. In particular, Crawford (1978: 64–70) compiled resemblances in Algonquian languages for the following glosses (with the names of their original sources added in parentheses):

(9) 'bobcat', 'lynx', 'wildcat:' †**pešo** ("píshu" (Gatschet), "pishu" (Read)); cf. Menomini **pise'u**ˀ and **pishe'u** 'panther' (Walter James Hoffman), Cree **pisiw** (Albert Lacombe?), Ojibwa **pījyⁿ/pijîⁿ** 'lynx' (William Jones) or **bisîw** 'lynx' (Bishop Friedrich Baraga), Eastern Ojibwa **pesiw** 'lynx' (Leonard Bloomfield), Round Lake Ojibwa **pišiw** 'lynx' (Jean Hayes Rogers), the second part in Miami **wikwipinzhia** 'spotted

lynx' (Charles F. Voegelin), and Proto-Algonquian ***pešiwa** 'lynx' (Frank T. Siebert)[6]

'gourd-rattle', 'rattle', 'drum': †**šešekoše** ("shishikushi" (Gatschet)); cf. Ojibwa **jishigwan** 'rattle' and **jishigwe** 'rattlesnake' (Baraga), Nipissing **cicikwan** 'gourd-rattle' and **cicikwe** 'rattlesnake' with **c** as equivalent to [š] (Jean André Cuoq), Menomini **ssisi'kwan** 'rattle, of gourd or tin, [whose] contents usually consist of grains of corn, or gravel' and **sik'si?kwan** 'flat drum or tambourine' (Hoffman), Plains Cree **sīsīkwanisak** 'Little Rattles' [name of a dancers' society] and **sīsīkwanak** 'rattles' (Bloomfield), Cree **sisikwan** 'small bag of tied up parchment, in which are confined some small stones; instrument shaken with cadence in the incantations' (Lacombe), Hudson Bay Cree **šišikwap** and possibly **šišikwak** 'instrument of gambling' (Marshall Hurlich), and Shawnee **θeeθiikwaaniki** 'rattle' (Voegelin).[7]

'persimmon': †**peakemena** ("piakímina" (Gatschet)); cf. Miami **piakimini** or **piakimina** 'persimmon' (Voegelin), Ojibwa **pâshkiminassigan** 'sweetmeats, preserves' (Baraga), Nipissing **packiminasigan** 'preserves' and **packimin** 'broken seeds,' crushed fruit (Cuoq), the

---

[6] Further compare Lake St John Montagnais **pišow** 'lynx, bobcat,' Penobscot **pə̀so** 'lynx, bobcat' (Aubin 1975: 131), and St Francis Abenaki **pezó** 'wild cat, lynx' (Day 1964); but contrast Fox **pešiwa** 'lynx, bobcat,' Shawnee **pešiwa** 'lynx, bobcat' (Aubin 1975: 131), and Miami-Illinois †**pinšiwa** 'bobcat, cat' (Costa 1992: 26).

[7] Voegelin (1937–1940: 315, 317) also listed **ši?šiikwa** 'speckled gourd, gourd, rattle' for Shawnee and **šišikwia** 'rattle snake (black)' for Miami. Further note St Francis Abenaki **sizihkwá** 'rattlesnake' (Day 1964), Menomini **si:qsekwan** 'bottle, quart, rattle' (Bloomfield 1975: 242), Delaware (Lenape) **sheshekwan** 'rattle made of gourd-skin' (Friederici 1960: 172), Miami-Illinois †**siihšiikwani** ~ †**šiihšiikoni** 'gourd, cup' (Costa 1993 MS) and Miami-Illinois **šiihšiikweewa** ~ **šiihšiikwia** 'massassauga, rattlesnake' (Costa 1992: 27). However, the form corresponding closest to Mobilian Jargon †**šešekoše** phonologically is apparently Menomini **si:qsekuahsεh** 'bottle' (diminutive; Bloomfield 1975: 242).

Intriguingly, the historical attestations of "sicicouet," "sisyquoy," "sysyquoy," and "cicikoics" in contrast to those of "chichicoya," "chichicoir," "chichicois," "chychycouchy," "chichikois," "chichakois," "Chichicoüas," "chichikoué," and "schischikué" for 'gourd-rattle' (Crawford 1978: 65–6) may reveal not so much the sound correspondence between the voiceless alveolar fricative and its palatalized variant in Algonquian languages as much more the characteristic variation of **s**–**š** in Mobilian Jargon (see Sects. 4.1 and 8.2). What lends support for this interpretation is the fact European explorers, settlers, and travellers—although perfectly aware of the phonemic contrast between /s/ and /š/ in their own languages, including French, English, and German—recorded this variation for a period of at least a century and a half; they did not systematize its spelling to either **s** or **š**, as one might have expected them to do. In a more daring moment, the usually cautious Crawford hinted at such an interpretation without however espousing it expressly: 'Because of the frequent occurrence of the variant forms of this Algonquian word in the literature, it may be supposed that, if any Algonquian word entered Mobilian [Jargon], the word for rattle did. However, there is no documentation for this. It apparently did not enter Louisiana French. It is not one of the Algonquian words in Read's list of Indian words taken into Louisiana French' (Crawford 1978: 66–7). The systematic nature of variability in these attestations provides some suggestive if hardly conclusive evidence that they represent Mobilian Jargon.

Cree root **pâsk** 'to open, to make an opening, to burst, to shatter' and perhaps **pâsiminân** 'dried seed' (Lacombe).[8]

'uproar', 'racket', 'hubbub'/'war-whoop': †**sasak(o)ya**, †**sasak(o)wa**, and/or possibly †**sakak(o)wa** (?; "sacacuya" (Gatschet), "sacacoua" and "sasacoua" (Read, identifying these words only as Louisiana French)); cf. Nipissing **sasakwe** 'to utter shrill cries (but cries of joy)' (Cuoq) and Ojibwa **sassâkwe** 'shout with joy' (Baraga), or Nipissing **sakwatam** 'to utter cries' (Cuoq) and Plains Cree **sākuwä-** or **sākōwä-** 'whoop' (Bloomfield)[9]

An early recording of 'gourd-rattle' in the form of "Chichicoüas" with the variable glosses of 'calabash, gourd' occurs with other attestations clearly identifiable as Mobilian Jargon by their semantactically reduced phrases (see Dumont de Montigny 1753: i. 193, 203–6). Reconstituted as †**šešekowa**, this variety also matches corresponding Algonquian terms more closely than Gatschet's recording. None the less, the evidence for this and the other three Algonquian-derived terms for indigenous phenomena convinced Crawford that the French had acquired them directly from Algonquian Indians in Canada or from Algonquian guides and interpreters accompanying them on their explorations down the Mississippi River. On their arrival in Louisiana, the French had simply continued using these Algonquian terms, presumably also in their interactions with the local indigenous population. According to Crawford, Mobilian Jargon thus could not have been the immediate source for these Algonquian loan-words in Louisiana French.

Other Algonquian words in Louisiana French have an equal claim to

---

[8] For Miami-Illinois, Costa (1993 MS) has reconstituted †**pyaakimini** (sg) and †**pyaakimina** (pl), related to Proto-Algonquian ****pya:kimini** 'cranberry' (Goddard 1982: 24). For further cognates, note Menomini **piakemen** 'cranberry' (Bloomfield 1975: 216) and Powhatan **passi:min** 'persimmon' (Siebert 1975: 367).

According to Georg Friederici (1960: 516), the word for 'persimmon' in Illinois, Miami, and related dialects supposedly derived from Mobilian Jargon, and was a "corrupted" form of *persimmon* in Delaware, Nipissing, and Cree **pasimen** and **pasimenan**. Probably relying on Gatschet's attestation, Friederici offered no support for his explanation, which is erroneous in light of the comparative evidence.

[9] Following a suggestion by Claude Medford, Crawford (1978: 69, 120 n. 54) also considered a similarity of the Mobilian Jargon word for 'war-whoop' to Muskogee **sasv'kwv** [sa:sákwa] 'goose,' and observed in a footnote: 'Haas maintains that the dissimilarity in meaning prevents the Creek form from being construed as a borrowing from Algonquian. Citing Choctaw **šalaklak** and Cherokee **sa:sɂ**, she observes that other languages besides Creek have similar words for "goose" (personal communication). Haas may be right. However, I am more reluctant than she is in rejecting the possibility of borrowing. It is not outside the realm of possibility that the Creeks, perhaps through the contact with the Shawnees, may have made a connection between the sounds geese make and those denoted by Algonquian **sasakwa**.' Medford (personal communication) thought that a flock of several hundred geese sounded like human war-whoops.

Mobilian Jargon as their medium of southward diffusion, and include those two identified by Read:

(10) 'leggings': "mitasses" (Read 1940: 548)[10]

'pecan nut': "pacane;" cf. Cree **pakan** 'nut,' Ojibwa **pakan** 'nut, walnut,' Ojibwa **pagan** 'hazel nut' (Read 1963 [1931]: 99)[11]

Crawford could not find any supporting evidence for these or other Louisiana French words of Algonquian provenance in Mobilian Jargon, and suggested a similar history for them as for the first four glosses. Yet, as he also recognized (Crawford 1978: 63, 70), the lack of attestations for these words in Mobilian Jargon does not rule out their one-time occurrence in the pidgin, which could have adopted them from Louisiana French.

However, Crawford found two other words in Mobilian Jargon with Algonquian resemblances, suggesting a possible northern origin: 'hominy' (discussed by Crawford under 'sagamité') and 'money.' His argument for the first item still depended on whether its historical source, the *Essai* by the anonymous author (Anonymous 1862 MS), described some Western Muskogean language or Mobilian Jargon. While the anonymous author had attested both "Sacamité" and "Sonac" for 'hominy' and 'money' respectively (Anonymous 1862 MS: 51,58), Crawford found independent evidence only for the second, in fact recorded it as [sunak] or [sǝna:k] and as the variant realization of [šɔ:nɛ] from modern speakers of Mobilian Jargon. For 'hominy,' he located easy corresponding forms in Ojibwa and Cree; but for 'money,' with its variable realizations, he identified more divergent resemblances in Nipissing, Ojibwa, Menomini, Cree, Miami, and still other Algonquian languages (Crawford 1978: 71–4):

(11) 'hominy' ('sagamité'): †**sakamete** ("sagamité" (Anonymous), "sacamité" (Read)); cf. Nipissing **-agami** 'beverage, potion, liquid for drinking' as in **kijagamite** 'the liquid is hot' (Cuoq), Round Lake Ojibwa **kiša:kamite:** 'it is hot (liquid)' (Rogers), Cree **kisâgamisuw** and **kisâgamitew** 'it is hot (liquid)' (Lacombe), and Plains Cree

---

[10] For corresponding forms, Friederici (1960: 417) has offered **mitas(s)** in Eastern, Central, and Northwestern Algonquian languages, **muttásash** and **metásash** in Natick, **mitass** and **metos** in Ojibwa and Cree, and **mitiq?san** in Menomini. Also, contrast St Francis Abenaki **nemedás** 'my legging, my legging, my stocking' (Day 1964), Miami-Illinois †**nitaahsi** 'my legging' (Costa 1993 MS), and Shawnee **mateta** 'leggings, pants' (Voegelin 1937–40: 354).

[11] Furthermore, note Cree and Menomini **paka:n** 'large nut,' Abenaki **pagaïn** 'nut,' Abenaki **pagôn** 'walnut,' but contrast Fox **paga:ni** 'large nut,' Shawnee **paka:ni/paka:na** 'nut,' Miami **pakani** 'nut' (Aubin 1975: 126), Miami-Illinois †**pakaani** 'nut, pecan' (Costa 1993 MS), and St Francis Abenaki **bag⁵n** 'nut, butternut, walnut' (Day 1964).

According to Mary Haas, Muskogee similarly borrowed **paká:na** from Shawnee, but developed a different gloss, that of 'peach' (Martin 1994: 15–16).

kisākamis 'heat it as liquid' and **kisākamisikan** 'tea-kettle' (Hans C. Wolfart).

'money': **sonak** ("sonac" (Anonymous)) ~ **šonak** ~ **šone** [šɔ:nɛ] (Crawford); cf. Nipissing **conia** 'money' with **c** for [š] (Cuoq), Ojibwa **joniia** /šo:nya:/ 'money' and **joniiag** /šo:niya:k/ 'silver pieces' (Baraga), Round Lake Ojibwa **šo:niya:hka:** 'money is plentiful; it's "treaty time"' (Rogers), Eastern Ojibwa **šo:neya:** 'money' (Bloomfield), Menomini **su:niyan** 'silver, money, coin, dollar' (Bloomfield) or **Shu'nïen**, **Ssu'nien**, and similar renderings 'money' (Hoffman), Cree **sooneyow** /so:niya:w/ and **sooneyan** 'money, silver,' **sooneyas** /so:niya:s/ 'shilling, small silver coin,' and **sooneyowuˊkāsew** /so:niya:wahke:siw/ 'silver fox' (Edwin A. Watkins) or **soniyaw** 'silver,' **soniyâwiw** 'it is of silver,' **soniyans** 'small piece of silver,' **soniyâwikamik** 'bank,' and **soniyâwakkesiw** 'silver fox' (Lacombe), Plains Cree **sō niyāw** or **sōniyāwa** 'money' (Wolfart), Miami **šoli** or **šolia** 'money' and **wapikišolia** 'silver ring' (Voegelin), Fox /šo:niya:hi/ 'money' (Frank T. Siebert), and Penobscot /sòlsis/ 'medal, medallion, silver amulet' (Siebert).[12]

Since a search for documentation of 'money' in Louisiana and Canadian French produced no results, Crawford argued that this word—unlike other Algonquian loans, including the attested word for 'hominy'—had entered Mobilian Jargon directly from some Algonquian language(s) on contact between Louisiana and northern Algonquian-speaking Indians; such direct language contact had presumably occurred on occasions of northern Indians accompanying French explorers on their southward expeditions. According to Frank T. Siebert (in Crawford 1978: 74), Algonquian Indians had in turn borrowed the word for 'money, silver' from sixteenth-century Spanish **sol** 'silver coin' (also 'sun, day'), **jornal** 'earnings, wages,' and most probably American Spanish **jola** 'money' (with **j** pronounced as [š] at that time rather than as [x] of modern Spanish). For Siebert, **jola** was "a portmanteau form or blend of Sp. /joya/ *gem, jewell, piece of gold or silver*, and /gola/ or /golilla/ *gorget*, giving such portmanteau forms as /šola/ and /šoliya/'" (in Crawford 1978: 74). It is not clear how Siebert understood the specifics of borrowing for this Spanish loan. On the one hand, he thought that eastern Algonquians had directly adopted it from Spaniards on the Maine coast in the sixteenth century; on the other, and in apparent contradiction, he suspected that the Spanish term for 'money' and 'silver' had indirectly passed from Mobilian Jargon into Illinois and Miami, whence it had entered the other Algonquian languages.[13]

[12] In addition, consider Kickapoo **sooniaah-** 'money' (Voorhis 1988: 118), and contrast Miami-Illinois †**šooli** as reconstituted by Costa (1993 MS).

[13] "Exotic" loans such as 'money' in Mobilian Jargon have attracted rather intriguing expla-

Following up on Crawford's research, I consulted former speakers of the pidgin for surviving evidence of these Algonquian loan-words, and also tapped their memories for any indication of the various Louisiana French terms of Algonquian and, in one instance, Iroquoian provenance in Mobilian Jargon. These included: "açmine" 'pawpaw fruit,' often mistaken as "jasmine," and its tree "açminier" or "jasminier" (< Illinois **rassimina**); "babiche" 'rawhide' (< Algonquian **sisibab** 'cord' or **sisibabish** 'a little cord'); "batiscan" 'mild oath to express surprise, regret, scorn, or discontent' (< Montagnais **patiscan** 'vapor, light mist'); "mataché" 'spotted' (< Algonquian?); "micoine" 'shoveler duck' (< Algonquian **emikwan** 'wooden spoon'); and "ouaouaron" 'bullfrog' (< Huron **ouaraon** and Iroquois **wararon**) as listed by Read (1963 [1931]: 79–81, 90–1, 95–9).

My attempts at attesting these words in Mobilian Jargon failed in every instance except one. Surviving speakers of Mobilian Jargon recognized Gatschet's and Read's Algonquian loans other than "shishikushi," yet considered all except one to be Louisiana French, not Mobilian Jargon. They also confirmed Read's list of Louisiana French terms of northern origin, but recognized them as exclusively Louisiana French. The only word in the entire list of alleged Algonquian loans that my consultants could still remember as part of the pidgin lexicon was **sonak** or **šonak**, yet without the other variant form [šɔ:nɛ] recorded by Crawford. Significantly, all surviving speakers of Mobilian Jargon remembered 'money,' recalled it among the very first words, and also repeated it most often, as if it served as a kind of lexical identification marker for Mobilian Jargon. But none of the consultants identified it as an Algonquian or some other foreign loan. Rather, **sonak** or **šonak** in Mobilian Jargon appears to have related forms in several Muskogean languages: Choctaw **asonak** 'a vessel made with brass or tin,' Chickasaw **asonnak/aso:nak** 'tin,' Koasati **ocona** 'machine, metal,' Alabama **ocona/ocana** 'tin,' Apalachee **ocona niko watka** 'lightning' (with **niko watka** meaning 'ray of sun'), Seminole **kocuni** 'iron,' Mikasuki **koconi** 'metal,' and Hitchiti **kocon-i** 'iron' (Munro, forthcoming: 'metal'). Although these similarities suggest a common origin, they need not be true cognates, but could

nations of their origin. Ian Hancock (personal communication) has suggested Romani **sunakai** 'gold' as another possible etymology, in which case the likely source were early French Rom ("Gypsy") immigrants to Louisiana, usually known as *Bohémiens* (Hiram F. Gregory, personal communication). Whereas Mobilian Jargon **sonak** and its variable pronunciations are phonologically closer to the Romani word for 'gold' than the Spanish term for 'money, silver,' the first shows greater semantic difference from its Mobilian Jargon counterpart than the second. There also remain questions about the sociohistorical circumstances under which the pidgin would have adopted a word of Romani origin. Notwithstanding, the study of language contact cannot disregard such derivations, however distant and unlikely they may appear at first sight. The basic sociolinguistic underpinning of pidginization is the recognition that several peoples of very different linguistic and cultural backgrounds, occasionally originating in the most distant parts of the globe, came into contact with each other, and compromised in their interactions, including linguistic borrowings.

have been borrowings of the same or related words into several Muskogean languages. Resemblances suggestive of an area-wide loan-word also
occur in Catawba **sɔnu'** 'money' (Speck 1934: 38, 39) and in Cherokee
sö:nɪ̠kt?a' 'beads' (Mooney 1932: 164).[14]

Unquestionably Algonquian in origin is the Mobilian Jargon word
papo(s) or **papoš** 'baby, child,' attested in the 1930s as "papoose" by the
Louisiana naturalist and humanist Caroline Dormon in her notes on Mobilian Jargon (Dormon n.d. MS: 10) and occurring in Louisiana French and
English as well (see Trumbull 1872: 27–8). Those individuals who remembered this word thought it to be variably French, Choctaw, or some other,
unidentified American Indian language in origin, and could not agree as to
its source. They were also unable to determine in what, if any, respects it
differed in meaning from †**alla** 'child, baby,' **atoše** 'baby,' **oše** 'child,' and
posko(š) or **poškoš** 'baby, child.' At any rate, Mobilian Jargon **papos** and its
variants were practically identical in both form and meaning to corresponding forms in Eastern Algonquian languages of New England, especially **pápoos**, **papoós**, and **poupous** in Natick and presumably some related
form in Mohegan-Pequot (Friederici 1960: 479), **pápūs** in Narragansett
(Gatschet 1973 [1879]), and similar words in other Eastern Algonquian languages and even Delaware Jargon, an Algonquian-based pidgin (Prince
1912: 522).

Still another example of Algonquian origin is "manggasin" or possibly
"mauggasin" 'shoe,' which Ezra Stiles, a minister and educator from Connecticut and later president of Yale College, recorded from a surveyor
named Selden, a former captive of the Osage or possibly Oto Indians on
the Missouri river, in 1794 (Stiles 1794 MS; 1980 [1794]; cf. Sherwood 1983:
440–1). The vocabulary does not represent a Siouan or perhaps some
Algonquian language of the region, but clearly proves to be Mobilian
Jargon, as determined on the basis of both lexical, morphological, and sociolinguistic information (see Sherwood 1983: 441 n. 11; for further discussion of this document, see Sect. 9.3). Reconstructed †**māgasin** (?) or rather
its variant †**mogasin** (?) resembles corresponding forms attested widely in
all major Algonquian languages: Cree **maskisin**, Menomini **mahkɛ:sen**,
Ojibwa **makkisin**, and Penobscot **maksən** (Aubin 1975: 85). Among other
corresponding forms, there are Mahican **máksen** 'shoe' (Masthay 1991: 125),
Munsee **máhksən** 'shoe' (Goddard 1982: 28), Powhatan **mahkesen** 'shoe,
moccasin' (Siebert 1975: 381), St. Francis Abenaki **mahkessén** 'moccasin'
(Day 1964), and Miami-Illinois †**mahkisini** 'shoe' (Costa 1993 MS).

Several speakers of Mobilian Jargon also recalled **nešken** 'eye,' for which
there exist independent historical attestations as "nichekine" (Anonymous

---

[14] The Catawba and Cherokee resemblances were brought to my attention by Jerry King,
who also remembered an old Catawba man using **sɔnu?** to refer to 'bead' (personal communication).

1862 MS: 41). According to Haas (1958: 245), the equivalent form **niškin** in Choctaw was related to Proto-Central Algonquian ***-ški:nšekw-** 'eye' and ***neški:nšekw-i** 'my eye' and to Ojibwa **niški:nšik** or Delaware **nəʼškinkw** 'my eye,' but not to other Central Algonquian languages such as Fox, Cree, Menomini, or Shawnee because of substantial linguistic differences from the first.[15] Further, note Powhatan **neski:nsek** 'my eye' (Siebert 1975: 338), Munsee **nəskí:nčəkw** 'my eye' (Goddard 1982: 45), as well as Miami-Illinois †**nihkiinšikwi** 'my eye' (Costa 1993 MS), and contrast Mahican **nʔskétschok** 'my eye' (Masthay 1991: 62). On the other hand, there existed an apparent cognate in the form of **iškin** in Chickasaw (Munro, forthcoming) and an equivalent word in Mobilian Jargon, "esquen" (Bourgeois 1788: 297) or †**ešken**. In explaining these striking similarities, Haas considered either common origin or borrowing; the latter option entails the question of whether Mobilian Jargon played a role in its diffusion.

In addition, David J. Costa (personal communication) has recognized a resemblance of Miami-Illinois †**-čiihči** 'sinew, nerve' (Costa 1993 MS) to Mobilian Jargon †**čeašwa** (?) 'nerve' as reconstituted from "tchiachoi" (Anonymous 1862 MS: 41). As related contrasts serve Kickapoo **oceehci** 'sinew,' Menomini **neci:ʔtan** 'my sinew' and the derived root **oci:ʔt-** 'sinew,' and Munsee **wčéht** 'tendon, sinew' (Goddard 1982: 20).

Yet another word of ultimate Algonquian origin may be †**beyāka** 'chicken hawk, hawk,' reconstituted from "bihanca" (Anonymous 1862 MS: 29). Haas (1958: 247) has observed a close resemblance between Proto-Muskogean ***kʷiya:nkak** and Proto-Central-Algonquian ***ki/aya:Hkw-a** 'gull' or its plural ***ki/aya:Hkw-aki** (with **H** representing an unspecified initial member in a consonant cluster), which she has interpreted in terms of borrowing without, however, indicating its direction. Related Algonquian forms are Miami-Illinois †**kinwalaniihsiwa** ~ †**kinwalaniihsia** ~ †**kilwanaliihsia** 'hawk' (Costa 1992: 23). On the other hand, there are corresponding words in Muskogean languages such as **biyãkak** in Choctaw, **biyakka** in Koasati, **biyãk** in Alabama, and **kiya:kka** in Muskogee (Munro, forthcoming), for which Geoffrey Kimball (personal communication) has suggested the Proto-Muskogean form ***kʷiyakkaka** (with neither long vowel nor nasalization) and whose similarity to the Proto-Central-Algonquian word for 'gull' he attributes to onomatopoeia rather than borrowing.

The discussion of Algonquian loan-words demonstrates that modern recordings, while incomplete, are consistent with historical attestations, and thus relieves Crawford (1978: 71) of his concern about the validity of the anonymous *Essai* as a historical source. By extension, one cannot dismiss other historical attestations as simple fantasies of a nineteenth-century

---

[15] Haas did not discuss these differences, which probably related to the absence of a medial nasal. Compare Fox **neški:šekwi**, Cree **niski:sik**, and Menomini **neske:hsek** 'my eye' (Aubin 1975: 107) as well as Shawnee **(-)ʔškiišekwi** 'eye' (Voegelin 1937–40: 314).

anthropologist (Gatschet), a Romance linguist (Read), or a naturalist (Dormon), but may place more trust in their historical attestations, even if circumstantial. What lends credibility to their data is their very "innocent" nature, their incidental occurrence among other linguistic, ethnographic, or nature-related observations gained "in the field" in Louisiana. The three scholars did not provide any details on how they gathered these Algonquian words, but may well have heard them still spoken in Mobilian Jargon before these dropped from use. Modern speakers have since offered erroneous folk etymologies for these words as in the case of **papo(s)** or **papoš**, or simply could no longer remember them.

Currently, several entries remain uncertain as Algonquian loans in Mobilian Jargon; others appear less disputable. A list of Mobilian Jargon words with definite and tenuous Algonquian resemblances includes the following entries (with question marks following those that remain uncertain in terms of either attestation or reconstitution):

(12) 'baby', 'child': **papo(s)** ("papoose" (Dormon)) ~ **papoš**

'bobcat', 'lynx', 'wildcat': †**pešo** ("pishu" (Gatschet); "pishu" (Read))

'chicken hawk', 'hawk': †**beyãka** ("bihanca" (Anonymous))?

'eye': **nešken** ("nichekine" (Anonymous)) ~ †**ešken** ("esquen" (Bourgeois))?

'gourd', 'calabash'/'gourd-rattle'/'rattle'/'drum': †**šešekowa** ("chichi-coüas" (Dumont de Montigny)) ~ †**šešekoše** ("shishikushi" (Gatschet))

'hominy': †**sakamete** ("sacamité" (Anonymous); "sacamité" (Read))

'leggings': †**metas** (?; "mitasses" (Read))

'moccasin', 'shoe': †**mãgasin** (?; "manggasin" (?) (Stiles)) or †**mogasin** (?; "mauggasin" (?) (Stiles))

'money': **sonak** ("sonac" (Anonymous)) ~ **šonak** ~ **šone** [šɔ:nɛ] (Crawford)?

'nerve': †**čeašwa** (?; "tchiachoi" (Anonymous))

'pecan nut': †**pakan** (?; "pacane" (Read))

'persimmon': †**peakemena** ("piakímina' (Gatschet))

'uproar', 'racket', 'hubbub', 'war-whoop': †**sakak(o)ya** (?; "sacacuya" (Gatschet), †**sasak(o)wa** (?; "sasacoua" (Read)), and/or possibly †**sakak(o)wa** (?; "sacacoua" (Read))

There also remain several unidentified words and phrases in Mobilian Jargon open to an explanation of an Algonquian provenance. A vocabulary such as that gathered by the surveyor Selden (Stiles 1794 MS; 1980 [1794];

cf. Sherwood 1983: 440–1) among the Oto or Osage on the Missouri River may fortuitously broaden the search for sources of its unidentified entries and make etymologies from neighboring non-Muskogean groups including Algonquians more likely.

Any of these Algonquian loans in Mobilian Jargon raises the question of how they entered the pidgin, and may offer noteworthy insights into its history. Conceivably, there were several routes by which Mobilian Jargon could have incorporated Algonquian words:

(*a*) in communication with Acadians ("Cajuns") and other European Americans who had learned some Algonquian language, a contact language based on it, or simply a few words of either in northeastern North America before emigrating to Louisiana after the mid-eighteenth century and who extended their linguistic skills to contact with Louisiana Indians;

(*b*) on visits by Algonquian Indians accompanying French explorers, missionaries, and traders (independent *coureurs de bois* and licensed *voyageurs*) on their expeditions down the Mississippi River from the late seventeenth century on, in which case Mobilian Jargon borrowed words

(i) indirectly from Canadian French explorers, as maintained by Read (1963 [1931]: 101–2) for 'bobcat'/'lynx'/'wildcat' and for 'uproar'/'racket'/'hubbub'/'war-whoop' (if he thought of the latter word to occur in Mobilian Jargon also) and as reasoned by Crawford (1979: 63–75) for all Algonquian words in his listing because of the presence of similar terms in Canadian and Louisiana French except for 'money;' and

(ii) directly from native guides and interpreters, as presumed by Read (1963 [1931]: 99–106; 1940: 548) for his own list of Algonquian loans in Mobilian Jargon and as argued by Crawford (1978: 72) for 'money' because of the absence of similar terms in Canadian or Louisiana French;

(*c*) from direct contacts between Southeastern Indians and southern Algonquian Indians without any European intermediaries, specifically between Mobilian Jargon speakers and

(i) Algonquian-speaking immigrants to the South such as the Shawnee; and

(ii) southern Algonquians of Virginia and North Carolina; and

(*d*) from direct contacts between Southeastern Indians and northern Algonquian Indians without any European intermediaries, specifically between Mobilian Jargon speakers and northern Algonquians on Mobilian Jargon's northern border in the central and upper Mississippi River valley.

These alternative explanations are not equally plausible, nor does any single one necessarily apply to all Algonquian loans in Mobilian Jargon or exclude another explanation.

The probability that Acadians or other European immigrants of northeastern North America were the transmitters of Algonquian loans into Mobilian Jargon is limited; there are but a few that show any close linguistic similarity to corresponding words in Eastern Algonquian languages, the Native American languages to which Acadians would have been exposed before emigration. One example might be 'moccassin'/'shoe.' This word first appeared in Mobilian Jargon on the word list by the surveyor Selden, a former captive among the Oto or Osage Indians on the Missouri River in the late 1780s, who had contacts with people in New England, probably including Algonquian Indians (see Sherwood 1983: 440–1 and (84) in Sect. 9.3). The loan also shows close resemblances in Algonquian languages of the Great Lakes region, serving as alternative sources. Another borrowing of Northeastern Algonquian origin could have been 'baby'/'child' with its corresponding forms in Algonquian languages of the Atlantic coast. Yet similar forms in Delaware Jargon (Prince 1912: 522), Chinook Jargon on the Northwest Coast (Chamberlain 1891: 261), and English (Chamberlain 1902: 252) suggest its wide spread across much of North America without the necessary help of Acadians and via other, perhaps multiple channels of transmission.

Various other Algonquian words in Mobilian Jargon—namely, 'bobcat'/'lynx'/'wildcat,' 'gourd'/'calabash'/'(gourd-) rattle/drum,' 'hominy,' 'leggings,' 'pecan nut,' 'persimmon,' and 'uproar'/'racket'/'hubbub'/'warwhoop'—disqualify as loans introduced by Acadian immigrants, simply because attestations for these words occur in records on colonial Louisiana in the early eighteenth century. They belong to a period before the first Acadian immigrants or subsequently English-speaking Northeasterners set foot into Louisiana in the second half of the century (see Crawford 1978: 64–72; Read 1963 [1931]: 97–106). Single instances, specifically 'persimmon,' also exhibit greater similarity to Miami-Illinois than any other Algonquian language. A third, if weaker, argument against any significant Algonquian input into Mobilian Jargon by Acadians rests on the fact that there exist no attestations for Mobilian Jargon terms corresponding to those Algonquian words that Acadians introduced into Louisiana French.

Contacts between northern and southern Indians along the Mississippi as part of European explorations were a more likely route for the transmission of several Algonquian words into Mobilian Jargon, as already recognized by Read and Crawford. 'Money' with its apparent ultimate source in Spanish, 'bobcat'/'lynx'/'wildcat,' and possibly 'moccassin'/'leggings' and 'shoe' suggest the sociohistorical context of the fur and hide trade, in which both Northeastern and Southeastern Indians were deeply engaged during colonial periods and in which Mobilian Jargon served as a primary interlingual medium (see Sect. 10.2).

There are few indications for any direct borrowings by Mobilian Jargon from any of the Algonquian-speaking peoples of southeastern North America, including Shawnee immigrants, for none of the attested Algonquian words in the pidgin except possibly for 'gourd'/'calabash'/'(gourd-) rattle'/'drum' shows close or exclusive resemblance to known equivalent forms in southern Algonquian languages or Shawnee. Haas (1958: 245) has excluded Shawnee as the source for 'eye.' Likewise, Shawnee provides a less satisfactory source for most other Algonquian-derived words in Mobilian Jargon than languages of the Great Lakes area, as judged by their phonological and other grammatical similarities. Another possible Algonquian loan, *açmine* and its variant form of *jasmine* in Louisiana French, apparently exhibits a closer resemblance to Virginia Algonquian or Powhatan /assi:min/ 'pawpaw' (Siebert 1975: 365) than to Illinois **rassimina**, which David J. Costa (1993 MS) has alternatively reconstituted as †**ahsiimini** (sg.) and †**ahsiimina** (pl.); but in this case, there are no claims for a corresponding word in Mobilian Jargon.

Pending better comparative data or actual historical records, the most convincing explanation is the direct transmission of words from adjoining Algonquian languages in the Great Lakes area into Mobilian Jargon. What speaks for such a route is the fact that most Algonquian loans in Mobilian Jargon apparently derived from one or more Central Algonquian languages and, in a few instances, specifically from Miami-Illinois, whose speakers were the immediate northern neighbors of Southeastern Indians. This interpretation receives additional support from the recognition that terms as 'eye' are basic words and others refer to distinctly indigenous phenomena, namely '(chicken) hawk,' 'hominy,' 'pecan nut,' 'persimmon,' '(gourd-) rattle/drum,' and 'uproar'/'racket'/'hubbub'/'war-whoop.' These loans— unlike possible fur-trade terminology such as 'bobcat'/'lynx'/'wildcat,' 'leggings,' 'moccassin', 'shoe,' and 'money'—do not relate to a single semantic domain or a specific sociohistorical context, much less to any intermediary role by European explorers, traders, or settlers and, with it, European contact. The most intriguing of all these words is 'eye,' which—if confirmed as an Algonquian loan—leaves us with an enigma. Why would Western Muskogeans such as the Chickasaw and Choctaw, but not apparently their eastern relatives, have borrowed a word for such a basic concept for which they undoubtedly had their own term at one time? Did this loan or the native word that it replaced (perhaps as a result of word tabooing) represent some abstract quality of supernatural significance such as the eye in pre-European Mississippian symbolism (Howard 1968: 26) that once linked Algonquians and Western Muskogeans? Other Mobilian Jargon words of Algonquian origin, among them especially '(chicken) hawk,' 'uproar'/'racket'/'hubbub'/'war-whoop,' 'gourd/calabash/(gourd-) rattle/drum,' and even 'bobcat'/'lynx'/'wildcat,' may similarly echo Mississippian themes, related to warfare and the ceremonial complex (see Howard 1968; Hudson 1976: 77–97).

Crawford's explanation for the diffusion of most Algonquian loans via French Canadian explorers is unsatisfactory in the end, for there remains a need to clarify the narrower sociolinguistic parameters for the transmission of these loans into Mobilian Jargon. French explorers and traders could indeed have picked up one or the other Algonquian word from Native Americans of the wider Great Lakes area or from native guides and interpreters who accompanied them on their southward explorations, and might then have introduced them into Mobilian Jargon either directly or indirectly via Louisiana French. Yet Crawford's arguments leave some inconsistencies and nagging questions regarding the Algonquians' precise role in their contacts with Southeastern Indians. Why would the evidence for a single direct Algonquian loan in Mobilian Jargon be limited to 'money,' a word supposedly of European origin? What kept northern and southern Indians from exchanging words—in the literal as well as extended sense? On the other hand, why did Southeastern Indians borrow, by other routes, basic words as for 'baby'/'child,' possibly 'eye,' and various indigenous plants and animals, for which they probably had their own terms?

The primary scenario for the southward transmission of Algonquian words may have been the reverse of what Crawford suggested for most— via Mobilian Jargon rather than French, on the grounds that the pidgin already existed in the earliest periods of French colonial explorations in the Gulf region and French was not established at the time (see Chapter 9). In this case, French was the end rather than the vehicle of transmission. That neither Louisiana nor Canadian French came to adopt any form corresponding to Mobilian Jargon 'money' was due to the fact that this word referred to a European device, for which French speakers did not require a new term. This hypothesis need not preclude Crawford's arguments for some northern borrowings via French as a second, alternate route.

These explanations still leave unanswered some questions about the transmission of Algonquian loan-words into Mobilian Jargon. Closer examination provides no reason for supposing that Algonquians, and especially Algonquian interpreters to the French, remained silent in contact with their southern hosts, even if one could argue against any systematic contact between the two groups before the Europeans' arrival. As Crawford undoubtedly acknowledged, linguistic differences *per se* could hardly have kept Native Americans of the greater Mississippi valley from communicating with each other. That Algonquians aided the French on their expeditions down the Mississippi River actually suggests familiarity by Great

Lakes Indians with the territory and its peoples to the south. Archaeological evidence likewise warrants no assumption for linguistic reticence or other restraints by Algonquians in contact with Southeastern Indians during pre-Columbian times; on the contrary, it suggests regular and systematic contact between the Gulf Coast and the Great Lakes region along the Mississippi River and its tributaries, especially as part of the Mississippian Complex (see Brown, Kerber, and Winters 1990).

Southeastern Indians probably borrowed Algonquian words as a result of direct contact and without any European intermediary, and already did so in pre-Columbian times. Not only has Algonquian constituted the most widespread language family in native North America, and covered much of the Northeast; Algonquians were also the immediate neighbors of Southeastern Indians, including Muskogeans and Siouans in the area of the confluence of the Ohio and Mississippi Rivers (for an illustrative map of the geographic distribution of the Algonquian and Muskogean language families, see Haas 1958: 236). Algonquian peoples, moreover, showed historical prominence with several contact media of their own, some of which were probably interrelated: Delaware Jargon and other Algonquian-based contact languages on the Atlantic Coast; a lingua franca based on Shawnee; Central Algonquian *koinés* based on Eastern Ojibwa (Algonquin or Nipgissing), Ottawa, Southwestern Ojibwa (Chippewa), and Cree; and French Cree known as Métis, Mitchif, or Métif (see Sects. 2.3 and 12.4).[16] These wide-ranging means of intertribal communication made Algonquian Indians well-prepared interpreters and guides for French explorers in the Great Lakes area, the Mississippi valley, and beyond.

Any of the Algonquian lingua francas, but especially those of the Great Lakes region that served as prime contact languages for Algonquian interpreters accompanying European explorers could then have provided a medium of transmission for Algonquian loan-words into Mobilian Jargon.

---

[16] On the other hand, there is no indication for any other means of intertribal communication such as a crosslingual sign language, which—in place of a spoken contact medium—might have discouraged the spread of Algonquian loans into Southeastern Indian languages. The major sign language among North American Indians, that of the Plains Indians, did not extend eastwards into the Woodlands according to Allan R. Taylor (1975: 331–3, 368); his single reference to the use of hand signs among Atakapa, as attested by the eighteenth-century traveller Jean Bernard Bossu (Taylor 1975: 331; see Bossu 1768: ii. 151, 1962: 192), does not provide strong evidence for a sign language in use among Louisiana Indians. The attested hand signs were probably part of Mobilian Jargon (see Sect. 8.6). Similarly, there exists no evidence for a comparable non-linguistic medium among Great Lakes Indians (Rhodes 1982: 1 n. 2), who were the primary source of Algonquian loans in Mobilian Jargon. Altogether, the Plains Indian sign language could hardly have competed with existent native lingua francas if it developed after the first explorations by Europeans, as argued by Taylor (1975: 330–2) and William J. Samarin (1987). The picture changes with any claims to a pre-European existence of the sign language (Wurtzburg and Campbell 1995), but still requires confirmation of its usage east of the Mississippi River.

These would have become part of its lexicon only via a linguistic detour, after first "piggybacking" on an Algonquian contact medium. They further explain the predominance of Ojibwa, Nipissing, and Cree words among the closest resemblances for the Algonquian loans in Mobilian Jargon rather than words of neighboring Illinois or Miami (with similar forms only for 'nerve' and 'persimmon').

Michael Silverstein (1973 MS: 15–16) has already recognized linguistic influences of the Illinois and other Algonquians of the upper Mississippi valley among Siouans and Caddoans farther south, and has attributed a dominant influence to Algonquian languages of the upper Mississippi drainage. But, contrary to Silverstein's argument, evidence for any Algonquian-based lingua franca, much less for a few Algonquian loan-words in southern Siouan and Caddoan languages, does not preclude the presence or even the predominance of Mobilian Jargon in the area. While unquestionably in competition, two or more native contact media could have coexisted and even overlapped in their geographic ranges, as was apparently the case with Algonquian-based and other indigenous contact media in eastern North America (see Sect. 12.4). Just as Mobilian Jargon extended as far north as the lower Ohio and Missouri River valleys in the eighteenth century, any Algonquian-based lingua franca of the Illinois Indians or the Great Lakes area possibly reached into the lower Mississippi valley. But linguistic exchanges between Algonquian and Southeastern Indians would not have been one-way affairs. In contact with their northern neighbors, Southeastern Indians probably adopted as much Algonquian as Great Lakes Indians learned Mobilian Jargon. Research on one or the other Algonquian contact medium may yet bring forth loan-words of Muskogean and perhaps other Southeastern origin, which would serve as indirect evidence for this suggestion.

While satisfactory answers are still wanting, basic words of Algonquian origin in Mobilian Jargon open up the discussion to considering the pidgin not just as a receiver of northern loan-words, but also as a medium of their transmission into Muskogean languages. What complicates the assessment of Algonquian loan-words in Mobilian Jargon is the fact that, as a pidgin, it could substantially change the composition of its vocabulary over time, depending on the speakers' first languages, their sociopolitical status, and their influence on the pidgin. Possibly, Algonquian Indians once had a greater impact on Mobilian Jargon, with additional words from their native languages in its vocabulary, than the evidence indicates today. As the Algonquians' impact waned over time, speakers of other languages could easily have replaced Algonquian loans with equivalent words of their own by partial relexification. For this reason, some early Algonquian loans need not have survived in modern recordings of Mobilian Jargon, just as but a few words of Chickasaw origin endured.

5.5. *Lexical Aspects of Compounds*

If Mobilian Jargon always had a fairly limited vocabulary (as suggested by some historical observers), its speakers could take recourse for lexical expansion by compounding—that is by the combination of two or more otherwise independent words into a single one with a regular order and a meaning of its own.

At times, it is difficult to determine the distinctive use of compounds in contrast to structurally equivalent phrases consisting of the same constituent words without extensive comparative information, which requires some caution in the application of the concept of *compound* to historical data. But the anonymous author of the *Essai* already recognized the significance of compounds in Mobilian Jargon when sketching its grammar (Anonymous 1862 MS: 8–9; see also the quotation in Preliminaries to Part II). After some incidental comments about compounds here and there, the description of Mobilian Jargon's basic characteristics closed with the following observations:

Le mot *Sipi* [**sepe**] qui littéralement veux dire vieux, prend une étrange acception dans les locutions suivants, reproduites dans le cours de cet ouvrage.

Tatliba-Sipi [**taɬepa sepe**]—mille, et litteralement: vieux cent, semblerait indiquer que le nombre est devenu pour eux incommensurable—*tamaha-Sipi* [†**tamaha sepe**], grande ville, vielle ville, semble emporter la même signification. Le nom de Mississipi lui-même dans la terminaison est *sipi* vieux, parait confirmer ceque nous avançons: attendu le nombre de ses tributaires et sa superiorité relative sur eux— C'est aussi ce qui, probablement, a fait interprêter son nom par celui de: père des eaux.

On ne peut guère donner un sens absolu au mot *oulou* [†**holo**], qu'en reproduisant ici les divers mots composés dont il fait partie et qui sont contenus dans le vocabulaire, les voici: *na-oulou* [**nahol(l)o**], race blanche—*nitack-oulou* [**net(t)ak hollo**] dimanche, *oké-oulou* [†**oke holo**] eau bénite, *Sainti-oulou* [†**sēte holo**]—serpent-à-sonnette, serpent à qui ils croient une puissance imaginaire. *tchita-oulou* [†**ešt aholo**] le diable ou l'esprit malfesant.—*tchita* est quelquefois dit pour *Shibah* qui signifie méchant.—On peut voir par ces differentes applications on peut s'assurer que ce mot n'est employé par les Indiens que pour les choses qui pour eux, sont en dehors de leur comprehension, ou de la vie réelle et materielle dans laquelle ils ont l'habitude de se mouvoir et d'agir.

Nous reproduirons ici quelques unes des différentes acceptions de *pasca* [**paska**], comme nous venons de la faire pour *oulou*.—*Pasca* seul, veut dire pain, *loquefe-pasca* [†**lokfe paska**] brique, *pichik-pasca* [†**pešek paska**] fromage. *tallai-pasca* [†**tale paska**]—une pierre.—*chide-pasca* [†**ešt paska** (?)], des cartes à jouer—*louquecé-pasca* [†**lokse paska**] écaille de tortue—

Pasca, dans pain et brique semblerait vouloir dire, une pâte durcie au feu; dans fromage du lait solidifié; dans écaille de tortue, la croûte dure qui recouve l'animal, dans *tallai-pasca* un pain de pierre et dans *chide-pasca*, cartes à jouer quelque chose de plus substantiel que le papier.

Tallai [**tale**] a aussi differentes significations, il s'applique en général, à toutes les matières dures, ainsi on le voit toujours employé avec les modifications que l'on trouvera dans le tableau ci-contre, pour designer les metaux et les pierres. [*sic*]; (Anonymous 1862 MS: 72–4).[17]

The person who added the alphabetically organized vocabulary sections to the *Essai* (Anonymous 1862 MS: 75–137)—somebody other than the original author, as evident from the substantially different handwriting— likewise considered compounding important; he or she extracted from the vocabulary what were among the most productive compounding elements and listed these separately in the appendix (Anonymous 1862 MS: 138–44) (see (13)).[18] As illustrated by more than twenty-five accompanying exam- ples for **ete** and by numerous instances for the other entries (Anonymous

---

[17] 'The word *sipi* [**sepe**], which literally means old, has an odd meaning in the following phrases, reproduced in the course of this work.

Tatliba-Sipi [**taɫepa sepe**]—a thousand and literally an old hundred, would seem to indicate that the number has become incommensurable for them—*tamaha-Sipi* [†**tamaha sepe**], large town, old town, seems to carry the same meaning. The name of [the] Mississippi in its ending is *sipi* old, [and] seems to confirm what we suggest: given the number of its tributaries and its superiority in comparison to them—That is also what has probably led to the interpretation of its name as the father of waters.

One can hardly assign an absolute meaning to the word *oulou* [†**holo**], which recurs here as a part of various words contained in the vocabulary; these are: *na-oulou* [**nahol(l)o**], white race—*nitack-oulou* [**net(t)ak hollo**] Sundary, *oké-oulou* [†**oke holo**] holy water, *Sainti-oulou* [†**sēte holo**]—rattlesnake, a snake to which they assign an imaginary power. *tchita-oulou* [†**ešt aholo**] devil or evil spirit.—*tchita* is sometimes said instead of *Shibah*, which means wicked.— From this varying usage, one can certainly see that this word is used by the Indians only for things that are beyond their comprehension or the real or material life in which they are used to moving around and behaving.

Here we note a few different expressions with *pasca* [**paska**], as we have just done for *oulou*.—*Pasca* alone means bread, *loquefe-pasca* [†**lokfe paska**] brick, *pichik-pasca* [†**pešek paska**] cheese. *tallai-pasca* [†**tale paska**]—a stone.—*chide-pasca* [†**ešt paska** (?)] playing cards—*louquece-pasca* [†**lokse paska**] tortoise shell—

Pasca in bread and brick would seem to mean a paste hardened in fire, in cheese solidified milk, in tortoise shell the hard shell that covers the animal, in *tallai-pasca* a piece of stone, and in *chide-pasca* playing cards more substantial than paper.

Tallai [**tale**] also has different meanings; it usually applies to all hard things; thus, one always sees it used in those modifications that one will find in the table opposite to designate metals and stones' (author's translation; the discussion of compounds is missing in the English trans- lation by Anonymous (n.d. MS)).

While quite perceptive about compounding in Mobilian Jargon, the anonymous author erred in the analysis of a few examples. The interpretation of "Mississippi" partly in terms of "*Sipi*" or **sepe** is based on a folk etymology. This toponym, actually of Algonquian origin and meaning 'large river' with "-sippi" referring to 'river' (Green and Millward 1971: 40, 43, 47), has no his- torical relationship to Choctaw **sipi** 'old.' Moreover, the anonymous author's observations regarding "*tchita*" rely on an incorrect morphological analysis of †**ešt aholo**, and there exists no other attestation for "*Shibah*" as a synonym for "méchant."

[18] In the English translation of the *Essai*, the list of principal compounds appears immedi- ately after the text (Anonymous n.d. MS: 59–64), and precedes the actual vocabulary sections rather than following it as in the French original. While continuing the use of a characteristic French-based transcription, the English translation also amends minor errors of alphabetical arrangement in the French version.

(13) Compounds including	Semantic domains
čokha ~ čokka ("tchouka") 'house'	different kinds and parts of buildings
†**elbak** ("elback") 'hand, arm'	different parts of the arm and hand, 'finger ring'
et(t)e ("ité") 'tree, wood'	different kinds and parts of trees, forest, various things made of wood
ey(y)e ("ihié") 'foot'	different parts of the foot
haše ("atchi") 'sun, month'	'sun,' 'moon,' different times of day, cardinal directions
hat(t)ak ("attack") 'person, people'	different kinds of humans
lokfe ("loquefé") 'dirt, earth, ground'	'dust,' 'brick,' agricultural tools such as 'shovel' and 'plow'
lowak ("lowack") 'fire'	'flame,' 'match,' 'burn'
nahele ("nahilé") 'morning, tomorrow'	'early morning,' 'the day after tomorrow'
†**nane** ("nanni") 'fish'	different kinds of fish, 'scale,' tools of fishing
nešken ("nichekine") 'eye'	miscellany relating to the eye
oke ("oké") 'water'	different kinds and aspects of water, 'ice,' various consumable liquids, 'gallon'
oske ("houski") 'reed, cane'	'sugar-cane,' 'blowgun,' 'arrow'
†**pene** ("pinni") 'boat, canoe'	'ship,' 'steamboat'
pešek ("pichik") 'milk'	'milk,' various milk products
soba ("souba") 'horse'	'mare,' 'stallion,' 'foal,' 'donkey,' 'mule,' 'hoof,' different parts of riding gear
†**takõ** ("taconte") 'peach'	different kinds of fruit
tale ("tallai") 'stone, rock, metal, iron'	different kinds of stone and metal, 'chain,' 'blacksmith'
tanãpo ("tananbo") 'gun'	different kinds and parts of guns
ta(y)ek ("taïk") 'female, woman'	women of different ethnic groups, 'prostitute,' 'pregnant'

1862 MS: 138–44), most of these compounding elements assumed initial position of lexical compounds, but some also occurred in secondary position, depending on the grammatical functions of their constituents as well as on their roles as topics and comments (see Sect. 5.6).

Significantly, most of the anonymous author's compounding elements survived into modern times, as the last speakers of Mobilian Jargon could still remember them independently and without any suggestive aid from earlier attestations. For two of the reconstituted words, †**elbak** 'hand, arm' and †**nane** 'fish,' I recorded Alabama-Koasati derived equivalents, namely **elbe** 'hand' and **łało** 'fish,' which as compounding elements were undoubtedly just as productive as the synonyms based on Chickasaw and Choctaw. There remain only †**pene** 'boat' and †**takõ** 'peach' in the above list of compounding elements for which no modern recordings or equivalent forms were available any longer. For the first, there is a good historical reason: a rapid decline in the use of boats as major vehicles of transportation (ranging from dug-outs to steamships) with a corresponding increase in travel and delivery over land by such means as train and automobile.

The Mobilian Jargon–English vocabulary, drawing on modern as well as reconstituted data (see Drechsel, 1996), reveals several additional compounding elements. Among the most proudctive with at least five recorded instances were the listings in (14). Three of those compounding elements, namely **(a)kãka** and **kãkã**, **net(t)ak**, and **wak(a)**, were regular nouns, and as such functioned just like other nominal components in compounds as those in (13). The other three the listings in (14) differed in their grammatical functions among compounding elements; **-(e)kšo** operated as a negative and evidently as Mobilian Jargon's only suffix, †**eska** as a verb and the single recorded instance producing verbal compounds, and †**ešt** as an instrumental, perhaps a prefix. Still other compounding elements worked as adjectives and apparently as adverbs.

(14) Compounds including	Semantic domains
(a)kãka ~ kãkã 'chicken'	varieties and parts of chicken, other fowl (e.g. 'turkey'), 'chicken hawk'
-(e)kšo NEG	antonyms
†**eska** 'to do, to make'	specific actions described in terms of verbal compounds
†**ešt** INSTR	various tools and means in the broadest sense
net(t)ak 'day'	different days of the week
wak(a) 'cattle, cow'	different cattle, various milk products

Among the most important compounding elements in Mobilian Jargon was the negative marker **-(e)kšo**, as already recognized by the author of the *Essai* (Anonymous 1862 MS: 8–9; see also Crawford 1978: 78, 90). Speakers could generate antonyms for adjectives by simply adding **-(e)kšo**:

(15) **alokpa** 'sharp' + **-(e)kšo** NEG → **alokpakšó** 'dull'

    alotá 'full' + **-(e)kšo** NEG → **alotakšó** 'empty'

    četó 'big' + **-(e)kšo** NEG → **četokšó** 'small, little'

    čokmá 'good' + **-(e)kšo** NEG → **čokmakšó** 'bad'

    faláya 'long' + **-(e)kšo** NEG → **falayakšó** 'short'

    lawá 'much' + **-(e)kšo** NEG → **lawakšó** 'little, few, scarce, rare'

    sepe 'old' + **-(e)kšo** NEG → **sepekšó** 'new, young'

In modern recordings, **-(e)kšo** closely fused with the stem of the preceding morpheme, whence the initial dash and the deletion of the first vowel of the negative marker. Haas (1975: 260) has described this phonological process with the vowel deletion rule in (16). Lending additional and perhaps the

(16) $\#V_2 \to \emptyset \, / \, V_1\underline{}$

    (with V_1 standing for the final vowel of the adjective and V_2 for the initial one of the negative marker)

strongest support for interpreting these constructions as single units is their highly regular stress pattern, which is rather unusual in light of the alternating prominence in Mobilian Jargon (see Sect. 4.4). As indicated in (15), stress occurred regularly on the final syllable of the entire negative compound constructions irrespective of their length, although usually three or four syllables long. The highly regular pattern of antonym constructions might even lead one to construe the negative marker as a suffix, were it not for that fact that **(e)kšo** also occurred as an independent grammatical element, simply meaning 'no' or 'not.'

The interpretation of antonym constructions as compounds is further justified on semantic and psychological grounds. The last speakers of Mobilian Jargon conceived of antonym constructions as single units and psychologically real, as in the case of other compounds. Among the lexical items remembered best and still used most were the antonyms **čokma** 'good' and **čokmakšo** 'bad,' and it probably was no accident that the author of the *Essai* (Anonymous 1862 MS: 9) had likewise recorded "tchoucouma" and "tchoucouma-(e)kcho" as an exemplary pair. For an alternative, independent antonym for 'good,' he or she presented "Poulou" and "Opoulou" (?; Anonymous 1862 MS: 47), reconstitutable as †**(ok)polo** (?) 'bad, ugly.' In addition, there were a few other independent antonyms describing elementary properties such as **oše** 'small, little,' **kanome** 'a little bit,' **hemeta** 'young,' **yoškolole** 'short,' and †**hemona** 'new.' Yet the last speakers of Mobilian Jargon had great difficulty in recalling antonyms for 'good' or other properties without **-(e)kšo**; independent antonyms did not occur widely in Mobilian Jargon, at least not in its recent history.

By historical indications, the range of application for the negative marker for antonym constructions applied not only to adjectives, but to other words as well, thus providing additional evidence for its productivity. The author of the *Essai* (Anonymous 1862 MS: 8, 20, 85, 93) suggested that **-(e)kšo** in fact applied to all words, and illustrated the observation with examples for two nouns and a verb:

(17) **ãłe** 'truth' + **-(e)kšo** NEG → †**ãłe ekšo** ("antle-ekcho") 'lie'
  mõgola 'friend' + **-(e)kšo** NEG → †**mõgola ekšo** ("mangoula-ekcho") 'enemy'
  tokafa 'to explode, to shoot' + **-(e)kšo** NEG → †**tokafa ekšo** ("toukafa-ekcho") 'to misfire'

In these instances, speakers did not delete the initial vowel in **-(e)kšo** or V_2 in Haas's rule above. The author of the *Essai* (Anonymous 1862 MS: 9, 50, 95) recorded the negative's initial vowel also for the above examples of **čokmakšo** 'bad' and **sepekšo** 'new, young' and other instances including †**tanãpo četo ekšo** 'pistol' (literally: 'gun-big-not') as "tchoucouma ekcho," "Sipi-ekcho," and "Tananbo tchito ekcho" respectively. There is further, independent evidence for the retention of the initial vowel in **-(e)kšo** in historical attestations of regular negative constructions (see (37) in Sect. 6.2).

Early attestations suggest greater variability in the pronunciation of **-(e)kšo** than is obvious from modern recordings. Haas's deletion rule thus requires minor modification to account for the anonymous author's evidence and to make it read as a variable rule (see (18)). This kind of

(18) $\#V_2 \rightarrow (\emptyset) / V_1$___

alternation was perfectly consistent with other known phonological variations in Mobilian Jargon (see Sect. 8.2). Information on any applicable sociohistorical conditions is missing; however, the vowel deletion rule by Haas apparently describes a recent development that arose around or after the turn of the century and perhaps was a form of linguistic calcification as a result of language obsolescence.

Another unique compounding element in Mobilian Jargon is †**eska** 'to do, to make,' attested solely in historical documentation, and it was the only one to result in compounds with an unequivocal verbal function. Its difference in function is evident not only from its gloss, but also from its position with compound phrases, for †**eska** always followed the nouns or adjectives

with which it formed compounds, as illustrated in the following examples
(see Anonymous 1862 MS: 108, 117, 121, 133, 135):

(19) †**alota** 'full' + †**eska** 'to make' → †**alota eska** ("allouta-eska") 'to
  fill'

  †**čolok** 'hole' + †**eska** 'to make' → †**čolok eska** ("tchoulouque-
  eska") 'to make a hole'

  †**holesso** 'speckled, written; book' (?) + †**eska** 'to make' → †**holesso
  eska** ("houlisso eska") 'to write'

  †**lača** 'wet' + †**eska** 'to make' → †**lača eska** ("latcha-eska") 'to wet'

  †**tas(a)nok** 'stone' + **lowak** 'fire' + †**eska** 'to make' → †**tas(a)nok
  lowak eska** ("tas-nouk-lavak-eska") 'flint'

These constructions exhibit essentially the same pattern. Whereas the last
example †**tas(a)nok lowak eska** 'flint' was a noun phrase, it actually consisted of the noun †**tas(a)nok** 'stone' and the verb phrase †**lowak eska** 'to
make a fire;' the latter in turn is analyzable as a sequence of the noun **lowak**
'fire' and †**eska** 'to do, to make.' Superficially, compounds with †**eska** would
not differ from regular verb phrases except that they functioned syntactically and semantically as inseparable units, which qualifies them as compounds and renders them comparable to noun incorporation.[19]

Like †**eska**, the third among the extraordinary compounding elements,
the instrumental †**ešt**, is attested only in the anonymous author's *Essai*,
which lists more than twenty instances, among them the following (see
Anonymous 1862 MS: 50, 52, 58):

(20) †**ešt** INSTR + **ačefa** 'to wash' → †**ešt ačefa** ("tatchifa") 'soap'

  †**ešt** INSTR + **hõsa** 'to shoot' (?) → †**ešt hõsa** ("chetehonsa") 'dart'

  †**ešt** INSTR + **pesa** 'to see, to look' + **nešken** 'eye' → †**ešt pesa nešken**
  ("ichit-pissa-nichekine") 'glasses, spectacles'

  †**nane** 'fish' + †**ešt** INSTR + **albe** 'to kill' (?)[20] → †**nan(e) ešt albe**
  ("nanni-shtelbé") 'fishhook'

---

[19] In the vocabulary, the author (Anonymous 1862 MS: 15, 138, 140–3) further included
examples that at first glance look like verbal compounds analogous to the phenomenon of
noun incorporation in Mobilian Jargon's source languages (see (38) in Sect. 6.2). Yet unlike
the verbal compound constructions with †**eska**, these examples are solely verb phrases including objects, which—separated by a subject in a full sentence—would not be morphologically
continuous like compounds (see Sect. 5.6).

[20] Mobilian Jargon **albe** probably derived from Western Muskogean **abi** 'to kill,' including
the "passive" infix **-l-** (Heather K. Hardy, personal communication; see Munro 1984: 443 n. 7,
446 n. 10). Although this infix appeared in selected other examples such as **holčefo** 'name,'
there is no evidence that it functioned as a separate, productive morpheme in Mobilian Jargon,
unlike its analogous forms in Western and other Muskogean languages (see n. 3). Instead, the
pidgin had quite possibly incorporated the word for 'fishhook' and others as a whole without
adopting corresponding morphological distinctions; for comparison, note the Choctaw compound **na̱n(i) isht a̱lbe** 'fishhook' (Byington 1915: 45).

oke 'water' + †**ešt** INSTR + **alpesa** 'to measure' → †**oke ešt alpesa**
("oké ichetal-alpissa" with an insignificant reduplication of "al")
'gallon'

As indicated by considerable variations in the spellings for †**ešt**, the author
did not recognize their common form or function; instead, he or she apparently considered its various occurrences as parts of larger units that did not
share any morphological feature.[21] None the less, reconstitution of what at
first sight would appear to be no more than a set of several distinct syllables has been possible on the basis of the large number of samples and
modern comparative evidence in the form of the instrumental prefix **išt-** in
Choctaw and Chickasaw (see Munro, forthcoming: 'take').

Mobilian Jargon †**ešt** stood out in terms of not only its productivity, but
also its morphological functions. The absence of any attestation for †**ešt** as
an independent unit in Mobilian Jargon and comparative data in Western
Muskogean suggest that this compounding element similarly functioned as
a prefix, specifically as an instrumental nominalizer (Pamela Munro, personal communication). This inference would be in accord with the historical attestations for the variable deletion of the initial vowel and even the
consonant **š**, as, for example, in "tatchifa" in (20), if such deletions and
accompanying phonological fusions had not been quite common in Mobilian Jargon at large (see Sect. 8.2) and they provided satisfactory evidence
for affixation. Much less can this interpretation rely on some regular stress
pattern comparable to that evident in antonym constructions with the negative suffix **-(e)kšo** (see (15) above). The de-emphasized or even deleted
initial syllable in some of these compounds vary with those retaining an
initial vowel as in "ichet-" or †**ešt** right after "oké" or †**oke** 'water,' including a distinct final vowel, as in the last example given in (20). These observations and the analytic nature of Mobilian Jargon grammar in contrast to
the morphologically synthetic Muskogean and other Southeastern Indian
languages favor an interpretation of the instrumental as an independent
compounding element. †**ešt** apparently functioned like a noun with the
gloss of 'instrument' or 'implement,' which also accounts for compounds
with a more abstract meaning such as †**ešt aholo** 'sorcerer, witch, devil' (literally: 'supernatural instrument or implement'). Like this example, compounds with †**ešt** usually operated as nouns as judged by their context at
the sentence level. The only attested exceptions were the verb †**hekčk ešt
abe** (?; "Hiquinquichetabé" [Anonymous 1862 MS: 17]) 'to poison' and the
adjective †**ešt ayope** ("Steillé-houpé" [Anonymous 1862 MS: 45]) 'last.' In

---

[21] For additional examples with original transcriptions and equivalents in source languages,
see the following glosses in the English–Mobilian Jargon section of the pidgin's vocabulary
(Drechsel, 1996): 'broom,' 'button,' 'clock,' 'cork,' 'ell,' 'fishing line,' 'fork,' 'key,' 'last' (adj.),
'lock' (n.), 'playing card,' 'plow'/'furrow'/'row,' 'poison' (v.), 'scissors,' 'shovel,' 'sorcerer'/'witch'/'devil,' 'spoon,' 'watch' (n.), and 'whip' (n.).

the first instance, †**ešt** and **abe** 'to kill' formed a noun phrase as part of a larger verb phrase; in the second, it is not clear whether the instrumentalizer was truly productive or whether Mobilian Jargon adopted the Choctaw phrase **isht aiopi** (Byington 1915: 202, 488) as a whole.

One might even consider as compounds numbers larger than 'ten,' if Mobilian Jargon speakers perceived them as units with their own meanings. With the exception of monolexemic **taɬepa** 'hundred,' these numbers consisted of two or more figures, with the larger preceding the smaller one(s) in sequences of thousands, hundreds, tens, and units and with the intermediate connective **awa** 'and' distinguishing digits from multipliers:

(21) **pokole** 'ten' + **awa** 'and' + **čaf(f)a** 'one' → **pokole awa čafa** 'eleven'
pokole 'ten' + **tokolo** 'two' + **awa** 'and' + **čafa** 'one' → **pokole tokolo awa čaf(f)a** 'twenty-one'
taɬepa 'hundred' + **čafa** 'one' → **taɬepa čafa** 'one hundred'
taɬepa 'hundred' + **sepe** 'old' + **čafa** 'one' → **taɬepa sepe čafa** 'one thousand'

These examples demonstrate that speakers of Mobilian Jargon would have had little difficulty in expressing themselves numerically and that, counter to Anonymous (1862 MS: 73), they could even formulate the thousands with ease. Numbers obviously were not limited to two lexical components, but could include three, four, and possibly more, as expected in larger, complex numbers. Although not confirmed in either a historical documentation or a modern recording, a figure like '1,111' was presumably *****taɬepa sepe (čafa) awa taɬepa (čafa) awa pokole awa čafa**.

Multiple compounds were not limited to numbers; they also occurred in non-numerical constructions, as illustrated by the anonymous author's example of †**tanãpo četo ekšo** 'pistol' cited earlier and by the following instances (see Anonymous 1862 MS: 28, 30, 34, 55):

(22) †**fočoš** 'duck' + **četo** 'big' + **-(e)kšo** NEG → †**fočoš četoekšo** ("foutious-tchito-ekcho") 'teal'
haše 'sun' + **lašpa** 'hot' + †**etola** 'to lie down' + †**olase** 'near' → †**haše lašpa etola olase** ("atchi-lachepa-etoulla-aulassé") 'evening'
netak 'day' + **ẽla** 'other, else' + **meša** 'after' → **netak ẽla meša** 'the day before yesterday'
netak hollo 'Sunday' + **tokolo** 'two' + **meša** 'after' → **netak hollo tokola meša** 'Tuesday'
soba 'horse' + †**anõka** 'inside; within' + †**pataɬpo** 'saddle' → †**soba anõka pataɬpo** ("souba-anonka-patalpo") 'saddle blanket'
soba 'horse' + **haksobeš** 'ear' + **falaya** 'long' → †**soba haksobeš falaya** ("souba-arsoubiche-falaya") 'donkey, mule'

wak 'cow' + **peše** 'to milk, to suck, to nurse' (?) + **neha** 'fat grease'
→ **wak peš neha** 'butter'

As evident from the above sets of examples, most complex compounds are reconstituted—a fact that indicates their greater use in Mobilian Jargon's better days than recently. The lack of modern evidence makes it difficult to determine the precise grammatical functions for constituents of some examples—especially **anõka** in †**soba anõka pataɫpo** and **peš** in **wak peš neha**—and their internal hierarchies or phrase structures. Other examples, however, suggest that a second modifier including the negative **-(e)kšo** and **meša** 'way off, way out, after,' interpretable either as an adverb or postposition, followed the element that it modified.

Perhaps the most convincing evidence for compounding as a productive and psychologically real process in Mobilian Jargon were loanblends—that is compounds that drew constituent elements from different languages. Most compounds showed few internal differences with respect to the etymology of their constituent elements, in fact revealed resemblances primarily to Western Muskogean, just like the vocabulary in general. Yet there are several examples that illustrate compounds blending lexical elements from different, even unrelated languages, as in the following instances:

(23)   **akãka** 'chicken' (< Western Muskogean) + **čoba** 'big' (< Alabama, Apalachee, Koasati) → **akãka čoba** 'turkey'

eno 'I' (< Alabama, Chickasaw) + **elap** 'he, she, it, they; his, her, its, their' (< Choctaw) → †**eno elap** 'my'

eske 'mother' (< Koasati) + **čome** 'like' (comp.; < Western Muskogean) → †**eske čome** 'aunt'

†**ešt** INSTR (< Western Muskogean) + †**alpesa** 'enough, right' (< Koasati, Alabama) → †**ešt alpesa** 'ell'

kafe 'coffee' (< Spanish, French) + **oše** 'small, little' (< Western Muskogean) → **kafe oše** 'ground coffee'

kato 'cat' (< Spanish) + **nagane** 'male' (< Western Muskogean) → **kato nagane** 'tomcat'

oke 'water' (< Alabama, Koasati) + †**čolok** 'hole' (< Western Muskogean) + †**kale** 'spring, well' (< Western Muskogean, Alabama, Koasati) → †**oke čolok kale** ("oké tchoulouque-calé") 'well' (n.)

palke 'fast, quick' (< Alabama, Koasati) + **ekšo** NEG (< Western Muskogean) → †**palke ekšo** ('palké-ekcho') 'slow, gentle'

skale 'bit' (coin worth 12¹/₂ cents; < French < Dutch) + **tokolo** 'two' (< Alabama, Koasati, Western Muskogean) → **skale tokolo** 'quarter' (coin)

sok(h)a 'pig, hog' (< Alabama, Koasati) + **nepe** 'meat' (< Western Muskogean) → **sok(h)a nepe** 'pork'

hattak 'person' (< Western Muskogean) + **losa** 'black' (< Western Muskogean) + **tayyi** 'female, woman' (< Alabama, Koasati) → **taklosa tayye** 'African-American woman, Black woman' (Geoffrey Kimball, personal communication)

One might argue that compounds with a European-derived constituent such as **kafe**, **kato**, or **skale** do not qualify as truly mixed compounds; although originally borrowed from European languages, these words supposedly behaved no longer like loans with their integration into the lexica of Southeastern Indian languages. But this synchronistic argument ignores the possibility that Mobilian Jargon served as the very medium by which these loans diffused (see (94) in Sect. 12.3), in which case compounds like the above suggest possible historical examples. Numerous other mixed compounds also demonstrate that speakers of Mobilian Jargon apparently observed few restrictions in blending words from different languages into new compounds, even if they preferred to draw on their native tongues.

As is evident from the cited examples, compounding applied to all major grammatical categories, including nouns, verbs, and adjectives, and covered a variety of semantic domains. Among these, only some 120 entries or about a third of the entire body of compounds applied to items introduced by Europeans or other post-Columbian phenomena; most semantic domains of compounds suggest no obvious European influence, and consisted of items of local nature (stones, plants, animals, and so on), food, kin terms, social categories, and miscellany, among the latter also two names for Mobilian Jargon. Altogether, compounds made up as much as 29 per cent of the pidgin's entire vocabulary, both reconstituted and recently recorded. If one also takes potentially debatable examples (such as compound numbers and other instances) into consideration, their overall percentage increases to over a third of the lexicon.

5.6. The Structure of Compounds

Compounds in Mobilian Jargon do more than illustrate an aspect of its lexicon; they provide pointers to the pidgin's broader grammatical patterns. Although its speakers exhibited considerable creativity in generating neologisms, compounding constituents of diverse grammatical functions (including nouns, adjectives, verbs, the negative **-(e)kšo**, and the instrumental †**ešt**) did not occur in free order, but reveal aspects of Mobilian Jargon's syntax.

If a compound consisted of two nouns, the modifier preceded the key or head noun:

(24) **nešken** 'eye' + **oke** 'water' → †**nešken oke** ("nichekine-oké" (Anonymous 1862 MS: 62)) 'tear'

soba 'horse' + **ey(y)e** 'foot' → †**soba eye** ("souba-ihié" (Anonymous 1862 MS: 131)) 'hoof'

sok(h)a 'pig' + **nepe** 'meat' → **sok(h)a nepe** 'pork'

tanče 'corn' + **paska** 'bread' → **tanče paska** 'cornbread'

In contrast, compounds with an adjective as modifier showed the reverse order in a second major type of compounding patttern:

(25) **čanalle** 'wheel' + **lašpa** 'hot' → **čanalle lašpa** 'car, automobile'

hat(t)ak 'person' + **losa** 'black' → **hat(t)ak losa** 'African American, Black'

†**kostene** 'spirit, ghost' + **četo** 'big, large' → †**kostene četo** ("coustiné tchito") 'Great Spirit, god, God' (Le Page du Pratz 1758: ii. 326)

oke 'water' + **sepe** 'old' → **oke sepe** 'ocean'

paska 'bread' + **čampole** 'sweet' → **paska čampole** 'cake'

As the anonymous author of the *Essai* already noticed and illustrated with several supporting examples in the listing of animals (Anonymous 1862 MS: 26–32), **nakne/nagane** 'male' or **ta(y)ek** 'female' likewise occurred in the position of the adjective if gender needed specification:

(26) **hat(t)ak** 'person' + **nakne** 'male' → **hat(t)ak nakne** 'man'

hat(t)ak 'person' + **ta(y)ek** 'female' → **hat(t)ak ta(y)ek** 'woman'

soba 'horse' + **nagane** 'male' → **soba nagane** 'stallion'

wak 'cattle, cow' + **nagane** 'male' → **wak nagane** 'bull'

When **nakne/nagane** or **ta(y)ek** functioned as a noun with the meanings of 'man' or 'woman' respectively, it assumed the same position in compounds as other nouns, depending on their status as either modifier or head element. Thus, there are examples that at first sight appear to contradict the order in (26), but in reality reveal the characteristic noun–adjective pattern:

(27) **ta(y)ek** 'woman' + **homma** 'red' → **ta(y)ek homma** 'Indian woman'

ta(y)ek 'woman' + **losa** 'black' → **ta(y)ek losa** 'African–American woman'[22]

---

[22] There are no attestations for corresponding compounds with **nakne** or **nagane** 'man' as head, probably because the major single-term ethnonyms such as **(a)sovaš** 'Indian' and **nahol(l)o** 'white' usually implied male gender.

Similarly, the head preceded the modifying element in compounds with verbs, for which the anonymous author's *Essai* (1862 MS: 53, 57) supplied some historical evidence:

(28) †**ayonaša** 'chair' + **benele** 'to sit (down)' → †**ayonaša benele** ("ahounacha-bénilé") 'chair, seat'

†**elbak** 'hand' + **tõla** 'to lie' (?) → †**elbak tõla** ("elback tonla") 'finger ring'

With the verb as modifier of the preceding noun, these compounds repeat the pattern of compounds with the instrumental †**ešt**, and resemble the order of constituents in compounds with †**eska** 'to do, to make.' Yet these surface similarities cannot hide substantial differences in their overall grammatical role as compounds. The examples in (28) and those with †**ešt** (see (20) above) served as nouns, whereas compounds with †**eska** (see (19) above) principally operated as verbs.

A comparison of various types of compounds yields a common pattern irrespective of their overall grammatical functions or the etymology of their constituents. See (29).[23] In summary, the head or key element preceded the modifier in a left-headed pattern unless the latter was a noun, for which the reverse order applied. Adjectives and verbs similarly followed nouns and the instrumental †**ešt**, as did the negative marker **-(e)kšo** and adverbs or postpositions. In other words, modifying elements branched out to the right except for nominal modifiers, which bifurcated in the opposite direction. Significantly, this pattern suggests a functional equivalence for verbs and adjectives, a hypothesis that receives further support if one interprets †**ešt** to have operated as a noun.

The formula in (29) describes the basic order of any two or more contiguous constituents in Mobilian Jargon compounds, and proves useful in understanding complex ones. But it cannot account for simple antonym constructions with nouns as heads, compounds consisting of an adjective and †**eska** 'to do, to make,' or complex numbers, except that they shared the predominant pattern of the modifying elements branching out to the right. There is also a historical example of complex compounds that apparently deviates from this pattern: "souba-arsoubiche-falaya" (Anonymous 1862 MS: 28, 30–1) or †**soba haksobeš falaya** 'donkey, mule' in (22). Fol-

(29)

Noun$_2$	$\left\{ \begin{array}{c} \text{Noun}_1 \\ \text{†ešt} \end{array} \right\}$	$\left\{ \begin{array}{c} \text{Adjective} \\ \text{Verb} \end{array} \right\}$	$\left\{ \begin{array}{c} \text{Adverb/} \\ \text{Postposition} \\ \text{-(e)kšo} \end{array} \right\}$

[23] Following standard linguistic conventions, brace brackets require a choice of one of the two or more vertically arranged items.

lowing the formula in (29), one would instead expect †**haksobeš falaya soba**, in which case the noun phrase consisting of the noun **haksobeš** 'ear' and **falaya** 'long' modified the presumed key noun **soba** 'horse.' There is no satisfactory answer to resolve this discrepancy except to propose in this case that Native American speakers considered **haksobeš** 'ear' rather than **soba** 'horse' as the head noun, or alternatively to suggest an error by either the anonymous author of the *Essai* or the Creole source.

Beyond obviously closer ties of the negative marker **-(e)kšo** to its head, the order of compounding constituents in (29) offers no clues about the internal constituency or hierarchy of compounds with more than two lexical elements. From a semantic perspective, compounds such as †**tas(a)nok lowak eska** 'flint' in (19), †**nane ešt albe** 'fishhook' and †**oke ešt alpesa** 'gallon' in (20), and †**soba haksobeš falaya** 'donkey' in (22) suggest a closer relationship between the second and third components, which as a phrase then relate to the first lexical constituent. Other complex compounds apparently exhibit a mirror hierarchy. In †**ešt pesa nešken** 'glasses, spectacles' of (20), the nominalizer †**ešt** and the verb **pesa** 'to see, to look' form a unit, and in turn modify the subsequent key noun **nešken** 'eye,' to be understood as something like 'the-one-to-see-with eyes' or 'seeing eyes.' The identical hierarchical pattern seems evident in **netak ẽla meša** 'the day before yesterday' of (22) with ([noun + adjective] + adverb/postposition [?]), although the constituents of this compound reflect grammatical categories different from the preceding example. In the same set of examples, †**haše lašpa etola olase** 'evening' may even be analyzable as a compound consisting of a noun phrase with a noun and adjective plus a verb phrase with a verb and an adverb or a postposition. Still other complex compounds such as †**soba anõka patałpo** 'saddle blanket' and **wak peš neha** 'butter' in (22) first require clarification regarding the precise grammatical functions of their constituents **anõka** and **peš** respectively to answer the question of their internal structure, left unresolved without a substantial set of modern comparative data. The currently available evidence, however, points to alternating patterns, depending on the grammatical functions of their constituents.

6

Syntax

6.1. General Aspects

Following conventional, perhaps almost stereotypical wisdom, North American Indian languages distinguished themselves by polysynthesis— that is by the incorporation of several stems and affixes into one-word phrases or sentences (see e.g. Mithun 1983). At the opposite end on the scale of morphological synthesis and in sharp contrast to this type of grammatical pattern appear pidgins with their fundamentally analytic structure. Like Eskimo Jargon, Chinook Jargon, Delaware Jargon, and other Native American contact media, Mobilian Jargon generally lacked affixations or inflections; its speakers determined the grammatical functions of words by their position within a phrase or sentence, that is word order, and also from the sociolinguistic context.

The position of words in phrases and sentences permits the distinction of several syntactic categories: (1) the predicate (Pred) and the verb (V); (2) the noun (N) and noun phrase (NP); (3) modifiers such as adjectives (Adj) and adverbs or adverbials (Adv), applied to nouns and verbs respectively; (4) various verb markers pertaining to negation (NEG), modality (MOD), tense (PAST), and probably others; (5) personal and possessive pronouns (Pers, Poss) and demonstrative pronoun (Dem); (6) relative and interrogative pronouns (Rel, Ques); (7) postpositions; and (8) independent words of approval, acknowledgement, exclamation, interjection, etc. Mobilian Jargon speakers also recognized the following major categories of grammar: the subject in the form of both nouns (S) and pronouns (s); direct and indirect objects (O_1 and O_2 respectively); and any other sentence segment (X) such as adverbs or adverbial phrases.

This listing probably contains all the major types of syntactic functions and grammatical distinctions in Mobilian Jargon. Yet documentation of only a few single instances for some of these categories leaves open the possibility for others. In particular, there remains the question of some tense-aspect marker other than **taha** PAST, such as the conditional and the future. The anonymous author of the *Essai* (Anonymous 1862 MS: 9; see the quotation in Preliminaries to Part II) only described the future tense as expressed by a reference to the prospective point in time and by the repetition of the verb.

The present chapter offers a description and analysis of the basic phrase and sentence structure of Mobilian Jargon, ranging from the least to the most complex constructions, from one-word utterances to embedded clauses.

6.2. *Simple Utterances and Phrases*

Utterances in Mobilian Jargon could simply consist of single terms or short phrases, specifically greetings, exclamations, short questions, and words of acknowledgement and agreements. They did not constitute sentences with explicit noun and verb phrases, but were pragmatically equivalent to full sentences:

(30)	**šla, mogola.**	'Hello, friend.'
	nanta?	'What?'
	o, čokma yama.	'Oh, good indeed.'
	yamma	'Yes'

Listing these single-word utterances and short phrases might appear super-fluous were it not for the fact that they played an important role in Mobil-ian Jargon, a second language. Short expressions were prevalent among speakers lacking fluency, and predominated among those who could remember but bits and pieces of the pidgin in modern times. These brief utterances, rendering the pidgin rather formulaic at times, may even have reflected some conversational or discourse restriction characteristic of Southern Indians. This interpretation draws on the observations of Le Page du Pratz on Mobilian Jargon in the first half of the eighteenth century, when Mobilian Jargon was well established and still in wide use. His description at times suggests a rather reduced use of the pidgin, which resulted in his recording of primarily short utterances such as the above (for further dis-cussion, see Sects. 7.3 and 9.3). Although the available data remain insuffi-cient for a definite conclusion, there is considerable ethnographic evidence for **yam(m)a** 'yes, right, alright, indeed; this, that (in response to "Which one?")' to have played this very role in recent Mobilian Jargon conversa-tions. The Coushatta of southwestern Louisiana and their neighbors appar-ently used this single expression so often with each other that it came to be identified with the pidgin and to serve as a major name for it. Speakers of Mobilian Jargon presumably were sayers of **yam(m)a**, as a few suggested independently (see Sects. 9.1 and 10.4).

Whatever the range and nature of simple utterances in Mobilian Jargon, its speakers did not shy away from using more complex constructions, including a variety of sentence structures as evident from noun, adjectival, negative, verb, and other phrases.

Phrases consisting of two nouns exhibited a pattern in which the modifying noun preceded the key noun as in noun–noun compounds:

(31) **eske** 'mother' + †**anakfe** 'brother' → †**eske anakfe** 'mother's brother, maternal uncle'

nane 'fish' + †**hakšop** 'skin' → †**nane hakšop** 'fish scale'

sapõtak 'mosquito' + **čokha** 'house' → **sapõtak čokha** 'mosquito net'

tamaha 'town' + **olčefo** 'name' → **tamaha olčefo** 'name of town' (Crawford 1978: 85)

Replacing modifying nouns, personal or demonstrative pronouns in noun phrases similarly occurred in initial position:

(32) **eno** 'my' + **haksobeš** 'ear' → **eno haksobeš** 'my ear'

(e)šno 'your' + **ĕke** 'father' → **(e)šno ĕke** 'your father'

yako 'this' + **netak** 'day' → **yako netak** 'this day, today'

In agreement with this pattern is another phrase for 'today:'

(33) **hemaka** 'now' + **neta** 'day' → **hemaka neta** 'today'

The order of this singular example suggests an interpretation of **hemaka** 'now' as a temporal demonstrative, comparable in grammatical function to that of **yako** 'this, that; here, there.'

In contrast, modifying elements such as adjectives, adverbs, and negatives followed the sentence element that they modified. Thus, adjectives in noun phrases characteristically appeared after nouns as in corresponding compound constructions (see (25) through (27) in Sect. 5.6):

(34) **čokka** 'house' + **sepe** 'old' → **čokka sepe** 'old house'

łało 'fish' + **četo** 'big' → **łało četo** 'big fish'

tayek 'woman' + **čokma** 'good' → **tayek čokma** 'good woman'[1]

Likewise, adverbs modifying adjectives took second position:

(35) **čokma** 'good' + **fena** 'very' → **čokma fena** 'very good'

kapassa 'cold' + **kanome** 'a little' → **kapassa kanome** 'a little cold'

lašpa 'hot' + **lawa** 'much' → **lašpa lawa** 'very hot'

The same order of modified and modifier applied to **-(e)kšo** NEG, which—as in antonym constructions (see (15) through (18) in Sect. 5.5)—occurred after the word to be negated:

(36) **aša** 'to have' + **-(e)kšo** NEG → **ašakšo** 'do not have'

tana 'to know' + **-(e)kšo** NEG → **tanakšo** 'don't know'

Historical attestations provide independent corroboration for this pattern:

---

[1] Adjectives in the same position could likewise function as predicates. The examples of (34) could thus read also as 'The house is old,' 'The fish is big,' and 'The woman is good' respectively (for further discussion, see Sect. 6.3).

(37) "tĕne áksho" 'don't know' (Gatschet 1885 MS: 24)/†**tana ekšo** (?)
     "Yokepa iksho" 'not calm' (Johnson and Leeds 1964: 24, 25)/
     †**yokepa ekšo** ~ †**yekopa ekšo** (including metathesis)

Verb phrases with objects or other supplements reflected a pattern similar in form to that of noun phrases with a verb or a predicate (as, for instance, in (28) and (34) above), in that the verb or the predicate occurred in final position in both instances. Yet the formal similarity of verb phrases with noun phrases in Mobilian Jargon was superficial due to the limited possibilities of two-word combinations, and cannot hide fundamental syntactic differences between them—with noun phrases branching to the right and verb phrases to the left. The author of the *Essai* (Anonymous 1862 MS: 15, 138, 140–3) already listed numerous examples of verb phrases, in which a noun phrase or an equivalent element such as an adjective preceded the verb:

(38) **ete** 'wood' + †**čãle** 'to cut, to chop' → †**ete čãle** ("ité-tchanfé"/"chanlé") 'to chop wood'
     hat(t)ak 'person' + **bole** 'to beat, to strike' → †**hat(t)ak bole** ("attack-boulé") 'to beat (up)/strike a person'
     lokfe 'earth, ground' + **bašle** 'to cut' → †**lokfe bašle** ("loquefé-bachelé") 'to plow' (literally: 'to cut the earth')
     lowak 'fire' + †**ɫalle** (?) → †**lowak ɫalle** (?) ("lowack-hallé") 'to boil' (literally: 'to boil over fire')
     nane 'fish' + †**halale** 'to pull, to draw' → †**nane halale** ("nanni-allalé") 'to catch fish, to fish'
     oke 'water' + **elle** 'to die' → †**oke elle** ("oké-ellé") 'to drown' (literally: 'to die in water')
     †**pene** 'boat' + †**malele** 'to run' → †**pene malele** ("pinni-malilé") 'to row' (literally: 'to run [on] a boat')
     soba 'horse' + **benele** 'to sit' → †**soba benele** ("souba-bénilé") 'to ride (on horseback)' (literally: 'to sit [on] a horse')
     soba 'horse' + †**tabakale** 'to gallop' → †**soba tabakale** ("souba-tabakhalé") 'to gallop (on horseback)'

Some of these verb phrases may well have served as idioms, in which case there arises the question of whether they functioned as verbal compounds comparable to those with †**eska** 'to do, to make' (see (19) in Sect. 5.5). But there currently is no evidence that the above verb phrases constituted morphologically coherent, indivisible phrases, that—in other words—they maintained their structural integrity as single syntactic units like compounds. On the assumption that Mobilian Jargon speakers could insert lexical elements within these verb phrases with little or no restriction, they conceivably generated constructions such as *ete *lawa* **čãle** 'to chop much wood' or *nane *eno* halale 'I catch fish' (with italics identifying the inserted

(39)

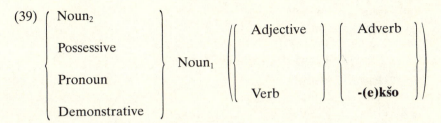

items and with the initial asterisk indicating that these are reconstructed samples without any modern or historical attestation). Support for such reasoning comes from one of the anonymous author's illustrations, actually an entire sentence. For "soif" or 'thirst,' the author of the *Essai* (Anonymous 1862 MS: 103, 141) gave "Oké-no-bana," which—reconstituted as †**oke (e)no bana**—really means 'I want water' (word-for-word translation: 'Water I want'). In this case, the speaker inserted the pronoun **(e)no** for 'I' between the initial object and the verb, which disqualifies the verb phrase *oke bana 'to want water, to be thirsty' as a compound.

Nominal, adjectival, negative, and verb phrases (incorporating nouns, pronouns, adjectives, verbs, adverbs, and the negative in various combinations) revealed an overall pattern analogous to that of compounds. As with the latter, modifying elements in short phrases branched out to the right except for nominal modifiers plus possessive pronouns and the demonstratives **yako** and **hemaka**, which bifurcated in the opposite direction (see (39)). Aside from obviously closer ties between the adverb or the negative and the predicate, the available data are no longer detailed or comprehensive enough to suggest an internal hierarchy for multiple-word phrases; the constituent structure probably altered depending on meaning, like that of compounds.

The structural similarity of regular phrases to compounds with comparable lexical elements suggests a structural and historical relationship between the two, but cannot hide their less obvious differences. Phrases differed from structurally analogous compounds in that the first lacked the established meanings and the grammatical impermeability of the latter with their calcified structure. Regular phrases, among them especially verb phrases, did not necessarily maintain their integrity as a syntactic unit, but permitted the insertion of grammatical elements from outside the phrase, of which a prime example is pronouns in full sentences.

6.3. Full Sentences

In full sentences with a noun and a verb phrase, the subject preceded the verb:

(40) **ešno   benele.**
    you   sit
    2 sg/pl   V
    '(You) sit (down)!' (invitational imperative)

    lašpa   mente.
    heat   come
    N   V
    'The heat (summer) arrives.'

This pattern of subject–verb also applied to predicate constructions, in which the predicate consisted of an adjective or noun. In this case, it would appear to be more economical to consider the adjective or noun as equivalent to a verb or as a verbal rather than to posit a zero copula, for many words in Mobilian Jargon could occur in two or all of the three major grammatical categories of verb, noun, and adjective, as already observed (see Sect. 5.1):

(41) **pošno   nokowa.**
    we   angry
    Pers   Pred
    'We are angry.'

    eno   poškoš   lawa.
    my   child   many
    Poss   N   Pred
    ⎣_____⎦
            S
    'I have many children.' (Literally: 'My children are many.')

    eno   nagane   hemeta.
    I   man   young
    Pers   N   Adj
            ⎣_____⎦
            Pred
    'I am a young man.'

If the verb of a sentence needed modification, the modifying element consisting of one of the verb markers (PAST, MOD, or NEG) or an adverb usually followed the actual verb:

(42) **lap   čokma   -kšo.**
    it   good   NEG
    Pers   Adj   NEG
    ⎣_____⎦
            Pred
    'It is not good.'

eno	noše	taha.
I	sleep	PAST
Pers	V	PAST

V

'I slept.'

šno	sepe	lawa.
you	old	very
Pers	Adj	Adv

Pred

'You are very old.'

eno	mente	yako.
I	come	here
Pers	V	Adv

V

'I come here.' (Possibly: 'I have come here.')

ešno	albe	banna?
you	pay	want
Pers	V	MOD

V

'Do you wish to pay?'

Adverbs or adverbial phrases that modified the entire sentence, however, occupied the initial position in a sentence, and expressed such qualifications as time, place, quantity, manner, and instrumentality:

(43)
meša	eno	benele.
over	I	sit
Adv	Pers	V
Adv	s	V

'I sit down over there.'

"Pilla-ino-noha."

†pel(l)a	eno	nowa.
away, off	I	walk
Adv	Pers	V
Adv	s	V

'I walk away.'[2]

(Anonymous 1862 MS: 22)

[2] The gloss of French *flâner* or English 'doing nothing' (Anonymous 1862 MS: 14) is erroneous.

eltən	pošno	aya.
Elton	we	go
N	Pers	V
Adv	s	V

'We go to Elton.'

eno	cokha	eno	falama	banna.
My	house	I	return	want
Poss	N	Pers	V	MOD

| Adv | s | V |

'I want to return to my house/home.'

ašobolle	eno	hopone.
fireplace	I	cook
N	Pers	V
Adv	s	V

'I cook (it) in the fireplace.'

yako	netak	pošno	aya.
this	day	we	go
Dem	N	Pers	V

| Adv | s | V |

'We go today.'

palke	eno	aya.
fast	I	go
Adv	S	V

'I go fast.'

bašpo	eno	bašle	taha.
knife	I	cut	PAST
N	Pers	V	PAST

| Adv | s | V |

'I done cut (it) with a knife.'   [*sic*]

The initial position was also home to objects. When a sentence included a direct object, it preceded the subject, which in turn came before the verb and consisted only of pronouns in the following instances:

(44) neta	eno	hoyo.
bear	I	hunt
N	Pers	V
O	s	V

'I hunt bear.'

šonak	lawa-kšo	eno	aša.
money	much-NEG	I	have
N	Adj-NEG	Pers	V

| O | | s | V |

'I have (a) little money.'

poškoš	točena	lap	aša.
child	three	she	have
N	Adj	Pers	V

| O | | s | V |

'She has three children.'

yama		eno	anõpole.
Mobilian Jargon		I	speak
N		Pers	V
O		s	V

'I speak Mobilian Jargon.'

yako	lap	aša.
that	he	has
Dem	Pron	V
O	s	V

'He got something.'

pleša	eno	banna.
work	I	want
N/V	Pron	V
O	s	V

'I want work.'/'I want to work.'

In their word order, these sentences match examples recorded by James M. Crawford and a historical instance by the anonymous author of the *Essai*:

(45)
kafe	no	banna.[3]
coffee	I	want
N	Pers	V
O	s	V

'I wish (some) coffee.'
(Crawford 1978: 82)

[3] For reasons of consistency, I have represented Crawford's transcription of the vowels [i] and [u] as **e** and **o** respectively in this and the following examples (see Sect. 4.1).

tamaha	olčefo	eno	hakalo	banna.
town	name	I	hear	want
N₂	N₁	Pers	V	MOD

$$\underbrace{\text{N}_2 \quad \text{N}_1}_{\text{O}} \quad \underset{\text{S}}{} \quad \underbrace{\phantom{\text{hakalo banna}}}_{\text{V}}$$

'I want to hear the name of the town.'
(Crawford 1978: 85)

anõpa	eno	tana-kšo.
language	I	know-NEG
N	Pers	V-NEG
O	s	V

'I don't know (his) language.'
(Crawford 1978: 87)

"Oké-no-bana."

†oke	(e)no	bana
water	I	want
N	Pers	V
O	s	V

'I am thirsty.' (Literally: 'I want water.')
(Anonymous 1862 MS: 103, 141)

I did not record any simple sentences including an indirect object and comparable to English 'I pay you'; nor have I yet found any historical attestation for such a construction. But like any direct object or adverbial phrase, a single indirect object probably assumed initial position, if another construction with both a direct and indirect object provides any indication (see (51) in Sect. 6.4).

As already suggested by the last example in (42), speakers of Mobilian Jargon followed the same word order as that of assertions in questions requiring **yam(m)a** 'yes' or **(e)kšo** 'no' as answer. Without inverting any phrases, yes–no questions differed from assertions only by a rising intonation towards the end. Thus, an individual might ask:

(46)
yamma	šno	tana?
Mobilian Jargon	you	know
N	Pers	V
O	s	V

'Do you know Mobilian Jargon?'

kafe	šno	banna?
coffee	you	want
N	Pers	V
O	s	V

'Do you want (some) coffee?'
(Crawford 1978: 82)

tamaha	**olčefo**	**ešno**	**tana?**
town	name	you	know
N₂	N₁	Pron	V

O   s   V

'Do you know the name of the town?'

In inquiries equivalent to *Wh*-questions in English, the interrogative similarly occurred in initial position like sentence-level adverbials and objects, and took a secondary, adjectival position after a noun in accordance with the pidgin's standard noun-phrase pattern only in questions equivalent to English *Which* plus a noun:

(47)
katema	**šno**	**eya?**
where	you	go
Ques	Pron	V
Adv	s	V

'Where do you go?'[4]

nanta	**lap**	**anõpa**	**taha?**
what	she	say	PAST
Ques	Pron	V	PAST

O   s   V

'What did she say?'

katome	**šno**	**albe?**
how much	you	pay
Ques	Pron	V
O	s	V

'How much do you pay?'

hatak	**nanta?**
human	what/which
N	Ques

'Who?'

poškoš	**katome**	**ešno**	**aša?**
child	how many	you	have
N	Ques	Pers	V

O   s   V

'How many children do you have?'

---

[4] In her notes on "Choctaw," Caroline Dormon (n.d. MS: 2) recorded the same sentence as "Cotteema ïshnõ ïyä?" with the translation of 'Where are you going?'

There are no recordings of complex imperative, exclamatory, or other constructions, which might reveal an alternative structure. But it is reasonable to infer that these other constructions followed the same pattern by the mere fact of its pervasiveness in assertions and questions and because of the limited number of theoretically feasible and unambiguous options.

6.4. Complex Constructions

Most of the examples that Crawford and I could still record from the last speakers of Mobilian Jargon in the field barely exceeded two or three arguments; more complex structures were rather rare in our sets of recordings. To some extent, the prevalence of simple sentences in our data reflects the basic nature of Mobilian Jargon, that of a contact medium. On the other hand, these limited data also resulted from language death, as complex constructions became less common with Mobilian Jargon's decline. In the past, fluent speakers undoubtedly used complex constructions more frequently than the current corpus of data indicates, and could express elaborate semantic relationships beyond two or three arguments. When there was a need to express some additional idea, there were various options at hand.

In the syntactically most simple form, speakers of Mobilian Jargon could add any new information in a separate juxtaposed sentence that shared the same base with the preceding sentence, repeating old information. For instance, two such constructions could share an identical subject and verb and differ only in one argument, as (48) illustrates. Such "compounding" of two minimal-pair sentences, or parataxis, apparently was quite common at one time. For example, the anonymous author of the *Essai* (Anonymous 1862 MS: 26) rendered 'I dream' as "Ino-nocé-ino-pissa," which, reconstituted, reads as †**eno** *nose*; **eno** *pesa* and which literally translates as 'I sleep; I see.' In this instance, the two juxtaposed sentences present a relationship between two arguments not only at some superficial syntactic level, but also on an underlying, semantic basis, and in fact describe another concept, that of dreaming, in terms of two arguments.

(48) *paska*	**eno**	**bašle**;	*bašpo*	**eno**	**bašle**.
bread	I	cut	knife	I	cut
N	Pron	V	N	Pron	V
O	s	V	Adv	s	V

'I cut (the) bread with a knife.'

Mobilian Jargon moreover permitted the incorporation of a third argument or element at the end of a sentence, at least in the form of an adverb:

(49) **netak   ela   eno   mente   mona.**
      day   other   I   come   back
      N   Adj   Pron   V   Adv

          Adv   s   V
      'On another day, I come back.'

pelašaš   eno   topa   lawa.
yesterday   I   sick   very
Adv   Pers   Adj   Adv

Adv   s   Pred
'Yesterday I was very sick.'

kafe   no   banna   fena.
coffee   I   want   very much
N   Pron   V   Adv

O   s   V
'I want coffee very much.'

katema   eno   nowa-kšo   fena.
anywhere   I   travel-NEG   really
Adv   Pers   V–NEG   Adv

Adv   s   V
'I do not really travel anywhere.'[5]

katema   šno   pleša   hemaka?
where   you   work   now
Ques   Pron   V   Adv
Adv   s   V   Adv
'Where do you work now?'

In these examples, the posterior position of the second adverbs suggests a closer semantactic relationship between these and the predicate, presumably modifying the preceding verb or adjective rather than the full sentence. The only instance possibly not fitting this pattern is the final utterance, in which **hemaka** 'now' apparently modifies the entire sentence rather than specifically the verb. If confirmed, this exceptional pattern could be due to the need to preserve the initial position of the interrogative **katema**.

At first impression, the constructions in (49) might suggest some constraint against the fronting of more than one sentence constituent

---

[5] This sentence is an unpublished example that James Crawford (personal communication) recorded from Arzelie Langley.

(50) **nante**   **fʊt**   **trabəl**   **eno**   **aša.**
     another   foot   trouble   I   have
     time
     Adv N_2 N_1 Pers   V

     Adv   O   s   V
     'Another time, I have a foot ailment.'

(51) **ešno**   **sonak**   **točena**   **eno**   **albe.**
     you   money   three   I   pay
     Pers   N   Adj   Pers   V

     O_2 O_1 s   V
     'I pay you three dollars.'

preceding the subject. Yet this case did not apply in all instances, as is evident in a third type of "complex" construction, in which an adverb preceded the object (see 50)). This example is all the more interesting for the reason that its speaker, an African–American neighbor of the Coushatta near Elton (Louisiana), borrowed *foot trouble* from his first language without any hesitation, and integrated it into his pidgin sentence as if this loan from English had already been part of the regular Mobilian Jargon vocabulary, thus giving a firsthand illustration of the process of lexical replacement as it undoubtedly occurred on repeated occasions before. Structurally, English-derived *foot trouble* with its right-headed pattern matched the internal order of noun$_2$–noun$_1$ compounds or noun phrases in Mobilian Jargon.

In still another instance (51), we find both an indirect and direct object in initial position. Following the standard pattern of a Mobilian Jargon noun phrase including a possessive pronoun (as illustrated in (32) in Sect. 6.2), one might be inclined to interpret **ešno sonak točena** as a noun phrase including the initial possessive pronoun **ešno** 'your' or as 'your three dollars.' Yet such an interpretation, while possible, appears unreasonable because it would not fit the context in which I recorded this utterance. The speaker, who addressed the author, explicitly stated he would pay the indicated amount for a desired item.

Sentences with two arguments preceding the subject were comparatively rare in the corpus of Mobilian Jargon utterances that Crawford and I could still record. But the pidgin permitted truly complex constructions with multiple arguments either by parataxis or in a single sentence. Crawford (1978: 82, 94, 97; personal communication) recorded samples with subordinate clauses from the late Arzelie Langley, a Choctaw medicine woman among the Louisiana Coushatta and one of the last fluent speakers of Mobilian

Jargon. These constructions followed the same basic syntactic principles as those of simple utterances; the embedded clause simply occurred in the initial position usually assigned to an object or adverbial phrase:

(52)

nanta	šno	banna,	šno	čõpa.
what	you	want	you	buy
Rel	Pers	V	Pers	V
O	s	V		

| X | | s | V |

'You buy what you want.'

katema	oya	lap	nowa	banna,	lap	aya.
where	all over	he	travel	want		he	go
Rel	Adv	Pers	V	MOD		Pers	V

Adv | s | | V

| X | | s | V |

'He goes wherever he wants to travel.'

yako	hatak	pake	lap	mente,	eno	yokpa	fena.
this	man	afar	he	come	I	glad	very
Dem	N	Adj/Adv(?)'	Pers	V	Pers	Pred	Adv

focused(?) S | (Adv?) | s | V | s | | V

| O | | s | V |

'I am very glad that this man (from) afar comes (here).'/'. . . that this man comes (here from) afar.' (?)

The subordinate clause **yako hatak pake lap mente** in the last example presents two interrelated problems of grammatical analysis in so far as the noun phrase **yako hatak** 'this man' occurred in initial position, followed by **pake** 'far' and the copied pronoun **lap** 'he.' There are also questions of interpretation with respect to the grammatical function of **pake** 'far, afar' between the initial noun phrase and the pronoun. In one explanation, one might consider **pake** as an adverb, preceded by a full noun phrase and followed by a pronoun that subsequently copied the initial noun phrase. In this case, we would have a single instance of a full subject preceding an adverbial phrase, which would suggest a different word order for constructions with overt nouns as subjects, that is SXV and by extension SOV. In a second interpretation preferable for its simplicity, we read the subordinate clause **yako hatak pake lap mente** as '(That) this remote man comes here' with **pake** 'far' functioning as an adjective that modified the noun **hatak** 'man' in the standard noun–adjective sequence.

However, there is little doubt about an instance of pronoun copying in the case of **yako hatak (pake)** and the pleonastic **lap**, which can refer only to the preceding noun phrase in this otherwise unambiguous example. At the very least, the speaker could have added the pronoun for clarification, and might inadvertently have done so because of Crawford, who had just begun research on Mobilian Jargon. From the recording context, there may also be some indication for focusing or explicit emphasis in the initial noun phrase, in which case Langley expressed her pleasure about the visit by Crawford instead of some other person. Following these arguments, the final example in (52) need not suggest a word order different from that of constructions with pronoun subjects; with such structural highlighting, the subject's actual position could still be indicated by the pronoun rather than the noun.

6.5. Basic Structure and Word Order: SOV or OSV?

As attested in numerous modern and historical recordings, Mobilian Jargon exhibited a highly regular, but distinctive word order for multi-argument sentences with pronouns as subjects (see (53)). This formula can be reduced to XOsV or X/OsV, where X stands for a second, indirect object, an adverbial, or even an entire embedded sentence in the initial object position, O for a direct object, lower case s for a pronominal subject, and V for a verb. The phrase structure of Mobilian Jargon sentences thus branched out to the left as well as the right with the pronominal subject assuming a middle position.

The OsV word order was the norm for sentences with a pronoun subject in Mobilian Jargon, and is evident from an overwhelming majority of the examples that Crawford and I recorded. Thus, they preclude an analysis of the recordings in terms of any stylistic or discourse-conditioned change in the order of sentence constituents, be it focusing, topicalization, or some other structural means of emphasis and highlighting. Focusing, if confirmed in the final example of (52), actually exhibited a word-order pattern that differed from that of (53), but did not contradict it. Altogether, there were only a few utterances with a variable word order that disagreed with the OsV pattern. In all these exceptions, speakers immediately corrected their sentences to match the above rule, or else exhibited confusion about the proper word order in Mobilian Jargon when quizzed further. Sociologically, they belonged to the youngest and oldest generations to remember any of

$$(53) \quad \left\{ \begin{array}{l} \left\{ \begin{array}{l} O_2 \\ \text{Adv} \quad O_1 \end{array} \right\} \\ \text{subordinate clause} \end{array} \right\} \quad s \quad V$$

the pidgin, which possibly indicates that they either had never learned it fully or were no longer certain of their memories.

OsV seems to be a rather unusual word order for a pidgin, because one would expect a more common linguistic denominator as the basic grammatical pattern of a linguistic and social compromise in a multilingual environment. Equally noteworthy is the fact that almost all sentences with a second argument in the form of an object, an adverbial phrase, or even an embedded clause show pronouns as subjects rather than overt nouns. This observation raises the question as to the basic word order of sentences with two or more arguments including a full subject noun; it is these constructions rather than sentences with pronominal subjects that usually define the basic word order of a language.

Just as the last example in (52) reveals some uncertainty about its interpretation, there is little unequivocal evidence to resolve the issue of nominal subjects in multiple-argument constructions. Neither Crawford nor I have recorded any exemplary transitive sentences with overt nouns as subjects from the last Mobilian Jargon speakers. My attempts at formally and informally eliciting such constructions in my field inquiries have been fruitless; I have not been any more successful in finding any sentences with an overt noun plus a second argument in the form of an object or an adverbial phrase, much less an embedded clause, in historical documents. Just as challenging as the question of Mobilian Jargon's basic word order may thus be an explanation for its largely missing documentation in both modern and historical recordings.

By all indications, complex sentences with nouns as subjects were possible in Mobilian Jargon, which had intransitive and other two-argument sentences with nominal subjects. There is no conceivable reason why speakers of an established pidgin with a history of no less than two and a half centuries should have omitted such constructions. Interpreting the absence of noun subjects in multiple-argument constructions in terms of grammatical simplicity or as characteristic of a "simplified" or "reduced" form of Muskogean would do injustice to Mobilian Jargon in view of its complex multiple-argument constructions. Conversely, the diverse sociohistorical contexts in which it served as an interlingual medium (see Chapters 9 and 10) were intricate enough to warrant sentences with clearly identifiable full subjects and additional arguments.

Circumstantial evidence and educated guesses suggest two mutually exclusive basic word orders for Mobilian Jargon. For one, subject nouns preceded any second argument, and took the initial position with SOV or SXV as fundamental semantactic pattern (with capital S representing nominal subjects). In this case, constructions with pronoun subjects and their characteristic word order of X/OsV would be mere surface variations of underlying SOV, following the model of Muskogean and other Gulf languages. Alternatively, nominal subjects occupied the same position as pronominal ones in analogy to X/OsV, and immediately followed any objects, adverbial phrases, or even entire subordinate clauses, thus providing X/OSV.

If there existed substantial variation in word order as standard in Mobilian Jargon, one would expect major historical observers to have made reference to it or at least to have expressed confusion about its grammar at one point or another. In particular, the author of the quite detailed *Essai* (Anonymous 1862 MS) should have made mention of any major syntactic variation, but did not do so. Similarly, Antoine Simon Le Page du Pratz, author of *Histoire de la Louisiane* (1758) and an early perceptive source on Mobilian Jargon, would have left some clue to an alternating word order based on his own knowledge. Instead, he solely observed about "la Langue vulgaire" that "elle s'apprend mieux par l'usage que par principes" (Le Page du Pratz 1758: ii. 323) or 'it is easier to learn by practice than by rules' (Le Page du Pratz in Crawford 1978: 44); he would hardly have made this observation had there been a regular alternation between OsV and SOV, foreign to Europeans and requiring some explanation. Nor are there any suggestions of any confusion about the pidgin's word order such as one would expect from an OsV–SOV alternation. Any substantial misunderstandings between Indians and non-Indians due to a variable word order would directly contradict the distinct impression that historical documents leave us about European and African immigrants of various nationalities making wide use of the Indian pidgin without any unusual problems of communication (see Crawford 1978 and Chapter 9).

The hypothesis of SOV and SXV as basic word order for Mobilian Jargon can draw on the last, ambiguous example in (52), if **yako hatak pake lap mente** is interpreted as a sentence with a subject noun phrase followed by an adverbial, reading as '[that] this man comes [here from] afar.' For a possible additional example, I recorded an apparent SOV sentence in (54) as part of a joke song (see (60) in Sect. 7.3 for further details). Yet there remain major unresolved issues in interpreting this song. I could no longer identify the meanings of all constituents and their grammatical functions with certainty, for the person who remembered it, a Tunica-Biloxi woman near Marksville in central Louisiana, did not recall any of the pidgin's grammar or lexicon. Then, there is the question of poetic license in a formal, ritualized context such as this joke song accompanied by dances. Why did this example not meet Mobilian Jargon's other grammatical standards, including a possessive pronoun accompanying **bolokfa** 'nose' and the past-tense

(54) **sapõta(k)**   **bolokfa**   **belesõ** (?)
      mosquito   nose (?)   sting (?)
      'a mosquito stung (his) nose (?)'

(55) **eno   patassa   banna.**
    I   sunfish   want
    s   O   V
    'I want sunfish.'

participle **taha** for the verb? Perhaps a third example consists of a Coushatta Indian's quotation of what a Black neighbor supposedly uttered with pronominal subject (see (55)). Did the non-Indian neighbor derive this sentence from an underlying SOV word order by simply extending it to constructions with pronoun subjects? Although this explanation appears attractive, the Coushatta—a middle-aged man who knew only a few words of Mobilian Jargon—possibly misquoted his neighbor.

Such isolated examples with their many ambiguities constitute at best poor evidence for multiple-argument sentences, including an overt nominal subject in initial position, and former speakers could not help resolve these problems of analysis. On my most recent visit to Louisiana, in summer 1989, I pursued the question of basic word order in Mobilian Jargon again, and addressed it among others to Ernest Sickey, a multilingual Coushatta Indian with native competency in Koasati and Choctaw, whose grandmother had spoken Mobilian Jargon fluently and who had retained some passive knowledge of the pidgin. His first response to my questions was that Mobilian Jargon—like Koasati and Choctaw—followed SOV; but he could not provide me with any examples. When I offered him a hypothetical, potentially confusing sentence such as **hatak homma hatak hatta abe* ('person-red + person-white + kill') for interpretation and alerted him to the absence of any morphological features identifying grammatical function, he was uncertain about the meaning, and rejected SOV as the pidgin's basic word order.

Although the Coushatta consultant could not give me an answer, he did provide me with a possible clue as to why neither Crawford nor I were able to record Mobilian Jargon constructions with full nouns any longer and why historical records similarly lack reliable examples. If Mobilian Jargon's basic word order had been SOV, the accompanying alternation of SOV and OsV would have been confusing to speakers without corresponding models of grammar, especially to Europeans, Africans, and other immigrants. Yet most striking would have been the problem of subordinate clauses in a grammar with SOV as basic word order. To maintain consistency, did Mobilian Jargon permit the insertion of a subordinate clause between the nominal subject and the verb? Alternatively, did sentences with a nominal subject and a subordinate clause follow a word order different from SOV? In either case, this scenario would have discouraged the use of multiple-argument constructions with nominal subjects, and would have led to their early decline and obsolescence.

On the other hand, if Mobilian Jargon's basic word order was OSV, the kind of multiple-argument utterances to survive the longest would have been constructions with pronominal subjects. They agreed in their structure with corresponding sentences in Choctaw, Koasati, and other Muskogean or Gulf languages, which continued to serve as linguistic models or targets. In contrast, multiple-argument sentences with nouns as subjects occurring between adverbials or objects and the verb would have disagreed with the basic SOV pattern of the last speakers' native languages, namely Choctaw, Koasati, Alabama, and Tunica, and would have been prime candidates for early oblivion. Sentences with nominal subjects and objects in Mobilian Jargon apparently provide another dramatic case history of the impact of language death on grammatical description (see Mithun 1990*a*).

The second proposal for Mobilian Jargon's basic word order, that of X/OSV, receives support from its extended history of at least 250 years, if not longer (see Chapter 9) and a relatively stable syntax with little seman-tactic variation (see Sect. 8.4). Its morphologically analytic structure simply lacked the necessary formal machinery to identify the grammatical func-tions of sentence parts other than by word order, its overriding syntactic principle, and would have discouraged from the outset any major variation in word order—such as between SOV and OsV—for reasons of commu-nicative expediency. Following this argument, Mobilian Jargon speakers had no choice but to apply the same pattern in complex constructions with nominal subjects as in sentences with pronominal subjects in order to avoid major and repeated miscommunications or confusions. How otherwise would speakers resolve conflicting interpretations of a hypothetical example such as ****hatak homma hatak hatta abe** ('person-red' + 'person-white' + 'kill') as either 'The Indian kills the white man' or 'The white man kills the Indian' if not by word order? Such reasoning must have applied especially to multi-argument sentences or constructions with subordinate clauses, in which a variable word order would have made the identification of the subject, objects, and adverbials without morphological markings difficult if not impossible. Reliance on a single word-order pattern must have been most important in contact situations between Indians and non-Indians, the latter of whom spoke typologically very different lan-guages from the first and had no linguistic models by which to interpret any hypothetical SOV–OsV alternation in Mobilian Jargon.

Inferences for a non-varying word order in Mobilian Jargon receive further support from various forms of other, internal linguistic evidence. In sentences containing three arguments, the indirect object or the adverbial modifying the entire sentence regularly preceded the direct object, which in turn led the way for the subsequent pronominal subject and the verb. Unlike Muskogean and other Gulf languages with their rather complex system of stems and affixes in alternating order plus infixes, Mobilian Jargon did not exhibit any corresponding variations in the sequence of pronouns and verb, but maintained a strict sV order in all recorded instances (for a comparison, see Sect. 12.1); the only known exception is an instance recorded by Antoine Simon Le Page du Pratz and best explained in terms of interference from his primary language French rather than a Muskogean vernacular (see Sect. 8.4). Instead of functioning as affixes bound to a verbal stem, the pidgin's pronouns served as truly independent pronouns and sentence parts, which etymologically derived from their counterparts in Muskogean languages rather than pronominal affixes (see (91) in Sect. 12.1). By this fact, pronouns assume a more significant role than that of a surface variation in determining word order, and may in fact be syntactically equivalent to nouns.

There may yet be some indirect support for OSV in Mobilian Jargon from the analysis of its compounds and complex phrases in that they bear some suggestive implications of a formal analogy (see Sects. 5.6 and 6.2). To determine their basic word order, one can focus on the essentials of the formula in (29) and (39), ignoring pronouns, demonstratives, adjectives, adverbials, and the negative **-ekšo**. If we further consider the instrumental **ešt** as equivalent to a key noun and the adjective to a verb, for which the anonymous author of the *Essai* has provided some historical evidence, the word-order formula for the structure of lexical compounds and complex phrases, reduced to the indispensable elements, is as shown in (56). In other words, the modifying noun preceding the key or head noun and the verb in final position present a pattern that exhibits a formal analogy to the suggested word order of OSV in that the second noun branched out to the left, but the verb to the right. Compounds thus demonstrate not only that a combination of two arguments in two nouns and a verb was possible, but also that arguments occurred with the head noun at the center preceded by the modifier and followed by the verb. The analogy between (56) and proposed OSV is most convincing if Noun$_2$ in the formula is a patient genitive rather than an agentive genitive. In suggesting a structural parallel between (56) and proposed OSV, one need not presume the same underlying pattern, for questions arise regarding their internal hierarchies. However, there are several arguments that justify considering a formal analogy between these constructions as more than just accidental or superficial. Compounding and the formation of complex phrases, like other constructions beyond the level of a single word in Mobilian Jargon, relied on word order, thus belonged to the same domain of grammar, that of syntax. The incorporation of verbs in lexical compounds and noun phrases, resembling full sentences, strengthens the case further. On the basis of this reasoning, speakers of Mobilian Jargon

(56) Noun$_2$ Noun$_1$ Verb

should have found little formal dificulty in accepting a basic word order in which the object preceded a nominal subject noun in full sentences. Conceivably, they recognized on their own a formal similarity between multiple-part compounds, noun phrases, and full sentences, just as they apparently made no syntactic distinction between adjectives and predicates. With no formal means of distinguishing between different kinds of constructions, speakers of the pidgin could not identify a hypothetical example such as ****čokfe heše hata** ('rabbit, sheep' + 'hair' + 'white') as either a compound phrase in terms of 'white wool,' a regular noun phrase with the literal meaning of 'white rabbit hair' (including the ambiguities in the constituent structure of the corresponding English form), or as a full sentence, 'The rabbit's hair is white' or 'The wool is white.' Yet, irrespective of its semantactic interpretation, the overall message of ****čokfe heše hata** remained the same with the larger linguistic and social contexts as resources to resolve remaining ambiguities. Any differences in meaning would have been minor when compared to the confusion accompanying the earlier example of ****hatak homma hatak hatta abe** ('person-red' + 'person-white' + 'kill') if interpreted by an alternating word order depending on whether speakers intended a compound or noun phrase with the meaning of 'the white murderer of Indians' or a full sentence with an order other than OSV. Should Mobilian Jargon have permitted or required the interpretation of transitive sentences with nominal subjects in terms of SOV ('The Indian kills the white man') rather than OSV ('The white man kills the Indian'), the first kind of word order would not only have been the source of fundamental misunderstandings with possibly fatal consequences for somebody generalizing OsV to sentences with nouns as subjects, but it would also have conflicted regularly with an accurate interpretation of compounds and complex phrases in terms of Noun$_2$–Noun$_1$–Verb. Confusions would expectedly have been so severe to have attracted the attention of one or the other of the more perceptive historical observers, among them Le Page du Pratz, the Rouquette brothers, or Swanton, for which there exists no record or other indication. In short, the evidence from compounds and complex phrases supports a formally analogous word order of OSV in so far as misunderstandings arising from a confusion of the two types of constructions would have been fewer and less serious than in an alternative situation of SOV leading to the incorrect interpretation of compounds and complex phrases in terms of Noun$_1$–Noun$_2$–Verb. Mobilian Jargon speakers could easily permit some ambiguity in the interpretation of multiple-part phrases as to the kind of construction (compounds, noun phrases, or full sentences) without misunderstanding each other, but could have ill afforded any variable subject–object word order for simple reasons of communicative efficiency.

Finally, there remains the question of why speakers of Mobilian Jargon might have selected highly marked OSV over unmarked SOV. Most conversations in Mobilian Jargon in its functions as a contact medium in day-to-day affairs likely related directly to either the speaker, the hearer, or the immediate environment. The explicitness of the context in conversation would therefore have favored the use of personal pronouns for the subjects, probably a known entity or old information in many instances. Consequently, there would initially have been little need for the use of nouns in subject position; they served primarily to express new information, as found for example in an object position. If a noun nevertheless occurred in subject position, it expressed—more likely than not—new information, in which case speakers would have neglected expressing old information as it might occur in the position of an object in transitive constructions. This scenario could have fostered personal-pronoun constructions and an OsV pattern, eventually generalized to OSV, if Muskogean and other Gulf languages served as the original models for Mobilian Jargon.

Because of its hypothetical nature, the question of basic word order in Mobilian Jargon remains unresolved at this time. Whereas I argued exclusively for X/OSV in my doctoral dissertation (Drechsel 1979: 85–94) and have used it as evidence for the pre-European existence of Mobilian Jargon (Drechsel 1984), I have since assumed a less insistent position about its word order, because SOV with SXV appears as a theoretically feasible, although less convincing alternative. However, if confirmed by some hitherto unknown documentary evidence, the SOV–OsV variation would only render the pidgin more Muskogean or Gulf in its basic pattern rather than less, and would not contradict the hypothesis of Mobilian Jargon's pre-European origin (see Chapter 11 and Sects. 12.1 and 12.2).

7

Semantics and Beyond

7.1. General Aspects

While a grammar and lexicon can account for much of meaning in Mobilian Jargon, there are two aspects that do not neatly fit the descriptive-analytical frame used thus far and that merit closer attention as part of the pidgin's wider linguistic structure—semantic domains and discourse. However disparate at first sight, these linguistic features are part of semantics, and—more than any other—reflect Mobilian Jargon's uses by illustrating how it meshed with the sociocultural context. The topics of semantic domains and discourse, together with the subsequent chapter on linguistic variation, build a convenient bridge to an examination of the pidgin's extralinguistic aspects.

7.2. Semantic Domains

The discussion of Mobilian Jargon's lexicon and especially its compounding elements (see Chapter 5) has already disclosed a considerable variety of semantic domains, which is also evident from the *Essai sur quelques usages et sur l'idiôme des Indiens de la Basse Louisiane* (Anonymous 1862 MS). Its author organized the description of Mobilian Jargon primarily according to semantic categories rather than syntactic or lexical ones, and distinguished in particular:

- pronouns and verbs, the latter of which the author divided into a general category and verbs of "body actions" such as 'to bite,' 'to dream,' and 'to laugh' (chapter 2);
- animals (chapter 3);
- celestial bodies, seasons, cardinal points of directions, periods of time, and weather (chapter 4);
- numbers (chapter 5);
- ethnic variation, body parts, and kinship terms (chapter 6);
- words of qualification and colors (chapter 7);
- other.nouns (chapter 8);
    arms, hunting and fishing equipment;
    food and other articles of daily use;

household ware and house utensils;
harnessing gear for horses;
trees and small plants;
clothing, ornaments, and other personal items;
items relating to:
    trade;
    animals and products derived from them;
    fire;
    disease, death, and medicine;
    navigation;
    community and larger environment; and
    miscellany.

Similarly, Mobilian Jargon verbs permit a division into major semantic categories beyond the anonymous author's vague distinction, although these are hardly rigid and there is much overlapping between individual categories:

- subsistence and household (e.g. 'to cook,' 'to gather,' 'to sweep,' and 'to wash');
- movement and travel (e.g. 'to go,' 'to ride,' 'to dance,' and 'to swim');
- trade (e.g. 'to buy,' 'to lend,' 'to measure,' and 'to sell');
- cognition (e.g. 'to believe,' 'to forget,' 'to know,' and 'to speak'); and
- miscellany (e.g. 'to bark,' 'to explode,' 'to shave,' and 'to snow').

The category with the largest number of entries covered subsistence and household, which we could undoubtedly divide further if we had access to full information on the range of meanings and application of these verbs. The entries next highest in frequency were verbs concerning movement and travel as well as trade, whereas the number of verbs was comparatively small for the remaining two domains. However, the most difficult to place in any specific semantic category are words of qualification. While many of them were adjectives particularly useful in the description of specific human traits (e.g. 'blind,' 'deaf,' 'naked,' and 'smart'), others referred to general qualities that could relate to anything (e.g. 'bad,' 'long,' 'new,' and 'ugly').

This classification into major semantic domains can hardly meet the standards of modern lexicographical analysis, if applying them to the *Essai* retroactively were in fact appropriate. Nevertheless, the anonymous author captured the major categories in Mobilian Jargon's lexicon and their semantic diversity remarkably well. A comparison of the vocabulary with modern lexical evidence (see Drechsel, 1996) reveals no major new semantic category. The primary lexical differences found in more recently recorded data pertain to modern items such as 'automobile' and perhaps also 'cigarette' on the one hand and to traditional native utensils and concepts such as 'busk,' 'gourd rattle,' and 'stickball game' on the other.

With some rearrangements, refinements, and additions, the anonymous author's classification actually extends to the entire Mobilian Jargon vocabulary, including modern attestations:

- humans
    - body parts and functions
    - health, disease, medicine, and death
    - gender and age
    - kinship and family
    - occupations
    - ethnic diversity
- natural environment
    - plants and trees
    - animals—wild and domesticated
    - waters
    - celestial bodies
    - periods of time
    - seasons
    - weather
- subsistence and work
    - food and drink
    - hunting, fishing, and gathering
    - gardening and farming
    - occupations
- home and community
    - clothing, ornaments, and other personal articles
    - tools, weapons, and other utensils
    - furniture and other houseware
    - shelter and housing
    - community at large
- Miscellany
    - travel, transportation, and trade
    - entertainment and games
    - conflict, defense, and warfare
    - morals and religion
    - colors
    - numbers

This classification remains largely arbitrary, and makes no claims at being emic. The available lexical data for Mobilian Jargon simply are not detailed or precise enough to permit an analysis in accordance with semantic-field theory or ethnoscience. Even if they were, the above categories present only scant details about the conceptual world of its speakers, for a secondary and auxiliary medium hardly shaped their cognition possibly as did their first languages.

Yet both the anonymous author's and modern vocabularies of Mobilian Jargon are sufficiently rich to reveal considerable conceptual complexity. The above semantic categories give a reliable indication of the various kinds of sociolinguistic contexts in which speakers used the pidgin—among them subsistence and work, home and community, travel and trade. These semantic dimensions demonstrate Mobilian Jargon's use in everyday affairs and its highly utilitarian nature; they also relate directly to the multilingual contact situations among linguistically diverse Southern Indians as well as between them and immigrant groups (Europeans, Africans, and their descendants), as indicated in the ethnographic and ethnohistorical record (see Chapters 9 and 10). The focus of the lexical diversity referring to the speakers' immediate environment—both natural and human—and their daily lives further reflects one of Mobilian Jargon's other functions, that of a linguistic buffer (see Sect. 10.3).

The predominance of terms for tangible phenomena in Mobilian Jargon does not mean that its speakers were incapable of expressing abstract notions or ideas; occasional terms pertaining to morals, religion, and the supernatural world clearly prove otherwise, as did the speakers' great ingenuity in circumscribing any new topic of conversation, creating new compounds, or making use of borrowings for an extra reserve. In 1700, the French Jesuit priest Paul du Ru (1700 MS: 46; 1934: 32) recorded a Houma councilman making a reference to a supernatural being in the first unquestionable attestation of Mobilian Jargon (see 57).

Two or three decades later, Le Page du Pratz (1758: ii. 322, 326) learned much about the religion and other traditions of his Natchez hosts by using the pidgin with the superior of their temple guards:

Je fus charmé de tenir un homme, qui mieux que tout autre pouvoit me donner les instructions que je souhaitois sur leur Religion, sur leur Temple que j'avois vû dès

(57) "Jeheno,   Yno,   nanhoulou   toutchino   atchota[1] [*sic*]."
    †**šno**   **eno**   **nãholo**   **točeno**   **ačofa**(?)
    you   I   white man   three   one
    'You [the Great Spirit], I, and the white man, [we] three, [are] one.'

---

[1] The "t" in "atchota" is probably a misspelling of what must have been the graphically similar "f", as pointed out by T. Dale Nicklas (personal communication). The original French translation by du Ru (1700 MS: 46) reads as follows: "Toy [,] dit il [,] moy [,] luy [,] nous ne serons qu['un."

les premiers jours de mon arrivée, & du feu éternel que l'on y conservoit. Ce qui me faisoit encore un grand plaisir, c'est qu'il sçavoit la Language vulgaire [Mobilian Jargon]; j'avois par ce moyen beaucoup plus de facilité [than in Natchez].   (Le Page du Pratz 1758: ii. 322)[2]

As if to prove his point and to illustrate compounding in Mobilian Jargon, Le Page du Pratz even offered two words to describe 'God':

Je voulois d'abord sçavoir du Gardien du Temple ce que lui & les Compatriotes pensoient de Dieu. Dans la Langue vulgaire *Coustiné* signifie *Esprit; tchito, grand;* & comme tous les Naturels, quelque Langue qu'ils parlent, employent le mot *grand* Esprit, pour exprimer le mot de Dieu, je lui demandai en sa Langue Natchez ce qu'il pensoit du *grant Esprit* . . .   (Le Page du Pratz 1758: ii. 326)[3]

One word is reconstitutable as †**kostene** 'ghost, spirit,' and the other has a modern corresponding form in **četo** 'big, large.' Following Le Page du Pratz, the word for 'god' or 'God' thus was †**kostene četo** 'Great Sprit.' That he asked the temple guardian in Natchez rather than in Mobilian Jargon gives no indication of any linguistic shortcoming for the latter, but is left unexplained.

Both linguistic data and historical evidence then contradict the suggestion by Crawford (1978: 39) that Mobilian Jargon was lexically deficient with respect to conveying Natchez history, which he apparently based on a misinterpretation of Le Page du Pratz's relevant passages (for further discussion, see Sect. 9.3).

7.3. Samples of Discourse: A Monologue, a Song, and Historical Attestations

A knowledge of Mobilian Jargon not only helped me in locating surviving speakers, activating their memories, and setting up a more conducive environment for my field research (see Sect. 3.2). Learning a limited repertoire of small talk also provided me with a sense of discourse in the pidgin, even if most of these conversations—usually taking place at the beginning of an interview, before I had an opportunity to request permission to tape it

---

[2] 'I was delighted to encounter a man who, better than any other, could give me the instructions that I sought about their religion, their temple that I had seen from the first days of my arrival, and the eternal fire kept in it. What further pleased me greatly was that he knew the common language [Mobilian Jargon]; I had greater fluency in this medium [than in Natchez]' (author's translation).

[3] 'I first wanted to know from the temple guardian what he and his fellow countrymen thought about God. In the common language, *Coustiné* means *Spirit; tchito, great*; and since all the natives, whatever language they speak, use the word great *Spirit* to express the word God, I asked him in his Natchez language what he thought of the *great Spirit* . . .' (author's translation).

or to set up the recording equipment—went unrecorded and I could only take down parts of them later from memory. This experience still furnished me with a basis by which to interpret other bits and pieces of discourse in Mobilian Jargon—a short account by Arzelie Langley, a song or parts thereof by Tunica-Biloxi (with such considered just a special genre of speech), and bits and pieces of historically attested discourses. If these examples offer limited insight into the overall structure of Mobilian Jargon, they present some valuable details about conversation in the pidgin from an ethnographic and historical perspective.

After first providing a list of words and their meanings in Mobilian Jargon, the Coushatta medicine woman of Choctaw ancestry, Arzelie Langley, recited the following monologue to James M. Crawford (personal communication):

(58)   **eno**   **eya**   **bana.**   **eno**   **čokha**   **eno**   **falama**   **banna.**
       I   go   want   My   house   I   return   want
      'I want to go. I want to return to my home.'

      eno   **čokha**   **eno**   **aya**   **banna.**
      My   house   I   go   want
      'I want to go to my house.'

      anõte **neta** **tokolo** **nahele** **meša** **ma** **anõte** **no** **mente . . .**
      again   day   two   tomorrow after there/ again I   come
                                                  back
      'Two days after tomorrow, I come back.'

      eno   **čokha**   **eno**   **aya**   **taha.**   **eno**   **falama . . .**   **eno**   **falama.**
      My   house   I   go   PAST   I   return   I   return
      'After going (to my) home, I return . . . I return.'

      eno   **čokka**   **eno**   **mente . . .**
      My   house   I   come
      'I come to my house . . .'[4]

      eno   **yemmekšo . . .**
      I   believe-NEG
      'I don't believe . . .'[5]

      yako   **hatak**   **katema**   **lap**   **mente?**
      this   man   where   he   come
      'Where does this man come from?'[6]

---

[4] It is not clear whether, in this case, Arzelie Langley referred to her original Choctaw home or to the house among the Coushatta where Crawford recorded this sentence. The latter seems more likely from the context and the intermittent translations offered by her granddaughter Rosaline Langley.

[5] This sentence appears as an incomplete construction.

[6] **yako hatak** in this instance related to Crawford, and probably was a focused subject as in other examples below (also see the discussion concerning the third example in (52) above).

tamaha   olčefo   eno   hakalo   banna.
town   name   I   hear   want
'I want to hear the name of (his) town.'

[unintelligible]   **ayome**
                      married/marriage
'. . . married/marriage . . .'[7]

yako   hatak   čokmakšo.
this   person   good-NEG
'This person is bad . . .'

yako   hatak   pake   lap   mente,   eno   yokpa   fena.
this   man   afar   he   come   I   glad   very
'I am very glad that this man (from) afar comes (here).'/'. . . that this man
comes (here from) afar.' (?)

yako   hatak   ačokma   fehna.
this   man   good   very
'This man is very good.'

katema   oya   lap   nowa   banna,   lap   aya.
where   all over he   travel   want   he   go
'He goes wherever he wants to travel.'

eno   čokha   eno   aya   banna.   eno   aya   bana.
my   house   I   go   want   I   go   want
'I want to go (to my) home. I want to go.'

eno   nowakšo . . .   eno   nowakšo.
I   travel-NEG   I   travel-NEG
'I don't travel . . . I don't travel.'

eno   čokha   eno   eyakšo.
My   house   I   go-NEG
'I don't go (to my) home . . .'

[unintelligible]   **lap   aya   banna**   [unintelligible]
                      she   go   want
'She wants to go . . .'[8]

In referring to Crawford in these instances, Arzelie Langley did not address him directly with the second person singular pronoun, but used the third person as if speaking to another person—most likely her granddaughter, who translated Choctaw and Koasati explanations into English on her behalf.

[7] On the one hand, the context might suggest that Langley also wanted to know whether Crawford was married; on the other, the subsequent negative assessment, which appears out of context and contradicts later, positive statements about Crawford, makes no obvious sense, unless it referred to a third person. In that case, she may have been talking about her husband or perhaps even herself, as she in fact does later.

[8] In this and the following sentence, the third person pronoun **lap** clearly refers to Langley, who probably introduced it in analogy to her granddaughter's use of the third person in her intermittent English translations.

lap   aya   [unintelligible]   **lap   kaneya.**
she   go   she   lost
'(Anywhere) she goes . . . she (gets) lost.'

katema   õya   eno   nowa   banna.   eno   nowa   banna.
anywhere   all   I   walk   want.   I   walk   want
'I want to walk allover. I want to walk.'

eno   eye   čokmakšo
My   foot   good-NEG
'My foot is bad/My feet are . . . bad.'

katema   eno   nowakšo   fena.
anywhere   I   travel-NEG   really
'I do not really travel anywhere.'

eno   noškobo   õya   čokmakšo,   čokmakšo,   čokmakšo.
My   head   allover   good-NEG   good-NEG   good-NEG
'My head allover is bad, bad, bad.'

yako   hatak   lap   kaneya   falama   lap   mente?
this   man   he   leave   back   he   come
'Does this man, (once) gone, come back?'

This discourse is quite artificial inasmuch as there was only one partner speaking the language with intermittent translations into Koasati and English interrupting its flow; these also explain Langley's use of the third person in reference to Crawford and herself, and may account for some of the repetitions, otherwise acceptable in pidgins and perhaps also due to the speaker's advanced age and poor health. However, this account demonstrates that Mobilian Jargon was not limited to utilitarian purposes such as trade.

With a wide range of topics also came a variety of dispositions displayed by speakers of Mobilian Jargon, which were not always congenial, but could take an outright hostile and racist turn. In one instance, a European–American speaker apparently confronted a Native American neighbor, probably a Coushatta, with the utterance in (59) (Geoffrey D. Kimball, personal communication). There is no record of how Louisiana Indians reacted to such insults. However, the same individual was said also to express vulgarisms in Mobilian Jargon at funerals, which would make older women in the audience still able to understand them turn away to hide their chuckle.

A sample of Mobilian Jargon larger than a single utterance moreover survived in so-called joke songs, of which Claude Medford and a few individ-

(59) **comme   homma   mente,   pačotle!**
buttocks   red   come   wrestle
'Come (here), red ass, (and) wrestle!'

uals among the Tunica-Biloxi in Marksville still remembered one with some text, but little of its meaning:

(60) **tale hata   besa   čokma,   hoyã, hoyã, ...**
      silver   see   good   VOCABLES
      'To see silver (coins?) is good.'/'Silver looks good.'

      tak(a)losa   tamaha   na   tahã,   noweya, noweya ...
      black person   town   reach,   PAST   VOCABLES
                                    get
                                    there
      'A black person went to town(?)'

      ... sapõta(k)   bolokfa   belesõ (?) ...
      mosquito   nose (?)   sting (?)
      '(and) a mosquito stung (his/her) nose (?)'

      taek   sepe   (hene)   hattak sawa   hene
      woman   old   VOCABLE   ape   VOCABLE
      'an old woman ... an ape ... (?)'

      ape   losa   šno   aya-kšo   rehkən (?)   hatta   šno   mayokoba (?) ...
      body   black   you   go-NEG   hole in   white   you   like
                                                 a tree
      'you don't go with a black body (person), you like a white hole'

      čoka komə̃sa   šno   aya-kšo.
      jail   you   go-NEG
      'you don't go to a jail'[9]

Evidence of Mobilian Jargon from other sources allowed the identification of most words and their glosses; but there remain some questions of interpretation, especially as regards the phrase of **sapõta(k) bolokfa belesõ** (?; see (54) in Sect. 6.5).

Similarly, Mary R. Haas (1950: 165) had apparently obtained some limited text to a song in Mobilian Jargon when recording the Raccoon Dance in Tunica in the 1930s:

They [the Tunica, Biloxi, and Choctaw Indians in the Marksville area] dance the Raccoon (Dance). When they have danced four dances, (the dance) is over. (As) they dance, they jump. While they are singing his [i.e. Raccoon's] song in that way, they jump. "wi-ha, wi-ha, wi-ha, etc., wi-hi-ya-ha, wi-hi-ya-ha," they (sing and) stop. "hu-ya-ne, etc., ho-wi-a, etc.," they sing and jump. "hik-na-wi-hya-ne, etc., ni-kui-ča-da-la, etc.," (they sing) and walk (as) they dance. "we:-ha:, etc.," they (sing and) jump again. "yo:-hi:," they say. (Then) they stop.

---

[9] I received some help from Geoffrey Kimball and Pamela Munro in interpreting this song, which my Native American consultants quite possibly understood fully, but perhaps did not wish to translate for me because of supposedly vulgar connotations.

Without pursuing further analysis, Haas commented about the untranslated items merely that "These are for the most part meaningless syllables. Some words of the now extinct Mobilian trade jargon may, however, be occasionally interspersed" (Haas 1950: 165 n. 2). An example may be "wi-ha" and its equivalent with lengthened vowels "we:-ha:," reconstitutable in the context of a dance as †**weha** 'move' on the basis of Choctaw/Chickasaw **weha** 'to move' (Munro, forthcoming). Other syllables likewise recall familiar Western Muskogean etymologies, but can call on far less convincing comparative evidence.[10]

Like Arzelie Langley's account, joke and other songs in Mobilian Jargon unmistakably demonstrate its use in other than purely utilitarian contexts, and may even have incorporated some special poetic features. These songs constituted part of a long-standing pantribal repertoire among Louisiana and other Southeastern Indians, who performed it at intertribal gatherings and stickball games in the Marksville area as late as the 1920s and in the Kinder-Elton area as recently as the 1940s. Major participants were not only Haas's source of Tunica, Sesostrie Youchigant of part Biloxi ancestry, but also Arzelie Langley and other prominent Southeastern Indians of the period (see Levine 1991).

Moreover, fragments of conversations in Mobilian Jargon are available in historical sources. In his *Histoire de la Louisiane*, Le Page du Pratz (1758) was the first to leave us a detailed, although incomplete, description of short conversations in what clearly appears as the pidgin (see Sects. 8.4 and 9.3).[11] In particular, Le Page du Pratz portrayed encounters between Native Americans and French on the road and a Frenchman's visit to a Native American home with focus on their greetings:

Quand les Naturels recontrent des François qu'ils connoissent ils leur tendent la main, la serrent un peu inclinant un peu la tête & leur disent toujours en leur Langue [Mobilian Jargon in this case]: "te voilà, mon ami"; si on n'a rien de sérieux à leur dire, ou si eux-mêmes n'ont rien de conséquence à proposer, ils poursuivent leur chemin.

S'ils vont au même endroit que les François, qu'ils rencontrent ou qu'ils joignant, ils ne le dépasseront jamais, à moins qu'ils ne soient pressés pour quelques choses qui en valent bien la peine; dans ce cas ils passent à quelques pas de la personne, et ne rejoignent le chemin que lorsqu'ils sont un peu éloignés.

Lorsqu'on entre chez eux, ils disent le mot de salutation, *ichla mongoula* **[ešla**

---

[10] Elsewhere in her Tunica texts, Haas (1950: 23, 83, 85, 121) included samples of what she identified as "archaic Tunica" or "nonsense syllables," but that—at closer examination with better comparative materials—may prove to be part of the same intertribal text materials, perhaps with a Tunica parlance, as the Mobilian Jargon songs.

[11] The subsequent discussion of Le Page du Pratz's description essentially follows the section "Two Exemplary Historical Scenes of Speaking in Mobilian Jargon" of my paper on ethnohistory of speaking (Drechsel 1983b: 170–3), supplemented by some modifications.

mõgola], qui signifie ce que je viens de dire, *te voilà mon ami*; ils donnent la main & disent de s'asseoir* en montrant un lit qui sert à cet effet. Ils laissent reposer la personne qui arrive & attendent qu'elle parle la premiere, parce qu'ils présument que l'on doit être essoufflé d'avoir marché, & personne n'ose interrompre le silence qui régne alors dans la cabanne.

Dès que celui qui est arrivé commence à parler, la femme apporte à manger de ce qu'ils ont tout prêt. Le maître dit: "*Apas-Ich* [†**apa(s) eš**], manges["]: il faut prendre de ce qu'ils présentent, à la vérité si peu que l'on veut; parce qu'autrement ils s'imagineroient qu'on les méprise; après ces petites cérémonies, on parle de ce qu'on veut leur traiter, ou de ce qu'on désire qu'ils fassent.

　* *Chpénélé* [†**(e)š benele**], assis-toi.

(Le Page du Pratz 1758: iii. 6–7)[12]

Thus, when meeting Native Americans and speaking Mobilian Jargon, the French had to observe native rules of conversation by attending to little ceremonies before they could begin business. The common greeting and welcome, **(e)šla mogola**[13] 'Hello, friend,' survived into modern times (see (30) in Sect. 6.2), and was quite formulaic, as greetings so often are and as an Acadian speaker of Mobilian Jargon still noted in recent years. How the French responded is not evident from Le Page du Pratz's description; apparently any conversation could ensue afterwards. On visits to Native

---

[12] 'When the natives meet French whom they know, they hold out the hand, and press it a little while inclining the head a bit and always say to them in their language [Mobilian Jargon in this case]: "There you are, my friend." If they have nothing important to tell them or they themselves have nothing of consequence to offer, they keep going.

If they have the same destination as the French whom they meet or join, they would never pass unless pressed for time on account of some urgent matter. In this case, they would pass some steps from the [nearest] person, and return to the trail only when they are some distance away.

When one is at their home, they say the word of greeting, *ichla mongoula* [**ešla mõgola**], which means what I have just said, *There you are, my friend*. They shake hands, and tell you to sit down* by pointing to a bed that serves this purpose. They let the arriving person rest, and wait until he speaks first, because they presume that one must be out of breath from having walked; nobody dares to break the silence that then prevails in the hut.

As soon as the one who has just arrived starts speaking, the woman brings food that they have ready to hand. The master of the house says: "*Apas-ich* [†**apa(s) eš**], eat!" One has to take some of what they offer, however little one desires, because they would otherwise think that one scorns them. After these small ceremonies, one talks about what one wants to bring up with them or what one wishes them to do.

　* *Chpénélé* [†**(e)š benele**], sit down!' (own translation).

[13] **mogola** or **mõgola**, which Mary Haas (1975: 259) traced back to Alabama **am-okla**, 'my friend,' but could equally derive from the first person singular possessive prefix **am-** in Muskogean languages (Booker 1980: 34–5) and Choctaw **oklah** 'people' or Chickasaw **okla** 'town' (Munro, forthcoming: 'town'), simply means 'friend' (without any possessive pronoun) in Mobilian Jargon. Note the nasalization of the first vowel in Le Page du Pratz's sample, which resulted in a partial morphological convergence of French, Alabama, and/or Western Muskogean in Mobilian Jargon. In accordance with their possessive pronoun "mon" [mɔ̃], French speakers of Mobilian Jargon likely reinforced, although hardly originated, this case of nasalization, which must have led Le Page du Pratz to write "mongoula" and to translate it as '*my* friend' (for etymologies, see 'friend' and 'hello' in Drechsel, 1996).

American homes, the hosts strongly encouraged their guest first to eat some of the readily offered food by saying †**apa(s) eš** 'You eat!' (for a discussion of the variation in the position of the pronoun **eš** 'you,' see Sect. 8.4). Even if the visitor did not feel like eating, custom dictated that he first helped himself to a little food so as not to offend his hosts.[14] After these preliminaries, the visitor could proceed to talk about the purpose of his call.

In addition to these scenes of speaking, Le Page du Pratz (1758: iii. 7–8) provided some supplementary ethnographic observations on the general speech behavior of Louisiana Indians in the early eighteenth century. When Native Americans, whatever their number, conversed with each other, there was always only one person speaking at a time; never did two persons talk simultaneously. If somebody in the gathering had to say something to another person, he did it in a low voice so that the rest could not hear. Any unruly children were taken aside, and even their scolding was not to interrupt a conversation among adults. When a question required an answer or an issue was up for debate in council meetings, everyone kept silent for a while, spoke when it was his turn, and never cut another person short.[15] This custom made it hard for the Native Americans to contain their laughter when they saw several French men and women in company, conversing with each other and speaking at the same time. For almost two years, Le Page du Pratz observed, and wondered about, Louisiana Indians stifling their laughter on such occasions, until he pressed his Native American companion for a satisfactory answer. After begging Le Page du Pratz not to get angry at him, the Native American replied in Mobilian Jargon: "nos gens disent que quand plusieurs François sont ensemble, ils parlent tous à la fois comme une volée d'oyes" (Le Page du Pratz 1758: iii. 8).[16] Le Page du Pratz unfortunately did not record this sentence in its Mobilian Jargon original; nor did he leave any clues as to whether these rules of discourse applied only to the native languages of Louisiana Indians such as the Natchez whom he knew best or to Mobilian Jargon as well. However, this passage followed shortly after Le Page du Pratz's earlier remarks, which suggests that the native conversational practice of a single speaker applied to Mobilian Jargon as well, just as Native Americans probably observed it. In this case,

---

[14] More than two centuries after Le Page du Pratz's initial observation, I had a similar experience among the Coushatta. When a host invited me to his home, he strongly urged me to help myself to some food, although I had just eaten dinner and was not the least hungry. His explanation was that I always had to have enough in my stomach so as not to starve on my way to the afterworld, should I die right then and there.

[15] Similarly, an elderly Louisiana Choctaw whom I interviewed about Mobilian Jargon once reminded me to grant him some time to think about my question, and warned me in no uncertain terms about interrupting him in his answer as unacceptable behavior among his people.

[16] 'our people say that when several French are together, they speak all at the same time like a flock of geese' (author's translation).

Indian and non-Indian speakers of Mobilian Jargon must regularly have misunderstood each other with respect to the pidgin's proper use. If not even as perceptive and empathetic an observer as Le Page du Pratz had been aware of the speaker's right to the floor, other Europeans, most of whom were less sympathetic or understanding towards native peoples, probably kept violating their single-speaker rule, as Europeans usually extended their own manners of discourse to Mobilian Jargon.

Another scene with Mobilian Jargon as the prime medium including two short phrases was reported by the anonymous author of the *Essai* in a discussion of the Native Americans abhorrence of slavery:

Ils [the Native Americans] poussent même l'horreur qu'ils ont pour l'esclavage, jusqu'à faire le sacrifice de leur vie plutôt que d'en supporter même l'accusation. En voici un example: la confiance placée à juste tître en celui de qui elle est rapportée permettrait d'en garantir l'authenticité.

Une jeune sauvagesse parlant très bien le français avait été employée chez un habitant des Avoyelles pour faire l'ouvre du ménage. Elle était d'une grande intelligence, elle s'acquittait de ses devoirs, lavait et cousait aussi bien que la meilleure domestique eut pu le faire. Malgré cet état avancé de civilisation, elle avait conservé, à l'égard de l'indépendance et de la domesticité toutes les idées de sa caste.

Un jour un indien de sa tribu lui reprocha sa profession en lui disant; *Youka yamah, hauffa-hia-eska* [†**yoka, yama, hofahya eska**]; esclave oui, tu l'es, et cela ne te fait pas honte? Humiliée de l'insulte et du reproche qui venait de lui être fait, elle s'empara, d'une corde et alla se pendre à une poutre de la maison d'école. La pauvre femme était si fermement résolue à mourir, qu'on remarqua que ses pieds, par un leger effort, pouvaient toucher la terre et la sauver ainsi de la mort. [*sic*]   (Anonymous 1862 MS: 12–13 n. 4)[17]

Without doubt, the sample speech by the unidentified Native American woman in Avoyelles Parish north of Opelousas in the mid-nineteenth century is Mobilian Jargon, for it can be easily reconstituted as †**yoka, yama, hofahya eska**, rendered literally as 'Slave, yes indeed, shame make' or more freely 'You are a slave indeed; you have brought shame onto yourself.'[18] But

---

[17] 'Such is their [the Native Americans'] horror of slavery that they will rather sacrifice their life than suffer themselves to be accused of being in that condition. Here is an example: such is our confidence in the person who related it to us that we are ready to guarantee its authenticity.

A young indian girl who spoke french very well, was employed by a planter in the Parish of Avoyelles to do household work. She was very intelligent and performed her duty admirably and had much skill in sewing and washing. Notwithstanding her progress in civilization she still retained for slavery and the condition of a servant the feelings common to her cast.

One day, an Indian of her tribe reproached her with her condition in life, adressing these words: *Youka yamah, hauffa-hia-eska* [†**yoka, yama, hofahya eska**]—slave, thou art, and are you not ashamed of it? mortified at the insult and at the reproach offered her, she took a rope and went out and hung herself to a beam of the school house. Such was the resolution of this woman to die, that it was observed by a slight effort her feet could have touched the ground & thereby save her life.' [*sic*]   (Anonymous MS n.d.: 11–12 n. 4).

[18] Note that there is no question mark in the Mobilian Jargon original, which appears only

it is not obvious why a man of "her tribe" addressed the woman in the pidgin instead of their native language. His choice of Mobilian Jargon could have stemmed from a combination of any of the following reasons:

(*a*) The Indian man and woman belonged to one of the many multitribal, multilingual communities that existed in the mid-nineteenth century throughout Louisiana. Anonymous (1862 MS: 2, 3, 8) listed several mutually unintelligible and even unrelated languages among the speakers' first languages: Choctaw (Muskogean), Opelousa (unidentified), Atakapa (Gulf isolate), Natchitoches (by all indications Caddoan), Alabama (Muskogean), and Biloxi (Siouan). Avoyelles Parish was also the home to Taënsa (unidentified), Tunica (Gulf isolate), and probably others (see Drechsel and Makuakāne 1982*b*: 87–92). If the Native American man and woman spoke different first languages, Mobilian Jargon was their principal and perhaps only common medium.

(*b*) The man wished to humiliate the woman in his choice of the medium, by making sure that a larger audience (including either the anonymous author or his Creole consultant) could overhear and understand him in a situation outside the Native Americans' own community.

(*c*) As reported in other instances (see Chapter 9 and Sect. 10.3), Indians simply avoided using their first languages in the vicinity of non-Indians, and resorted "in public" to the pidgin instead. This inference draws support from the fact that the author of the *Essai*, although perceptive about the lexicon of Mobilian Jargon, revealed no fundamental understanding of its true functions and remained unaware about Louisiana's sociolinguistic complexities.

Unfortunately, the *Essai* offers no further clues that would resolve this sociolinguistic puzzle. Its author did not even record whether and how the women responded verbally to the male member of her community. But she obviously understood him; otherwise, she would hardly have committed suicide—by hanging herself, a manner of ending one's life considered suitable only for slaves and despised by Native Americans.

Some historical sources have documented the use of Mobilian Jargon without much linguistic attestation of a lexical or grammatical nature, but provide some pragmatic information in translation. Such documentation allows only limited conclusions because of problems of translation, ethnographic-historical accuracy, and poetic license (including apparent embellishments); in the absence of other texts, it remains the best evidence available about the nature of longer discourse in the pidgin.

One such instance demonstrates that Mobilian Jargon was not necessar-

---

in the French and English translations. The context suggests this question to have been a rhetorical one, which I have translated here as an affirmative statement.

ily limited to short utterances or brief exchanges, but served as the medium for extensive speeches. For the year 1720, Jean Bernard Bossu, a French naval officer, reported on peace negotiations by a Chitimacha delegation with the French in what was undoubtedly Mobilian Jargon. Not only had numerous contemporary French observers already attested the pidgin to the Chitimacha in their interlingual interactions (see Sect. 9.3); but Jean Baptiste Le Moyne, Sieur de Bienville and *de facto* governor of Louisiana at the time, also responded "en langue Vulgaire qu'il parloit avec facilité" (Bossu 1768: i. 36, possibly quoting Le Page du Pratz 1758: i. 113) or 'in the common language [i.e. Mobilian Jargon], which he spoke with ease' (in Crawford 1978: 32). The specific circumstance for the Chitimacha Indians' speech was their desire for truce with the French, who had attacked them for their alleged murder of Abbé de S. Côme, a missionary. The Chitimacha, dressed in their best finery and announcing their mission by singing the song of the calumet, came to New Orleans to turn over the murderer's head as demanded by de Bienville and to present the peace pipe to him (Bossu 1768: i. 29–30). On this occasion, the head of the Chitimacha party addressed de Bienville:

"que je suis content de me voir devant toi, il y a long-temps que tue es faché contre notre Nation; nous nous sommes informés de ce que disoit ton coeur, & nous avons appris avec joye qu'il vouloit nous donner de beaux jours."

Ils [the Chitimacha] s'assirent ensuite à terre, appuyant leur visage sur leurs mains, le Porte parole sans doute pour se recueillir & pour prendre haleine avant de prononcer sa harangue, les autres pour garder le silence; dans cet intervalle on avertit de ne point parler, ni rire pendant la harangue, parce qu'ils prendroient cela pour un affront.

Le porte parole, quelques momens après, se leva avec deux autres; l'un remplit de tabac la pipe du Calumet [,] l'autre apporta du feu, le premier alluma la pipe; le porte parole fuma, puis il essuya la pipe & la présenta à Monsieur de Bienville pour en faire autant; le Gouverneur fuma & tous les Officiers qui composoient sa Cour, les uns après les autres, suivant leur rang; cette céremonie finie, le vieillard Orateur reprit le calumet, le donna à M. de Bienville afin qu'il le gardât. Alors le porte parole resta seul debout, & les autres Ambassdeurs se r'assirent auprès du présent qu'ils avoient apporté au Gouverneur; il consistoit en peaux de Chevreuils and en quelques autres Pelleteries, toutes passées enblanc en signe de paix.

Le porte parole ou Chancelier, étoit revêtu d'une robe de plusieurs peaux de martres cousues ensemble; elle étoit attachée sur l'épaule droite & passoit sous le bras gauche; il se serra le corps de cette robe, and commença sa harangue d'un air majestueux, en adressant ainsi la parole au Gouverneur. "Mon coeur rit de joie de me voir devant toi; nous avons tous entendu la parole de paix que tu nous as fait porter: le coeur de toute notre nation en rit de joie jusqu'à tressaillir; les femmes oubliant à l'instant tout ce qui s'est passé, ont dansé, les enfants ont sauté comme de jeunes chevreuils. Ta parole ne se perdra jamais; nos coeurs & nos oreilles en sont remplis, & nos descendans la garderont aussi long-tems que *l'ancienne parole* durera;* comme la guerre nous a rendus Pauvres, nous avons été contraints de faire une chasse générale pour t'apporter de la pelleterie; mais nous n'osions nous éloigner, dans la crainte que les autres nations n'eussent pas encore entendu ta parole; nous ne sommes même venus qu'en tremblant dans le chemin, jusqu'à ce que nous eussions vu ton visage.

Que mon coeur & mes yeux sont contents de te voir aujourd'hui. Nos présents sont petits, mais nos coeurs sont grands, pour obéir à ta parole; quand tu nous commanderas, tu verras nos jambes courir & sauter comme celles des Cerfs pour faire ce que tu voudras."

Ici l'Orateur fit une pause; puis élevant sa voix, il reprit son discours avec gravité.

"Ah! que ce soleil est beau aujourd'hui, en comparaison de ce qu'il étoit quand tu étois faché contre nous; qu'un méchant homme est dangereux! tu sçais qu'un seul a tué le chef de la priere† dont la mort a fait tomber avec lui nos meilleurs guerriers; il ne nous reste plus que des vieillards, des femmes & des enfants qui te tendent les bras comme à un bon pere. Le fiel qui remplissoit auparavant ton coeur, vient de faire place au miel, le grand Esprit n'est plus irité contre notre nation; tu as demandé la tête du méchant homme; pour avoir la paix, nous te l'avons envoyée.

Auparavant le Soleil étoit rouge, les chemins étoient remplis d'épines & de ronces, les nuages étoient noirs, l'eau étoit trouble & teinte de notre sang, nos femmes pleuroient sans cesse la perte de leurs parens & n'osoient aller chercher du bois pour préparer nos alimens, nos enfans crioient de frayeur; au moindre cri des oiseaux de nuit, tous nos guerriers étoient sur pieds; ils ne dormoient que les armes à la main, nos Cabanes étoient abandonnées & nos champs en friche, nous avions tous le ventre vuide, & nos visages étoient allongés; le gibier fuyoit loin de nous; les serpens sifloient de colere, en allongeant leurs dards; les oiseaux qui perchoient près de nos habitations sembloient par leur triste ramage, ne nous chanter que des chansons de Mort.

Aujourd'hui le soleil est brillant, le Ciel est clair, les nuages sont dissipés, les chemins sont couverts de roses, nos jardins & nos champs, seront cultivés, nous offrirons au grand Esprit les premices de leurs fruits, l'eau est si claire que nous y voyons notre image, les serpens fuyent, ou plûtôt sont changés en anguilles, les oiseaux nous charment par la douceur & l'harmonie de leurs chants, nos femmes & nos filles dansent jusqu'à oublier le boire & le manger, le coeur de toute la nation rit de joie, de voir que nous marchons par le même chemin, que toi & les François: le même soleil nous éclairera: nous n'aurons plus qu'une même parole, & nos coeurs ne seront plus qu'un: qui tuera les François nous le tuerons, nos Guerriers chasseront pour les faire vivre, nous mangerons tous ensemble; cela ne sera-t-il pas bon, qu'en dis-tu, mon Père?" A ce discours prononcé d'un ton ferme & assuré, avec toute la grace & la décence, & méme, si on peut le dire, toute la Majesté possible, M. de Bienville répondit en peu de mots, en langue Vulgaire [Mobilian Jargon] qu'il parloit avec facilité; il lui dit qu'il étoit bien aise de voir que sa Nation avoit retrouvé l'esprit; il les fit manger, mit en signe d'amitié sa main dans celle du Chancelier ou porte parole, & les renvoya satisfaits.

* C'est ainsi que les Sauvages nomment la tradition.

† C'est ainsi qu'ils appellent nos Missionnaires. [*sic*]

(Bossu 1768: i. 30–6)[19]

Bossu (1768: i. p. x, 49–54, 194–9, 230–4; ii. 30–8, 47–64, 78–9, 132, 144, 147–8, 149–151) reported other encounters in Mobilian Jargon as the prime

[19] ' "I am happy to be in your presence. You have been angry with our nation for a long time. We have learned with joy what your heart has been saying, that it wishes to grant us happy days." They then sat on the ground, resting their heads in their hands. The spokesman must have done this in order to recover his breath before beginning his speech; the others, to help them remain silent. In the meantime, everyone was warned not to talk or to laugh during the speech, since the Indians would consider that an affront.

After several minutes, the spokesman and two others arose; one of the two filled the pipe with tobacco and lighted it with fire supplied by the other. The spokesman smoked; then he wiped the pipe and presented it to Monsieur de Bienville. The Governor smoked as did all his officers, taking their turn according to rank. After the ceremony, the old orator took the calumet and handed it to Monsieur de Bienville to keep. The spokesman was the only one to remain standing, while the other emissaries sat near the presents they had brought for the Governor. There were skins of deer and other animals, all colored white as a peace symbol.

The spokesman was dressed in a robe made of several marten skins sewed together, fastened over his right shoulder and passing under his left arm. He wrapped the robe around his body, and with a great deal of majesty he began the speech which he addressed to the Governor.

"My heart laughs with joy because I am in your presence. We have all heard the words of peace which you have sent us. The hearts of all our nation laugh with joy. Our women, forgetting for a moment all that happened, danced and our children leaped like young deer. Your words shall never be forgotten. They fill our hearts and our ears, and our descendants will remember them as long as the ancient word* will last. Since the war made us poor, we had to have a great hunt to bring you skins, but we did not dare wander too far in case the other nations had not yet heard your words. We came trembling on the path until we saw your face.

How happy are my heart and my eyes to see you today. Our gifts are small but our hearts are big and ready to obey your words. When you command us, you will see our legs run and jump like the legs of stags to carry out your orders."

Here the orator paused. Then, raising his voice, he continued gravely.

"Ah, how much more beautiful the sun is today than when you were angry with us! How dangerous a bad man is! You know that just one man killed the prayer chief,† whose death caused our best warriors to fall with him. There remain only the old men, the women, and the children who stretch out their arms to you as to a kind father. The gall which formerly filled your heart has been replaced by honey. The Great Spirit is no longer angry with our nation. You asked for the head of the evil man. We sent it to you in order to have peace.

The sun was red before, the paths were full of thorns and brambles, the clouds were black, the water was troubled and stained with our blood, our women wept constantly over the loss of their relatives and did not dare to go off in search of firewood to prepare our meals, our children cried out in fright. All our warriors jumped up at the slightest cry of the night birds, they slept with their arms within reach, our huts were abandoned and our fields lay fallow. We all had empty stomachs and drawn faces, game fled from us, the snakes hissed in anger and showed and bared their fangs; the birds, perched in trees near our villages, seemed to sing only songs of death.

Today the sun is bright, the sky is clear, the clouds are gone; the paths are covered with roses; our gardens and our fields will be cultivated, and we shall offer their first fruits to the Great Spirit. The water is so clear that we can see our faces in it; the serpents flee or, rather, have changed into eels; the sweetness and harmony of the birds' song charm us, our wives and our daughters dance and forget to eat and drink. The hearts of the entire nation laugh with joy to see us walk on the same path with you and the French; the same sun will light us, we shall speak with one voice, and our hearts will be one. We shall kill those who will kill the

medium, as suggested by their sociolinguistic circumstances and single words with attested equivalent forms in the pidgin (see Bossu 1768: i. 160, 217; ii. 30, 36, 153). Unfortunately, he provided no further evidence in the form of a name, morphosyntactic data, or sociolinguistic information that permits identification of Mobilian Jargon with certainty.[20]

Another example provides a sense of the diversity of topics in Mobilian Jargon conversations. After reporting the death of the Natchez chief named Tattooed Serpent in 1725, Jean Benjamin François Dumont de Montigny, a young French lieutenant and settler, quoted in translation the response that a Tioux war chief had given to a Frenchman in Mobilian Jargon:

S'il est vrai, comme tu le dis, que le Serpent piqué soit mort, son frere le grand Chef de guerre se tuera; car ils se sont promis l'un à l'autre que si le grand Chef de guerre mouroit le premier, son frere ne pleureroit point, mais se tueroit avec un couteau; & que si au contraire le Serpent piqué mouroit le premier, le grand Chef du guerre ne pleureroit point, mais se casseroit la tête d'un coup de fusil. Ainsi il est bon, François, que tu parles à tes Chefs: car s'il se tue, ses femmes mourront avec un grand nombre de Guerriers; & *cela est beaucoup de valeur.**

   * C'est-à-dire, *c'est dommage.* [*sic*]

                       (Dumont de Montigny 1753: i. 212–13)[21]

French; our warriors will hunt food for them, and we shall all eat together. Will that not be good? What do you say to this, Father."

This speech, delivered in a firm and assured tone with eloquence and propriety and even, if it can be said, with all possible majesty, was answered briefly by Monsieur de Bienville, who spoke the Indians' language [Mobilian Jargon] rather fluently. He told the spokesman that he was very pleased that the nation had come once again to its senses. He had the emissaries fed, and, as a sign of friendship, shook hands with the spokesman. The Indians were sent off satisfied.

                       (Bossu 1962: 25–8)

* This is what the savages call *tradition.*
† This is what they call our missionaries.

[20] Caution is appropriate in the interpretation of Bossu's documentation, for he also reported encounters with Indians farther north, specifically "Mitchigamias" and "Kaos" and even recorded two phrases: "*indagé ouai panis*, c'est-à-dire, je suis indigne de vivre, je ne mérite plus de porter le doux nom de pere" and "*tikalabé, houé ni gué*, c'est à dire, nous te croyons, tu as raison" (Bossu 1768: i. 134–8, 154–9, 219–22). In English, these sentences apparently meant 'I do not deserve to live; I am unworthy of the name of "father" ' and 'We believe you. You are right" (Bossu 1962: 73, 109). The evidence is not interpretable as Mobilian Jargon, but suggests to John Koontz (personal communication) some unidentified Siouan language of the Mississippi valley with "some oddities."

In his second book describing a third voyage to Louisiana, Bossu (1777) similarly provided several speeches in translation and single words interpretable as Mobilian Jargon. To conclude so with confidence requires better evidence, which is missing in this case. Bossu also mentioned the "Akanças" (Quapaw) and "Illinois" Indians whom he had visited, and it is not clear from either linguistic or extralinguistic indications whether he referred to their own languages, lingua francas based on them, or possibly Mobilian Jargon.

[21] 'If it is true, as you say, that Tattooed Serpent is dead, his brother, Great War Chief, will kill himself; for they are pledged to each other so that if the great war chief would die first, his brother would hardly mourn, but would kill himself with a knife; and if, on the other hand, Tattooed Serpent would die first, the great war chief would hardly mourn, but would shoot

The Frenchman whom Dumont de Montigny cited was most likely Antoine Simon Le Page du Pratz, who had witnessed Tattooed Serpent's death and had served as Dumont de Montigny's prime source of information (see Crawford 1978: 39–40).

According to another historical document, Mobilian Jargon provided the channel for extensive and quite complex negotiations. For the year 1742, a Frenchman by the name of Antoine Bonnefoy reported an encounter with northern Alabama, British traders, and Chickasaw near present-day Memphis (Tennessee), in which they used Mobilian Jargon. His account reads as follows in translation:

They [Alabama Indians] questioned me much, taking me for an enemy, and fearing that I had come to lay a snare for them and to take from them some scalps, as had happened to them a short time ago. I spoke to them in French and Mobilian [Jargon], which, after two hours of questions, caused them to make up their minds who I might be and where I came from.   (Bonnefoy in Mereness 1916: 253)

During the time that I was in the council-house, the English came and gave me their hands, inquiring in the Chicachas language respecting my adventures, and how I had been able to come where I was. I told them in the Mobilian language, which they understood, that having been taken by the Cherakis in December, I had escaped from their villages a month before, and that I had been compelled, after having lost my two comrades, who had escaped with me, to take my flight in the direction of the Alibamons, being no longer in a state to proceed to the Illinois, as had been our first plan. They took me to their store-houses, where they gave me to eat, and wished to engage me to follow them to Carolina, which I refused to do, and returned to the cabin of my savage. Then the 15 Chicachas came to see me, and asked me the same questions as the English had just asked [presumably also in Mobilian Jargon]. They then asked why the French did not give them peace, saying that the Chactas vexed them continually. To all this I replied that they ought not to expect peace until they had driven the English from their villages; that moreover it could not be true that they wished peace, since they struck at us every day. They assured me that with the exception of a party of young people, which had acted con- trary to the consent of the nation, the last year at Pointe Coupée [on the lower Mis- sissippi], they were a people who had struck no blow; that I could see clearly that those which had been ascribed to them had been inflicted by the Cherakis. I told them that in that case it would be necessary to make known to the Great French Chief the dispositions which they wished me to understand that their nation enter- tained: First, by driving out all Englishmen, and secondly by settling the Natchéz in the environs of the Rivière à Margot upon the Missisipy, and breaking forever with the English, because as long as they received them they would engage the Indians always in some enterprise against us. To this they agreed. I smoked with them the same day, and the next, which was the *28th of May*.   [*sic*]   (Bonnefoy in Mereness 1916: 254–5)

himself in the head. Thus, it is good, Frenchman, that you speak to your chiefs; for if he kills himself, his wives will die with a large number of warriors; and *that is worth a great deal*.*

* That is to say, *it is a pity*' (author's translation).

The main actors speaking Mobilian Jargon in this historical scene were Bonnefoy, several Alabama and British, and apparently Chickasaw. Bonnefoy also spoke French with the Alabama, perhaps to convince his hosts of his national identity. Most interestingly, Bonnefoy used Mobilian Jargon not only with Native Americans, but with the British, as they presumably did with him, either because neither party knew the other's language, or possibly out of courtesy towards their Alabama hosts and the Chickasaw visitors so as to avoid any appearance of deception towards the Native Americans.

Along with this historical attestation of an exchange in Mobilian Jargon, another document indicates that the pidgin could be the medium of encounters between two or more unfriendly or even hostile parties. In 1752, Macarty Mactigue, the French commandant of the Illinois post at Kaskaskia near Ste. Geneviève on the middle Mississippi, reported in a letter written in rather mangled French to Pierre de Rigaud de Vaudreuil, then Governor of Louisiana, that

Elle [an African–American slave woman] Vit En même temp un Sauvage qui Luy parla mobiliens, ne voulant pas Luy repondre, La mis En Jouë Surquoy [.] Elle Luy dit En mobiliens pourquoy me Tuë tu [.] Le Sauvage dit tu disois que tu ne Savois par parler [Mobilian Jargon]. La negresse Sans fut [.] Et Le Sauvage Ledit Lusignans [an Indian slave] Revint La nuit à La maisons ches La negresse [.] Et Luy parla devant trois autres negres de Bienvenus des chose Et d'autre, Lusignans S'informant de chaque chose Et demandat Son mary, Jl deffendit á La negresse de dire quelle L'avoit vuë qui La turoit S'il avoit des nouvelles . . ." [sic] (Mactigue in Pease and Jenison 1940: 756)[22]

In the same letter, Mactigue reported a hostile verbal confrontation between French and Indians between the area of the confluence of the Wabash with the Ohio River and the latter's junction with the Mississippi, in which the Native Americans addressed the French party in Mobilian Jargon:

M. Leonardy Revint Le deux de decembre ayant Estée Jusqu'a La petite prairie né vit riens ayant Laissee par En haut une partie de voyageurs: Le nommee Boserons Et Sa Bande Estant á La mine De fert audessous du ouabaches qui foncés un Tierssont de Salaisons Le 13 9bre Lorsqun nommée Delisle apperçut une piᵣaugue qui derivoit avertis ce premier de ne pas faire de Bruit[.] JL repondit Bon Se Sont

---

[22] 'At the same time she [an African–American slave woman] saw an Indian who spoke to her in Mobilian [Jargon] and who when she did not answer laid hold of her [actually: he took aim at her]. On that she said to him in Mobilian [Jargon], "Why do you kill me?" The Indian said, "You said you could not talk it." The negress ran away; the Indian and Lusignans [an Indian slave] came that night to the cabins where the negress was and talked to her before three other negroes of one thing and another, Lusignans learning about everything and asking for her husband. He forbade the negress' telling that she had seen him, saying he would kill her if he found she had told' (Mactigue in Pease and Jension 1940: 756).

de nos gens Et continuë[.] Les Sauvages Qui venoient droit a L'ensse ou Jils auroient put faire Leur decharge prirent aussytot L'autre côtee Du fleuve S'appercevant du Bruit[.] Et L'ors quil furent passes Jls Leurs crierrent En mobiliens[:] viens nous avons deux de tes frerres Et tuee un ferent trois crie de mort[.] Les francois disent[:] mis a terres nous verons á te Les disputer[.] JL mondit qu'ils auroient Biens donnee áprés Sils nussent crains quils ne tuassent Les prison- niers. [*sic* plus punctuation]   (Mactigue in Pease and Jenison 1940: 758–9)[23]

We have no further details about the content of their conversations in Mobilian Jargon, which obviously concerned day-to-day matters in at least the first instance. However, this document confirms that the pidgin proved convenient even in less than amicable circumstances, and offers the first his- torical evidence that, among the immigrants to North America, it was not just Europeans, but also Africans who spoke Mobilian Jargon. Moreover, Mactigue's letter attests the use of Mobilian Jargon as far north as the lower Ohio River and the area south of St. Louis on the Mississippi.

As judged by these examples of discourse, conversations in Mobilian Jargon were not limited to utilitarian purposes such as those of trade, but extended to a variety of topics, as evident from the diversity of its lexicon, and even included a repertoire of intertribal songs with poetic features. At times, dis- course in Mobilian Jargon was limited to single formulas, short utterances, and brief exchanges; on other occasions, it could consist of longer conver- sations and full speeches. Furthermore, the pidgin served as a medium in hostile as well as friendly encounters. The variety of examples for discourse indicates that there were few, if any, restrictions on the topics or contexts for Mobilian Jargon's use.

---

[23] 'M. Leonardy returned December 2, having been as far as the Little Prairie and seen nothing. He left a party of *voyageurs* above. The man named Bosseron and his company were at the iron mine below the Wabash heading a cask of salted meat, when on November 13 a man called Delisle saw a pirogue appraoching. He warned the other to make no noise. He answered, "Good, they are our own people," and went on. The Indians who were coming straight to the cove where they could have fired on them, immediately on hearing the noise went to the other side of the river. Once they had passed by they cried out in Mobilian [Jargon], "Come to us, we have two of your brothers prisoners and have killed another." They made the death cry three times. The French cried out [presumably also in Mobilian Jargon], "Come on shore, and we will dispute them with you." They told me that they would have pursued if they had not been afraid that the prisoners would have been killed' (Mactigue in Pease and Jenison 1940: 758–9). Apparently the first to refer to this most valuable historical source on Mobilian Jargon was Michael Silverstein (1973 MS: 34); but Crawford (1978: 102 n. 15) recognized it as an important historical reference to Mobilian Jargon as well.

8

Linguistic Variation

8.1. General Aspects

Previous discussion has already made repeated references to linguistic variation at all levels of description and analysis of Mobilian Jargon. Considerable alternation existed in its phonology so as to invalidate the monosystemic concept of phoneme. The pidgin also exhibited differing proportions in the etymological sources of its vocabulary over time and space. There are even hints for some alternation in syntax, semantics, and discourse as well.

Linguistic variation in Mobilian Jargon was not an epiphenomenon resulting from language obsolescence, but was very much part of the pidgin, reflecting influences from the speakers' diverse first languages. For want of a demographically representative set of data across time and space that would permit a variationist analysis, the present chapter presents a consolidated discussion of variation in Mobilian Jargon, which proves useful in interpreting its history.

8.2. Phonological Variation and Processes

Mobilian Jargon exhibited variation in its pronunciation in the form of an accent, which fluctuated according to foreign-language learning skills as well as first-language background. In articulating consonants, some speakers might add or miss a feature such as voicing, aspiration, or lateralization as compared to others; furthermore, the pronunciation of distinctive vowels, limited to three, could substantially vary in height, tenseness, and lip-rounding, and occasionally revealed nasalization or diphthongization.

Modern recordings of Mobilian Jargon, including those by Crawford (1978: 77–8), attest the following alternations among the most frequent and common ones:

(61) Degemination of consonants:
      ačaffa ~ **ačafa** 'one'
      bessa ~ **besa** 'to see'
      eyye ~ **eye** 'foot'
      hannale ~ **hanale** 'six'

hattak ~ **hatak** 'person, people, man; human'
kapassa ~ **kapasa** 'cold; winter, ice'
nettak ~ **netak** 'day'
sokko ~ **soko** 'muscadine'
yamma ~ **yama** 'yes, right, alright, indeed; this, that; Mobilian Jargon'

(62) Voicing of consonants such as **p** and **k**, the latter especially before an epenthetic vowel (see (71) below):

alokpa ~ **alokba** 'sharp'
mokla ~ **mogola** 'friend'
nakne ~ **nagane** 'male, man'
pokne ~ **pogone** 'grandmother'
tohbe ~ **tohobe** 'white'

(63) Secondary aspiration of stops and affricates, characteristic of speakers of English:

kapassa ~ **kʰapʰassa** 'cold'
kate ~ **kʰatʰe** 'cat'
papos ~ **pʰapʰos** 'baby, child'
tanče ~ **tʰančʰe** 'corn'

(64) Variation of the affricates **č** and **c**, which—unlike their sibilant counterparts—did not constitute separate basic sounds:

četo ~ **ceto** 'big, large'
čokəma ~ **cokəma** 'good'
čokfe ~ **cokfe** 'rabbit'

(65) Variation between the sibilants **s** and **š**, although both occurred also as phonemically distinct fricatives, as in the varieties spoken by Choctaw and probably Chickasaw (see Sect. 4.1; cf. Crawford 1978: 123 n. 1, 12):

kapas(s)a ~ **kapaša** 'cold'
lokse ~ **lokše** 'turtle, tortoise'
losa ~ **loša** 'black'
noskobo ~ **noškobo** 'head, neck'
ose ~ **oše** 'small, little'
papos ~ **papoš** 'baby, child'
soba ~ **šoba** 'horse'
sokha ~ **šokha** 'pig, hog'
sonak ~ **šonak** 'money'

(66) Variation between **ł** and **sl, šl**, or even **š**, the latter reflecting the **s** ~ **š** alternation of (65), but occurring primarily, perhaps exclusively, in lects of those who did not speak a Southeastern Indian language with the marked lateral fricative:

lowak ɬáfa ~ lowak šláfa 'match'

ɬaɬo ~ slašo/šlašo 'fish'

†ɬokata ~ †šlokata ("schloukoatta" (Anonymous 1862 MS: 55)) 'whip' (n.)

taɬape ~ taslape/tašlape 'five'

Indicative of this variation is also the observation by a non-Indian neighbor of the Coushatta Indians that he knew the word for 'fish,' but that it was too hard to pronounce (Geoffrey D. Kimball, personal communication).

(67) Nasalization and concurrent backing of central vowel in final syllable as characteristic of French speakers:

čokma ~ čokmã/čokmɔ̃ 'good'

homma ~ hommɔ̃ 'red'

yama ~ yamɔ̃ 'yes, right, alright, indeed; Mobilian Jargon'

(68) Variation between nasals and l, as attested by Nicolas Louis Bourgeois (1788: 296–7) in particular and the influence of a corresponding variation in Western Muskogean (see Haas in Crawford 1978: 124 n. 14):

†elbak ("elback" (Anonymous 1862 MS: 39)) ~ †embak ("imbóc" [Bourgeois 1788: 297]) 'hand'

†napeš (?; "napiche" (Bourgeois 1788: 297)) ~ †lapeš ("lapiche" [Anonymous 1862 MS: 59]) 'horn'

noškobo/noskobo ~ †loškobo ("louche coubo" (Bourgeois 1788: 297)) 'head, neck'

†sõlaš ("sonlache" (Anonymous 1862 MS: 40)) ~ †sonaš (?; "sounac" (Bourgeois 1788: 297)) 'tongue'

tanãpo ~ talambo ("talambo" [Bourgeois 1788: 296]) 'gun'

(69) Epenthesis of glides:

kanea ~ kaneya 'gone, lost; to go away, to leave'

taek ~ tayek 'female, woman, lady, wife, girl, Indian woman'

teak ~ teyak 'pine'

(70) Diphthongization, characteristic of English speakers:

lawakšo ~ lawakšoⁿ 'little, few, scarce'

ponola ~ poⁿnoⁿla 'cotton'

(71) Epenthesis of a vowel, usually of the same quality as the preceding one or schwa, frequently accompanied by voicing of the intermediate consonant (see (62) above):

čokma ~ čokəma 'good'

haklo ~ hakalo 'to hear' (Crawford 1978: 85) ~ hakolo 'to hear, to listen, to understand'

mokla ~ mogola 'friend'

nakne ~ nagane 'male, man'

pokne ~ pogone 'grandmother'

(72) Coalescence of the final and initial vowels in two juxtaposed words, as already evident in constructions, especially compounds, with the negative **-(e)kšo** and the instrumental †**ešt** (see Sect. 5.5):

(a)kãka oše ~ **(a)kãk oše** 'chicken egg'
tanãpo oše ~ **tanãp oše** 'pistol'

(73) Aphaeresis, as indicated in the instrumental †**ešt** (see (20) in Sect. 5.5) and the word for 'chicken egg' in (72):

ačaffa ~ **čaffa** 'one'
ačokma ~ **čokma** 'good, well'
anõte ~ **nãte** 'again, another time'
ekšo ("ekcho" [Anonymous 1862 MS: 62]) ~ **kšo** ("kcho" (Anonymous 1862 MS: 32); "qshaw" (Dresel 1920–1: 407)) 'no, not'
eno ~ **no** 'I'
†**epešek** ("hi-pichik" (Anonymous 1862 MS: 40)) ~ †**pẽšek** ("pingic" (Bourgeois 1788: 297)) 'breast, teat'
ešno ~ **šno** 'you'
okčak(k)o ~ **čak(k)o** 'blue, green'
†**oke lowak** ("oké-lowack" (Anonymous 1862 MS: 51)) ~ †**ke lowak** ("que loac" 'to drink spirits/brandy' (Bourgeois 1788: 296)) 'brandy, spirits, whiskey'

Words and phrases from various historical sources as well as modern recordings of Mobilian Jargon suggest additional phonological variations and processes, among them: (*a*) the palatalization of **k**; (*b*) the variation of **k** and **t** as in **kapas(s)a** and **tapas(s)a** 'cold;' (*c*) metathesis for both consonants and vowels as in **ašekšo** and **akšešo** 'unavailable' and in †**takoba** and **toboke** 'belly' (Hiram F. Gregory, personal communication); (*d*) vowel assimilation as in **eško** and **oško** 'to drink' and (*e*) apparent syncopation including the deletion of the accompanying glide as in **bayok** 'bayou, creek, river' and †**bok** 'bayou' ("bouk houk" (Anonymous 1862 MS: 60)), with Mobilian Jargon preserving an archaic pattern. However, these instances were incidental, and require further evidence to confirm systematic patterns.

Phonological variations suggest specific linguistic or social conditions for several instances. The **s–š** variation was characteristic of Mobilian Jargon speakers whose native languages (such as Koasati and Alabama) did not make a phonological distinction between these two sounds, whereas Choctaw and likely Chickasaw Indians retained it in the pidgin from their first languages. Corresponding alternations were less distinct and occurred less frequently for the affricate counterparts of **c** and **č**, probably because there did not exist as much conflict between the phonological systems of the Mobilian Jargon speakers' first languages, even with the characteristically palatalized sibilants of Southern English. The most noteworthy phonological variation was the variable pronunciation of ɬ as **sl**, **šl**, or even **š**, which typically occurred in the Mobilian Jargon speech of those whose primary languages lacked the lateral voiceless fricative, mostly non-Indians. By comparison, aphaeresis was a fairly widespread phonological process common to speakers of Muskogean languages. Other phonological alternations in the pidgin again were typical of non-Indian speakers: the variable degemination of consonants; the secondary aspiration of stops and affricates, as recorded specifically for speakers with English as their native tongue; the nasalization and backing of the central vowel in final syllables, as evident in French speakers' Mobilian Jargon; and diphthongized vowels, again reflecting the influence of English speakers. For still other variations, information is too meager to permit any conclusions about their linguistic or extralinguistic contexts. Among these are the voicing of consonants, the variation between nasals and **l**, the epenthesis of glides and vowels, the coalescence of vowels between two words, as well as the poorly attested phonological alternations and processes. However, if the better attested instances give any indication, most if not all of these variations were examples of "interference" from the speakers' first languages, thus making pronunciation or "accent" a key element in giving away the linguistic and ethnic identity of its speakers.

8.3. Lexical Variation and Replacement

Borrowing from the lexicon of one's first language or possibly others could easily occur in Mobilian Jargon, resulting in lexical replacement as already illustrated in (50) of Section 6.4. When asked about his well-being, an elderly African–American neighbor of the Coushatta Indians, speaking English as his first language, inserted not only one, but two compounds from his native tongue in this instance:

(74) **eno   topa   kanome.   stomak   trabəl   eno   aša…**
I   sick/hurt   a little   stomach   trouble   I   have
                                                   (ache)
'I am sick a little. I have a stomach ache.'

nante   fʊt   trabəl   eno   aša
another time   foot   trouble (ailment)   I   have
'Some other time, I have a foot ailment.'

Similarly, in a sentence recorded by Crawford (1978: 94), another African–American speaker chose the French or English loan **segaret** 'cigarette' instead of the more generic term **hakčomak** 'tobacco,' although he was quite aware of the latter and observed the standard OsV word order of Mobilian Jargon:

(75) **segaret   eno   banna**.
     cigarette   I   want
     'I want a cigarette.'

One's first inclination might be to explain lexical replacement in terms of language death—on the presumption that the last speakers of Mobilian Jargon increasingly borrowed corresponding words from their first languages with the pidgin's decline. But these speakers inserted English and French loan-words without any hesitation and with perfect ease, as if they had already been part of the regular Mobilian Jargon vocabulary. Likewise, other non-Indian speakers displayed variable vocabularies of Native American terms with the same glosses—some with more Choctaw words and others with more Koasati terms, depending on who had originally taught them the pidgin and with whom they primarily used it. Native American speakers remembered similar borrowings in Mobilian Jargon with loan-words from any of the many possible source languages, including Koasati, Alabama, Tunica (such as **rehkən** (?) 'hole [in a tree]' in (60) in Sect. 7.3), French, and undoubtedly others. So what at first sight appear as borrowings were very much part of the variable, easily expansive vocabulary of Mobilian Jargon.[1]

A closer examination of the Mobilian Jargon lexicon, especially entries with two or more equivalent forms, quickly demonstrates that lexical replacement was not peculiar to the pidgin's recent decline, but must have been a widespread process throughout its existence, as is also evident from historical documentation. Lexical variation made up a substantial portion of the entire recorded vocabulary with some 200 sets of real or apparent synonyms, many of them with multiple variants, and applied to all semantic domains. Were this figure to include entries just described in terms of phonological variations or to apply to multiple entries consisting of compounds and their reduced varieties (such as †**foše heše** '(bird) feather' ~ †**heše** 'feather'), the portion of lexical variants in the vocabulary would be substantially higher.

Synonyms could be of various kinds in Mobilian Jargon. Whereas a few multiple entries in the lexicon may have reflected synonymy original to a particular source language, especially Choctaw as the dominant source for the pidgin's recorded lexicon, others originally had distinct meanings in the source languages, only to shed their semantic differences and apparently to

---

[1] Such lexical replacements recall the numerous words that J. V. Powell (1990) has found in Chinook Jargon, but that are usually missing in existing vocabularies—among them regionalisms, European lapses, "crude" terms including body references and sexual slang, argot related to particular activities (such as religious or domestic terminology), and other lexical items that never caught the attention of Chinook Jargon lexicographers.

assume a common meaning in Mobilian Jargon, as in the following instances (see Drechsel, forthcoming, for further details and Munro, forthcoming, for comparative Muskogean data unless noted otherwise):

(76) 'ball': †**lõbo** ("lonbo" (Anonymous 1862 MS: 61); < Choctaw **lõbo** 'round', Chickasaw **lombo** 'whole, round') ~ †**towa** ("touha" (Anonymous 1862 MS: 63): < Choctaw **towa**, Chickasaw **toʔwaʔ**)

'bed': †**anose** ("a-nocé" (Anonymous 1862 MS: 54); < Western Muskogean **nosi** 'to sleep') ~ †**topa** ("toupoua" (Bourgeois 1788: 296); < Chickasaw/Muskogee/Oklahoma Seminole **topa** 'bed', Choctaw **topah** 'bed', Seminole **topa** 'table'

'devil': †**est aholo** ("tchita-oulou" (Anonymous 1862 MS: 62); < Choctaw **išt-ahollo** 'witch', Chickasaw **išt-aholloʔ** 'witch') ~ †**šolop** ("shouloupe" (Anonymous 1862 MS: 62); < Mississippi Choctaw/Chickasaw **šolop** 'ghost')

'lend' (v.), 'loan' (v.): **peta** ("pita" (Anonymous 1862 MS: 17); < Western Muskogean **ipita** 'to feed') ~ †**empota** ("anpouta" (Anonymous 1862 MS: 20); < Choctaw **impota** 'to lend, to loan' [Byington 1915], Chickasaw **ĩ pota** 'to lend' [Humes and Humes 1973]) ~ **pota** (< Choctaw **pota** 'to borrow, to take, to transfer by way of borrowing or lending' [Byington 1915])

'Mobilian Jargon': **anõpa ẽla** (< Chickasaw **anompa** 'word, language,' Choctaw **anõpa** 'word, language' + Chickasaw **ĩla** 'different') Choctaw **ĩlah** 'different one' ~ **yam(m)a** (< Western Muskogean **yamma-**'that') ~ **yoka anõpa** (< Western Muskogean **yoka** 'captured' + Chickasaw **anompa** 'word, language,' Choctaw **anõpa** 'word, language')

'night': †**nenak** ("ninack" (Anonymous 1862 MS: 34); < Western Muskogean **ninak** 'night') ~ **opeya** (< Choctaw **oppiya** 'evening') ~ **tanka** (< Koasati **tanka** 'darkness, afternoon,' Alabama **tanka** 'dark')

'people': **hat(t)ak** ("atta(c)k" (Anonymous 1862 MS: 39); < Western Muskogean **hattak** 'person') ~ **okla** (< Choctaw **oklah** 'people,' Chickasaw **okla** 'town') ~ **ola** Alabama/Koasati **o:la** 'town'

'worker:' †**tõksale** ("tonkcelé" (Anonymous 1862 MS: 46); < Western Muskogean **toksali** 'to work') ~ †**yoka** ("youka" (Anonymous 1862 MS: 47); < Western Muskogean **yoka** 'captured')

A few entries in Mobilian Jargon consisted of pairs of words and their negated antonyms (for negative constructions, see the discussion accompanying examples (14) to (18) in Sect. 5.5):

(77) 'bad': **(a)čokmakšo** (< Choctaw **(a)cokma** 'good,' Western Muskogean **cokma** 'good' + Western Muskogean **ik-š-o** 'to be none') ~
†**okpolo** (?; "opoulon" or "opoulou" (Anonymous 1862 MS: 47); <
Choctaw **okpulo** 'bad; evil')

'empty': **alotakšo** (< Mississippi Choctaw **alota** 'full' + Western
Muskogean **ik-š-o** 'to be none') ~ †**tošole** ("toucho-oulé," "toucho-
oullé" (Anonymous 1862 MS: 47); < Choctaw **tosholi** 'to pour out'
(Byington 1915))

'lie' (n.): †**ā+e ekšo** ("antlé-ekcho" (Anonymous 1862 MS: 109); <
Apalachee **ā+i** 'law,' Western Muskogean **ā+i** 'true' + Western
Muskogean **ik-š-o** 'to be none') ~ †**holabe** ("oulabbé" (Anonymous
1862 MS: 62); < Choctaw **holabi** 'to tell a lie')

'new': **sepekso** ("sipi-kcho" (Anonymous 1862 MS: 47); < Choctaw
sipi 'old' + Western Muskogean **ik-š-o** 'to be none') †**hemona**
("imouneha" (Anonymous 1862 MS: 47); < Choctaw **himonna**,
Chickasaw **himonna?**)

'short': **falayakso** (< Choctaw **falaya** 'long' + Western Muskogean
ik-š-o 'to be none') ~ **yoškolole** (< Choctaw **yushkololi** (Byington
1915))

'small, little': **četokšo** ("tchito-kcho" (Anonymous 1862 MS: 47); <
Choctaw **cito** 'big' + Western Muskogean **ik-š-o** 'to be none') ~
†**esketene** ("îskîtî'nî" (Swanton 1911: 32); < Choctaw **iskitini**) ~ **ose**
(< Apalachee **osi** 'child') ~ **oše** (< Choctaw **oši** 'son,' diminutive in
compounds, Chi **oši?** 'son,' diminutive in compounds)

'young': **sepekšo** (< Choctaw **sipi** 'old' + Western Muskogean **ik-š-
o** 'to be none') ~ †**aneta** (?; "amita" (Anonymous 1862 MS: 46); <
Koasati **anihta**) ~ **hemeta** (< Western Muskogean **himitta**)

Yet most synonyms in the pidgin reflected the influence of the speakers'
different first languages, as illustrated by the following examples:

(78) 'African American,' 'black' (n.): **atloča** (< Koasati) ~ **hat(t)ak losa**
(< Western Muskogean) ~ **tak(a)losa** (< Alabama, Chickasaw)

'afternoon': **opeya** (< Choctaw) ~ **tanka** (< Alabama, Koasati)

'axe': **čafe** (< Alabama, Koasati) ~ **(e)škefa** (< Choctaw) ~ †**oskefa**
("osquifa" (Anonymous 1862 MS: 54); < Chickasaw)

'baby': **atoše** (< Alabama, Koasati) ~ **papo(s)** (< Algonquian) ~
posko(š) (< Western Muskogean)

'belly': †**takoba** ("tacauba" (Anonymous 1862 MS: 41); < Western
Muskogean) ~ †**ekfe** (?; "icpir" (Bourgeois 1788: 297); < Alabama,
Koasati)

'big': **četo** (< Choctaw) ~ **čoba** (< Alabama, Koasati, Apalachee)

'bird': †**foše** ("fouchi" (Anonymous 1862 MS: 30); < Chickasaw) ~ **hoše** (< Choctaw)

'black': **loca** (< Alabama, Koasati) ~ **losa** (< Western Muskogean)

'buffalo': **yanasa** (< Alabama, Koasati, Muskogee) ~ †**yanaš** (?; "lianache" (Bourgeois 1788: 296); < Western Muskogean) ~ †**yanaše** "hianaché" (Anonymous 1862 MS: 28); < Tunica (loan), Hitchiti, Mikasuki (?))

'day': **neta** (< Alabama, Koasati, Muskogee) ~ **net(t)ak** (< Western Muskogean)

'ear': **hakčo** (< Alabama, Koasati) ~ **haksobeš** (< Choctaw)

'eye': †**ešken** ("esquen" (Bourgeois 1788: 297)) < Chickasaw < Algonquian?) ~ **nešken** ("nichekine" (Anonymous 1862 MS: 41); < Choctaw < Algonquian?) ~ **teɬe** (< Alabama, Koasati)

'fat,' 'grease': †**bela** ("billa" (Anonymous 1862 MS: 51); < Western Muskogean) ~ †**neya** ("nihia" (Anonymous 1862 MS: 51); < Alabama, Choctaw)

'fish' (n.): **ɬaɬo** (< Alabama, Koasati, Muskogee) ~ **nane** (< Western Muskogean)

'friend': †**babešele** (< Alabama) ~ **mokla** (< Alabama, Koasati, Western Muskogean)

'hand': †**elbak** ("elback" (Anonymous 1862 MS: 39); < Chickasaw ~ **elbe** (< Alabama, Koasati)

'hot': **lašpa** (< Western Muskogean) ~ **lokba** (< Alabama)

'hundred': **čokpe** (< Koasati, Muskogee, Hitchiti) ~ **taɬepa** (< Western Muskogean, Alabama)

'Indian': **(a)sovaš** (< French) ~ **hat(t)ak (ape) homma** (< Western Muskogean)

'lie down': **blaka** (< Alabama, Koasati) ~ **et(t)ola** (< Western Muskogean) ~ **taške** (< Western Muskogean)

'mother': **eske** (< Koasati) ~ **eške** (< Western Muskogean) ~ **mama** (< English) ~ **mamã** (< French)

'name': **(h)olčefo** (< Koasati) ~ **hoɬcefo** (< Chickasaw)

'nose': **besane** (< Alabama, Koasati) ~ †**bešak(a)ne** ("béchak-ané" (Anonymous 1862 MS: 41); < Choctaw)

'rain' (n.): **moyba** (?; < Western Muskogean) ~ **oyba** (< Alabama/Koasati) ~ **õba** (< Western Muskogean) ~ **welba** (< Choctaw?)

'road,' 'way': **hena** (< Western Muskogean) ~ **hene** (< Alabama, Koasati)

'sharp': **(h)alokpa** (< Alabama, Koasati, Chickasaw) ~ †**halopa** ("alloupa" (Anonymous 1862 MS: 15); < Western Muskogean)

'silver': †**plata** ("plata" [Dresel 1920–1: 407] < Spanish) ~ **tale hat(t)a** (< Western Muskogean)

'snake': **čento** (< Alabama, Koasati) ~ **sente** (< Western Muskogean)

'tree,' 'wood': **et(t)e** (< Western Muskogean) ~ **et(t)o** (Alabama, Koasati, Muskogee)

'turkey': **akãk(a) četo** (< Western Muskogean + Choctaw) ~ **akãka čoba** (< Western Muskogean + Alabama, Koasati, Apalachee) ~ **faket** (< Choctaw)[2]

'water': **oka** (< Western Muskogean) ~ **oke** (< Alabama, Koasati)

'watermelon': **čokše** (< Alabama, Koasati) ~ **okčak(k)o** (?; < Choctaw, Alabama, Koasati 'green, blue') ~ **šokše** (< Choctaw) ~ **talakče** (< Koasati)

'woman': **(hat(t)ak) ta(y)ek** (< Western Muskogean) ~ **taye** (< Alabama, Koasati)

These sets of synonyms reflect but a limited range of the lexical variation that must once have existed for Mobilian Jargon in other communities and that better historical samples would undoubtedly confirm for earlier times. Short of obtaining representative specimens of Mobilian Jargon vocabularies for various communities and different periods and while taking into consideration the inherent statistical distortions of short word lists, the next best option to providing a more accurate sense of lexical variation in Mobilian Jargon is a statistical comparison of the etymological compositions of its two major vocabularies, each containing several hundred entries: (1) the word list by the anonymous author of the *Essai* for the area of Opelousas in south-central Louisiana in the early 1860s, and (2) the modern lexicon gathered in the greater vicinity of Elton, west and northwest of Opelousas, more than a century later (including a few single entries by James M. Crawford, Hiram F. Gregory, and Geoffrey D. Kimball). A comparison of these two vocabularies with respect to their etymological composition appears in Table 8.1,[3] which yields several interesting observations about the lexical

---

[2] The last speakers of Mobilian Jargon avoided **faket** [fʌkɪt] because of an interlingual taboo, specifically because of the vulgar connotations in its English homophone, which undoubtedly contributed to the lexical variation for 'turkey.'

[3] The following classification relies on the comparison of Mobilian Jargon words with resemblances in various likely source languages (see Drechsel, forthcoming), and employs categories suggested by Munro (1987a) in her new classification of Muskogean languages, but without adopting the historical implications of its genetic relationships. These categories are: Choctaw, Chickasaw, and Western Muskogean (Choctaw and Chickasaw); Alabama-Koasati and South-

composition of Mobilian Jargon over just a limited geographic area in south-central Louisiana and during a period of no more than a century.

First, there is a difference of more than 20 per cent for Western Muskogean elements in the two vocabularies. With an incidental phrase of Choctaw, "S(i)abana" 'to desire, to want' or †s(i)a bana 'I want' (Anonymous 1862 MS: 17, 84; see Munro 1993), the larger number of words with resemblances in Choctaw or general Western Muskogean in the anonymous author's vocabulary, adding up to more than 75 per cent of the entire vocabulary, lends support to the suggestion that the anonymous author's principal source of information, a Creole, had learned Mobilian Jargon from speakers of Choctaw or some closely related dialect. Independent historical evidence confirms the existence of Choctaw communities in the Opelousas area at the time (see Drechsel and Makuakāne 1982*b*: 21–3, 66–7).

On the other hand, the larger number of Eastern Muskogean elements in the modern vocabulary as compared with the anonymous author's— while still few when contrasted with the number of Western Muskogean-derived entries—adds up to a difference of almost 14 per cent. Similarly, one can observe an analogous, if smaller, difference in the number of resemblances of Mobilian Jargon words to corresponding forms in both Eastern and Western Muskogean languages. These differences relate directly to the fact that most of the modern vocabulary originates from speakers among the Coushatta near Elton and their neighbors, a community including not only Koasati, but also Alabama together with Choctaw, French, and English.

As expected, Mobilian Jargon further exhibits a lexicon with substantial percentages of terms with resemblances in more than one language, although at varying rates. This conclusion applies especially to Western Muskogean, Alabama-Koasati, and Western Muskogean and Alabama-Koasati. The figures for most other categories are too small to permit any conclusions beyond three rather general observations. First, this table con-

western Muskogean (Alabama-Koasati and Western Muskogean); Western Muskogean and individual Eastern Muskogean languages; other Native American Languages (including Algonquian and Tunica); European (Spanish, French, and English); compounds with composite etymologies; and uncertain or unidentified etymologies.

If a word exhibits a close similarity to more than one of the related languages, it appears under the appropriate family category such as Muskogean. These broader categories do not suggest that the Mobilian Jargon word necessarily exhibited a resemblance to corresponding terms in *all* of the family's languages. This methodological liberty was necessary in order to avoid an overly diversified list of categories and subcategories, which with their small numbers of entries would not only have confuted such a statistical approach, but would also have defeated the purpose of offering an impression of Mobilian Jargon's variable lexical composition. For example, the number of entries for individual European languages was far too small and statistically insignificant to permit separate categories for Spanish, French, and English; instead they appear under the category of European.

TABLE 8.1. *Etymological compositions of two major vocabularies*

Lexical Resemblances in Mobilian Jargon with:	Anonymous' Vocabulary of 1862		Modern Vocabulary	
	Number of entries	Percentage of vocabulary	Number of entries	Percentage of vocabulary
Choctaw	270	28.72	84	14.89
Chickasaw	23	2.45	11	1.95
Western Muskogean	417	44.36	210	37.23
Subtotal Western Muskogean	710	75.53	305	54.08
Alabama	3	0.32	10	1.77
Koasati	5	0.53	27	4.79
Alabama-Koasati	7	0.74	36	6.38
Alabama-Koasati and any other Eastern Muskogean language	2	0.21	16	2.84
Subtotal Eastern Muskogean	17	1.81	89	15.78
Choctaw or Chickasaw and any Eastern Muskogean language	14	1.49	14	2.48
Western Muskogean and Alabama	23	2.45	15	2.66
Western Muskogean and Koasati	2	0.21	2	0.35
Western Muskogean and Alabama-Koasati	47	5.00	41	7.27
Western Muskogean and any other Eastern Muskogean language	26	2.77	17	3.01
Subtotal Western Muskogean and Eastern Muskogean	112	11.91	89	15.78
Other Native American languages (Algonquian, Tunica)	1	0.11	4	0.71
European languages	4	0.43	15	2.66
Compounds with Mixed Etymologies	35	3.72	26	4.61
Uncertain, Partially Identified, and Unidentified Entries	61	6.49	36	6.38
TOTAL	940	100	564	100

firms the decline of Chickasaw elements in Mobilian Jargon since the mid-nineteenth century, as already noted in Section 5.3. Second, the portion of non-Muskogean elements was small in both vocabularies, and amounted to less than 1 per cent of the entire lexicon. Third, as one would expect with the growing influence of European languages and especially English in Native American communities, words of European origin have increased over the past century, although only slightly so. Fourth, compounds whose composite parts have resemblances in different languages were comparatively few in number in the nineteenth century as well as recently, and may never have exceeded 5 per cent of the entire vocabulary.

The above comparison has two serious limitations with respect to any claims to being representative of the overall lexical variation in Mobilian Jargon over time and space. For one, the anonymous author's vocabulary and the modern lexicon together embody but a limited sample of Mobilian Jargon for two communities—Opelousas and Elton—separated by a distance of no more than thirty miles and a period of only about a century. Moreover, both sets of lexical data with all their differences clearly reveal the dominant influence of Western Muskogean, in that speakers of Choctaw served as their direct or indirect sources. The two major vocabularies thus do not comprise information for the Mobilian Jargon's full geographic range across much of the central South or its extended history of at least 250 years, if not longer; specifically, they lack data for communities with less or no distinctive influence from Western Muskogean (see Sects. 8.5 and 9.2).

These limitations suggest a still greater range of lexical variations when one takes into consideration the pidgin's full geographic range of distribution, its entire history, and the sociolinguistic differences among the member groups in the contact speech community. Because Mobilian Jargon spread to numerous other communities speaking diverse, even unrelated, languages and these came to serve as additional lexical sources, it must have absorbed a wider vocabulary than is evident from either the anonymous author's or the modern vocabulary. For this reason, the above comparison does not permit any conclusions about the etymological composition of Mobilian Jargon's lexicon in other communities or at earlier times.

A better perspective on the full range of lexical variation in Mobilian Jargon is available only from incidental documentary evidence. Such historical observations often provide no more than impressionistic information about Mobilian Jargon, but they offer valuable clues to the pidgin's etymological composition in different communities and at various points in time.

In 1858, about the same time when the anonymous author of the *Essai* made his or her observations, Thomas S. Woodward (1939 [1859]: 79), an American settler and trader to Louisiana, described the Mobilian Jargon of Texas as "a mixture of Creek, Choctaw, Chickasay, Netches and Apelash." Not only did he observe Chickasaw influences (see Sect. 5.3); but by his explicit references to Creek (possibly including Muskogee) and Apalachee, Woodward presented Mobilian Jargon as more Eastern Muskogean than its conventional portrayal as an essentially Western Muskogean pidgin, and further suggested elements from Natchez (Gulf isolate), otherwise unattested.

Such a divergent characterization raises the question of how reliable Woodward was as an observer. When mentioning the Texas Indians, he could simply have referred to the Alabama-Coushatta east of Livingston, and might have mistaken Alabama and Koasati elements as influences from related Muskogee. But with considerable experience in Creek Indian affairs in Georgia and Alabama (J. J. Hooper in Woodward (1939 [1859]: 3–4), Woodward was less subject to flights of fancy than many of his contemporaries. During his earlier years among Creek Indians in Georgia and Alabama, he had learned some of their language (Woodward 1939 [1859]: 148), which allowed him to recognize Eastern Muskogean elements. Woodward (1939 [1859]: 20–1) even recorded a compound of apparent Muskogee origin, and left some perceptive observations about the variable pronunciations of the voiceless lateral fricative, reminiscent of modern phonological variations in Mobilian Jargon:

I know a number of words in their language . . . and names of things and places that are not spoken or pronounced as they were when I first knew them. This has been occasioned by the whites not being able to give the Indian pronunciation, and the Indians in many cases have conformed to that of the whites. A horse, for instance, is now called Chelocko by the whites who speak Indian, and by most of the Indians; but originally it was Echo Tlocko, signifying a Big Deer—Echo is a deer and Thlocko is something large. The first horses the Creeks ever saw were those introduced by the Spaniards, and they called them big deer, as they resembled that animal more than any other they knew—this is their tradition, and I am satisfied that it is correct.

The variable attestations for the Muskogee word for 'horse' as pronounced by Creek and non-Indian speakers, "Echo T(h)locko" and "Chelocko," may be reconstituted as †**ečo łakko** (< Alabama/Koasati/Muskogee/Seminole **ico** 'deer' + Muskogee/Oklahoma Seminole **-łakko** 'big' (Munro, forthcoming)) and †**š(ə)loko** (Silverstein 1973 MS: 39) or †**č(ə)loko**[4] respectively,

---

[4] Silverstein (1973 MS: 39) has suggested †**š(ə)loko** on the assumption that Woodward's sequence of the first four letters in "Chelocko" were his rendition of the lateral fricative [ł], in which case the compound for 'horse' was reduced to the same word as that for 'big.' Yet, following Woodward's use of the letters *c* and *h* in the Creek pronunciation of the word for 'deer,' the *Ch* in the second form more likely represented a voiceless alveopalatal affricate, in which case there simply occurred aphaeresis (rather than a deletion of the initial compounding element for 'deer') and a possible merger of the alveolar affricate with the lateral fricative, perceived as [ł]. Both phonological processes were quite common in Mobilian Jargon (see Sect. 8.2). In contrast, Silverstein's explanation entails the questionable assumption of the deletion of the initial element, which constitutes the compound's head or key in this case. In Mobilian Jargon, there is no reliable evidence for variable forms of compounds without the key or

with the characteristic phonological variation for the later fricative [ɬ] (see
(66) in Sect. 8.2). Woodward (1939 [1859]: 22–3, 78, 107–8) displayed a
broader knowledge of Muskogean with a few other words. Of special interest is the native name for the Creek chief Black Warrior, "Tustanugga
Lusta," which Woodward (1939 [1859]: 78) considered as related to Tusca
Loosa, "a mixed word of Creek and Choctaw." Whereas the second name
derives from Choctaw **taška** 'warrior' and **losa** 'black' and is a poor example
of language "mixture," Woodward was correct in recognizing a historical
relationship to "Tustanugga Lusta" (< Muskogee **tastanaki** 'warrior' +
lasti: 'black;' for Muskogean derivations, see Munro, forthcoming), by which
he demonstrated a knowledge of Choctaw or some other Western Muskogean language. Unfortunately, Woodward provided no clues as to whether
these words were a sample of pidginized Muskogee *per se*, as Michael Silverstein has proposed for 'horse,' or possibly Mobilian Jargon. The characteristic pattern of the variable pronunciation of [ɬ] identifies Woodward's
word for 'horse' with reasonable certainty as either pidginized Muskogee
or Mobilian Jargon, an inference that does not apply to his other Muskogean words without further supporting information. However, Woodward's
comparative knowledge of Muskogee and Western Muskogean leaves little
doubt about the accuracy of his observations about Creek or Muskogee elements in Mobilian Jargon.

   The linguistic data also match available sociohistorical information.
Although Woodward did not further identify the Texas Indians, there
indeed existed a Creek community on the Penwau Slough and Kickapoo
Creek west of Livingston until a few years ago (see Marsh 1974: 306–13).
Erroneously identified as Kickapoo (Algonquians), these Creek were
descendants of one or more member groups of the former Creek Confederacy, spoke Muskogean and perhaps other Southeastern Indian languages,
and were closely associated with local African Americans.[5] Since Mobilian
Jargon reached well into eastern Texas (see Sect. 10.1), it was probably

head element; historical documents and modern recordings only attest absent modifiers, either
adjectives or second nouns, in variable forms of compounds, as e.g. in †**foše heše** ("fouché-
hiché" (Anonymous 1862 MS: 59)) ~ †**heše** ("hiché" (Anonymous 1862 MS: 116)) 'bird
feather' (< 'bird' + 'feather, body hair, fur'), **haksobeš falaya** ~ **haksobeš** 'mule' (Geoffrey
Kimball, personal communication; < 'ear' + 'long'), †**et(t)e te(y)ak** ("ité-tyiak" (Anonymous
1862 MS: 56)) ~ **te(y)ak** 'pine' (< 'tree, wood' + 'pine'), **poškoš nakne** ~ **poškoš** 'son' (Crawford 1978: 83; < 'child, dear baby' + 'male'). From this perspective, the second reconstitution
appears preferable to the first.

   [5] The probable source for this confusion is the fact that there also was a group of Kickapoo
Indians along the Sabine River in eastern Texas in the early nineteenth century. Like other
eastern Indians (including Creek), these Kickapoo came to serve as a buffer against raids by
Plains Indians and against the westward expansion by the United States into Texas. It is not
clear what relationship the Creek and Kickapoo of eastern Texas had with each other; but a
group of modern Kickapoo has had quite close ties to an Afro-Seminole community (including descendants of Creek) near Nacimiento in Mexico, close to the American border (see
Latorre and Latorre 1976).

(79) †no,　kšo,　　　　papešelõ;　plata,　plata,　čokəma　fena.
　　　no　not(hing)　friend　　silver　silver　good　very/fine (?)

common also among these Creek—in their associations with African–American neighbors, the nearby Alabama-Coushatta, and non-Indians, as well as possibly within their own community, if multilingual. Elements of Muskogee, Apalachee, and Natchez other than Choctaw and Chickasaw presumably reflected the varying influences of the community's member groups onto Mobilian Jargon.

Like Woodward in Texas, but some twenty years earlier, a German traveller and poet by the name of Gustav Dresel (1920–1921: 407) quoted an Alabama as saying to him in Mobilian Jargon in response to an offer of paper money: "No, Qshaw, Papeshille; plata, plata, shoke me fina;" or "That is nothing, man, silver, silver is fine, good the sterling." Dresel's example may be reconstituted as shown in (79). The translation of the reconstituted version, 'No, (that is) not(hing), friend; silver, silver (is) very good,' fits Dresel's remarkably well. The only essential difference concerns "Papeshille" or †**papešele**, which he interpreted as 'man.' Why he did so becomes evident from the use of the same word in another context. Dresel (1920–1: 371) quoted a Coushatta friend as saying "You good man, you good papeshillo, you Dutchman," and must have interpreted "papeshillo" as a simple lexical replacement of English 'man.' Although erring in this instance, Dresel had good reason to draw this inference, because such lexical replacements occurred quite frequently in Mobilian Jargon. However, †**papešelo** with its voiceless bilabial stops and its apparent ending of **-o** was a Hispanicized rendering of widely used †**babešele** 'brother, friend,' deriving from Alabama **iba:pisi:li** 'be a friend to' (Munro, forthcoming: 'sibling'[6]). Of special interest in this historic sample of Mobilian Jargon, but hardly surprising for Dresel's period, are Spanish influences. The most obvious one is the Spanish loan-word †**plata** 'silver,' for which another speaker might have equally used the Choctaw-derived version **tale hat(t)a**, literally 'white stone.' Yet a speaker familiar with Spanish could misinterpret **fena** 'very, really, especially' as the feminine form of Spanish *fino* 'fine'

---

[6] Here, acknowledgement is due to Joe Dillard, who with all his monogeneticist inclinations for the origin of pidgins and creoles was skeptical about Spanish or some other, related source for "papeshillo" and drew my attention back to Mobilian Jargon. Because of the obvious Hispanic flavor of Dresel's sample, I had first turned to Spanish and other Romance languages for possible corresponding forms for "papeshillo"—with little success beyond such questionable instances as Spanish "papacito," meaning 'little father.' The current interpretation of "papeshillo" as simply a Hispanicized version of †**babešele** remains the most convincing. Later, I found this word in varying forms to be one of the better attested terms of Mobilian Jargon in other historical documentation, as if it had served as a lexical identity marker for the pidgin (see (84) and (87) as well as the discussion preceding (86) in Sect. 9.3). Yet I have not come across any indication that †**babešele** ever came to function as a name for Mobilian Jargon as **yam(m)a** 'yes, right, alright, indeed; this, that' did.

in accordance with the feminine gender of the foregoing noun **plata**, and would still be able to understand the gist of this utterance. In this context, even the initial "no" in the above quotation could have been Spanish rather than English.

This document has raised questions of historical accuracy. Did Dresel simply enhance the literary style of his diary with a stereotypic rendering of Indian speech? The translator of Dresel's diary into English, Max Freund (in Dresel 1954: 140–1), already addressed the issue of poetic license, and had some Alabama or Coushatta of eastern Texas examine Dresel's sample. The Native American recognized it as accurate and still in colloquial use in the vicinity of the Alabama-Coushatta Reservation near Livingston as late as the 1930s! Oral history similiarly indicates a partially Hispanicized variety of Mobilian Jargon in use among people of Choctaw, Lipan Apache, and Spanish descent in Sabine Parish in western Louisiana until a few decades ago (Hiram F. Gregory, personal communication), for which surviving Choctaw loans in the local Spanish are still an indication.

If Dresel's attestations for the Alabama-Coushatta are reliable, there exists little reason to doubt another of his observations, which applied to the speech of Native Americans in Adams County around Quincy in present-day west-central Illinois and is of some significance: "Diese Indianer, die meist französisches Blut in sich haben, kauderwelschen Französisch und Indianisch durcheinander" (Dresel 1920–1: 348).[7] Dresel did not name this *Kauderwelsch* or lingo, nor did he identify the Native Americans, which might give us a clue to what they spoke. Did he again refer to Mobilian Jargon, perhaps without realizing a relationship between this lingo and that of the Alabama-Coushatta because of varying influences from European and Native American languages in their vocabularies? If this question appears far-fetched at first, it is perfectly justified in light of the fact that Mobilian Jargon extended as far north as southern Illinois and as far northwest as 500 miles upstream on the Missouri River from its confluence with the Mississippi during at least the second half of the eighteenth century (see Sect. 10.1).

Indication for precisely such a variety with a greater share of French loanwords is given by Claude C. Robin, who described Mobilian Jargon for Louisiana in the early nineteenth century in the following terms: "Quelques mots de français qu'ils [the Indians] entendaient, quelques mots de leur langue qu'un de nos engagés savait, et beaucoup de signes que les sauvages ont l'art de rendre avec une expression singulière, furent nos interprètes" (Robin 1807: ii. 304).[8]

---

[7] 'These Indians, most of whom have some French blood in their veins, jabber a mixture of French and Indian' (Dresel 1954: 15).

[8] 'Some French words that they [the Indians] understood, some words of their language that one of our enlisted men knew, and many gestures that the savages artfully produce with a remarkable expression were our interpreters' (author's translation).

The information on lexical variation in Mobilian Jargon farther back into history remains anecdotal, but worth considering. During his sojourn in Louisiana from 1784 until 1798, the French traveller Louis Narcisse Baudry des Lozières observed phonological and lexical variations for "la langue des chactas et des chicachas" or 'the language of the Choctaw and Chickasaw,' identifiable as Mobilian Jargon because of its easy acquisition, its "mixed" nature, and its great geographic range of more than 1,200 miles around. By implication, some of these variations displayed contributions by the Chickasaw; but Baudry des Lozières left no details: "Il n'y a souvent de différence que dans le plus ou moins de force de la prononciation, ou dans quelques mots que les gestes auxquels les sauvages sont beaucoup accoutumés expliquent intelligiblement aux louisianais qui en ont l'habitude" (Baudry des Lozières 1802: 267).[9] With his repeated references to Mobilian Jargon as a form of Chickasaw, Le Page du Pratz in his *Histoire de la Louisiane* (1758: ii. 218, 219, 242) likewise suggested a substantially greater Chickasaw component in the pidgin's lexicon in early eighteenth-century Louisiana (see Sect. 5.3).

There are probably other, similar instances of lexical variations attested in historical documents pertaining to once greater Louisiana and beyond. In his book *The Mobilian Trade Language*, Crawford (1978: 110 n. 53) argued judiciously that the use of an apparent Natchez phrase in Antoine Simon Le Page du Pratz's conversation with Natchez Indians, "**Noco**, je ne sçais," was "not irrefutable proof that the conversation was in Natchez. One cannot rule out the possibility that the word has entered the variety of Mobilian [Jargon] spoken by the Natchez and by those who dwelled among them." If the phrase †**noko** indeed meant 'I don't know,' it was either Natchez-influenced Mobilian Jargon or pidginized Natchez rather than standard Natchez, the latter of which renders this phrase as ʔicokʷaːt taːʔaː; alternatively, Le Page du Pratz conceivably mistranslated †**noko**, which appears closer to Natchez **nacoko** 'he knows' (Geoffrey D. Kimball, personal communication; cf. Van Tuyl 1980: 89). Of interest in this context is also an older Houma woman's phrase in what may be Mobilian Jargon, "nakio' " or †**nakeo** for 'You do not know anything' as recorded by John R. Swanton (1911: 29) some 150 years later. A comparison of Le Page du Pratz's attestations identified as Natchez with more recent recordings of the same language (see Van Tuyl 1980) shows other substantial differences between them.

In extension of Crawford's argument, many attestations of single Indian words in historical and ethnographic documents of greater Louisiana would probably turn out to be Mobilian Jargon rather than the first language of

---

[9] 'There often is only a difference in more or less intensity in pronunciation or in some words; the gestures to which the Indians are much accustomed explain these words intelligibly to the Louisianians, who are used to them' (author's translation).

some Native American group as presumed by their authors, and may imply still more lexical variation. However, this proposition is ultimately difficult to prove without supporting evidence in the form of linguistic and preferably semantactic data, identification by name, or other reliable, extralinguistic clues.

The currently available data are sufficient to confirm a greater range of lexical variation in Mobilian Jargon than is evident from modern lexicographic information. Historical sources suggest partial lexical replacements with "loan-words" from various languages, determined by sociolinguistic factors such as the speakers' native-language backgrounds and their audience. Partial lexical replacement could recur over time, as it did with lects exhibiting variable portions of Chickasaw, Alabama, Koasati, other Eastern Muskogean and Gulf languages (including Muskogee and Tunica), Algonquian, Spanish, French, and English. Among these, European loans never assumed any substantial portions of Mobilian Jargon's lexicon until the pidgin's replacement; they have received special attention only because Europeans could identify them easily, just as they interpreted native vocabulary in terms of European etymologies as probably in the case of Dresel's "fina."

8.4. Semantactic Variation

In contrast to the attested variations in the phonology and lexicon of Mobilian Jargon, its syntax (including morphology as evident from compounds) exhibited little variation. Modern recordings present a semantactically stable pidgin with a set word order except for a few single variable examples with sOV or sVO, apparently the result of interference from the speakers' first languages in language obsolescence rather than standard expressions of a functional medium. If there existed any substantial variation in Mobilian Jargon's syntax, it probably applied only to the word order of multiple-argument constructions with nominal and pronominal subjects, as already suggested in terms of alternative analyses of SOV and OSV (see Sect. 6.5). There are no clues to any greater semantactic variation in historical documents of Mobilian Jargon; most early attestations in fact conform remarkably well with modern observations about its grammar.

Yet there remains a single and curious instance of historical word-order variation in need of closer examination: Le Page du Pratz's description of a historical discourse for the early eighteenth century in his *Histoire de la Louisiane* (1758: iii. 6–7). In a sample of historical discourse already discussed in Section 7.3, Louisiana Indians invited Frenchmen into their homes by saying "Chpénélé" or †**(e)š benele** 'You sit down!' followed by "Apasich" or †**apa(s) eš** 'You eat!' While the lexical variation of †**eš** and **ešno** 'you' is well within the expected range and the first is even explainable as a short form of the latter, the alternating order of pronoun and verb in these two phrases comes as a surprise in light of both modern as well as other historical recordings, and provides a serious challenge to claims of a stable grammar, if this sample indeed represents Mobilian Jargon.[10]

One could simply ignore Le Page du Pratz's observations by dismissing them as questionable, as several anthropologists with interest in Native Americans of southeastern North America have done by relying on an incomplete and poor translation of his book (see Le Page du Pratz 1975 [1774]). But his description, more sympathetic towards native peoples than most of his contemporaries or even subsequent generations of observers, has proved a rich early document for the study of Southeastern Indians in general and Mobilian Jargon in particular, and merits closer scrutiny.

On the assumption that the author's observations are fundamentally accurate, there first arises the question of whether these passages perhaps describe some Muskogean language proper instead of Mobilian Jargon, for he did not explicitly identify these samples as part of the pidgin. What suggests an alternative interpretation is an apparent example of the interchanging order of subject pronoun affixes and verb in Muskogean languages depending on person and number, if not his use of the personal prefix **iš-** for the second person singular, occurring in Choctaw and other Muskogean languages, in place of the independent pronoun for the second person singular such as **ešno** 'you' (see Haas 1946). With a greater influence from a Western Muskogean language than even recent varieties spoken by Choctaw Indians, Le Page du Pratz's recordings could conceivably serve as evidence for what Silverstein (1973 MS: 29–32) and Crawford (1978: 28–9) have described as Western Muskogean, a presumably non-pidginized lingua franca similar to Choctaw in its structure and spoken by several different groups of the lower Mississippi region, among them non-Muskogeans such as Biloxi and Chitimacha. Arguments for such a Western Muskogean contact medium provided the basis for Crawford's case against the presence of Mobilian Jargon in early colonial Louisiana and, by extension, against its aboriginal, pre-European existence.

At length, Silverstein and Crawford could draw on little or no evidence in support of their hypothesis. The principal linguistic source used by Crawford for their argument, an example of "Bayogoula" by the Jesuit priest Paul du Ru (1700 MS: 46/1934: 32; see (57) in Sects. 7.2 and 9.3), does not describe some non-pidginized form of Western Muskogean, but provides the first unquestionable linguistic attestation of Mobilian Jargon, as indicated by its analytic sentence structure and social context. Significantly, du

---

[10] The following passages again rely to a considerable extent on the section "Two Exemplary Historical Scenes of Speaking in Mobilian Jargon" of my paper on the ethnohistory of speaking (Drechsel 1983*b*: 170–3).

Ru's recording of 1700 preceded Le Page du Pratz's observations, made during the period of 1718 to 1734, by two to three decades, and undermines not only Silverstein's and Crawford's hypothesis, but also their arguments against the existence of Mobilian Jargon in early French Louisiana.

Rejecting du Ru as evidence for the Western Muskogean hypothesis does not dismiss it altogether, but would require an extended sociolinguistic explanation for the existence of another, distinct Muskogean-based lingua franca spoken in the same location and during the same period as Mobilian Jargon. If one were still to insist that, instead of du Ru's attestation, it was the one of Le Page du Pratz that represented Western Muskogean, closer examination also yields several linguistic and extralinguistic arguments against such an interpretation. First, the pronominal affix for the second person singular **iš-** in Choctaw and corresponding forms in other Muskogean languages, such as **is-** in Class-I verbs of Koasati, are specifically prefixes, and—unlike the pronoun in Le Page du Pratz's recording of "Apasich"—do not alternatively assume a postverbal position (see Haas 1946; Booker 1980). Most importantly, the author of *Histoire de la Louisiane* was considerably less familiar with Muskogeans than with either the Chitimacha or Natchez; he did not live among the Choctaw or some other Muskogean people for any extended period, and would hardly have had an opportunity to learn any of their languages. If by accident it still was Choctaw Indians who had provided the author with the above speech samples, these would have been in Mobilian Jargon rather than any of the Indians' native languages, as Le Page du Pratz (1758: ii. 219) confirmed elsewhere: "Pour ce qui est des Chat-kas, je pense qu'étant venus après les autres & en très grand nombre, ils ont conservé leur Langue en partie, dans laquelle ils entremêlent quelques mots de la Langue Tchicacha [i.e. Mobilian Jargon]; quand ils m'ont parlé, c'étoit en cette dernière Langue."[11] On the other hand, the author was quite intimate with the Chitimacha and Natchez, among whom he had resided for many years and who were the source of most of his observations. The two groups spoke two so-called Gulf isolates quite different from Muskogean languages and mutually unintelligible with them or each other, but used Mobilian Jargon with the French and Le Page du Pratz. He had learned much of the pidgin from his Chitimacha slave and his Natchez hosts (Le Page du Pratz 1758: i. 85–6; ii. 321–2). Thus, the Muskogean-derived phrases "Chpénélé" and "Apas-ich" represent, with reasonable certainty, Mobilian Jargon rather than Western Muskogean.

This conclusion still requires an explanation for the variable pre- and postverbal position of †**(e)š** 'you.' Although vaguely reminiscent of Musko-

---

[11] 'As for the Choctaw, I think that, having come after the others and in very great number, they have in part retained their language, into which they intersperse some words of the Chickasaw language [Mobilian Jargon]; when they spoke to me, it was in this latter language' (author's translation).

gean pronominal prefixes and suffixes, this pattern recalls a characteristic of French grammar instead. Reflexive verbs such as *s'asseoir* 'to sit down,' the equivalent of Le Page du Pratz's first example, demand a switch for the pronoun from a preverbal position in the declarative mood to a postverbal position in imperative constructions as in *Assis-toi!*, translated word for word into English as 'Seat yourself!' The same pattern of the pronoun's alternating pre- and postverbal positions appears in †**eš benele** 'You sit down!' and †**apa(s) eš** 'You eat!' with a difference. Le Page du Pratz did not render the first phrase *†**benele eš** as one would expect from a word-to-word translation of French *Assis-toi!* 'Be seated!,' but used a form corresponding to the invitational imperative in French non-reflexive verbs as in *Tu manges!* 'Eat!'; on the other hand, the equivalent verb for the second example in French, *manger* 'to eat,' is not reflexive. It is then as if Le Page du Pratz committed a flip-flop change of French imperative patterns in the corresponding Mobilian Jargon forms. He apparently confused the imperative forms for 'to sit down' and 'to eat,' in which case †**apa(s) eš** simply is a loan translation based on the pattern of imperatives in French reflexive verbs. This interpretation receives further support from another peculiarity, the epenthetic consonant **s**, which corresponds to the final *s* in the second person singular of French verbs, pronounced only if the following word begins with a vowel or glide as in this sample, and thus reflects a morphophonological feature of French. The hypothesis of Le Page du Pratz's apparent confusion of the verb and pronoun order in these instances becomes perfectly reasonable in light of the fact that it took the author more than twenty years to publish his *Histoire de la Louisiane* after he had left Louisiana in 1734; in the mean time, his memory could easily have lapsed with respect to the word order in Mobilian Jargon, as was the case with younger and older members among its last speakers.

In short, Le Page du Pratz presented a variety of Mobilian Jargon that reflects a greater influence from French grammar (including morphophonology) rather than Western Muskogean and illustrates his claim that the pidgin "s'apprend mieux par l'usage que par principes" (Le Page du Pratz 1758: ii. 323) or 'is easier to learn by practice than by rules' (see Le Page du Pratz in Crawford 1978: 44). His single phrase consisting of a verb followed by a pronoun remains a grammatical idiosyncrasy due to interference from French and a confusion in his memory; it has no matching attestation in either historical or modern recordings, nor does it give any clues about the position of nouns in multi-argument sentences.

Linguistic variation in Mobilian Jargon undoubtedly extended beyond syntax and semantics to discourse. Regrettably, the available evidence, both historical and modern, reveals little else beyond the fact that French and other non-Indians must have regularly broken native rules of conversation, acting like a flock of geese (see Sect. 7.3).

8.5. A Broader Perspective: The Lingua Francas Creek and Apalachee as Eastern Varieties

The discussion on lexical variation in Mobilian Jargon has already recognized lects of Mobilian Jargon with influence from Muskogean languages other than Western Muskogean—that is Choctaw or Chickasaw. A prominent example was Woodward's description of a variety among Texas Indians in the mid-nineteenth century as "a mixture of Creek [Muskogee], Choctaw, Chickasay, Netches, and Apelash," an assessment that is convincing with his comparative knowledge of Muskogee and some Western Muskogean language, illustrated with several words and alternating pronunciations of the voiceless lateral fricative [ɬ]. Although Woodward did not identify his Muskogean samples as Mobilian Jargon or alternatively as pidginized Muskogee (see Sect. 8.3), his observations are interpretable as a Muskogee-based interlingual medium. There are various linguistic and historical indications for a lingua franca Creek, spoken among member groups of the Creek Confederacy in Alabama, Georgia, and Florida in the eighteenth and nineteenth centuries, next to another, apparently related contact language based on Apalachee. His reference to Creek and Apalachee influences open the question of whether and how Mobilian Jargon was related to the lingua francas Creek and Apalachee.[12]

As in the case of Mobilian Jargon, there were only occasional references to the lingua francas Creek and Apalachee available in the linguistic and anthropological literature until recently (see Crawford 1978: 6–7; Drechsel 1979: 45–51, 132–5; Silverstein 1973 MS: 17, 28–9, 37, 39; Sturtevant 1971: 96, 103, 107, 112–13). Most of the information available on the lingua franca Creek or Muskogee has also been rather anecdotal in nature (see Drechsel 1983a). Aside from modern linguistic evidence for Eastern Muskogean "flavored" varieties of Mobilian Jargon by speakers of Alabama and Coushatta, the best data consist of incidental sociolinguistic and historical observations about the lingua francas Creek and Apalachee, which none the less are suggestive in the context of what is now known about Mobilian Jargon.

The first to recognize the lingua franca Creek as a distinct phenomenon, William C. Sturtevant (1971: 96) has described it as follows:

---

[12] This section presents suggestions about the relationship of Mobilian Jargon in a regional sociolinguistic context presented earlier (Drechsel 1976b, 1983a), with better support including some limited linguistic data.

Muskogee was the internal language of the majority of towns and the lingua franca between towns. But there was a large minority of towns whose internal language was Hitchiti (in the same family, but not mutually intelligible with Muskogee). There were also Alabama- and Koasati-speaking towns (two more Muskogean languages, or perhaps two quite distinct dialects of one language), and, at least in late times, towns of languages whose other speakers were outside the Creek orbit (including some non-Muskogean languages). Because of the preponderance of Muskogee-speaking towns and the use of this language for inter-town communication, there was a tendency for non-Muskogee-speaking towns to replace their distinctive languages with Muskogee. This happened in many Hitchiti towns, and the town of Tukabahchee, for example, may originally have spoken Shawnee, an Algonquian language.

Unfortunately, Sturtevant has not provided any further linguistic details about the lingua franca Muskogee or Creek[13]—except perhaps a list of eighteen words of Spanish origin (Sturtevant 1962: 51). As determined by phonological evidence, Muskogee was the medium by which most of these Spanish loans entered other Southeastern Indian languages, including Choctaw, Chickasaw, and Cherokee (Sturtevant 1962: 52–4), and even shared several identical or similar words with Mobilian Jargon: Muskogee **aló:so, aló:sa** and Mobilian Jargon **onos(e), onoš(e), honoš** 'rice;' Muskogee **ʔcołákko** and Mobilian Jargon †**ečo łako** ("echo t(h)locko"), †**č(ə)loko/š(ə)loko** ("chelocko" (Woodward 1939 (1859): 21)) 'horse;' Muskogee **ispá:ni** and Mobilian Jargon †**spane** ("spanié" (Anonymous 1862 MS: 131)) 'Spaniard;' and Muskogee **wá:ka** and Mobilian Jargon **wak(a)** 'cow.'

Other traces of this Muskogee-based medium may have survived in Oklahoma Cherokee charm songs, which recall pantribal songs in Mobilian Jargon. Although interpretable in Cherokee, these songs were apparently of Creek origin, and appeared to Creek consultants as a "corrupted" Muskogee structure with a mixed vocabulary ("macaroni text") including Cherokee, Muskogee, and possibly Natchez words, in so far as they are identifiable (see Kilpatrick and Kilpatrick 1967). Remaining uncertainties in interpretation first require further inquiry into the linguistic data to make a reliable comparative source.

In discussing dialect variation in Muskogee proper, Mary Haas (1945) may already have provided some modern linguistic clues about the lingua franca Creek. In particular, she noticed different types of phonological variations—such as [t] – [ł], [c] – [k], [m] – [w], and others—that she did not

[13] Following Sturtevant (1971: 97–8), I continue using the distinction between *Muskogee* and *Creek* to refer to Muskogee-speaking communities and the larger political alliance ("confederacy") of Muskogee with other, non-Muskogee peoples respectively. There is no synecdochical error in the continued use of *Creek* or its extension to non-Muskogee Indians, counter to recent objections by Joel W. Martin (1991: 7). All present references to the Creek or their lingua franca are explicitly synecdochical; any redefinition in terms of "Muskogee" would only project an inappropriate sociopolitical and linguistic uniformity that did not apply.

interpret as recent dialect divergences from a previously homogeneous language, but as "a hodgepodge from many sources" (Haas 1945: 72) represented by the linguistic diversity of the Creek Confederacy:

In other words one is led to suspect that many of these words represent a substratum of a former Muskogean (though non-Muskogee) dialect. And this becomes even more apparent when other Muskogean languages are brought in for comparison.

In some cases the number of different forms of one word recorded among Muskogee speakers exceeds the number recorded from all the other extant Muskogean languages taken together. (Haas 1945: 72)

The most important point to be noted here is that for the most part the types of variation between the different dialects of Muskogee resemble the types of variation found between the different Muskogean languages. Of equal significance is the fact that the study of the Muskogee dialects has helped uncover cognates and sound correspondences between the Muskogean languages and has thereby increased our knowledge of Proto-Muskogean. (Haas 1945: 74)

In this description, Haas acknowledged non-Muskogee neighbors, but explained similarities to their languages in terms of survivals from a common ancestral form of Muskogean following the classic tree model of language diversification in historical linguistics, and left unanswered the question of how these disparate phonological variations developed in Muskogee. An alternative, integrated explanation interprets these variations in Muskogee as elements of superstrata influences that resulted from language contact between Muskogee and other languages within and without the linguistically diverse Creek Confederacy. Rather than indicating variations of some common Muskogean proto-form, Haas's "hodgepodge" makes greater sense as survivals of different varieties of Muskogee that various non-Muskogee and possibly even non-Muskogean groups once spoke as a second language or a lingua franca. This explanation receives support from sociolinguistic information provided by Haas. Among the languages spoken by the member groups of the Creek Confederacy, she not only listed Muskogee, Alabama, Coushatta or Koasati, Hitchiti, and Mikasuki (all Muskogean), plus Shawnee (Algonquian) as recognized by Sturtevant; she also included Apalachee (Muskogean), Natchez (Gulf isolate), and Yuchi (isolate; Haas 1945: 69). Several variable Muskogee forms closely resembling Choctaw (Haas 1945: 73–4) specifically indicate the influence of a Western Muskogean language in Muskogee and perhaps even a one-time presence of some Western Muskogeans in the Creek Confederacy.

Early documentation indeed confirms regular, if at times less than amicable relations between the Creek and their western neighbors, the Choctaw and Chickasaw (see Booker, Hudson, and Rankin 1992: 411, 432). A retrospective examination of relevant historical records also reveals several references to a lingua franca Creek, displaying Western Muskogean and other elements.

A major source is the narration by George Stiggins, an agent of part-Natchez descent raised among the Creek with a knowledge of Natchez, Muskogee, and Cherokee (Stiggins 1873–4 MS: 65. 2–3). In observations about several member groups among the Creek in the early 1870s, Stiggins (n.d. MS: 66. 2/Stiggins in Nunez 1958: 20) noted that the Creek Indians called the Alabama "*che lok cul ga*, which is a man that uses an imperfect or mixed language,"[14] and suggested a connection to the Chickasaw and Choctaw by their linguistic similarities. In Stiggins's opinion, Alabama was "a mongrel of both [Alabama and Choctaw] and no doubt was adulterated since the connection of the Alabamas with the Creek tribes as they had no grammatical rule to retain in its original stile or purity [*sic*]" (Stiggins n.d. MS: 66. 2/Stiggins in Nunez 1958: 20).[15] He further reported that

while in the assemblies they [Alabama chiefs] use the Creek tongue, but in their local concerns they use their own tongue or Language, they are tenacious of their private self government seldom associating with any other Indians, the [national?] tongue they speak is similar to and can be understood by the Choctaws, Chickasaws, Hitchities and Cowasadas [Coushatta], which five bodies in time may have been one nation, detached by some circumstance and separated finally.   (Stiggins n.d. MS: 66. 3/Stiggins in Nunez 1958: 21)

Similarly, Stiggins (n.d. MS: 66. 13/Stiggins in Nunez 1958: 30–1) considered Hitchiti as "a mixed tongue" like Alabama. In recognizing a resemblance to Western Muskogean and Hitchiti, he might simply have referred to the "genetic" position of Alabama between Muskogee and Western Muskogean, in accordance with a conventional tree model of the Muskogean language family. Yet its members were truly distinct, mutually unintelligible languages, and Stiggins's suggestion for their mutual intelligibility does not make sense, unless he referred to different, but mutually intelligible lects of the Creek "national tongue" or the lingua franca Creek with varying portions of Hitchiti, Alabama, Koasati, and even Western Muskogean elements.

Almost a century earlier, William Bartram, an observant naturalist from Philadelphia, had recognized the lingua franca Creek in comparable terms, and implied a significant role for Western Muskogean and other languages:

The Muscogulge tongue being now the national or sovereign language, the Chicasaws, Chactaws, and even the remains of the Natches, if we are to credit the Creeks and traders, being dialects of the Muscogulge; and probably, when the Natches were

[14] "*che lok cul ga*" recalls Muskogee **celokv'lkē** 'Cherokee Indians,' speakers of an Iroquoian language, or even **celokhokv'lke** 'people of another language' (Loughridge and Hodge 1964 [1890]: 112 with **v** standing for a short low central vowel), neither of which gives any necessary indication for incomplete language learning or linguistic mixture, however.

[15] In this quote, the crucial word "adulterated" in the original (Stiggins n.d. MS: 66, 2) appears only as "[illegible]" in the printed version by Nunez (1958: 20). There are several other differences between the manuscript and printed version, most of them insignificant.

sovereigns, they called their own the national tongue, and the Creeks, Chicasaws, &c. only dialects of theirs. It is uncertain which is really the mother tongue. (Bartram 1958 [1791]: 294)

The Muscogulge language is spoken throughout the confederacy, (although consisting of many nations, who have a speech peculiar to themselves) as also by their friends and allies, the Natches. The Chicasaw and Choctaw the Muscogulges say is a dialect of theirs.   (Bartram 1958 [1791]: 330)

His inclusion of Natchez, an isolate of Gulf distantly related to Proto-Muskogean and mutually unintelligible with any of its modern descendants, makes unlikely an explanation of "Muscogulge" in terms of Muskogee or some other Muskogean language proper, and again suggests the lingua franca Creek instead. Significantly, Bartram (1958 [1791]: 293) recognized two towns on the Coosau River, namely "Abacooche" and "Natche," as speakers of "Chicasaw" or a related dialect among Muskogee and other languages spoken in the Creek Confederacy. In interpreting Bartram's observations, John R. Swanton confirmed the presence of "a town of Chickasaw Indians among the Creeks of Coosa River" (Swanton in Bartram 1958 [1791]: 414), but dismissed the possibility that the Abacooche and Natche towns had spoken some form of Chickasaw, without giving any reason for doubting Bartram's account or considering "Chickasaw" as Mobilian Jargon in this case. Swanton thought that "the dialect which Bartram attributes to the Abacooche and in part to the Natche town was undoubtedly Natchez, though some Chickasaw may have mingled with these Indians" (Swanton in Bartram 1958 [1791]: 414) without offering any supporting evidence or reasoning for his hypothesis. Alternatively, Bartram simply referred to the lingua franca Creek with Chickasaw- and Choctaw-influenced varieties. The multilingual environments of the Creek Confederacy, including widely disparate elements like Natchez, further suggest a pidginized structure for the lingua franca Creek. Unfortunately, Bartram's description of "Muscogulge" as "very agreeable to the ear, courteous, gentle and musical" as well as "r"-less (Bartram 1958 [1791]: 330) gives no clues about its overall linguistic structure; it could apply equally to Muskogee or any contact medium based on it.

In recording his observations for about the same period, the French brigadier Louis [LeClerc de?] Milfort (1802: *avis*) attributed his poor writing in French to his continued use of some (unspecified) foreign language and "un jargon épouvantable" ('a terrible jargon'), while living among Creek Indians for twenty years. But he did not care to describe this jargon, and listed only a few terms and names, most of Muskogee origin.

For the mid-eighteenth century, James Adair, an Irish-born trader among the Cherokee and Chickasaw, attested the lingua franca Creek in quoting a second-hand, but apparently reliable source:

I am assured by a gentleman of character, who traded a long time near the late Ale-bahma garrison, that within six miles of it, live the remains of seven Indian nations, who usually conversed with each other in their own different dialects, though they understood the Muskohge language . . .   (Adair 1968 [1775]: 267)

Accompanied by an Indian "astrologer" (probably a Chickasaw medicine man), Adair also experienced an encounter with some Creek Indians among whom he applied his knowledge of "Chickkasah," presumably Mobilian Jargon. Adair told his companion that he "did not understand the Muskohge dialect, nor did they much of the Chickkasah language" (Adair 1968 [1775]: 273), which Silverstein (1973 MS: 34) has interpreted as evidence against the extension of Mobilian Jargon to the Creek Indians. However, a careful reading of Adair's quotation suggests that the Creek Indians, speaking Muskogee in one form or another, actually understood a considerable amount of Chickasaw or Mobilian Jargon. That the two parties indeed communicated with each other by a common linguistic medium ensues from Adair's subsequent comments:

I [Adair] told them [the Creek Indians], before my removal to my night quarters, that he [Adair's Chickasaw companion] was almost their countryman, by a residence of above twenty years among them,—their chieftain therefore readily addressed him, and according to what I expected, gave me an opportunity of decently retir-ing. But when he expected a formal reply, according to their usual custom, our astro-logical interpreter spoke only a few words, but kept pointing to the river, and his wet clothes, and to his head, shaking it two or three times; thereby informing them of the great danger he underwent in crossing the water, which gave him violent a head-ach, as to prevent his speaking with any pleasure. I laughed, and soon after endeavoured to persuade him to go over a little while to their camp, as I had done, and by that means, he might know better their present disposition . . . [*sic*]   (Adair 1968 [1775]: 274)

In other words, it was the headache of Adair's companion rather than the lack of a common medium that kept him from giving a long speech. How could the "astrologer" even join the Creek and learn more about their dis-position without at least some knowledge of their language, presumably the lingua franca Creek? Instead of suggesting a lack of comprehension between the Creek Indian party and a speaker of Chickasaw or Mobilian Jargon, this passage by Adair reads as if he only pretended to his compan-ion not to understand any Muskogee in order to find an excuse to retire early for the night. While Adair did not offer any evidence for the presence of Western Muskogean elements in the lingua franca Creek, his observa-tions do not preclude such either, counter to Silverstein's interpretation.

For the 1730s, there are other attestations for language contact between Western Muskogeans and the Creek. In 1734, James Oglethorpe, founder of the British colony of Georgia, offered the following information:

As for their Language they [the Creek Indians] have two kinds, One which is a vulgar Dialect, different in each Town, the other a general Language common to the Creek Nations [,] the Chactaws [,] and the Blew Mouths, which if thoroughly searched into would (I believe) be found to be the radical Language of all America. In this Language are the Songs which contain their History and sacred Ceremonies ...

I had the Lord's Prayer translated into their general Language of which I send you a Copy. The New England Bible is in the Dialect of a particular Nation that lived where Boston now is and of no use but to that particular Nation.   (Oglethorpe in Jones 1966: 515)

Of special interest is Oglethorpe's confirmation of ceremonial songs in the lingua franca Creek and its intelligibility to Choctaw Indians; but his translation of the prayer remains to be found.

For the same period and locale, reports on immigrants from Salzburg to Georgia, collected by their pastor Samuel Urlsperger, provided some further linguistic impressions on the contact medium, including selected words:

Buchstaben haben sie [the Creek Indians] gar nicht. Ihre Sprache aber soll in allem nur etwa tausend *primitiua* haben, und am bequemsten mit Griechischen Buchstaben geschrieben werden können, weil einige Wörter aus dieser Sprache darin befindlich, und verschiedene Buchstaben in keiner andern als der Griechischen Sprache ausgesprochen werden können. Die Herren Prediger haben sich einige Wörter aus ihrer Sprache sagen lassen, und mit Griechischen Buchstaben also angezeichnet: τύτκα das Feuer, ἀσσε die Sonne, ξύκκο das Haus, ςιλλιπάικα der Schuh, ἁψαγίκα die Strümpfe, ἰψὅκα der Hund.

... Sie glauben ein oberes Wesen, so sich über alles ausbreite, und welches sie gemacht habe. Dieses nennen sie Sotolycate, das ist, der, welcher droben sitzt, so sie auch anbeten, und ihm dancken, dass er sie gemacht habe.   (Philipp Georg Friedrich von Reck in Urlsperger 1735: 192)[16]

Wir haben uns zwar von den Indianern selbst, die sehr gern zu uns kommen, viele Wörter sagen lassen, die wir in ein Büchlein zusammen getragen haben. Es finden sich aber hieben diese Schwierigkeiten: 1) Dass man nichts mehr als die Benennungen solcher Dinge von ihnen erfahren kann, die man ihnen vorzeiget, z.B. Brodt, *Appalásko*, Fleisch, *Suck-hah*, Hand, *Tzeuky* &c. Hingegen *verba adjectiua*, u.s.f. weiss man von ihnen, weil sie wenig oder nichts von der Englischen Sprache verstehen, nicht zu erfragen, daher man die Worte nie zusammen setzen lernet, wo man nicht von iemanden eigentlichen Unterricht bekommt. 2) Sie sprechen die meisten

---

[16] 'They do not have any letters at all. But their language is said to have only about one thousand primitive words. Supposedly these can be written most conveniently in Greek letters because their language contains some Greek words and some of the sounds cannot be expressed with any letters other than Greek. The two pastors have let them pronounce some of the words from their language and have written them down with Greek letters as follows: tutka—the fire, ásse—the sun, tsukko—the house, tillipaika—the shoe, hapsalika—the socks, ipseka—the dog. [*sic*]

... They believe in a Superior Being that is everywhere and which has made them. They call it Sotolycate, that is the one who sitteth above. They pray to it and thank it for having made them' (Urlsperger 1968: 147).

Wörter so dunkel und in der Kehle aus, dass man die *Vocales* und *Consonantes* nicht allezeit fassen und mit unsern Buchstaben völlig ausdrucken kann. Fraget man ein Wort gar zu oft, so schämen sie sich entweder, und schweigen gar still, oder fangen an überlaut und lange zu lachen, dass hernach nichts anzurichten ist. Ich habe es auch schon etliche mal erfahren, dass, wenn ich die Worte, die ich mir sagen lassen, andern Indianern in der folgenden Zeit vorgelesen, sie gedachte Worte ganz anders ausgesprochen haben, dass ich daher nicht gewusst, wer recht hat, der erstere oder der letztere. Wie mir vorkommt, hat die Sprache unserer Indianer vieles in Häufung der *Consonantium* und Endigung der Worte mit der Wendischen oder Polnischen Sprache gemein... (Johann Martin Boltzius and Israel Christian Gronau in Urlsperger 1738: 282)[17]

A colonist acquaintance by the name of Monsieur Savy, who had lived for three years among Indians several hundred miles up on the Savannah River, described their language as poor; the Indians had to employ one word to express some ten different things, as Savy argued without, however, leaving any examples (Urlsperger 1738: 345). Another, unnamed and older gentleman, who was to serve as a teacher of the Indian language to the Salzburgers, had only learned so much as to understand and answer questions concerning daily matters such as food, drink, and trade (Urlsperger 1738: 372). Yet the Salzburgers' reports did not just mention a reduced vocabulary and functional restrictions for the lingua franca Creek, but also observed considerable variation in the medium's pronunciation, and offered several words.

Comparative evidence permits the reconstitution of most of the Salzburgers' small vocabulary (with entries in original Greek spelling appearing here in equivalent Roman orthography for easy comparison (see Sturtevant 1994: 141)):

(80) 'bread': "Appalásko" or †**appalásko**; cf. Choctaw **pallaska** vs. Muskogee/Oklahoma Seminole **pa:kk-ita** 'rise (of bread),' Hitchiti/Mikasuki **palast-i**, Alabama **paspa**, Alabama/Koasati **pa:pa** 'bread' (child speech), Alabama **paskocomali** 'blue bread,' and Choctaw/Chicka-

---

[17] 'From the Indians themselves, who like to visit us, we have acquired many words which we have collected in a little book. But this presents a number of difficulties. 1) One can learn from them only the names of objects which can be shown to them, e.g., bread *appalásko*, meat, *suck-hah*, hand, *tseuky*, etc. But verbs, adjectives, etc. cannot be learned from them because they know little or nothing about the English language. Thus one cannot learn to put the words properly together without regular instruction from someone. 2) Most of the words they pronounce so low and so far back in their throats that it is often impossible to distinguish the vowels and consonants or to express them with our letters. If one asks too often for the same word, they either become bashful and silent or they start to laugh so long and loud that nothing can be done afterwards.

Several times I have found, on reading some of the words I had learned to some other Indians, that the latter pronounced them quite differently and I did not known who was right, the first or the last. It seems to me that the language of our Indians resembles that of the Wends or Poles in its endings and its manner of bunching consonants' (Urlsperger 1969: 30).

saw **paska** (Munro, forthcoming) plus Muskogee **apáski** parched meal' and **apataká** 'flat cake' (Sturtevant 1994: 143)

'dog': "ipsouka"/"ifoua" or †**efa** (?) < Muskogee/Seminole/Oklahoma Seminole/Koasati/Alabama **ifa** vs. Hitchiti/Mikasuki **i:f-i**, Choctaw **ofi**, Chickasaw **ofi**? (Munro, forthcoming)

'fire': "tútka" or †**totka**; cf. Muskogee/Oklahoma Seminole **to:tka** vs. Alabama/Koasati **tikba**, Choctaw **tikbici** 'to poke the fire' (Munro, forthcoming)

'Great Spirit,' 'God': "Sotolaycate" or †**sotolaykate**; cf. Muskogee †**soto(h)laykatí: (sota-oh-leyk-atí:** (sky-on above-sit (sg.)-quotative)) 'he (it is said) sits above on the sky' (Karen Booker in Sturtevant 1994: 140 n. 4)

'hand': "Tzeuky" or †**cenke** (?; with "u" as a likely misspelling of "n"); cf. Muskogee **cínki** 'your hand' (Sturtevant 1994: 143) vs. Hitchiti/Mikasuki **ilb-i**, Alabama/Koasati **ilbi**, Chickasaw **ilbak**, Choctaw **ibbak** (Munro, forthcoming)

'house': "xúkko"/"zukkoo" or †**coko**; cf. Muskogee/Seminole/Oklahoma Seminole **coko**, Apalachee **coko** 'dwelling,' even Choctaw **cokka** and Chickasaw **cokka**? vs. Hitchiti/Mikasuki **cik-i**, Alabama **i:scokóoli** 'house with a dirt floor,' and Apalachee **cik** 'house' (Munro, forthcoming)

'meat': "Suck-hah" or †**sokha**; cf. Muskogee/Seminole/Oklahoma Seminole/Alabama/Koasati **sokha** 'pig, hog,' even Choctaw **šokha** 'pig, hog' and Chickasaw **šokha**? 'pig, hog' vs. Hitchiti/Mikasuki **sok-i** 'pig, hog' (Munro, forthcoming)

'shoe': "sillipáika" or †**stellepayka**; cf. Muskogee **istillipayka** 'shoe' (< **isti** 'person' + **ili** 'foot, leg' + **payk** 'one put inside' + **a** 'nominalizer' (Booker in Sturtevant 1994: 140 n. 4))

'stockings,' 'leggings': "hapsatika"/"afatika," or †**hafateka** (?); < cf. Muskogee **hafatí-hka** 'leggings' < Muskogee **hafi** 'thigh' + **ati:hk** 'more than one put inside' + **a** 'nominalizer' (Booker in Sturtevant 1994: 140 n. 4)

'sun': "hásse"/"asse" or †**hase**; cf. Muskogee/Seminole/Oklahoma Seminole **hasi**, Oklahoma Seminole **hasi:**, Hitchiti/Mikasuki **ha:s-i** and Alabama/Koasati **hasi** 'sun, month,' and even Choctaw **haši**; Chickasaw **haši**? (Munro, forthcoming)

That most of the above terms show resemblances in Muskogee or the closely related dialect of Seminole hardly comes as a surprise. Of greater interest are words that resemble not only Muskogee or Seminole, but also other Muskogean languages such as that for 'house' in Apalachee and those for 'meat' and 'sun' in Alabama and Koasati. In the latter instances, the cor-respondences of [s] in Eastern Muskogean languages with [š] in Western Muskogean (Choctaw and Chickasaw) constituted but a minor variation, which would hardly have prevented mutual understanding (for examples of the **s–š** variation in Mobilian Jargon, see (65) in Sect. 8.2). Even more intriguing is the apparent Choctaw source for 'bread,' for which Sturtevant's Muskogee resemblances are far less satisfactory, just as there may exist better resemblances for 'dog.' However, a comparison of the above word list with corresponding terms in Mobilian Jargon demonstrates that the entries for at least 'bread,' 'house,' 'meat,' and 'sun'—four out of ten words—were easily intelligible to speakers of Mobilian Jargon with Choc-taw or Chickasaw as their first language. This conclusion is conservative, because Southeastern Indians were traditionally multilingual. Speakers of Mobilian Jargon with a Western Muskogean language as their native tongue frequently possessed some knowledge of Eastern Muskogean languages such as Alabama or Koasati, and thus would have had little difficulty in understanding additional words.

The immediate source for some of the Salzburgers' words was not Creek or other Indians, but fellow settlers. By its spelling, 'Great Spirit'/'God' came from an English source, quite possibly Oglethorpe (Sturtevant 1994: 142). Absent initial aspiration in the words for 'stockings'/'leggings' and 'sun' as it occurs in one set of entries (see Sturtevant 1994: 141) suggests a French source such as the already mentioned Monsieur Savy, who would not have recognized word-initial [h] unlike the German-speaking Salzburger immi-grants. Yet these mixed sources also raise the possibility that some entries come from different languages and do not represent a single medium.

Ultimately, Urlsperger's data remain too meager to determine conclu-sively whether the vocabulary with its Muskogee, Western Muskogean, and possibly other sources represents Muskogee plus a few single loan-words, or a true *Mischsprache* ('mixed language'). Nor is the available evidence sufficient to resolve the question of pidginization. Contrary evidence might consist of "Tzeuky" or †**cenke** (?) '(your) hand,' interpreted to include the Muskogee pronominal prefix **ci-** for inalienable possession, and possibly complex compounds such as 'Great Spirit'/'God' and 'shoe.' On the other hand, there was conceivably an independent possessive pronoun †**ce** 'your.' The lingua franca Creek—like modern Mobilian Jargon—could also have adopted compound phrases and possibly even †**cenke** (?) as entire units, in which case the latter had lost any possessive implications and simply meant 'hand.'[18]

---

[18] At any rate, Urlsperger's attestations, clearly identified as "Creek," cannot serve as lin-guistic evidence for Yamasee or its classification as a Muskogean language, as recently pro-posed by George A. Broadwell (1991). He ignored the non-Muskogee elements, and neglected to take into consideration the broader sociolinguistic circumstances of his linguistic informa-

Still fewer data are available on the lingua franca Apalachee, and would be unsatisfactory by themselves; but they become suggestive in the context of the lingua franca Creek and Mobilian Jargon at large.

In 1710, a French ship's carpenter by the name of Pénicaut characterized the Apalachee language as follows: "il faut avouer qu'ils [the Indians] n'ont rien de sauvage que le langage, qui est meslé de la langue des Espagnols et des Alibamons" (Margry 1876–1886: v. 487).[19] But according to Henry R. Schoolcraft (1852: 34), this intertribal medium was like Muskogee, and Juan Ortiz, interpreter of the sixteenth-century Spanish explorer Hernando de Soto, supposedly used such a lingua franca Apalachee as a major means of communication with various Southeastern Indian groups. These incidental observations about the intertribal medium assume greater importance when one considers Geoffrey Kimball's recent description of Apalachee proper, a language that—unlike other Muskogean languages—lacked true case suffixes for nouns except for a few survivals and that principally distinguished their grammatical functions by word order, as reconstitutable from a letter written in 1688 to Charles II of Spain (Kimball 1987: especially 139). Its comparatively analytic structure has even led Kimball (personal communication) to wonder whether the Apalachee materials represented "a legitimate daughter of Proto-Muskogean" or rather a creole, presumably deriving from an Apalachee-based pidgin. Do the numerous lexical similarities between Apalachee (traditionally classified with Alabama and Koasati) and Western Muskogean (see Kimball 1988) perhaps serve as further evidence for an earlier pidginization? Whether or not this suggested contact medium based on Apalachee and Alabama was part of the lingua franca Creek, there appears little doubt that the Apalachee had a linguistic impact on their neighbors as indicated independently by Woodward's inclusion of Apalachee elements in the Mobilian Jargon of Texas Indians in the mid-nineteenth century (see Sect. 8.3).

There may be yet earlier although less persuasive evidence for a principally Muskogee- or Apalachee-based contact medium—that is an eastern variety

tion, although he recognized the possibility of Muskogean borrowings for other alleged Yamasee words examined by Albert S. Gatschet and John R. Swanton (Broadwell 1991: 267–8). Several differences in his transcription of the linguistic material between his source in English translation and the German original also indicate that Broadwell did not consult the latter, which might have led him to an alternative interpretation. Currently, the classification of Yamasee as a Muskogean language is premature in the absence of clearly identifiable evidence, especially morphosyntactic data. While no less suggestive, Monsieur Savy's description of the language as poor and its apparent functional restrictions point to the lingua franca Creek rather than Muskogee proper, and leave open the latter's historical affiliation; for the Yamasee could have spoken any other language as their "mother tongue" (for a similar assessment of Broadwell's interpretation, see Sturtevant 1994).

[19] 'one must admit that they [the Indians] have nothing savage other than their language, which is a mixture of Spanish and Alabama' (author's translation).

of Mobilian Jargon in Spanish Florida of the sixteenth century. The relevant source is a memoir by Hernando de Escalante Fontaneda, who was
shipwrecked in Florida as a boy and lived for about seventeen years among
Indians in the mid-sixteenth century. He spent an extended period as a
captive among the Calusa in the south of the peninsula and afterwards
apparently two years among the Apalachee on the northwestern coast, and
recorded his experiences upon his return to Spain in 1575. Evidently,
Fontaneda learned four native languages of Florida, from which he explicitly excluded those of the Ais and Jeaga on the Atlantic coast, but which
supposedly included Calusa and possibly Timucua and Apalachee
(Fontaneda 1973 [1944]: 31, 70; see David O. True's comments in Fontaneda
1973 [1944]: 13–14). Along with various ethnographic observations that
were remarkably detailed for the period, he took down numerous native
names and terms, but neglected to provide translations for most of his
recordings or even the languages' names.

Attempts to determine the source of Fontaneda's words have remained
largely fruitless to date. Buckingham Smith (in Fontaneda 1973 [1854])
found apparent resemblances in Choctaw with the help of native speakers,
and made the following observation about some of Fontaneda's terms and
names: "My monitors say, that all these words are eminently Chahta in their
sounds, but that sometimes they are too imperfectly preserved to be understood, or that their sense can be detected only in part" (Smith in Fontaneda
1973 [1854]: 52 n. 29S[mith]). Albert S. Gatschet (1969 [1884]: 14, 67), who
selected Timucua and Muskogee for comparison, later suspected Carib as
another source for Fontaneda's words. John R. Swanton (1922: 28–31), too,
differed with Smith's derivations, but came to support his conclusion by
similarly preferring Choctaw as probable relative:

My belief that a connection existed between the Calusa language and Choctaw does
not rest mainly on the particular interpretations he [i.e. Smith] gives of Calusa
names for in such matters it is very easy to go astray. I rest my case rather on the
general appearance of the names, and some of their terminations, on Bell's mention
of a Caloosahatchee town inhabited by "Choctaws" and reference in at least one
other place to a Choctaw band among the Seminole. If you compare Smith's
attempts to interpret the Calusa words by means of Choctaw with Gatschet's similar
attempt by the use of Creek, I think you will feel that Smith has had much greater
success.   (Swanton in Fontaneda 1973 [1944]: 41 n. 13Sw[anton])

As Swanton (1922: 29, 30) suggested elsewhere, several interpretations by
Smith and Gatschet are superficial, others even improbable. On the other
hand, Swanton's own reasoning is not on much more solid ground, owing
to the data's limitations. All three scholars have proposed translations of
single words without access to glosses or at least an unquestionable identification of the samples' languages—at best a problematic endeavor because

of the casual projection of doubtful meanings into unidentified terms, resulting in questionable translations. Our limited knowledge of the native languages of early colonial Florida has not made the interpretation of Fontaneda's terms any easier.

Among the words and names offered by Fontaneda, there is only one that includes any reliable clue to its meaning: the ethnonym of "Cañegacola" or "cañogacola" for a native group in central Florida "que quiere desir jente bellaca sin Respeto" [*sic*], or 'which means a people without respect, skillful with the bow' (Fontaneda 1973 [1575]: 31, 36, 71, 74). On the basis of Fontaneda's translation, Swanton (in Fontaneda 1973 [1944]: 42, n. 13Sw[anton]) suggested a Hitchiti origin for this name; but, as is evident from a confusion with another term presented in pair, he must have intended Choctaw as the source—on the basis of Choctaw **oklah** 'people' and Chickasaw **okla** 'town' (see Mooney 1900: 182–3; Swanton 1922: 29–30; cf. Munro, forthcoming: 'town'). The same Western Muskogean root would be consistent with Fontaneda's gloss "jente," and can draw on numerous other, comparable ethnonyms for Southeastern Indians with the meaning of 'people:' Apalachi*cola*, Bayo*goula*, Ofo*goula*, Pasca*goula*, and Pensa*cola* (see Swanton 1946: 31, 216–18). For an alternative interpretation, Geoffrey Kimball (personal communication) has suggested a possible Apalachee etymology: †**akola** 'people' or perhaps 'non-Apalachee people' as reconstituted on the basis of such Florida place names as "sabacola" and "pansacola" as well as Proto-Muskogean ***okola**. Both derivations clearly contrast with Hitchiti/Mikasuki **okl-i** and Alabama/Koasati **o:la** (Munro, forthcoming: 'town'), and identify a western influence from either Apalachee or even Western Muskogean in central Florida of early colonial times, when Muskogean influences were far less widespread than later after the immigration of Muskogee, Hitchiti, Mikasuki, and other Creek Indians, to become Seminoles in the eighteenth century.

These derivations raise the question of how to explain Apalachee- or Choctaw-like terms in early historic Florida. As convincing as the examples with the **-kola** endings and possibly other lexical instances may be for the presence of western influences in early historic Florida, they obviously provide no evidence for Mobilian Jargon by themselves. A few instances *per se* might simply reflect the survival of Apalachee or Western Muskogean words as lexical borrowings in a foreign environment. The latter alternative in fact seems to have been the case for several Western Muskogean-derived names of Southeastern Indian groups whose native languages need not even have been Muskogean (such as those of the Atakapa and possibly even the Houma).

Better evidence for pidginization consists of some indication for morphosyntactic reduction, which indeed appears in Fontaneda's description of the Florida Indians' speech as "abbreviated" when compared with Spanish.

After a chief, presumably representing the Calusa, had tested Spanish captives for their linguistic skills by telling them "seletega," Fontaneda (1973 [1944]: 34) translated it for them as 'Run to the look-out, see if there be any people coming!' and further observed that "Abrebian mas en la palabra que nosotros los de la florida," or 'they of Florida abbreviate their words more than we' (Fontaneda 1973 [1545]: 34, 73). Fontaneda did not elaborate his claim. In the absence of better evidence, such an "abbreviation" could possibly be the result of European deficiencies in describing and analyzing the grammar of the native languages of Florida. An interpretation of Fontaneda's Native American data in terms of Mobilian Jargon, as already suggested by James Mooney (1900: 187) and as attractive as such would appear in light of the currently available data, remains inconclusive at this time.

A first glance might lead one to view any such contact media as linguistic entities separate from Mobilian Jargon, by analogy with the conventional historical-linguistic division of the Muskogean language family into eastern and western branches (see Haas 1941*a*). This view would also continue an earlier tradition of thought that posited "Muskogee" or "Creek" on the one hand and "Mobilian," "Chickasaw," "Choctaw," on the other, designating the lingua franca Creek and Mobilian Jargon respectively as "mother" or ancestral languages.

Following the classificatory division between Eastern and Western Muskogean languages, Silverstein (1973 MS: 34, 39) has insisted that the Creek Indians were not part of the Mobilian Jargon community; but breaking with the tradition culminating in the classification of Muskogean languages, he has also surmised that a pidginized form of Muskogee "intergraded" with Mobilian Jargon. Silverstein (1973 MS: 28–9) has further maintained that the lingua franca Apalachee merged with Mobilian Jargon in the early eighteenth century when the Apalachee moved from Spanish settlements in Florida to Fort Mobile under French rule. Several linguistic and historical considerations indeed indicate that, sociolinguistically, the lingua francas Creek and Apalachee were not entities separate from Mobilian Jargon, but intertwined with it extensively in a single speech community.

For one, there was a close overlap of the major member groups in the Mobilian Jargon speech community with those of the lingua francas Creek and Apalachee, as evident from the linguistic-ethnic identification of their speakers. Mobilian Jargon and the lingua franca Creek shared at least Choctaw, Chickasaw, various Creek communities, Alabama, Koasati, and Apalachee (all Muskogeans except perhaps for some linguistically unidentified Creek communities) plus Natchez, speaking a Gulf-isolate language. Among those groups who spoke the lingua franca Creek or Apalachee, but not apparently Mobilian Jargon, there were only Abihka, Blew Mouths, Hitchiti, Mikasuki, Muskogee, Shawnee, Yamasee, and Yuchi. Significantly, these groups, except the Muskogee, were not sociopolitically dominant among the Creek to suggest any varieties of the lingua franca Creek principally based on any of these languages. Muskogeans played a greater sociopolitical role, and extended farther north, during the period of Spanish explorations in the sixteenth century than conventionally recognized (for a recent sociolinguistic-ethnohistorical review, see Booker, Hudson, and Rankin 1992). People of Creek ancestry have also persisted among the Coushatta of Louisiana and the Alabama-Coushatta of eastern Texas— among the very families who had remembered Mobilian Jargon until recently (Claude Medford, personal communication).

By all indications, Muskogean grammar and lexicon thus dominated over less influential non-Muskogean elements in the lingua francas Creek and Apalachee, as they did in Mobilian Jargon, and kept "foreign" elements from assuming any major formative part beyond loan-words. By virtue of the fact that Muskogean constitutes a family of closely related languages, comparable in its diversity to that of Romance languages, speakers of the lingua francas Creek and Apalachee shared with those of Mobilian Jargon a common substrate with fundamentally the same grammar, including similar phonologies and an identical word order. The grammars of the various Muskogean substrate languages are sufficiently alike to result in a structural convergence among them in pidginization. In other words, the speakers of the lingua francas Creek and Apalachee would have developed grammars similar to that of Mobilian Jargon, even if one could demonstrate that they developed independently from each other—an isolationist conclusion with little justification in light of extensive ethnographic and archaeological evidence for areal contacts (see Chapters 10 and 11).

The major linguistic differences between Mobilian Jargon and the lingua francas Creek and Apalachee would probably have been lexical in nature, reflecting the different etymological compositions of their vocabularies, which resulted from the varying contributions by their speakers' first languages. By currently available indications, the lingua franca Creek exhibited a stronger Eastern Muskogean and specifically Muskogee influence in its lexicon, in contrast to Mobilian Jargon with its substantial portion of Western Muskogean elements. As judged by the close relationship of Apalachee to Alabama and Koasati (Kimball 1987: 162) and by many lexical similarities to Western Muskogean languages (see Kimball 1988), the lingua franca Apalachee would probably have taken a middle position between Mobilian Jargon defined narrowly and the lingua franca Creek.

Yet even the most western variety of Mobilian Jargon must always have shared a substantial lexicon of mutually recognizable cognates with the most eastern variety of the lingua franca Creek. A review of the Mobilian

Jargon vocabulary for lexical resemblances in Muskogee yields the following exemplary list of identical or near-identical terms that a speaker of the
lingua franca Creek should have understood without difficulty (for Muskogean resemblances, see Munro, forthcoming, unless noted otherwise):

(81) 'bag', 'saddle bag', 'pocket': †**šokča** ("tchouktcha" (Anonymous
1862 MS: 58)); cf. Choctaw/Chickasaw **šokca** 'sack' and Alabama/
Koasati/Muskogee/Seminole/Oklahoma Seminole **sokca** 'sack'

'bed': †**topa** ("toupoua" (Bourgeois 1788: 296); cf. Chickasaw/
Muskogee/Oklahoma Seminole **topa**, Choctaw **topah**, Seminole
topa 'table'

'body': **ape**; cf. Choctaw **api**, Chickasaw **api?**, Muskogee **api** 'corn-
stalk,' Seminole **api** 'stalk,' Mikasuki **a:p-i**

'bone': †**fone** ("founi" (Anonymous 1862 MS: 41)); cf. Choctaw/
Oklahoma Seminole **foni**, Chickasaw **foni?**, Muskogee **-foni**,
Hitchiti/Mikasuki **-fo:n-i**

'brain'/'marrow': †**lope** ("loupé" (Anonymous 1862 MS: 39, 40)); cf.
Choctaw **lopi**, Chickasaw **lopi?**, Alabama/Koasati/Hitchiti/Mikasuki
lopi 'liver,' Muskogee/Oklahoma Seminole **-lopi** 'liver'

'buffalo': **yanasa** (Crawford 1978: 82); cf. Alabama/Koasati/Musko-
gee/Oklahoma Seminole **yanasa**

'butter': **wak (em)peš neha**; cf. Spanish "vaca" 'cow' + Muskogean
im- third person dative or alienable possessive (Booker 1980: 34–35;
Haas 1958: 250) + Choctaw/Chickasaw **pisi** 'to nurse,' Alabama/
Koasati **pisi** 'to nurse; breast,' Muskogee/Oklahoma Seminole **ipisi**:
'breast' + Koasati/Chickasaw **niha** 'fat, grease,' Alabama/Koasati
ni:ha 'fat, grease,' Muskogee/Oklahoma Seminole **niha:** 'fat, grease'

'cat': **kate**; cf. also Alabama/Koasati/Muskogee **kati** < Spanish *gato*

'cow': **wak(a)**; cf. Alabama/Koasati/Muskogee/Seminole **wa:ka**,
Chickasaw **wa:ka?**, Choctaw **wa:k** < Spanish "vaca"

'day': **neta**; cf. Alabama/Koasati **nihta**, Muskogee/Seminole **nitta**
'day'

'fat', 'grease' (n.) (2): †**neya** ("nihia" (Anonymous 1862 MS: 46); cf.
Alabama **niya**, Choctaw **niya** 'to be fat,' Koasati/Chickasaw **niha**,
Alabama/Koasati **ni:ha**, Muskogee/Oklahoma Seminole **niha:**

'fish' (n.): **łało ~ slašo ~ šlašo**; cf. Alabama/Koasati/Muskogee/
Seminole **łało**

'handle' (n.): †**ape** ("appé" (Anonymous 1862 MS: 54)); cf. Mississippi Choctaw/Hitchiti **api**, Mikasuki **a:pi** 'stalk, handle,' Muskogee
im-api (including the possessive **im-**)

'horse': †**ečo ɬako** ("echo t(h)locko" (Woodward 1939 [1859]: 21))
~ †**č(ə)loko/†š(ə)loko** ("chelocko" (Woodward 1939 [1859]: 21)); cf.
Muskogee/Seminole/Alabama/Koasati **ico** 'deer' + Muskogee/
Oklahoma Seminole -**ɬakko** 'big,' Mississippi choctaw **ɬãko** 'strong'

'hundred': **čokpe**; cf. Koasati **cokpi** 'hundred,' Muskogee/Seminole/Hitchiti **cokpi**- 'hundred'

'hurt' (v.): **topa**; cf. Choctaw/Chickasaw **hottopa** 'hurt'; Chickasaw/Muskogee/Oklahoma Seminole **topa** 'bed,' Choctaw **topah** 'bed' (cf. Crawford 1978: 92)

'itch' (n.): †**waško** ("ouacheko" (Anonymous 1862 MS: 60)); cf. Choctaw **waško** 'to hurt from scratching,' Chickasaw **waško** 'chigger,' Koasati/Oklahoma Seminole **wasko** 'chigger,' Muskogee **wa:sko** 'chigger,' Alabama **wasko** 'itchy'

'lard': †**šok(h)a neya** ("chouka-nihia" (Anonymous 1862 MS: 51)); cf. Choctaw **šokha** 'hog,' Chickasaw **šokhaʔ** 'hog,' Alabama/Koasati/Muskogee/Seminole **sokhaʔ** 'hog' + Alabama **niya** 'fat, grease,' Choctaw **niya** 'to be fat,' Koasati/Chickasaw **niha** 'fat, grease,' Alabama/Koasati **ni:ha** 'fat, grease,' Muskogee/Oklahoma Seminole **niha**: 'fat, grease'

'milk' (n.): **wak peše ~ peše** ("piché" (Anonymous 1862 MS)); cf. Spanish "vaca" 'cow' + Choctaw/Chickasaw **piši** 'to nurse,' Alabama/Koasati **pisi** 'to nurse; breast,' Muskogee/Oklahoma Seminole **ipisi**: 'breast'

'milk' (v.): †**peše** ("piché" (Anonymous 1862 MS: 26)); cf. Choctaw/Chickasaw **piši** 'to nurse,' Alabama/Koasati **pisi** 'to nurse; breast,' Muskogee/Oklahoma Seminole **ipisi**: 'breast'

'Mobilian Jargon': **čahta ~ šata**; cf. Alabama/Koasati/Choctaw **cahta** 'Choctaw,' Chickasaw **cahtaʔ** 'Choctaw,' Muskogee **ca:hta** 'Choctaw'

'mouth': **čokhalbe**; cf. Alabama/Koasati **icokhalbi**, Mikasuki -**cokhalb-i** 'lips,' Seminole **cokhaɬpi** 'lips,' Muskogee **cokaɬpi** 'lips'

'opossum': †**šokhata** ("choukata" (Anonymous 1862 MS: 30)); cf. Choctaw **šokhata**, Chickasaw **šokhataʔ**, Alabama/Koasati **sokhatka**, Muskogee/Seminole **sokha-hatka**

'otter': †**ošan** ("oushanne" (Anonymous 1862 MS: 29)); cf. Choctaw **ošan**, Koasati/Muskogee/Seminole **osana**, Hitchiti/Mikasuki **osa:n-i**

'palmetto': †**tala** ("tala" (Anonymous 1862 MS: 56)); cf. Choctaw **talah**, Alabama/Koasati/Muskogee/Seminole **ta:la**

'pig', 'hog': **sok(h)a ~ šok(h)a** ("chouka" (Anonymous 1862 MS: 29)); cf. Alabama/Koasati/Muskogee/Seminole **sokha**, Choctaw **šokha**, Chickasaw **šokhaʔ**

'pigeon': †**pače** ("patché (Anonymous 1862 MS: 30)); cf. Choctaw/ Alabama/Koasati/Muskogee/Oklahoma Seminole **paci**, Chickasaw **paci**?, Hitchiti/Mikasuki **pac-i**

'sick': **topa** ("toupa" (Anonymous 1862 MS: 136); "to'pa" (Swanton 1911: 32)); cf. Choctaw/Chickasaw **hottopa** 'hurt'; Chickasaw/ Muskogee/Oklahoma Seminole **topa** 'bed,' Choctaw **topah** 'bed' (cf. Crawford 1978: 92)

'Spaniard': †**spane** ("spanié" (Anonymous 1862 MS: 131)); cf. Koasati **spani**, Choctaw **špa:ni**, Muskogee/Alabama **ispa:ni**, Chickasaw **ošpa:ni**? < Spanish "español" 'Spanish'

'sun', 'month': **haše**; cf. Choctaw **haši** 'sun,' Chickasaw **haši**? 'sun,' Alabama/Koasati **hasi** 'sun, month,' Muskogee/Seminole **hasi** 'sun,' Hitchiti/Mikasuki **ha:s-i** 'sun'

'that', 'there': **ma**; cf. Alabama/Koasati/Muskogee/Oklahoma Seminole/Mikasuki **ma** 'that'

'tooth': †**note** ("noutté" (Anonymous 1862 MS: 40)); cf. Choctaw/Chickasaw/Oklahoma Seminole **noti**, Muskogee **-noti**, Hitchiti/Mikasuki **-no:t-i**, Alabama/Koasati **innoti**, Alabama **nati**

'tree', 'wood': **et(t)o**; cf. Alabama/Koasati **itto**, Muskogee/Seminole **ito**

Mobilian Jargon probably shared numerous other words with the lingua francas Creek and Apalachee.

Widely overlapping ranges and similar, closely related linguistic repertoires speak against a "separatist" interpretation of Mobilian Jargon and the lingua francas Creek and Apalachee, and do not support the assumption for two or three fundamentally distinct contact media within one and the same, larger contact community. Instead, the different terms merely submit different varieties of a single linguistic system consisting of a continuum of interrelated lects with varying Eastern and Western Muskogean proportions in their lexica, just as modern recordings show vocabularies with varying etymologies for Mobilian Jargon and several different names for it (see Sects. 8.3 and 9.1). By this reasoning, the lingua francas Creek and Apalachee were eastern varieties of Mobilian Jargon, or the latter a western extension of the first two.

The distinction between these varieties of a *greater* Mobilian Jargon roughly corresponds to the eastern and western branches of the Muskogean language family—with two significant differences. The concepts of eastern and western varieties in Mobilian Jargon neither imply a genetic relationship between them, nor do they suggest any rigid separation in terms of grammar or possibly even lexicon. The differences between narrowly defined Mobilian Jargon and the lingua francas Creek and Apalachee

as part of one system of intertwined lects may well have been more geographic and social in nature than linguistic, and the distinction between
them nominal rather than substantive. This conclusion matches recent historical-linguistic descriptions of the Muskogean language family in terms of
intertwined dialects and as a linguistic area, notwithstanding the substantial differences in its internal classification (see Nicklas 1994; Martin 1994).
However, the following discussion continues using these names for the
purpose of distinguishing these geographic varieties, while alternatively
referring to them as varieties of Eastern and Western Mobilian Jargon.

8.6. Nature and Range of Variation

The inclusion of the lingua francas Creek and Apalachee in Mobilian Jargon
as part of one larger contact medium substantially extends its geographic
and social boundary and, by implication, its linguistic and especially lexical
variation. For at least 250 years and over a geographic range covering much
of central southeastern North America, Mobilian Jargon must have exhibited a greater range of linguistic variation than the recently collected data
and historical documentation indicate.

Via its Creek varieties, Mobilian Jargon also had indirect ties to Seminole Pidgin (English?) and Afro-Seminole Creole. Recognized from a
sociopolitical perspective as separatist Creek Indians since the mid-
eighteenth century, the linguistically diverse Seminole of Florida (< Muskogee **simanóli ~ simalóni** < Spanish "cimarrón" 'wild, runaway') used a
Muskogee-based contact medium both among each other and with their
new neighbors, associated Africans as well as European traders and settlers,
and did so well into the twentieth century. For the years of 1836 to 1840, an
American brevet captain by the name of John T. Sprague (1964 [1848]: 99)
observed "a mixture of Indian and Spanish" among "Spanish Indians" of
southern Florida, who—as judged by their leader Chekika—were Calusa,
frequently misidentified as "Choctaw" according to Swanton (1946: 102).
Sprague (1964 [1848]: 268–9, 309, 507, 510, 512) also referred to the use of
"the Indian language" or "Seminole" by Spaniards and African Americans
with Florida Indians in the early 1840s, and listed Seminole, Mikasuki,
Creek, Tallahassee, Yuchi, and Choctaw or Calusa among the surviving
Florida Indians.[20] Alanson Skinner (1913: 63) similarly noted a trade jargon
composed of Muskogee, Spanish, and English among the Seminole of the
Everglades and Big Cypress in the summer of 1910, just as William C.
Sturtevant (1971: 112) later observed an incipient, partially Muskogee-

---

[20] As for Choctaw, there existed at least one community in northeastern Florida, the independent band of Ridaughts in the vicinity of Palatka south of Jacksonville, who had reportedly moved there in the early nineteenth century (Ridaught 1957).

based jargon in use by the Mikasuki with non-Indians. References to a traders' "patois" drawing principally on Muskogee and English vocabularies plus occasional samples, some rather stereotypical, appear in historical documentation as late as the 1930s (see e.g. Kersey 1975: p. vi, 35, 66–7, 75, 82, 90, 95, 99, 104, 110–11, 113–14, 120, 123, 136, 139, 178). Since the mid-nineteenth century, this contact medium had apparently become increasingly "relexified" with an English vocabulary in semi-autonomous communities of African associates near Seminole Indians. Descendants of Africans, Seminole and other Southern Indians eventually acquired, by way of creolization, some form of this Muskogee–English pidgin as their first language, which they continued to label "Creek" or "Seminole." Until recently, this so-called Afro-Seminole Creole survived in isolated communities on Andros Island in the Bahamas, in eastern Oklahoma, and in the area of Del Rio on the border of Texas and Mexico (Hancock 1980*a*, *b*). At this time, the lingua franca Creek, the Seminole Pidgin, and Afro-Seminole Creole still require better descriptive evidence to clarify their precise historical relationship.

Variation in Mobilian Jargon and related lingua francas throughout their history resulted from a variety of factors: (1) interference from many diverse native languages and a few immigrant ones (see Sect. 10.1); (2) different levels of competence in the pidgin for individual speakers; (3) knowledge of other second languages, serving as alternative resources for Mobilian Jargon; and (4) the pidgin's decline, which not only produced levelling, but also introduced replacements, especially from European languages.

  If the present grammar of Mobilian Jargon can no longer cover the full range of its linguistic variation, it can highlight several relevant, interrelated issues. Was linguistic variation in Mobilian Jargon greater or less during its decline than its prospering years? How representative are the description and analysis of modern Mobilian Jargon for earlier periods? Are problems of description and analysis compounded by the fact that Mobilian Jargon was a second language and has been out of regular use for some forty years? Or could its very nature as a pidgin maintain a creative component not present in first languages? In short, there exists a problem of superimposing generalizations on the basis of a temporally or geographically limited body of linguistic data, as had already become evident, for example, for the vowel-deletion rule in negative constructions (see (16) in Sect. 5.5) and as applies especially to the pidgin's phonology and lexicon.

  In spite of its nature as a true *Mischsprache*, its attested linguistic variation, and its name, Mobilian Jargon was a stable pidgin, as confirmed by a regular syntax. The present description and analysis then differs substantially from that of Chinook Jargon as presented by Michael Silverstein

(1972). His model presents the latter with a highly variable grammar including few established rules; Chinook Jargon exhibited different, even conflicting deep structures converging at its surface structure with all their
semantactic variations and varying interpretations in between. In contrast
to Mobilian Jargon with its established grammar, Chinook Jargon in
Silverstein's presentation was a true jargon or pre-pidgin, defined as a
makeshift, *ad hoc* linguistic response in rather restricted situations of interlingual communication (for an analysis in disagreement, see Hymes 1980:
405–18; Thomason 1983).

A consideration of the nature and extent of variation in Mobilian Jargon
must eventually confront the question of mutual intelligibility between its
different varieties. The information at our disposal, both modern and historical, permits only a limited examination of this issue. On the one hand,
recognizing the lingua franca Creek as part of Mobilian Jargon might imply
that their speakers did not understand each other fully or at all times, just
as the varieties at the opposite ends of an extended dialect continuum could
be mutually unintelligible for all practical purposes. On the other hand,
widespread multilingual competency among Southeastern Indians, characteristic also of Mobilian Jargon speakers, undoubtedly permitted a far
greater range of linguistic variation than was accessible to monolinguals
(see Chapter 10). Thus, the lingua franca Creek could have been mostly
understandable to Mobilian Jargon speakers of Louisiana and eastern Texas
with a knowledge of an Eastern Muskogean language such as Koasati and
Alabama; in reverse, speakers of the lingua franca Creek with exposure to
a Western Muskogean language such as Chickasaw or Choctaw should have
found little difficulty in following a conversation in its western variety.

To maximize understanding, speakers did not need to depend exclusively
on linguistic information, but also relied on facial expressions, hand signs,
and body language, which could make up for some deficiencies of expression. I still observed a few otherwise stereotypically stoic Louisiana Indians
using expressive faces, intensified gestures, and explicit body language when
speaking in the contact medium, apparently to enhance their linguistic communication. Remembering his family speak Mobilian Jargon, Ernest Sickey
(personal communication) described it as "an emotional language" that was
slow in comparison with Koasati or Choctaw and that at times—unlike
either—required more body language and hand signs for intelligibility.
Unfortunately, he could recall only one gesture—a kind of clapping with
the right hand hitting the left one crosswise and upside-down; each hand
strike emphasized a specific point when speaking or each number when
counting. The anonymous author of *Essai* already noticed that "le geste chez
l'Indien n'est pas la plus faible partie des discours" (Anonymous 1862 MS:
9) or 'gestures among the Indians by no means constitute the most unim-

portant part of speech' (Anonymous n.d. MS: 9). Other historical documentation likewise indicates that expressive gestures with Mobilian Jargon were common to Indians as well as non-Indians—among them the German traveller and poet Gustav Dresel (1920–1: 407; 1954: 65), who used sign language to reinforce his pidgin words and could thus communicate without an interpreter. In the early nineteenth century, the French traveller Claude C. Robin (1807: ii. 304) similarly noticed the Native Americans' adept use of gestures with what was probably Mobilian Jargon, just as another French visitor by the name of Louis Narcisse Baudry des Lozières (1802: 267) had observed their skills in gesturing while speaking Mobilian Jargon. According to James Adair (1968 [1775]: 274), his Chickasaw companion's interactions with the Creek, too, included pointing besides speech. Hand signs may even have been part of Mobilian Jargon as used by Atakapa Indians in the mid-eighteenth century (Bossu 1768: ii. 151/1962: 192).

PART III

Sociohistorical Aspects of Mobilian Jargon

Preliminaries

The chapters on semantics and linguistic variation have already made reference to the extralinguistic domain of Mobilian Jargon. Part III now offers a social history in the spirit of an ethnohistory of speaking, and includes a section on the lingua francas Creek and Apalachee in a broadly conceived notion of the pidgin.

Discussion first deals with the numerous names of Mobilian Jargon as possible keys of identification in early documents, then reviews historical attestations for both its eastern and western varieties, and traces its survival and decline (Chapter 9). Attention next turns to its geographic and social distribution, its communicative and meta-communicative functions, and the speakers' attitudes to the medium—all with an eye on its role in traditional Southeastern Indian societies (Chapter 10). By extending combined linguistic and sociohistorical findings back in time, the final chapter in this part addresses questions of Mobilian Jargon's origin, and explores pre-European roots in the pre-Columbian Mississippian Complex (Chapter 11).

Some of these topics have already intrigued James M. Crawford in his book *The Mobilian Trade Language* (1978), the first to examine the pidgin's history in any detail and to compile much of the relevant historical documentation. The present discussion relies on many of the same archival sources, which—supplemented by new linguistic, ethnographic, and historical evidence—have, however, lent the basis for an interpretation of Mobilian Jargon's early history and origin divergent from Crawford's.

9

History

9.1. The Identification of Mobilian Jargon in Historical Records:
Names and Extralinguistic Clues

A prime concern of historical research has been how to identify Mobilian
Jargon in historical records or ethnographies other than by linguistic and
specifically morphosyntactic characteristics. The basic means would appear
to be names used in designating the pidgin; but this conclusion has proven
unreliable due to the diversity and non-exclusivity of names for Mobilian
Jargon, some of which could refer at the same time to the native language
of a people or the people themselves or might yet have some other
reference.

In the early periods of its recorded past, European observers named the
pidgin primarily after a particular group of people among whom they first
heard it. With little awareness of the native linguistic diversity, non-Indians
identified the Mobilian Jargon with their hosts' first languages while
describing it as the most widespread or universal medium of the area. Thus,
one finds it identified as Bayogoula, Chickasaw, Choctaw, and by names of
still other native groups in the first irrefutable historical attestations. The
recognition of Muskogee-based and other eastern varieties as part of the
Mobilian Jargon speech community (see Sect. 8.5) entails still other names.
In the perception of Europeans, there must then have existed considerable
confusion about the sociolinguistic situation of Southeastern Indians, since
many of these peoples spoke Muskogean languages as their mother
tongues. While grammatically more complex than Mobilian Jargon, these
languages shared much lexicon with the pidgin of the same name, and could
not have been easily distinguishable to an uninitiated ear. Only once Europeans had developed a better understanding of the indigenous sociolinguistic situation did they introduce occasional specifications by adding
"trade" or by describing Mobilian Jargon as "la Langue vulgaire," with "vulgaire" simply meaning 'common' and possibly even 'popular' rather than
'vulgar' (Le Page du Pratz 1758: ii. 242, 321–3).

The name that came to prevail in historical records was *Mobilian* in one
form or another (see Sect. 10.1). The first to colonize the central lower
South, French explorers, officers, missionaries, traders, and settlers already
called the interlingual medium "(le) Mobilien" or "la langue mobilienne"—
perhaps as early as 1704, but at the latest in 1721 in the writings of Péni-

caut, a French ship's carpenter (see Crawford 1978: 101 n. 10). This name survived among French-speaking neighbors of the Tunica-Biloxi in and around Marksville in central Louisiana until recently. Meanwhile, by the turn of the twentieth century, anthropologists had already popularized the pidgin's name in the form of *Mobilian (trade) jargon* or *language* (Gatschet 1969 [1884]: 31, 95, 96; Mooney 1900: 15, 182, 187; Swanton 1911: 32, 38 ff.), possibly by analogy with better-known Chinook Jargon.[1]

Mobilian suggests some historical tie to Mobile, the major port city in modern Alabama, as well as its namesake, the Mobilian Indians, a now extinct native community that once enjoyed considerable recognition as ritual keepers of a permanent fire among Indians of the Gulf Coast (see Knight and Adams 1981: 185). The precise origin and etymology of *Mobilian* remain uncertain, for it need not have derived directly from the Indians of the same name. In spite of their sociopolitical status in early colonial Louisiana, the Mobilians vanished shortly as a distinct community, and there remains some doubt as to whether they exerted enough influence to lend their name to an intertribal medium extending across much of southeastern North America. Conceivably, the denomination *Mobilian* assumed significance only indirectly when the first French outpost in the area, named after the Mobilian Indians, developed into a center of commerce and the first capital of colonial Louisiana. In this case, it would have been French explorers and traders who, in the early eighteenth century, applied *Mobilian* to the major medium in the area at the time—Mobilian Jargon.

Tracing the etymology of *Mobile* proves even more elusive. The nineteenth-century historian Henry Sale Halbert (1899: 68–9; cf. Byington 1915: 262) derived the name from an old form of Choctaw **moeli**, "mo-we-lih" or "mo-be-lih," with the meaning of 'to skim, to row, to paddle,' suggesting transportation on water. By implication, Halbert's etymology alluded to travel on the many natural waterways of the lower South (creeks, bayous, and rivers) and even along the shore, which brought people speaking different languages into contact with each other and thus provided a favorable environment for a common interlingual medium such as Mobilian Jargon. However attractive, this etymological derivation remains unsatisfactory, as do numerous attempts at identifying the Mobilians and other Southeastern Indians as Muskogeans on the basis of their names. Such explanations fall short of sufficient or convincing linguistic evidence, open to multiple interpretations.

---

[1] However, Mobilian Jargon never came to be known by the corresponding name of *Choctaw Jargon*, *Chickasaw Jargon*, or *Creek Jargon*, which perhaps requires an explanation in light of the pivotal role of the Choctaw, Chickasaw, and Creek Indians in the history of southeastern North America. Swanton (1931: 1) attributed the lack of a name directly reflecting the Choctaw Indians' influence to being "poorly press agented"—an idle proposition.

Just as the authors of historical documents knew Mobilian Jargon by a variety of names, so did its last speakers call it by different terms, depending on their linguistic backgrounds or ethnic identities. Acadians and African Americans in the neighborhood of Elton in southwestern Louisiana simply termed the pidgin *the Indian language* or merely *Indian*, and occasionally specified it as *Choctaw*, as did those Coushatta neighbors who apparently had never learned any Choctaw. The ethnically diverse, part-Choctaw community of Clifton in west-central Louisiana, too, knew Mobilian Jargon as *Choctaw* (Hiram F. Gregory, personal communication), possibly the only Native American language that a few older individuals could still remember. Similarly, the Tunica-Biloxi in Marksville, central Louisiana, knew Mobilian Jargon as **húma ʔúlu** or the 'Houma's language' (Haas 1953: 219, 320) in reference to their language identified as Western Muskogean.[2]

The last speakers of Mobilian Jargon whom Crawford and I interviewed were more discriminating in naming the interlingual medium. An African American of southwestern Louisiana, who had learned some Koasati in addition to the contact medium, described Mobilian Jargon in its own terms as **anõpa ẽla** 'other/different/strange talk,' as recorded by Crawford (personal communication); **ẽla** in this instance might even have implied 'odd' and related meanings as in Choctaw **inla** (Byington 1915). On the other hand, Lessie B. Simon, a Choctaw woman near Oakdale in south-central Louisiana and one of the last fluent speakers of Mobilian Jargon, was most descriptive in terming it "broken or short-way Choctaw" in English. She also knew it by **yoka anõpa** 'servant/slave language' in her own language and the pidgin, for which neither she nor any other speaker would explain what **yoka** 'servant, slave' meant or how the pidgin had acquired this name. Most Indian speakers around Elton in southwestern Louisiana and Livingston in eastern Texas, however, called Mobilian Jargon "the broken, old, or lost language" in English and probably in French as well, or **yam(m)a** in their native languages of Koasati, Alabama, and Choctaw. This word means 'yes, right, alright, indeed,' used as a frequent marker of acknowledgment or approbation in pidgin conversations. In answer to the question of 'Which one?', **yam(m)a** could further mean 'this' or 'that,' which—following a pos-

---

[2] Whether or not the linguistic identity of the Houma was Western Muskogean as commonly assumed remains in doubt. The frequently cited evidence by Swanton (1911: 28–9) is open to interpretation in terms of either a Western Muskogean language or Mobilian Jargon, and leaves unanswered the question of whether the first might be just one among several languages spoken by the Houma, a highly diverse intertribal community at the time (see Swanton 1911: 291–2). The Muskogean etymology of their name (< Alabama/Koasati/Choctaw/Chickasaw **homma** 'red' (Munro, forthcoming)) is of no further help because an ethnonym for a community can derive from the neighbors' language or even a lingua franca; as evidence serve Muskogean-derived ethnonyms for numerous non-Muskogean Indian groups of southeastern North America (see Sect. 2.4).

sible folk explanation—served as a most useful linguistic device in trading or negotiation (Ernest Sickey, personal communication).

As suggested by the last speakers' many different names for Mobilian Jargon, almost each community knew it by its own term. Members of various linguistic and ethnic groups probably employed different names earlier and in initial contact situations as well; any resulting confusion would have quickly resolved from the pidgin's actual use, and there exist no ethnographic or historical hints for the erroneous identification of Mobilian Jargon among Native American speakers. Diverse names for indigenous languages and communities bewildered only non-Indians, often misled into believing that they referred to the first language of a native community instead of the interlingual medium (for further discussion related to this point, see Sect. 10.3).

Mobilian Jargon thus did not come to be known by a single name in either historical or ethnographic records, which at times left confusion about its identity and prevented its wider recognition as a single phenomenon in earlier research. Acknowledging a variety of names for Mobilian Jargon with the great linguistic and ethnic diversity of its speakers in fact entails some unexpected methodological complications. Just as reference to Mobilian Jargon by a single term was unproductive or even misleading in field research (see Sect. 3.2), names by themselves have not proven reliable enough for the pidgin's identification in historical records, and require supplementary information in the form of a descriptive specification such as *contact, trade,* or *intertribal* or some sociolinguistic evidence. With frequently absent linguistic evidence and ambiguous names, archival research has relied on broader clues for identifying Mobilian Jargon in historical records, specifically explicit references to: (1) functions as an interlingual medium; (2) its intelligibility among speakers of diverse and mutually unintelligible languages (including information on their identity that allows preclusion of some Muskogean language proper); (3) its geographic range extending beyond that of Muskogean languages and into that of other language families; and (4) any unusual characteristics such as the increased use of hand signs.

9.2. Historic Attestations of Eastern Mobilian Jargon (the Lingua Franca Creek)

Finding references to Mobilian Jargon by either linguistic or extralinguistic means has proved difficult in early documentation relating to southeastern North America, especially colonial Spanish records relating to Florida, most of which contain no substantive information on indigenous languages. The first possible document of Mobilian Jargon, namely Hernando de Escalante

Fontaneda's memoir of 1575 on Florida (1973 [1994]), offers little evidence that is more than suggestive (see Sect. 8.5). The earliest reliable, if still incidental observations currently date back only to the beginning of the eighteenth century.

During the period from 1706 to 1717, Francis Le Jau, a French-born Anglican missionary of the Society for the Propagation of the Gospel in Foreign Parts, recognized a lingua franca Creek as distinguished from one based on Shawnee (Algonquian):

the Language of our Southern Indians [i.e. the Creek] is understood in all the Southern parts of the half of this Continent at the least.   (Le Jau 1956 [1706–1717]: 41)

The Crick Indians Language, Nations that border near fflorida is also understood in the Southern parts; I have a promise of some Specimens of both Languages, with many observations which I hope will afford some Satisfaction . . .   [sic]   (Le Jau 1956 [1706–1717]: 68)

The Crick Indians Language is understood by many Nations namely the Yamousees; and I am still Confirm'd that the Savannock Language [the lingua franca Shawnee] is understood as far as Canada. These two General Languages have no manner of Affinity and each Nation has a Peculiar not only Dialect but Language, and yet the two Languages of the North and South called Crick & Saonock are understood by the respective Inhabitants the most part and most sensible of them. I'le send to You the Specimens in the manner You desire, and do all diligence to get them. I have desired the best of our Traders to help me, who Promise to do it.   [sic]   (Le Jau 1956 [1706–1717]: 87)

Le Jau's promised specimens remain wanting by all indications; but his observations suggest that the lingua franca Creek, spoken among others by the Yamasee (unidentified) and used by European traders, extended as far west as the Mississippi—that is well into the territory of Western Muskogeans.

The journals by Salzburger immigrants to Georgia dated between 1733 and 1737 (Urlsperger 1735: 192; 1738: 282, 345) confirmed the existence of the lingua franca Creek, and were among the first to provide a few words (see (80) in Sect. 8.5). Its speakers included not only unspecified Creek Indians, but also European traders and settlers, among them Salzburgers who had made an effort to learn the medium.

In 1734, the founder of the British colony of Georgia, James Oglethorpe (in Jones 1966: 515), similarly recognized a common intertribal language between different groups of Creek Indians, Choctaw, and Blew Mouths, which served as a medium of native myths, songs, and ceremonies. He thought it of it as "the radical [i.e. rudimentary] Language of all America," and had the Lord's Prayer translated into it, though without apparently leaving a copy. This reference suggests the use of the intertribal medium by missionaries among the Indians of the area, as Le Jau (1956 [1706–1717]: 35, 41) had already attested a similar use for the lingua franca Shawnee farther north.

Among prominent European colonists to have used a variety of Mobilian Jargon in contact with Creek Indians was the Irish-born trader James Adair (1968 [1775]: 273). With extensive experience among Southeastern Indians in the mid-eighteenth century, he left disappointingly few insights into the sociolinguistics of the multilingual Creek Indians and their neighbors, but hinted that the Chickasaw and Creek could communicate with each other via a variety of Mobilian Jargon (see Sect. 8.5).

Some sociolinguistic details came forth from the naturalist William Bartram (1958 [1791]: 294, 330), who described Muskogee as "the national or sovereign language" of the Creek, and Chickasaw, Choctaw, and surviving Natchez merely as dialects, apparently variants of the lingua franca Creek. He also named villages and languages of the Creek Confederacy during his travels among Southeastern Indians from 1773 to 1778 (see Table 9.1). This survey indicates a multilingual community of Southeastern Indians with different first languages and the lingua franca Creek as their common interlingual medium in most instances, which reflected the Muskogee Indians' sociopolitical dominance in the area. Bartram identified at least the following distinct language communities: Muskogee (Eastern Muskogean); "Chickasaw" (Western Muskogean or, more likely, western Mobilian Jargon); "Stincard" or some non-Muskogean language of low-status people as reported among the Natchez Indians; Yuchi (an isolate); probably several other Muskogean languages such as Alabama and Apalachee; and possibly Shawnee (Algonquian). There have been some doubts about Bartram's linguistic identification of a few Creek communities in his survey. John R. Swanton (in Bartram 1958 [1791]: 414) sweepingly dismissed the presence of "Chickasaw" among the Abacoche and Natchez, and suggested Natchez in its place, without providing any justification for his claim or considering Mobilian Jargon as an alternative explanation. A better answer to this incongruity in linguistic identification is an interpretation of Bartram's "Chickasaw" as a western variety of the pidgin, which the Abacoche (unidentified, possibly non-Muskogean) and the Natchez (non-Muskogean Gulf) employed in their communications with neighboring groups, including other Creek. Currently, there is no independent evidence for the linguistic affiliation of Abacoche that would resolve the question of whether this village spoke Chickasaw or perhaps some other language as their "mother tongue," which would then give us a clue about the nature of their "Chickasaw" speech. Yet, on the assumption that at least the Natchez spoke another language, presumably Natchez, as their mother tongue and "Chickasaw" only as a second language, we can identify the latter as Mobilian Jargon with reasonable certainty. By making this case, reading Bartram's

TABLE 9.1. *William Bartram's list of villages and languages of the Creek Confederacy*

Towns on the Tallapoose or Oakfuske river, viz.

Oakfuski, upper.	
Oakfuski, lower.	
Ufale, upper.	
Ufale, lower.	
Sokaspoge.	
Tallase, great.	These speak the Muscogulge or Creek
Coolome.	tongue, called the Mother tongue.
Chuaclahatche.	
Otasse.	
Cluale.	
Fusahatche.	
Tuccabatche.	
Cunhutke.	
Mucclasse.	Speak the Stincard tongue.
Alabama.	
Savannuca.	Speak the Uche [Yuchi] tongue.
Whittumke.	Speak the Stincard tongue.
Coosauda.	

Towns on the Coosau river, viz.

Abacooche.	Speak a dialect of Chickasaw.
Pocontallahasse.	
Hickory ground,	Speak the Muscogulge tongue.
traders name.	
Natche.	Speak Muscog. and Chickasaw.

Towns on the branches of the Coosau river, viz.

Wiccakaw.	
Fish pond,	
traders name.	Speak the Muscogulge tongue.
Hillaba.	
Kiolege.	

Towns on the Apalachucla[a] or Chata Uche river, viz.

Apalachucla.	
Tucpauska.	
Chockeclucca.	
Chata Uche.	
Checlucca-ninne.	Speak the Muscogulge tongue.
Hothletega.	
Coweta.	
Usseta.	
Uche.	Speak the Savannuca tongue.
Hooseche.	Speak the Muscogulge tongue.

TABLE 9.1. *Continued*

Chehaw.
Echeta.
Occone. ⎫ Speak the Stincard.
Swaglaw, great. ⎬
Swaglaw, little. ⎭

Towns on Flint river, comprehending the Siminoles or Lower Creeks.
Suola-nocha.
Cuscowilla or Allachua.
Talahasochte.
Caloosahatche.

___ Great island.	Traders name.
___ Great hammock.	Traders name.
___ Capon.	Traders name.
___ St. Mark's.	Traders name.
___ Forks.	Traders name.

The Siminoles speak both the Muscogulge and Stincard tongue.

Source: Bartram (1958[1791]): 292–4

ᵃ The element "-ucla" recalls Fontaneda's "-(a)cola" with the etymology of Choctaw **oklah** 'people', Chickasaw **okla** 'town', or Apalachee †**akola** 'people' or perhaps 'non-Apalachee people' (in contrast with Hitchiti/Mikasuki **okl-i** 'town' and Alabama/Koasati **oːla** 'town'), and again sugggests a western influence in terms of either Apalachee or even Western Muskogean (see Sect. 8.5).

"Chickasaw" as western Mobilian Jargon need not contradict the argument for a Muskogee-based variety; both apparently existed side by side, and merely reflected the linguistic diversity of the Creek and other Southeastern Indians. Nor does this interpretation impede the inquiry of remaining questions about the linguistic affiliation of other Creek.[3] Instead, Bartram's picture of the Creek Confederacy as an intertribal association of alloglos-

[3] Questions have also been raised about the linguistic identity of "Stincard", "Uche", and "Savannuca," about which Bartram (1958 [1791]: 294) added the following: 'As for those numerous remnant bands or tribes, included at this day within the Muscogulge confederacy, who generally speak the Stincard language (which is radically different from the Muscogulge) they are, beyond a doubt, the shattered remains of the various nations who inhabited the lower or maritime parts of Carolina and Florida from Cape Fear, West to the Mississippi. The Uches and Savannucas is a third language, radically different from the Muscogulge and Lingo, and seems to be a more Northern tongue; I suppose a language that prevailed amongst the numerous tribes who formerly possessed and inhabited the maritime parts of Maryland and Virginia. I was told by an old trader that the Savannuca and Shawanese speak the same language, or very near alike.' Swanton (in Bartram 1958 [1791]: 414) simply identified Stinkard as "dialects of Alabama and Koasati among the Upper Creeks and dialects of Hitchiti among the Lower Creeks." As Crawford (1978: 100 n. 9) has already pointed out, Swanton's interpretation remains puzzling in light of Bartram's description of Stinkard as "radically different" from

sic groups with considerable linguistic diversity lends support to the interpretation of the lingua franca Creek as a pidgin rather than just as phenomenon of bilingualism.

Relying on a part-Natchez ancestry and a comparative knowledge of
American Indian languages (including Muskogee, Natchez, and Cherokee),
the Creek agent George Stiggins made observations about the sociolinguistics of Creek towns in the 1810s. Just as the Alabama reserved their
native language for local concerns and spoke the intertribal medium in
public assemblies so that the Coushatta, Hitchiti, Choctaw, and Chickasaw
could understand (Stiggins n.d MS: 66. 3/Stiggins in Nunez 1958: 21), the
Natchez men

almost all converse in the Creek tongue with their families or not, tho' the women
can speak it fluently yet most generally in their own Common Concerns[.] And to
their Children they use their own native tongue, frequently in one house they use
both tongues without any detriment to their conversation or business[.]   (Stiggins
n.d MS: 66. 7/Stiggins in Nunez 1958: 25)

Similarly, the Abihka, residing among the Natchez, evidently spoke
Natchez in the home, but the intertribal medium outside of it. According to
Stiggins,

their present appellation is derived from their manner of approving or acquiesse-
ing a proposition tho' the national tongue is spoken by the tribe in all its purity yet
most notorious they assent or approbate what you may say to them in conversation
with the long aspiration a̅w̅ whereas the rest of the nation approbate or answer short
c̅a̅w̅s from their manner of answering or approbating so singular they got the name
of aw̲ bih̲ ka̲[;] moreover the rest of the Indians in talking of them and their tongue
aptly call it the aw̲ beh̲ ka̲ tongue, and never resort to the appelation of Ispocaga

Muskogee, in contrast to the closely related Eastern Muskogean languages such as Alabama,
Koasati, and Hitchiti. Crawford has proposed, in analogy to the Stinkards' role among the
Natchez, that the term "referred to tribes of low social status in the Creek Confederacy without
regard to the languages they spoke." I have alternatively considered an interpretation of
Bartram's "Stincard" in terms of either the lingua franca Creek or western Mobilian Jargon
in analogy to one of the latter's by-names, **yoka anompa** 'servant/slave language,' and on the
basis of the frequent association of pidgins with bondage. Yet this interpretation like Swanton's
neglects to address Bartram's recognition of the fundamental linguistic differences, for presumably neither variety of Mobilian Jargon differed so much from Creek to deserve the
description of "radically different." Incorporating both Bartram's and Crawford's arguments
it seems most reasonable to regard Stinkard as a non-Muskogean language of low-status communities that were part of the Natchez and other paramount chiefdoms of southeastern North
America in the early colonial period.

Bartram's identification of Yuchi and Shawnee would appear even more mysterious in light
of the fact that the Yuchi spoke an isolate language and the Shawnee were Algonquians. In
their case, he probably indicated no more than that these two groups spoke the same language,
if different from that of the Creek Indians, which may well have been a Shawnee-based lingua
franca (see Sect. 12.4).

[Creek] only in a national way. [*sic*] (Stiggins n.d MS: 66. 5–6/Stiggins in Nunez 1958: 23–4)

On the other hand, there were only a few Yuchi who reportedly cared to learn the lingua franca Creek:

in all their conversations among themselves or not they [i.e. the Yuchi] speak their own barbarous tongue in general, which is a quick gutteral stammering accent not very unlike the dying respiration of an Old Sow under the hands of a Butcher, the Uchie tongue is only spoken by the natives of the tribe, as there is not exceeding four or five instances of its being learnt and spoken by any one else; they are so attached to their own Tongue and mode of living that very few of 'em make any use of or can converse in the national tongue, which is said by the other tribes of the nation to be owing to the general dislike expressed and manifested against them, as well as to their wild roguish and insipid nature. [*sic*] (Stiggins n.d MS: 66. 4–5/Stiggins in Nunez 1958: 22–3)

For still other groups such as the Pacana, Stiggins could not ascertain whether they spoke a language of their own (Stiggins n.d MS: 66. 5/Stiggins in Nunez 1958: 23).

For the years between 1836 and 1838, a major-general of the US army, Ethan Allen Hitchcock (1930: 120), noted that:

The principal Indians of the Creek Nation are the Creeks properly so called or Muskogees, next the Uchees [Yuchi,] then the Hitchitees, the Notchez (Natchez), Coowarsarde [Coushatta] and Alabamas . . . These all have different languages, but the young people nearly all understand and speak the Creek language. All the Hitchitees speak the Creek, but the Uchees or many of them, do not speak the Creek.

Hitchcock (1930: 121) further remarked that the Natchez

have a distinct language, but speak Creek, or nearly all of them do. The Hitchitees may number two or three hundred but are much intermixed and have almost become Creeks.

The Uchees are more numerous, may be 800, and preserve their distinctive character more than any other band or tribe. Not many of them speak Creek and they intermarry but rarely with the Creeks.

At the time, the Yuchi stood aside linguistically and socially, as Bartram (1958 [1791]: 245) and Stiggins had already observed.

For about the same period and through 1840, John T. Sprague (1964 [1848]: 99, 268–9, 309, 507, 510, 512), an American brevet captain, observed the use of "the Indian language" or "Seminole" by Spaniards and African Americans with Florida Indians in the early 1840s. Among its native speakers, he recognized Seminole, Mikasuki, Creek, Tallahassee, Yuchi, and Choctaw or Calusa surviving in Florida.

Another source of evidence for an eastern variety of Mobilian Jargon was the American trader and settler Thomas S. Woodward (1939 [1859]: 20–1, 41, 79, 108, 148). He not only attested Muskogee influences in the Mobilian Jargon spoken by Creek and other Indians of eastern Texas in the 1850s; but he also listed among its speakers American traders and settlers (including himself) and African–American interpreters, who with their knowledge of English and "the Indian language" or Creek proved most adept in translation.

Historical attestations for the lingua franca Creek or other eastern varieties of Mobilian Jargon, small in number, became even fewer in the late nineteenth century. One among a few instances is a reference to Creek as a common medium among Alabama, Hitchiti, Yuchi, and Coushatta presumably in parts of the Indian Territory (now Oklahoma) in 1879 (Tuggle 1973: 36–7). This source gives no further details, and may be no more than a repetition of earlier information. If the number and quality of references to the lingua franca Creek are a reliable indication, it did not survive west of the Mississippi much longer. Indeed, there was a diminishing need for an indigenous contact medium with the native population east of the river, the disintegration of the traditional Creek Confederacy, and the removal of many remaining communities to the Indian Territory as a result of the growing encroachments by American settlers in the nineteenth century.

However, the lingua franca Creek persisted in the form of a Muskogee-based Seminole Pidgin in Florida, and was the major medium between the Seminole Indians and their African–American associates, many of whom served as skilled interpreters (see e.g. Porter 1971: 43–71, 96–121, 182–358, 369–460, 472–91). According to Alanson Skinner (1913: 63), this medium survived among the Seminole of the Everglades and Big Cypress as late as 1910:

In spite of the fact that the villages of the Everglades and Big Cypress Seminole are so little known to outsiders, the Indians themselves are quite familiar with the towns of the white men, and a few of the women, often go to Miami, Fort Lauderdale, Jupiter, and other towns to trade. Not more than two or three members of all the several bands can speak English well, but all the men make use of a trade jargon composed of Seminole [i.e. Muskogee], Spanish, and English, and this nondescript speech has a wide vogue among the white settlers, or "crackers," who dwell in the pinelands.

William C. Sturtevant (1971: 112) elaborated:

The Mikasuki, even though they were now in the majority, maintained the old Creek convention of using Muskogee for communicating with outsiders. Good evidence for this is the incipient jargon that was used between Indians and non-Indians in Florida until about 1920. All the Indian terms in this jargon were of Muskogee origin, despite the fact that the majority of its Indian users were native speakers of Mikasuki.

A recent ethnohistory of white traders among Seminole Indians in Florida has attested a mixed "patois" of Muskogee, Mikasuki, and English for the period of 1870 through 1930, nourished by the traders learning some "Seminole" and the Indians some English (Kersey 1975: 35, 66, 67, 75, 78, 82, 90, 99, 110). This study also includes some examples, most of which resemble stereotypical Seminole Pidgin English of little historical value as recordings of actual speech (see Sect. 2.3). By the 1950s, according to Sturtevant (1971: 112–13), the sociolinguistic situation changed:

> In most of the cases I observed of conversations between Mikasuki and Muskogee speakers, the language used was Mikasuki. The jargon had died, and one Mikasuki word had even been borrowed into local south Florida English: "chikee," meaning "Seminole house" (from **cikí·**, meaning 'house'). This is in contrast to the two earlier local borrowings from Muskogee, "sofkee," meaning "Seminole corn soup," from **sá·fki**; and "coontie," a wild cycad, genus **Zamia**, locally used for starch by both Indians and non-Indians, from **kontí·**.

Drawing on his extended contacts to Southeastern Indians including Seminole, the basket maker Claude Medford of part-Choctaw ancestry believed that Mobilian Jargon had survived in Florida until recently. I have not found any leads to confirm his suggestions over the years. Traces of the lingua franca Creek may only survive in Oklahoma Cherokee charm songs of Creek origin with their apparently "corrupted" Muskogee structure and mixed vocabulary of Muskogee, Natchez, and Cherokee (Kilpatrick and Kilpatrick 1967).

Since the mid-nineteenth century, this Seminole jargon had apparently adopted a growing English vocabulary by lexical replacement—with "Creek" vestiges perhaps surviving in some form or another in Afro-Seminole Creole (see Sect. 8.5). Its last speakers have been descendants of Africans, Seminole and other Southern Indians in isolated communities on Andros Island in the Bahamas, in eastern Oklahoma, and in the area of Del Rio on the border of Texas and Mexico (see Hancock 1980*a*, *b* for sociolinguistic surveys and Bateman 1990 for a contrastive historical study of these communities).

9.3. Historic Attestations of Western Mobilian Jargon (the Chickasaw-Choctaw Trade Language)

The first reference to Mobilian Jargon in colonial Louisiana did not appear until more than a century after what may have been the earliest documentation of the lingua franca Creek by Hernando Escalante de Fontaneda

(1973 [1944]) in Florida of the mid-sixteenth century. In 1699, one of the primary French explorers to the Mississippi delta area, Pierre Le Moyne, Sieur d'Iberville, noted briefly that "Les Oumas, Bayogoulas, Theloël, Taensas, les Coloas, les Chycacha, les Napissa, les Ouachas, Chotymachas, Yagenechito, parlent la mesme langue et s'entendent avec les Bilochy, les Pascoboula" (Margry 1876–86: iv. 184).[4] D'Iberville received this information from his brother Jean Baptiste Le Moyne, Sieur de Bienville, who had learned "Bayogoula" or Mobilian Jargon from his native guide within less than six weeks and who served as interpreter for d'Iberville among the above groups, the Acolapissa, the Choctaw, and Natchez, plus possibly three others that d'Iberville did not identify (Margry 1876–86: iv. 167, 412; see also Crawford 1978: 32).

While the Chickasaw and Choctaw were Muskogeans, the first languages of the Washa, the Chitimacha, the Biloxi, and Natchez were all non-Muskogean—Caddoan, a Gulf isolate, Siouan, and another Gulf isolate respectively. Although the lingustic affiliation can no longer be identified for all the groups that d'Iberville mentioned, some of the unidentified groups such as the Taënsa and probably others were not Muskogeans. John R. Swanton (1911: 22) thought the Taënsa spoke the language of the Natchez or a closely related dialect, because there was no need for the two groups to use Mobilian Jargon with each other. However, the linguistic diversity among the various groups, representing distantly related and unrelated language families, is sufficient to interpret d'Iberville's reference to a common language in terms of an intertribal medium. The fact that de Bienville took less than six weeks to learn "Bayogoula" further suggests a grammatically reduced form of language or a pidgin; with no grammars of related languages available at the time, even the most adept European polyglot could not have acquired Bayogoula proper in such a short time. The apparently dominant presence of speakers of Western Muskogean languages among the groups whom de Bienville and d'Iberville encountered—namely the Chickasaw, Choctaw, and supposedly the Houma, the Bayogoula, the Pascagoula, and the Acolapissa—further points to Mobilian Jargon. Some years later, the early French settler Antoine Simon Le Page du Pratz (1758: i. 90) actually observed de Bienville speaking "La Langue vulgaire" or Mobilian Jargon with facility. In 1720, the pidgin was also to serve as the medium of his peace negotiations with the Chitimacha, as recorded in translation by the French naval officer Jean Bernard Bossu (1768: i. 30–6; see Sect. 7.3).

In 1700, the French Jesuit priest Paul du Ru, accompanying the two French explorer brothers, confirmed these observations, and identified

---

[4] 'The Houma, the Bayogoula, the Theloël [= the Natchez?], the Taënsa, the Koroa, the Chickasaw, the Napisssa, the Washa, the Chitimacha, and the Yagenechito speak the same language, and made themselves understood with the Biloxi and Pascagoula' (author's translation).

"Bayogoula as the intertribal medium. Du Ru had already learned a vocabulary of fifty words from an elderly Bayogoula, and thought it to be rather meager without "R and D" (du Ru 1700 MS: 9–10/1934: 8–9; for the appropriate quotation, see the Preliminaries to Part II). Du Ru (1700 MS: 31) observed further that "je mattache a leur langue parceque cest une des plus etendues de ce pays–cy, il y a 8 ou 10 nations qui lentendent et la parlent" [*sic*].[5] Like de Bienville, du Ru could not have acquired Bayogoula proper as easily as he suggested, nor would he have commented on its meager structure in light of the rather elaborate morphology of Southeastern Indian languages. Significantly, he would not have mentioned its intelligibility among as many as ten tribes of the area, probably the very same ones to which d'Iberville had already referred and among which there were several non-Muskogean groups. A few pages later, du Ru (1700 MS: 46/1934: 32) in fact offered a sample of "Houma," which—according to d'Iberville—was the same as Bayogoula, but in fact presents the first unquestionable example of Mobilian Jargon: "Jeheno, Yno, nanhoulou toutchino atchota" or †**šno eno nãholo točeno ačofa** (?) 'You [the Great Spirit], I, and the white man, [we] three [are] one' (for details about the reconstitution of this example, see (57) in Sect. 7.2). This evidence convincingly establishes Mobilian Jargon some twenty to thirty years before Crawford's proposed date of origin, and undermines his Western Muskogean hypothesis (for further discussion, see Sect. 11.1).

By that time and during a period of about five years, a ship's carpenter by the name of Pénicaut (in Margry 1876–86: v. 442, 446, 462) had apparently learned a few native languages of Louisiana, among them Natchez, Natchitoches, and especially "le Mobilien, qui est le principal et qu'on entend par toutes les nations" 'Mobilian [Jargon], which is the main [language] and which is understood by all nations.' Included among its speakers were Acolapissa (unidentified) and Natchitoches (Caddoans). Pénicaut (in Margry 1876–1886: v. 480, 487) also observed two Frenchmen to have used "la langue mobilienne" ('the Mobilian language') with Alabama Indians (Eastern Muskogeans). Further, he described the Apalachee language as 'savage' and 'a mixture of Spanish and Alabama' (see Sect. 8.5). According to Crawford (1978: 34–8), Pénicaut could hardly have referred to Mobilian proper in this instance. But in light of du Ru's evidence and Pénicaut's own observations, it is not necessary to propose that the French ship carpenter referred to some non-pidginized lingua franca of Western Muskogean instead of Mobilian Jargon. His observations closely match those by d'Iberville and du Ru, and "Apalachee" may have been a reference to no more than an eastern variety of the pidgin.

---

[5] 'I devote myself to their language because it is one of the most widespread in this region. There are eight or ten tribes who understand and speak it' (du Ru 1934: 23).

Other observers of early colonial Louisiana made occasional remarks on Mobilian Jargon, most of them rather spare in content. At about the time of d'Iberville's visit, François Jolliet de Montigny, one among three missionaries making their way down the Mississippi River, noticed that

La langue des Chicachas était commune aux Kinipissas, aux Oumats et à plusieurs autres nations.

Enfin, les Tonicas, les Taënsas et les Natchez parlaient une même langue, mais elle différait et de celle des Chicachas et celle des Akansas.   (summarized in Gosselin 1906: 38)[6]

This quotation confirms at least one indigenous contact medium, possibly another. The first part may merely convey that the Quinipissa and Houma, about whose linguistic affiliation little or no conclusive information is available, was the same as Chickasaw; alternatively, "la langue des Chicachas" could again refer to Mobilian Jargon. In that case, the second part of the quote refers to a distinct variety or even a second lingua franca among the Tunica, the Taënsa, and the Natchez, among whom at least the first and the last spoke mutually unintelligible languages (Gulf isolates). Unfortunately, Montigny's observations are too sketchy to resolve this issue.

In 1704, a French priest by the name of Henri Roulleaux de la Vente (in Gosselin 1906: 39) observed that the Indian languages "sont si différentes qu'un village n'entend pas la langue d'un autre et qu'il n'y a que les Chatta dont la langue ait plus d'étendue et soit plus universelle."[7] There can be little doubt that he was referring to Mobilian Jargon rather than Choctaw. By that time, Europeans had gained a minimal sense of the diversity of the area's native languages.

A young French lieutenant and settler, Jean Benjamin François Dumont de Montigny, went a step further, and apparently considered Mobilian Jargon as a kind of "mother language," comparable to Latin as a lingua franca in Europe and best interpreted as the dominant medium in the area instead of a proto-language:

C'est a dire qu'il [the traveller] apprit differentes langues et surtout celle qui a la mere langue, car dans ce pays si grand et si vaste, rempli de nations si differentes, il y a veritablement une mere langue qui se parle par tout outre celle de la nation, ainsi que chez nous le Latin.   [*sic*]   (Dumont de Montigny 1747 MS: 430)[8]

---

[6] 'The language of the Chickasaw was common to the Quinipissa, the Houma, and several other nations.

Finally, the Tunica, the Taënsa, and the Natchez spoke an identical language, but it differed, from that of the Chickasaw and that of the Akansa [the Quapaw]' (author's translation).

[7] 'are so different that one village does not understand the language of the other and that there are only the Choctaw whose language covers a greater area and is more universal' (author's translation).

[8] 'That is to say that he [the traveller] learns different languages and above all the one that has the mother language; for in this land so big and vast, full of so many different nations,

A l'égard de leur [the Indians'] langue, je remarquerai, 1°. que comme on distingue pormi eux des Nobles & des Puants, chacun de ces deux ordres a aussi sa langue qui lui est particuliere; ensorte que pour signifier la même chose, les Grands and le Peuple se servent de mots qui n'ont aucune ressemblance; 2°. que quoique dans ce grand nombre de Nations qui habitent la Louisiane, chacune ait une langue qui lui est propre; il y a cependant une espéce de langue mere qui est générale pour toutes, & qui s'entend par-tout: c'est celle de la Mobile. Lorsqu'on la sçait, on peut voyager par toute cette Province sans avoir besoin d'interpréte. [*sic*]; (Dumont de Montigny 1753: i. 181–2)[9]

A reference to Mobilian Jargon even appears in a poem by Dumont de Montigny, entitled "Poème en vers touchant l'établissement de la province de la Louisiane, connue sous le nom de Mississipy avec tout ce qui s'y est passé de depuis 1716, jusqu'à 1741: le massacre des François au poste des Natchez, les Mœurs des Sauvages, leurs danses, leurs Religions, enfin ce qui concerne le pays en le général" (de Villiers du Terrage 1931). Although Dumont de Montigny did not name Mobilian Jargon, a comparison of the poem with his *Mémoires* leaves no doubt about the identity of the international language, as recognized by Crawford (1978: 50–1), and provides perhaps the best indication of how much the French had accepted Mobilian Jargon as Louisiana's language at that time:

Dans chaque nation, c'est différents langages,
C'est différentes mœurs et différents usages.
.   .   .   .
Ce qui peut étonner, parmi ce continent,
C'est qu'une même langage est, très certainement,
Connue en tout endroit, et, par cet avantage,
On peut se faire entendre en tout dans les villages.
(Dumont de Montigny in de Villiers du Terrage 1931: 395–6)[10]

---

there really is a mother language spoken everywhere besides that of the nation, just as Latin is among us' (author's translation).

[9] 'Regarding their [the Indians'] language, I would observe first that, as one distinguishes Nobles and Stinkards among them, each of these two classes has also its language, which is distinctive; [they are] such that to mean the same thing, the elite and the people use words that have no resemblance to each other; secondly, that although in this large number of nations that inhabit Louisiana, each has a language of its own; there is however a kind of mother language that is common to all and that is understood everywhere; it is the one of Mobile. When one knows it, one can travel through the entire province without need of an interpreter' (author's translation).

[10] In each nation there are different languages,
There are different customs and different habits.
.   .   .   .   .
That which can amaze, amid this continent,
Is that one very same language is, very certainly,
Known in every place, and, by this advantage,
One can make himself understood entirely in the villages.

(Crawford 1978: 50–1)

Dumont de Montigny further cited several words and phrases of Mobilian Jargon, identifiable by semantactically reduced constructions (such as the first and the last instances below) or by close association with such:

(82) "alouta la houa" or †**alota**   'I am full' (Literally: 'very
    lawa   full')

    "pasca" or **paska**   'bread'

    "attaque" or **(h)at(t)ak**   'human' (n.)

    "appa" or **apa**   'to eat'

    "attaqu'appa" or †**hat(t)ak apa**   'cannibal'[11]

             (Dumont de Montigny 1747 MS: 367, 378)

    "Chichicoüas" or †**šešekowa**   'calabash, gourd;
                             gourd-rattle'

    "Pocolé" or **pokole**   'ten'

    "honathea"   VOCABLE (?)

    "Iche-la" or **ešla**   'Here I am!' (Actually:
                             'Here you are!')

    "hom"   VOCABLE (?)

    "athiocma" or **ačokma**   'Yes, that is good.' (Actually:
                             'good')

             (Dumont de Montigny 1753: i. 193, 203–6)

Dumont du Montigny (1753: i. 212–13) moreover quoted in translation a Tioux war chief who responded to a Frenchman in Mobilian Jargon, but whose first language remains unidentified if distinct from Natchez (see Sect. 7.3).[12]

The Frenchman with whom the Tioux war chief conversed in Mobilian Jargon was probably another Louisiana settler, Antoine Simon Le Page du

---

[11] This phrase also served as the common ethnonym for the Atakapa Indians (Dumont de Montigny 1747 MS: 367, 378).

[12] Following another account by Dumont de Montigny (1753: ii. 194–5), Crawford (1978: 41) suggested Mobilian Jargon likewise as the medium by which six Natchez Indians passed as Choctaw in order to gain entry to a French garrison after the Natchez uprising in 1729. They then revealed their true identity by switching to their own language and by assassinating several French soldiers before being killed themselves. Although Crawford's hypothesis of Natchez disguising themselves as Choctaw by speaking the pidgin appears reasonable, it lacks supporting evidence. Dumont de Montigny neither specified the language of masquerade, nor did he provide linguistic or extralinguistic clues that warrant such an assumption. In light of references to bilingualism and multilingualism next to Mobilian Jargon, it is conceivable that the Natchez spoke Choctaw instead. One may further question whether the Natchez could have so easily fooled the French to accept them as Choctaw by speaking Mobilian Jargon, when they had used the medium with the newcomers before and when by that time some Europeans had come to recognize differences between Choctaw and the pidgin based on it (see the following discussion on the sociolinguistic observations by Antoine Simon Le Page du Pratz). In short, this instance leaves too many uncertainties to accept Dumont de Montigny's account as a convincing reference to Mobilian Jargon.

Pratz (1695?–1775), who had been Dumont de Montigny's prime source of information. The first to provide sociolinguistic data of any detail about the pidgin, Le Page du Pratz had already described it in a letter to the young lieutenant in similar terms:

Toutes ces Nations en général parlent un langage d'autant plus différent, qu'elles sont plus éloignées les unes des autres; & j'ai remarqué que ceux de ces Peuples qui sont voisins des Chicachas & des Chactas, ont beaucoup d'idiômes de ces deux grandes Nations, dont la langue est presque la même, à l'exception de la prononciation & de l'accent qui sont différens. (Le Page du Pratz in Dumont de Montigny 1753: i. 119)[13]

In his *Histoire de la Louisiane . . .* , Le Page du Pratz (1758: ii. 218) similarly observed that . . . "toutes les Nations qui sont dans les environs des Tchicachas, & que je viens de nommer, parlent la Langue Tchicacha, quoiqu'un peu corrompue, & ceux qui la parlent le mieux s'en font gloire."[14] Le Page du Pratz may have adopted some of his ideas from an older Yazoo Indian by the name of "Moncacht-apé," who considered the Chickasaw as his elders and as the source of "la Langue du Pays (la Langue vulgaire;) . . ." (Le Page du Pratz 1758: iii. 89) or 'the Language of the Country (the common language),' i.e. Mobilian Jargon.

However, Le Page du Pratz also relied on his own experiences and observations, for he lived among the Chitimacha and Natchez for many years, from 1718 until 1734, and made an effort to learn their languages (see Crawford 1978: 38–9). He spoke the pidgin to his slave, a Chitimacha woman, who had taught it to him (Le Page du Pratz 1758: i. 85–6). When Choctaw Indians addressed him, they likewise used Mobilian Jargon (Le Page du Pratz 1758: ii. 219). It moreover proved a most useful medium, when he approached the Natchez superior of the temple guardians to learn more about their religion, including their conception of "God" (Le Page du Pratz 1758: ii. 322, 326; see Sect. 7.2).

Le Page du Pratz found Mobilian Jargon present not only among the Chickasaw, the Choctaw, and their neighbors, the Chitimacha, the Yazoo (unidentified), and the Natchez, but also among the Tapoussa (unidentified), the Chakchiuma (unidentified), the Ofo (Siouan), the Taënsa (unidentified), the Natchitoches and other Caddoans, apparently the Acolapissa (unidentified), and all other Louisiana Indians (Le Page du Pratz 1758: i.

[13] 'All these nations generally speak a language that differs more as they are farther away from each other; I have noticed that those of these peoples that are neighbors of the Chickasaw and Choctaw have many idioms of these two large nations, whose language is almost the same with the exception of pronunciation and accent, which are different' (author's translation).
[14] 'all the nations that are in the vicinity of the Chickasaw and that I have just mentioned speak the Chickasaw language, although a bit corrupted, and those who speak it the best pride themselves on it' (author's translation).

85–6; ii. 219, 226, 242, 321). The 'common language' thus extended across much of colonial Louisiana, embracing the lower Mississippi River valley at the time. There was solely one group of people whom Le Page du Pratz (1758: ii. 321) did not find to speak much Mobilian Jargon—Natchez women:

La plûpart des Natchez parloient assez bien la Langue vulgaire, & et je la sçavois de façon à pouvoir me faire entendre pour ce qui regardoit les besoins de la vie & pour ce qui concernoit la Traite; mais je désirois aussi apprendre la Langue de cette Nation, pour être en état de parler aux femmes qui ne parlent point la Langue vulgaire, & qui souvent nous apportoient beaucoup de choses nécessaires à la vie . . .[15]

Le Page du Pratz offered no clue for this gender difference.

In learning Natchez as well as Mobilian Jargon, Le Page du Pratz was exceptional among European colonists and perhaps the earliest to gain a deeper understanding of the sociolinguistic complexities of colonial Louisiana. His knowledge of both Natchez, however limited, and Mobilian Jargon must have been the key to his comparison of the latter with the medieval contact medium of the Mediterranean, the lingua franca Sabir, in terms of sociolinguistic functions: "elle [Mobilian Jargon] est dans cette Province [Louisiana] ce qu'est la Langue Francque dans le Levant" (Le Page du Pratz 1758: ii. 242) or 'it [Mobilian Jargon] is in this province [Louisiana] what the lingua franca is in the Levant'. Notably, Le Page du Pratz drew only a sociolinguistic analogy in this comparison, and did not in fact ponder Mobilian Jargon's origin beyond citing the Yazoo Indian's opinion on its Chickasaw roots.[16]

Le Page du Pratz's observations have been subject to repeated misinterpretations, possibly due to erroneous readings of *vulgaire* as 'vulgar' (see, e.g. Jefferys 1760: 165) instead of 'common' or 'plebeian' and because of his reference to the neighbors of the Chickasaw taking pride in speaking their language the best. Among those to misread Le Page du Pratz was the eighteenth-century Irish trader James Adair (1968 [1775]: 210), who was rather sarcastic about "Monsieur Le Page du Pratz" and maintained that:

---

[15] 'Most Natchez speak the common language quite well, and I knew it sufficiently well to be able to make myself understood regarding the necessities of life and concerning trade; but I also wanted to learn the language of this nation in order to talk to the women, who do not speak the common language and who often brought us many things necessary for life . . .' (author's translation).

[16] In no fashion does this quote lend support to attempts at construing Mobilian Jargon as a "descendant" of the lingua franca Sabir, whence the technical term of lingua franca. It would seem unnecessary, even pointless, to make this argument, were it not for repeated and continuing, at times quite ardent attempts by monogeneticist theoreticians of pidgin-creole origins to claim the lingua franca Sabir as the proto-pidgin of all modern pidgins and creoles, including non-European ones (see Sect. 2.3).

According to him, the Chikkasah tongue [actually Mobilian Jargon] was the court language of the Missisippi Indians, and that it had not the letter *R*.—The very reverse of which is the truth; for the French and all their red savages were at constant war with them, because of their firm connection with the English, and hated their national name; and as to the language, they could not converse with them, as their dialects are so different from each other. I recited a long string of his well-known stories to a body of gentlemen, well skilled in the languages, rites, and customs of our East and West-Florida Indians, and they agreed that the Koran did not differ more widely from the divine oracles, than the accounts of this writer from the genuine customs of the Indian Americans.

Le Page du Pratz had made no mention of Chickasaw, much less Mobilian Jargon, as "the court language," if Adair intended anything other than diplomatic functions with this term. Counter to the Irish trader, there indeed occurred no [r] in the pidgin, as first observed by Paul du Ru (1700 MS: 10/1934: 9) at the turn of the eighteenth century and as confirmed in subsequent recordings; the only possible exceptions could have been varieties of Mobilian Jargon whose speakers (such as Europeans and perhaps Tunica) introduced loans with [r] from their own languages and pronounced them accordingly (see Sect. 8.3). Nor did linguistic differences or conflict keep the Chickasaw, other Southeastern Indians, and the French from communicating with each other. A careless reading of Adair's passage then has led to mistaken notions about Mobilian Jargon's social roles in relation to the Native Americans' first languages, as proposed by the nineteenth-century anthropologist Albert S. Gatschet (1969 [1884]: 39) for Natchez and the pidgin:

The scanty vocabularies which we possess of the Naktche language contain a sprinkling of foreign terms adopted from the Chicasa or Mobilian. Two languages at least were spoken before 1730 in the Naktche villages; the Naktche by the ruling class or tribe; the other, the Chicasa or trade language by the "low people;" and hence the mixture referred to. Du Pratz gives specimens of both. Naktche is a vocalic language, rich in verbal forms, and, to judge from a few specimens, polysynthetic to a considerable degree in its affixes.

Gatschet did not specify how Mobilian Jargon compared to Natchez in terms of its structure, and erred in assigning the two languages to particular classes—Natchez to the nobles and Mobilian Jargon to the Stinkards. There apparently existed considerable linguistic differences between the two classes (Le Page du Pratz 1758: ii. 324), but they were not those between Natchez and Mobilian Jargon, just as, by all indications, the primary language of the Stinkards among the Creek was not the lingua franca Creek (Bartram 1958 [1791]: 294; see n. 3). Mobilian Jargon was also far from being exclusive to Stinkards, as is evident from the language of the temple-guard superior, chiefs, medicine people, and other persons of high social status (see Crawford 1978: 100–1 n. 9; Silverstein 1973 MS: 88 n. 1; Swanton 1911:

182). In a vein similar to Adair's and Gatschet's misinterpretations is Crawford's assessment of Le Page du Pratz's passage about women and the pidgin as suggesting that "Mobilian [Jargon] was deficient in the terms and expressions" for the purpose of learning Natchez history (Crawford 1978: 39, 110 nn. 54, 55). Le Page du Pratz conveyed that he wished to learn Natchez only because the Natchez women with whom he wanted to converse hardly knew Mobilian Jargon; if they had spoken the pidgin, there would presumably have been no hindrance for him to inquire about things beyond the basic necessities of life, such as history and religon. That one could in fact discuss any topic, even the most abstract, in Mobilian Jargon, and that Le Page du Pratz thought so as well is evident from his discussion of his experience with the Natchez superior of temple guardians and the compound †**kostene četo** 'god, God' in the original's subsequent pages. It was precisely the superior's knowledge of the pidgin by which Le Page du Pratz could learn more about the religion and other intimate aspects of Natchez society.

Le Page du Pratz also offered a quite detailed, if incomplete, description of short discourses in Mobilian Jargon (see Sects. 7.3 and 8.4). Still, the author of *Histoire de la Louisiane* left many of the native terms and names, exhibiting modern corresponding forms in Muskogean languages or Natchez, unidentified as to their source. He further neglected to provide other linguistic details and to supplement his observations with a grammar or vocabulary. He apparently thought he had at least two good reasons; aside from being easier to learn through use rather than by grammatical rules, . . . "cette Langue n'est plus si nécessaire que dans le temps que je demeurois dans cette Province, parce l'on n'est plus si voisins ni en si grande relation avec les Naturels" (Le Page du Pratz 1758: ii. 323).[17] Crawford (1978: 44) adopted Le Page du Pratz's opinion as an indication for Mobilian Jargon's historic peak. But Le Page du Pratz's comparatively rich description only reflected his empathy and expertise in dealing with Louisiana Indians, matched by few contemporaries or successors. The nature and amount of historical information provided by a source thus need not be in any direct correlation with the object's historic strength and role—especially in view of the great sociocultural gap between the observer and the observed as it existed between Europeans and Native Americans.

As perceptive as Le Page du Pratz was about the sociolinguistic nature of Mobilian Jargon, he still underestimated its utility and vitality by two full centuries. As the author of a major source of information on Louisiana and

---

[17] 'this language is no longer as necessary as when I lived in this province because one is neither as close to nor in as frequent dealings with the natives' (author's translation)

the native peoples, he influenced the ideas that Europeans had of life in the colony. His bleak assessment of Mobilian Jargon's future may thus have caused visitors and settlers to cease paying much attention to it. By then, the pidgin was no longer the novelty that it formerly had been for the early explorers and settlers such as de Bienville, du Ru, and especially Le Page du Pratz; their successors simply took Mobilian Jargon for granted as "la Langue vulgaire." Perhaps more significantly, later settlers showed less interest in the Indians and less empathy towards them, when Louisiana began establishing itself as a colony and came to depend less on its native inhabitants (see Usner 1992). Compared with Le Page du Pratz's quite specific sociolinguistic observations, subsequent firsthand reports on Mobilian Jargon were meager, and remained so for more than a century. None the less, they contain some valuable supplementary information on who spoke Mobilian Jargon—and, occasionally, who did not—plus other sociolinguistic details.

In 1723, a party led by Diron d'Artaguette, travelling down the Mississippi, encountered a Chickasaw south of the Margot River (near present-day Memphis, Tennessee):

upon our left as we were drifting very close to shore, we perceived on the bank of the river a man who called us in the language of the Mobile to come to him. We asked him, at the same time taking up our guns, if he was a Chicachat [then customary foes of the French and allies of the British]. Our arms frightened him. He got behind a large tree and replied that he was a Chicachat.   (Mereness 1916: 85)

This verbal exchange allegedly ended with a few gunshots by the Chickasaw at the French.

Almost twenty years later, another Frenchman, Antoine Bonnefoy, reported in some detail an encounter with northern Alabama, British traders, and Chickasaw. The northern Alabama Indians, allied with the British, suspected Bonnefoy as an enemy, and questioned him extensively, as did the English and the Chickasaw; once convinced of Bonnefoy's harmlessness, his captors eventually let him go (Mereness 1916: 253, 254–55). In this instance, Bonnefoy used Mobilian Jargon not only with the Alabama and the Chickasaw, but also the British traders, who probably responded likewise—either because of the lack of some other common medium or out of courtesy towards their Alabama hosts and the Chickasaw visitors (for the quotation of the relevant passages and further discussion, see Sect. 7.3).

In 1745, the French ship *Superbe* under the command of a captain named Grenier landed at Matagorda Bay on the Gulf Coast of Texas in the mistaken belief that it was Florida. There, they met an unidentified Native American who pointed out their error, but—to their surprise—apparently did *not* speak Mobilian Jargon:

deux jours auparavant, un Sauvage comprenant quelques mots d'espagnol, à qui ils [members of the party including Spanish pilots] avaient demandé où se trouvait Pensacola, leur avait répondu: "Cinq jours", en montrant le couchant. Pourtant, le lieutenant du Hamel, qui parlait bien le mobilien, avait été fort étonné de ne point parvenir à se faire comprendre.   (de Villiers du Terrage and Rivet 1914–1919: 413)[18]

The source gave no further clues to the Native American's tribal identity, probably that of a neighboring community west of the Atakapa, nor did it indicate whether all members of his community were unable to speak Mobilian Jargon. Quite possibly, Indians of coastal Texas used a gestural code or a full sign language for interlingual communication in place of the pidgin (Wurtzburg and Campbell 1995).

However, Mobilian Jargon was fairly prominent among British traders of the South in the mid-eighteenth century, as is evident from James Adair's *History of the American Indians* (1968 [1775]). As a long-time trader among the Cherokee, Chickasaw, and other Southeastern Indians, Adair was undoubtedly familiar with the pidgin, and evidently used some reduced form of Western Muskogean of his own, especially with the Chickasaw, among whom he resided for many years during the period from 1744 until 1768.[19] That he came to disagree strongly with Le Page du Pratz's observations about the role of "Chikkasah" among the Natchez (Adair 1968 [1775]: 210; see his quotation above) was due to his misinterpretation of *Histoire*

---

[18] 'two days earlier, a savage understanding some words of Spanish, whom they [members of the party including Spanish pilots] had asked where they could find Pensacola, answered them: "Five days," pointing to the west. Even so, Lieutenant du Hamel, who spoke Mobilian Jargon well, had been greatly surprised that he had not succeeded in making himself understood [with the pidgin]' (author's translation). This Indian of the Texas Gulf Coast may have pointed to the west or the sunset figuratively to express 'day' rather than the direction for Pensacola, for there is no indication that he misunderstood the French–Spanish party or deliberately misled it into the opposite direction.

[19] Throughout his book, Adair provided numerous examples of "Choktah" and "Chikkasah," including words and short phrases, that show some resemblances to Western Muskogean as well as Mobilian Jargon, but also many differences from both. Committed to demonstrating the Indians' ancestry in Israel, Adair (1968 [1775]: 37–74) made a misguided and desperate attempt at explaining his linguistic samples in terms of Hebrew etymologies and grammar. This misconception probably misled him into projecting into his data imagined characteristic features of Hebrew inapplicable to both Western Muskogean and Mobilian Jargon, and renders his data suspect for philological reconstitution. Adair's bias towards Hebrew introduces problems of analysis comparable to those in the historical study of "American Indian Pidgin English" or AIPE (see Sect. 2.3). There exists insufficient evidence to argue for an interpretation of his "Choctah and "Chikkasah" linguistic data in terms of either Western Muskogean proper (Choctaw and/or Chickasaw), Mobilian Jargon, or perhaps even a third alternative—some incomplete, non-formalized version of Western Muskogean as learned by Adair. His attestations may in fact match the "broken" Choctaw offered by H. B. Cushman (1962 [1899] with numerous examples, apparently unintelligible to Choctaw Indians; see Sect. 12.1). Only a careful contrastive analysis of Adair's linguistic data with Choctaw and Chickasaw on the one hand and Mobilian Jargon on the other may eventually sort out any useful from fanciful information.

de la Louisiane and a prejudice against the French rather than firsthand experience. Adair apparently did not recognize the "Chikkasah" and the "Choktah" as fundamentally identical, but acknowledged Mobilian Jargon in the latter. In a surprising turn-around of his earlier observation of the supposedly poor relationships between the French and the Indians, he conceded, if quite reluctantly, that "... the French at Mobille, and some at New Orleans, could speak the Choktah language [Mobilian Jargon] extremely well, and consequently guide them much better than the English" (Adair 1968 [1775]: 285). Adair even communicated with French traders or colonists in writing and by employing Chickasaw couriers, to whom the French responded in Mobilian Jargon, via a female African interpreter:

Notwithstanding the bad treatment I had received; as I was apprehensive of the difficulties they would necessarily be exposed to, on account of their ignorance and haughtiness, I wrote to them [the French, in an unidentified language], by a few Chikkasah warriors, truly informing them of the temper of the Indians, and the difficulties they would probably be exposed to, from the policy of the French at Tumbikpe; and that though I had purposed to set off for South-Carolina, I would postpone going so soon, if they were of my opinion, that Mr. J. C——l (who joined with me in the letter) and I could be of any service to their mercantile affairs. They received our well-intended epistle, and were so polite as to order their black interpretess to bid our red couriers tell us, they thanked us for our friendly offer, but did not stand in need of our assistance. (Adair 1968 [1775]: 327)

Like Bonnefoy and the British traders among northern Alabama Indians some twenty years earlier, Adair's attestation points to Mobilian Jargon's range beyond colonial Louisiana or the French-influenced area of southern North America.

In 1752, Macarty Mactigue, the French commandant of the Illinois post at Kaskaskia (near Ste. Genevieve on the middle Mississippi), reported to Pierre de Rigaud de Vaudreuil, then Governor of Louisiana, a less than friendly encounter between an unidentified Native American man and an African slave woman, in which they used Mobilian Jargon and the Native American threatened to kill the woman. In the same letter, Mactigue also described a hostile confrontation between French and Indians in the area between the confluence of the Wabash with the Ohio River and the latter's junction with the Mississippi, in which the Indians addressed the French in Mobilian Jargon (Pease and Jenison 1940: 756–9; for quotations, see Sect. 7.3). This document confirms the pidgin's use by Africans in contact with Native Americans and as far north as the area on the Mississippi south of St. Louis and on the lower Ohio River, even in less than amicable circumstances.

A few years later in 1756, Choctaw Indians addressed Louis Billouart de Kerlérec, then Governor of Louisiana, as "*Tchakta youlakty mataha anke achukema,*" translated as "le Roy des Chactas, le plus Grand de la race des Youlabas et le très bon Père" (de Villiers 1923: 225) or 'the King of the Choctaw, the Greatest of the Yolaba race and the very good Father.' This title or phrase is not Choctaw as judged by the unusual occurrence of **taha,** a Western Muskogean verb or auxiliary meaning 'to end, to finish' or 'done, finished' (Pamela Munro, personal communication; see Munro, forthcoming). In this example, **taha** is not interpretable as such, but rather seems to function as a modifying element in the form of an adjective or a noun, which suggests that the example is Mobilian Jargon, reconstitutable as shown in (83). Also noteworthy is the particular use of †**āke** (< Muskogean **am-** first person singular possessive prefix (Booker 1980: 34–5) + Choctaw **īki** 'father', Chickasaw **inki**ʔ 'father' (Munro, forthcoming)). Unlike its Western Muskogean source, †**āke** probably meant only 'father' without a possessive in this instance, for the context of several Choctaw addressing the governor would presumably have required the first person plural pronoun (instead of its singular counterpart). This usage would have been consistent with that of kin terms in Mobilian Jargon in general. Yet, most interestingly, the Indians referred to the governor by what apparently was a Muskogee-derived or closely related word: †**holak(a)ti** (< Muskogee **holahtaki** 'former Creek town' (with metathesis) in contrast to Apalachee **holahta** 'chief,' Choctaw **hattak ī-holahta** 'one of the great Choctaw families' (Munro, forthcoming: 'chief')) instead of widely current †**mēko** 'chief.' This word has no obvious relationship to "Youlabas" that the French source gave in the accompanying translation and perhaps mistook as Yalobusha, the location of Chakiuma Indians (see Swanton 1911: 29).

In the early 1770s, Bernard Romans, a Dutchman who served as a surveyor for the British in Florida and Georgia, mentioned the use of Mobilian Jargon in northern and western Florida, extending from the Apalachicola River all the way to the Mississippi (Romans 1962 [1775]: p. xxxv, 1–2, 59). Based on his acquaintance of Southeastern Indian communities, he observed the Chickasaw as "being (although a small tribe) accounted the mother nation on this part of the continent, and their language, universally adopted by most, if not all the western nations [between the Apalachicola and Mississippi Rivers]." At first glance, Romans's sparse observation appears suspect as independent information, for he merely repeated the conventional wisdom of his time by referring to earlier French explorers. Yet closer examination suggests that Romans drew on his own

(83) †**čakta**	**holak(a)te**	**ma**	**taha**	**āke**	**ačokma**
Choctaw	chief	oh	perfect	father	good
			(one)		

'Oh, Chief of the Choctaw, the perfect one (and) good father'

observations. With quite detailed ethnographic sketches, he offered an English loan translation for 'silver' or 'white stone,' which Romans (1962 [1775]: 324) never identified as Mobilian Jargon, but which a non-Indian trader apparently uttered in conversation with Abihka Indians among Choctaw and which actually has a modern corresponding form in Mobilian Jargon **tale hat(t)a.** What in this instance matters more than the kind of information is its source: a European who was not French and looked at Mobilian Jargon from Florida, an eastern perspective. Significantly, Romans agreed with other observers.

Some time before 1776, a French traveller, Nicolas Louis Bourgeois (1788: 296–7), offered the first systematic, if small, vocabulary of Mobilian Jargon or "la langue des sauvages du Mississipi" [*sic*]. The author gave no further information on the source of his lexical data; but these words unquestionably represent Mobilian Jargon and not some Western Musko-gean language, as Crawford (1978: 113 n. 119) already recognized on the basis of morphosyntactic evidence in the form of a noun phrase with a possessive pronoun:

Bourgeois was careless in his transcriptions, often omitting initial sounds and sylla-bles. Also many errors appear to have been made by Bourgeois's compiler or printer. Allowing for all these errors of transcription and printing, I have been able to find resemblances for only slightly more than half the words in Bourgeois's vocabulary to words in Byington's Choctaw dictionary. Except for one word, "lianache," from French *la vache* (assuming *n* is an error for *v*), all the others may also be Choctaw or some other Western Muskogean language. They are Choctaw-like, but I cannot identify them. An interesting feature about many words is that Choctaw has *n* where Bourgeois has *l* and vice versa. One of the words in Bour-geois's vocabulary, "Talambo," is exactly like a Mobilian [Jargon] word which I col-lected (see PISTOL in the Vocabulary). One entry looks like "Nocté" for which the French is given as "La bouche" (the mouth). I believe the *c* in this word should be taken as *i*, giving *(i)no ité* "my mouth" (see I in Vocabulary). The replacement here of the pronominal prefix by the independent pronoun is exactly like what happens in Mobilian [Jargon]. Pilling identified the words collected by Bourgeois as Choctaw ("Bibliography," 11). In my opinion, they are Mobilian [Jargon], not Choctaw.

Crawford's argument requires one or two qualifications. Whereas Bour-geois was indeed careless in compiling this vocabulary, many of his record-ings without initial sounds or even syllables could well have reflected actual, quite widespread aphaeresis in Mobilian Jargon (see examples in (73) in Sect. 8.2). Recognizing this fact further strengthens Crawford's point, for Choctaw or some other Western Muskogean language with its pronomi-nal and other affixes would not have permitted the same extent of phonologi-cal variation without seriously hampering comprehension. An alternative source for "lianache" might be Western Muskogean **yanaš** 'buffalo,' (see Munro, forthcoming), in which case an explanation is necessary for the initial "l."[20]

During a twelve-month captivity among Native Americans named "Ozaws," "Ozawi," "Oh-zaws," or "Oh-taws" (the Osage or possibly the Oto, both Siouans), a surveyor called Selden learned a few Indian words and phrases that Ezra Stiles, a clergyman and educator in Connecticut and later president of Yale College, recorded in 1794 and identified as Mohegan-Pequot (Algonquian) of Long Island and southern New England (Stiles 1794 MS: 91–2, 109–10; cf. Stiles 1980 [1794]: 51 and Sherwood 1983: 440–1; the printed version is incomplete, and contains several errors). In reality, the vocabulary does not represent this Eastern Algonquian language or, for that matter, Osage or Oto;[21] by all identifiable lexical and morphosyntactic features, the vocabulary represents Mobilian Jargon, even if several entries remain uncertain in their reconstituted form and others unidentified at this time:

(84) "Baubasheelah" or †**babešele**   'good,' actually 'friend'
      "feah" or †**fe(h)na** (?)   'good', actually 'very,
                                           especially, better, best' (?)

      "Ex-Show" or †**ekšo**   'dead, wanting, missing,
                                           absent, & such
                                           negatives'

      "Seebáu" or †**soba** (?)   'horse'
      "Mauggasin"/"Manggasin" (?)   'shoes'
      or †**māgasen**/†**mogasen** (?)
      "Chiv-ze" or †**esse**[22]   'deer'
      "BaubiCheelah" or †**babešele**   'fellow' (?), actually 'friend'
      "fuchet" or †**faket**   'turkey'
      "Yaukilla(u)h finah" or †. . .   'the Greatest, Great Spirit,
      fena   God'

[20] As the present discussion does not depend on the presentation of Bourgeois's vocabulary, it does not appear here, but has been integrated into the main vocabulary under the glosses of: 'arm' (1), 'bead,' 'beard' (2), 'bed' (2), 'big' (1), 'blue,' 'brandy'/'spirits'/'whiskey,' 'breast'/'teat,' 'breechcloth' (2), 'broken,' 'buffalo' (2), 'bullet' (2), 'clothes' (1)/'dress,' 'cow' (3), 'deer,' 'dog' (3), 'drum' (1), 'ear' (2), 'eat,' 'eye' (1), 'flat,' 'foot' (1), 'gun' (1), 'hair' (2), 'hand' (2), 'head'/'neck' (2), 'horn,' 'knife' (3), 'liquor,' 'mouth' (2), 'my' (1), 'nose' (4), 'pipe' (2), 'pistol' (1), 'powder'/'dust' (2)/'gunpowder (2),' 'red,' 'scissors' (2)/'chisel,' 'shirt' (1)/'jacket,' 'shot' (2)/'lead shot' (2), 'stocking(s)' (2), 'stomach' (1)/'belly' (2), 'table,' 'tallow candle'/'dip candle,' 'thigh' (1), 'throat'/'neck' (3), 'tobacco' (1), 'tongue,' 'wildcat' (1), and 'wine' (2) (see Drechsel, 1996).

[21] John E. Koontz (personal communication) has confirmed from a Siouanist perspective that Stiles's sample did not resemble any Siouan language.

[22] The first two letters in "Chiv-ze" may simply reflect initial aspiration, as also perceived in "hisse" by the anonymous author of the major historical vocabulary of Mobilian Jargon (Anonymous 1862 MS: 29), who recorded distinct initial aspiration even though one would not expect a French speaker to have done so.

"Minta languah" or †**mente** . . .	'come here boy'
"Chikke-mau-feenah-baubicheelau" or †**čekəma fe(h)na, babešele**	'very good,' actually 'very good, friend'
"Mintau-lowa" or †**mente lawa** (?)	'come quickly or as fast as I do' (literally 'come fast' or perhaps 'really come')
"Lowah" or †**lawa** (?)	'do like me' (comparative; literally '(as) much'?)
"Mintau-zaauh-vaulah" or †**mente** . . .	'I came a good way hunting this morning.' (?)
"Eyo-chivze" or †**hoyo esse** (?)	'I killed a deer' (literally 'hunt deer'?)
"Lowah min'tau vee anza" or †**lawa mente** . . .	'go and do as I have done—get as many scalps as . . . my father . . .' (actually 'come much . . .'?)
"Yaukil(l)auh Exsho" or †**. . . ekšo**	'the greatest Evil power, Devil' or the negative of the word for 'god'

The first to identify this word list as Mobilian Jargon was David F. Sherwood (1983: 441 n. 11). He has already provided Choctaw correspondences for these reconstitutions except "Baubasheelah" and its variant spellings, "feah," and "Kam-po'ucha;" he has also compared "lowa" with Choctaw **olah** 'this way' in the phrase of "Mintau-lowa" or 'come quickly,' which, however, appears less convincing than the intensifier **lawa**. Sherwood (1983: 441 n. 11) has further recognized a word of clearly Algonquian origin, which had probably led to the earlier misidentification of the Selden's word list as Mohegan-Pequot: "Manggasin" or "Mauggasin" 'shoes,' reconstitutable as †**mãgasen** or †**mogasen** with corresponding forms in many Algonquian languages (see Sect. 5.4). There remain several terms with unidentified etymologies: "Keshau" 'bear;' "langah" 'boy;' "Kam-po'ucha" 'child, baby;' "Messau messa" 'to eat;' "Keevah" 'fire;' "Keevauh Koo" 'Fire will smoke;' "Yawkilah" 'great king, great man, warrior,' apparently also the name of an Osage chief in the form of "Yaukilauh;" "Kiv-'va-leh" 'house;' "Ki'ck-a" 'Indian corn;' "Zee-auh" 'light;' "Leeh" 'moon;' "Bre-h I" [?] 'salt spring;' "Zee-auh-feasch" 'sun;' "Le'ewah" 'wake' (?); and "Kallako" 'wor(l)d.'(?) Some may eventually prove the influence of native languages of eastern North America other than those already identified. However, the evidence that unquestionably identifies Stiles's word list as Mobilian Jargon consists of the negative "Ex-Show" and its variant spelling "Exsho;" support also derives from various short phrases reconstitutable in full or in part and exhibiting a lack of affixation or inflection. Stiles's word list thus confirms the use of Mobilian Jargon farther north than any other known document—among Siouans on the Missouri River some five hundred miles upstream from its confluence with the Mississippi, where Selden had reportedly learned and recorded these words and phrases.

In the years between 1794 and 1798, another French traveller, Louis Narcisse Baudry des Lozières, provided a concise assessment of Mobilian Jargon. He not only recognized a mixed lexicon with a variable pronunciation and vocabulary and the concurrent use of hand signs (see Chapter 8), but also estimated the pidgin's geographic range:

La langue des sauvages n'est pas aussi difficile qu'on se l'imagine. Il y a toujours une mère langue que l'on entend par-tout; par exemple la langue des chactas et des chicachas s'entend à plus de quatre cents lieues à la ronde, et les différens patois dont elle est mêlée ne sont pas assez dénaturés pour ne pas se ressentir de la mère langue dont ils dérivent.   (Baudry des Lozières 1802: 266–7)[23]

A range of more than four hundred *lieues* or leagues equaled some 1,200 miles around at a conservative definition of three miles per league, and would have covered an area extending from the Atlantic Coast to the Rocky Mountains with the Choctaw and Chickasaw at the center. In this case, the author vastly overestimated Mobilian Jargon's geographic range, or perhaps had in mind a *diameter* of 400 leagues rather a radius, which would match its geographic distribution deduced from all historical attestations quite closely (see Sect. 10.1). However, Baudry des Lozières provided a sense of the pidgin's wide-ranging utility.

In 1802, a French settler by the name of Berquin-Duvallon elaborated on Baudry des Lozières's assessment:

Le langage Mobilien est la langue-mère d'où dérivent les différens dialectes qu'emploient ces peuplades diverses, et au moyen de laquelle toutes peuvent s'entendre et se correspondre. Quoique la plupart des mots dont ces dialectes sont composés, étant entre-mêlés de voyelles, et n'abondant point en consonnes redoublées, ne soient pas rudes à l'oreille, ils semblent pourtant l'être, dans les bouches des sauvages, par un effet de leur prononciation sourde, inarticulée, et gutturale. Quant aux vocabulaires ou collections de mots isolés de ces dialectes, qui ont été, jusqu'à ce jour, publiés en français, anglais, espagnol, etc., tout ce que j'en puis dire de plus positif, est qu'il n'y faut ajouter presqu'aucune créance ni considération quelconque, attendu que la manière dont ces mots sont prononcés, et par conséquent écrits, dans chaque langue européenne, est différente l'une de l'autre, et s'écarte, plus ou moins,

___

[23] 'The language of the savages is not as difficult as one imagines. There always is a mother language that one understands everywhere; for example, the language of the Choctaw and Chickasaw [Mobilian Jargon] is understood more than four hundred leagues around, and the different dialects with which it is mixed are not sufficiently distorted in order not to bear the marks of the mother language from which they derive' (author's translation).

de la véritable prononciation, et qu'à bien dire un pareil répertoire de mots vagues et décousus, n'est que l'aliment d'une vaine curiosité, loin d'être un objet d'utilité réelle. (Berquin-Duvallon 1803: 191)[24]

Although focused on Mobilian Jargon's "descendant" languages, Berquin-Duvallon apparently applied his description also to the pidgin, if an abridged and questionable English translation that appeared within a few years after the French original (Berquin-Duvallon 1806; see also Crawford 1978: 113 n. 12) is any indication:

It [Mobilian Jargon] is not without melody, but rendered unpleasant to the ear by the harsh, inarticulate and guttural pronunciation of the savages. I have seen many vocabularies collected from the dialects of these people, but they are all so vague and distorted that they promote no useful purpose. (Berquin-Duvallon 1806: 95)

Berquin-Duvallon's description could indeed have applied to Mobilian Jargon. The supposed inarticulateness then referred to its phonological variation, and that of gutturalness perhaps to the mistaken identification of apical–veolar and lateral fricatives. The most convincing comment has been his observation about its tendency towards consonant–vowel alternation, which is evident more in Mobilian Jargon than other Southeastern Indian languages. As regards earlier vocabularies as sources, Berquin-Duvallon could have drawn on only a few instances, such as that by Bourgeois, and did not offer any better description, as far as is known. Berquin-Duvallon's comments ultimately provide no new information other than a measure of Mobilian Jargon's acceptance and significance in colonial Louisiana.

In a letter of 24 April 1802 addressed to the explorer William Dunbar in Natchez and accompanying vocabularies of Atakapa and Chitimacha, Martin Duralde, commandant of the Attacapas Post near present-day Opelousas in south-central Louisiana, gave two reasons for the difficulty of learning native languages, especially those of the Opelousa and Coushatta Indians:

[24] 'The Mobilian language is the mother tongue from which derive the different dialects that these diverse tribes use and by means of which all can understand and communicate with each other. Although the majority of words that make up these dialects, being intermixed with vowels and not abounding in reduplicated consonants, are not harsh to the ear, they seem all the same to be—in the mouth of the Indians and from an effect of their pronunciation—muted, inarticulate, and guttural. As to the vocabularies or collections of isolated words from these dialects that have been published in French, English, Spanish, etc. to date, the most positive thing that I can say about them is that one ought to give them hardly any credence or heed whatsoever, considering that the manner in which these words are pronounced and therefore written in each European language differs from case to case and deviates more or less from the real pronunciation and that to properly pronounce such collection of vague and desultory words only nurtures a vain curiosity, far from being an object of true usefulness' (author's translation).

l'une que ces nations ne Se communiquant avec les blancs qu'au moyen de la langue mobilienne commune, personne ne prend interêt à en connaître l'originaire; l'autre que quand on n'est pas certain Soi même du vrai original, on ne doit point l'exposer aux yeux des Savans.   [*sic*]   (Duralde 1802 MS: 2)[25]

This statement reveals Duralde's own insecurity about which language was which in the complex sociolinguistics of Louisiana, just as it indicates that Mobilian Jargon was the Native Americans' preferred medium in contact with colonists and presumably other outsiders.

Incidental references to Mobilian Jargon appeared in other sources of the period. For the same year, the newspaper *Moniteur de la Louisiane* mentioned a 30-year-old slave born in Senegal who could speak not only Spanish, French, and English, but also "Mobilian" (Fortier 1904: 219), confirming its use by African Americans.

From 1802 to 1806, another French visitor, Claude C. Robin, repeated much conventional wisdom about Mobilian Jargon, yet added the Talabouche Indians among its speakers, and emphasized its function as a diplomatic medium; according to Robin, the pidgin in fact was the means by which the larger groups had gained influence and status:

A travers ces grandes régions habitaient particulièrement les nombreuses nations des *Chactas*, des *Alibamons*, des *Chichacas*, des *Pascagoulas*, des *Biloccis*, des *Talabouches*, des *Mobiliens*. Il faut que ces nations, riveraines de la Mobile, fussent devenues puissantes et fameuses dès les siècles les plus reculés, puisque, quoique chacune d'elles parlât une langue particulière et très différente, elles avaient adopté pour langue commune la *Mobilienne*, qui, comme l'a été long-temps en Europe la langue latine, était devenue et est encore leur langue publique et politique.   (Robin 1807: ii. 54–5)[26]

In addition, Robin mentioned an encounter with some unidentified Native Americans on one of Louisiana's many rivers, during which the different parties drew on a few words of French, the Native Americans' language or likely Mobilian Jargon, and hand signs for mutual communication (see Sect. 8.3).

In 1803 and 1804, after the Louisiana Purchase, by which the United States obtained much of the territory between the Mississippi River and the Rocky Mountains, John Sibley, US Indian Agent at Natchitoches, sur-

---

[25] 'one being that, with these nations communicating with the whites only by means of the common Mobilian language, nobody takes an interest in knowing the original one; the other that, when one is not certain oneself about the true original, one must not expose this to the eyes of the scholars' (author's translation).

[26] 'Across these vast regions lived in particular the numerous nations of the Choctaw, the Alabama, the Chickasaw, the Pascagoula, the Biloxi, the Talabouche, and the Mobile. These nations, bordering the Mobile river drainage, must have become powerful and renowned many centuries ago, for although each of them spoke a particular and very different language, they had adopted as a common language Mobilian, which—as the Latin language once was in Europe—had become and still is their public and diplomatic language' (author's translation).

veyed Indian groups within the Red River drainage, and reported the following inventory-like assessment about their languages:

BOLUSCAS [Biloxi] . . . Their native language is peculiar to themselves, but speek Mobilian [Jargon], which is spoken by all the Indians, from the east side of the Mississippi . . .

APALACHIES . . . have their own language, but speak French and Mobilian [Jargon].

ALABAMAS . . . they speak the Creek and Choctaw languages, and Mobilian [Jargon]; most of them French, and some of them English . . .

PACANAS [unidentified] . . . their own language differs from any other, but speak Mobilian [Jargon] . . .

TUNICAS . . . Their native language is peculiar to themselves, but speak Mobilian [Jargon] . . .

PASCAGOULAS [unidentified] . . . speak Mobilian [Jargon], but have a language peculiar to themselves; most of them speak and understand French.

TENISAWS [Taënsa] . . . All speak French and Mobilian [Jargon] . . .

CHACTOOS [Chatot, unidentified and not to be confused with the Choctaw] . . . have their own peculiar tongue; speak Mobilian [Jargon]. [*sic*] (Sibley 1807: 724–5)

Sibley further noticed that, besides their native language, the Coushatta spoke Choctaw, which in this case cannot reliably be interpreted as Mobilian Jargon because Sibley distinguished between Choctaw and Mobilian Jargon among the Alabama. For several other groups (specifically the Natchitoches, Atakapa, Opelousa, Washa, Choctaw, and Arkansas), Sibley (1807: 724–5) made no mention of Mobilian Jargon. Yet his absence of references to the pidgin among these Native Americans hardly constitutes negative evidence; such in fact would contradict his initial statement that all Native Americans east of the Mississippi spoke Mobilian Jargon. Of greater interest is his observation that Mobilian Jargon persisted next to French among the Alabama, the Apalachee, the Pascagoula, and the Taënsa; some Alabama also knew English.

Sibley's survey eventually became the source for two other travel reports of the early nineteenth century. Henry Marie Brackenridge, a lawyer who had travelled in Louisiana in 1810 and 1811, listed under the heading of Biloxi most of the same Louisiana Indian communities as speaking Mobilian Jargon: Apalachee, Alabama, Pacana, Pascagoula, Tunica, plus Coushatta (Brackenridge 1962 [1814]: 82). Probably drawing on Adair's views, Brackenridge (1962 [1814]: 82) also described it as "the court language amongst the Indian nations of Lower Louisiana." Sibley's and Brackenridge's information then became the major source for a survey of Indian groups west of the Allegheny Mountains by John F. Schermerhorn (1814: 23, 26–7), who prepared it for the Society for Propagating the Gospel and listed many of the same groups among Mobilian Jargon speakers—only to disagree strongly with Sibley about linguistic differences among Louisiana Indians:

The last ten tribes [the six mentioned listed earlier plus the Biloxi, Coushatta, Taensa, and Choctaw] mentioned as distinct, and many of which, Silby observes, have a distinct language, though they speak the Mobilian [Jargon], have all emigrated from Missisippi territory and Georgia, and are or were parts of the Chactaws, or Creek Indians. What Silby observes, therefore, as to their possessing a language distinct from the Mobilian [Jargon], I apprehend is erroneous; for it is a fact that the Chactaws and Chickesaws speak the same language; and [Le Page] Du Pratz observes, that the Chickesaws and Alibamans speak the same language. But the Alibamans, says Dr. Silby, speak the Mobilian [Jargon]; of course, to those parts of the nation that have crossed over the Missisippi, the Mobilian [Jargon] is their former tongue, and not a different language, as Silby observes.   [*sic*] (Schermerhorn 1814: 27–8))

Manifestly, Schermerhorn understood few of the sociolinguistic complexities of Louisiana Indians that Sibley and others before him had begun to unravel, and demonstrated little personal experience in interacting with Louisiana Indians (see Crawford 1978: 55–6).

From 1810 until 1813, John Maley, another traveller through what then was the US Southwest, made incidental observations about Louisiana Indians along the Red River. On his visits to Coushatta, Caddo, and Choctaw Indians, he learned their language, which he identified as "Choctaw," but which differed little from tribe to tribe according to Maley (Flores 1972: 103, 160). In this case, he undoubtedly referred to Mobilian Jargon, and provided some linguistic evidence: "tompullu" or †**tãfola** 'hominy' among Coushatta and Caddo as well as "Chicamaw, Chicamaw, Chicamaw feenee" or †**čekama**, **čekama**, **čekama fenǝ** 'good, good, very good' among Coushatta Indians (Flores 1972: 57, 72, 93).

In the next decade, a resident of Natchitoches, J. H. Cosgrove, noted the use of Mobilian Jargon by clerks in local stores trading with Indians, presumably Caddo. Similarly, the "Indian language" was the medium of plantation owners in their interactions with native peoples (Kniffen, Gregory, and Stokes 1987: 96–7). Few details remain, however.

In 1826, a resident of Navasota northwest of Houston reported two basic words of Western Muskogean origin among the nearby Bidai Indians (possibly Atakapan): **púskus** 'boy' and **tándshai** 'maize' (Gatschet 1891: 39 n. 2). These words clearly have corresponding equivalences in Mobilian Jargon, **posko(š)** ~ **poškoš** 'baby, child' and **tanče** 'corn.' Rather than single loanwords, they possibly represented Mobilian Jargon, by the fact that they constituted basic vocabulary. The pidgin may indeed have extended even to the central Gulf Coast of Texas. For 1839, an observer by the name of J. O. Dyer (1917: 1) described an intertribal community speaking Karankawa (isolate), Tonkawa (isolate), Comanche (Uto-Aztecan), and other languages as follows: "The clan was a conglomeration of outcasts from neighboring tribes, who kept alive by begging, stealing, and fishing, and their language in 1839, [was] a jargon mostly of Spanish–English mixed with Indian dialects." Some suggestive evidence for this medium to have been Mobilian Jargon comes from an apparent Natchez or originally Muskogean loanword: Karankawa **lá-ak** 'goose' (Gatschet 1891: 77, 98) with its similarities to Natchez **laalak** (Haas 1956: 65), Choctaw/Chickasaw **šalaklak** (Munro, forthcoming), and Mobilian Jargon †**šalaklak**).

Between 1836 and 1838, a major-general of the US army named Ethan Allen Hitchcock (1930: 168, 174), learned from two sources that Biloxi in the Indian Territory (Oklahoma), originating from Texas, "can understand the Choctaw language, but their own tongue has so much changed that they can hardly be understood by the Choctaws." The limited intelligibility of the Biloxi's "Choctaw" to Choctaw Indians suggests that it was Mobilian Jargon instead, but that it was also in decline among the Choctaw of Oklahoma.

The period between 1837 and 1841 was the time when the German poet Gustav Dresel (1920–1: 407) observed how Texas and other Indians communicated with Europeans. In 1838, he recorded an Alabama of eastern Texas to have said: "No, Qshaw, Papeshille; plata, plata, shoke me fina," or †**no, (e)kšo, papešele; plata, plata čokəma fena** as a sample of a Hispanicized version of Mobilian Jargon (for further discussion, see Sect. 8.3). Dresel (1920–1: 371) further quoted a Coushatta's response: "You good man, you good papeshillo, you Dutchman." While Dresel had learned some Indian expressions and sign language, his Alabama host also spoke some Spanish and English. As reflected in these linguistic attestations, Mobilian Jargon coexisted with Spanish and English. Similarly, Dresel (1920–21: 348) had earlier observed some unidentified Indians north of St Louis in Adams County, Illinois, to mix French and "Indian" in their speech, and may have witnessed Mobilian Jargon in its northern extension. Although there exist no clues to corroborate the latter hypothesis, the translator of the English version, Max Freund (in Dresel 1954: 140–1), confirmed Dresel's example among the Alabama-Coushatta near Livingston in eastern Texas a century later, in the 1930s: "A particularly intelligent member of the tribe was invited by this editor to examine the Indian words and phrases quoted by Dresel in his diary . . . He declared them to be perfectly correct and still in colloquial use."

In 1840, a French traveller, Victor Tixier, encountered Choctaw some twenty miles "above New Orleans," and partook in their *sagamité* or hominy by invitation with the apparently proverbial, almost formulaic encouragement of "*Tchoukouman-finan,* ce qui voulait dire: C'est très bon" (Tixier 1844; 40)[27] or †**čokomã fenã** 'very good.' While Tixier did not care for the Choctaw's offering, he responded similarly out of courtesy. His pronunciation of the phrase made his hosts laugh.

In 1849, the ethnologist William Bollaert (1850: 277) reported that Lipan

---

[27] 'which meant: "It is very good" ' (Tixier 1940: 56).

Apache (Athapaskans) conversed in "Lipan-Hispano-English" with Texans, and provided an example with the all-present word for 'friend' in Mobilian Jargon: "'Bobachelo, Bueno, Very good' (My friend you are good, very good)." Later, the same word also appeared as "Boba-chela" with the gloss of 'comrade, friend' in a list of other alleged Lipan words, including one of apparent Algonquian origin, "kin-i-ki-nik" to refer to tobacco mixed with sumac (Bollaert 1850: 278). A variety in the form of "boba-shee-la (friend)" turned up again in an English conversation with a young Coushatta of the lower Trinity River, without the author recognizing any relation between them (Bollaert 1850: 282). Whereas Bollaert's linguistic examples are subject to closer examination, there exist some independent indications for the use of Mobilian Jargon among Lipan Apache. Not only did Lipan Apache live in eastern Texas, but they had also entered Louisiana as French and Spanish slaves, and—after liberation—had established themselves among Choctaw Indians and Hispanic settlers west of Natchitoches along the Sabine River (Kniffen, Gregory, and Stokes 1987: 65, 91, 94). Their descendants in Sabine Parish (see Van Rheenen 1987) remembered single words of Choctaw origin or Mobilian Jargon until recently.

For the mid-nineteenth century, François-Dominique Rouquette, a poet, described his experiences among native peoples in New Orleans and neighboring parishes, including a few encounters with speakers of Mobilian Jargon. He had grown up with his younger brother Adrien-Emmanuel around Choctaw earlier in the century when "there were more Indians [in the city] than there were either whites or blacks" (LeBreton 1947: 13). As children, the two Rouquette brothers—unlike most other non-Indians—had acquired Choctaw rather than Mobilian Jargon, evident from many of their attestations (see LeBreton 1947; Rouquette 1839, 1937–8 MS); but there are one or two instances that by their sociolinguistic contexts are interpretable in terms of Mobilian Jargon:

The flat-head [Choctaw] women are industrious, but the men have a horror of all manual labor. If you ask one of these natives why he does not work, he indignantly replies, "Am I a *iouca* [†**yoka**], a slave?"   (Rouquette 1937–8 MS: 13)

One day he [a man named Mische-an-hia or Vincent] came to the house of one of my friends. He was half drunk, jabbering as usual in a sort of polyglot dialect, a veritable babel of words, a mixture of French, Choctaw, Negro and Talapouche [unidentified]. He had a magnificent kerchief wound artistically around his head like a turban. 'Who gave you this present?' asked the planter. 'You!' 'How?' 'You, I tell you. I know you are my friend, my comrade, *mongoula finan* [†**mõgola fenã** 'friend really']. I took it on credit on your account at the merchant's over there; Tchoucoumau [†**čokoma** 'good']; it's all right, isn't it?' The planter laughed heartily at the simplicity of the savage, and answered him, in great seriousness: 'I appreciate this proof of your friendship. I see that you are interested in me." Once Vincent came back at his generous protector's (whose ordinary hunter he was) after a long absence. 'Ah! there you are, rascal,' said the white man, 'I have been without game for three months, and I heard that you were hunting for others.' 'My friend I have gone all over the country and I have found nothing better than you.' (Rouquette 1937–8 MS: 15)

The younger Rouquette, also a poet eventually to turn to ministry among Indians, was said to be the only non-Indian with sufficient knowledge of their language to disentangle the etymologies of local place names with a Choctaw origin. According to the New Orleans *Bulletin*, Adrien-Emmanuel, known by the Choctaw as Chahta-Ima or 'Choctaw-like,' remarked reportedly that "The Choctaws who lived (and some of them still live) about this city have many compound words, and they have become so corrupted, passing on into the French and Spanish tongues, they are difficult to recognize now" (LeBreton 1947: 328–9). Although Rouquette did not say so, many of these "corruptions" had resulted from pidginization in Mobilian Jargon, others from their transference as loans into European languages via the pidgin (for examples, see Sect. 12.3).

The 1850s were the years during which the author of *Essai sur quelques usages et sur l'idiôme des Indiens de la Basse Louisiane* (Anonymous 1862 MS), an anonymous resident of Opelousas, collected information on what William A. Read (1940: 546) erroneously identified as "virtually pure Choctaw," but what Crawford (1978: 57–8) recognized as Mobilian Jargon, as evident from its grammar and mixed vocabulary. An incidental phrase of Choctaw, "S(i)abana" 'to desire, to want' or †**sa bana** (?) 'I want' (Anonymous 1862 MS: 17, 84; see Munro 1993), and the predominance of Western Muskogean etymologies in the anonymous author's lexicon (see Sect. 8.3) indicates only that the Choctaw exerted greater influences in this variety of Mobilian Jargon and probably were the major native group in the area. The author's source was a Creole, a person of European and perhaps African ancestry born in America, who had long lived with Indians in the pinewoods of western Louisiana and reportedly spoke their language well (Anonymous 1862 MS: 1, 2), but who as a non-Indian probably did not learn Choctaw or some other, closely related Western Muskogean language. Although the manuscript's author left unnamed the described language, speakers were mentioned in the introduction:

La langue des Biloxi, une des tribus sauvages, qui habitaient le Sud de la Louisiane, est, avec la language Mobilienne, autre tribu qui habitait ce qu'on nomme aujourd'hui l'Etat de l'Alabama, l'idiôme le plus généralement en usage parmi les quelques Indiens vagabonds, qui restent de ces nationalités détruites et dispersées. (Anonymous 1862 MS: 2)

La plupart des Indiens, debris des tribus Chactaw, Opelousas, Attakapas, Natchitoches, Alibamon, Biloxi et autres n'ont maintenant pour ainsi dire plus de village. (Anonymous 1862 MS: 3)

Il est presque inutile de dire que l'idiôme dont on va s'occuper n'est que celui des tribus dont il est parlé au commencement de ce chapitre.   (Anonymous 1862 MS: 8)[28]

These groups spoke mutually unintelligible and even unrelated languages—Choctaw (Muskogean), Opelousa (unidentified), Atakapa (Gulf isolate), Natchitoches (Caddoan), Alabama (Muskogean), and Biloxi (Siouan); the medium that united them was Mobilian Jargon, as evident from other, independent sociolinguistic-historical evidence (see Sect. 10.1). The pidgin was in use in diverse situations, including one in which a man reproached a woman of the same community for her work as a servant. With her abhorrence of slavery characteristic of Indians, she took the man's accusation as a major embarrassment, and committed suicide, which she could have easily avoided upon a last-minute change of mind. The man's choice of Mobilian Jargon could have been due to any combination of reasons: the lack of a common first language in a truly multilingual community, a desire by the man to be overheard by a larger audience including speakers of different languages, or the public context of his interaction with the woman outside their own community (Anonymous 1862 MS: 12–13 n. 4; for a full discussion of this scene in Mobilian Jargon, see Sect. 7.3). The substantial amount of attention paid by the anonymous author to Indian stickball games and gambling (Anonymous 1862 MS: 8, 13–14) also suggests the use of Mobilian Jargon as a major medium at such events, as independently recalled by a few of the last speakers.

In 1858, the Louisiana settler and trader Thomas S. Woodward (1939 [1859]: 79; see also Sect. 8.3) encountered speakers of Mobilian Jargon in Texas. He recognized the pidgin and its role as a trade language from his earlier experiences among Creek Indians east of the Mississippi, which implies that Mobilian Jargon once extended east well beyond the immediate neighbors of the Choctaw and Chickasaw and into the territory of the Creek Confederacy. If Woodward overestimated Mobilian Jargon's geographic range in citing almost all of the country's tribes as its speakers, it was perhaps because he had in mind only the antebellum South at the time shortly before Secession or did not have a full understanding of the United States' vast size.

[28] 'The language of the Biloxi, one of the indian tribes that inhabited southern Louisiana, together with the language of the Mobilians, another tribe that inhabited what constitute now the state of Alabama, is the idiom the most in use among the wandering Indians who remain of those nationalities now destroyed and dispersed' [sic] (Anonymous n.d. MS: 3).

'The greater portions of the Indians, remnants of various tribes—the Choctaws, Opelousas, Attakapas—Alabama, Natchitoches, Beloxi and others possess no longer any villages' [sic] (Anonymous n.d. MS: 3).

'It is scarce necessary to say here that the idiom to which our attention will be given, is that of few tribes of whom mention has been made at the beginning of this chapter' [sic] (Anonymous n.d. MS: 8).

During 1885 and 1886, Albert S. Gatschet lent an ear to speakers of Mobilian Jargon while doing linguistic fieldwork on Atakapa and Biloxi in Louisiana. As part of his linguistic notes on Atakapa, Gatschet (1885 MS: 24–5) collected some twenty words and a few phrases with some distinctive morphosyntactic information that clearly identifies the language as Mobilian Jargon:

(85) "ishno ba'na" or †**ešno bana**   'you want'[29]
     "těne áksho" or †**tana ekšo** (?)   'do not know'

Gatschet simply called it "Mobilian," and mistakenly equated it with Choctaw. His source was Joe le Bleu in Lake Charles, whom he thought to be a Mobilian Indian (probably on the basis of the name given for the language), but who was more likely to have been an Atakapa. Similarly, Gatschet (1886 MS) recorded a few words of so-called "Chá?hta," apparently from a Biloxi at Lecompte, south of Alexandria in central Louisiana, but again appeared to be unaware of the fact that he was dealing with Mobilian Jargon rather than Choctaw. The author's visit to Louisiana could have been the very occasion for him to learn about the *Essai sur quelques usages et sur l'idiôme des Indiens de la Basse Louisiane* (Anonymous 1862 MS) and have given him the incentive to prepare its alphabetical indices. Eventually, Gatschet (1887: 412) did realize that many Southeastern Indians bearing Muskogean names—among them the Houma, the Washa, the Tohome, the Tangipahoa, and the Opelousa—spoke Mobilian Jargon, but were not necessarily Choctaw or Muskogean and could have spoken non-Muskogean languages like the Biloxi.

Around the turn of the century, the missionary family Chambers by accident learned more about the sociolinguistics of the Alabama-Coushatta Indians in eastern Texas:

The true tribal language is spoken only in the privacy of the Indians' homes. Where white people can hear them speak, they use a "trade" dialect, a common language used by a number of tribes for purposes of trade and communication [Mobilian Jargon]. The Reverend and Mrs. Chambers did not know there were two dialects used until their daughter Dorothy was six years old. She had learned to speak the language of the Indians [Alabama or Koasati], and one day in Livingston the Chambers family met a man who had been closely associated with the Alabama and Coushatta for several years and was said to speak their language. The man and Dorothy tried to talk to each other in the Indians' native tongue, but they could not understand each other. Dorothy's parents were disappointed, for they had been under the impression that she could speak the Indians' language. But they soon discovered that their daughter, who had been received into the Indians' homes, could

---

[29] Gatschet actually recorded 'I want' as the gloss for this phrase, based on a misunderstanding. While "ishno" or **ešno** means 'you,' the pronoun for 'I' was **eno** or—in his transcription—"ino."

speak their real language, whereas the man with whom she had tried to converse knew only their "trade" dialect. Dorothy (now Mrs. Dorothy Shill of Livingston) always held first place in the hearts of the Indians.   (Rothe 1963: 96)

This experience allowed the Chambers to unravel what Duralde had already suspected in his observations about the Opelousa and Coushatta Indians of Louisiana a century earlier.

Incidental references to Mobilian Jargon appeared in other sources dealing with Native Americans of Louisiana and eastern Texas. In 1905, a local resident of Cotile (present-day Boyce), northwest of Alexandria in central Louisiana, remembered that King Brandy, a Mississippi Choctaw (Hiram F. Gregory and Claude Medford, personal communications), had called her father "Good Bobbi Shele" (Barber 1966: 15) with "Bobbi Shele" reconstitutable as †**babešele** 'friend.' Similarly, in the early twentieth century, boys in the Kinder area in southwestern Louisiana knew an older Coushatta or Choctaw Indian by the name of Jake, who owned a peach orchard: "When the fruit was ripe, the boys would come and claim to be his friend. He used to tell people, 'When peaches are ripe, Jake is good *bobisheila*; when peaches are gone, Jake is no *bobisheila*.' (This Indian word means friend.)" (Johnson and Leeds 1964: 126). The authors reporting these instances undoubtedly referred to Mobilian Jargon in consistency with other, more detailed attestations. But they did not provide reliable evidence for any variety with a greater portion of English lexicon, for they probably took considerable poetic license by replacing native vocabulary other than the almost stereotypical †**babešele** 'friend' with English words and by hypercorrecting any unusual grammar as in the case of AIPE (see Sect. 2.3).

The pidgin even appears in the diary of the congregational minister Paul Leeds, who did missionary work among the Coushatta and Choctaw near Kinder and Elton in southwestern Louisiana in 1908: "Didn't go to prayer meeting. *Yokepa iksho. Couché 11:15*" (Johnson and Leeds 1964: 24, 25), with the intermediate phrase reconstitutable as †**yokepa ekšo** or †**yekopa ekšo** 'not calm, restless' (with metathesis of the initial two vowels). Why Leeds inserted a phrase in what he identified as Koasati and then switched into French is not evident; but as reflected by the characteristic morphosyntactic pattern of the negative construction, the supposed Koasati phrase actually was Mobilian Jargon, which suggests its use in Leeds's clerical work among the Coushatta and Choctaw. He apparently spoke with Coushatta Indians in a mixture of Mobilian Jargon, French, and English. Surprisingly, for a person who was supposedly a close friend of the Native Americans, Leeds revealed no sociolinguistic understanding of his congregation, and never learned Koasati.

John R. Swanton (1911: 32) demonstrated greater alertness of Mobilian

Jargon when he visited two brothers of Biloxi-Pascagoula descent during the same year. They could say little about their parents' languages, but one of the brothers remembered a few words and distinctive phrases learned from their father or mother:

(86) "Î'no î'nkê" or **eno ĕke**   'my father'
     "Î'no iskê" or **eno eske**   'my mother'
     "Tcîtokso' " or **četokšo**   'little'
     "Pû'skus tcîtokso' " or **poskos**   'babies' (literally: 'child' +
       četokšo   'little')

Swanton (1911: 32) interpreted these samples plus five single words of an obvious Western Muskogean source in the following terms:

Since these words are not Biloxi, it follows either that they belonged to the Pascagoula language, which would thus have been a Muskhogean dialect, or, what is more probable, to the Mobilian trade language. In the latter case, however, the fact that it was employed by a Biloxi and a Pascagoula in conversation is evidence that the languages of the two tribes were not enough alike to enable members of the two to converse easily.

Significantly, Swanton's recordings demonstrate not only the recent survival of Mobilian Jargon among the Biloxi (Siouans) and the Pascagoula (unidentified), but also the fact that it served as a convenient medium between spouses of different linguistic backgrounds. Swanton's data further raise the question of creolization for Mobilian Jargon, although there currently exists no substantial evidence for it.

In the late 1920s, a columnist of the monthly *The American Indian* by the name of John Madden (1928: 8) described Mobilian Jargon as "a means devised to use the root words common in the various kindred dialects" (i.e. Choctaw, Chickasaw, and perhaps other Muskogean languages), and thought that Mobilian Jargon survived among Choctaw and Chickasaw in southeastern Oklahoma. "I do not doubt but what there may be old people living around Tuskahoma and Tishomingo [Choctaw and Chickasaw respectively], who could make themselves understood among the Caddoes and Creeks in the old Mobilian dialect [Mobilian Jargon]" [*sic*] (Madden 1928: 8). Madden did not elaborate or provide any other information in support of his claim. His observations reveal little ethnographic or historical depth; they would be of greater interest only if he wrote about the pidgin from personal experience, for which there is little evidence.

Mobilian Jargon was still very much in use in the greater area of Natchitoches around 1930, when the Louisiana naturalist Caroline Dormon (n.d. MS) collected several pidgin words and phrases among examples of Choctaw, apparently from different individuals:

(87) "Eno-tike-chicka-ma-lawa" or   'My wife [is] plenty good (is
    †**eno tayek čekama lawa**   well).'
    "Eno-ish-no-bä-bi-she-le-lawa"   'I am your good friend.'
    or †**eno ešno babešele lawa**
    "Barbesheely ä chōk mo^n" or   '[You are my] good friend.'
    †**babešele ačokmã**
    "Cotteema ĭshnō īyä?" or   'Where are you going?'
    †**katema ešno eya?**
    "Läshpä ĭshnō?" or †**laSpa**   'Are you hot?'
    ešno?

Dormon neither expressed any awareness of the differences between Choctaw and Mobilian Jargon by keeping her recordings separate for each; nor did she offer sufficient sociolinguistic details that might help to sort out these two sets of data beyond obvious instances identifiable by their grammar such as the above.[30]

In the 1930s, while working on the Tunica language, Mary R. Haas (1975: 258) learned about "Mobilienne" from her consultant Sesostrie Youchigant, who could remember a few words of apparent Choctaw or Chickasaw origin. Haas (1950: 165) also recorded a few vocables in Mobilian Jargon that accompanied the Raccoon Dance, but did not explore leads for the pidgin's survival at the time because of other commitments (see Sect. 7.3).

In agreement with the American translator and editor of Dresel's journal, W. E. S. Folsom-Dickerson (1965: 94) attested the existence of Mobilian Jargon speakers among the Alabama-Coushatta near Livingston in eastern Texas as late as in the 1940s: "Many of the Indians, particularly those who have traveled in neighboring areas, speak a variety of languages and dialects. Due to their original geographical nearness to the Choctaw, many individuals have a smattering of this language" (Folsom-Dickerson 1965: 94). Mobilian Jargon had survived in spite of widespread bilingualism and multilingualism among Indians of the area, as exemplified by one individual with "a fair command of six languages: Alabama, Koasati, Choctaw [= Mobilian Jargon?], Spanish, French, and English" (Folsom-Dickerson 1965: 94).

9.4. Survival into Modern Times and Recent Decline

Historical attestations of Mobilian Jargon could easily lead one to conclude that Mobilian Jargon persisted only among the Alabama-Coushatta in

---

[30] For this reason, the above set of examples and the lexicon (Drechsel, 1996) incorporate only those entries of Dormon's recordings identifiable exclusively as Mobilian Jargon. I acknowledge the help of Pamela Munro in sorting out Choctaw from Mobilian Jargon.

eastern Texas and perhaps a few Indian communities in Louisiana. Although not exactly wrong, this inference requires some revision in light of findings from fieldwork, which presents a more complex picture. The search for surviving speakers of Mobilian Jargon took Crawford to the Alabama–Coushatta Reservation east of Livingston, the Coushatta near Elton (southwestern Louisiana), the Houma community in Dulac and an individual of Choctaw descent in Lacombe (both in southern Louisiana), and the Choctaw in Jena (central Louisiana). He could still record a few words of Mobilian Jargon from some Alabama and Coushatta Indians in Texas, yet met the most fluent speakers, among them the late Arzelie Langley, in the vicinity of Elton. He expected to find further Mobilian Jargon to survive in that community (Crawford 1978: 116–17 n. 167), as borne out by my own field research.

Mobilian Jargon indeed prevailed the longest among the Coushatta and their neighbors, Indians and non-Indians. About a dozen individuals among the Coushatta remembered single sentences and words, and provided quite detailed sociohistorical information. The most fluent speaker whom I could still record in the late 1970s was Lessie Simon, a Choctaw sharecropper, who lived north of Elton near Oakdale with ties to the Coushatta and the former intertribal community of Indian Creek south of Alexandria. According to these sources, the pidgin had still been regularly heard in the area well into the 1940s, perhaps the early 1950s, in a variety of social contexts: intertribal gatherings in the form of feasts, dances, and stickball games and interethnic contacts with both European–American and African–American neighbors on occasions such as trapping, share-cropping, and the Indians' employment in various functions (as guides to hunters and fishermen in the surrounding swamps and bayou country, farm hands and servants, workers in the local timber and oil industries, and so on). Through history, the Coushatta and their neighbors have distinguished themselves by their linguistic diversity. As a former haven for refugees from other Southeastern Indian groups, the Coushatta not only had adopted refugees from various smaller native groups in the tradition of Southeastern twin and multiple towns (see Drechsel and Makuakāne 1982*b*: 49–54; Kniffen, Gregory, and Stokes 1987: 83–105); but until recently, old and young also maintained three native languages in their community—Koasati, Alabama, and Choctaw—upon which Mobilian Jargon could feed as major sources. Significantly, the larger environs were multilingual as well, and included French-speaking Acadians ("Cajuns") and French Creole-speaking African Americans, plus the larger community of Southern and Black English.[31] The

---

[31] Louisiana has also harboured several German-speaking communities, some of which arrived with the first French colonists (see Deiler 1909). By all available indications, German never contributed significantly to the linguistic diversity of the community at large, as it apparently survived only within settings of the family and its speakers had adopted French and then

pidgin benefited from the competition between French and English, allevi-
ating some of the pressure against the Indians to abandon their native and
contact languages. The minority status of French in the United States may
even have made its speakers more sensitive towards other language communities and their potential role as allies. Another factor in the persistence
of Mobilian Jargon was its functions as a sociolinguistic buffer (see Sect.
10.3).

Single words and short phrases in Mobilian Jargon also occurrd to a few
individuals among the Tunica-Biloxi Indians near Marksville in the 1970s.
Two of them recalled a song or portions thereof, performed at intertribal
gatherings, but could no longer provide a full translation (see Sect. 7.3). The
only native language then to survive in the immediate area of Marksville
was Tunica in the memory of two individuals, remembering single words
and phrases. With Biloxi and any other native language already extinct for
decades (see Haas 1968: 77), the community adopted French and increasingly English as their first language. Claude Medford (personal communication) believed that his late friend Joseph Pierite, Sr., former chief of the
Tunica-Biloxi, had used Mobilian Jargon as recently as the 1960s on visits
to Southeastern Indian communities in Oklahoma, including the Caddo.
But Choctaw Indians of Jena argued that Pierite had always spoken
Choctaw proper with them, and there is no indication that, with the exception of one or two Louisiana-born Choctaw, Oklahoma Indians (among
them even Choctaw or Chickasaw) knew Mobilian Jargon during the past
sixty or seventy years.[32] The pidgin had already been in decline since the

English. Consequently, there exist no more than incidental attestations about Mobilian Jargon
speakers with German as their first language as in the case of the Salzburger immigrants to
colonial Georgia (Urlsperger 1735: 192; 1738: 282, 345, 372) and German visitors such as
Gustav Dresel (1920–1: 407) to Texas in 1838. Another German by the name of Brandenstein
reportedly became a full-fledged Indian and even a chief, and served as an interpreter between
German immigrants and his tribe in Pensacola around 1780 (Deiler 1909: 136). In this function, he could well have used Mobilian Jargon as his medium of translation, even on the
assumption that he had learned the first language of his Indian community and had transcul-
turated fully. However, the source does not name the language that Brandenstein used in interpreting, nor does it identify the native community that he had joined.

[32] Apparently lending support to Medford's suggestion, some Jena Choctaw reportedly
mistook examples of Mobilian Jargon that Crawford had recorded from Arzelie Langley as
"Choctaw 'with a French accent' " and with only a few different words (Hiram F. Gregory, personal communication). One need not, however, read this description as one of Choctaw proper
(as Gregory apparently has done); this characterization is precisely the kind that one could
expect from speakers of Choctaw to refer to Mobilian Jargon, especially if they heard only a
short portion, as was most likely the case under field conditions. On the other hand, one would
expect Pierite as a child raised among the Choctaw-Biloxi at Indian Creek in central Louisiana
to have acquired Choctaw proper rather than Mobilian Jargon and to have addressed the Jena
Choctaw in the first. If Pierite used Mobilian Jargon until the 1960s, he would have been a
truly extraordinary person, as he apparently was by other indications, and would undoubtedly
have retained the pidgin as a result of his many contacts with other Indian communities of the
South.

time when Mary Haas had carried out research on Tunica in the 1930s. Her consultant Sesostrie Youchigant still knew of "Mobilienne," and remembered two or three words of apparent Choctaw or Chickasaw provenance (Haas 1975: 258). Until about the 1920s, Marksville had been a hub of intertribal associations where Tunica, Biloxi, Ofo, and Avoyel gathered with other Native Americans such as Coushatta for dances and games. Like Lessie Simon, all of the last speakers of Mobilian Jargon among the Tunica-Biloxi had close ties to the intertribal community of Indian Creek to the south (Hiram F. Gregory, personal communication).

In other intertribal communities of central Louisiana, several persons could recall a few common words interpretable as either Mobilian Jargon or Choctaw proper, but no longer retained utterances whose morphosyntactic structure would have resolved this question. These individuals lived in Clifton, Ebarb, and Spanish Lake, former intertribal and interethnic communities in the greater triangle of Opelousas–Alexandria–Kinder, that once included Indian Creek as well. Although this area was also the home of Lipan Apache, former French and Spanish slaves (Kniffen, Gregory, and Stokes 1987: 65, 91, 94, 124), most people were of Choctaw or part-Choctaw descent, and could well have learned Choctaw rather than the pidgin. The only exception of confirmed Mobilian Jargon is a short phrase that Bob Ebarb recalled from his former work at the sawmill (Gregory, personal communication): **čokma fena. taboke baša**, literally 'Very good. Cuts belly' (with apparent metathesis of the two final consonants in †**takoba** 'belly'). This phrase was a translation of the hand sign of a slash across the belly with one's hand, used to signal agreement to cut wood in a noisy environment.

Mobilian Jargon did not survive among the Alabama-Coushatta in the area of Livingston in eastern Texas as long as among their Louisiana relatives, and had apparently begun to decline in the 1930s. Those few individuals who still remembered single words until recently were Coushatta of part-Choctaw descent with close ties to the Louisiana Coushatta. By all indications, there were no Alabama or other Indians, much less non-Indians, who retained much knowledge of the pidgin in the 1970s. Although the Texas Alabama-Coushatta and their Creek neighbors, too, had adopted refugees from neighboring groups, they did not keep as extensive intertribal ties as their Louisiana relatives, and spoke only two or three native languages, closely related Alabama, Coushatta, and perhaps Muskogee. At the same time, English made increasing inroads as both the primary second or even the first language, especially among the younger generations, due to pressures from the larger community of non-Indians.

Mobilian Jargon was no more viable among the Choctaw in Jena (central Louisiana), where there was only one older man who supposedly had once spoken it, but did not care to reminisce about it. Older members of the community still maintained Choctaw next to English, but apparently had little need for the pidgin. Most of their contacts with other Indian communities were with Choctaw of Mississippi and Oklahoma; conversely, most visitors were other Choctaw Indians passing through on their way back and forth between Mississippi and Oklahoma.

Nor is there any reliable indication for Mobilian Jargon's recent survival among the Choctaw of Mississippi, the Five Civilized Tribes of Oklahoma (Cherokee, Chickasaw, Choctaw, Creek, and Seminole), or other Southeastern Indian groups in that state, although most of these groups still spoke their native languages and Choctaw was the most viable one next to Cherokee. The Mississippi Choctaw had no recollections of the pidgin whatsoever, explainable by the fact that these Native Americans spoke only Choctaw or English. Among Oklahoma Indians, the only persons to know about Mobilian Jargon were two Louisiana-born Choctaw, who mentioned that they had never heard it in Oklahoma. All the various leads about local Indians or even non-Indians remembering the pidgin proved fruitless, just as subsequent inquiries with traditional Southeastern Indians such as the late Archie Sam of part-Natchez ancestry (see Drechsel 1987*c*) turned up no reliable clues. Familiar with Choctaw in Mississippi, Louisiana, and Oklahoma, Thurston Dale Nicklas (personal communication) has not found any evidence for the pidgin either. For many decades, English had been the intertribal medium in bilingual and multilingual speech situations, even in those that included two or more mutually unintelligible native languages at the exclusion of European tongues, and increasingly became the first and only language of younger generations of Native Americans. There are several closely interrelated reasons to account for the absence of Mobilian Jargon among Southeastern Indians in Oklahoma: For one, immigrants to the former Indian Territory have been culturally less conservative than many of their eastern relatives, especially those of Louisiana and Florida, and early adopted English as a new lingua franca among each other as well as with their other neighbors. Then, Removal had affected older people, the bearers of traditions, to a greater extent than younger ones, and had taken a heavier linguistic and cultural toll on displaced Southeastern Indians than commonly recognized. Moreover, the decline in the use of native languages resulted in reduced sociolinguistic complexity, which in turn decreased the need for Mobilian Jargon. Thus, the Southeastern Indians of Mississippi and Oklahoma demonstrate that viable indigenous languages, among them at least one major source for Mobilian Jargon, were no guarantee for the latter's survival.

As expected, there was no evidence for the recent use of Mobilian Jargon in communities that had long abandoned their indigenous language(s) for a European tongue (French, Spanish, or English) such as the Chitimacha, the Houma, various smaller Native American or part-Indian groups in

Louisiana, and the Creek in Alabama and eastern Texas. The decline of native languages undermined not only Mobilian Jargon's basic functions as a lingua franca, but also its resources for grammar and lexicon.

Today, a few individuals, most likely elderly Southeastern Indians, may still survive and remember some Mobilian Jargon. Yet there remain no more than suggestive traces, as indicated by an incident following my field research. In the early 1980s, an elderly Coushatta man objected when the preacher of the local Assembly of God church and some European–American worshippers reportedly identified Mobilian Jargon with the global language of Babel and with their speaking in tongues (of which they presumably were the only speakers). Their claim eventually dissipated on grounds of the elderly Coushatta's knowledge of the pidgin, which he had not shared with others for a while (Medford, personal communication). Attested vestiges of the pidgin endure nowadays only in the stereotypical phrase of **čokəma fehna** 'very good' in Mardi Gras songs by African Americans dressed up as Indians (Geoffrey D. Kimball, personal communication) and "chakimo fino" or "jagamo fino" in blues refrains (Anonymous 1983), confirming that African Americans once spoke the pidgin as well.

Mobilian Jargon clearly persisted the longest in intertribal, multilingual communities with two or more native languages, of which at least one was Muskogean, usually Choctaw. The proportions of etymologies in Mobilian Jargon's modern vocabulary (with most words deriving from Western Muskogean, specifically Choctaw, and a substantial number from Alabama and Koasati) reflect the sociolinguistic make-up of the late contact speech community remarkably well—except that there existed no known speakers with Chickasaw or an Algonquian language as their first language in recent history. Significantly, all the last pidgin speakers were fluent in two or more native and European languages. This fact suggests that bilingualism or multilingualism was not a recent development, but had already coexisted with Mobilian Jargon for decades or longer. However, the survival of French in Louisiana was probably a mitigating factor in Mobilian Jargon's decline. While perhaps inevitable, the pidgin's demise did not come about until much later than expected by the two early observers most intimately familiar with it; Mobilian Jargon survived for 200 years longer than predicted by Antoine Simone Le Page du Pratz (1758: ii. 323) and for about a century later than anticipated by the anonymous author of the *Essai* (Anonymous 1862 MS: 2).

10

Sociocultural Aspects

10.1. Geographic Range and Social Distribution

With their variable quality and limitations, historical attestations cannot offer a complete picture of the geographic range and social dissemination of Mobilian Jargon for its recorded history, much less its origin; the pidgin probably extended across greater distances to communities not mentioned here and over longer periods than documented by the presently available records. Yet a closer examination of historical and ethnographic historical attestations, arranged by individual communities (both larger as well as smaller ones), provides a cumulative picture of Mobilian Jargon's geographic distribution during its colonial and modern history with the following comparative ranges for its eastern and western varieties; see Fig. 10.1.

A bird's-eye view of Mobilian Jargon, based on a synthesis of early surveys in the eighteenth century (listed under *Larger areas* in Fig. 10.1), suggests a spread extending from colonial Georgia and northern Florida across much of colonial Louisiana and northwards along the Mississippi River to the lower Ohio and Missouri river valleys. Essentially the same geographic range for the pidgin emerges from a synthesis of the diverse historical records with sociolinguistic information on Mobilian Jargon in particular communities (listed under the headings of language families or comparable larger categories in Fig. 10.1). These boundaries also correspond remarkably well to what, around the turn of the century, James Mooney, Albert S. Gatschet, and Cyrus Thomas suggested as Mobilian Jargon's range, although without supportive documentation:

This trade jargon, based upon Choctaw, but borrowing also from all the neighboring dialects and even from the more northern Algonquian languages, was spoken and understood among all the tribes of the Gulf states, probably as far west as Matagorda bay and northward along both banks of the Mississippi to the Algonquian frontier about the entrance of the Ohio. (Mooney 1900: 187 n. 2)

The so-called Mobilian trade language was a corrupted Choctaw jargon used for the purposes of intertribal communication among all the tribes from Florida to Louisiana, extending northward on the Mississippi to about the junction of the Ohio. (Gatschet and Thomas 1907: 916)

This area was the home of several distinct language families, various distantly related and unrelated isolates, and numerous languages that until today have remained unidentified in terms of their historical affiliation. While some of the unidentified languages probably belonged to established language families, the long underestimated linguistic diversity of southeastern North America suggests others to represent unknown language families (see Sect. 2.1). Aside from these unidentified Southeastern Indian languages, the speech community of Mobilian Jargon included representatives of all the following linguistic units: the area's very own Muskogean and its distant Gulf relatives, namely the Atakapa, Chitimacha, Natchez, and Tunica; Caddoan; Siouan of the lower Mississippi River valley; Yuchi (isolate); and Lipan Apache (Athapaskan). Considering that Mobilian Jargon extended to the middle Mississippi River, the lower Ohio, and some five hundred miles up the Missouri in the eighteenth century, the pidgin probably reached also into neighboring Algonquian and northern Siouan communities, as indicated by Algonquian loan-words and Selden's vocabulary of Mobilian Jargon gathered among the Osage or Oto (Siouans).

Some suggestive, but unreliable support for Mobilian Jargon's spread farther north than is evident from historical records may derive from Muskogean-derived place names in non-Muskogean environments, mostly Algonquians and Siouans. A prime example would seem to be *Oskaloosa* in Missouri, northeastern Kansas, southeastern Iowa, and Illinois and *Oscaloosa* in Kentucky. Its source purportedly was the name of one of two wives of the Florida Seminole chief Osceola or that of the wife of the Iowa chief Mahaska or White Cloud, meaning 'black water' (Harder 1976: 440; Stewart 1970: 349; *The United States Dictionary of Places* 1988: 180), but it has also received various other, questionable translations (Rydjord 1968: 296–7). A better etymology consists of Choctaw **oski**/Chickasaw **oski**?/ Mobilian Jargon **oski**, all meaning 'reed, cane', plus Choctaw/Chickasaw/Mobilian Jargon **losa** 'black' (see Munro, forthcoming), which the inhabitants possibly adopted via Mobilian Jargon rather than calling themselves after some obscure wife of an Iowa or Seminole chief.[1]

---

[1] At best, place names provide tricky evidence for Mobilian Jargon's spread, and I consider the case of *Oskaloosa/Oscaloosa* only because of its occurrence in immediate non-Muskogean vicinities, suggesting the presence of speakers of a Muskogean language or presumably Mobilian Jargon among non-Muskogean peoples. An examination of place names within the range of Muskogean languages has offered no distinctive morphological clues that would identify some Muskogean language or Mobilian Jargon as their source. For example, the linguistic information accompanying a Chickasaw map of *c.*1723 (Waselkov 1989: 324–9, 341 n. 87) is interpretable in terms of both Western Muskogean and Mobilian Jargon, and thus is of no use in determining the latter's geographic range. Muskogean place names are also risky indicators for the one-time presence of Mobilian Jargon outside of the range of Muskogean languages, simply because names spread easily and widely beyond the range of its source language or neighboring areas. An illustrative example is the name of a major street in Honolulu, *Pensacola*, whose etymology derives from Apalachee (< Apalachee **păsak** 'hair' + **akola** 'people' (Geoffrey D. Kimball, personal communication)), Western Muskogean (<Choctaw **ippăši** 'hair

FIGURE 10.1. Comparative time ranges for eastern and western Mobilian Jargon

	1700	1750	1800	1850	1900	1950

Larger areas

Indians of Georgia and Alabama \\\\\\\\\\

Indians of the Mobile River drainage ////////////

Indians between Florida and the
  Mississippi River //////////////

Indians of Louisiana (within current
  state boundaries) /////////////////////////////////////...

Indians on the central Mississippi
  River //////

Indians on the lower Ohio River /

Indians on the Missouri River /

Indians of eastern Texas /////////////////...

Muskogeans and associates

Alabama //////////////////X/////X/////////...

Apalachee \   //

Coushatta ////X////X//////////...

Hitchiti \   \\\\\\

Mikasuki \   \\\\\\

Muskogee \\\\\\\\\\\\\\\\\\\\\\\\

Creek (i.e. Muskogee, other
  Muskogeans, and non-Muskogean
  associates) \\\\\\XXXXX\\\\\\\\\\   ...//

Seminole of Florida (i.e. Muskogee,
  Mikasuki, Hitchiti, and non-
  Muskogean associates) \....\\\\\\\\

Neighbors of the Creek (unidentified) \\\\\\\\

Chickasaw /////////XXXXX\\\\\\\   ..//

Choctaw /////XXXXXXXXXXXXX//////////...

Neighbors of the Chickasaw and
  Choctaw (Muskogeans and non-
  Muskogeans) ////////////   ..//

Speakers of Gulf isolates

Atakapa //////

Chitimacha //////

Natchez /////////X\\\\\\\\\\\\\

Tunica ///////////////////...

Caddoans

Caddo ////////////////   ..//

Natchitoches //////////////////...

Siouans

Biloxi //////////////////////////////////...

	1700	1750	1800	1850	1900	1950
Ofo	////					
Osage		/				
Speakers of other isolate languages						
Yuchi				\	\\	
Athapaskans						
Lipan Apache				/		
Linguistically unidentified groups						
Abacoche		/				
Abihka					\\	
Acolapissa	//////					
Bayogoula	/					
Blew Mouths		\				
Chakchiuma (= Houma?)		///				
Chatot (≠ Choctaw)		/				
Houma (Western Muskogean?)	/ . . .					
Koroa	/////					
Mobilians (Mobile)	//////////////////////// . . .					
Napissa	/					
Opelousa				//////. . .		
Pacana			//			
Pascagoula	//////////////////////////					
Quinipissa (= Napissa?)	/					
Taënsa	/////////////					
Talabouche (= Talapoosa?)			//			
Tapoussa (= Talapoosa?)		///				
Theloël (= Natchez?)	/					
Tioux (= Tunica?)		/				
Washa	/					
Yagenechito	/					
Yamasee	\\					
Yazoo	///					
Non-Indians						
Europeans and European Americans in general (speaking Spanish, French, English, and other European languages)		///XXXXXXXXXXXXXXXXXXXXXXXX/// . .				
French		///XXX////XX/. . .				
Acadians ("Cajuns")					. . .//. . .	
British	. . .///. . .					
Africans and African Americans		/////XX////X///////////// . . .				

Key:
\\\ eastern Mobilian Jargon ("the lingua franca Creek")
/// western Mobilian Jargon ("the Chickasaw-Choctaw trade language")
XXX Both varieties of Mobilian Jargon
. . . probably continuing from earlier times or surviving later

Mobilian Jargon's extension north along the Mississippi River and its tributaries into neighboring Siouan and Algonquian territories conceivably reflected the expansion of French and other European colonists along the Mississippi River and its tributaries during the eighteenth century. However, Fig. 10.1 reveals a more obvious development in the colonial history, the pidgin's southward push into Florida and its general westward movement across the Mississippi concomitant with the growing expansion by European colonial powers across eastern North America. Unless already spoken in central Florida or eastern Texas in early colonial times, Mobilian Jargon spread there with the dispersal of Southeastern Indians from their northern or eastern homelands in the eighteenth and nineteenth centuries.

In their sociolinguistic distribution, the eastern and western varieties of Mobilian Jargon shared a common core of the same speech communities (indicated by X in Fig. 10.1 if the two varieties overlapped in time, as they did in single instances for a period of almost 150 years from the mid-eighteenth to the late nineteenth century): Alabama, Coushatta, various Creek communities, plus Natchez as well as Choctaw and Chickasaw. On the periphery, the contact community consisted of additional languages that were only part of one or the other variety: Hitchiti, Mikasuki, Muskogee, and Yuchi in the east; Atakapa, Chitimacha, Tunica, plus Caddoan, Siouan, and apparently most unidentified languages in the west. All in all, Western Mobilian Jargon or "the Chickasaw-Choctaw trade language" extended across a wider area, and exhibited a greater internal diversity among its speakers' first languages, than the eastern variety or the lingua franca Creek. This observation suggests a correspondingly greater range of internal linguistic variation due to first-language interference in the west than in the east (see Chapter 8).

The peak periods for Mobilian Jargon in general as well as its western variety in particular were in the eighteenth century, if many of the linguistically unidentified groups presumably spoke distinct, perhaps even unrelated languages and if the speakers' sociolinguistic diversity as determined by the number of their first languages and different communities serves as a reliable indicator. By the measure of sociolinguistic diversity, the eastern variety of Mobilian Jargon or the lingua franca Creek apparently culminated in the nineteenth century; but this conclusion is less certain due to the smaller number of historical attestations and their uneven distribution, and requires better documentation. However, Mobilian Jargon declined

---

of the head,' Chickasaw **ippáši?** 'hair of the head' + Choctaw **oklah** 'people,' Chickasaw **okla** 'town' (Munro, forthcoming), or both. The Honolulu street received its name from a US warship that regularly visited the Hawaiian Islands in the nineteenth century and was christened after the city of the same name in the Florida panhandle, which in turn had been named after the Pensacola Indians (Daws 1968: 200–3; Pearce 1980: 61–4). It would obviously be ludicrous to deduce from this chain of names that Mobilian Jargon once was spoken in Honolulu.

first in eastern communities with the exception of the Seminole Indians of Florida, and survived the longest among western Southeastern Indians other than those of Oklahoma.

The vitality and wide spread of Mobilian Jargon across much of the South led many non-Indian immigrants to adopt it as the major medium in contact with native peoples. Among them were speakers of Spanish, French, French Creole, English, Black English, Creole English of the Caribbean, German, and even African languages, which added further to the area's sociolinguistic complexity. The community of non-Indian Mobilian Jargon speakers included explorers, interpreters, traders, settlers, missionaries, Indian agents, plantation owners, store clerks, and others who regularly interacted with Native Americans of the area. Among them were prominent individuals such as de Bienville, du Ru, Pénicaut, Le Page du Pratz, Adair, Woodward, Duralde, and Dresel. The pidgin may also have served as a convenient tool by which early anthropologists such as Gatschet, Mooney, and Swanton elicited information from native people by either acquiring basic conversational skills in Mobilian Jargon or employing interpreters using it.

While used extensively, Mobilian Jargon was not necessarilty known by everybody in a community or even an entire social segment of it, as was apparently the case with most women in Natchez society (see Le Page du Pratz 1758: ii. 321). On the other hand, there is no indication that the pidgin was exclusive to a particular group within a larger society. Mobilian Jargon was neither "the court language" among Louisiana Indians, if Adair misread Le Page du Pratz's account to refer to anything else than diplomatic functions; nor was it characteristic of the Stinkards among the Natchez, as Gatschet erroneously interpreted the same source (see Sect. 9.3). Among non-Indian parties on explorations or in colonial settlements, there were often only a few individuals competent in the pidgin, usually those referred to as interpreters.[2]

The use of Mobilian Jargon usually implied the presence or participation of Indians in a conversation; but it occasionally was the medium among non-Indians in interlingual encounters. In one instance, a Frenchman by the name of Antoine Bonnefoy spoke to hostile British traders in Mobilian Jargon (Mereness 1916: 254–5), for a variety of possible reasons: courtesy towards the Native Americans present, whom Bonnefoy deliberately wanted to overhear his conversation; avoidance of any appearance of deception towards the Native Americans; or, simply, lack of any other

---

[2] Michael Silverstein (1973 MS: 32–3) has interpreted Pénicaut (Margry 1876–86: v. 514) to contend that, on an expedition north of the Natchez in 1714, he was the only Frenchman who could communicate with Indians, presumably in Mobilian Jargon. In checking the original source, I have found that documentation does not support the conclusion, however reasonable, that Pénicaut was the only Frenchman capable of speaking with Indians or that he used Mobilian Jargon in this instance (see also Crawford 1978: 36–7).

common medium. According to a Coushatta consultant, Acadians ("Cajuns") and African Americans, speaking French and English, likewise resorted to Mobilian Jargon as a common medium until fairly recently.

There remains a major enigma with respect to the use of Mobilian Jargon in one major Southeastern Indian community—the Cherokee. Mooney (1900: 15, 182–3, 235) included the Cherokee within the contact community, and expected to find in Cherokee legends a "close correspondence with the myths of the Creeks and other southern tribes within the former area of the Mobilian trade language." He also derived their ethnonym, "Tsa'răgĭ' " or "Tsa'lăgĭ'," from Choctaw **choluk** or **chiluk** for 'pit' and 'cave' via the pidgin, for which there exists the corresponding word †**čolok** 'hole.' In an alternative and more convincing etymology, Swanton (1946: 217) derived the Cherokee's name from Muskogee **tciloki** 'people of a different speech,' and Munro (forthcoming) offers comparable ethnonyms for the Cherokee in several Muskogean languages: Muskogee **cala:kki**, Oklahoma Seminole **calakki**, Alabama/Koasati **calakki**, Choctaw **calakki**, and Chickasaw **calakki?**, with that in Alabama and Koasati also meaning 'gypsy.' Considering Mobilian Jargon's geographic range and functions as the area's major native lingua franca, one would indeed expect the Cherokee as a major group of Southeastern Indians and as speakers of an Iroquoian language to have used the pidgin in their communications with Muskogean and possibly other neighbors, in which case the Cherokee might have formed the northeastern boundary of Mobilian Jargon. The late Claude Medford (personal communication) even thought to have once heard the pidgin among Iroquois in upstate New York. This assertion is all the more startling, for Medford, who had a rich knowledge of various Indian communities in eastern North America and who was the first to alert Haas and Crawford to the survival of Mobilian Jargon (when already long thought extinct), was hardly subject to fancy. Yet, there has emerged no reliable historical, ethnographic, or linguistic documentation for Mobilian Jargon among the Cherokee or—for that matter—other Iroquoians until today. Attestations for the pidgin are even missing for western Cherokee who had extended interactions with Louisiana Indians in yearly hunting expeditions across the Mississippi as early as the second half of the eighteenth century, in trade relations with the Spaniards at New Orleans and Pensacola, and in relocations to northeastern Texas, former Osage territory in Arkansas, and eventually eastern Oklahoma in the early nineteenth century (see Everett 1990; Raymond D. Fogelson in Sturtevant 1962: 54; Thornton 1990; 43–4, 58–63, 83–7). Indicative is also the fact that Cherokee exhibits comparatively few loan-words of Muskogean origin (see Ballard 1983; 328, 332–3; Gatschet 1969 [1888]: 191–2) and even fewer with corresponding forms in Mobilian Jargon (see Sect. 12.3); while such need not presume Mobilian Jargon as their medium of transmission, their absence conforms with the absence of known historical attestations for Mobilian Jargon among the Cherokee or other Iroquoians.

Indications for the absence of Mobilian Jargon in other communities are of interest inasmuch as they help define its geographic boundaries. With but skimpy evidence for Mobilian Jargon on the Texas Gulf coast, the French document attesting an unidentified Indian at Matagorda Bay in 1745 who did not know the pidgin (de Villiers du Terrage and Rivet 1914–1919: 413) would fix the pidgin's western border in eastern Texas for early colonial periods before eastern groups immigrated. Nor are there any clues beyond incidental historical and oral references that Mobilian Jargon was in regular use among the Five Civilized Tribes (including the Cherokee, the Chickasaw, the Choctaw, the Creek, the Seminole) or by their associates (such as Alabama, Coushatta, and Natchez Indians) in Oklahoma in modern times. Similarly, the pidgin was apparently absent in the recent past of Southeastern Indians east of Louisiana such as the Alabama Creek, the Mississippi Choctaw, and other smaller native communities. The absence of Mobilian Jargon in these cases may simply be due to the rapid decline of truly multilingual communities, consisting of several native and immigrant languages. Ultimately, the lack of information does not constitute absolute negative evidence, as Crawford (1978: 21) already observed for Mobilian Jargon, and presents a weak case, even with complementary information and in consideration of the broader historical context.

10.2. Communicative Functions

The great linguistic diversity of indigenous southeastern North America, enhanced by an alloglossic immigrant population in early colonial times, provided the sociolinguistic context within which Mobilian Jargon functioned as a major lingua franca in the area. The pidgin thus served as a convenient interlingual medium both among native peoples and with colonial immigrants, as early observers already recognized when comparing it to the medieval lingua franca Sabir in the Mediterranean or Latin in Europe.

As a regional contact language, Mobilian Jargon operated as a major medium of translation in interlingual encounters, in which those who spoke it became interpreters for those who did not—a majority of Europeans, African dependants, and other immigrants in colonial times. To develop a body of skilled translators, the French placed cabin boys, government cadets, soldiers, and officers in Indian villages beginning with their earliest explorations of Louisiana around 1700 so that they might learn "the Indian language," usually Mobilian Jargon. Crawford (1978: 12–13) described this usage as follows:

The practice of placing French boys in the Indian villages to learn the native languages began within a few months after the first contacts were made with the Indians at Biloxi. The usefulness of these boys in the Indian villages, who at first were cabin boys from the ships, as interpreters for French officers and others in dealing with the Indians was such that Iberville requested the minister of the marine, Count de Pontchartrain, to permit him to take ten boys with him on his third voyage to Louisiana. Later on, Bienville chose intelligent men for this purpose from among the young cadets of the government. The cadets who maintained good conduct and progressed in learning the languages of the Indians with whom they lived were assured of advancement in the government. It was not only cabin boys and cadets who learned to speak the Indian languages, however; in addition, Bienville, several officers and men of the garrison became proficient in some of the languages. The most convenient circumstances for acquiring the native languages were those occasions when the food supplies of the garrison were low and when many officers and men, leaving a few to guard the fort, scattered themselves among the Indian villages to live with the Indians and to share their food, until the next ships arrived. These periods of living with the Indians often lasted several months.

On the basis of early references to interpreters, Crawford surmised that the French had acquired the native languages of various indigenous groups, which he took as evidence against the existence of a lingua franca in his discussion of the pidgin's origin (Crawford 1978: 21–9). Yet because Mobilian Jargon did not necessarily extend to every member in a particular community, even under the most ideal circumstances, there is no need to assume any contradiction or inconsistency between Mobilian Jargon's functions as a lingua franca and as a medium of interpretation, as Crawford (1978: 34, 47–50) recognized elsewhere. What he identified as native languages was, in most instances, solely Mobilian Jargon with different names (see Crawford 1978: 30–8).

There are several considerations in support of this conclusion. A residency of several months simply was not long enough for boys, much less adult men, to acquire proficiency in a native language, fundamentally different in its grammar from French. A longer stay in an Indian community, allowing youngsters to become competent in a native language, was not feasible. Such a change in residence with an interrupted exposure to French would have jeopardized not only their competency in the first language, but also their identity as French and their loyalty to the French government, both fundamental for their future role as interpreters and spies. However, short residencies among native peoples allowed French boys and men to learn Mobilian Jargon and to gain sufficient fluency in it to hold basic conversations with them. Even if French interpreters eventually began learning and using the first language of a native community, they continued to depend and rely on Mobilian Jargon with other native groups and in multilingual situations.

This very situation applied to Jean Baptiste Le Moyne, Sieur de Bienville, who had supposedly learned "Bayogoula" from his native guide within less than six weeks and who served as interpreter for his brother Pierre Le Moyne, Sieur d'Iberville, on their explorations as early as 1699. "Bayogoula" allowed de Bienville to talk to the Bayogoula plus other, linguistically diverse groups—the Houma, the Theloël [= Natchez?], the Taënsa, the Koroa, the Chickasaw, the Napissa, the Washa, the Chitimacha, the Yagenechito, the Biloxi, the Pascagoula, the Acolapissa, the Choctaw, the Natchez, and apparently three unidentified communities (see Margry 1876–1886: iv. 167, 184, 412). What Crawford (1978: 12, 32–3) interpreted to be Bayogoula proper actually was Mobilian Jargon, with "Bayogoula" serving as no more than just another name for the pidgin (see Margry 1876–1886: iv. 422). Indications for Mobilian Jargon's twofold function as lingua franca and medium of interpretation further emerge from later documents of colonial Louisiana such as those of the Mississippi Provincial Archives of the 1730s (Rowland and Sanders 1927), which make frequent references to interpreters for a period when the French already used Mobilian Jargon widely. Interpreters at Indian posts used it in several tasks: diplomatic missions, negotiations, presentation of speeches on behalf of French officials, intelligence gathering (spying), military preparations for native allies, and trading (Galloway 1987).

Historical and ethnographic records attest the use of Mobilian Jargon in a variety of sociocultural contexts.

For one, Mobilian Jargon was the language of voyages, in which Southeastern and other Indians engaged enthusiastically and over great distances, often several hundred miles and even farther than a thousand. Native people travelled by using both land trails and natural waterways, including the Mississippi, its tributaries, and other major streams and rivers, and did so for various purposes: foraging and hunting expeditions; visits to friendly associates; trips to intertribal ballgames, dances, and seasonal gatherings; diplomatic missions; war raids; and other ventures. As suggested by "Chickasaw-Choctaw trade language" and related descriptions including "trade," Mobilian Jargon was also the medium of regional exchange among Indians of greater Louisiana and their neighbors, Indians and non-Indians alike. Neither travel over great distances nor interregional trade was a colonial phenomenon; both had already occurred in pre-Columbian times, and had extended from the Gulf Coast to the Great Lakes and from the Atlantic Coast to the Rocky Mountains (Tanner 1989). Before the arrival of Europeans, Southeastern Indians participated in an extensive trade of both exotic natural resources (such as salt, various rocks and minerals, copper, sea shells, and pearls) and manufactured products (especially ornaments and prestige goods, including shell beads, long-nose god maskettes, copper

plates, and non-functional stone-ax heads) in an exchange network covering much of eastern North America (Brown, Kerber, and Winters 1990).
Drawing on this indigenous infrastructure, Southeastern Indians and Europeans of colonial times developed a thriving trade in domestic and imported
goods, which included deer skins and furs, guns and tools, and ornaments
among many other commodities (see e.g. Waselkov 1989). Mobilian Jargon
was at the very heartland of this extensive network of land and water routes
across eastern and central North America (see Tanner 1989: 8).

In another function, Mobilian Jargon was "the public and diplomatic
language" among the Indians of "western Florida" or Louisiana (Robin
1807: 55). It was frequently used in hostile as in peaceful encounters, including extensive negotiations (see Mereness 1916: 85: 254–5; Pease and
Jenison 1940: 756, 759). The pidgin also functioned as a quasi-official lingua
franca in multilingual political alliances, including the Creek Confederacy,
other pantribal associations among Southeastern Indians, plus numerous
twin and multiple towns related by kinship at the clan moiety level and
across language boundaries (see Knight 1990; Willis 1980). With increasing
encroachments and the westward push by Europeans and their American
descendants, many Southeastern Indians found refuge with relatives and
former allies farther west, especially in Louisiana—with the result of per-
petuating the institution of multilingual intertribal communities through
the nineteenth and into the twentieth century (see Drechsel and Makuakāne 1982*b*; Kniffen, Gregory, and Stokes 1987; 83–105). Thus, Mobilian
Jargon was never limited to interactions between Indians and non-Indians,
but functioned throughout recorded history as an established medium
among Southeastern Indians, who rarely dwelt in a monolingual environment outside of their immediate kin group.

One of Mobilian Jargon's many names, **yoka anõpa** 'slave/servant
language,' indicates that it functioned as a lingua franca in bondage—that is
between masters and vassals or servants and probably among the latter if
they spoke different languages. In one instance, the anonymous author of the
Essai (1862 MS: 12–13 n. 4) described a specific situation involving the use
of Mobilian Jargon in servitude, in which a Native American man
reproached a woman of his community for submitting to slavery (for details,
see Sect. 7.3). In another case, the pidgin was the language of convention for
the former master of Le Page du Pratz's female Chitimacha slave, acting as
interpreter when at first Le Page du Pratz could communicate
with the woman only by signs (Le Page du Pratz 1758: i. 82–3, 85–6). Both
situations   involved   Native   American   slaves   and   European   or
European–American masters; but Mobilian Jargon undoubtedly was the
primary medium between Native American masters and African slaves as
well. In a practice inspired by European colonists, Native Americans
acquired African slaves on raiding parties of European settlements and by

purchase; other Africans ran away from their European masters in search of greater freedom and a better life among Native Americans, who often conferred to their wards considerable liberties, at times even positions of influence and leadership, as was the case among the Seminole in particular (see Foster 1935; McLoughlin 1974; Porter 1971: 42–71, 154–358; Willis 1971 [1963]). The Southeast became the only area north of Mexico where Native Americans and Africans intermingled in substantial numbers, although Europeans and their American descendants pursued a firm policy of *divide et impera* towards Native Americans and Africans in constant fear of a joint uprising. During their residence among Southeastern Indians, Africans usually acquired either the language of their masters or hosts in some form or Mobilian Jargon, an experience that made them skilful interpreters engaged even by European and American colonists (see e.g. Adair 1968 [1775]: 327; Pease and Jenison 1940: 756; Woodward 1939 [1859]: 108). As **yoka anõpa**, Mobilian Jargon also continued in the native tradition of aboriginal bondage, which Southeastern Indians had practiced with war captives of hostile tribes—with the difference that these vassals, if not killed, played the role of pets rather than of servants or hard laborers. However, at no time are there any indications for the pidgin to have been exclusive to subordinates or Stinkards, as erroneously claimed by Gatschet (1969 [1884]: 39).

In addition to travel, trade, diplomacy, and bondage, there were other occasions for intertribal and interethnic encounters and thus for the use of the pidgin: games, gambling, dances, and ritual gatherings. In the midnineteenth century, the anonymous author of the *Essai sur quelques usages et sur l'idiôme des Indiens de la Basse Louisiane* (1862 MS: 8, 13–14) described a stickball game including betting in which Choctaw and Alabama engaged and evidently used Mobilian Jargon. Tunica-Biloxi Indians near Marksville in central Louisiana and Coushatta farther south similarly remembered intertribal dances back in the 1920s and 1940s respectively (for details including a song in Mobilian Jargon, see (60) in Sect. 7.3). On such occasions, Mobilian Jargon took on religious functions according to the late part-Choctaw basket maker Claude Medford, who repeatedly indicated that the pidgin tied into traditional medicine and religion (Medford, personal communications). Native medicine men and women, frequently operating on a pan-tribal basis and travelling from one Indian community to another as late as the early twentieth century, were said to employ Mobilian Jargon as a special medium in their functions, just as one of its last truly fluent speakers, Arzelie Langley, did (Kniffen, Gregory, and Stokes 1987: 268; see also Langley's account in (58) in Sect. 7.3). Further clues for this suggestion occur in incidental historical references to the pidgin's use by religious leaders such as the superior of the Natchez temple guards (see Le Page du Pratz 1758: ii. 326). Any such ritualistic usage of Mobilian Jargon would suggest a non-utilitarian significance not usually associated with a contact medium; but until today, details on this subject have been difficult to obtain, probably because of its rather sensitive nature.

As part of a regional infrastructure, Mobilian Jargon was a convenient vehicle by which Europeans and their American successors not only established contact with native peoples, but maintained relations with them. In examining Indian–French relations, Andrew C. Albrecht (1946: 332) attributed the success of *coureurs de bois* or independent traders among Native Americans of the lower Mississippi valley directly to their knowledge of Mobilian Jargon. Christian missionaries similarly made use of the pidgin in their attempts at converting Native Americans. Around 1908, a congregational minister by the name of Paul Leeds apparently employed Mobilian Jargon in his proselytizing efforts among Coushatta and Choctaw near Kinder and Elton in southwestern Louisiana, as suggested by an entry in his diary where he misidentified the pidgin as "Koasati" (Johnson and Leeds 1964: 24, 25). Mobilian Jargon had moreover been the medium of conversations on religion, teachings of the catechism, and probably sermons by the French Jesuit priest Paul du Ru (1934 [1700]: 32, 48, 56) among Louisiana Indians two centuries earlier. Unfortunately, no prayer or song book, much less a book of the Bible, has come forth in translation to leave details about the pidgin's role in Christian proselytizing.

Mobilian Jargon might be heard in still other contexts. An African–American neighbor of the Coushatta remembered how his grandfather, following the tradition of other African–American interpreters, had used the pidgin with Indians in translating and writing letters in French or English on their behalf. A German American recounted how his father and uncle often relied on Mobilian Jargon when they defended Coushatta Indians in court and needed to translate on their behalf. Until at least the 1940s, the pidgin further served as an appropriate medium for many Louisiana Indians when they found employment outside their communities in various occupations—as scouts, trappers, fishermen, share-croppers, homesteaders, farm laborers, timbermen, offshore workers in the oil industry, domestic servants, or guides to hunters and anglers in the swamps and bayous.

The pidgin was not limited to the "public" domain, and was used in Native Americans' homes as well. The widely respected medicine woman of Choctaw ancestry, Arzelie Langley, used Mobilian Jargon in treating people, who would visit her at home and included members of her own community (Coushatta and Choctaw near Elton), non-Indian neighbors, and residents from other native communities, at times as far away as Oklahoma. Her grandson Ernest Sickey (personal communication) remembered a ritualized use of Mobilian Jargon even among kin and friends, who had employed it as a medium of greetings, introduction, friendly teasing, and joking before switching into Koasati, Choctaw, or perhaps even French.

The pidgin specifically served as a convenient means of communication in intertribal families. Evidence for this function derives from several unmistakable Mobilian Jargon words and phrases (with focus on the semantic domains of home and kin) that Swanton (1911: 31–2) recorded in 1908 from a man of Pascagoula and Biloxi descent near Livingston, Texas. Because his parents had probably spoken mutually unintelligible languages (with Pascagoula remaining unidentified and Biloxi classified as Siouan), we can infer with reasonable certainty that the spouses had spoken Mobilian Jargon with each other. Another indication for its role as a home language derives from the fact that almost all of its last Native American speakers came from intertribal families. Until recently, Mobilian Jargon may similarly have been in use in interethnic homes in which at least one partner was a Native American and still spoke his or her native language. Yet there are no indications for the creolization of Mobilian Jargon; apparently, children first acquired their parents' native language(s), French, and/or English, as the Pascagoula-Biloxi man had done.

Mobilian Jargon exhibited functional pervasiveness in all kinds of sociolinguistic contexts. This observation, together with the pidgin's linguistic characteristics (including a stable grammar and a large lexicon), points to a well-established contact medium that could serve in practically any bilingual or multilingual circumstances and with few if any restrictions on subject matter, as already suggested by du Ru (1700 MS: 46, 1934 [1700]: 32) and Le Page du Pratz (1758: ii. 321–2). The pidgin's recorded history of at least two and a half centuries, its extensive geographic range, as well as the prominence of Muskogean and other Native American elements (in contrast to just a few European loan-words) further indicate a truly indigenous institution of considerable age. These very characteristics made Mobilian Jargon a convenient medium for European newcomers and colonists, their African attendants, and eventually their American creole descendants in their interactions with Southeastern Indians. That there remain few detailed historical descriptions of Mobilian Jargon used exclusively among Native Americans is due to the fact that the authors of relevant historical documents were all Europeans or Americans of European ancestry. Few newcomers other than Le Page du Pratz with a comparative knowledge of the pidgin, Chitimacha, and Natchez possessed the necessary sociolinguistic breadth and empathy to grasp the true role of Mobilian Jargon. A full understanding of the pidgin's functions in traditional native societies can come only from a detailed firsthand account by a Southeastern Indian who not only possessed a knowledge of several native languages in addition to that of Mobilian Jargon, but had learned to write. Such a document still awaits discovery. Under these circumstances, it is perfectly understandable, if perhaps ironic, that it took a Native American, Claude Medford, to recognize Mobilian Jargon's persistence well into the twentieth century and to alert American linguists of its survival.

10.3. Meta-Communicative Functions

The recognition of Mobilian Jargon's communicative functions and especially the fact that, until a few decades ago, non-Indians took pains to learn it as well, comes close to acknowledging a larger role of the Indians in the history of the South. Native peoples have indeed been of greater importance economically and sociopolitically than commonly recognized hitherto. Not only did Indians assist Europeans in "exploring" and, inadvertently, in colonizing the South with their knowledge of the environment, adaptive forms of subsistence, and other skills and expertise; but during the colonial period, they also proved important associates of one or the other European power, usually in alliance against a competing one (as in the case of the Choctaw, who joined the French against the British and their Chickasaw allies). Native peoples further played a key role in the fur and hide trade, and non-Indians early came to appreciate other goods of theirs, ranging from the spice of sassafras (*filé*) for gumbo and other dishes to herbs for medicine, from dug-out boats to basketry. Southern Indians have continued providing invaluable services to the larger community, especially on the farm as well as in the timber and oil industries (see Kniffen, Gregory, and Stokes 1987). One farmer of Elton appreciated the nearby Coushatta Indians as the best and most reliable field laborers he had ever employed.[3]

To interpret Mobilian Jargon as a straight reflection of the Indians' influence or social position in modern Louisiana and neighboring states would, however, be at odds with the area's sociolinguistic and political realities. In particular, there are several, albeit interrelated considerations to keep in mind:

(*a*) At the latest beginning with the late colonial period or American rule, Southern Indians have been a small minority in a society controlled by immigrants speaking European languages. The native population has not exerted any sociopolitical or economic control in the area for almost two centuries, if not longer.

(*b*) There has existed widespread racism, latent and open, by the European–American majority towards the native population. The former has consistently withheld equal rights from the latter, and has even denied their status as Native Americans by regarding them as "colored," formerly

---

[3] Much of the discussion in the current section previously appeared in an essay in honor of the late creolist John E. Reinecke (Drechsel 1987*b*).

subject to slavery, in spite of obvious phenotypical, sociocultural, and linguistic differences from their African–American neighbors.

(*c*) All of the last speakers of Mobilian Jargon were at least bilinguals, and many of the Indians were true multilinguals with fluency in three, four, or even more languages. While the European and African Americans among them usually spoke local varieties of French and English as their first languages, the Indians were competent in Choctaw, Koasati, and/or Alabama plus at least French or English, frequently both. By all available indications, such bilingual and multilingual skills were not a recent phenomenon among Southern Indians that one might presume to have increased with the decline of Mobilian Jargon; rather, the ability to speak more than one native language and perhaps a European one has had a long history among Indians of greater Louisiana (as indicated throughout the historical documentation of Mobilian Jargon) just as among the Creek, their associates and neighbors (see e.g. Miller 1978: 613–14, Sherzer 1976: 253). Mobilian Jargon existed side by side with native bilingualism and multilingualism.[4]

(*d*) A life history of at least 250 years appears unusually long for a contact medium—that is a second and auxiliary language—and especially for a non-European pidgin in rapidly changing sociohistorical circumstances with growing and dominant European–American influences that also affected Southeastern Indians. This point gains significance in light of the fact that even so perceptive an observer of Louisiana Indians and Mobilian Jargon as Antoine Simon Le Page du Pratz (1758: ii. 323) predicted its declining importance and, by implication, its obsolescence two centuries before its actual demise.

Any one of these factors could thus cast doubt on Mobilian Jargon's chances for survival into the first half of the twentieth century; in combination, they would make it even less likely. To explain the pidgin's longevity depends on a consideration of other than purely communicative roles or so-called *meta-communicative functions*, although such would appear outright contradictory to the nature of a contact medium.

Meta-communicative functions of language occur, for instance, in phatic communion, in which the participants converse with each other for the primary purpose of being sociable and keeping their channels of communication open, as in chit-chat and gossip (Malinowski 1936: 314–15).

---

[4] The former Creek agent and Louisiana settler, Thomas S. Woodward, who reported about Mobilian Jargon, also recognized special foreign-language learning skills among the Indians: 'Indians in almost every instance learn our language quicker than we learn theirs, particularly our pronunciation. An Indian, if he speaks our language at all, almost invariably pronounces it as those do from whom he learns it. If he learns it from a white man that speaks it well, the Indian does the same; if he learns it from a negro he pronounces as the negro does. You may take the best educated European that lives, that does not speak our language, and an Indian that does not speak it; let both learn it; if the Indian does not learn so much, he will always speak what he does learn more distinctly than the European' (Woodward 1939 [1859]: 21).

Whether and to what extent Mobilian Jargon served purposes of phatic communion is difficult to determine today. Le Page du Pratz's observations on the carefully orchestrated speech behavior of Louisiana Indians—rules about one person speaking at a time in contrast to the "unruly" simultaneous conversations by the French "like a flock of geese" (Le Page du Pratz 1758: iii. 8)—speak against such a meta-communicative function, as would my own experiences of contrived conversations by Louisiana Indians. On the other hand, chit-chat and phatic communion seemed perfectly possible in Mobilian Jargon, as judged by the opinion of its last speakers.

Ethnographic and ethnohistorical evidence exists for other meta-communicative functions of the pidgin. When continuing Crawford's research in the field, I encountered little difficulty in learning (about) Mobilian Jargon, and found almost all of its last speakers readily willing to assist me in my research in otherwise quite closed native communities. Except for two or three persons reportedly once competent in the pidgin, all consultants took pleasure in recalling the pidgin, instructing me in it, and providing me with such related ethnographic or historical information as they could still remember. With all my anthropological curiosity and inquisitiveness about Mobilian Jargon, I did not receive any indication that I was invading the private spheres of these former speakers. Not only had the pidgin once been the appropriate medium between Louisiana Indians and outsiders such as myself, but addressing former speakers in a sentence or two of Mobilian Jargon helped to break the ice in initial contacts and to clarify the intention of my research subject. Some even expressed pleasant surprise and curiosity about where I had learned to speak "Indian" (see Sect. 3.2). Yet the same individuals turned visibly reluctant to co-operate when I inquired about their native languages or other traditions.

My experience was by no means unique. A few years earlier, Arzelie Langley had generously shared her knowledge of Mobilian Jargon with Crawford, but was not willing to teach him Choctaw. Lifelong African–American and European–American neighbors of the Coushatta, among them even speakers of Mobilian Jargon, lacked any true understanding of its structural-functional relationship to the Indians' native languages or even an awareness of their existence. Some of these individuals claimed to have once known everything that there was for them to learn about their Indian neighbors, including their "language" (used in the singular and referring to Mobilian Jargon). The same individuals also expressed doubt when told of their neighbors' true sociolinguistic complexities, and dismissed my claims to additional native languages (Choctaw, Koasati, and Alabama) as fancy.

The experiences of modern non-Indians with Mobilian Jargon closely match attestations concerning the pidgin's use in historical documents. Around the turn of the century, an American trader who spoke Mobilian

Jargon could not communicate with the 6-year-old missionary daughter Dorothy Chambers, who as a child was privileged to acquire Alabama or Koasati in the intimacy of the Indians' homes (see Rothe 1963: 96). Linguistic reticence about one's native language may be the explanation of why, in the mid-nineteenth century, an Indian of Avoyelles Parish addressed a woman of his community in Mobilian Jargon rather than their first language (Anonymous 1862 MS: 12–13 n. 4). For the same reason, Martin Duralde, Commandant of the former Atacapas Post near present-day Opelousas in 1802, reported that Mobilian Jargon was the preferred medium of Opelousa and Coushatta Indians in communication with colonists, and expressed uncertainty about identifying the native languages of southcentral Louisiana (Duralde 1802 MS: 2). Many other observers—including the trader James Adair, the anonymous author of the *Essai*, the congregational minister Paul Leeds, and even the anthropologists Albert S. Gatschet and John R. Swanton—missed understanding the sociolinguistic complexities of Southeastern Indians in full or in part, because they lacked a comparative knowledge of the Indians' primary languages and the pidgin (for details, see Sect. 9.3). In this light, it is no longer a surprise that, in examining the anonymous author's *Essai*, William A. Read (1940) similarly failed to recognize its subject matter as Mobilian Jargon instead of Choctaw.[5]

The same sociolinguistic situation once applied to the eastern variety of Mobilian Jargon or the lingua franca Creek in Florida according to the following observation by William C. Sturtevant (1971: 112):

An occasional attentive observer recognized that the Seminole spoke Muskogee or "Creek" ... But hardly any outsider was aware until well into the twentieth century that another language was also spoken—when in fact, some two-thirds of the Florida Indians speak the dialect of Hitchiti, which, by a transferral of the Oklahoma terminology, has been called "Mikasuki" in English since about 1920 ... Even [Clay] MacCauley, the first ethnographer of the Florida Seminole, did not discover this; his Mikasuki linguistic and ethnographic informant gave him only Muskogee forms.

In this case, "Creek" was not standard Muskogee, but what Sturtevant described in the same passage as an "incipient jargon" with a predominant Muskogee vocabulary in use between Indians and non-Indians until around 1920. A majority of these Indians were native speakers of Mikasuki rather than mutually unintelligible, albeit related Muskogee.

Indians of Louisiana, eastern Texas, and Florida have traditionally been protective and private, at times even secretive, regarding their heritage; they

---

[5] Documented misidentifications in the reverse direction, that of Choctaw or some other Southeastern Indian language with Mobilian Jargon, occurred to my knowledge in only one instance, Albert Gallatin's *A Synopsis of the Indian Tribes within the United States East of the Rocky Mountains* (1973 [1836]: 100–1). This case was obviously due to his limited knowledge of both Choctaw and Mobilian Jargon.

have regularly withheld opportunities for non-Indian outsiders to learn their native languages since at least the early nineteenth century, if not earlier, and put Mobilian Jargon in front as if they went into hiding behind it. Southeastern Indians later adopted fewer Europeans or American descendants into their communities, as judged by the number and quality of historical accounts of life among them. Only rarely did they open up their communities to non-Indians, as they had done in the case of empathetic settlers like Le Page du Pratz in the early eighteenth century and did again with the young girl Dorothy Chambers and persistent linguists such as Mary R. Haas and Morris Swadesh. As recently as 1989, a middle-aged Coushatta of a former Mobilian Jargon-speaking family, who successfully related to the larger non-Indian society, frowned upon any extrovert behavior by members of his community such as even that of increasingly popular imitations of Plains Indian dancing at powwows. Under these circumstances, it is perhaps no accident that, until recently, only a few systematic grammars or full ethnographies were available for Southeastern Indians. Moreover, this observation raises the question of whether linguistic reticence towards outsiders by Southeastern Indians explains another, older sociolinguistic phenomenon—the small number of loan-words among native languages of the area (see Sect. 12.3).

As a rationale for their linguistic restraint towards outsiders and their insistence on Mobilian Jargon, Louisiana Indians simply argued that their languages were too diffcicult for non-Indians to learn; African and European Americans with some Native American ancestry believed that they had learned "the Indian language" or Mobilian Jargon more easily and better than people without any Indian heritage. The Indians' linguistic reticence has yet another explanation in recent history, and directly reflects their geographic and social withdrawal into marginal and inaccessible areas such as dense forests, bayou country, and swamp lands after the Louisiana Purchase in 1803. When at the time the United States acquired vast territories west of the Mississippi River, they increasingly pushed eastern Indians farther west into Louisiana and beyond, with their displacement culminating in the Removal of the Five Civilized Tribes (Cherokee, Chickasaw, Choctaw, Creek, and Seminole) to the Indian Territory (now Oklahoma). Under the continued threat of removal and the official American policy of lumping all non-white groups into one and the same category of "colored people" irrespective of their actual ethnic identity, remaining Southeastern Indians hid in the wilds of the South ranging from Florida to eastern Texas, and thus escaped deportation and renewed slavery (see Perdue 1988; Williams 1979). The experience of Louisiana Indians in the nineteenth century closely resembles that of Creek Indians of diverse linguistic backgrounds who withdrew into the swamps of Florida and came to be appropriately known by the collective name of Seminoles (< Muskogee

simanóli ~ **simalóni** < Spanish *cimarrón* 'wild, runaway'; for historical discussions, see Drechsel and Makuakāne 1982*b* and Sturtevant 1971).

In this sociohistorical context, Mobilian Jargon took on at least three
meta-communicative functions other than possibly that of phatic communion: (1) a medium of social equality in pan-tribal, multilingual communities: (2) a sociolinguistic marker of identity for Louisiana and other
Southern Indians: and (3) a linguistic and sociocultural buffer against undue
outside influences on native societies.

As a linguistic compromise of Muskogean and possibly other Southeastern Indian languages, Mobilian Jargon was a socially acceptable intertribal
medium in multilingual native communities ("twin or multiple towns"),
as have existed throughout the South in post-Columbian periods, in part
as a result of European–American encroachments (see Willis 1980). As
"nobody's language" reflecting influences from a variety of languages, the
pidgin avoided obvious linguistic preference, and thus social dominance, of
one native group over another in bilingual and multilingual situations;
Mobilian Jargon as a comparatively impartial medium provided a balance
in the rapidly changing social relationships among diverse native communities and their non-Indian neighbors.

Mobilian Jargon further helped to assure the identity of Louisiana
and other Southern Indians as native peoples—in contrast to the predominant perception of them as "colored" by many Southerners of European
ancestry. Linguistic evidence, even in the form of a second language such
as Mobilian Jargon, has left less doubt about the Indians' true identity
among their non-Indian neighbors than other traditions of theirs. Some
older Louisiana Indians recollected that generations ago community elders
had saved themselves from bondage by demonstrating fluency in Mobilian
Jargon.

At the same time that it functioned as a contact medium, Mobilian Jargon
also served as a linguistic and sociocultural buffer, even barrier, against
unwelcome European–American intrusions. By using an indigenous
medium, Louisiana and other Southern Indians—intentionally or
inadvertently—led outsiders such as traders, settlers, missionaries, teachers,
government officials, and even anthropologists to believe that they spoke
"*the* Indian language" of the area, and provided them with limited access
to their native societies. Yet as a secondary medium, Mobilian Jargon
restricted a stranger's exposure to the Indians' native languages, and
deflected attention from their societies by maintaining an air of mystique,
even secrecy, about them. Without access to the Indians' primary languages,
even the most linguistically adept missionary, teacher, or government official could gain no more than a limited understanding of their societies, much
less exert any substantial influence on them. Acting as a shield, Mobilian
Jargon thus interposed social distance to non-Indians, and reconfirmed

ethnic boundaries and the identity of Southern Indians. In protecting native communities from undue outside incursions, the pidgin helped to preserve their privacy and their cultural integrity, and provided some resilience in the survival of their traditions, including indigenous languages, just as these contributed to Mobilian Jargon's persistence.

10.4. *Attitudes towards Mobilian Jargon*

If few non-Indians ever learned about the sociolinguistic diversity of South-eastern Indians and, with it, the structural-functional differences between Mobilian Jargon and its source languages, the missing awareness was perhaps a blessing in disguise. With attention on Mobilian Jargon as either the principal language of Southeastern Indians or "the Indian language" of Louisiana, Europeans and their American descendants accepted the pidgin as they rarely approved other native languages in the area. Neither the last non-Indian speakers nor early observers showed a negative set of mind with regard to Mobilian Jargon. Even the first reliable attestation of Mobilian Jargon by the Jesuit Paul du Ru, who found it "rather meagre" (du Ru 1934 [1700]: 8), made no further negative comment about it, and demonstrated the feasibility of a conversation on an abstract topic such as a supernatural theme with the Houma councilman's utterance.

With a true understanding of Mobilian Jargon's role, European observers might have been less sympathetic, as they in fact were in the case of the so-called American Indian Pidgin English (see Sect. 2.3). The first non-Indian with a deeper understanding of the sociolinguistic complexities of greater Louisiana, Le Page du Pratz (1758: ii. 218–19, 242), described Mobilian Jargon in comparative terms as 'the Chickasaw language, although a bit corrupted' and 'the common language,' often interpreted as "broken Chickasaw (or Choctaw)." Le Page du Pratz also used the French term *vulgaire*, not in the sense of 'vulgar' or 'plebeian,' but simply as 'common' and possibly in contrast to the written word (*la langue écrite*), without discernible negative connotations. Apparently, he intended his observation of "ceux qui la parlent le mieux s'en font gloire" (Le Page du Pratz 1758: ii. 218) or 'those who speak it the best pride themselves on it' to apply to Mobilian Jargon rather than just Chickasaw proper.

Recent Native American speakers, who had a comparative understanding of Mobilian Jargon in relation to their native languages, betrayed no aversion or other negative disposition towards the pidgin because of its linguistic form or functions. Some Coushatta perceptively characterized Mobilian Jargon as a "mixed" language with elements of Choctaw, Koasati, Alabama, and perhaps a few single European words, but revealed no objection to it. Similarly, Louisiana Choctaw who simply called it a "broken or short-way Choctaw" did not consider it an "adulterated" or substandard version of their own language, but accepted it as a legitimate medium for interactions with outsiders, and had apparently used it without any reservation. The best supportive clue comes from the fact that Louisiana Choctaw Indians, whose language served as a major linguistic source for Mobilian Jargon and who were among its last fluent speakers, had themselves adopted it in their encounters with speakers of other languages; in other words, they did not respond in Choctaw, as we might have expected them to do if they stigmatized the pidgin based on their language.

Another indication of Mobilian Jargon's full acceptance derives from one of its many names, **anōpa ēla** 'other/different/strange language,' by which Louisiana Choctaw recognized its distinctness. In the minds of Tunica-Biloxi who could still remember some Mobilian Jargon, it was nobody's language and as such a neutral medium. Songs including ethnic allusions, performed at intertribal dances and games near Marksville (see Sect. 7.3), supposedly lost much of their biting sarcasm in Mobilian Jargon, and did not offend the dignity of either the performer(s) or the audience (Claude Medford, personal communication). The same inference possibly applied to offensive and vulgar language as documented for a European–American speaker (see (59) in Sect. 7.3).

Beyond such detached or even nonchalant attitudes, several former speakers, Indian and non-Indian alike, remembered Mobilian Jargon quite fondly as a most practical medium and "a handy language;" they expressed pride in their former ability to communicate with alloglossic Indians over a vast region. According to former Indian speakers, Mobilian Jargon had come about as a result of contact among native peoples speaking mutually unintelligible languages and requiring a common medium in their regular interactions. In recalling Mobilian Jargon, Indians displayed no embarrassment, but felt quite at ease, laughed a lot, and even found parts comical, whether because of its former association with joke songs, slightly unnatural and uncomfortable speech situations of its use at the time, or my stumbling attempts at speaking it. Ernest Sickey (personal communication), a multilingual who had spoken some Mobilian Jargon as a child, even recalled it with affection in an uncharacteristically emotional tone of voice. The pidgin was a "warm and personal" language used with relatives and friends, and it expressed endearment and respect. Even the ritualized use of Mobilian Jargon in teasing and joking with relatives and friends never intimated a loss of courtesy, but simply entailed a different kind of thinking, and had taken on almost an aura of sacredness for Sickey. Analogously, Medford (personal communication) suggested, on the basis of his extensive consultations with elders in various traditional Indian communities of the eastern United States, that speaking Mobilian Jargon had demanded a positive disposition and carried prestige, that once it had even been the privilege of the élite in traditional Southeastern Indian societies. In support of his proposition, Medford referred to another common name of Mobilian Jargon among the Alabama and Coushatta, **yam(m)a** 'yes, right, alright, indeed.' He thought this word reflected the positive attitudes expected of political and other leaders in their interactions with neighboring tribes and allies, as appears evident from the frequent use of **ačokma** 'good' or variant forms in discourse. According to Maggie Poncho, an Alabama woman of eastern Texas, those best suited to learn and speak the pidgin were children, who exhibited a positive disposition towards strangers and could "get the ball rolling" in interlingual contact (Medford, personal communication). Sickey's and Medford's views match the fact that all its last Indian speakers had once distinguished themselves socially by playing prominent roles as political officers, religious heads, or medicine people in their native societies, and echo historical documents with repeated references to political and religious leaders speaking Mobilian Jargon. The same suggestion ensues even from members of the Coushatta Assembly of God church having mistaken the pidgin as the global language of Babel and as speaking in tongues in the early 1980s (Medford, personal communication).

On the other hand, the description of Mobilian Jargon as **yoka anõpa**— literally 'servant/slave language'—would suggest an association with indigenous traditions of bondage, poorly documented, or more likely with slavery of the colonial South, which native peoples feared for good reasons as they had repeatedly been its victims. Apparently in disagreement with Medford, Hiram F. Gregory has construed **yam(m)a** as a hyperpolite response used especially with non-Indians and corresponding to an obsequious 'Yes, sir' in English. This word in its French-influenced variable pronunciation, [yamɔ̃], denoted 'Indian' with the racist connotations of *sauvage*, as used by Acadians near Marksville in reference to the Tunica-Biloxi. Lessie B. Simon, a Choctaw woman and one of the last speakers of Mobilian Jargon, observed: "One has to be careful how one talks to whites" (Gregory 1982: 19, 36–7; see also Kniffen, Gregory, and Stokes 1987: 97) None the less, Simon, like other older Louisiana Indians, always enjoyed reminiscing in and about the pidgin, and never showed any contempt for it.[6]

Even those two or three individuals who reportedly spoke Mobilian Jargon but were unwilling to teach it to me did not explain their indisposition to co-operate in terms of some negative attitude towards Mobilian Jargon. The only Native Americans ever to express disdain of the pidgin were a few Choctaw of Jena (Louisiana) and Mississippi as well as Southeastern Indians of Oklahoma, all of them middle-aged or younger, who were fluent in Choctaw, Chickasaw, or some other Muskogean language, but

---

[6] To resolve what still appears to be a paradox, I wondered whether I had perhaps misheard **yoka anõpa** as **yokpa anõpa** 'happy language'; but the available recordings contain no [p] after [k], and this noun phrase violates the standard word order of noun and adjective, by which one would have to expect *anõpa yokpa** instead.

apparently had never heard Mobilian Jargon before. In listening to tape recordings, they understood single words and short phrases, but regularly exhibited confusion and misinterpreted longer utterances, out of which they could make little sense by their own accounts. These individuals expressed utter disbelief in Mobilian Jargon, and took it to be a made-up corrupted version of their languages; some even suggested that I was the victim of a carefully staged hoax by Louisiana Indians.[7] Significantly, these negative reactions to Mobilian Jargon came from outsiders, who were not aware of its functions, communicative or other; they apparently were secondary rationalizations, directly related to the decline of Native American languages among Southeastern Indians and the pidgin.

[7] Such a joke might indeed have been in the tradition of Southeastern Indians. Yet, rather than construing a hoax as a mean trick, one would have to take it in its proper sociohistorical context as a means of cultural self-defense (see Sect. 10.3) and as an extraordinary example of linguistic creativity, which would only make the study of Mobilian Jargon all the more intriguing and interesting.

11

Questions of Origin

11.1. Origin and Development: Pre-European or Post-Contact?

Prior discussion has deliberately avoided the question of Mobilian Jargon's origin and development because of the topic's elusiveness. Any answer is by its very nature speculative, and must draw on the broadest possible range of information, including extralinguistic data and findings from archaeology with some intelligent guesses. Only such a comprehensive approach can tackle the issue of Mobilian Jargon's origin, specifically whether the pidgin was the product of European colonialism or reflected indigenous, pre-Columbian sociopolitical conditions.[1]

This question already occupied the minds of nineteenth-century scholars, who assumed Mobilian Jargon to have been in use during the earliest periods of European explorations in southeastern North America in the early sixteenth century. The botanist Thomas Nuttall (1905 [1821]: 358) as well as the anthropologists Henry R. Schoolcraft (1852: 344) and James Mooney (1990: 182, 187) surmised that Juan Ortiz, a survivor from an early Spanish expedition led by Pánfilo de Narváez who had joined that of Hernando de Soto as interpreter, had been able to communicate with Indians from Florida to the Mississippi River by speaking Mobilian Jargon or the lingua franca Apalachee. Mooney (1990: 235) expected "to find close correspondence with the myths of the Creeks and other southern tribes within the former area of the Mobilian trade language," by which he intimated its pre-European existence. Students of colonial Louisiana—among them the ethnologist Albert S. Gatschet (1969 [1884]: 31, 36) and the Alabama historian Peter Joseph Hamilton (1910 [1897]: 51)—similarly assumed the presence of Mobilian Jargon at the time of the earliest French explorations in the late seventeenth century.

Americanists of the first half of the twentieth century did not challenge their predecessors. They too regarded the pidgin as a native institution, and implicitly affirmed its aboriginal existence and pre-European origin. To John R. Swanton (1911: 26, 38, 46), any attestation of Mobilian Jargon served as an indicator of aboriginal linguistic differences between Indian communities for which he had no other linguistic information. He explained

[1] This section draws on an earlier essay (Drechsel 1984), but incorporates new evidence and additional arguments (see Drechsel 1994a).

the many Muskogean-derived names for Louisiana Indians (as applied especially to non-Muskogeans such as the Atakapa and others, including those with the ending of *-ougoula* or *-oucoula* 'people') in terms of Mobilian Jargon, a convention that the French colonists had simply adopted from the Indians (for further discussion, see Sect. 12.3). In discussing Indian loans in Louisiana French, William A. Read (1963 [1931]: 77–8, 99, 101–3, 105–6; 1940: 548) likewise assumed the pidgin to have been the vehicle of transmission for several Algonquian-derived terms: *mitasses* 'leggings,' *pacane* 'pecan nut,' *pichou* 'bob-tailed wild cat,' *plaquemine* 'persimmon fruit,' and *sagamité* 'hominy.' Read did not explain how he arrived at his conclusions, but cited *mitasses* and *plaquemine* as examples attested in Louisiana before the arrival of the first Acadian ("Cajun") immigrants in the mid-eighteenth century; these people with a part-Algonquian heritage thus could not figure as prime carriers for Algonquian loans into Louisiana French and Mobilian Jargon. Read's conclusion implies the presence of Mobilian Jargon at the arrival of the French, and suggests a pre-European existence for it, unless one argued for the pidgin's development as a result of the first French explorations from the Great Lakes area to the Gulf of Mexico in the late seventeenth century (for a review, see Crawford 1978: 16–21).

In his survey of American Indian contact media, Michael Silverstein (1973 MS: 29–32) rejected the notion of pre-European Mobilian Jargon as an idea lacking proof or even contradicted by evidence. He also objected to the use of this thesis as an integral part of ethnological arguments, and warned against the danger of circularity in the search for linguistic relationships. Silverstein specifically referred to an example in which Swanton (1911: 22) argued for the mutual intelligibility and thus the similarity of the Taënsa and Natchez languages by relying on the lack of any indications for the use of Mobilian Jargon among speakers of those two languages. Silverstein has also dismissed Muskogean-based names as valid pointers to the presence of a related pidgin, and interpreted d'Iberville's sociolinguistic observations about different groups speaking the same language to indicate a large Western Muskogean dialect area rather than a pidgin. According to Silverstein, Mobilian Jargon was not attested until 1704, namely in Pénicaut's *Relation* (Margry 1876–1886: v. 442), and came about from increasingly intimate contacts between various Western Muskogean groups and French colonists, providing the necessary linguistic diversity for pidginization.

After reviewing the evidence in support of Mobilian Jargon's pre-European existence, Crawford (1978: 21–9) similarly rejected the hypothesis, and presented several counter-arguments: (1) the absence of any mention of a lingua franca in the documents of the earliest European explorers, especially in conjunction with (2) observations of a great native linguistic diversity and (3) attestations of bilingualism and the use of translators or even hand signs in interlingual situations; (4) absent records of systematic and intimate contacts among the Indians of the Mississippi valley or specifically regular interactions between Southeastern Indians and Algonquians that would have abetted an intertribal medium and Algonquian loans; and (5) limitations of the first close relations by the French with the native population of Louisiana to speakers of Western Muskogean languages. While Crawford (1978: 21) recognized the "absence of any mention of a lingua franca" as insufficient to disprove its aboriginal existence, he reckoned that at least a few early European observers would have noted the presence of a widespread lingua franca if it had existed at the time of their arrival.

Crawford (1978: 16–17) also considered as most unlikely the hypothesis by nineteenth-century anthropologists that de Soto's interpreter Ortiz had spoken Mobilian Jargon. Instead, he had probably learned Timucua while living among Florida Indians for some ten to twelve years, and had just served as a link in a chain of several translators. Like Silverstein, Crawford interpreted the first sociolinguistic observations by French explorers in terms of a common but non-pidginized Western Muskogean language as distinguished from Mobilian Jargon with its own structural-functional characteristics. These counter-arguments convinced Crawford that Mobilian Jargon had come about in post-Columbian times and specifically as a result of French colonialism in the lower Mississippi valley, as also suggested by the pre-eminence of French documentation for the pidgin (Crawford 1978: 30–50).

One might raise still other arguments against Mobilian Jargon's pre-European origin not considered by Silverstein or Crawford. There was too large a gap of time, some 160 years, between the Europeans' earliest attested visit to the interior of southeastern North America, that of de Soto in 1539, and the first reliable attestations of the pidgin. Advocating a geographic overlap of Mobilian Jargon, if narrowly defined as the Chickasaw-Choctaw trade language, with colonial Louisiana would further suggest that the French provided the stimulus for the pidgin's origin.

Yet these counter-arguments do not hold up on closer inspection. Muskogean-based ethnonyms are indeed poor indicators for the presence or origin of Mobilian Jargon, but equal caution is necessary in using them as a source of information for the linguistic and ethnic affiliation of people with such names. In fact, there is no linguistic or other evidence for the Western Muskogean hypothesis. It was solely by dint of a few historical attestations of linguistic similarities among Louisiana Indians, especially those by Pierre Le Moyne, Sieur d'Iberville (Margry 1876–86: iv. 184, 442, 514, 521) and by

Paul du Ru (1934 [1700]: 8–9, 23) around 1700 plus their Western Musko-gean ethnonyms and a few isolated words, that Silverstein and Crawford argued for several Louisiana Indian groups to have spoken the same lan-guage as Chickasaw and Choctaw. The native languages of many Indian groups assumed to be Western Muskogeans following ethnological con-vention—among them the Acolapissa, the Bayogoula, the Houma, the Pascagoula, the Quinipissa, the Tohome, and the Yakgenechito—have remained unidentified, because there exists no linguistic evidence of unequivocal descriptive-analytical quality. In particular, Silverstein and Crawford have lacked morphosyntactic data that would permit an answer to the crucial question of whether any of these groups spoke Western Muskogean as their native language or another, possibly unrelated lan-guage plus Mobilian Jargon as a second language. Using ambiguous lexical data without morphosyntactic information in support of the Western Muskogean hypothesis, while arguing against the pre-European existence of Mobilian Jargon, only means falling into the very trap of circularity against which Silverstein has warned. Considering unidentified Louisiana Indians as Western Muskogeans without a solid linguistic foundation a priori precludes a possible alternative interpretation in terms of Mobilian Jargon, which is what one expected to demonstrate in the first place.

Diagnostic linguistic evidence in fact exists in a specimen of so-called "Western Muskogean" or "Houma," the first unquestionable linguistic attestation of Mobilian Jargon, as reported by the Jesuit priest Paul du Ru (1700 MS: 46; 1934 [1700]: 32) in 1700: "Jeheno, Yno nanhoulou totchino atchota" or †**šno eno nãholo točeno ačofa**(?). 'You [the Great Spirit], I, and the white man, [we] three are one' (see Sects. 7.2 and 9.3). Because of its "meagre" nature (du Ru 1700 MS: 10; 1934 [1700]: 8) or analytic structure, this example cannot be interpreted as Western Muskogean such as Choctaw or Chickasaw, which exhibit considerable morphosyntactic synthesis in the form of affixation; but it matches modern evidence of Mobilian Jargon per-fectly. On the basis of this or similar evidence, we cannot determine what the Houma actually spoke as their first language, and the same negative conclusion appears to hold true for other Louisiana Indian groups prema-turely identified as Western Muskogeans. Du Ru's observations about lin-guistic similarities among some ten tribes closely parallel those by fellow explorers d'Iberville and de Bienville, whom he accompanied on their expe-ditions in the Mississippi delta area. This observation suggests that d'Iberville and de Bienville, too, referred to Mobilian Jargon rather than to any Western Muskogean language, a conclusion supported by the observa-tion that de Bienville learned so-called "Bayogoula" within six weeks and that his brother included some non-Muskogeans on his list of speakers

(Margry 1876–1886: iv. 167, 184, 412). If de Bienville indeed did so, "Bayogoula" could hardly have been full-fledged Western Muskogean, with a grammar totally alien to Europeans and a complex morphosyntactic structure, about which no information was available at the time. The extraordinarily short period within which de Bienville acquired "Bayogoula" then argues by itself for an "incomplete," "reduced," or pidginized variety even if he had been the most adept adult polyglot (see Sect. 9.3). This conclusion lends further, if indirect support to the consideration that each of the groups frequently cited as Western Muskogeans—among them the Acolapissa, the Bayogoula, the Houma, the Pascagoula, the Quinipissa, the Tohome, and the Yakgenechito—could have spoken some language other than Western Muskogean as its "mother tongue." Such reasoning is fully justified in light of the great linguistic diversity and the many other linguistically unidentified groups in southeastern North America (see Sect. 2.1).

Du Ru's attestation of Mobilian Jargon undermines Silverstein's and Crawford's other arguments as well. The absence of any mention of a lingua franca can be explained by the fact that European observers of Louisiana Indians before Le Page du Pratz lacked the comparative understanding of the Indians' languages and the sociolinguistic sophistication necessary for distinguishing a contact medium from its speakers' first languages. For most non-Indians. Mobilian Jargon was simply "*the* Indian language"—an idea reinforced by the pidgin's buffer function (see Sect. 10.3). The fact that early observers neglected to provide an elaborate description of Mobilian Jargon suggestively reflected its wide acceptance as *la langue vulgaire* or 'the common language' of greater Louisiana. The pidgin simply required no further attention in their minds. Had there been more early observers to recognize the true functions and value of Mobilian Jargon as a lingua franca, it might quite possibly have received more attention. Occasional references to great linguistic diversity hardly alter these conclusions, and in some instances may only reflect individual names by which different groups knew Mobilian Jargon in recent history (see Sect. 9.1). If one postulated the pidgin's origin in colonial times and specifically in the early eighteenth century, one would in fact expect to find a greater number of alternate names for Mobilian Jargon at that time than later, when it supposedly had become established and its speakers agreed on fewer terms by which to refer to it.

Attestations of hand signs, bilingualism, and interpreters do not provide any better evidence against the pre-European existence of Mobilian Jargon, for the simple reason that these means of interlingual communication co-occurred with the pidgin. Hand signs often accompanied discourse in Mobilian Jargon (see Sect. 8.6). The pidgin was also the second language of many biliguals and multilinguals, and served as a medium of native translators (see Sect. 10.2); colonial French documents in fact make frequent references to interpreters in the eighteenth century, when Mobilian Jargon was already well established (see e.g. Rowland and Sanders 1927). Multilinguals and translators spoke primarily the languages of their immediate neighbors rather than those of more distant contacts, and did not usually share a language in encounters with people outside their customary range of interaction, in which case a regional contact medium such as Mobilian Jargon came in handy. In reviewing the hypothesis of a pre-European origin for various American Indian pidgins, including Mobilian Jargon, Sarah G. Thomason (1980: 191 n. 14) has presented a similar argument in response to Crawford:

One historical possibility that he does not, in my opinion, take seriously enough is that Mobilian [Jargon] *was* used in a restricted area before the Europeans came— as a trade pidgin spoken by some Muskogean tribe(s) and other tribes they dealt with, but not as a lingua franca over its entire later territory. That is, I think he is mistaken in his apparent belief that all pidgins function as extended lingua francas, used outside the context of vocabulary-base language trade situations.

Thomason's functional point would apply especially if long-distance contacts of pre-Columbian Southeastern Indians had been limited to trade.

Arguments against the pre-European existence of Mobilian Jargon even fail with references to chain interpretation, a burdensome arrangement in which European explorers depended on several translators lined up according to their ability to speak with each other, as apparently attested for de Soto's exploration of 1539 to 1543. There are two major reasons to consider. For one, de Soto took a route considerably farther east and north than previously believed, and paid visits to the Cherokee and their neighbors, including speakers of Muskogean, Siouan, and other languages such as Yuchi (Booker, Hudson, and Rankin 1992). He thus travelled into present-day North Carolina and Tennessee, beyond the historically attested range of Mobilian Jargon. The great diversity of the languages that de Soto's expedition encountered probably necessitated a chain of interpreters, even if Ortiz or any of de Soto's other translators spoke Mobilian Jargon. Similar circumstances evidently applied to Juan Pardo's expedition from 1566 to 1568, when his interpreter's knowledge of a Muskogean language, probably a lingua franca, did not suffice upon entering Cherokee-speaking towns in the Blue Ridge Mountains, and they had to resort to multiple translators (Booker, Hudson, and Rankin 1992: 425). Secondly and perhaps more significantly, chain interpretation may have served Southeastern Indians as a form of passive resistance, a use ignored by historians and anthropologists until today. By insisting on an unnecessarily complicated arrangement of multiple translations, native peoples could hope to slow down, if not bring to halt, the foreign usurpers without showing any outright hostility towards them.

Crawford's fourth presumption about the absence of regular and systematic contact among the Indians of the Mississippi valley and between Southeastern Indians and northern Algonquians is contradicted by archaeological evidence, which has revealed a pre-European network of long-distance interactions across much of eastern North America, reaching from the Atlantic Coast to the Rocky Mountains and from the Gulf of Mexico to the Great Lakes (see Brown, Kerber, and Winters 1990). Given socio-politically complex, multilingual chiefdoms among Southeastern Indians of the sixteenth century, Karen M. Booker, Charles M. Hudson, and Robert L. Rankin (1992: 442 n. 19) see "no reason to restrict the formation of simplified contact languages to the colonial period," and in fact consider both the lingua franca Creek and Mobilian Jargon (narrowly defined) among the languages already spoken by Southeastern Indians during the first Spanish explorations.

Evidence for area-wide contacts also weakens Crawford's final argument for initial contacts by the French to have been limited to Western Muskogeans, for it does not hold up in view of early French explorations to non-Muskogean peoples including Biloxi (Siouan), Chitimacha (Gulf), and most likely others such as Natchez (Gulf) and Taënsa (linguistically unidentified, but reported to have spoken a dialect of Natchez).

Nor do other arguments against the pre-European existence of Mobilian Jargon have any more validity. The explanation for missing references to it in Spanish records may simply be a matter of absent documentation. Conceivably, Spanish documents omitted to distinguish and record instances of Native American contact languages just as they appear remarkably negligible about the linguistics of southeastern North America. Until today, archival research on Mobilian Jargon has yielded surprisingly poor findings even in records for Louisiana under interim Spanish rule in the eighteenth century, when the pidgin was already in existence and French observers regularly attested it in some detail. However, additional and better Spanish documentation may yet confirm the use of Mobilian Jargon in early sixteenth-century Florida and by Ortiz.[2]

A closer examination of Mobilian Jargon's geographic range puts to rest its interpretation as an epiphenomenon of French colonialsim. Historical

---

[2] All of the Spanish documents that I have examined are remarkably vague or outright silent with respect to the sociolinguistics of native peoples, and have proved even less satisfactory in quality than the sixteenth-century memoir by Hernando de Escalante Fontaneda (1973 [1944]; see Sect. 8.5). Still, Hiram F. Gregory and Meinhard Schuster (personal communications) suspect that there exists a wealth of Spanish documents with relevant linguistic and ethnographic information only waiting to be uncovered.

records confirm that the pidgin was never limited just to Native Americans who had come under French colonial influence, but extended across the borders of greater Louisiana into the neighboring, frequently hostile colonial territories of Spain and Britain, including among others Caddoans in Spanish-ruled northestern Texas as well as Chickasaw and Creek under British influence from the pidgin's earliest recorded history on (see Sect. 10.1). The claimed ontogenetic link of Mobilian Jargon's origin to the French colony also withers with the recognition of the lingua franca Creek as an eastern variety of the pidgin (see Sect. 8.5). In the end, its survival in modern Louisiana longer than elsewhere relates to serveral factors—the Native American speakers' withdrawal into marginal areas, their reticence towards non-Indian outsiders, their cultural conservatism, and a multilingual area in which French was only one among several languages (see Sect. 9.4). That the best historical attestations of Mobilian Jargon have turned up in French accounts seems less an indication of its geographic range or a clue to its colonial origin than a reflection of the quality of colonial documentation.

As far as Mobilian Jargon's origin and development are concerned, early observations of the sociolinguistics of colonial southeastern North America, taken at their face value, are of limited worth, and may even be outright misleading if we disregard the broader sociohistorical context. Many early European references to Southeastern Indian languages, in particular to Muskogean ones, applied to Mobilian Jargon rather than to any of the Native Americans' first languages, as determined by independent data avoiding the problem of circularity. The first European to begin disentangling some sociolinguistic complexities of southeastern North America was Antoine Simon Le Page du Pratz (1758), who acquired the necessary comparative understanding from his extended residence among Chitimacha, Natchez, and probably other Louisiana Indians (see Sect. 9.3). His experiences suggest that early European observers and Americanist scholars following in his steps have continuously underestimated the great linguistic diversity of southeastern North America.

These arguments against the aboriginal, pre-European existence of Mobilian Jargon then present a weak case for its post-Columbian origin, much less the Western Muskogean hypothesis, and serve merely to highlight the poverty of early historical documentation for the pidgin. Significantly, Silverstein and Crawford have also overlooked several fundamental questions related to Mobilian Jargon's origin. Why, in the first place, did European explorers and settlers make any effort to adopt the medium of peoples whom they considered subordinates, savages, even animals? Why did Mobilian Jargon not become relexified into a predominantly European-based contact medium early in colonial history? Why did the lexical replacement with a European vocabulary take place only about two centuries later, when its eastern variety known as the lingua franca Creek apparently developed into Seminole Pidgin English (see Sect. 8.5)? Why had Spanish, French, and English not simply replaced Mobilian Jargon at the latest by the early nineteenth century?

These questions raise a major enigma about Southeastern Indians, for the sociolinguistics of Mobilian Jargon does not match the social history of European colonists submitting, enslaving, decimating, and removing the native population. An answer to this sociolinguistic-sociopolitical discrepancy is all the more crucial in light of the fact that Spanish, French, and English, although frequently pidginized and creolized, became the dominant languages of colonized non-European peoples elsewhere in the Americas and did so early in their colonial history.

The only solution appears to be that Mobilian Jargon already existed across extended regions and among most native peoples of southeastern North America at the time of the first contact with Europeans; in other words, it had originated in "prehistoric" times. In this case, native peoples competent in Mobilian Jargon conveniently extended its use to the European newcomers rather than embracing any of their languages as contact media. Conversely, learning widely used Mobilian Jargon proved more practical, if not economical, for early European explorers and colonists than superimposing their own languages onto the native population. Once Mobilian Jargon was established also as an interethnic medium in greater Louisiana, later immigrants and their American descendants had much greater difficulty in changing the sociolinguistic realities, even once they had acquired full political control. At no point would there have been a need for Europeans to recognize its true functions as a pidgin; they could have used it in their misguided belief that it was the only indigenous language and that it suited the presumably simple-minded Indians better than their own "civilized" languages.

Neither the rejection of Silverstein's and Crawford's counter-arguments nor questions about the discrepancy between the sociolinguistic facts and sociopolitical realities qualify as evidence for the pre-European origin of Mobilian Jargon. My doctoral dissertation convinced Crawford with my interpretation of du Ru's and contemporary attestations in terms of Mobilian Jargon rather than Western Muskogean (Crawford, personal communication), but we still wavered with respect to the pre-European origin of Mobilian Jargon because of less than satisfactory arguments for or against it (Drechsel 1979: 111–17). Conceivably, Mobilian Jargon could have originated in contact between Southeastern Indians and European colonists, and reflected political control by Southeastern Indians and especially Muskogeans in the early colonial South. Yet this hypothesis again raises the unresolved question about the absence of Mobilian Jargon's lexical replacement with Spanish, French, or even English vocabularies as the Europeans gained political dominance.

In examining further evidence, I have come to argue in favor of Mobilian Jargon's pre-European existence (Drechsel 1984, 1994a). There are four major considerations in support of this finding: (1) its indigenous grammatical structure; (2) its wide usage or functional pervasiveness with few, if any, limitations as to sociocultural contexts; (3) its persistence against replacement by European (contact) languages; and (4) its geographic range during colonial periods, which was at the center of the pre-Columbian paramount chiefdoms known as the Mississippian Complex. In combination, these characteristics suggest that Mobilian Jargon was not a secondary or incidental product of colonial origin, but a well-established, native institution before the Europeans' arrival.

First, Mobilian Jargon was not a hodgepodge of predominantly Native American or primarily Muskogean words, but shows a distinct grammatical pattern without structural parallels in any of the known languages of colonial immigrants to North America. The pidgin's word order of X/OsV and possibly a rare concomitant of X/OSV (see Sect. 6.5) echoes characteristic Muskogean and even Proto-Muskogean morphosyntactic patterns of pre-European provenance. The linguistic parallel becomes evident in a comparison of Mobilian Jargon word order with the system of subject prefixes for active verbs in Proto-Muskogean and in a model of pre-Proto-Muskogean verbal conjugation with preceding personal pronouns, as suggested by Mary R. Haas (1964: 331; 1969: 54–5). In her reconstruction, the majority of the Proto-Muskogean and pre-Proto-Muskogean subject pronouns preceded the verb (for further details, see Sect. 12.1). This pattern points to a sequence of subject prefix and active verb as their basic word order, in distinct contrast to patterns of alternating verbal prefixes and suffixes in modern Muskogean languages. On the assumption that objects and perhaps adverbial phrases introduced Proto-Muskogean and pre-Proto-Muskogean verbal constructions in analogy to the pattern of their modern descendant forms, the pre-European word order would have been Os-V, serving as an early model for Mobilian Jargon. Its X/OsV thus appears as a linguistic compromise among typologically similar Muskogean languages and possibly even Gulf isolates. If, however, one rejects this assumption in favor of an alternative word order for Proto-Muskogean and pre-Proto-Muskogean constructions, one has to find an answer to the question of why Mobilian Jargon speakers chose such a consistent and highly marked pattern as X/OsV in light of their variable Muskogean and other Gulf models. There appears to exist no obvious or satisfactory solution.

If one accepts the arguments in favor of the initial position of objects and perhaps adverbial phrases, the pronominal root of Mobilian Jargon's proposed basic word order of X/OsV and possibly X/OSV further indicates that the pidgin developed with pronominal constructions rather than with sentences containing nouns as subjects. This inference could have a basis in fact. In the early developmental stages of Mobilian Jargon, conversations did not need to address abstract topics, but probably dealt with the day-to-day interpersonal affairs and the immediate environment of its speakers and audience. The subject, either a known entity or familiar information to the audience, could then be easily expressed by tacit person deixis—that is by a pronoun rather than a full noun.

Haas's comparative data with correspondences in Mobilian Jargon word order yet suggest a greater time depth for its history than even nineteenth- and early twentieth-century anthropologists assumed; according to this interpretation, the pidgin had a past of many centuries, going back to Proto-Muskogean times. But over an extended history with changing sociopoliti- cal conditions, Mobilian Jargon could have undergone lexical replacement, which would have affected pronouns as well. For this reason, such recon- structive reasoning cannot depend on phonological correspondences between subject pronouns in Mobilian Jargon and their Proto-Muskogean or pre-Proto-Muskogean counterparts, unlike conventional historical-linguistic reconstructions, and remains highly speculative.

The second argument in favor of the pre-Columbian existence of Mobil- ian Jargon relies on two interrelated extralinguistic characteristics—its role as a dominant interlingual medium in traditional Southeastern Indian soci- eties and its use by native diplomats and the native sociopolitical élite, with few or no restrictions and without obvious negative dispositions by former speakers (see Chapter 10). That the pidgin was an indigenous institution may also transpire from early French descriptions of it as "the mother lan- guage," which Southeastern Indians reportedly understood as a language of common ancestry (see Sect. 9.3). In short, Mobilian Jargon does not repli- cate the sociolinguistics of other contact media or pidgins, especially those based on European languages, with their frequently limited range and neg- ative attitudes by those in control. Mobilian Jargon appears quite unique in these regards, explicable in terms of long-term aboriginal traditions rather than as the outcome of European contact.

Third, the survival of Mobilian Jargon into modern times against all odds similarly indicates strong traditional underpinnings with a long history. As already observed, the sociolinguistics of Southeastern Indians does not mirror the sociopolitical realities of European–American colonialism. If Mobilian Jargon resulted from contact with Europeans, one would have to explain why, in speaking the pidgin, Southeastern Indians evinced a neutral or positive attitude towards colonists, whom they clearly recognized as usurpers shortly after contact. One would further expect the native popu- lation with a positive disposition towards Europeans to have made a matching effort to adopt Spanish, French, or English as their new lingua franca, which native interpreters had learned since first contact. The discrepancy between the ongoing role of Mobilian Jargon as an interethnic medium into the mid-twentieth century and European–American sociopolitical domination since the early eighteenth century—a time gap of more than two centuries—appears resolvable only if we recognize Mobilian Jargon as an aboriginal institution, which Europeans adopted as a convenient linguistic infrastructure for their own purposes after arrival in southeastern North America. Embracing the indigenous lingua franca was simply easier for Europeans and their American followers than superimposing their own languages on a native population of great linguistic diversity. This conclusion gains strength in light of the findings that European colonial powers did not fully control the greater Mississippi valley until the end of the eighteenth century (see Usner 1992) and developed little understanding of the indigenous sociolinguistics (see Sect. 10.3).

The fourth point for the pre-Columbian origin of Mobilian Jargon relies on geography, with its cumulative range covering much of the middle South, especially along the Mississippi River and its tributaries, as determined from early colonial attestations (see Sect. 10.1). This area overlaps quite closely with the core of the Mississippian Complex, a network of pre-Columbian paramount chiefdoms in the greater Mississippi valley, which formed more or less stable intertribal, multilingual alliances with the first rudiments of a complex society in North America.[3] The overlap in geographic distribution between the Mississippian Complex and colonial Mobilian Jargon in the eighteenth century might be purely accidental on the grounds that the Mississippi River and its tributaries served as prime routes for native travel and for European explorations, were it not for some other considerations. The Mississippian Complex was the dominant force in defining much of pre-Columbian southeastern North America as a culture area with common characteristics ranging from subsistence to sociopolitical organization and from religion to the arts (see Hudson 1976 and Swanton 1946).[4] Yet the widespread sociocultural uniformity of pre-Columbian Southeastern Indians did not match their great linguistic diversity, surpassed in North America only by native California and the Northwest Coast, and including representatives of all major language families of eastern North America, distantly related as well as unrelated isolates, and numerous unidentified languages (see Sect. 2.1). The great linguistic diversity of Southeastern

---

[3] I owe the observation of similar geographic ranges for Mobilian Jargon and the Mississippian Complex to Hiram F. Gregory.

[4] In my own experience, a Seminole of Florida on visit in Oklahoma sang along to a set of songs that I had recorded among Louisiana Indians, as if they were his own. He insisted that the songs were part of his own community's tradition and that he had had no contacts, direct or indirect, with Louisiana Indians, from whom he could have acquired them.

Indians in contrast with their sociocultural uniformity then presumes some common medium of interlingual communication—bilingualism and multilingualism among neighboring groups, and a lingua franca at a regional level and for long-distance relations. This scenario would be sufficient for pidginization to occur without input by Europeans. Mobilian Jargon may in fact be the only solution to the persistent incongruity between the sociocultural uniformity and linguistic diversity among Southeastern Indians, to which both Americanist ethnologists and linguists have paid insufficient attention to date, probably due to the mutual isolation of their academic fields.

Taken alone, none of these arguments can make a strong case for the pidgin's pre-European origin; but in combination, they provide a convincing foundation for this hypothesis. Although speculative, this line of reasoning provides a plausible explanation for how pre-Columbian Southeastern Indians interacted with each other before the Europeans' arrival. In the absence of better or contradictory evidence, the hypothesis of Mobilian Jargon's pre-European origin deserves further examination in the sociohistorical context of the Mississippian Complex, as reconstructed on the basis of archaeological data and vestiges of ethnographic evidence among post-Columbian descendants.

11.2. Mobilian Jargon as the Lingua Franca of the Mississippian Complex?

The archaeology and ethnohistory of pre-Columbian Southeastern Indians cannot yield any information on how they spoke with each other. Yet the study of their extended past lends a sociohistorical framework for exploring Mobilian Jargon's role as a pre-Columbian lingua franca.

At the center of "prehistoric" southeastern North America was the Mississippian Complex, also known as Southeastern or Southern Ceremonial Complex and Southern Cult, among other names.[5] It consisted of a more

---

[5] I prefer and retain the term *Mississippian Complex*, although not fashionable currently, because it implies a multi-faceted system of different interacting parts, namely smaller member groups with traditions of their own (see Brown 1976); other designations focus unduly on the South or religion, suggest a sociocultural monolith that it was not, or carry negative implications, as in the case of *cult*. For simplicity's sake, I call its peoples Mississippians—with the explicit understanding that the term refers to diverse pre-Columbian inhabitants of the greater Mississippi valley, the drainage of the Mississippi River, rather than the modern state of Mississippi.

The following paragraphs draw substantially on recent synopses on the Mississippian Complex by James B. Griffin (1990) and Bruce D. Smith (1985). For further information, there is a growing literature available on the subject, (for major recent contributions, see e.g. Dye and Cox 1990; Emerson and Lewis 1991; Galloway 1989; Smith 1978, 1990, 1992).

or less integrated network of paramount chiefdoms across much of the eastern deciduous woodlands, with its heartland in the central Mississippi valley. Sometimes presumed descendants of a Meso-American civilization because of superficial cultural similarities, Mississippians formed the most complex sociopolitical organizations in native North America from at the latest AD 900 into the period of first European explorations in southeastern North America in the sixteenth century. None the less, the Mississippian Complex did not constitute a civilization or complex society in the anthropological sense; member groups lacked the sociopolitical integration of a state consisting of urban centers with extensive supportive surrounding areas, and they dealt with each other as much through armed conflict as through economic co-operation and trade.

Mississippian settlements were usually located in major river floodplains on levees or bluffs. They exploited fertile environments for growing crops, gathering natural products of the bottomlands, forests, and swamps (fruit, berries, nuts, seeds, roots, and tubers) and drawing on other natural resources such as fish, migrating waterfowl, and game. The major form of subsistence was intensive agriculture with the cultivation of various crops, including maize, beans, squash, and other cultigens—with maize assuming the major portion, up to 50 per cent of their diet. Mississippians distinguished themselves not only by superior farming methods, but also by sophisticated technology, numerous innovations, and a rich artistry as attested by diverse artefacts: chipped flint, ground and polished stone, engraved and excised shells, elaborate ceramics, and embossed copper plates. As determined by the attention that Mississippians devoted to their arts and crafts, skilled artisans probably enjoyed considerable recognition and perhaps a special social status.

Fertile environments and extensive reliance on food production (in contrast to hunting and gathering) yielded a considerable surplus. This condition supported a substantial growth in population, and led to an increasingly sedentary lifestyle and growing permanent settlements, ranging from hamlets of extended families to towns with several thousand inhabitants. Over time, pre-Mississippian societies developed from small separate sociopolitical entities to extensive regional networks of interrelated peer communities, in which farmsteads and subsidiary villages fed natural and other resources to larger communities or towns. These regional polities eventually formed paramount chiefdoms, hierarchical societies with ranked communities, in which towns exerted a dominant role as political and ceremonial centers, evident from larger public housing (such as council houses), town squares, and earthen platform or temple mounds. At various times, major regional centers of political and religious power emerged at Moundville near Tuscaloosa (Alabama) and at Cahokia east of St. Louis, with populations as large as 2,000 to 5,000, in the latter case perhaps even up to 10,000, during their peak periods. A growing population and larger sedentary aggregations also resulted in increased social differentiation and stratification with emergent classes of commoners and an élite, as reflected in differences in burial practices, diet, and health. The élite consisted of centralized political authorities in control of resources and a religious leadership in charge of elaborate ceremonial traditions, as suggested by a rich iconography on artefacts.

Increasing numbers of people, competition for limited resources, the development of larger polities, and growing social fragmentation and stratification led to much strife within and between regional associations of villages and towns. Although Mississippians undoubtedly acted out some differences by contests and games (such as chunkey), archaeological evidence of fortified settlements, projectile points in human bones, other injuries resulting from violence, and scenes of conflict on various artefacts also attests a tradition of armed conflict and native warfare, and even suggests the existence of war captives, vassals, and an élite of warrior chiefs. Bellicose groups apparently threatened weaker communities, which in response formed intertribal political alliances for their defense. In the end, sociopolitical integration among Mississippians remained rather fragile, and did not give rise to a true urban society comparable to those of the Aztec, Maya, or Inca Indians in Central or South America.

Americanist archaeologists and ethnologists have long been puzzled by the question of how the pre-Columbian Mississippians developed considerable sociocultural uniformity and expanded the so-called Southeastern Ceremonial Complex across much of central North America within a period of only a few hundred years. This question, although still unanswered, has led archaeologists to suggest various models of diffusion-interaction and cultural colonization (see Smith 1984).

A major integrating factor among Mississippians was trade, which placed them right at the center of an elaborate network of exchange across eastern North America, extending from the Atlantic coast to the Rocky Mountains and from the Gulf of Mexico to the Great Lakes. This topic led James B. Griffin, dean of eastern North American archaeology, to the following observation:

Trade of raw materials and of manufactured goods was one of the main threads that helped to produce and integrate the southeastern Mississippian societies. While little archaeological evidence exists for trade in salt, the concentration of ceramics used in salt evaporation found around salt springs and the known Early Historic records certify to the probability of this condiment being traded. Large marine gastropods, especially the *Busycon* whelks found along the south Atlantic and Gulf coasts, furnished cups for the Black Drink purification purgative ceremony before meetings of the "tribal" council. These shells were also fashioned into beads, pendants, and circular cutout sections that were used as gorgets. These latter objects were engraved with designs representing various concepts of their complex ritual and religious belief. The Mill Creek flint quarries in Union County, Illinois, produced the raw materials for hundreds of flint hoes in a variety of shapes. The Crescent quarries on the southwestern outskirts of St. Louis furnished an excellent white flint, out of which was made not only projectile points but also flint maces 12 to 14 inches (30 to 36 cm) long that were used as symbols of status and authority. Pottery vessels with distinctive forms made for different functions and embellished with engraved or painted decoration can be recognized as regional products. Engraved shell gorgets of distinctive areal or individual style appear far outside their usual territory. Embossed copper plates with a variety of symbolic meanings represent trade in copper from sources in the Lake Superior Basin and the southern Appalachians, and some trade activity of these finely decorated plates also took place. The large reddish sculptured human figures and human effigy pipes, once thought to have been made of Arkansas bauxite, are now believed to have been made in the Cahokia area perhaps out of Missouri fire clay, which is found a short distance north of Rolla, Missouri. Other pipe forms in Late Mississippian times, such as the catlinite disk pipe or various distinctive style of Protohistoric Cherokee forms, were extensively traded.   (Griffin 1990: 9–10)

Griffin also considered the possibility of the trade of wood and food, albeit difficult to document in the archaeological record, and presumed the latter to have occurred primarily at times of local droughts, floods, and other natural disasters such as tornadoes or hurricanes. While Griffin (1990: 10–11) expressed doubt about exchange occurring at regular established intervals and about the existence of a class of traders, he thought that "trade was one of the activities that served both to reflect and to produce the distinctive 'world' view that identifies most of the southeastern Mississippian societies as a large interacting culture area." (Griffin 1990: 11). Given its significance and wide range, trade among Mississippians and with their neighbors surprisingly has not received much systematic attention until recently, and still remains poorly understood according to the authors of a recent essay on this subject (Brown, Kerber, and Winters 1990). This topic would hardly be of much concern if many indications did not point to an elaborate network of established trading relations extending across much of eastern North America, with major corridors along the Mississippi River and its tributaries.

The sociocultural uniformity of Mississippians cannot hide geographic and temporal variations that may reflect greater differences among them than is evident from the archaeological data. Within the Mississippian Complex, there existed several regions, each with its own political and ceremonial center and with distinct traditions, as reflected in part by their material culture and symbolism. Foremost among their differences were their languages.

Americanist scholars, relying on the idea of one nation, one language from their own experience and extending it to one culture complex, one language family, have traditionally thought of the pre-Columbian Mississippians as Muskogeans, and have identified them with specific groups (for a recent example, see Booker, Hudson, and Rankin 1992: 435). One anthropologist, Marion Johnson Mochon (1972), has even used lexical reconstruction to argue that—by greater differentiation of the semantic domains of subsistence, economy, sociopolitical organization, and world view—Muskogean languages matched archaeological interpretations of Mississippian culture better than the comparatively underdifferentiated vocabularies of Siouan languages of the Mississippi valley. She recognized cognates and possible cognates for vegetable foods, the basic domesticate of corn, hoe technology, male leadership, concerns with solar movements, and purification in Choctaw and Muskogee (Muskogean) in contrast to a minimal set of cognates pertaining to food, shelter, and basic numbers in Biloxi, Ofo, and Osage (Siouan). Regrettably, the lexical data available for the different languages are uneven in quantity and quality. Moreover, the author neglected to take into full consideration the problem of language death and other sociolinguistic complications, related for example to elicitation; she also ignored other of the area's major language families and isolates for comparison without giving any justification for their omission (see Mochon 1972: 478–83). Mochon's data and reconstructions thus show at best that there could indeed have been Muskogeans among the Mississippians, but cannot exclude from them Mississippi Siouans, Algonquians, Caddoans, or speakers of still other Southeastern languages.

There are other considerations that speak against the exclusive identification of the Mississippian Complex with the Muskogean language family. Conspicuous among these is a fundamental chronological contradiction between the development of the Mississippian Complex around AD 900 and the Muskogeans' migrations into southeastern North America in late pre-European times (as suggested by mythology)—a discrepancy that no revision of the Muskogean-migration model backwards in time by several centuries can resolve satisfactorily (Smith 1984: 21–5). If the distribution of native languages in the Southeast in early colonial times provides any clues as to their range before contact with Europeans, there also appears to be little or no correlation with archaeological sites. As judged by early European observations of colonial descendants, Mississippians included the Natchez (Gulf) and linguistically unidentified affiliates, Muskogeans, Siouans, probably Caddoans and the Illinois (Algonquians), and perhaps the Cherokee (Iroquoians) among others.

There remains no cogent reason for assuming that the Mississippians were speakers of only one language or a single linguistic family; by all available indications, they spoke a diverse range of languages, some of which were not mutually related. Even by conservative estimates, the Mississippians probably included members of all known families in the area plus several unidentified and extinct languages—the premiss for the enigma of great linguistic diversity and sociocultural uniformity among Southeastern Indians. The question then arises of how the Mississippians, speaking different languages, interacted in trade and other contact situations. And how did these pre-Columbian peoples come to develop similar societies without abandoning their linguistic diversity?

The archaeological record of the Mississippian Complex suggests a variety of possible bilingual and multilingual contexts: extensive and widespread trade of diverse natural resources and products across much of eastern North America; competition between neighboring villages in the form of games and raids; intertribal religious and other ceremonies; intergroup diplomacy and alliances; multilingual complex chiefdoms; enslavement of captives from raids on neighboring communities; and possibly even some form of indigenous conquest.

This reconstruction of broad Mississippian sociolinguistic conditions looks similar to ethnographic and historical observations of Southeastern Indians, but finds support in the archaeological records, which are reliable and detailed enough to escape the trap of circular reasoning. If there existed any major differences between pre-Columbian Mississippians and their post-Columbian descendants in their sociolinguistics, they applied to the range and diversity of bilingual and multilingual interactions, which were more intensive and extensive among the first than the latter, not less as is often surmised. There were larger native populations, a greater linguistic diversity among them, and probably more frequent and institutionalized interactions as a result of their closer sociopolitical integration into paramount chiefdoms in pre-Columbian times than after contact with Europeans. That event not only introduced new diseases with epidemic effects, resulting in a rapid decline of the native population, a concurrent sociopolitical disintegration, and the obsolescence of many indigenous languages; it also led to a decline of the overall system of intertribal networks. New intertribal alliances in response to the crisis (see Willis 1980) and the arrival of alloglossic Europeans and Africans could hardly make up for the lost pre-Columbian sociolinguistic complexity, even as there arose new contexts for the continuous use of an already existent lingua franca.

If Mississippians had limited their intertribal relations to the exchange of raw materials and a few artefacts, one could reasonably interpret it in terms of silent trade as attested in small societies. But taciturn interactions between speakers of different languages would have had serious limitations on trade as institutionalized and far-reaching as that among the Mississippians, and would simply have been unworkable in other contexts. Griffin (1990: 10) surmised, probably by analogy to the early historical situation, that native traders dealt with each other by relying on a knowledge of several languages. This assumption would seem quite reasonable for interaction among members of neighboring communities as observed in colonial times, although one cannot help wondering now whether interlingual interaction took place via Mobilian Jargon as well. A knowledge of two or more languages would have been sufficient to enable a community's dealings with its immediate neighbors, but would have quickly met its limits in long-distance interactions because of the area's great linguistic diversity. Bilingualism and multilingualism provide an unsatisfactory model of understanding interlingual interactions among paramount chiefdoms of Mississippians, unless they included a regional lingua franca.

An elegant answer to this problem would be the use of Mobilian Jargon as the Mississippian lingua franca, whether in trade or other interlingual interactions. The pidgin in some form comparable to attestations in early documents would have suited well as a contact medium among pre-Columbian Mississippians speaking different languages, and could have served in other contexts than just those mentioned. As attested historically, Mobilian Jargon would clearly qualify in this role if one could take the listing of Choctaw and Muskogee words related to subsistence, economy, sociopolitical organization, and world view by Mochon (1972) as a reliable linguistic indicator for the Mississippian Complex. Out of the total of 108 terms in Mochon's list, the pidgin's historically attested vocabulary (with a smaller number of entries than the other languages except Ofo) could match a majority of words and in many instances with two or multiple entries—at least seventy-six corresponding or equivalent terms, in contrast to the lower numbers of comparable entries in Osage (seventy), Ofo (thirty-nine), and Biloxi (forty-six) as listed by Mochon (1972: 483–98).[6]

---

[6] Mobilian Jargon could specifically match words or equivalent compounds for at least the following concepts (arranged by Mochon's semantic domains and occurring more than once in some instances): 'plant'/'to plant,' 'wild potato,' 'corn,' 'beans,' 'squash,' 'field,' 'farm,' 'soil,' 'to hoe,' 'to till,' 'to harvest,' 'pottery'/'pot,' 'bowl,' 'plate,' and 'bottle' (food production); 'artisan,' 'tribute'/'tax,' 'to trade,' 'to buy,' 'to sell,' 'to purchase,' 'market'/'market place,' and 'measure' (production and distribution); 'nation,' 'tribe,' 'camp,' 'village,' 'town,' 'city,' 'people,' 'household,' 'clan'/'lineage,' 'noble,' 'lord,' 'chief,' 'artisan,' 'tributary people,' 'rich,' and 'poor' (settlement and social category); 'governor,' 'kingdom,' 'chief,' 'armor,' 'battle,' 'to war,' 'warrior,' 'tributary people,' and 'law' (polity); 'to build,' 'house,' 'bone house,' and 'temple' (public construction); 'sun,' 'moon,' 'month,' 'menses,' 'eclipse,' 'planet,' 'week,' 'year,' 'deity'/'god,' 'medicine,' 'priest,' 'ball ground,' 'one,' 'two,' 'three,' 'eleven,' 'twelve,' 'thirteen,' 'ten,' 'twenty,' 'thirty,' 'one hundred,' 'one thousand,' and 'the period of "Fire Extinguished" ' (world view). The available, but incomplete historical documentation of the pidgin's lexicon cannot confirm any equivalent or corresponding terms for thirty-two other terms: 'grindstone' and 'dish' (food production); 'to barter' (production and distribution); 'class' and 'rank' (settlement and social category); 'to rule,' 'assembly,' 'council,' 'council house,' 'to arm,' 'war chief,' and 'to conquer' (polity); 'builder,' 'council house,' 'mound,' and 'mountain' (public construction); 'world,' 'hour,' 'religion,' 'to fast,' 'January,' 'February,' 'March,' 'April,' 'May,' 'June,' 'July,' 'August,' 'September,' 'October,' 'November,' and 'December' (world view). Whether or not Mobilian Jargon once had words for these concepts, its speakers could easily have borrowed

Such a pre-Columbian variety of Mobilian Jargon would not necessarily have had to resemble modern lects closely; it could have exhibited considerable differences from the historically attested examples, especially with respect to the lexicon. The possibility of repeated lexical replacements render misleading any assumptions that pre-European Mississippians spoke a predominantly Muskogean-based variety of Mobilian Jargon; there is no need to apprehend the reintroduction of the Mississippian–Muskogean identification through the backdoor. Any Mississippian variety would probably have reflected the influence of its speakers' first languages in phonology and lexicon, if not syntax. Assuming that pre-Columbian Mississippians spoke other than just Muskogean languages, we would expect Mississippians speaking Natchez to have shown substantial Natchez elements in their version of the pidgin, ancestors of the Biloxi and Ofo some Siouan-influenced varieties, and people of Cahokia perhaps an Algonquian-colored lect, the latter of which could also have been the source of one or the other Algonquian loan. Mobilian Jargon, as we know it in its modern forms, possibly occurred only in Muskogia's heartland, the greater region of Moundville in what is today Alabama. We must even be prepared to recognize that the different varieties were not always mutually intelligible and that Mobilian Jargon was not the only contact medium in the Mississippian Complex.

Like its colonial varieties, a pre-Columbian Mobilian Jargon need not have been subject to any structural-functional restrictions, and would have met all the communicative demands of Mississippians; for all practical purposes, its speakers could have held conversations with each other on any topic and in any context. Mobilian Jargon easily suited established protocol requirements for paramount chiefs, their representatives, and their subordinates in their mutual interactions (see Chapter 7). Interlingual interactions apparently included elaborate formal greetings, and applied to food and housing, marriage alliances, guides and burden bearers, and transportation by canoe, as well as other services and tributes (Smith and Hally

or created them anew and as necessary. (For comparison, see also the discussion on the pidgin's semantic domains in Sect. 7.2 and Drechsel, 1996.) The pidgin's rate in meeting corresponding or equivalent words could thus have been substantially higher.

Mochon's conclusion that Muskogean languages lexically matched Mississippian culture better than other Southeastern Indian languages might even suggest indirect support for Mobilian Jargon as the lingua franca of the Mississippian Complex. By this argument, the similarities between the Choctaw and Muskogee words on the one hand and Mobilian Jargon on the other possibly resulted from the latter serving as a source for new lexicon as well as exerting a conservative role. Yet such reasoning lacks foundation because of considerable lexical variation and the possibility of repeated lexical replacements in the pidgin, and only runs an undue risk of circularity. There remains considerable doubt about the applicability of lexical-reconstructive methodology, developed in the tradition of the comparative method and based on the tree model of language diversification, to contact languages because of widespread borrowing. For this reason, this line of inquiry is not pursued any further here.

1992). The pidgin could even have served as a medium of political control that paramount chiefs used in establishing and reasserting their authority over their alloglossic subjects by periodic visits in place of a complex system of infrastructure and redistribution (see Smith and Hally 1992: 107–8). Conversely, Mobilian Jargon could have functioned as the language of vassals, if one of its modern names, **yoka anõpa** 'slave/servant language,' serves as any indication.

Linguistically, Mobilian Jargon closely matched the sociopolitical integration of paramount chiefdoms—by nature dynamic and flexible, but also rather fragile societies; the pidgin provided a common medium, while allowing its speakers to maintain their native languages and with them their social identities, just as in colonial and recent periods (see Sect. 10.3). Pressures towards a single national language would have increased only if the Mississippian Complex had developed into a state-level society, in which case a corresponding sociolinguistic centralization might have resulted in the selection of one language over others or possibly the creolization of Mobilian Jargon, replacing other already existing languages. The Mississippian Complex did not emerge into a civilization in the anthropological sense, and there is currently no indication of the creolization of Mobilian Jargon. However, it may have been one among few vestiges of the Mississippian Complex that survived until recently. Even if perhaps never uttered by Mississippians, modern Mobilian Jargon words of post-contact origin like *bayou* apparently provide as much of a historical link to this society as its mounds, artefacts, and bones.

In short, Mississippians were linguistically diverse enough, and interacted with each other on a sufficiently regular basis across great distances and in a variety of contexts, to warrant fully the hypothesis of an interlingual medium in use among them. Southeastern Indians did not have to wait for the arrival of European explorers and colonists to develop Mobilian Jargon. Still, the pidgin's pre-European origin and its identification with the Mississippian Complex remain hypotheses in need of conclusive historical evidence. Such may yet come forth. Perhaps we can hope to find a document of the earliest contact of Europeans, specifically Spaniards, with Southeastern Indians, referring to the long-term, pre-Columbian use of an established lingua franca among Mississippians speaking diverse languages and providing supportive sociolinguistic details such as the structure, functions, and geographic range of the intertribal medium.

PART IV

Mobilian Jargon in a Broader Perspective

Preliminaries

The foregoing description and analysis now permit an examination of Mobilian Jargon or, rather, its western variety in a comparative perspective, directing attention to broader methodological and theoretical issues.

Of prime concern is a comparison of the pidgin's grammar with the linguistic pattern of the related Muskogean languages. Consideration is also due to the relationship of Mobilian Jargon to other Southeastern Indian languages, explored below in terms of shared areal-typological features and lexical diffusion. With Mobilian Jargon as a possible model, discussion then surveys other indigenous lingua francas in southeastern North America. These subjects provide a framework for assessing contact-induced linguistic convergence among the area's native languages (Chapter 12).

Mobilian Jargon contributes to a wider comparative dimension in the study of non-European non-standard languages, especially other Native American pidgins, and bears major implications for Native American linguistics, pidgin and creole studies, the ethnology of North American Indians and the history of eastern North America—with methodological and theoretical ramifications. Appraising these implications underscores the significance of language contact in Americanist historical linguistics, and provides a convenient means of summarizing this book's major findings (Chapter 13).

Language Convergence in Southeastern Indian Linguistic Diversity

12.1. Mobilian Jargon and Muskogean Languages

The frequent misidentification of Mobilian Jargon as either Choctaw, Chickasaw, or even Muskogee by Europeans suggests a close historical relationship and much structural similarity between any of these languages and the pidgin, and calls for a comparison of Mobilian Jargon with Muskogean and possibly other Gulf languages. A contrast recognizing differences as well as shared patterns helps further clarify the pidgin's precise nature.

Among their most obvious resemblances, Mobilian Jargon and Muskogean languages exhibit fundamentally the same inventories of basic sounds and similar phonologies. The pidgin's phonemic inventory even looks like that of Proto-Muskogean as reconstructed by Mary Haas (1941*a*: 42; 1969: 34). This parallel was not the result of any survivals of Proto-Muskogean phonology in the pidgin, but instead was due to the common underlying sound system of Muskogean languages with only a few highly marked sounds. In exceptional instances such as the lateral fricative [ɬ], Mobilian Jargon speakers, depending on their native-language backgrounds, could, however vary their articulations as [sl], [šl], or even [š] (see (66) in Sect. 8.2). In contrast to Muskogean languages, Mobilian Jargon also exhibited a considerably greater range of variation in the pronunciation of vowels, specifically in the tongue position (tongue height and frontness), which likewise reflected the influence of the speakers' diverse first languages.

Other differences in the phonologies of Mobilian Jargon and Muskogean languages related to their distinct morphosyntactic patterns. With virtually no inflection and affixation, Mobilian Jargon was typologically analytic, and revealed few widespread morphophonological processes, limited primarily to aphaeresis and coalescence of the final and initial vowels in two adjacent words (see Sect. 8.2). In comparison, Muskogean languages have been typologically more synthetic, and have exhibited a correspondingly more complex morphology, including an elaborate system of prefixes, infixes, and suffixes and accompanied by a fairly diversified morphophonology. For example, while Mobilian Jargon employed independent personal pronouns to indicate possession, Muskogean languages have used possessive affixes, and have distinguished between alienable and inalienable possession, not attested in the pidgin. Differences are also evident in negative constructions. Mobilian Jargon used the **-(e)kšo** as single established suffix, added to adjectives, verbs, and even nouns in antonym and other negative constructions with their characteristic stress on the final syllable in an otherwise highly variable pattern of prominence. In contrast, negative constructions in Muskogean languages have exhibited discontinuous-affix constructions with quite complex morphophonemic patterns (see e.g. Haas 1975: 259–60).

In its lexicon, the pidgin reflected the dominant influence of Muskogean source languages. As "the Chickasaw-Choctaw trade language," Mobilian Jargon shared a substantial amount of its vocabulary with Western Muskogean languages; in the form of the lingua franca Creek, it presumably drew much of its lexicon from Muskogee and other Eastern Muskogean languages. A comparison of the pidgin vocabulary with Proto-Muskogean (see Haas 1958) reveals numerous resemblances, which are due to similarities with its modern descendant languages and cannot serve as evidence for the pre-European origin of Mobilian Jargon because of the possibility of intermittent lexical replacements. Unlike its lexical source languages, the pidgin showed much greater variation in its lexical sources and thus a greater diversity in its etymology, and was a true *Mischsprache* or mixed language, including several unmistakable borrowings from northern Algonquian languages.

Mobilian Jargon shared much of its phrase structure with Muskogean languages. The structure of compounds and noun phrases in the pidgin, $N_2 + N_1$ and N + Adj, is identical to corresponding constructions in Muskogean languages, quite possibly because Mobilian Jargon originally incorporated them as full phrases without analysis of their composite parts.

Similarities between Mobilian Jargon and Muskogean languages are far less obvious with respect to syntax, specifically their sentence structure, including word order. At first sight, X/OsV and possibly X/OSV of Mobilian Jargon appear unrelated to standard SOV in Muskogean languages. Their difference initially suggested a search for OSV languages in southeastern North America and surrounding areas as possible models for the unique word order of Mobilian Jargon. However, findings have proved inconclusive, even disappointing, for there exists no evidence for any OSV language in the Southeast or in any of the immediately adjacent areas, including the Caribbean. Those Southeastern Indian languages that present any substantial documentation on syntax have not revealed any corresponding basic or unmarked word order. The single remaining possibility would be an extinct instance that has not been documented, but whose existence is unlikely in light of the overall rarity of OSV.

Mobilian Jargon and Muskogean languages do exhibit similarities in word order at a less obvious underlying level, which explains the failure to recognize them at first glance. The answer is in the verbal system of Muskogean and other Gulf languages rather than the word-order pattern of some real or imaginative OSV language. The key to the puzzle lies in a comparison of constructions with pronoun subjects in Mobilian Jargon and Muskogean as well as other Gulf languages. They show a striking structural analogy, as illustrated with examples from Choctaw and Chickasaw, two closely related Western Muskogean languages often assumed to have been the historical model for Mobilian Jargon:[1]

(88) Mobilian Jargon: ***hattak   ešno   pesa   taha.**
                            man   you   see   PAST
      Choctaw   **hattak   iš-   pisa   tuk.**
                            man   2 sg. actor   see   PAST
                                            (nominative)
'You saw a man.' (Jacob, Nicklas, and Spencer 1977: 65)

      Mobilian Jargon: **oka   eno   banna.**
                            water   I   want
      Choctaw: **oka   sa-   banna   -h.**
                            water   1 sg.   want   predicative
                                       accusative
                                       (patient)
'I want water./I am thirsty.' (Davies 1986: 4)

      Mobilian Jargon: ***talowa   eno   emehakse   taha.**
                            song   I   forget   PAST
      Chickasaw: **talowa?   am-   alhkaniya   -tok**
                            song   1 sg. dative   forget   PAST
                                       ("subject" of
                                       experiencer
                                       verbs)
'I forgot the song.' (Munro and Gordon 1982: 85)

---

[1] The asterisk below does not indicate ungrammatical examples following transformational convention, but marks reconstructed sentences in Mobilian Jargon to match Choctaw and Chickasaw counterparts word for word. Although not recorded in actual speech, the sentences given in Mobilian Jargon follow the grammatical rules of historical and modern examples.

Some of the Western Muskogean grammatical categories in (88) and (90) as well as in the accompanying discussion have been supplemented or reglossed by related ones for reasons of comparability, and do not necessarily reflect the authors' own terminology.

According to Pamela Munro and Lynn Gordon (1982: 83), speakers of Western Muskogean use pronominal prefixes in constructions with the second person singular of "active" verbs, the first and second person singular of "patient" verbs, and all three singular persons of "experiencer" verbs, possibly preceded by an object or adverbial phrase. Similarly, Haas (1946: 326–7) described Choctaw active verbs and one of the three active verb classes in Koasati, an Eastern Muskogean language, as exhibiting a pattern of verbal prefixes for the second-person singular and plural subject pronouns as well as the first-person plural subject pronoun (with the first-person singular subject pronoun consisting of a suffix and the third-person subject, singular and plural, remaining morphologically unmarked). Haas (1946: 331; 1969: 54–5) even suggested the same pattern for one of the three active-verb classes in Proto-Muskogean and for the conjugation of active verbs in pre-Proto-Muskogean except for the third person, reconstructed as zero (see (89)). The pronominal system of three other verb classes in Muskogean languages and Proto-Muskogean—marking patient, dative, or alienable possessor, the negative, and other "hypothetical" constructions—analogously consists of prefixes (Booker 1980; Munro 1993). Reconstructions of the Muskogean verbal pronouns ultimately appears to be related to an analogous grammatical pattern in two Gulf isolates, specifically subject prefixes in Natchez auxiliaries and Tunica periphrastic constructions (Haas 1956: 71–2; 1977*b*), and may even have parallels in sentence constructions of Biloxi, a neighboring Siouan language (Rankin 1986: 81–2 n. 1). These constructions except instances with a first-person singular suffix in active verbs exhibit a pattern in which an independent subject, a direct or indirect object, an adverbial phrase, or even an entire clause evidently preceded the verb with a prefixed pronoun, in contrast to varying patterns of alternating prefixes and suffixes in the descendant Muskogean languages. On the assumption that objects and probably also adverbial phrases introduced Proto-Muskogean and pre-Proto-Muskogean verbal constructions, analogous to the pattern of their modern descendant forms,

(89) Proto-Muskogean		pre-Proto-Muskogean
1st sg.	*-**li**	*verb stem + **li**
2nd sg.	***iš**-	***iš** + verb stem
3rd sg.	*∅	*verb stem
1st pl.	***il(i)**-	***ili** + verb stem
2nd pl.	***haš(i)**-	***haš** + verb stem
3rd pl.	*∅	*verb stem

we can surmise that the basic order of ancestral Muskogean constructions with pronominal subjects was Os-V and could have served as an early syntactic model for Mobilian Jargon. The characteristic OsV word order of Mobilian Jargon would thus follow a "prehistoric" pattern of distinctly Proto-Muskogean and even pre-Proto-Muskogean verbal paradigms. Analogous patterns between Muskogean languages and Mobilian Jargon also applied to the syntax of complex constructions. For example, subordinate switch-reference marked clauses in Chickasaw "almost always precede their main clauses" (Payne 1980: 116), which with their "expectancy-raising" function provided a model for the characteristic pattern of subordinate clause-s-V in complex constructions of Mobilian Jargon (see Sects. 6.4 and 6.5). In light of this evidence, other explanations seem far less satisfactory, since they would have to answer the question of why Mobilian Jargon speakers chose as model the highly marked word order of X/OsV and possibly X/OSV over less marked variables in Muskogean and Gulf languages.

All these similarities cannot hide fundamental syntactic differences between Mobilian Jargon and Muskogean languages, as is evident from a few contrastive examples of simple constructions with the same meanings and corresponding vocabularies in the pidgin and its presumably dominant source, Western Muskogean:

(90) Choctaw:

	chi-	**bashli**	**-li**	**-tok**
	2 sg.	cut	1 sg.	PAST
	accusative	V	nominative	
	(patient)		(active)	
Mobilian Jargon:	***ešno**	**eno**	**bašle**	**taha.**

'I cut you.' (Davies 1986: 15)

Choctaw:	**pi-**	**pisa-**	**h.**[2]
Chickasaw:	**po-**	**pisa.**	
	2 pl.	look	
	patient	V	
Mobilian Jargon:	***pešno**	**lap**	**pesa.**

'He looks at us.' (Munro 1987b: 122)

	is-	**sa-**	**bi**	**-tok.**
Chickasaw:	2 sg.	1 sg.	kill	past
	agent	patient	V	
	(active)			
Mobilian Jargon:	***eno**	**ešno**	**abe**	**taha.**

'You killed me.' (Payne 1982: 366)

	iti	**chĭ-**	**chãli**	**-li**	**-tok.**
Choctaw:	wood	2 sg.	chop	1 sg.	PAST

---

[2] Identified as a predicative in (88) and in the final example below, final **-h** in Choctaw verbs is archaic by all indications; it apparently "seems to add no meaning, and is hard to gloss" (Munro 1987b: 121).

	dative	V	nominative (active)	
Mobilian Jargon:	*ešno	ete	eno	**čăle**	**taha.**

'I chopped wood for you.' (Davies 1986: 41)

Choctaw:	**ofi**	**sa-**	**banna**	**yimmi**	**-li**	**-h.**
	dog	1 sg. accusative (patient)	want V	believe	1 sg. nominative (active)	predicative
Mobilian Jargon:	*ofe	eno	**banna**	eno	**yemme.**	

'I believe I want a dog.' (Davies 1986: 71)

By all available historical and modern evidence, speakers of the pidgin adhered to a rigid word order due to the lack of morphological machinery to identify different grammatical functions for sentence parts, which would otherwise have permitted variations in sentence patterns. Without some means of formally marking case, speakers of Mobilian Jargon had little option but to apply the same word order in constructions with nominal subjects as in those with pronominal ones in order to avoid major misunderstandings and confusion (as exemplified by the few late speakers who, under the influence of their native languages, were no longer certain about the pidgin's grammar and could only remember traces; see Sect. 6.5). Mobilian Jargon also made no known distinction among different classes of verbs, specifically active, patient, and experiencer verbs, and did not exhibit any of the ergative-like or antipassive features of Western and other Muskogean languages; nor did the pidgin reveal any evidence of nominal case markings, a switch-reference system, or a fairly elaborate set of pronouns characteristic of the complex grammars of Western Muskogean languages (see Munro and Gordon 1982). Unlike in Muskogean languages, subject pronouns in Mobilian Jargon functioned as true grammatical subjects, although not necessarily as agents. Significantly, they also derived etymologically from independent and full pronouns in Muskogean languages rather than their corresponding pronominal affixes and—in the case of the third person, left unmarked in Muskogean languages—from a reflexive pronoun (see Munro, forthcoming; cf. Haas 1975: 259):

(91) **eno** 'I' < Alabama/Chickasaw **ino** 'I'
    (e)šno 'you' (sg., pl.) < Choctaw **išno-** 'you' (sg.), Chickasaw **išno?** 'you' (sg.), Alabama/Koasati **isno** 'you' (sg.)
    (e)lap 'he, she, it, they' < Choctaw **ila:p** 'oneself, by oneself', Chickasaw **ila:po?** 'oneself, by oneself'
    pošno 'we' < Chickasaw **pošno** 'we', Alabama **posno** 'we'

In Muskogean languages, independent pronouns with the same grammatical function—unlike pronominal affixes—do not show any preverbal–

postverbal variation; nor do they occur in intermediate position between the object and verb, although some clearly show an etymological relationship to their affixed counterparts (as in the case of the second person singular **išno** and **iš-** in Western Muskogean). The word-order pattern characteristic of independent full pronouns in Muskogean languages then did not serve as model for the lexically related pidgin. If it had done so, Mobilian Jargon speakers would have generated sOV and—by extension to constructions with nominal subjects—presumably SOV as basic word order.

In spite of structural homologies to Muskogean and other Gulf languages, Mobilian Jargon differed fundamentally from them in both morphology and syntax, and demonstrates substantial structural independence from its source languages. Whereas pronominal affixes merely present a surface variation of underlying sOV in Muskogean languages, OsV was basic to Mobilian Jargon, and exhibited little, if any, transformational depth. If Mobilian Jargon speakers once projected OsV onto multiple-argument constructions with nominal subjects, their basic word order would have been OSV, and the differences between the pidgin and its source languages even greater. This inference appears eminently reasonable in view of Mobilian Jargon's consistent word-order pattern in contrast to the preverbal–postverbal variation of Muskogean languages and its use of full and independent pronouns instead of pronominal affixes.

In short, Mobilian Jargon was not simply a "broken," "stripped," "corrupted," or "reduced" version of Choctaw, Chickasaw, or some other Muskogean language bereft of its morphology. It exhibited a grammar of its own that, with all its characteristic Muskogean features, differed substantially from that of its source languages. Reduced forms of Choctaw and Chickasaw as illustrated by James Adair (1968 [1775]) in *The History of the American Indians* show few similarities to Mobilian Jargon, and were the result of his incomplete knowledge of Chickasaw and Choctaw as much as his desperate attempt at explaining the origin of Native Americans in Israel by the linguistic evidence. Similarly, examples of "broken" Choctaw as cited by H. B. Cushman in his *History of the Choctaw, Chickasaw, and Natchez Indians* (1962 [1899]) not only differ substantially from standard Choctaw equivalents and spurious etymologies (T. Dale Nicklas, personal communication), but also exhibit few grammatical resemblances to Mobilian Jargon apart from occasional examples of XsV word order. In fact, Cushman (1962 [1899]: 114) made a revealing observation about his knowledge of Choctaw:

I have frequently met, here and there, a few Choctaws in Texas bordering on Red River . . . With each different little band I tried to introduce a conversation only to be disappointed; and though I addressed them in their own native language, I could only obtain a reply in a few scarcely audible monosyllables [quite likely Mobilian Jargon].[3]

All in all, the syntactic similarities between Mobilian Jargon and Muskogean languages are superficial enough to render one of the pidgin's many names, **anõpa ẽla** 'other/different/strange language,' quite appropriate. The substantial linguistic differences also explain why speakers of Choctaw and other Southeastern Indian languages considered Mobilian Jargon largely unintelligible beyond single words or short phrases, unless they had learned it as a second language or had deduced its distinctive grammar from extended exposure. Profound dissimilarities between Mobilian Jargon and Muskogean languages further account for the misinterpretations of and the confusion about longer pidgin utterances as well as accompanying negative reactions by younger Southeastern Indians who had no knowledge of it (see Sect. 10.4). Conversely, Muskogean languages remained unintelligible to speakers of Mobilian Jargon beyond single words and without further learning.

It is reasonable to surmise an analogous situation of historical affinity with substantial grammatical differences and basic mutual unintelligibility for the eastern variety of Mobilian Jargon (the lingua franca Creek) in relation to Muskogee and other Eastern Muskogean languages, although supportive evidence is lacking at this time.

12.2. Mobilian Jargon and the Language Area of Southeastern North America

The role of Mobilian Jargon as a major regional lingua franca extending beyond Muskogeans suggests that it reflected influences from languages of their neighbors; conversely, one would expect it to have had an impact on these other Southeastern Indian languages in some form.

Short of individually comparing Mobilian Jargon with each of the numerous native languages of the area, any examination of mutual interrelations can only draw on a contrast with areal-historical features of Southeastern Indian languages for determining possible shared traits of distinctive or marked quality. If not widespread and common to other languages, these

---

[3] On other occasions, Choctaw Indians apparently addressed Cushman in what appears to be Pidgin English (Cushman 1962 [1899]: 120), which raises further questions about the adequacy of his knowledge of Choctaw or recalls a situation similar to W. Gilmore Simms's rendering of the "most musical Catawba" in "Indian-English" (see Sect. 2.3 above). In either case, reservations about the accuracy of these and other observations by Cushman (such as his etymologies of Indian names) discourage further examination of his attestations of "Choctaw" here. Perhaps Cushman learned Mobilian Jargon first, and then acquired an inadequate form of Choctaw that made little sense to its native speakers and also differed from Mobilian Jargon.

features suggest a historical relationship in the form of linguistic retention, diffusion, or innovation, in any of which the pidgin could have had a part. Such shared marked features manifestly reintroduce the problem of distinguishing substrata from superstrata influences and their direction—a fundamental methodological issue of historical linguistics still in need of a satisfactory solution.

Joel Sherzer's *An Areal-Typological Study of American Indian Languages North of Mexico* (1976: 202–18) serves as a major source of contrastive linguistic data for Southeastern Indian languages. A typological comparison of Mobilian Jargon with his data, however, carries along some inadvertent limitations. For one, areal research in Americanist linguistics has focused on phonology and morphology, due to limited comparative information on syntax, semantics, and sociolinguistic aspects (Sherzer 1976: 13). By excluding Caddoan and southern Algonquian languages, Sherzer (1976: 202) has also espoused a narrower definition of southeastern North America than is accepted generally (Crawford 1975a; Haas 1971, 1973; see Sect. 2.1) or is advisable in light of Mobilian Jargon's range into the neighboring areas of Caddoans, Siouans, and likely Algonquians.[4]

A comparison of areal-typological features of Southeastern Indian languages with Mobilian Jargon presents numerous common features in phonology (with parentheses enclosing shared absent or negative areal-typological traits—of minimal significance in determining historical relationships—together with any relevant contrastive information; see Sherzer 1976: 202–10 and Table 12.1). Some areal-typological features relating to the sound systems of Southeastern Indian languages require revision. By reconstituting five vowels for Timucua, Julian Granberry (1987: 11, 57) has rejected his earlier reconstruction of a three-vowel system, thus removing the language from areal affiliation with Muskogean for this feature. Geoffrey Kimball (personal communication) considers nasalized vowels in Muskogean languages as independent developments rather than a family trait, and rejects them as a central areal trait of the Southeast. The **s/š** opposition extends to Chickasaw. On the other hand, Muskogean, Natchez, and

---

[4] Regrettably, one cannot simply remedy this shortcoming by including comparative information from Sherzer's chapters on the neighboring areas of the Plains and the Northeast (see Sherzer 1976: 168–201) due to a focus on different areal features specific to these areas and due to the rather cursory nature of the attestations for wider regional ties. In examining the relationship of Caddo to its eastern neighbors, Wallace Chafe (1983: 245) has confirmed a void when he observed that "the influence of Muskogean languages on Caddo (or vice versa) is a subject still to be explored." Similarly, the areal relationships between Muskogean languages on the one hand and Algonquian and Siouan on the other require closer attention. Regna Darnell together with Sherzer (Darnell and Sherzer 1971: 27) has described an apparent enigma between regular sound correspondences of Southeastern Indian languages with Algonquian and their grammatical similarities to Siouan. Sherzer's survey is thus in need of systematic updating in light of newly gathered data, recent analyses, and perhaps redefined geographic areas—a major task that may suggest some significant revisions.

TABLE 12.1. *Areal-phonological features of Southeastern Indian languages and Mobilian Jargon*

Southeastern American Indian languages	Mobilian Jargon
1-1-1 vowel system in Muskogean, probably a family trait, and a 2-1 vowel system in Timucua, which with the three-vowel system of Muskogean variation is an areal trait of the Muskogean–Timucua region (in contrast to five-vowel systems in Chitimacha, Atakapa, Natchez, Siouan, and Tuscarora, six-vowel systems in Yuchi and Cherokee, and a seven-vowel system in Tunica versus absent four-vowel systems and absent mid and high central vowels)	1-1-1 vowel system with considerable allophonic variation, including occasional schwa
Nasalized vowels in Muskogean, Yuchi, Siouan, and Iroquoian, a family trait of Muskogean, Siouan, and Iroquoian and apparently a central areal trait of the Southeast (plus some predictable voiceless vowels in Iroquoian languages versus absent phonemic pitch)	Nasalized vowels, original to the area, but perhaps reinforced by French
One series of voiceless stops in Biloxi, Timucua, and Gulf isolates except Chitimacha and one series of voiceless stops plus **b** in Muskogean except Muskogee, an areal trait of the Gulf-Timucua region (in contrast to a voiceless-voiced two-stop series in Iroquoian, Ofo, and Catawba, a voiceless-glottalized two-stop series in Chitimacha, and a voiceless-voiced-glottalized three-stop series in Yuchi versus absent four-stop series)	One series of voiceless stops plus **b**, with insufficient evidence for the phonology of the Muskogee-based variety of Mobilian Jargon or the lingua franca Creek
Labial stop order in all Southeastern Indian languages other than Iroquoian; dental stop and 'k' orders in all Southeastern Indian languages (plus **c/č** in Chitimacha and Yuchi and **kʷ** in Natchez and Timucua versus absent **ṭ, tθ, q,** and **qʷ**)	Labial and dental stop and 'k' orders
One series of voiceless fricatives in all Southeastern Indian languages except Yuchi and Ofo, a central areal trait of the Southeast and probably a family trait of Gulf and Iroquoian (in contrast to a voiceless–voiced fricative series in Ofo and a voiceless–glottalized fricative series in Yuchi versus absent series of voiceless–voiced–glottalized fricatives and pharyngeal fricatives)	One series of voiceless fricatives

TABLE 12.1. *Continued*

Southeastern American Indian languages	Mobilian Jargon
Labial or bilabial fricatives in Muskogean, Timucua, Yuchi, Ofo, Biloxi, and Tuscarora, a family trait in Muskogean, a central areal trait of the Southeast, and probably the result of contact with Muskogean in Timucua, Yuchi, Ofo, Biloxi, and Tuscarora	**f**
s/š opposition in Choctaw (but in no other Muskogean language), Tunica, Chitimacha, Ofo, Biloxi, Yuchi, and Catawba, a regional areal trait of the Southeast	**s/š** opposition in the Mobilian Jargon of at least Choctaw and various European speakers
h, a whole areal trait of the Southeast (plus **θ** in Tuscarora, **x** in Biloxi, Tutelo, Yuchi, and Tuscarora versus absent **ḍ, z, xʷ, x̣, x̣ʷ, ɣ, ɣʷ,** and **hʷ**)	**h**
l in Muskogean and all Gulf isolates except Chitimacha, Timucua, Yuchi, Ofo, and Cherokee, a central areal trait of the Southeast and probably a family trait of Gulf	**l**
ł in all Muskogean languages, Atakapa, Yuchi, and Cherokee, a family trait of Muskogean, a Muskogean-centered regional areal trait of the Southeast, and probably the result of contact in Yuchi (plus **tł** and **tl** in Cherokee, **lʔ** and **łʔ** in Yuchi versus absent **tłʔ, lʸ,** and **łʸ**)	**ł**, with alternate, less marked articulations such as the clusters of **šl** and **sl** in the speech of Europeans
nasals (plus **n** in Atakapa, voiceless nasals in Natchez, Cherokee, and Tuscarora, and glottalized nasals in Yuchi versus absent **nʸ**)	**m** and **n**
r in Tunica, Timucua, Tuscarora, and Catawba (plus voiceless **r** in Tuscarora and Catawba, regional areal traits of the Tuscarora–Catawba region and **l/r** opposition in Tunica and Timucua versus glottalized **r**)	**r** attested only in single words of Tunica or European origin

Tunica shared the retroflexion of sibilants, also adopted by Quapaw (Dhegiha Siouan) as well as other indigenous languages along the Missouri River as far north as Kickapoo (Algonquian; see Rankin 1988: 644) and attested in Mobilian Jargon in the form of **ṣ** and **ç̣**. An updating or systematic revision of the above listing in light of findings gathered since its publication would undoubtedly suggest other necessary changes.

Drawing on Mary R. Haas (1953: 229; 1956: 65), William L. Ballard (1985) has observed correspondences among the syllables **sa, ša,** and **la** and their occurrence in combination or reduplication among several related and unrelated Southeastern Indian languages, as evident especially for 'goose': Choctaw **šalaklak,** Alabama and Koasati **salakla,** Muskogee sasʌ kwʌ or [sâ:sákwa], Cherokee **sasa,** Yuchi **šalala,** Natchez **la:lak,** Tunica **lálahki,** and Tonkawa **xilik** (in contrast to Mobilian Jargon **šalaklak**). Ballard (1985: 339–40) has further noted that "Cher[okee] and Cr[eek] are more similar than Cr[eek] is to its kin Choc[taw] and Koa[sati], which, in turn, looks like Yuchi, Tunica, and Tonkawa." Other examples illustrate similar syllable correspondences among various Southeastern Indian languages, including Catawba and Shawnee. Ballard has interpreted such syllable correspondences as an area-wide form of sound symbolism related to images of birds (especially goose and eagle), lizards, snakes, rattling, and possibly the moon, characteristic of the Mississippian Complex. Analogous to the complex of **sa/ša/la** correspondences is the widespread syllable **ya** referring to the semantic domain of 'mouth' and mouth-related phenomena such as 'lips, teeth, tongue, language; to eat, to speak, to sing,' evident in many native languages of North America and especially those of the Southeast, including Choctaw, Alabama, Muskogee, Atakapa, Chitimacha, Tunica, Biloxi, Ofo, Osage, Catawba, and Yuchi (see Crawford 1975*b*: 271–6). Among these, all except Catawba also spoke Mobilian Jargon in either an eastern or western variety. Crawford's examples include only one item with a corresponding form in Mobilian Jargon: **yaya** 'to cry, to weep' (< Choctaw **ya:ya**); but the pidgin furnished other instances, foremost among them one of its names, **yam(m)a,** which—while deriving from Choctaw and Chickasaw **yamma-** 'that'—probably reinforced the association between **ya** and 'mouth.'

In addition to areal-typological features of sound, Sherzer (1976: 210–18) compiled comparative data for the morphology of Southeastern Indian languages (with parentheses again enclosing shared absent or negative areal-typological traits or any relevant contrastive information; see Table 12.2). According to Robert L. Rankin (1988: 642), Siouan languages of the Ohio and the central Mississippi River valleys, Algonquian, and Muskogean languages have moreover had in common a quinary counting systems for the numerals of 'six' to 'ten,' which speakers of Mobilian Jargon used as well.

In examining Southeastern Indian languages, T. Dale Nicklas (1979) has recognized various other grammatical similarities, which reflect some striking correspondences in the syntax of Mobilian Jargon (see Table 12.3). To Nicklas (1979: 46), the numerous similarities among Southeastern Indian languages of the area, especially between Gulf and Siouan, are evidence for a lengthy pre-European association with each other. Notably, the languages of southeastern North America that do not conform to these

Southeastern American Indian languages	Mobilian Jargon
(Overtly marked nominal case system in Muskogean [except Apalachee], Tunica, and Biloxi, a Muskogean-centered regional areal trait)	Cases determined by word order
Independent possessive pronouns in Chitimacha (preposed to nouns) and Atakapa (in contrast to mostly prefixed possessive pronouns in Muskogean, Tunica, Yuchi, Siouan (for inalienable nouns in Biloxi, Ofo, and Catawba), and Iroquoian, a family trait of Siouan, Iroquoian, and a central areal trait of the Southeast in contrast to suffixed possessive pronouns for alienable nouns in Ofo, Biloxi, and Catawba)	Independent possessive pronouns, preceding nouns
(Plurality marked in pronouns of probably all languages of the Southeast, apparently a family trait of all language families and an areal trait of the whole area)	Number evident from the context or expressed with a specific figure
(Overtly marked nominal plural in languages of the Southeast)	A noun's number evident from the context; if necessary, plural marked by **lawa** 'many, much' or a number following the noun
Nominal incorporation in Muskogean, Natchez, and Cherokee	Vestiges of non-productive noun incorporation (?)
Prefixes of subject person markers in Muskogean (in most paradigms and for most persons), Natchez, Siouan, Yuchi, and Cherokee, a family trait in Muskogean and other Gulf languages, Siouan, and Iroquoian and a central areal trait of the Southeast (in contrast to suffixes of subject person markers for some persons in some paradigms in Muskogean, Chitimacha, Atakapa, and for active verbs in Tunica, a Gulf-centered regional areal trait of the Southeast and perhaps a Gulf-centered family trait versus the absence of subject person markers as exclusively independent pronouns)	Independent subject personal pronouns, preceding the verb
Tense-aspect suffixes in all languages of the Southeast, a whole areal trait and probably a family trait of all language families of the Southeast (in contrast to some tense-aspect prefixes in Cherokee and Tuscarora)	Independent past-tense marker **taha**, following the verb

TABLE 12.3. *Areal-syntactic features of Southeastern Indian languages and Mobilian Jargon*

Southeastern American Indian languages	Mobilian Jargon
Predominant word order of SOV, with main verbs preceding auxiliaries and relative clauses following the modified noun	OsV with main verbs preceding auxiliaries and relative clauses following the modified noun; SOV or OSV
Dominant order of noun, adjective, and numeral with the demonstrative taking either initial or final position; postpositions	Order of noun, adjective, and numeral with the demonstrative occupying initial position; postpositions
Negation by prefixes, suffixes, a combination of both, or postposed adverbs	Negation by suffix

and other patterns are Cherokee (Iroquoian) and Tutelo (Siouan), neither of which was within Mobilian Jargon's attested geographic range. Perhaps most significantly, the pidgin's word order of OsV mirrors grammatical patterns of not only Muskogean languages (see Sect. 12.1), but Biloxi (Nicklas 1991: 535; Rankin 1986: 81–2 n. 1), other Siouan languages of the Mississippi valley, and Yuchi (Nicklas, personal communication), and apparently Caddoan languages (Wallace Chafe, personal communication) as well. Similarly, Munro (1993: 376) has recently come to consider the pronominal agreement system of active verbs in Muskogean languages as an areal phenomenon of the Southeast shared by Tunica, local Siouan languages, and even Cherokee, which in cases preceded by a direct or indirect object again matches the characteristic semantactic pattern of Mobilian Jargon.

On the other hand, the comparison of Mobilian Jargon with areal-historical traits of various Southeastern Indian languages reveals several conspicuous differences. The comparative material currently at disposal indicates that Mobilian Jargon lacked the following major grammatical functions or categories: distinction of alienable–inalienable possession; reduplication of nominal stems as distributives and plurals; masculine–feminine gender distinctions in nouns or pronouns; inclusive–exclusive plural and dual pronouns; visible–invisible distinction in demonstratives; locative suffixes in nouns; reduplication of verbal stems signifying distribution, repetition, etc.; evidential and locative-directional markers (see Sherzer 1976: 211–15). Furthermore, Mobilian Jargon did not employ positional verbs such as for 'to sit,' 'to stand,' and 'to lie' as auxiliaries of location and continued action (see Rankin 1977; Watkins 1976). Nor did the pidgin show any evidence of the following features: pluralization by

pronominal affixes rather than suppletion, either with a combination of prefixes and suffixes, as among languages of the Atlantic Coast (including
Algonquian) and Siouan languages, or with contiguous affixes, as among
languages farther west; verbal prefixes for the associative, the reciprocal,
and the dative cases; the element **-ki-** in the numeral 'five'; the distinction
of four basic motion verbs (including not only direction, but also motion in
transit and arrival); gender differences in discourse (men's and women's
speech); or the first-person inclusive (see Nicklas 1979). Also absent in
recordings of Mobilian Jargon are nominative versus oblique markings in
noun phrases, verb stem suppletion for number, and switch-reference
marking for conjoint sentences (see Rankin 1986: 80–4; 1988: 642–5). All
the grammatical distinctions, expressed by affixation in Southeastern Indian
languages, probably reflect the overall morphosyntactic difference of typologically analytic Mobilian Jargon in comparison to its synthetic sources. If
the pidgin expressed these grammatical categories, it apparently articulated
them by alternative means.

In sum, a comparison of Mobilian Jargon with Southeastern Indian areal-
historical traits yields several common linguistic characteristics and structural correspondences, especially at the levels of phonology and syntax:

(*a*) Muskogean regional traits: 1-1-1 vowel system (with the difference
      that Mobilian Jargon permitted considerably greater variation
      including occasional mid-central vowels); one series of voiceless
      stops plus **b**; and **ɬ**.

(*b*) central areal traits: possibly nasalized vowels; **s/š** opposition;
      retroflexion of sibilants; one series of voiceless fricatives including **f**;
      l; prefixation of verbal subject markers (corresponding to indepen-
      dent subject personal pronouns preceding the verb in Mobilian
      Jargon);

(*c*) whole areal traits: **h**; labial and dental stop and 'k' orders (except
      labials missing in Iroquoian); tense-aspect verbal suffixes (corre-
      sponding to the past-tense marker **taha** following the verb), and pos-
      sibly the **sa/ša/la** and **ya** correspondences.

Mobilian Jargon further exhibited a correspondence with a possible Gulf
trait of independent possessive pronouns, preposed to nouns in Chitimacha,
and a change from suffixation to prefixation for ownership pronominals as
in Muskogean and much of Siouan, although both affixed them as well. The
pidgin may even have displayed vestiges of non-productive noun incorporation comparable to Muskogean, Natchez, and Cherokee. Moreover,
Mobilian Jargon and many Southeastern Indian languages shared the same
basic word orders with respect to the following sentence parts: noun, adjective, numeral, and demonstrative; noun and modifying relative clause; verbs
and auxiliaries; and negation by postposed suffix or adverb. If OsV in

Mobilian Jargon derived from SOV in Muskogean and perhaps other Gulf languages (see Sect. 12.1), there also existed a close, if less obvious relationship between these two word orders. Characteristically, all of these shared similarities are Muskogean or even Gulf in nature, and none reflects any conspicuous non-Gulf features or other "exotic" influences.

While some distinctive areal features among Southeastern Indian languages are due to common origin or retention reinforced by contact, others are the result of linguistic diffusion. Sherzer (1976: 217) concluded that Biloxi, Ofo, Yuchi, Timucua, and Tuscarora developed labial or bilabial fricatives as a result of contact with Muskogean languages, just as the development of Yuchi ł was probably due to contact with neighboring Southeastern Indians, presumably also Muskogeans. Crawford (1975*b*) made no attempt at explaining the wide spread of **ya** in terms of language contact, just as Nicklas (1979) recognized areal influences among the various Southeastern languages mostly without specifying the direction of influence. However, Ballard (1985) has construed the **sa/ša/la** complex of syllable correspondences as evidence of language contact of which the core would again have been Muskogean languages. Rankin (1986; 1988: 644–5) has since attributed the development of some grammatical features in Biloxi, Quapaw, and other Siouan languages (such as sibilant retroflexion) to contact with Muskogean and possibly other Gulf languages. In an abstract to an unpublished paper, Rankin (1980: 45) has considered specifically Mobilian Jargon as a source for sibilant retroflexion among Southeastern Indian languages. When examining linguistic provinces within southeastern North America, Nicklas (1994) has similarly recognized Muskogeans and other Gulf Indians as major players in their interactions with other groups. He has tellingly presented the Choctaw and the Muskogee at the opposite ends of a regional dialect continuum of Muskogean, in regular face-to-face interaction with non-Muskogeans, and has portrayed their languages as "the most innovative" in the family and as "simplifications of the type one might expect from the absorption of other [non-Muskogean] peoples" (Nicklas 1994: 9).

In his overall assessment of areal traits in relation to southeastern North America as a culture area, Sherzer (1976: 252–3) has given only limited significance to language contact beyond an incidental recognition of bilingualism and multilingualism in intertribal confederacies. This reading is overly conservative in light of the growing number of areal features among Southeastern Indian languages and beyond, marked parallel features in Mobilian Jargon, and new archaeological evidence for large native populations and greater sociopolitical integration in alloglossic paramount chiefdoms among pre-Columbian Southeastern Indians, all of which point to extensive interlingual contact. In terms of its communicative patterns, the Southeast resembles more closely the greater Northwest Coast, including the Plateau with its extended network of interlingual contacts (see Sherzer

1976: 229–37), than the Northeast or the Plains as suggested by Sherzer (1976: 253).[5]

The present findings suggest a role for Mobilian Jargon in the area's extended history, corroborating its pre-Columbian origin; structural parallels in areal features and the pidgin's grammar would also confirm its proposed Muskogean basis. Still, caution is due in drawing such conclusions. Whether one understands Mobilian Jargon only in terms of a narrowly defined Western Muskogean variety ("the Chickasaw-Choctaw trade language") or accepts a broader definition including the lingua franca Creek, its phonology and lexicon do not necessarily make highly reliable domains for comparison with areal features for *long-term* agreements because of great variability and easy replacement by partial relexification, characteristic of so many pidgins. As a morphophonological feature, the syllabic patterns of Southeastern Indian languages, matched by only a few attested examples in Mobilian Jargon, provide no better indicator. Conceivably, Mobilian Jargon could once have had quite a different phonological, syllabic, and lexical composition, with a substantial portion of some Gulf isolate language such as Natchez. Such a variety would not necessarily have reflected areal features of Southeastern Indian languages in the same fashion as recent evidence. Following this reasoning, areal similarities with Mobilian Jargon could be due to the fact that recordings for both Southeastern Indian languages and Mobilian Jargon originate from speakers with the same or similar linguistic backgrounds and did not include a truly representative variety of the pre-Columbian speech communities. In short, the pidgin's phonological and lexical features carry little time depth in historical reconstruction because of its variable nature as a contact medium; they do not demonstrate the stability that historical linguists take for granted in cognates with their sound correspondences in reconstructions of "genetically" related languages.

The more promising domain for examining historical ties between areal features of Southeastern Indian languages and Mobilian Jargon appears to be word order, in the assumption that the syntax, once established, exhibited a fairly stable pattern for communicative efficiency, as indicated by the available information. With OsV and semantactic variability at a minimum, Mobilian Jargon reveals a basic word order widely shared by the area's native languages (Muskogean, Gulf isolates, Mississippi Valley Siouan, and Caddoan). These morphosyntactic similarities crosscut several language families, and are sufficiently marked to exclude explanations in terms of either universality, common origin, or accidental similarity. Yet even word order cannot serve as conclusive evidence for Mobilian Jargon's pre-Euro-

---

[5] A similar revision may well be necessary for northeastern North America with accumulating evidence for greater linguistic diversity, Delaware Jargon, and other indigenous lingua francas (see Sect. 12.4) such that its conclusions apply to eastern North America at large.

pean origin; it is historically and theoretically conceivable for Southeastern Indians to have developed a pidginized compromise based on shared grammatical patterns after the arrival of Europeans (see Sect. 11.1).

Areal-historical traits cannot fully determine the proportion of "diffusional cumulation" in relation to "archaic residue" (Swadesh 1951) without better comparative data or carefully defined criteria for identifying particular linguistic processes. Nor do patterns shared by Southeastern Indian languages and Mobilian Jargon demonstrate conclusively that the latter played a central role in the area's linguistic history. Much less can such research currently offer any means by which to measure time depth for areal features or resolve the question of the pidgin's origin. None the less, areal traits of southeastern North America show that Muskogean and probably Gulf isolates influenced other native languages of southeastern North American substantially, be it by the retention or the innovation and diffusion of areal traits, and did so over extended periods. Some striking patterns in word order suggest Mobilian Jargon as a potential medium with both conservative and diffusional-innovative functions.

12.3. Mobilian Jargon as a Medium of Lexical Diffusion

Among those words that Southeastern Indians borrowed from each other or from their neighbors, several passed probably through Mobilian Jargon. Borrowings via the pidgin are difficult, if not impossible, to distinguish from direct loans because of the lack of distinctive phonological features; but there are several other indications that the principal medium of lexical diffusion among Southeastern Indians was Mobilian Jargon. For one, the majority of lexical borrowings across language-family boundaries were Muskogean in origin (with thirty-one entries), in contrast to substantially lower figures for common Southeastern loan-words with origins in other languages or language families (Siouan: nineteen; Yuchi: twelve; Cherokee: nine; Tunica: five; Atakapa: five; and Shawnee: three; see Ballard 1983: 328). The primary centers of distribution for both indigenous and foreign loan-words were the Creek and Choctaw Indians (Martin 1994) in accordance with the prominence of the pidgin's eastern and western varieties, which passed on borrowings to other languages. In comparison to the other Southeastern Indian languages, Choctaw and Muskogee also disclose the largest percentages of European loans and the highest convergence rates between loans and items of native lexical acculturation (loan translations, extension of native vocabulary to new referents, and coining), although these have remained considerably lower than the corresponding percentages and convergence rates for all other culture areas of North America except the Plains (see Brown 1994: 97–9, 102). Moreover, various of the clearly

identifiable borrowings have corresponding forms in Mobilian Jargon, refer
to truly foreign phenomena, and display a wide distribution in several of
the area's languages, which reduces the feasibility of explanations in terms
of dispersal via neighborly bilingualism.

Borrowings that probably spread via Mobilian Jargon, at times even
beyond its attested range (as to the Cherokee, Catawba, and Karankawa),
included the following terms, showing varying degrees of phonological and
syllabic correspondences:

(92) 'buffalo': Tunica **yániši** 'bovine,' **yániškáši** 'original bovine,' Natchez
      yanasah, Cherokee **yahnsã** (Haas 1953: 279–80); Biloxi **yanasa'** ~
      yŭnisa' ~ **yĭnisa'** ~ **nsa** (Dorsey and Swanton 1912: 293; Haas 1968:
      82) < Choctaw/Chickasaw **yanaš**, Alabama/Koasati/Muskogee/
      Oklahoma Seminole **yanasa** (Haas 1968: 82; Munro, forthcoming);
      cf. Mobilian Jargon †**yanaše** ~ **yanasa**[6]

      'goose': Natchez **la:lak**, Tunica **lálahki** 'wild goose,' Yuchi **šalala**,
      Karankawa **la-ak** (Haas 1953: 229; Haas 1956: 65), Cherokee **sasa**
      (Ballard 1985: 339)[7] < Choctaw/Chickasaw **šalaklak**, Alabama/
      Koasati **salakla** (Munro, forthcoming); cf. Mobilian Jargon †**šalaklak**

      'milk': Tunica ɔ́**ndetiši** (Haas 1953: 292), Natchez **washtánshu** 'milk'
      (Van Tuyl 1980: 92), and possibly Yuchi **toši** (Crawford 1979: 346,
      347) < Choctaw/Chickasaw **piši** 'to nurse,' Alabama/Koasati **pisi** 'to
      nurse; breast,' Muskogee/Oklahoma Seminole **ipisi:** 'breast,'
      Choctaw/Chickasaw **ipišik** 'breast' (?; Munro, forthcoming), cf.
      Mobilian Jargon **wakatiši** 'milk' (Haas 1953: 292), **(wak) peše(k)**
      'milk,' and **(wak)peše** 'milk'

---

[6] Allan R. Taylor (1976: 166) explored the origin of the similar Southeastern Indian words
for 'buffalo' as loans from Athapaskan languages: Lipan Apache **iyándi** (with **-nd-** deriving
from Proto-Athapaskan *****n**), similar Athapaskan terms with a common verb root meaning 'to
eat, to graze,' or Navajo **ayáni ła?** 'buffalo, a buffalo, some buffalo' (with the enclitic particle
ła? serving as an indefinite determiner). He, however, regarded the late arrival of Athapaskans
in the Southern Plains around AD 1,200 as a problem in explaining the widespread diffusion
of the word for 'buffalo' in Southeastern Indian languages. Alternatively, Taylor proposed
Caddoan etymologies: Caddo **tanaha?**, Wichita **ta:rha**, Kitsai **tánaha**, Pawnee **taraha?**, and
Arikara **tanáha?**, for which he stipulated the phonological shifts *[y] > [t] and *[s] or *[š] >
[h] after their eastern neighbors had borrowed the Caddoan word(s) for 'buffalo.' He apparently preferred the latter explanation on grounds of the bison's primary habitat and the Caddoans' long-term home in the Plains (Taylor 1976: 166).
   Mobilian Jargon could still have been the primary medium by which Southeastern Indian
languages adopted either type of western loan for 'buffalo,' if one accepts phonological shifts
such as those proposed by Taylor as regular processes of language contact. Caddoan or even
Athapaskan etymologies for Mobilian Jargon †**yanaše** (?) and **yanasa** gain attraction in light
of the fact that the pidgin once included not only Caddo and other Caddoans (such as the
Natchitoches Indians), but also Lipan Apache among its speakers (see Sect. 10.1). What may
further appear as unlikely short-term shifts at first sight would be feasible with the hypothesis of Mobilian Jargon's pre-Columbian origin, offering greater time depth.

[7] Haas and Ballard also list Tonkawa **xilik**, excluded here because of its rather far-fetched
and possibly accidental resemblance.

'money': Choctaw **asonak** 'a vessel made with brass or tin,' Chickasaw **asonnak/aso:nak** 'tin,' Alabama **sonok** 'money,' **ocona/ocana**
'tin,' Koasati **ocona** 'machine, metal,' Apalachee **ocona niko watka**
'lightning' (with **niko watka** meaning 'ray of sun'), Seminole **kocuni**
'iron', Mikasuki **koconi** 'metal,' and Hitchiti **kocon-i** 'iron' (Munro
forthcoming: metal), Catawba **sənu'** 'money' (Speck 1934: 38, 39),
Cherokee **sö:nɪkt?a'** 'beads' (Mooney 1932: 164) < Algonquian . . .
(see Sect. 5.4)

One among few widespread loan-words without a corresponding entry in
Mobilian Jargon is 'woodpecker' (see Ballard 1983: 329), which quite possibly existed in the pidgin as well, but has remained unattested so far. Still
other borrowings show closer correspondences to Muskogee. They possibly
spread via the eastern variety of Mobilian Jargon or the lingua franca
Creek, with independent comparative evidence yet to be found in support
of this hypothesis. Mobilian Jargon also shared other, less widespread
borrowings of Muskogean origin with non-Muskogean languages, in whose
diffusion it may however have played no more than a limited role.[8]

In addition, Mobilian Jargon probably was the medium by which many
common ethnonyms and place names of Muskogean and especially Western
Muskogean origin came into use for both Muskogean and non-Muskogean
communities across much of southeastern North America (see Anonymous

---

[8] Among them are: 'bullfrog,' 'frog': Natchez **hánanai, ananá-i** (Van Tuyl 1980: 72), Cherokee **kanuna** (Feeling 1975: 142) < Alabama/Koasati **hanono** (Munro, forthcoming), cf. Mobilian Jargon **hanono**; 'hundred' (1): Cherokee **tsukwi** (Nicklas 1979: 48), Timucua **čupi**
(Granberry 1987: 43, 101) < Muskogee/Seminole/Hitchiti **cokpi-**, Koasati **cokpi**, cf. Mobilian
Jargon **čokpe**; 'hundred' (2): Biloxi **tsipa** (Nicklas 1979: 48) < Choctaw/Chickasaw **taɬipa**
'hundred,' Alabama **taɬɬi:pa/tahɬipa**: 'hundred,' cf. Mobilian Jargon **taɬepa**; 'nine': Biloxi **tckanɛ**
with syncopation of the initial vowel and **n** corresponding to **l**, absent in Biloxi (Nicklas 1979:
48; Rankin 1986: 80) < Koasati **cakkali**, Alabama/Koasati/Choctaw **cakka:li**, Chickasaw
cakka?li (Munro, forthcoming), cf. Mobilian Jargon **čak(k)ale**; 'owl': Ofo **apho'** (Dorsey and
Swanton 1912: 321) with metathesized vowels, if its resemblance to Muskogean languages
is not due to onomatopoeia (as suggested by Haas 1968: 2) < Chickasaw **ho:pa/hopah**,
Alabama/Koasati/Chickasaw/Muskogee/Oklahoma Seminole **opa**, Choctaw **opah**, Chickasaw
o:pa (Munro, forthcoming); cf. Mobilian Jargon †**hopa**; 'peach': Biloxi **tokonâ'** ~ **tkâ'nâ**
(Dorsey and Swanton 1912: 276)/**tkana** (Rankin 1986: 80); Ofo **akô"ti** (Dorsey and Swanton
1912: 320) < Choctaw **takkon** (Munro forthcoming); cf. Mobilian Jargon †**takō**; 'robin': Tunica
wišk?ohku (Haas 1953: 277); Catawba **wispɔkpɔk** (Matthews and Red Thunder Cloud 1967:
23) < Choctaw **biškoko** (Munro, forthcoming; cf. Mobilian Jargon †**beškoko**; 'salt': Yuchi **dabi**
(Crawford 1988: 159), Timucua **api** 'salt, ashes, powder' (Granberry 1987: 43, 96) <
Alabama/Koasati/Chickasaw **hapi**, Choctaw **hapih** (Crawford 1988: 159; Munro, forthcoming),
cf. Mobilian Jargon **hape**; and 'wildcat': Cherokee **koé/kuhé** 'wild-cat' (Gatschet 1969 [1888]:
191), **gvhe** 'bobcat' with **v** representing a short low central vowel, nasalized in Cherokee
(Feeling 1975: p. ix, 126) < Choctaw/Alabama/Koasati/Apalachee **kowi** 'mountain lion,
panther,' Chickasaw **kowi?** 'mountain lion, panther' (Munro, forthcoming), cf. Mobilian Jargon
†**kowe**. Absent evidence for the widespread distribution of these words beyond one or two
neighboring non-Muskogean languages and their occurrence in languages to which Mobilian
Jargon apparently did not extend (such as Catawba, Cherokee, and Timucua; see Sect. 10.1)
reduce the likelihood that the pidgin served as the medium of diffusion. These borrowings
probably were direct loans.

1862 MS: 144; Haas 1953: 184; Read 1963 [1931]: 156–8; Swanton 1911: 38, 46, 258; 1946: 94, 120, 141, 216–19; for a comparative Muskogean vocabulary, see Munro, forthcoming, unless indicated otherwise):

(93) Acolapissa < Choctaw/Chickasaw **haklo** 'to heart' + Choctaw/Chickasaw **pisa** 'to see'

Apalachicola < Apalachee **abalahci** 'other side [of the river]' + Apalachee **akola** 'people' or perhaps 'non-Apalachee people' (Geoffrey D. Kimball, personal communication), Choctaw **oklah** 'people,' Chickasaw **okla** 'town'

Atakapa < Choctaw/Chickasaw **hattak** 'person' + Choctaw/Chickasaw **apa** 'to eat' (= 'cannibal')

Atchafalaya < Choctaw **hacca** 'river' + Choctaw **falaya** 'long'

Bayogoula < Choctaw **bayuk** 'bayou' (Read 1963 [1931]: 82) + Choctaw **oklah** 'people,' Chickasaw **okla** 'town'

Bogalusa < Choctaw **bok** 'brook, creek, stream' (Byington 1915), Chickasaw **bok** 'river' (Humes and Humes 1973) + Choctaw/Chickasaw **losa** 'black'

Bogue Chitto < Choctaw **bok** 'brook, creek, stream' (Byington 1915), Chickasaw **bok** 'river' (Humes and Humes 1973) + Choctaw **cito** 'big'

Bogue Falaya < Choctaw **bok** 'brook, creek, stream' (Byington 1915), Chickasaw **bok** 'river' (Humes and Humes 1973) + Choctaw **falaya** 'long'

Chakchiuma < Choctaw **šakcih** 'crawfish,' Chickasaw **šakci** 'crawfish' + Alabama/Koasati/Choctaw/Chickasaw **homma** 'red'

Chinchuba < Louisiana Choctaw **cincoba** 'alligator'

Choula < Muskogee/Alabama/Koasati/Chickasaw **cola** 'fox,' Choctaw **colah** 'fox'

Houma < Alabama/Koasati/Choctaw/Chickasaw **homma** 'red'

Mogulasha < Muskogean **am-** first-person singular possessive (Booker 1980: 34–5) + Alabama/Koasati **-okla** 'friend,' Choctaw **oklah** 'people,' Chickasaw **okla** 'town' + Choctaw/Chickasaw **ãša** 'to dwell, to be located'

Ofogoula < Choctaw **ofi** 'dog,' Chickasaw **ofi?** 'dog' + Choctaw **oklah** 'people,' Chickasaw **okla** 'town'

Okelousa < Alabama/Koasati **oki** 'water' + Choctaw/Chickasaw **losa** 'black'

Opelousas < Choctaw **aba** 'up,' Chickasaw **aba?** 'up' (?) + Choctaw/Chickasaw **losa** 'black' (= 'hair people'?; see Haas 1953: 229)

Pacana < Creek/Oklahoma Seminole **paka:na** 'peach' < Shawnee **paka:na** 'nut' (Mary Haas in Martin 1994: 15–16)

Pascagoula < Choctaw/Chickasaw **paska** 'bread' + Choctaw **oklah** 'people,' Chickasaw **okla** 'town' (Haas 1953: 184, 244)

Pensacola < Apalachee **pãsak** 'hair' (Kimball, personal communication), Choctaw **ippãši** 'hair of the head', Chickasaw **ippãši?** 'hair of the head' + Apalachee **akola** 'people' or perhaps 'non-Apalachee people' (Kimball, personal communication), Choctaw **oklah** 'people,' Chickasaw **okla** 'town'

Shongaloo < Choctaw **šãkolo** 'cypress'

Tangipahoa < Choctaw **tãci**, Chickasaw **tanci?** 'corn' + Choctaw/Chickasaw **ayowa** 'to pick, to gather' (?)

Tassenocogoula < Choctaw **tassannok** 'flint' + Choctaw **oklah** 'people,' Chickasaw **okla** 'town'

Yakna-Chitto [Yagenechito] < Choctaw **yakni** 'land,' Chickasaw **yahni?** 'land' (?) + Choctaw **cito** 'big'

Whiskey Chitto < Choctaw **oski** 'reed,' Chickasaw **oski?** 'reed, cane' + Choctaw **cito** 'big'

Most of the compounding elements of these ethnonyms and place names have corresponding or equivalent forms in Mobilian Jargon, and there exist others that appear distinctly Muskogean in origin, but whose etymologies are incomplete or uncertain. Ultimately, the interpretation of ethnonyms and place names is fraught with various methodological complications (see Booker, Hudson, and Rankin 1992). These names only denote a general impact by Muskogean peoples in southeastern North America, probably via Mobilian Jargon; but it is impossible to sort out those names that diffused via the pidgin from direct borrowings (see Crawford 1975*a*: 34). For this reason, Muskogean ethnonyms and place names are not reliable indicators of the pidgin's geographic spread, much less of its pre-European existence (see Silverstein 1973 MS: 29).

However, Mobilian Jargon was the probable medium by which various Southeastern Indian languages adopted loan-words from Spanish, French, and possibly English, as indicated by the following few examples with corresponding terms in the pidgin:

(94) 'bit': Alabama/Choctaw **iskali** 'bit, money,' Alabama/Koasati/Choctaw **skali** 'bit, money' (Munro, forthcoming), Atakapa **skale'** 'bit, 12½ cents, escalin' (Gatschet and Swanton 1932: 108), Quapaw **skádi** 'money, measure generally' (Rankin 1988: 643), Ofo **ska'lo** 'escalin, bit, twelve and a half cents' (Dorsey and Swanton 1912: 329), Tunica **téskalahki** 'bit, escalin' (Haas 1953: 268) < French

"escalin" 'shilling' < Dutch "schelling" (worth 12¹/₂ cents); cf. Mobilian Jargon †**skale** ("skúlli" (Gatschet 1885 MS: 24))

'cat': Choctaw **kato(s)**, Alabama/Koasati/Muskogee **kati** (Munro, forthcoming); Biloxi **kətu** (Haas 1968: 78), Timucua **gato** (Granberry 1987: 103, 133) < Spanish "gato"; cf. Mobilian Jargon **kato/kate**

'coffee': Alabama/Koasati/Choctaw **kafi**, Muskogee **ka:fi**, Mikasuki **ka:f-i**, Chickasaw **ka:fi?** (Munro, forthcoming); Biloxi **kafi/kuxi** (Haas 1968: 78); Tunica **ka?fi**, Natchez **ka:Wih**, Chitimacha **kahpi** (Haas 1947: 146–8); Caddo **kapí:** (Chafe 1983: 247) < Spanish/French "café"; cf. Mobilian Jargon **kafe**

'cow': Alabama/Koasati/Muskogee/Oklahoma Seminole **wa:ka**, Chickasaw **wa:ka?**, Choctaw **wa:k**, Mikasuki **wa:k-i** (Munro, forthcoming), Hitchiti **wá:ka** (Sturtevant 1962: 51); Biloxi **wa:ka** (Haas 1968: 78); Catawba **wəde**, Yuchi **wedi** (Ballard 1983: 332); Caddo **wá:kas** 'cattle' (Chafe 1983: 247) < Spanish "vaca"; cf. Mobilian Jargon **wak(a)**

'hat': Choctaw **shapo** (Byington 1915: 328) < French "chapeau"; cf. Mobilian Jargon **šapo**

'nickel': Choctaw/Alabama/Koasati **pikayo** (Munro, forthcoming), Tunica **píhkayu/píkayun(i)** (Haas 1953: 245), Quapaw **ppikkáyõ** (Rankin 1988: 643), Biloxi **pûkĭyû⁗** 'five cents, nickel' (with metathesis; Dorsey and Swanton 1912: 250) < Louisiana French "picayune" < French/Spanish "picaillon" 'farthing'; cf. Mobilian Jargon **pekayo**

'rice': Koasati/Muskogee/Oklahoma Seminole **alo:so**, Muskogee **alo:s(w)a**, Mikasuki **alo:s-i** (Munro, forthcoming), Hitchiti **alo:s-** (Sturtevant 1962: 51), Chickasaw **ha:loši?/ha:lõši?**, Alabama **o:nosi**, Choctaw **onoš**, Louisiana Choctaw **honoši** (Munro, forthcoming) < Spanish "arroz"; cf. Mobilian Jargon **onos(e)/onoš(e)**

'Spaniard': Koasati **spani**, Choctaw **špa:ni**, Muskogee/Alabama **ispa:ni**, Chickasaw **ošpa:ni?** (Munro, forthcoming), Hitchiti **ispa:n-** (Sturtevant 1962: 51), Tunica **?íspani** (Haas 1953: 290) < Spanish "español" 'Spanish'; cf. Mobilian Jargon †**spane** ("spanié" (Anonymous 1862 MS))

In reverse, Mobilian Jargon was the immediate source via which numerous words of Native American origin entered Louisiana French and eventually English. Examples are several words of Algonquian origin that do not suggest any necessary European mediatory role in their transmission into Mobilian Jargon, but possibly originated from direct contact between Southeastern Indians and their northern neighbors and that transferred then into Louisiana French (see Sect. 5.4):

(95) 'bobcat', 'lynx', 'wildcat': Louisiana French "pichou" (Read 1963 [1931]: 101–2) < Mobilian Jargon †**pešo**

'hominy': Louisiana French "sacamité" (Read 1963 [1931]: 105–6); < Mobilian Jargon †**sakamete**

'leggings': Louisiana French "mitasses" (Read 1940: 548; 1963 [1931]: 97–8) < Mobilian Jargon †**metas** (?)

'pecan nut': Louisiana French "pacane" (Read 1963 [1931]: 99) < Mobilian Jargon †**pakan** (?)

'persimmon fruit': Louisiana French "plaquemine" (Read 1963 [1931]: 103) < Mobilian Jargon †**peakemena**

'uproar', 'racket', 'hubbub', 'war-whoop': Louisiana French "saca-coua"/"sasacoua" (Read 1963 [1931]: 103–4) < Mobilian Jargon †**sakak(o)ya,** †**sasak(o)wa,** and/or possibly †**sakak(o)wa**

Other Native American loan-words that probably entered Louisiana French via Mobilian Jargon reveal a Western Muskogean and specifically Choctaw etymology:

(96) 'bayou', 'creek', 'river': Louisiana French "bayou" 'bayou, sluggish water' (Read 1963 [1931]: 82) with variant spellings of "bayouc" and "bayouque" in the eighteenth century (Baudry des Lauzières 1802: 175; Le Page du Pratz 1758: i. 45; Margry 1876–1886: v. 387) < Choctaw **bayuk** (Jacob, Nicklas, and Spencer 1977: 21; Read 1963 [1931]: 82), Choctaw **bok** 'brook, creek, stream' (Byington 1915), Chickasaw **bok** 'river' (Humes and Humes 1973); cf. Mobilian Jargon **bayok**

'bowfin', 'mudfish': Louisiana French "choupique" 'bowfin, swamp fish' (Read 1963 [1931]: 88) < Choctaw **shupik** 'mudfish' (Byington 1915); cf. Mobilian Jargon **šopek** 'bowfin, mudfish'

'bread': Louisiana French "pasqua" (spelling?; Claude Medford, personal communication) < Choctaw/Chickasaw **paska**; cf. Mobilian Jargon **paska**, possibly also the medium for Biloxi **apasko^n/apasko/apasku** 'bread' (Haas 1968: 82)

'flatfish', 'sunfish', 'perch': Louisiana French "patassa" 'sunfish,' erroneously termed 'perch' (Read 1963 [1931]: 101) < Choctaw **patassa**, Chickasaw **patassa**? 'perch'; cf. Mobilian Jargon **patassa**

'muscadine': Louisiana French "soco" 'Southern Fox grape, berry of the muscadine' (Read 1963 [1931]: 106) < Choctaw **sokko**; cf. Mobilian Jargon **sok(k)o**

'raccoon': Louisiana French "chaoui" (Read 1963 [1931]: 87–8) < Choctaw **šawi,** Chickasaw **šawi**?; cf. Mobilian Jargon **šawe** 'red sumac': Louisiana French "bachoucta" 'dye made from the foliage of the South, Upland, or Scarlet Sumac' (Read 1963 [1931]: 81) < Choctaw **bašokča**; cf. Mobilian Jargon †**bašokca**

'watermelon': Louisiana French "chouquechi" 'cushaw' (Read 1963 [1931]: 89) < Choctaw **šokši**; cf. Mobilian Jargon **šokše**

'woman', 'wife', 'lady'/'Indian woman': Louisiana French "taïque" 'squaw,' often used derogatorily (Read 1963 [1931]: 107) < Choctaw **ti:k** 'female, woman', Chickasaw **-ti:k** 'female, woman,' Alabama/Koasati **tayyi** 'female, woman' (Munro, forthcoming); cf. Mobilian Jargon **ta(y)ek** 'female; woman, lady, wife, girl, Indian woman'

'woman's clothes': Louisiana French "alconand"/"acolan" (with apparent metathesis) 'petticoat' (Read 1963 [1931]: 80) < Choctaw **ạlhkuna** 'gown, dress for a lady' (Byington 1915); cf. Mobilian Jargon †**alkona**

Several considerations, linguistic as well as non-linguistic, strongly suggest an indirect transmission of these loan-words via Mobilian Jargon rather than a direct borrowing from a native language into Louisiana French. Not only was the pidgin the established medium between central Southeastern Indians and historic immigrants (see Sect. 10.2); but Louisiana French exhibited only two loan-words of Western Muskogean origin without any attested corresponding forms in Mobilian Jargon: "cantaque" 'smilax' < Choctaw **kãtak**, Chickasaw **kantak** 'briar' (Read 1963 [1931]: 84) and "sacli" 'trout, bass' < Choctaw **saklih**, Chickasaw **sakli?** 'trout' (Munro, forthcoming).[9]

All the attested loan-words of Western Muskogean origin date back to early colonial times at the beginning of the eighteenth century. In **bayok** and **ta(y)ek**, Mobilian Jargon even preserved the archaic Choctaw forms of **baiyok** and **taiyek**, which modern speakers contracted to **bok** and **tek** respectively (see Jacob, Nicklas, and Spencer 1977: 21). All these borrow-

---

[9] Actually, one can reasonably surmise that Mobilian Jargon once included corresponding entries of †**kantak** 'smilax, briar' and †**sakle** 'trout, bass' or some related forms in its lexicon as well; but such an assumption still requires confirmation by some independent historical attestation.

There is another word whose history might suggest a role for Mobilian Jargon: *okay* or *OK* in American English; but closer inspection cannot uphold it. In one among numerous undocumented etymologies, this word supposedly derived from Choctaw **hoke**, a final particle of assertion or affirmation (see Byington 1915: 158) or similar forms, in which case it would have been reasonable to consider Mobilian Jargon as the medium as in the case of established Western Muskogean loans. Yet no corresponding entry exists for Mobilian Jargon, and all indications point the origin of this Americanism to Martin van Buren's struggle for re-election to the presidency from 1839 to 1840, as determined by Allen Walker Read (for a recent review of this etymology with counterarguments extending to any Choctaw derivation, see Cassidy 1981).

ings refer to indigenous phenomena that early French explorers and settlers encountered in their contact with native peoples, but for which they had no terms of their own and needed to borrow words. As a measure of their acceptance and wide spread, modern speakers of Louisiana French have erroneously taken these words as French in origin, and even Acadians ("Cajuns") who remembered some Mobilian Jargon no longer recognized their Native American etymology.

A review of loan-words that probably diffused via Mobilian Jargon shows fewer corresponding entries in Southeastern Indian languages than in European ones. The pidgin also mediated more Native American words into French and other European languages than European loan-words into Native American languages. If numbers of shared loan-words were reliable indicators, the pidgin played a smaller role as a medium of lexical diffusion among Southeastern Indians than in their contact with European immigrants. This conclusion corresponds to the observation of surprise by Mary Haas (1947: 146) that there existed but a few French loan-words in Tunica, a comparatively well-studied language and representative case, whose speakers used Mobilian Jargon as well. Similar restrictions applied to lexical borrowing among the native languages, if numbers are an indication. In the comparative listing of words for plants, animals, tribes, and other culture-specific phenomena in various Southeastern Indian languages by William L. Ballard (1983: 332–4), there are only some thirty terms identifiable as true loan-words, while others are cognates or reveal accidental or questionable similarities. Recent research on lexical borrowings in Southeastern Indian languages has produced no better results (see Martin 1994), but confirms the low rates of European loans in the native languages of the Southeast in comparison to those of other culture areas in North America (see Brown 1994: 97–9, 102).

These findings may at first appear contradictory in view of the decline of indigenous languages, initiated presumably by extensive borrowing and eventually resulting in their replacement by Spanish, French, and English. The small number of widespread loan-words in Southeastern Indian languages even seems odd, given a long history of mutual contacts from early pre-Columbian times and common traditions. The absence of large-scale lexical borrowing would actually serve as an argument against any significant sociolinguistic and historical role of Mobilian Jargon and certainly against its pre-European origin.

These conclusions would hold if one viewed Mobilian Jargon solely in utilitarian terms as a medium of interlingual communication. Yet the limited evidence for loan-words in this case can be readily explained by the pidgin's meta-communicative functions as a sociolinguistic and sociocultural buffer (see Sect. 10.3). In many instances, lexical borrowing did occur in Mobilian Jargon without necessarily extending to its speakers' first languages. The

pidgin's role as a barrier against lexical borrowing apparently applied especially to smaller communities, for whom Ballard (1983: 325, 328–9) has
found greater resistance to lexical borrowing, as evident in smaller numbers
of loan-words in comparison to those of larger groups. In the widely shared
areal culture of Southeastern Indians, native languages apparently served
as major marks of social identity without necessarily hampering interlingual communication, made possible by widespread multilingualism and
contact media such as Mobilian Jargon.

Were it not for problems of circularity in argumentation, the resistance
against the widespread adoption of loan-words would lend indirect support
to the argument that Mobilian Jargon served as a linguistic and sociocultural buffer as much as an interlingual medium. The very "purity" of Southeastern Indian languages, reflecting a void of foreign influences in contrast
to their speakers' cultural uniformity, was possible only with the presence
of co-existent Mobilian Jargon in its central role as an interlingual medium.
Without a similar sociolinguistic institution, Southeastern Indian languages
would undoubtedly have been under greater pressure to converge among
each other, with processes of linguistic diffusion more or less mirroring the
widespread adoption of non-linguistic traditions. The absence of any extensive lexical borrowing among Southeastern Indian languages might even
suggest that the pidgin's buffer function was a long-term indigenous
phenomenon rather than just a response to American colonialism and
racist policies of the nineteenth century—potentially another clue for the
pre-European origin of Mobilian Jargon.

12.4. Other Native American Contact Languages of Greater Southeastern North America

As a major interlingual medium of southeastern North America, Mobilian
Jargon raises the question of other indigenous contact media in the area, in
which case it may serve as a model for their study. The discussion on the
pidgin's variation has already included the lingua francas Creek and
Apalachee as Eastern Muskogean varieties (see Sect. 8.5). As in these cases,
modern linguistic data for other Native American lingua francas in the area
are sparse or non-existent; but the ethnographic and historical literature
does contain incidental references to a few unrelated indigenous contact
languages.[10]

For the early nineteenth century and for today's four-state area of Oklahoma, Texas, Louisiana, and Arkansas, the ethnologist John R. Swanton

---

[10] This section draws in part on earlier surveys by Crawford (1978: 5–7) and Silverstein
(1973 MS: 12–13, 21–8).

(1911: 7), following the US Indian agent John Sibley, mentioned a Caddo trade language, presumably spoken among alloglossic Caddoan groups and perhaps in contact with their Muskogean, Siouan, and Plains Indian neighbors. Currently, there are no details available about the linguistic structure or social history of Caddo as a lingua franca.

Daniel G. Brinton (1859: 134–5) argued for Timucua of northeastern Florida as an indigenous lingua franca throughout much of the peninsula in the early seventeenth century. He based his finding on sociolinguistic observations by the missionary Francisco Pareja, who had apparently experienced no difficulty in speaking Timucua to neighboring groups of different linguistic backgrounds. Unfortunately, Brinton did not provide further supportive information. Julian Granberry (1987: 20–1, 26–55) has since described Timucua as a creolized blend of Macro-Chibchan, Arawakan, Muskogean, and other languages, without, however, specifying its preceding process of language convergence.[11]

Another native contact medium was apparently based on the language of the Shawnee Indians, a widely scattered group of Algonquians who in colonial times wandered across much of eastern North America from the Ohio River valley and even Pennsylvania as far south as Georgia and eastern Texas. In the early eighteenth century, the French-born Anglican missionary Francis Le Jau (1956 [1706–1717]: 11, 19, 41, 68–9, 73, 87) learned from a trader about "Savannah," "Saonah," or "Savannock," and described it as "fine smoth [*sic*] and easy to be got." The missionary called it "the transcendent language of America," apparently understood from colonial Carolina to Canada, and compared it not only with Latin and Arabic as international languages, but also with the lingua franca Creek of Southeastern Indians. Because of its easy intelligibility and extensive use, Le Jau engaged European traders with knowledge of the lingua franca Shawnee to help him translate the Lord's Prayer in a first step towards the Native Americans' conversion to Christianity, and he sent one of several versions to his superiors in England, published by John Chamberlayne (1715: 89) and again by Edmund Fry (1799: 258). There exist other, incidental mentions of a possible lingua franca Shawnee. An early source on Creek as intertribal medium, the naturalist William Bartram (1958 [1791]: 245, 294) also made a reference to the "Uches" (Yuchi) speaking "Savannuca" or "Shawanese." Several decades later, Thomas S. Woodward, who made pertinent observations about Mobilian Jargon and especially its eastern variety

---

[11] In describing the Tawasa dialect of Timucua as "a blend of both Timucuan and Muskogean characteristics," Granberry (1987: 20) drew an analogy to "the same kind of creolization that we see in the neighboring Mobilian 'jargon'." This reference suggests that Granberry understands *creolization* simply as language mixture rather than in the technical linguistic sense, as there are no indications that Mobilian Jargon creolized or became the first language of a community.

(see Sect. 8.3), similarly suggested Yuchi's mutual intelligibility with
Shawnee (Woodward 1939 [1859]: 39–41), presumably via a common
medium based on the language of the influential Shawnee. While John R.
Swanton (in Bartram 1958 [1791]: 414) simply dismissed Bartram's association of the Yuchi with the unrelated Shawnee as an error, Albert S.
Gatschet (1969 [1884]: 22–3, 143) had attempted to resolve the enigma by
suggesting two conflicting interpretations. On the one hand, he derived
"Savannuca" from Muskogee "Sawanógi" or 'dwellers upon Savannah
river' without making any claims about their linguistic affiliation, and contrasted this topographical etymology with "the Algonkin work sháwano
south," from which he derived the Shawnee's ethnonym; on the other hand,
he thought of the Sawanogi as " 'Sháwanos,' a town settled by Sháwano-
Algonkins [i.e. Shawnee], but belonging to the Creek confederacy" and
hosting some Yuchi. Yet, as recently pointed out by Bruce L. Pearson
(1987), the etymology of "Shawnee" (< Shawnee **ša:wano** ~ **ša:wanwa**
'Shawnee') is not identical with that of "Savannah," a topographical term
borrowed by English from Carib or Taino via Spanish. "Savannah" and
related forms simply referred to Indians of the Carolina grasslands, and
included native groups other than the Shawnee, such as their immediate
neighbors, the Creek. However, the explicit contrast by early observers
between Shawnee as an intertribal medium and the lingua franca Creek
precludes any interpretation of the first in terms of the latter or a confusion of the two. A preliminary examination of Le Jau's translation of the
Lord's Prayer confirms this conclusion, and a comparison of it with more
recent versions, three of them reprinted and discussed by J. Hammond
Trumbull (1873: 92–7) and another published by Thomas Alford (1929: 11
[Matt: 6: 9–13]), reveals little of the complex morphology common to
Algonquian languages. In an attempt at analyzing Le Jau's version, Trumbull (1873: 98) assigned some of the vocabulary to Algonquian languages,
including Shawnee, but considered a greater part to be Iroquoian "as if [it]
had been made up from some Iroquois dialect, half-understood by the
translator." Curiously, he also derived one word, **heyring**, from English
"heaven," supplemented with the locative suffix **-ng**, which he did not find
in Shawnee, although there exist corresponding suffixes indicating place in
various Algonquian languages such as **-enki** (see Aubin 1975: 24). Trumbull
concluded that Le Jau's translation did not represent any single native language, and named the language "Pseudo-Shawano." Relying on the argument of the comparatively small number of Shawnee settlements, Crawford
(1978: 99 n. 5) has expressed doubt about the existence of a Shawnee lingua
franca in southeastern North America, and did not take into consideration
broader sociopolitical factors such as the Shawnee's role in organizing intertribal resistance against American expansion under the leadership of
Tecumseh. Until today, a review of the linguistic data in light of modern,

more comprehensive comparative data has still been wanting, but may eventually confirm a lingua franca based in part on Shawnee, which Le Jau used for a possible word-for-word translation of the prayer from English or some other European language. Such an interpretation would match the Shawnee's long-term intertribal friendships with various groups east of the Mississippi River, including Delaware and Kickapoo (Algonquians), Seneca-Cayuga and Cherokee (Iroquoians), Biloxi and Quapaw (Siouans), Anadarko, Caddo, and Hainai (Caddoans), and Creek, Seminole, and Choctaw (Muskogeans) among others (see Howard 1981: p. xiii, 19).

For the mid-eighteenth century, James Adair, trader among the Cherokee and Chickasaw, mentioned a "mixed language" used between the once powerful and numerous Catawba and their neighbors in the Piedmont area of upper South Carolina and adjacent North Carolina northeast of the Creek Indians. According to Adair (1968 [1775]: 224–5), this contact medium was made up of more than twenty different "dialects or languages," among which he mentioned the following: Catawba (distant relative of Proto-Siouan), which apparently served as the "court" or standard language; Wataree (unidentified); Eno (Siouan?); Chowanoc (Algonquian?); Congaree (Siouan?); Natchez (Gulf); Yamasee (unidentified); and Coosa (unidentified). By Adair's indications, speakers of the lingua franca Catawba drew on linguistic elements from three or four different language families, possibly even more. Unfortunately, there are no other known attestations that confirm or elaborate Adair's observations.

The language of the Tuscarora, once a sizable and influential group of Iroquoians in eastern North Carolina, likewise functioned as a lingua franca, understood by at least some members of every adjacent alloglossic community such as the Pamlico (Algonquians) and the Woccon (Siouans). In the early eighteenth century, the English explorer John Lawson (1967 [1709]: 233–9) recorded a vocabulary of almost 200 entries and a few phrases. He further described this "Indian Jargon" to be imperfect in its moods and tenses and so deficient that the Indians could not express themselves with any elegance; apparently they barely understood each other, and younger members could not follow the elders' abbreviated speech in councils and debates (Lawson 1967 [1709]: 239). However, Lawson's vocabulary consisted of everyday expressions, numbers, and words related to the trade in hides and European goods, the latter suggesting the use of the lingua franca Tuscarora also in contact with Europeans.

Still farther north in the early eighteenth century, linguistically diverse Indians of south-central Virginia apparently spoke a common medium associated with the influential Occaneeche (Occaneechi) Indians. On a visit with them, the local historian Robert Beverley (1855 [1722]: 148, 157) compared their general language to the intertribal medium of Algonquin among Great Lakes Indians and to the lingua franca Sabir of the Levant; he further observed "broken and imperfect sentences," and mentioned the medium's use in religious ceremonies similarly to Latin in the Catholic mass. The nineteenth-century ethnologist Horatio Hale (1883: 12–13) equated the lingua franca Occaneeche with Tutelo (Siouan), and may have been accurate in his assumption short of supporting evidence. Recently, Edward P. Alexander (1971) discovered a small vocabulary of so-called Saponey (Saponi), recorded by a young Irish veteran by the name of John Fontaine at Fort Christanna in southern Virginia around 1716. Many words are Siouan in origin, close to Tutelo; but most numbers are Algonquian except for one or two identified as Iroquoian, and several entries remain unidentified (see Alexander 1971: 309–13). Especially noteworthy is the similarity of the word for 'six' in Saponey ("Quiock," probably an incorrect copying of "Ouiock"), Pamlico ("Who-yeoc"), and the lingua franca Tuscarora ("Houeyoc"), whose etymology is Tuscarora (see Alexander 1971: 310, 312 n. 71, Goddard 1972, and Lawson 1967 [1709]: 233). This vocabulary represents a mixed vocabulary collected from Indians of different linguistic backgrounds or, more likely, an intertribal contact medium rather than Saponey proper. By all indications, "Saponey" was not exclusive to the Indians of the same name, but was also the language of their affiliates, namely Occaneeche (Siouans), Stenkenocks (Algonquians?), Meipontski (Algonquians?), Tutelo, and possibly other Indians, which helps to explain their conflicting linguistic classifications. In early 1700, these groups had all fled from marauding Iroquois to Fort Christanna, and probably used Saponey as the basis for an interlingual medium. Moreover, this lingua franca Saponey apparently served as a trade language, as suggested by numerous references to exchange in the vocabulary and by the role of Fort Christanna as a trading center for Occaneeche and other Virginia Indians at the time (Alexander 1971: 304–7). If the Occaneeche and Saponey Indians in fact were closely related associates, "Saponey" was a variety of the lingua franca Occaneeche.

There are incidental references to a lingua franca in use among the member groups of the Powhatan confederacy of the Virginia coastal plain. In 1844, a clergyman by the name of E. A. Dalrymple collected a vocabulary of a few numbers and additional terms among the Pamunkey Indians, once a dominant tribe of the Powhatan. Surprisingly, these words do not resemble the vocabularies of Algonquian or other languages in the area, and have remained unidentified except for the numeral 'one' with its similarity to equivalent forms in Powhatan and Delaware (Howell, Levy, and Luckenbach 1979). This instance recalls the case of Nanticoke (Eastern Algonquian), spoken by the neighbors of the Powhatan Indians across the Chesapeake Bay, who borrowed the numerals 'one' through 'ten' from Mandingo-speaking African slaves (Brinton 1887). While the Mandingo loans in Nanticoke do not provide etymologies for Dalrymple's unidentified entries, they suggest the possibility of borrowings from other, distant languages. Curiously, Dalrymple's word list also present both l and r as apparently distinctly variable sounds, whereas Eastern Algonquian languages have exhibited either /l/ or /r/, but not both. However meager, these features point to a possible contact medium (Howell, Levy, and Luckenbach 1979: 79–80) or "jargonized Powhatan" (Goddard 1977: 41) rather than Pamunkey proper, an Eastern Algonquian language. Some indirect support for a Pamunkey or Powhatan Jargon comes forth from the fact that, as a result of early, prolonged, and close contacts by English speakers with Virginia Indians,

Powhatan is the source of more loans into English than any other single Algonquian language. These loanwords include the English terms: *chinquapin, chum, hominy, matchcoat, moccasin, muskrat* (a loanblend), *opossum, persimmon, pone* (and *corn pone* as a loanblend), *puccoon, raccoon, terrapin, tomahawk, tuckahoe,* and *wicopy* (*Dirca palustris* L.). All or most of them entered English during the first two decades of contact and probably before the outbreak of hostilities in 1622. (Siebert 1975: 290)[12]

On the northernmost border of southeastern North America, there existed Delaware Jargon, an indigenous contact language of New Netherland in the early seventeenth century between the Delaware Indians (including the Munsee, the Unalachtigo, and the Unami) and their associates. It, too, served as primary medium in early contacts by the Delaware Indians and their affiliates with European immigrants, especially Dutch colonists and later Swedish and English settlers, with the fur trade as a major activity. Delaware Jargon was a genuine pidgin with a lexical base in Unami, a dialect of Delaware or Lenape (Algonquian), but included words from other languages such as Natick, a dialect of Massachusett (Algonquian), and a few single "loan-words" from European languages (including Spanish, Dutch, Swedish, and English). Delaware Jargon exhibited little inflectional or derivational morphology and limited morphosyntactic redundancy, but revealed distinct syntactic patterns of negative–subject–predicate constructions and object–verb as predominant word order, shared by the area's Algonquian and Iroquoian languages (Prince 1912; Thomason 1980). Sarah G. Thomason has interpreted these areal-typological characteristics of Delaware Jargon as evidence for its pre-Columbian existence, and has placed it in the sociohistorical context of Algonquian–Iroquoian

---

[12] In contrast, "Other Algonquian loans in English are mostly from various New England and northeastern languages and include: *caribou* (from Micmac), *moose, sachem* (from Narragansett), *sagamore* (from Abenaki), *skunk, wampum,* and *wigwam* (from Abenaki). Some others are from various central Algonquian languages, all of them of a much later date: *pecan, pemmican* (from Cree), *totem* (from Ojibwa), and *wapiti* (from Shawnee). No loanwords from English into Powhatan have been recorded, but there probably were some" (Siebert 1975: 290–91).

contact, in particular a loosely organized alliance of eastern Algonquian groups led by the Delaware in opposition to Iroquois Indians. By some historical indications, the Delaware and other Algonquians used the pidgin as a sociolinguistic buffer behind which they could withdraw, and misled Europeans into thinking of the pidgin as Delaware proper (Goddard 1971: 15–16; Thomason 1980: 182–6).[13]

This sketchy survey points to several indigenous contact languages in southeastern North America apart from Mobilian Jargon and its varieties, including the lingua franca Creek. Some of these non-Muskogean-based contact media were probably related to each other. By the available evidence, Delaware Jargon in both structure and function resembled Algonquian-based lingua francas in the area, such as possibly interrelated Pidgin Massachusett in New England and Powhatan Jargon of Virginia (see Goddard 1977: 41). There are also incidental references to similarities, such as shared vocabulary, a distinct variation of l and r, and perhaps even the semantic domain of numbers, that hint at some lexical and perhaps grammatical interrelations between these lingua francas, as if they formed blends of variable Siouan–Algonquian–Iroquoian proportions in a larger contact-language chain along the Atlantic Coast not unlike the eastern and western varieties of Mobilian Jargon. This interpretation remains a conjecture in need of substantiation with systematic comparative data, quite possibly non-extant today.

No attestations exist for the survival of most of these non-Muskogean contact media in their original forms beyond the eighteenth century; they presumably yielded to "American Indian Pidgin English" (AIPE) with the expanding colonization of the Atlantic Coast by the English (Leechman and Hall 1955; Goddard 1977, 1978; Miller 1967). To the extent that AIPE was not just a figment of the European colonists' imagination, it was a kind of European foreigner talk with the Indians, characterized by stereotypical hypercorrections, and did not truly represent their speech. Before fully adopting English, the Indians of the Atlantic Coast undoubtedly continued responding in varieties of their traditional contact media with substantial native vocabularies, while gradually adopting a growing body of English loan-words via lexical replacement (Drechsel 1976a: 70–4). When first proposed, this interpretation could not draw on much evidence other than a small shared vocabulary of obvious Algonquian origin such as *papouse*, *squaw*, *tomahawk*, and **netap** 'friend' or the variation of l and r, a feature common to Delaware Jargon and AIPE. This model of language contact has

---

[13] For some useful supplementary information of a sociohistorical nature on the contacts between Native Americans and the Dutch in the seventeenth century, consult Feister (1973). This study, however, falls short on understanding their sociolinguistic interactions, and overlooks such basic sources as J. Dyneley Prince's essay on Delaware Jargon (1912).

since received support from suggestive evidence in the cases of Pidgin Massachusett and Powhatan Jargon (Goddard 1977: 41), possibly the present-day English of the Wesort or Piscataway Indians (Algonquians) of southern Maryland (Gilbert 1986), Tidewater Pidgin of Virginia (Miller 1986 MS), and even Seminole Pidgin (see Sect. 8.6).

The Atlantic contact media of eastern North America did not survive as long as Mobilian Jargon. This fact not only explains the fuller documentation of the latter, but also indicates several factors for its survival: (1) the greater political power by interior groups such as the Choctaw, Chickasaw, and the Creek as remnants of the Mississippian Complex than coastal groups, except perhaps the early Delaware; (2) the earlier, more destructive impact of European colonialism on native coastal communities as compared with interior groups, resulting in the earlier replacement of native contact media by European-based ones (including some forms of AIPE); and (3) a difference in colonial policy between the British and their American descendants on the one hand and the French on the other, with the French conceding a greater role and thus greater recognition to the native population, quite possibly because of the first two factors. This perspective also helps explain the quite close association perceived of Mobilian Jargon with the French during colonial periods.

13

Conclusions: Methodological and Theoretical Implications

13.1. Mobilian Jargon in Comparison with
Other Native American Pidgins

An initial cost-benefit estimate might not lead one to commit any substantial expenditure of time and resources to historical and field research on Mobilian Jargon, a secondary sociolinguistic phenomenon of non-European origin and, at that, no longer in use. What may initially appear as a search for a needle in a haystack has actually yielded a fairly comprehensive case study of what—if not outright ignored—has traditionally been treated from an almost exclusively European perspective. In short, Mobilian Jargon bears comparative sigificance, and its description and analysis offer a fresh and broader angle of language contact in American Indian languages.

The present study first offers a comparative perspective for other Native American pidgins, especially Chinook Jargon of the Pacific Northwest Coast, the only other instance described in any substantial detail. A contrast of these two pidgins immediately engenders numerous differences; these apply to their sound systems, grammars including word orders, lexica, and other aspects, and clearly reflect the influence of their speakers' native languages. Significantly, the description and analysis of Mobilian Jargon disagrees with a paradigm that, in a major essay in *Language*, Michael Silverstein (1972) has suggested for Chinook Jargon: a multi-level variable system of convergent, but ambiguous surface utterances interpretable in terms of the reduced grammars of its speakers' first languages such as highly divergent Chinook (ergative) and English (accusative). In adopting such a "macaronic" model of language contact, Silverstein has presented speakers of Chinook Jargon as simply echoing the different grammars of their first languages, and has argued against Chinook Jargon as a separate linguistic entity except for a common interlingual vocabulary. By implication, he also favors a recent origin for it, presumably the result of contact with Europeans, although he has not suggested a necessary logical link between his model and a claim for colonial origin.

Drawing on the underlying phonologies of the speakers' first languages, Mobilian Jargon, like Chinook Jargon, exhibited considerable phonological variation, which suggests the concept of *interlingual archiphoneme* for discussions of language contact rather than the inadequate, even inappropriate monosystemic concept of phoneme (see Sects. 4.5 and 8.2). Yet in contrast to Chinook Jargon as presented by Silverstein, Mobilian Jargon, with all its variation in both phonology and lexicon, exhibited a single underlying grammar at the level of syntax, which displayed a characteristic Muskogean and Gulf pattern and which even Europeans adopted in attempting to speak "the Indian language." The difference between Silverstein's analysis of Chinook Jargon and that of Mobilian Jargon becomes evident when one considers the latter's basic word order. X/OsV and possibly X/OSV would not be relatable to a European language such as Spanish, French, or English other than in a belabored manner, such as by postulating a grammar of focused, topicalized, or other object-fronted sentences as the fundamental underlying paradigm. For Mobilian Jargon, a Silversteinian model of variability, joining divergent underlying structures at the surface level following principles of implicational universals, would also require some special and rather tortuous explanation for what would strike speakers of European languages as an anomalous, if not outright unacceptable word order.

While Silverstein has presented Chinook Jargon as a jargon—that is a highly variable pre-pidgin with multiple underlying grammars—Mobilian Jargon does not meet this definition; it was a stabilized pidgin with a distinct, comparatively consistent grammar that cannot be reduced to the grammatical principles of its source languages, notwithstanding many obvious structural correspondences to Muskogean and other Gulf languages. A comparison of Chinook Jargon and Mobilian Jargon then suggests two typologically distinct Native American contact media (see Drechsel 1981: 99–101, 105) or else a need for the re-examination of Silverstein's analysis of Chinook Jargon, however ingenious it may be as a model of initial pidginization or jargonization.

In response to a manuscript version of Silverstein's essay, Terrence S. Kaufman (1971: 277), drawing on a broader range of text materials, has already argued for a uniform, formal grammar of Chinook Jargon, which its speakers had learned along with the lexicon as in any other situation of foreign-language learning, albeit incompletely. Taking a broader sociolinguistic and historical perspective, Dell Hymes (1980: 405–18) has likewise questioned Silverstein's analysis of Chinook Jargon as "a virgin situation," and has cited native standards of grammar in its long-established use in intertribal trade and in its formal adoption by European missionaries and merchants. According to Hymes, Chinook Jargon had to be learned like other established contact media, and probably stemmed from indigenous institutions of exchange, bilingual marriages, and multilingual villages among Northwest Coast Indians plus some form of slavery among the

Chinook—by all indications before the arrival of the first Europeans. Similarly, William W. Elmendorf (personal communication; see Elmendorf 1939 MS) and Sarah G. Thomason (1983) have rejected Silverstein's interpretation of Chinook Jargon by interpreting it instead as a genuine, full-fledged pidgin; its grammar not only differed from the speakers' native languages in non-simplificatory ways, but also exhibited a regular pattern of its own, applicable even to the pidgin's phonology. Thomason has further presented marked features of Chinook Jargon as characteristic typological traits of Northwest Coast native languages, which suggest predominantly indigenous sociolinguistic environments and support the hypothesis of a pre-European origin.

In contrast to Silverstein's multi-level "macaronic" interpretation, the alternative view of Chinook Jargon receives indirect support on typological grounds from the analysis of Mobilian Jargon. Typologically, these two Native American pidgins in turn resemble a third case, Delaware Jargon (see Thomason 1980). Like the first two contact languages, Delaware Jargon exhibits a distinct grammar with a uniform syntax. This observation need not suffer from the application of a Silversteinian analysis to the sound system—to the extent that the phonology of a pidgin, a second language, usually reveals influences from the speakers' first languages in more distinctive and lasting ways than other aspects of grammar. Nor does a conventional interpretation change by the attestation of lexical variation, for the simple reason that speakers borrowed words from their first and other languages without affecting the analytic grammars of these pidgins. Quite possibly, the interpretation of the lingua francas Creek and Apalachee as eastern varieties of Mobilian Jargon (see Sect. 8.5) also has an analogy in Nootka Jargon as a variety of Chinook Jargon or as part of a single Northwest Coast Indian pidgin rather than two separate contact media as proposed by William Samarin (1988). Ultimately, convention and convenience would argue against carrying this argument to its logical conclusion and renaming Mobilian Jargon, Chinook Jargon, Delaware Jargon, and other similar cases of stable American Indian pidgins as *Choctaw Pidgin*, *Chinook Pidgin*, *Delaware Pidgin*, and so on; capitalized *Jargon* simply remains part of their name without the typological implications of a highly variable pre-pidgin as now understood in linguistics.

Notwithstanding obvious substantive differences in lexicon and grammar, especially phonology and word order, Mobilian Jargon, Chinook Jargon, and Delaware Jargon share several structural, functional, and historical characteristics (see Drechsel 1981 for a preliminary sociolinguistic typology). Characteristic linguistic resemblances include:

   (*a*)   variable phonologies, syllable structures, and vocabularies, at least in
            the cases of Mobilian Jargon and Chinook Jargon, with alternations

occurring especially in the pronunciation of highly marked sounds and complex consonant clusters;

(*b*) parsimonious vocabularies consisting of generically defined, grammatically and semantically ambiguous, polysemous lexical entries and expandable by metaphorical extension, compounding, and borrowing by demand;

(*c*) "mixed" lexica with entries from predominantly native, frequently diverse and distant native sources for basic vocabularies and only a small number of European or other non-American loan-words for cultural borrowings;

(*d*) analytic sentence structures with little morphophonological "machinery" in the form of affixations or inflections and with limited morphosyntactic redundancy, but quite stable grammars with word order as the prime means for identifying the grammatical functions of sentence elements;

(*e*) primarily short utterances and sentences, with evidence for some subordination and complex constructions in at least Chinook Jargon and Mobilian Jargon;

(*f*) substantially conventionalized grammars with their own distinctive rules and characteristically indigenous word-order patterns, clearly reflecting the determinant influence of the areas' native languages in the form of marked grammatical features; no evident impact from languages of post-Columbian immigrants;

(*g*) linguistic variation limited largely to the phonology and the lexicon, which reflected the influence of speakers' first lanuages;

(*h*) close structural-functional affinities with interrelated, seemingly distinct varieties such as Nootka Jargon in the case of Chinook Jargon, the lingua francas Apalachee and Creek in relation to Mobilian Jargon, and Pidgin Massachusett and Powhatan Jargon with respect to Delaware Jargon.

Chinook Jargon, Mobilian Jargon, and Delaware Jargon further have in common several extralinguistic features:

(*i*) American Indians' animated use of body language, including gestures and facial expressions, in at least Chinook Jargon and Mobilian Jargon, contrasting with a traditionally sparing reliance on body language in their first languages;

(*j*) use in diverse interlingual contexts: kin, community, and intertribal gatherings; fur and hide trade; political alliances; European explorations and colonizations, including the conversion of the native population to Christianity; the employment of Native Americans by Europeans in various functions and apparently even the enslavement of native peoples;

(*k*) functions as indigenous lingua francas among linguistically diverse native groups, especially across great distances; use also as interethnic contact media and trade languages between indigenous peoples and post-Columbian immigrants (Europeans and other ethnic groups, among them Africans in eastern North America and Hawaiians as well as Asians on the continent's western shore) with a geographic distribution along coastal areas and major waterways of North America into their interiors;

(*l*) use not only for purely communicative purposes, but also in narration and other forms of poetic expression, pleasure, and amusement, plus possibly as means to promote social distance, especially in master–slave communication, in at least Chinook Jargon and Mobilian Jargon; sociolinguistic buffers in the case of Mobilian Jargon, apparently Delaware Jargon, and possibly Chinook Jargon;

(*m*) coexistence with other crosslingual compromises in occasionally overlapping sociolinguistic niches: (1) bilingualism and multilingualism in native languages, in use in the speakers' own communities of intermarrying groups and with immediate neighbors; (2) employment of interpreters in contact with distant visitors, with indigenous pidgins as major media; and (3) use of European languages in contact with immigrants;

(*n*) utilization in colonial times and—in the case of Chinook Jargon and Mobilian Jargon—into the twentieth century, but no evidence for systematic, large-scale creolization; and

(*o*) multiple suggestive evidence for the pre-European origin of these native pidgins, drawing on structural-functional arguments and explanations of pre-Columbian sociolinguistic conditions.

These patterns also apply in part to a fourth, less well-described indigenous pidgin of North America, namely Eskimo Jargon (see Stefánsson 1909), and suggest corresponding features in still other, poorly documented American Indian pidgins. In particular, indications for buffer functions in Delaware Jargon similar to those in Mobilian Jargon (see Thomason 1980: 185) raise questions about comparable roles for other Native American contact media, and may explain the largely absent creolization of major Native American pidgins. The adoption of a pidgin as a community's first language apparently occurred only in Chinook Jargon where children grew up with the pidgin as their main language in the linguistically and ethnically heterogeneous Grand Ronde Reservation in northwestern Oregon (see Hymes and Hymes 1972; Zenk 1984, 1988). Yet the description and analysis of such a nativized Chinook Jargon suggest no more than a limited or secondary creolization in that this pidgin never became the exclusive language, unlike pidgins in other communities. It existed side by side with various Native American languages, French, and English, and drew on indigenous languages as prime resources for its lexicon and grammar. Secondary or gradual creolization differs typologically from the abrupt creolization of a highly variable pidgin or a true jargon with the rapid adoption of a new grammar, as Derek Bickerton (1981, 1984) has proposed for various Caribbean pidgins and Hawaiian Pidgin. Some creolization may also have occurred with Europeanized versions of Native American pidgins, as in the cases of Seminole Pidgin English and perhaps Anglicized versions of Delaware Jargon, about which few details are, however, available. All in all, there never developed integrated multilingual communities in which Native American pidgins became the principal media, adopted by younger generations as their prime or sole languages as in plantation communities of North America dominated by European immigrants and African slaves. Instead, many native peoples have succeeded in maintaining greater independence from the larger society than immigrant groups, and have sometimes retained their indigenous languages with it. These issues again underscore the need for examining language contact in a broader than utilitarian perspective with its prevalent focus on communication.

The most controversial aspect of these Native American contact media remains their origin. Both linguistic and sociohistorical evidence in the form of native grammatical patterns, established traditions of intertribal interactions including long-distance trade, and the apparent sociopolitical integration of diverse groups into multilingual chiefdoms in pre-Columbian times strongly suggest the existence of Chinook Jargon, Delaware Jargon, and Mobilian Jargon before the Europeans' arrival in America. This inference is not conclusive, and requires further sociohistorical evidence for confirmation. Arguments principally based on linguistic traits including word order, as applied by Thomason (1980, 1983) to Delaware Jargon and Chinook Jargon, are of limited value. Although she expects crosslingual compromises resulting from contact with Europeans to have reflected some influences of their languages, a pidgin's linguistic pattern is actually an issue that is methodologically and theoretically separate from the question of its origin (Drechsel 1984: 141–2). Without rekindling the unnecessary Saussurean distinction between synchrony and diachrony, one might reasonably argue that Delaware Jargon, Chinook Jargon, and Mobilian Jargon came about as a result of contact with Europeans, but reflected an initial position of control by Native Americans over the early colonists. By this reasoning, the latter were initially in the minority, rather inept in their new environment, and at the Native Americans' mercy, which is why they left no linguistic mark on these Native American pidgins except single "loan-words." Such indeed is the argument of Gillian Sankoff (1980: 145–6), who has proposed a kind of inertia to explain the persistence of Chinook Jargon and other non-European contact media in European colonial situations; supposedly, indigenous lingua francas came about as a result of contact with Europeans and continued in use only by virtue of their existence. Yet Sankoff makes no effort to explain the remarkably long persistence of Chinook Jargon (with a history of at least 150 years), let alone that of Mobilian Jargon (with a minimum of 250 years); nor has she considered exploring the possibility of pre-Columbian existence for non-European pidgins. In a variation of Sankoff's arguments, one could further think of the Europeans' arrival as the very event that induced increased interlingual communication among native peoples and thus led to pidginization, without necessarily entailing an active role for Europeans in the pidgins' formation *per se*. However, as Thomason (1983: 866–7) has already convincingly argued for Chinook Jargon, it is difficult to imagine Europeans as disengaged and silent actors, when in fact they set up trading posts or factories and sent missionaries among native peoples with the explicit goal of establishing contacts with them for the purpose of trade, religious conversion, and political control.[1]

There is one feature common to Chinook Jargon, Mobilian Jargon, Delaware Jargon, and still other Native American contact media that might serve as a further proposition for their post-Columbian origin, namely their location in coastal areas (see (*k*) above). Accordingly, their very geography suggests contact with peoples from overseas, presumably Europeans in colonial times. This argument would first seem to receive support by the lack of attested indigenous contact languages in the Southwest, but then does not fare well in light of an apparently similar shortage in linguistically highly diverse California, under Spanish administration since the late eighteenth century. There is a better explanation instead. With rich natural resources and an advantageous infrastructure, coastal areas of North America traditionally supported larger populations of considerable sociopolitical complexity (such as paramount chiefdoms), and developed extensive linguistic diversity by both internal differentiation and immigration over thousands of years (see Gruhn 1988). Peoples of coastal areas of North America did not have to wait for Europeans to develop interlingual compromises. In fact, more or less stable pidgins appear to have been direct linguistic reflections of multilingual, but sociopolitically rather fragile chiefdoms as they existed especially in northwestern and eastern North America.

---

[1] William S. Samarin (personal communication) still disagrees with this assessment, and has suggested the Europeans' use of native or part-native intermediaries, sometimes known as *métis*, as a further argument against the pre-Columbian origin of Native American contact media. Yet these intermediaries either would have made use of already existing indigenous media in their interactions with distant groups, or alternatively would have passed on European elements in cases of post-Columbian pidginization by drawing on their own interlingual experiences with Europeans. Significantly, Europeans did not rely exclusively on *métis* in their interactions with Native Americans; they also dealt with them directly. Samarin's counterargument thus changes little in the overall picture presented here.

That no comparable pidgin developed in California would relate directly to the absence of sociopolitical integration of alloglossic peoples into large peer polities such as chiefdoms or complex chiefdoms (see Drechsel 1993 MS).[2]

Irrespective of their origins and histories, Chinook Jargon, Delaware Jargon, and Mobilian Jargon shared numerous sociolinguistic traits that call for an explanation. The source languages for these pidgins were historically and structurally too divergent (see Campbell and Mithun 1979*a*) to produce similar linguistic compromises simply by chance. Nor is there any evidence for direct historical ties among speakers of these Native American pidgins to suggest stimulus diffusion, just as the distinct grammars and lexica of the pidgins' sources languages preclude considering regular contact or a common origin among them. Instead, structural, functional, and even historical similarities among Chinook Jargon, Mobilian Jargon, and Delaware Jargon are typological in nature. Their resemblances indicate strategies of interlingual communication common among many Native Americans as well as among other peoples. The conclusion of independent, but convergent developments does not falter in light of incidental linguistic evidence of contact between speakers of two different contact languages, as the Algonquian "loan-words" might indicate for Mobilian Jargon and some Algonquian-based lingua franca of the Great Lakes area (see Drechsel 1985).[3]

The structural-functional similarities between Mobilian Jargon, Delaware Jargon, Chinook Jargon, and even Eskimo Jargon demonstrate the need for systematic typological research on a broader sociolinguistic scale beyond the traditional focus by Americanist linguists on phonology and morphology. Typologies of Native American languages must still extend systematic attention to syntax, semantics, and sociohistorical aspects, and readdress questions of interrelations between linguistic and culture area in a broad sociolinguistic frame (see Sect. 12.2).

[2] None of these arguments has convinced Samarin (1986) about Chinook Jargon's origin. He has rejected the pre-Columbian hypothesis by questioning the validity of the pidgin's early attestations, Thomason's linguistic arguments, and Hymes's sociohistorical explanation, and has suggested European colonialism as its source. In place of early Chinook Jargon, Samarin (1988) has proposed a prior so-called Nootka Jargon, presumably also the result of European contact, for which he has provided no substantive linguistic evidence and whose relationship to Chinook Jargon still requires clarification. According to Thomason (1983: 859–61), documentation of some European linguistic influences in Nootka Jargon confirms its post-Columbian origin, but also suggests that it succeeded Chinook Jargon, not the reverse as frequently maintained. None the less, Nootka Jargon could simply have been a variety of Chinook Jargon with a predominantly Nootka vocabulary by the fact that Nootka Indians spoke this pidgin.

[3] For a more "exotic" instance, note Hawaiian "loan-words" in Chinook Jargon and Eskimo Jargon, which, however, would not support the conclusion that either came about under the influence of Pidgin Hawaiian, much less Hawaiian Pidgin English (Drechsel and Makuakāne 1982).

Comparison of the structural-functional features of Native American pidgins suggests a possible direction to such an expanded sociolinguistic typology. Contact media provide an ideal focus because of obvious connections between linguistic and extralinguistic aspects, although sociohistorical aspects are vaguer than linguistic categories and thus more difficult to classify. Different levels of linguistic description and analysis—phonology, morphology, syntax, and semantics—not only interrelate, as in the case of the pidgins' analytic morphosyntactic structure and their speakers' reliance on word order as the prime principle of grammatical organization; but linguistic features can also serve as indicators of the speakers' first languages and hence their identities as members of particular communities, and point to other extralinguistic aspects such as sociocultural functions. Specifically, semantic fields of the lexicon suggest domains of use and primary functions such as those of a trade language; predominant syntactic patterns appear to mark politically prominent groups. A broader consideration of linguistic and sociocultural aspects further offers clues to origins, proposed as pre-European in the cases of Chinook Jargon, Delaware Jargon, and Mobilian Jargon on the basis of distinctive indigenous grammatical patterns and pre-Columbian sociolinguistic contexts. Examination of these pidgins in the wider context of areal-typological features promises correlations, as already suggested in the case of Mobilian Jargon in southeastern North America, and provide the basis for a comprehensive sociolinguistic typology embracing social dialects (such as baby talk as well as women's and men's speech), non-pidginized contact languages (e.g. Métis and Trader Navaho), bilingualism and multilingualism, and so on (see Drechsel 1981: 106–8).

13.2. Linguistic Convergence and Pidginization in Americanist Linguistics

For broader theoretical implications, this book first bears on the study of Native American languages, principally those of southeastern North America, and portrays a major Native American pidgin, long thought extinct among only few other known instances. Of special interest are Mobilian Jargon's unique word order of X/OsV and possibly X/OSV, surprising by dint of not only its existence, but also its occurrence in a pidgin. Other distinctive characteristics are its functions as a sociolinguistic buffer and its extended history with plausible roots in the pre-Columbian Mississippian Complex.

The grammar of Mobilian Jargon leaves no doubt about its word order for sentences with pronominal subjects, confirmed independently by Crawford as well as in historical documentation. OsV is derivable from the pro-

nouns prefixed to verbs in Muskogean and other Gulf languages with analogous patterns of Os-V in terms of substrata influences (see Sect. 12.1), a
standard form of explanation in the study of pidgins and creoles. Nevertheless, there remains some question about a corresponding word order of
OSV for sentences with nouns as subjects. In initial reactions, some linguists
have attempted to explain the unusual word order of Mobilian Jargon in
terms of stylistic or discourse-conditioned variation in the sequence of sentence constituents—be it focusing, topicalization, or some other structural
means of emphasis and highlighting. This proposition has proved unsatisfactory simply because of the predominance of sentences with OsV order
with only a few, highly variable and easily explainable exceptions (see Sect.
6.5). Other scholars have questioned the accuracy of the syntactic data for
Mobilian Jargon, on grounds that OSV was extremely rare if existent (see
Greenberg 1963: 61), or have altogether rejected its existence as a basic
word-order pattern (see e.g. Pullum 1977: 259–65). In recent years, some linguists, one of whom had originally denied the existence of OSV languages,
have complied a catalogue of object-initial languages, and have confirmed
at least four examples of unmarked OSV word order in native languages
of the Amazon drainage area in Brazil, plus possibly another in Haida of
western Canada and southwestern Alaska (Derbyshire and Pullum 1981:
205–12; Pullum 1981: 151–2; cf. Egg 1990). These comparative data for OSV
languages do not make it easier to derive Mobilian Jargon's word order historically; for such an explanation either predicates the existence of some
OSV language in southeastern North America, unattested so far, or long-
distance historical ties across the Caribbean to South American languages
or across western North America to the Haida—rather far-fetched by
any historical criteria. In an answer closer at hand, recognition of the
pronoun–verb system of Muskogean and perhaps other Gulf languages as
the likely sources for Mobilian Jargon's pattern of OsV in fact renders obsolete any further search for some real or imaginary OSV language as its paradigm of origin. Yet if Mobilian Jargon also exhibited OSV as its basic
sentence pattern, it gains significance for the discussion of word order and
linguistic typology by providing one among possibly other historical scenarios for how this pattern, however, rare, came about. Following this
model, OSV became the basic word order of a first language by the creolization of a pidgin with a comparable syntactic pattern, and was the result
of language contact rather than some internal linguistic process of language
change (such as drift), and again points to the need for a broader perspective in Americanist linguistics. This reasoning is consistent with recent findings for word order to exhibit—counter to conventional wisdom—little
"genetic" stability and strong areal influences (see Nichols 1992: 93–5,
105–9, 166–73, 195–6, 245–6; cf. Thomason and Kaufman 1988: 54–5).

That this hypothesis need not be as far-fetched as it may appear initially becomes evident from a similar, although more variable case of language contact, a Creole–American Indian pidgin of Suriname known as Ndjuká-Trio Pidgin. Like Mobilian Jargon, Ndjuká-Trio Pidgin exhibits OsV or XsV in sentences with pronominal subjects; but constructions with nominal subjects display SOV and SXV following the model of Carib languages, including Trio (Huttar 1982: 3–4; Huttar and Velantie n.d. MS: 5–10). At first sight, the structural similarity of sentences with pronominal subjects in Ndjuká-Trio Pidgin and Mobilian Jargon appears so striking as to lend itself as a model for the analysis of the Mobilian Jargon word order in terms of OsV variable with SOV. Their apparent resemblances might even suggest a historical relationship between the two pidgins to creolists prone to perceive linguistic and sociohistorical ties across great distances among various Caribbean and circum-Caribbean creole societies. A closer examination of Ndjuká-Trio Pidgin discloses significant structural differences from Mobilian Jargon, and raises major questions about its role as an example for a syntactic reanalysis of the latter, not to mention serious doubts about historical ties between the two American Indian pidgins. Unlike Mobilian Jargon, Ndjuká-Trio Pidgin displays major variations in the word order of constructions with pronominal subjects. It allows not only OsV, but also sOV as e.g. in **pumi so trángamee oto wani** ('I-?-hard-game/meat-want') for 'I want meat very much.' Likewise, a questioned object equivalent to English 'What . . . ?' can precede or follow the pronoun subject. These and other syntactic variations in Ndjuká-Trio Pidgin closely emulate the grammar of Trio (Huttar and Velantie n.d. MS: 4–5, 6). The superstrate language manifests its dominant influence in the Ndjuká-Trio Pidgin syntax directly, whereas Muskogean languages did so more obliquely in Mobilian Jargon with its invariable pronoun–verb order. The great range of syntactic alternations among constructions with pronominal subjects and, along with them, between OsV and SOV in Ndjuká-Trio Pidgin may simply reflect a short history in contrast to Mobilian Jargon's comparatively rich past of at least 250 years. Although George L. Huttar and Frank J. Velantie (n.d. MS: 1–3, 14) have suggested a time span of up to two centuries for the contact between Africans and American Indians and hence for their interlingual medium, recorded attestations of Ndjuká-Trio Pidgin extend back only for about 100 years, and may describe a variable pidgin, a jargon, rather than a stabilized pidgin. Typological linguists will be interested in learning whether Ndjuká-Trio Pidgin is going to stabilize by developing a grammar with less word-order variation and what its dominant sentence pattern will be.

In a second major implication, historical-sociolinguistic research of Mobilian Jargon has added to our appreciation of the linguistic and social diversity of Southeastern Indians. Both grammatical and sociolinguistic clues in various purported documents of Choctaw, Chickasaw, and other related Muskogean languages show beyond doubt that they do not describe any of these languages, but refer to Mobilian Jargon, and thus leave unidentified the first languages of its speakers. Although these could have been Choctaw or Chickasaw, there exists an equal chance that the sources spoke other, possibly even unrelated indigenous languages. In the past, an uncritical interpretation of historical Mobilian Jargon data with their obvious Muskogean features even led to the unfounded conclusion that Mobilian proper, for which there exists no independent linguistic evidence, was Muskogean (see e.g. Swanton 1946: 151). Conversely, many Americanist linguists and anthropologists have referred to the pidgin as "Mobilian" as if it were identical with the language of that name (see e.g. Crawford 1978; Haas 1975; Munro 1984; Rankin 1980: 45; Silverstein 1973 MS: 29–39; Taylor 1981: 175, 184–5; Willis 1980: 100; York 1982). Manifestly, the buffer function of Mobilian Jargon camouflaged much of the linguistic and social diversity of Southeastern Indians who spoke it. Recognition of the pidgin's true linguistic and sociocultural role thus argues for a greater linguistic variety among Southeastern Indians than Americanists acknowledged until recently (see e.g. Crawford 1975*a*; Haas 1979), even if Mobilian Jargon's buffer function no longer permits a reconstruction of the full sociolinguistic complexity of southeastern North America. Awareness of the greater sociolinguistic diversity moreover renders the classification of Southeastern languages more complex. The discussion of Mobilian Jargon in light of their areal-typological characteristics (see Sect. 12.2) may even provide clues to current classificatory problems—such as the subdivision of Muskogean language family (see Hardy and Scancarelli 1993; Nicklas 1994) or the precise position of Apalachee within the family (see Kimball 1987, 1988)—by helping to sort out areal from "genetic" features.

Like Chinook Jargon, Delaware Jargon, and other Native American contact media, Mobilian Jargon establishes that pidginization was a significant process of language change in the history of Native American languages, and demonstrates it for the Southeast. This process was not random or disorderly; rather, it occurred repeatedly and under mostly identifiable sociolinguistic and historical conditions with discernible patterns. The hypothesis of Mobilian Jargon's pre-European origin specifies further that pidginization was not an incidental process in recent Native American linguistic history, associated with European and especially French colonialism; instead, Mobilian Jargon apparently originated in the sociohistorical contexts of indigenous, pre-Columbian "intertribal" interactions, especially those of the Mississippian Complex—only to serve European and European–American expansionist ambitions after contact almost as well as a European-based medium.

Native American pidgins and other contact media dramatically reintroduce the issue of linguistic convergence into Americanist linguistics with its predominantly diversificationist models of language change. Along with other instances of Native American language contact, Mobilian Jargon challenges the almost unreserved confidence in the reconstructive methods of conventional historical linguistics and in the tree model of language change, exemplified at its extreme by Joseph Greenberg's *Language in the Americas* (1987), which has reduced the diverse native languages of North America via so-called mass or multilateral comparison to three megafamilies (Eskimoan-Aleutian, Na-Dene or Athapaskan, and Amerindian). Not only did this pidgin hide sociolinguistic complexities with consequences for classification (as already mentioned); it also raises serious questions about projecting the tree model back into earliest "prehistory" without recognizing linguistic convergence in various forms (similarities due to language contact as well as historical accidents and universal linguistic processes) or resolving the problem of distinguishing "genetic" from areal-typological relationships.

13.3. Native American Languages in the Study of Pidgins and Creoles

The findings relating to Mobilian Jargon are of relevance to research on language contact in general and on pidgins and creoles in particular. The present study exemplifies a case of pidginization of non-European languages, conventionally assumed to have been a linguistic process that occurred in the context of European colonialism and involved principally European languages. Together with other comparable instances, Mobilian Jargon also establishes pidginization of North American Indian languages as a recurrent process rather than an exception, as erroneously suggested in previous discussions of Chinook Jargon, which served as the single well-documented and recognized instance of Native American pidginization until recently.

Differing in many important ways from other pidgins, Mobilian Jargon presents several aspects, both linguistic and sociohistorical, worthy of the creolists' closer attention. First, Mobilian Jargon conclusively puts to rest the idea that pidgins reflect universal or near-universal patterns of grammar by default, as maintained until a few years ago (see e.g. Givón 1979; Kay and Sankoff 1974); they may actually exhibit highly marked features of superstrate languages ranging from the lateral fricative [ɬ] to the word order of OsV and possibly OSV. This observation is not new or particularly surprising, but it remains an important reminder in the description and analysis of pidgins and creoles. As Sarah G. Thomason and Terrence Kaufman (1988: 54–5) have argued, "The evidence we have collected does not support the often implicit assumption, in the literature on word order change, that word order patterns constitute a fundamental 'deep' structural feature relatively impervious to foreign influence. On the contrary, word order seems to be the easiest sort of syntactic features to borrow or to acquire via language shift." Johanna Nichols (1992: 93–5, 105–9, 166–73, 195–6, 245–6) has since demonstrated a low "genetic" stability for word order on a comparative basis. For this reason, speakers of Mobilian Jargon could easily have extended its marked features to other aspects of its grammar, as by applying its Muskogean-derived OsV pattern by analogy to sentences with nouns as subject and thus creating OSV as standard word order. However, the description and analysis of Mobilian Jargon does not support a multi-level "macaronic" model of initial pidginization or jargonization as developed by Silverstein (1972) for comparable Chinook Jargon.

Of further interest to students of pidgins and creoles is the fact that Mobilian Jargon provides an example of pidginization that did not creolize, except perhaps in the case of an Anglicized variety of the lingua franca Creek or Seminole Pidgin English, whose precise historical ties are still nebulous (see Sects. 8.6 and 9.2). All the last speakers of Mobilian Jargon used it as a second language only, without abandoning their native language(s). The pidgin served as a medium in intertribal and interethnic marriages (see Sect. 10.2), but never became the exclusive language of a household or a larger community, and children acquired the first language(s) of their parents as their mother tongue(s). Evidence is absent also for the limited creolization of an indigenous variety of Mobilian Jargon as observed for Chinook Jargon on the Grand Ronde Reservation (Hymes and Hymes 1972; Zenk 1984, 1988). Evidently, multilingual Southeastern Indian communities never integrated linguistically to the extent that the pidgin became the dominant medium, thus forcing younger generations to adopt it as their prime or sole language and resulting in creolization. Instead, native communities succeeded until recently in maintaining greater independence from the larger society than other, immigrant groups, and have retained several indigenous languages with the pidgin. In this process, Mobilian Jargon played an important role serving not only as a medium for communication across language boundaries, but also as a sociolinguistic buffer behind which Native Americans could withdraw while maintaining their threatened identity (see Sect. 10.3). Indications for similar roles by Delaware Jargon and possibly Chinook Jargon (see Sect. 13.1) raise the questions of whether the sociolinguistic buffer function applied to still other, perhaps even non-American pidgins, and to what extent it explains the absence of creolization. These issues again underscore the need for examining pidginization in a broader perspective than in traditionally utilitarian terms with focus on communication.

Significantly, with its range extending to the Gulf Coast, Mobilian Jargon was well within the borders of a major pidgin-creole-speaking area—the Caribbean and circum-Caribbean, considered as "classic" by creolists.

Sadly, native contact media in this area have received little attention from Caribbeanist creolists in their traditional preoccupation with grand Atlantic and even global schemes of pidgin-creole development. Symptomatically, the author of a major survey of the region's pidgins and creoles, Douglas Taylor (1977), who has had extensive experience in the study of Native American languages as well, covered these side by side with pidgins and creoles, but omitted any systematic discussion of the indigenous peoples' role in the latter's development.

With its sociohistorical significance in the lower South, Mobilian Jargon further calls for a re-examination of the role of Native Americans in North America. At this time, it is not entirely clear if and how Mobilian Jargon related to European-based pidgins or creoles on the northern rim of the greater Caribbean; but the lexical replacement of its eastern variety or the lingua franca Creek with an English vocabulary and concurrent semantactic changes, eventually resulting in Seminole Pidgin (English?) and Afro-Seminole Creole (see Sect. 8.6), offers a scenario that may prove fruitful in other instances. This Seminole pidgin-creole requires more linguistic and sociohistorical attention—hampered in part by methodological limitations due to hypercorrections, stereotyping, and poetic license as in the case of so-called American Indian Pidgin English (see Sect. 2.3). However, one point is clear. Rather than presuming a unidirectional transmission of some European language to Indians, possibly via Africans, the sociolinguistics of indigenous and immigrant languages in the Americas should recognize a complex give and take—perhaps even a greater take by newcomers than give in early colonial periods, as indicated by the many Native American lingua francas preceding Atlantic pidgins-creoles. This conclusion applies not only to Europeans, but also to Africans and their American descendants, who in their contact with the native population played diverse historical roles in southeastern North America—among them as the Indians' captives and slaves, maroons, allies, traders, and interpreters (see Forbes 1988; Foster 1935; Porter 1971). As attested throughout colonial records, African Americans in these functions learned native languages in some form or another, and even came to serve as translators for European colonists, before Indians adopted some Atlantic pidgin-creole or European languages. That few obvious Native American traces have survived in European-based pidgins and creoles of the greater Caribbean may simply be due to the lack of creolization of Native American pidgins, by which they could have been "fossilized." Still, this explanation does not reduce the significance of Native Americans or their contact media in the history of language contact during colonial periods.

Most importantly, the arguments for the pre-European origin of Mobilian Jargon suggest that pidginization was not exclusively associated with European expansion and colonialism, but occurred in other sociohistorical settings such as indigenous interregional trade and the overall integration of linguistically diverse communities into paramount chiefdoms, as it apparently happened in the case of the Mississippian Complex (see Chapter 11). This finding does not imply that Mobilian Jargon or other Native American pidgins failed to serve European colonialist purposes; quite on the contrary, Europeans made extensive use of indigenous lingua francas, including Mobilian Jargon, as part of an already existent pre-Columbian infrastructure. For this reason, it would be erroneous to exclude consideration of Native American pidgins and other contact languages from colonial American history, as for instance George Lang (1991) has done for the Canadian fur trade. He curiously favors some French- or perhaps even English-based pidgin-creole as the prime interethnic medium of licensed and independent traders (*voyageurs* and *coureurs de bois*) in place of indigenous contact languages such as Algonquin, Métis, and Chinook Jargon, although there exists plenty of evidence for them throughout Canada from colonial into modern times (see Sect. 2.3).

The present study then dissociates the process of pidginization from an exclusive association with European colonialism, without downplaying the Europeans' historical burden of colonialism in America with its attendant epidemic diseases, genocide, exploitation, and racism. Non-European contact media such as Mobilian Jargon confirm a far wider spread as well as a greater time depth for indigenous pidgins and—by implication— perhaps creoles than even creolists have conventionally acknowledged (Bright 1973; Drechsel 1976a, 1977; Silverstein 1973 MS; Taylor 1981). Consequently, Native American pidgins take on a greater role in the study of language contact and change in America at large.

13.4. Linguistic Persistence in Americanist Anthropology and History

Just as linguists have frequently ignored the broader sociocultural context of language in their preoccupation with linguistic structure, anthropologists have avoided linguistic questions, however central to their own extralinguistic concerns; historians have generally demonstrated even less interest in matters relating to language. Yet as a sociohistorical phenomenon, Mobilian Jargon carries several implications of significance for Americanist ethnology, ethnohistory, and possibly archaeology.

First, the pidgin constitutes undisputable evidence for the presence of Native Americans in the South today—counter to the widespread assumption in the social sciences that the area's Native Americans have all been victims of genocide, westward removal, or else acculturation and full absorption into the larger population. Although not all of its last speakers were Native Americans and it is competence in an indigenous language rather than knowledge of a pidgin that has determined the identity of a Native American community, Mobilian Jargon could obviously not have persisted without the presence of the area's Native American languages, which provided continuing linguistic and sociocultural reinforcement and new resources for its survival. The pidgin's existence also offers indirect confirmation for the vitality of Southeastern Indian languages and, by extension, their speakers' native traditions until recently. In its functions as a sociolinguistic buffer, Mobilian Jargon is a salient example of Native American resilience from at least the early nineteenth century, reminiscent of revitalization movements, conscious and organized attempts at reviving native traditions while adapting to new sociopolitical conditions (see Drechsel 1976a: 65; for revitalization movements, see La Barre 1971). If Mobilian Jargon ever served in such a role among Southeastern Indians, it was fairly late in colonial periods, perhaps only beginning with the American take-over of greater Louisiana in 1803, and was never the original cause for the pidgin's development.[4]

As an indicator of societal multilingualism and in its functions as a sociolinguistic buffer, the pidgin further implies greater social diversity, and accordingly more complexity in language-and-culture relationships, among Southeastern Indians than conventionally recognized. Mobilian Jargon calls in question the simplistic one-to-one identification of a language group with a particular society, as is still customary in much of Americanist anthropology. Instead, it suggests bilingual and multilingual communities with rather complex sociolinguistic arrangements, whose members need not have shared a knowledge of the same languages and required a regional medium. Mobilian Jargon functioned as a highly adaptable medium in sociopolitically rather unstable and fragile societies, as was the case with the chiefdoms and paramount chiefdoms of southeastern North America. The pidgin not only was a direct reflection of partnerships among larger kin groups such as clans and moieties (Knight 1990), which often crisscrossed linguistic boundaries; it also mirrored the sociopolitical phenomenon of non-kin-based alliances such as twin and multiple towns, which brought together different Southeastern Indian groups in response to disasters (crop failure, epidemic diseases, and defeat in conflict) and which resulted in bilingual and multilingual communities in both recent history and apparently pre-Columbian times (Willis 1980). Cognizant of Mobilian Jargon's historical role, William S. Willis, Jr. (1980: 100, 102) has already suggested that

twin towns helped spread pidgin languages. If so, the popularity of Mobilian [Jargon] as a lingua franca in the eighteenth century need not be explained entirely in terms

---

[4] In no fashion does such reasoning lend support to the unfounded idea that the Mississippian culture, alternatively known as Southern Cult, itself was a revitalization movement (for discussion, see Brown 1976: 130–1).

of commercial and political relations between Indians and whites . . . If ethnic and sociopolitical unity did not exist in multiple mound sites, then these prehistorical settlements also encouraged the linguistic processes of diffusion, bilingualism, polylingualism, and pidginization.

In other words, Mobilian Jargon was an instance of linguistic peer-polity interactions—that is, regular and systematic relationships between politically autonomous, alloglossic groups across a larger area. As such, it offers an insight into a sociopolitical phenomenon that is characteristic of chiefdoms in particular and that has recently received increased attention from anthropologists for its role in the development of more complex sociopolitical organizations up to the formation of states (see Renfrew and Cherry 1986).

Mobilian Jargon's use by non-Indians and its survival into the mid-twentieth century further gives credence to a greater role of the native population in the recent history of the South and especially that of Louisiana than social scientists, including anthropologists and historians, have traditionally acknowledged or than is evident from the Indians' present-day economic and sociopolitical marginality. This inference applies irrespective of whether one postulates a post-Columbian or pre-European origin for Mobilian Jargon. In the first case, European colonists deferred to Native American ways of communication in their linguistic compromises because the indigenous population still maintained considerable control; in the second, the colonists adopted from the native population a language that was already part of the existing infrastructure, if only for reasons of convenience. In either model, the pidgin reflects a history of the colonial South that involved mutual concessions as well as unresolved conflicts—a history that cannot be reduced to Removal and Civil War and that is in dire need of revision to include the native population in a systematic fashion. To interpret the post-Columbian history of Southeastern Indians in terms of Southern plantation culture, as Theda Perdue (1988) has done, is to present a skewed picture. If presumably Southeastern Indians had just been irresponsive victims of racist Southern society, they would have adopted some European language in pidginized or non-pidginized form in place of Mobilian Jargon and their native languages. Instead, the pidgin presents an alternative, more complex scenario that assigns a central role to the native population and that matches findings in Southern colonial history as recently presented by Daniel H. Usner, Jr. (1992) for greater Louisiana in the eighteenth century. Mobilian Jargon actually appears to mirror interethnic sociopolitical realities surprisingly well.

Yet the hypothesis of pre-Columbian origin proposes a much longer history for Mobilian Jargon than is evident from historical records, and interprets its unique word order and surviving loan-words like *bayou* in

French and English as much a reflection of the Mississippian Complex as "prehistoric" archaeological remains such as conch shells, pottery, and mounds with their distinctive ceremonial motifs (see Howard 1968). The suggested model of Mobilian Jargon's pre-European existence also offers an elegant solution to a long-standing, but frequently disregarded puzzle in the ethnology of Southeastern Indians: great linguistic diversity, yet considerable sociocultural uniformity from the Atlantic Coast to the western rim of the Mississippi valley (Crawford 1975*a*: 1–2; see also Hudson 1976; Swanton 1946). How did the native peoples of southeastern North America come to adopt a full range of common cultural traits, but maintain numerous mutually unintelligible, even unrelated languages? Why was there no more linguistic uniformity corresponding to the sociocultural homogeneity of Southeastern Indians? The answer to this enigma is in Mobilian Jargon. While enabling native peoples to retain different languages and, with them, separate social identities, the pidgin served as a convenient medium of interlingual communication and sociocultural diffusion for everything ranging from material culture to beliefs, as James Mooney (1900: 235) already suggested for mythology. Interpreted as the major lingua franca of the Mississippian Complex, Mobilian Jargon provides a model of how alloglossic member groups interacted with each other and with neighboring communities at close and large distance—a poorly understood topic in need of systematic attention, as evident from surveys of the area's infrastructure (Tanner 1989) and long-distance interregional trade (Brown, Kerber, and Winters 1990).

Perhaps more than any other linguistic phenomenon of southeastern North America, Mobilian Jargon corroborates the need for, Americanist anthropologists and other social scientists to reintegrate linguistics into their inquiries. With the increasing specialization of anthropology's subfields over the past decades, cultural anthropologists, ethnohistorians, and archaeologists have regularly overlooked languages as a major part of culture and history. It is a sad but indicative fact that many recent anthropological publications on Southeastern Indians, while emphasizing their interdisciplinary nature, have neglected to incorporate findings from linguistics (see e.g. Dye and Cox 1990; Emerson and Lewis 1991; Galloway 1989; Paredes 1992; Smith 1990; Wood, Waselkov, and Hatley 1989). Also, the discussion of a topic as eminently sociolinguistic as that of interpreters (see e.g. Galloway 1987; Kawashima 1989; Lang 1991) has often overlooked multilingualism, indigenous contact media, and other phenomena of language contact, and has paid surprisingly little attention to the particular languages spoken by them, the native population, and colonists beyond recognizing obvious language barriers.

By drawing on linguistic findings in their research, not only can nonlinguistic anthropologists and historians obtain answers to some of their own questions; but cultural anthropology, ethnohistory, and archaeology may conversely help resolve linguistic problems that rely on extralinguistic, sociohistorical evidence. Anthropologists, among them ethnohistorians and archaeologists in particular, may further develop different sociohistorical scenarios for language contact that are not limited to colonial explorations and trade, but include indigenous peer-polity interactions as evident in interregional trade and paramount multilingual chiefdoms. In particular, a better understanding of the sociopolitical complexity of pre-Columbian Southeastern Indians should help specify the conditions in which Mobilian Jargon could have developed as part of the Mississippian Complex. The social sciences can thus make a major contribution to an integrated sociolinguistic theory of language change.

13.5. *A Philology and an Ethnohistory of Speaking of Non-European Non-Standard Languages*

The present case study of Mobilian Jargon illustrates the feasibility of systematic historical-sociolinguistic research with focus on both non-European and non-standard aspects, and introduces greater time depth, an expanded basis of description and analysis (inclusive of extralinguistic aspects), and a broader comparative foundation. Early documentation for Mobilian Jargon exhibits a higher quality than a cursory comparison with recent linguistic and ethnographic data gathered in field research would suggest, and permits the reconstruction of key linguistic and extralinguistic features: a substantial vocabulary, single phrases, and important sociohistorical relationships. In other instances, limited early linguistic evidence is sufficiently detailed to permit the reconstitution of selected aspects by examining internal clues for regularities in pattern, comparative evidence from lexically related source languages, and information on the observers' first languages, just as a critical analysis of different documentary sources relating to the same sociohistorical aspects frequently permits at least a partial restoration of the large historical picture.

Differing in substance from historical studies of predominantly European-based contact languages, archival research on Mobilian Jargon and comparable indigenous lingua francas demonstrates feasibility. By and large, documentary research on Mobilian Jargon is untrammeled by the methodological problems of the study of so-called American Indian Pidgin English (AIPE), a purportedly English-based pidgin-creole whose historical attestations are difficult to interpret because of hypercorrections, stereotyping, and poetic license (see Sect. 2.3). The accuracy of historical documentation relating to Mobilian Jargon has been suspect in only a few cases, such as James Adair's *History of the American Indians* (1968 [1775]) with his comparisons of "Choktah" and "Chikkasah" with Hebrew in a desperate attempt at demonstrating the Indians' ancestry in Israel (see Sect. 9.3).

Supplemented by modern evidence, historical documentation and reconstruction justifies a philology of historical language-contact phenomena and a historical sociolinguistics or an ethnohistory of speaking. Such an approach specifically relies on the reconstitution of early linguistic documentation by triangulation with modern comparative evidence in Mobilian Jargon or its source languages, and reconstructs the broader sociohistorical environment of the pidgin's use by examining who spoke what and under what circumstances. A combined philology-ethnohistory of Mobilian Jargon not only enriches synchronic descriptions and analyses by adding time depth and illuminating the broader sociohistorical context, but can also determine the effects of language obsolescence on the structure and functions of Mobilian Jargon and perhaps resolve questions of its origin.

A broadly defined historical sociolinguistics shows promise for other, comparable cases of Native American contact media for which there exist modern descriptions and analyses. A prime example is Chinook Jargon (see e.g. Harris 1985; Zenk 1988). Native American lingua francas recorded by linguists and anthropologists using current techniques (as in the cases of Mobilian Jargon and Chinook Jargon) further suggest the applicability of the same principles of historical research to indigenous contact languages that did not survive into modern times. With linguistic and ethnographic field research no longer possible in these cases, the only means of keeping them from passing into total oblivion is a systematic examination of historical data. A combined philological-ethnohistorical approach should prove reasonably productive in historical research on Southeastern Indian lingua francas other than Mobilian Jargon, Algonquian-based contact media including Delaware Jargon, and likely others (see Sect. 12.4). We should expect equal success in a historical sociolinguistics of non-European non-standard languages outside of North America, among which a prime example is Pidgin Hawaiian attested in various nineteenth-century records (see Roberts 1995). Ethnohistories of speaking can thus raise the hope of establishing a comparative basis for the study of historical sociolinguistic phenomena as suggested by preliminary typological research (see Sect. 13.1).

Yet a philological approach to the study of contact languages has methodological implications that differ from those of conventional historical linguistics. While the tree model of language diversification indicates a greater number of shared features for an ancestral language than for comparable modern ones, a perspective that incorporates language convergence must in contrast postulate greater linguistic diversity in earlier forms. Language contact logically implies a linguistic compromise that resulted from language differences, and reveals an inverse relationship between linguistic similarities and differences as compared with phenomena of "regular" language change. This conclusion applies not only to creoles in which an ancestral pidgin has become institutionalized as the first language of a community, but also to the process of pidginization itself because of the possibility of great linguistic variation and lexical replacement, reflecting the speakers' varying native-language background and changing sociopolitical realities over space and time.

This fact, together with the very nature of contact media as second languages, specifically indicates that reconstructions of their lexica, including philological reconstitutions, have little validity for retrospective projections extending far back in time or across space, beyond the lifespan of the recorded speakers or their community and neighbors. The lexical composition of a contact medium may reveal many clues about its immediate past or contiguous communities (such as the native-language backgrounds of its speakers), but does not permit *per se* conclusions about its remote history or any distant members of its speech community, much less the medium's origin. A recorded item could easily have had a very different or possibly even unrelated earlier form because of intervening lexical replacement over time and space. Therefore, the supposed absence of Chickasaw elements in Mobilian Jargon, as surmised by Pamela Munro (1984), does not support the conclusion that the pidgin lacked Chickasaw elements in earlier stages, much less that the Chickasaw Indians played no role in its formation. Although few linguistic traces of Chickasaw survived in modern Mobilian Jargon, linguistic and sociohistorical evidence indeed suggests that it had once included a larger vocabulary from this language, before its speakers stopped using the pidgin and lost influence (see Sects. 5.3 and 9.3). Such reasoning also lends part of the justification for considering the lingua franca Creek as an eastern variety rather than a distinct contact medium (see Sect. 8.5). Recognizing lexical replacement as a possible process in Mobilian Jargon's history at last obliges us to refrain from making undue projections about its early lexical composition without considering other aspects. Conceivably, the vocabulary of early Mobilian Jargon need not even have been principally Muskogean, but could have originated from other Southeastern Indian languages such as Gulf isolates with little resemblance to the modern lexicon. So to reconstruct the history and origin of a contact medium of considerable age such as Mobilian Jargon solely on the basis of recent lexical materials would be a futile endeavor. For the same reason, any attempt at a historical affiliation for Mobilian Jargon must a priori fail if it draws principally on the etymological composition of its lexicon in the fashion of conventional comparative linguistics.

In contrast, we can expect greater reliability for extended reconstructions of diagnostic aspects of Mobilian Jargon's grammar such as basic word order than of its lexicon or phonology. Although pidginization implies radical semantactic changes, sentence patterns in a pidgin, once stabilized, evidently remained rather inflexible and more conservative than its comparatively volatile phonology and lexicon, and reflected less interference from the speakers' first languages. To reduce confusion in interlingual communication, speakers of an established pidgin such as Mobilian Jargon relied by all available indications on a rather rigid word order, which was the single most important means of identifying the grammatical functions of sentence constituents in the absence of other grammatical markers (such as affixes). Mobilian Jargon's word order of X/OsV, reflecting surviving traces of Muskogean and possibly Gulf morphology, thus gives better clues to the pidgin's long-term history than its recent lexical composition or its modern phonology, and serves as one among several arguments in support of the pre-European hypothesis.

Yet reconstructions relying on the basic semantactic structure of a pidgin are not without methodological problems. As already evident from the previous discussion of Mobilian Jargon's origin, I do not fully share Thomason's confidence in word order and other structural characteristics as the principal indicators of pre-European origin for indigenous contact media such as Delaware Jargon and Chinook Jargon (Thomason 1980, 1983). Not only does a sentence pattern change over time like any other aspect of language; but Mobilian Jargon could theoretically have developed as a linguistic compromise with an underlying Muskogean or Gulf pattern after the Europeans' arrival in North America. In light of other sociohistorical facts, this conclusion appears unwarranted for Mobilian Jargon as well as Chinook Jargon and Delaware Jargon, yet remains contestable without conclusive evidence. The questions that these linguistic issues raise reconfirm the need for taking the extralinguistic context into consideration in an integrated historical sociolinguistics or ethnohistory of speaking.

A combined sociolinguistic-ethnohistorical approach should not settle on language-contact phenomena; but it ought to extend to the study of Southeastern Indian language history at large, as explored in a recent study of place names and multilingualism in sixteenth-century southeastern North America (Booker, Hudson, and Rankin 1992).

13.6. *Towards a Comprehensive, Integrated Model and Theory of Language Change*

Contact languages such as Mobilian Jargon raise questions about the tree model of language diversification as well as the pervasive belief in some language-internal mechanism, frequently known by the more or less mysterious concept of *linguistic drift*, as the prime motivation for language change. This focus has unfortunately led historical linguists to concentrate principally on typological limitations, implicational universals, and constraints based on naturalness, to search for more and more formal ways of linguistic description and analysis, and to adhere to an increasingly atomistic perspective at the expense of considering the broader sociohistorical context of language change.

As Sarah G. Thomason and Terrence Kaufman have elaborately argued in *Language Contact, Creolization, and Genetic Linguistics* (1988) by drawing in part on Mobilian Jargon's counterparts Chinook Jargon and Delaware Jargon, language change—whether in the form of diversification or convergence—does not principally rely on system-internal stimuli, but is the result of sociocultural factors. These can easily override linguistic drift, evident in pressures toward the generalization of a prevalent pattern in response to structural imbalances within a language. Conversely, there is no reason for assuming a language to operate in a sociocultural vacuum and to do with no more than a minimum of change; any presumed systemic balance in a language would be easily undermined by its speakers' creativity, encouraging innovation and thus change. Whether a community preserves, changes, or abandons its language or specific speech forms depends on external circumstances such as social status, prestige, and power.

Sociocultural factors manifest themselves especially in language contact, including borrowing, language shift, pidginization, and creolization, which as various samples of linguistic compromise and language "mixture" of diverse linguistic elements reflect interactions between different communities across language boundaries. Although not always obvious, sociocultural factors also operate in "regular" language change, and are even present in language maintenance, which in order to prevail likewise relies on some external authority, be it simply "tradition."

With the erroneous assumption of "regular" language change operating in sociocultural isolation often comes the misconception that supposedly unusual linguistic processes such as pidginization and creolization necessarily lead to an acceleration in language change. Such need not be the case. In its historical role as a sociolinguistic buffer, Mobilian Jargon suggests that, in this case, language contact not only resulted in linguistic innovation, but also exerted a protective, conservative function that actually reduced the impact of language contact and helped to maintain the native languages in Mobilian Jargon-speaking communities. An increased rate of language change then would not necessarily be the logical consequence of language contact; rather, it depends on external factors—that is the sociocultural context. At first sight, this finding would ironically seem to speak against a model of language change incorporating language contact as well as sociocultural factors, and seemingly strengthens the tree model. In reality, such a conclusion would overlook the presence and importance of Mobilian

Jargon or any other comparable contact medium that had an impact on language change in the speakers' first languages.

Following the hypothesis of Mobilian Jargon's pre-Columbian origin, pidginization, if not possibly creolization, need not be the exclusive product of European colonization, but also occurred in non-European, non-state societies. Accordingly, European explorations of southeastern North America and the fur and hide trade did not provide the original sociopolitical stimulus for the pidgin's origin, although Mobilian Jargon came to serve as a convenient and useful medium in these contexts as well. By implication, this scenario suggests a more frequent occurrence of language-contact processes such as pidginization than conventionally acknowledged in the history of Native Americans, especially if we recognize a once greater linguistic diversity in pre-Columbian times and various contexts for interlingual contact, which again are sociohistorical rather than purely linguistic conditions.

Recognition of linguistic convergence as a major factor in a theory of language change implies that historical linguists cannot rely exclusively on the tree model of language diversification or the comparative method in its conventional "genetic" definition. Along with evidence for various forms of language contact such as borrowings, linguistic interference, and areal features, Mobilian Jargon serves as a prime example for linguistic confluence, best integrated with linguistic divergence of the *Stammbaum* or family tree in a *Stammbusch* or 'stembush' model. The representation of related linguistic branches merging again after separation recognizes language convergence, including language contact, as a significant process, and has first appeared in Americanist linguistics for native languages of California because of their intertwined historical relationships (see Callaghan 1990: 121 and Gamble 1988: 60). By the analogy that bushes do not grow as a high as trees, "bushy" historical reconstructions may have the disadvantage of not being extensible as far back in time as tree models; but they make it up with greater historical accuracy. Although Americanist linguists and especially students of Southeastern Indian languages have yet to accept such a perspective fully, we can already draw on a solid foundation in anthropological linguistics, foremost the Boasian tradition, that at various times has taken the first steps towards incorporating language contact in understanding language change and its sociocultural environment.

The historical sociolinguistics as conceived here calls for an explicit understanding of all major processes of language change as well as the identification of their extralinguistic conditions, still understood poorly for want of systematic comparative information. While arguing for sociocultural factors as primary determinants of language change, Thomason and Kaufman (1988: 4, 36, 46, 94) have made no claim to an explicitly sociolinguistic approach, as they are fully aware of the difficulty of generalizing about the extralinguistic context of language change. None the less, historical linguistics must extend its comparative approach to the more difficult task of determining the sociocultural conditions of language change in general and language contact in particular, as Mobilian Jargon and other instances of Native American lingua francas suggest.

References

ADAIR, JAMES (1968 [1775]), *The History of the American Indians Particularly those Nations Adjoining to the Mississippi, East and West Florida, Georgia, South and North Carolina, and Virginia*, with a new introduction by Robert F. Berkhofer, Jr. (New York: Johnson Reprint Corporation).

ALBRECHT, ANDREW C. (1946), 'Indian–French Relations at Natchez,' *American Anthropologist*, 48 NS: 321–54.

ALEXANDER, EDWARD P. (1971), 'An Indian Vocabulary from Fort Christanna, 1716,' *Virginia Magazine of History and Biography*, 79: 303–13.

ALFORD, THOMAS (1929), *The Gospel of Our Lord and Savior Jesus Christ According to Matthew* (Xenia, Oh.: Aldine Publishing Company).

ANONYMOUS (1862 MS), 'Essai sur quelques usages et sur l'idiôme des Indiens de la Basse Louisiane' (MS, Special Collections, Howard-Tilton Memorial Library, Tulane University, New Orleans).

ANONYMOUS (n.d. MS), 'An Essay on the language on the Indians of Lower Louisiana' [*sic*] (MS Collection, Gilcrease Museum, Tulsa, Oklahoma [English trans. of Anonymous 1862 MS]).

ANONYMOUS (1983), [Note on 'English World-Wide: A Journal of Varieties of English'], *The Carrier Pidgin*, 11: 4.

ARMISTEAD, S. G., and GREGORY, H. F. (1986), 'French Loan Words in the Spanish Dialect of Sabine and Natchitoches Parishes,' *Louisiana Folklife*, 11: 21–30.

AUBIN, GEORGE F. (1975), *A Proto-Algonquian Dictionary* (National Museum of Man Mercury Series, Canadian Ethnology Service Paper No. 29; Ottawa: National Museums of Canada).

AUROUX, SYLVAIN (1984), 'L'Affaire de la langue taensa,' in Sylvain Auroux and Francisco Queixalos (eds.), *Pour une histoire de la linguistique amérindienne en France*, special edition of *Amérindia: revue d'ethnolinguistique amérindienne*, 6 (Paris: AEA), 145–79.

AXTELL, JAMES L. (1990), 'Humor in Ethnohistory,' *Ethnohistory*, 37: 109–25.

BAILEY, CHARLES-JAMES N. (1973), *Variation and Linguistic Theory* (Arlington, Va.: Center for Applied Linguistics).

BAKKER, PETER (1988), 'Basque Pidgin Vocabulary in European–Algonquian Trade Contacts,' in William Cowan (ed.), *Papers of the Nineteenth Algonquian Conference* (Ottawa: Carleton University), 7–15.

—— (1989), ' "The Language of the Coast Tribes is Half Basque": A Basque–American Indian Pidgin in Use between Europeans and Native Americans in North America, ca. 1540–ca. 1640,' *Anthropological Linguistics*, 31: 117–47.

—— (1991), ' "La lengua de les tribus costeras es medio vasca." Un pidgin vasco y amerindio utilizado por europeos y nativos americanos en Norteamérica, h.

1540–h. 1640,' *Anuario del seminario de filologia vasca "Julio de Urquijo,"* 25: 439–67.

BALLARD, W[ILLIAM] L. (1983), 'Lexical Borrowing among Southeastern Native American Languages,' in Frances Ingemann (ed.), *1982 Mid-America Linguistics Conference Papers* (Lawrence: Department of Linguistics, University of Kansas), 325–34.

—— (1985), '*sa/ša/la*: Southeastern Shibboleth?,' *International Journal of American Linguistics*, 51: 339–41.

BARBER, PATSY K. (1966), *Historic Cotile* (Baptist Message Press).

BARNHILL, VIRON L., and REINECKE, GEORGE F. (1989), 'Indian Trade Languages,' in Charles Reafan Wilson and William Ferris (eds.), *Encyclopedia of Southern Culture* (Chapel Hill, NC: University of North Carolina Press), 787–8.

BARTELT, GUILLERMO (1991), 'American Indian English: A Phylogenetic Dilemma,' in Francis Byrne and Thom Huebner (eds.), *Development and Structures of Creole Languages: Essays in Honor of Derek Bickerton* (Amsterdam: John Benjamins), 29–39.

BARTELT, GUILLERMO, PENFIELD-JASPER, SUSAN, and HOFFER, BATES (1982) (eds.), *Essays in Native American English* (San Antonio: Trinity University Press).

BARTRAM, WILLIAM (1958 [1791]), *The Travels of William Bartram*, naturalist's edition, ed. with commentary and an annotated index by Frances Harper (New Haven: Yale University Press).

BATEMAN, REBECCA (1990), 'Africans and Indians: A Comparative Study of the Black Carib and the Black Seminole,' *Ethnohistory*, 37: 1–24.

[BAUDRY DES LOZIÈRES, LOUIS NARCISSE] (1802), *Voyage à la Louisiane, et sur le continent de l'Amérique septentrionale, fait dans les années 1794 à 1798 . . .* (Paris: Dentu).

BAUMAN, RICHARD (1974), 'Speaking in the Light: The Role of a Quaker Minister,' in Richard Bauman and Joel Sherzer (eds.), *Explorations in the Ethnography of Speaking* (London: Cambridge University Press), 144–60.

B[ERQUIN]-DUVALLON (1803), *Vue de la colonie espagnole du Mississipi, ou des provinces de Louisiane et Floride Occidentale, en l'année 1802, par un observateur résident sur les lieux* (Paris: Imprimerie expéditive).

—— (1806), *Travels in Louisiana and the Floridas, in the Year, 1802, Giving a Correct Picture of Those Countries*, trans. from the French, with notes, by John Davis (New York: I. Riley & Co.).

BEVERLEY, ROBERT (1855 [1722]), *The History of Virginia, in Four Parts*, repr. from the author's second rev. edn. London, 1722 (Richmond, Va.: J. W. Randolph).

BICKERTON, DEREK (1975), *Dynamics of a Creole System* (London: Cambridge University Press).

—— (1981), *Roots of Language* (Ann Arbor: Karoma).

—— (1984), 'The Language Bioprogram Hypothesis,' with peer commentary, *Behavioral and Brain Sciences*, 7: 173–221.

—— and ODO, CAROL (1976), *Change and Variation in Hawaiian English*, Final Report on National Science Foundation Grant No. GS-39748, i. *General Phonology and Pidgin Syntax* (Honolulu: Social Sciences and Linguistics Institute, University of Hawai'i at Mānoa).

BLOOMFIELD, LEONARD (1975), *Menomini Lexicon*, ed. Charles F. Hockett (Milwaukee Public Museum Publications in Anthropology and History, No. 3; Milwaukee: Milwaukee Public Museum Press).

BLOUNT, BEN G., and SANCHES, MARY (1977) (eds.), *Sociocultural Dimensions of Language Change* (New York: Academic Press).

BOAS, FRANZ (1888), 'Chinook Songs,' *Journal of American Folk-Lore*, 1: 220–6.

—— (1892), 'The Chinook Jargon,' *Science*, 19: 129.

—— (1933), 'Note on the Chinook Jargon,' *Language*, 9: 208–13.

BOLLAERT, WILLIAM (1850), 'Observations on the Indian Tribes in Texas,' *Journal of the Ethnological Society of London*, 2: 262–83.

BOOKER, KAREN M. (1980), 'Comparative Muskogean: Aspects of Proto-Muskogean Verb Morphology' (Ph.D. diss., Department of Linguistics, University of Kansas) (Ann Arbor: University Microfilms International).

——, HUDSON, CHARLES M., and RANKIN, ROBERT L. (1992), 'Place Name Identification and Multilingualism in the Sixteenth-Century Southeast,' *Ethnohistory*, 39: 399–451.

BOSSU, [JEAN BERNARD] (1768), *Nouveaux voyages aux Indes Occidentales; contenant une relation des differens peuples qui habitent les environs du grand fleuve Saint-Louis, appellé vulgairement le Mississipi; leur religion; leur gouvernement; leurs mœurs; leurs guerres and leur commerce* (Paris: Le Jay).

—— (1777), *Nouveaux voyages dans l'Amérique septentrionale, contenant une collection de lettres écrites sur les lieux, par l'auteur, à son ami, M. Douin, chevalier, capitaine dans les troupes du roi, ci-devant son camarade dans le nouveau monde* (Amsterdam: Changuion).

—— (1962), *Travels in the Interior of North America, 1751–1762*, trans. and ed. by Seymour Feiler (Norman: University of Oklahoma Press).

BOURGEOIS, NICOLAS LOUIS (1788), *Voyages intéressans dans différentes colonies françaises, espagnoles, anglaises, &c . . .* (London: J. F. Bastien).

BRACKENRIDGE, HENRY MARIE (1962 [1814]), *Views of Louisiana Together With a Journal of a Voyage Up the Mississippi River, in 1811* (Chicago: Quadrangle Books).

BRANDT, ELIZABETH, and MACCRATE, CHRISTOPHER (1982), ' "Make Like Seem Heep Injin:" Pidginization in the Southwest,' *Ethnohistory*, 29: 201–20.

BRIGHT, WILLIAM (1973), 'North American Indian Language Contact,' in Thomas A. Sebeok (ed.), *Current Trends in Linguistics*, x. *Linguistics in North America*, pt. III, *Native Languages of North America* (The Hague: Mouton), 713–26.

—— (1984), 'The Classification of North American and Meso-American Indian Languages,' in William Bright, *American Indian Linguistics and Literature* (Berlin: Walter de Gruyter), 3–29.

—— and SHERZER, JOEL (1976), 'Areal Features in North American Indian Languages,' in William Bright, *Variation and Change in Language: Essays by William Bright*, sel. and intro. by Anwar S. Dil (Stanford, Calif.: Stanford University Press), 228–68.

BRINTON, DANIEL G. (1859), *Notes on the Floridian Peninsula, its Literary History, Indian Tribes and Antiquities* (Philadelphia: Joseph Sabin).

—— (1887), 'One Certain Supposed Nanticoke Words, Shown to Be of African Origin,' *The American Antiquarian and Oriental Journal*, 9: 350–4.

BROADWELL, GEORGE A. (1991), 'The Muskogean Connection of the Guale and Yamasee,' *International Journal of American Linguistics*, 57: 267–70.

BROWN, CECIL H. (1994), 'Lexical Acculturation in Native American Languages,' with comments, *Current Anthropology*, 35: 95–117.

BROWN, JAMES A. (1976), 'The Southern Cult Reconsidered,' *Mid-Continental Journal of Archaeology*, 1: 115–35.

——, KERBER, RICHARD A., and WINTERS, HOWARD D. (1990), 'Trade and the Evolution of Exchange Relations at the Beginning of the Mississippian Period,' in Bruce D. Smith (ed.), *The Mississippian Emergence* (Washington: Smithsonian Institution), 251–80.

BYINGTON, CYRUS (1915), *A Dictionary of the Choctaw Language*, edited by J. R. Swanton and H. S. Halbert (Bureau of American Ethnology Bulletin 46; Washington: Government Printing Office).

CALLAGHAN, CATHARINE A. (1990), 'Proto-Costanoan Numerials,' *International Journal of American Linguistics*, 56: 121–33.

CAMPBELL, LYLE, and GODDARD, IVES (1991), 'Summary Report: American Indian Languages and Principles of Language Change,' in P. Baldi (ed.), *Patterns of Change—Change of Patterns: Linguistic Change and Reconstruction Methodology* (Berlin: Mouton de Gruyter), 15–30.

CAMPBELL, LYLE, KAUFMAN, TERRENCE, and SMITH-STARK, THOMAS C. (1986), 'Meso-America as a Linguistic Area,' *Language*, 62: 530–70.

—— and MITHUN, MARIANNE (1979a) (eds.), *The Languages of Native America: Historical and Comparative Assessment* (Austin, Tex.: University of Texas Press).

—— —— (1979b), 'Introduction: North American Indian Historical Linguistics in Current Perspective,' in Lyle Campbell and Marianne Mithun (eds.), *The Languages of Native America: Historical and Comparative Assessment* (Austin, Tex.: University of Texas Press), 3–69.

CASSIDY, FREDERIC G. (1961), *Jamaica Talk: Three Hundred Years of the English Language in Jamaica* (London: Macmillan & Co.).

—— (1981), '*OK*—Is It African?,' *American Speech*, 56: 269–73.

CHAFE, WALLACE (1983), 'The Caddo Language, its Relatives, and its Neighbors,' in James S. Thayer (ed.), *North American Indians: Humanistic Perspectives* [in Memory of James H. Howard] (Papers in Anthropology, 24; Norman: Department of Anthropology, University of Oklahoma), 243–50.

CHAMBERLAIN, A. F. (1891), 'Words of Algonkian Origin' [in Chinook Jargon], *Science*, 18 (457): 260–1.

—— (1902), 'Algonkian Words in American English: A Study in the Contact of the White Man and the Indian,' *Journal of American Folk-Lore*, 15: 240–67.

CHAMBERLAYNE, JOHN (1715) (ed.), *Oratio dominica in diversas omnium fere gentium linguas versa et propiis cujusque linguae characteribus expressa, una cum dissertationibus nonnullis de linguarum origine, variisque ipsarum permutionibus* (Amsterdam: D. and D. Goerei).

COSTA, DAVID J. (1992), 'Mami-Illinois Animal Names,' *Algonquian and Iroquoian Linguistics*, 17: 19–44.

—— (1993 MS), 'Miami-Illinois Dictionary' (MS, Berkeley: Department of Linguistics, University of California).

CRAIG, BETH (1991), 'American Indian English,' *English World-Wide*, 12: 25–61.

CRAWFORD, JAMES M. (1975a), 'Southeastern Indian Languages,' in James M. Crawford (ed.), *Studies in Southeastern Indian Languages* (Athens, Ga.: University of Georgia Press), 1–120.

—— (1975b), 'The Phonological Sequence *ya* in Words Pertaining to the Mouth,' in James M. Crawford (ed.), *Studies in Southeastern Indian Languages* (Athens, Ga.: University of Georgia Press), 265–83.

—— (1978), *The Mobilian Trade Language* (Knoxville, Tenn.: University of Tennessee Press).

—— (1979), 'Timucua and Yuchi: Two Language Isolates of the Southeast,' in Lyle Campbell and Marianne Mithun (eds.), *The Languages of Native America: Historical and Comparative Assessment* (Austin, Tex.: University of Texas Press), 326–54.

—— (1988), 'On the Relationship of Timucua to Muskogean,' in William Shipley (ed.), *In Honor of Mary Haas: From the Haas Festival Conference on Native American Linguistics* (Berlin: Mouton de Gruyter), 157–64.

CRAWFORD, JOHN (1983) (ed.), *The Mitchif Dictionnary, Turtle Mountain Chippewa Cree* (Winnipeg: Pemmican Press).

CUMMINS, LIGHT TOWNSEND, and JEANSONNE, GLEN (1982) (eds.), *A Guide to the History of Louisiana* (Westport, Conn.: Greenwood Press).

CUSHMAN, H. B. (1962 [1899]), *History of the Choctaw, Chickasaw and Natchez Indians*, ed. Angie Debo (Stillwater, Okla.: Redlands Press).

DARNELL, REGNA (1971a), 'The Powell Classification of American Indian Languages,' *Papers in Linguistics*, 4: 71–110.

—— (1971b), 'The Revision of the Powell Classification,' *Papers in Linguistics*, 4: 233–57.

—— and HYMES, DELL (1986), 'Edward Sapir's Six-Unit Classification of American Indian Languages: The Search for Time Perspective,' in Theodora Bynon and F. R. Palmer (eds.), *Studies in the History of Western Linguistics in Honor of R. H. Robins* (Cambridge: Cambridge University Press), 202–44.

—— and SHERZER, JOEL (1971), 'Areal Linguistic Studies in North America: A Historical Perspective,' *International Journal of American Linguistics*, 37: 20–8.

DAVIES, WILLIAM D. (1986), *Choctaw Verb Agreement and Universal Grammar* (Dordrecht: D. Reidel Publishing Company).

DAWS, GAVAN (1968), *Shoal of Time: A History of the Hawaiian Islands* (New York: Macmillan).

DAY, GORDON M. (1964), 'A St. Francis Abenaki Vocabulary,' *International Journal of American Linguistics*, 30: 371–92.

DE REUSE, WILLEM J. (1988), 'Studies in Siberian Yupik Eskimo Morphology and Syntax' (Ph.D. diss., University of Texas; Ann Arbor: University Microfilms International).

DE VILLIERS, MARC (1923), 'Notes sur les Chactas d'après les journaux de voyage de Régis du Roullet (1729–1732),' *Journal de la Société des Américanistes de Paris*, NS 15: 223–50.

——— (1931), 'L'établissement de la province de la Louisiane avec les mœurs des sauvages, leurs danses, leurs religions, etc.: Poème composé de 1728 à 1742 par Dumont de Montigny,' *Journal de la Société des Américanistes de Paris*, NS 23: 273–440.

DE VILLIERS DU TERRAGE, MARC, and RIVET, P. (1914–19), 'Les Indiens du Texas et les expéditions françaises de 1720 et 1721 à la "Baie Saint-Bernard",' *Journal de la Société des Américanistes de Paris*, NS 11: 403–42.

DEILER, J. HANNO (1909), *The Settlement of the German Coast of Louisiana and the Creoles of German Descent* (Philadelphia: Americana Germanica Press).

DERBYSHIRE, DESMOND C., and PULLUM, GEOFFREY K. (1981), 'Object-Initial Languages,' *International Journal of American Linguistics*, 47: 192–214.

DILLARD, J. L. (1972), *Black English: Its History and Usage in the United States* (New York: Random House).

——— (1975), *All-American English: A History of the English Language in America* (New York: Random House).

——— (1976), *American Talk: Where Our Words Came From* (New York: Random House).

——— (1985), *Toward a Social History of American English* (Berlin: Mouton Publishers).

——— (1992), *A History of American English* (London: Longman).

DORMON, CAROLINE (n.d. MS), [Various untitled notes on Choctaw and Mobilian Jargon] (MS, Caroline Dormon Collection, Cammie G. Henry Research Center, Watson Memorial Library, Northwestern State University of Louisiana, Natchitoches).

DORSEY, JAMES OWEN, and SWANTON, JOHN R. (1912), *A Dictionary of the Biloxi and Ofo Languages* (Bureau of American Ethnology Bulletin 47; Washington: Government Printing Office).

DOUAUD, PATRICK C. (1985), *Ethnolinguistic Profile of the Canadian Metis* (Canadian Ethnology Service Paper No. 99; Ottawa: National Museum of Man).

DRECHSEL, EMANUEL J. (1976a), ' "Ha, now me stomany that!" A Summary of Pidginization and Creolization of North American Indian Languages,' in J. L. Dillard (ed.), *Socio-Historical Factors in the Formation of the Creoles*, special issue of the *International Journal of the Sociology of Language*, 7 (The Hague: Mouton), 63–81.

——— (1976b), 'Possible American Indian Influences in Afro-Seminole Creole: A Study in Ethnolinguistic Methodology,' in George N. Cave (ed.), *New Directions in Creole Studies*, conference preprints (Turkeyen: University of Guyana, Department of English).

——— (1977), 'Historical Problems and Issues in the Study of North American Indian "Marginal" Languages,' in William L. Leap (ed.), *Studies in Southwestern Indian English* (San Antonio: Trinity University Press), 131–40.

——— (1979), 'Mobilian Jargon: Linguistic, Sociocultural, and Historical Aspects of an American Indian *lingua franca*' (Ph.D. diss., Department of Anthropology, University of Wisconsin-Madison; Ann Arbor: University Microfilms International).

DRECHSEL, EMANUEL J. (*cont.*) (1981), 'A Preliminary Sociolinguistic Comparison of Four Indigenous Pidgin Languages of North America (with Notes towards a Sociolinguistic Typology in American Indian Linguistics),' *Anthropological Linguistics*, 23: 93–112.

—— (1983*a*), 'The Question of the *lingua franca* Creek,' in Frances Ingemann (ed.), *1982 Mid-America Linguistics Conference Papers* (Lawrence, Kan.: Department of Linguistics, University of Kansas), 388–400.

—— (1983*b*), 'Towards an Ethnohistory of Speaking: The Case of Mobilian Jargon, an American Indian Pidgin of the Lower Mississippi Valley,' *Ethnohistory*, 30: 165–76.

—— (1984), 'Structure and Function in Mobilian Jargon: Indications for the Pre-European Existence of an American Indian Pidgin,' *Journal of Historical Linguistics and Philology*, 1: 141–85.

—— (1985), 'Algonquian Loanwords in Mobilian Jargon,' *International Journal of American Linguistics*, 51: 393–6.

—— (1986), 'Speaking "Indian" in Louisiana: Linguists Trace the Remnants of a Native American Pidgin,' *Natural History*, 95(9): 4–13.

—— (1987*a*), 'On Determining the Role of Chickasaw in the History and Origin of Mobilian Jargon,' *International Journal of American Linguistics*, 53: 21–9.

—— (1987*b*), 'Meta-Communicative Functions of Mobilian Jargon, an American Indian Pidgin of the Lower Mississippi River Region,' in Glenn G. Gilbert (ed.), *Pidgin and Creole Languages: Essays in Memory of John E. Reinecke* (Honolulu: University of Hawaii Press), 433–44.

—— (1987*c*), 'The Natchez Way,' *The Chronicles of Oklahoma*, 65: 174–81.

—— (1988), 'Wilhelm von Humboldt and Edward Sapir: Analogies and Homologies in their Linguistic Thoughts,' in William Shipley (ed.), *In Honor of Mary Haas: From the Haas Festival Conference on Native American Linguistics* (Berlin: Mouton de Gruyter), 225–64.

—— (1993), 'Basic Word Order in Mobilian Jargon: Underlying SOV or OSV?,' in Anthony Mattina and Timothy Montler (eds.), *American Indian Linguistics and Ethnography in Honor of Laurence C. Thompson* (University of Montana Occasional Papers in Linguistics, No. 10; Dallas: Summer Institute of Linguistics), 343–67.

—— (1993 MS), 'Indigenous Pidgin Languages, Coastal Chiefdoms, and the Pre-Colonial History of North America,' paper delivered at the Second International Conference: 'Oceans in World History' and 'Indigenous Peoples in World History,' Honolulu, 24–7 June 1993.

—— (1994*a*), 'Mobilian Jargon in the "Prehistory" of Southeastern North America,' in Patricia Kwachka (ed.), *Perspectives on the Southeast: Linguistics, Archaeology, and Ethnohistory* (Southern Anthropological Society Proceedings, No. 27; Athens, Ga.: University of Georgia Press), 25–43.

—— (1994*b*), 'The Philology of Non-European Pidgins: The Case of Mobilian Jargon,' *California Linguistic Notes*, 24: 51–62.

—— (1996), 'An Integrated Vocabulary of Mobilian Jargon, a Native American Pidgin of the Mississippi Valley', *Anthropological Linguistics*, 38: 248–354.

—— and MAKUAKĀNE, T. HAUNANI (1982a), 'Hawaiian Loanwords in Two Native American Pidgins,' *International Journal of American Linguistics*, 48: 460–7.

—— —— (1982b), 'An Ethnohistory of 19th Century Louisiana Indians,' *A Report Prepared for the National Park Service* (Norman: Department of Anthropology, University of Oklahoma).

DRESEL, GUSTAV (1920–1), 'Texanisches Jahrbuch,' in *Jahrbuch der Deutsch– Amerikanischen Historischen Gesellschaft von Illinois*, 20–1: 338–476.

—— (1954), *Gustav Dresel's Houston Journal: Adventures in North America and Texas 1837–1841*, trans. and ed. Max Freund (Austin, Tex.: University of Texas Press).

DU RU, PAUL (1700 MS), 'Journal d'un voyage fait avec M. d'Iberville de la rade des Billochis dans le haut du Mississipi avec un detail de tout ce qui s'est fait depuis ce temps jusqu'au depart du vaisseau . . .' (MS, Edward E. Ayer Collection, Newberry Library, Chicago).

—— (1934), *Journal of Paul du Ru (February 1 to May 8, 1700), Missionary Priest to Louisiana*, trans. with Intro. and Notes from a MS in the Newberry Library by Ruth Lapham Butler (Chicago: The Caxton Club).

DUMAS, BETHANY K. (1981), [Review of] *The Mobilian Trade Language* by James M. Crawford, *International Journal of American Linguistics*, 47: 262–4.

DUMONT DE MONTIGNY, JEAN BENJAMIN FRANÇOIS (1747 MS), 'Memoire De Lxx Dxx Officier Ingenieur, Contenant les Evenemens qui se sont passés à la Louisiane depuis 1715 jusqu'à présent ainsi que ses remarques sur les moeurs, usages et forces des diverses nations de l'Amerique Septentrionale et de ses productions' (MS, Edward E. Ayer Collection, Newberry Library, Chicago [printed in paraphrase in Dumont de Montigny 1753]).

DUMONT [DE MONTIGNY, JEAN BENJAMIN FRANÇOIS] (1753), *Mémoires historiques sur la Louisiane, contenant ce qui y est arrivé de plus mémorable depuis l'année 1687, jusqu'à présent . . .* (2 vols.; Paris: C. J. B. Bauche).

DURALDE, MARTIN (1802 MS), [Letter from Opelousas to William Dunbar, 24 April 1802] (MS, American Philosophical Society, Philadelphia).

DYE, DAVID H., and COX, CHERYL ANNE (1990) (eds.), *Towns and Temples along the Mississippi* (Tuscaloosa, Ala.: University of Alabama Press).

DYER, J. O. (1917), *The Lake Charles Atakapas (Cannibals): Period of 1817 to 1820* (Galveston, Tex.: J. O. Dyer).

EGG, MARKUS (1990), 'Zur Typologie subjektfinaler Sprachen,' *Linguistische Berichte*, 126: 95–114.

ELMENDORF, WILLIAM W. (1939 MS), 'Field Notes on Chinook Jargon Spoken by a Twana' (MS).

EMERSON, THOMAS E., and LEWIS, R. BARRY (1991) (eds.), *Cahokia and the Hinterlands: Middle Mississippian Cultures of the Midwest* (Urbana, Ill.: University of Illinois Press).

EVERETT, DIANNA (1990) *The Texas Cherokee: A People between Two Fires, 1819–1840* (Norman, Okla.: University of Oklahoma Press).

FEELING, D. (1975), *Cherokee-English Dictionary*, ed. William Pulte (Tahlequah, Okla.: Cherokee Nation of Oklahoma).

FEISTER, LOIS M. (1973), 'Linguistic Communication between the Dutch and Indians in New Netherland 1609–1664,' *Ethnohistory*, 20: 25–38.

FERGUSON, CHARLES A., and DEBOSE, CHARLES E. (1977), 'Simplified Registers, Broken Language, and Pidginization,' in Albert Valdman (ed.), *Pidgin and Creole Linguistics* (Bloomington: Indiana University Press), 99–125.

FLANIGAN, BEVERLY OLSON (1981), 'American Indian English in History and Literature: The Evolution of a Pidgin from Reality to Stereotype' (Ph.D. diss., Indiana University, Bloomington).

FLORES, DAN L. (1972) (ed.), 'The John Maley Journal: Travels and Adventures in the American Southwest, 1810–1813' (MA thesis, Northwestern State University of Louisiana, Natchitoches).

FOLSOM-DICKERSON, W. E. S. (1965), *The White Path* (San Antonio: Naylor Company).

FONTANEDA, HERNANDO DE ESCALANTE (1973 [1944]), *Memoir of D? d'Escalante Fontaneda Respecting Florida Written in Spain, about the Year 1575*, translated from the Spanish with Notes by Buckingham Smith, Washington 1854, and edited by David O. True (Miami: University of Miami and the Historical Association of Southern Florida).

FORBES, JACK D. (1988), *Africans and Native Americans: Color, Race and Caste in the Evolution of Red-Black Peoples* (Oxford: Basil Blackwell).

FORTIER, ALCÉE (1904), *A History of Louisiana*, ii. *The Spanish Domination and the Cession to the United States 1769–1803* (New York: Manzi, Joyant & Co., Successors).

FOSTER, LAURENCE (1935), 'Negro–Indian Relationships in the Southeast' (Ph.D. diss., Department of Anthropology, University of Pennsylvania, Philadelphia).

FRIEDERICI, GEORG (1960), *Amerikanistisches Wörterbuch* und *Hilfswörterbuch für den Amerikanisten: Deutsch–Spanisch–Englisch* (2nd edn., Hamburg: Gram, De Gruyter & Co.).

FRY, EDMUND (1799), *Pantographia; Containing Accurate Copies of All the Known Alphabets in the World; Together with an English Explanation of the Peculiar Force of Power of Each Letter: to Which are Added, Specimens of All Well-Authenticated Oral Languages; Forming a Comprehensive Digest of Phonology* (London).

GALLATIN, ALBERT (1973 [1836]), *A Synopsis of the Indian Tribes within the United States East of the Rocky Mountains, and in the British and Russian Possessions in North America* (New York: AMS Press).

GALLOWAY, PATRICIA (1987), 'Talking with Indians: Interpreters and Diplomacy in French Louisiana,' in Winthrop D. Jordan and Sheila L. Skemp (eds.), *Race and Family in the Colonial South* (Jackson, Miss.: University Press of Mississippi), 109–29.

—— (1989) (ed.), The Southeastern Ceremonial Complex: Artifacts and Analysis. *The Cottonlandia Conference* (Lincoln, Nev.: University of Nevada Press).

GAMBLE, GEOFFREY L. (1988), 'Reconstructed Yokuts Pronouns,' *Diachronica*, 5: 59–71.

GATSCHET, ALBERT S. (1885), 'Ata'kapa Language. Gathered at Lake Charles, Louisiana, January 1885' (MS, Bureau of American Ethnology Manuscript 239-a-b [ATTACAPA], National Anthropological Archives, Smithsonian Institution, National Museum of Natural History, Washington, DC).

—— (1886), 'Words and Sentences of the Biloxi Language, Siouan Family. Obtained at Lecompte, Rapides Parish, Louisiana, in October and November 1886' (MS, Bureau of American Ethnology Manuscript 933-a [BILOXI], National Anthropological Archives, Smithsonian Institution, National Museum of Natural History, Washington, DC).

—— (1887), Letters to the Editor, *Science*, 9: 411–13.

—— (1891), *The Karankawa Indians, the Coast People of Texas* (Archaeological and Ethnological Papers of the Peabody Museum, vol. i, No. 2; Cambridge, Mass.: Peabody Museum of American Archaeology and Ethnology).

—— (1969 [1884]), *A Migration Legend of the Creek Indians with a Linguistic, Historic and Ethnographic Introduction* (Brinton's Library of Aboriginal American Literature, No. 4; New York: Kraus Reprint Co.).

—— (1969 [1888]), *A Migration Legend of the Creek Indians*, ii. *Tchikilli's Kasïhta Legend in the Creek and Hitchiti Languages with a Critical Commentary and Full Glossaris to Both Texts* (transactions of the Academy of Science of St. Louis, 5; New York: Kraus Reprint Co.).

—— (1973 [1879]), 'Narragansett Vocabulary Collected in 1879,' *International Journal of American Linguistics*, 39: 14.

—— and SWANTON, JOHN R. (1932), *A Dictionary of the Atakapa Language, Accompanied by Text Material* (Bureau of American Ethnology Bulletin 108; Washington, DC: Government Printing Office).

—— and THOMAS, CYRUS (1907), 'Mobile,' in Frederick Webb Hodge (ed.), *Handbook of American Indians North of Mexico* (Bureau of American Ethnology Bulletin, 30; Washington, DC: Government Printing Office), 916.

GILBERT, GLENN G. (1986), 'The English of the Brandywine Population: A Triracial Isolate in Southern Maryland,' in Michael B. Montgomery and Guy Bailey (eds.), *Language Variety in the South: Perspectives in Black and White* (University, Ala.: University of Alabama Press), 102–10.

GIVÓN, TALMY (1979), 'Prolegomena to Any Sane Creology,' in Ian F. Hancock (ed.), *Readings in Creole Studies* (Ghent: E. Story-Scientia), 3–35.

GODDARD, IVES (1971), 'The Ethnohistorical Implications of Early Delaware Linguistic Materials,' *Man in the Northeast*, 1: 14–26.

—— (1972), [Brief mention of] 'An Indian Vocabulary from Fort Christanna, 1716' by Edward P. Alexander, *International Journal of American Linguistics*, 38: 220.

—— (1973), 'Philological Approaches to the Study of North American Indian Languages: Documents and Documentation,' in Thomas A. Sebeok (ed.), *Current Trends in Linguistics*, x. *Linguistics in North America*, pt. III, *Native Languages of North America* (The Hague: Mouton), 727–45.

—— (1977), 'Some Early Examples of American Indian Pidgin English from New England,' *International Journal of American Linguistics*, 43: 37–41.

—— (1978), 'A Further Note on Pidgin English,' *International Journal of American Linguistics*, 44: 77.

—— (1982), 'The Historical Phonology of Munsee,' *International Journal of American Linguistics*, 48: 16–48.

GOLLA, VICTOR (1992), [Untitled note on the origin of *kemosabe*], *SSILA Newsletter*, 11(3): 5–6.

GOLOVKO, EUGENI V., and VAKHTIN, NIKOLAI B. (1990) 'Aleut in Contact: The CIA Enigma,' *Acta Linguistica Hafniensia*, 22: 97–125.

GOSSELIN, AMÉDÉE (1906), 'Les Sauvages du Mississippi (1698–1708) d'après la correspondance des missionaires des missions étrangères de Québec,' *Compte rendu du congrès international des américanistes* (Québec), 1: 31–51.

GRANBERRY, JULIAN (1987), *A Grammar and Dictionary of the Timucua Language* (Anthropological Notes, 1; Horseshoe Beach, Florida).

GRAY, PATTY (1994), 'Mednyj Aleut: Language Contact in the North Pacific,' *Journal of Pidgin and Creole Languages*, 9: 109–13.

GREEN, EUGENE, and MILLWARD, CELIA (1971), 'Generic Terms for Water and Waterways in Algonquian Place-Names,' *Anthropological Linguistics*, 13: 33–52.

GREENBERG, JOSEPH (1963), 'Some Universals of Grammar with Particular Reference to the Order of Meaningful Elements,' in Joseph Greenberg (ed.), *Universals of Language* (Cambridge, Mass.: MIT Press), 58–90.

—— (1987), *Language in the Americas* (Stanford: Stanford University Press).

GREGORY, HIRAM F. (1982), *Road to Recognition: A Study of Louisiana Indians 1880–Present. A Report Prepared for the National Park Service* (Natchitoches: Department of Social Sciences, Northwestern State University of Louisiana).

GRIFFIN, JAMES B. (1990), 'Comments on the Late Prehistoric Societies in the Southeast,' in David H. Dye and Cheryl Anne Cox (eds.), *Towns and Temples Along the Mississippi* (Tuscaloosa, Ala.: University of Alabama Press), 5–15.

GRUHN, RUTH (1988), 'Linguistic Evidence in Support of the Coastal Route of Earliest Entry into the New World,' *Man*, 23 NS: 77–100.

GUMPERZ, JOHN J., and HYMES, DELL (1972) (eds.), *Directions in Sociolinguistics: The Ethnography of Speaking* (New York: Holt, Rinehart and Winston).

GURSKY, KARL-HEINZ (1969), 'A Lexical Comparison of the Atakapa, Chitimacha, and Tunica Languages,' *International Journal of American Linguistics*, 35: 83–107.

HAAS, MARY R. (1941a), 'The Classification of the Muskogean Languages,' in Leslie Spier, A. Irving Hallowell, and Stanley S. Newman (eds.), *Language, Culture, and Personality: Essays in Memory of Edward Sapir* (Menasha, Wis.: Sapir Memorial Publication Fund), 41–56.

—— (1941b), 'The Choctaw Word for "Rattlesnake",' American Anthropologist, 43 NS: 129–32.

—— (1945), 'Dialects of the Muskogee Language,' *International Journal of American Linguistics*, 11: 69–74.

—— (1946), 'A Proto-Muskogean Paradigm,' *Language*, 22: 326–32.

—— (1947), 'Some French Loan-Words in Tunica,' *Romance Philology*, 1: 145–8.

—— (1949), 'The Position of Apalachee in the Muskogean Family,' *International Journal of American Linguistics*, 15: 121–7.

—— (1950), *Tunica Texts* (University of California Publications in Linguistics 6(1): 1–174; Berkeley and Los Angeles: University of California Press).

—— (1953), *Tunica Dictionary* (University of California Publications in Linguistics 6(2): 175–332; Berkeley and Los Angeles: University of California Press).

—— (1956), 'Natchez and the Muskogean Languages,' *Language*, 32: 61–72.

—— (1958), 'A New Linguistic Relationship in North America: Algonkian and the Gulf Languages,' *Southwestern Journal of Anthropology*, 14: 231–64.

—— (1968), 'The Last Words of Biloxi,' *International Journal of American Linguistics*, 34: 77–84.

—— (1969), *The Prehistory of Languages* (The Hague: Mouton).

—— (1971), 'Southeastern Indian Linguistics,' in Charles M. Hudson (ed.), *Red, White, and Black: Symposium on Indians in the Old South* (Southern Anthropological Society Proceedings, No. 5; Athens, Ga.: University of Georgia Press), 44–54.

—— (1973), 'The Southeast,' in Thomas A. Sebeok (ed.), *Current Trends in Linguistics*, x. *Linguistics in North America*, pt. III, *Native Languages of North America* (The Hague: Mouton), 1210–49.

—— (1975), 'What is Mobilian?,' in James M. Crawford (ed.), *Studies in Southeastern Indian Languages* (Athens, Ga.: University of Georgia Press), 257–62.

—— (1976), 'Boas, Sapir, and Bloomfield,' in Wallace L. Chafe (ed.), *American Indian Languages and American Linguistics: The Second Golden Anniversary Symposium of the Linguistic Society of America* (Lisse: Peter de Rider Press), 59–69.

—— (1977*a*), 'Anthropological Linguistics: History,' in Anthony F. C. Wallace, J. Lawrence Angel, Richard Fox, Sally McLendon, Rachael Sady, and Robert Sharer (eds.), *Perspectives on Anthropology 1976* (Special Publication of the American Anthropological Association, No. 10; Washington: American Anthropological Association), 33–47.

—— (1977*b*), 'From Auxiliary Verb to Inflectional Suffix,' in Charles N. Li (ed.), *Mechanisms of Syntactic Change* (Austin: University of Texas Press), 525–37.

—— (1979), 'Southeastern Languages,' in Lyle Campbell and Marianne Mithun (eds.), *The Languages of Native North America: Historical and Comparative Assessment* (Austin, Tex.: University of Texas Press), 299–326.

HAGEDORN, N. L. (1988), ' "A Friend to Go Between Them:" The Interpreter as Cultural Broker during Anglo-Iroquois Councils, 1740–70,' *Ethnohistory*, 35: 60–80.

HALBERT, HENRY S. (1899), 'Choctaw Indian Names in Alabama and Mississippi,' *Transactions of the Alabama Historical Society 1898–9*, 3: 64–77.

HALE, HORATIO (1848), 'The "Jargon" or Trade Language of Oregon,' *Transactions of the American Ethnological Society*, 2: 62–70.

—— (1883), 'The Tutelo Tribe and Language,' *Proceedings of the American Philosophical Society*, 21: 1–47.

—— (1890), *An International Idiom: A Manual of the Oregon Trade Language or 'Chinook Jargon'* (London: Whittaker).

HALLOWELL, A. IRVING (1965), 'The History of Anthropology as an Anthropological Problem,' *Journal of the History of the Behavioral Sciences*, 1: 24–38.

HAMILTON, PETER JOSEPH (1910 [1897]), *Colonial Mobile: An Historical Study Largely from Original Sources of the Alabama-Tombigbee Basin and the Old South West, from the Discovery of the Spiritu Santo in 1519 until the Demolition of Fort Charlotte in 1821* (rev. edn.; Boston: Houghton Mifflin).

HANCOCK, IAN F. (1972), *A List of Place Names in the Pacific North-West Derived from the Chinook Jargon: With a Wordlist of the Language* (Vancouver: Vancouver Public Library).

HANCOCK, IAN F. (*cont.*) (1977), 'Recovering Pidgin Genesis: Approaches and Problems,' in Albert Valdman (ed.), *Pidgin and Creole Linguistics* (Bloomington, Ind.: Indiana University Press), 277–94.

—— (1980*a*), 'Texan Gullah: The Creole English of the Brackettville Afro-Seminoles,' in J. L. Dillard (ed.), *Perspectives on American English* (The Hague: Mouton), 305–33.

—— (1980*b*), 'The Texas Seminoles and their Language,' *African and Afro-American Studies and Research Center Papers*, Series 2.

—— (1986), 'On the Classification of Afro-Seminole Creole,' in Michael B. Montgomery and Guy Bailey (eds.), *Language Variety in the South: Perspectives in Black and White* (University, Ala.: University of Alabama Press), 85–101.

HARDER, KELSIE B. (1976) (ed.), *Illustrated Dictionary of Place Names: United States and Canada* (New York: Van Nostrand Reinhold).

HARDY, HEATHER and SCANCARELLI, JANINE (1993) (eds.), [Special number on Muskogean languages,] *International Journal of American Indian Languages*, 59: 371–496.

HARRIS, BARBARA P. (1985), 'Klahowiam Mr Smis: Context of Culture as a Factor in the Interpretation of a Chinook Jargon Text,' *Anthropological Linguistics*, 27: 303–17.

HAYNES, LILITH M. (1977), 'Candid Chimaera: Texas Seminole,' in Bates Hoffer and Betty Lou Dubois (eds.), *Southwest Areal Linguistics Then and Now* (Proceedings of the Fifth Annual Southwest Areal Language and Linguistics Workshop; San Antonio: Trinity University), 280–90.

HITCHCOCK, ETHAN ALLEN (1930), *A Traveler in Indian Territory: The Journal of Ethan Allen Hitchcock, Late Major-General in the United States Army*, ed. and annotated by Grant Foreman (Cedar Rapids, Ia.: Torch Press).

HOIJER, HARRY (1973), 'History of American Indian Linguistics,' in Thomas A. Sebeok (ed.), *Current Trends in Linguistics*, x. *Linguistics in North America*, pt. III, *Native Languages of North America* (The Hague: Mouton), 657–76.

HOLM, JOHN (1988), *Pidgins and Creoles*, i. *Theory and Structure* (Cambridge: Cambridge University Press).

—— (1989), *Pidgins and Creoles*, ii. *Reference Survey* (Cambridge: Cambridge University Press).

HOWARD, JAMES H. (1968), *The Southeastern Ceremonial Complex and its Interpretation* (Missouri Archeological Society Memoir 6; Columbia: Missouri Archaeological Society).

—— (1981), *Shawnee! The Ceremonialism of a Native Indian Tribe and its Cultural Background* (Athens, Ga.: Ohio University Press).

HOWELL, BENITA J., LEVY, RICHARD, S., and LUCKENBACH, ALVIN (1979), 'What is Dalrymple's Pamunkey?,' *International Journal of American Linguistics*, 45: 78–80.

HUDSON, CHARLES (1976), *The Southeastern Indians* (Knoxville, Ten.: University of Tennessee Press).

HUMES, JESSE, and HUMES, VINNIE MAY (JAMES) (1973), *A Chickasaw Dictionary* (Norman, Okla.: The Chickasaw Nation).

HUTTAR, GEORGE L. (1982), 'A Creole–Amerindian Pidgin of Suriname,' *Society for Caribbean Linguistics, Occasional Paper* No. 15 (Kingston, Jamaica School of Education, University of the West Indies at Mona).

—— and VELANTIE, FRANK J. (n.d.), 'Ndjuká-Trio Pidgin' (MS).

HYMES, DELL (1961), 'Alfred Louis Kroeber,' *Language*, 37: 1–28.

—— (1964) (ed.), *Language in Culture and Society: A Reader in Linguistics and Anthropology* (New York: Harper and Row).

—— (1966), 'Two Types of Linguistic Relativity (with Examples from Amerindian Ethnography),' in William Bright (ed.), *Sociolinguistics: Proceedings of the UCLA Sociolinguistics Conference, 1964* (The Hague: Mouton), 114–67.

—— (1971), *Pidginization and Creolization of Languages*, proceedings of a Conference Held at the University of the West Indies, Mona, Jamaica, April 1968 (Cambridge: Cambridge University Press).

—— (1974), *Foundations in Sociolinguistics: An Ethnographic Approach* (Philadelphia: University of Pennsylvania Press).

—— (1980), 'Commentary,' in Albert Valdman and Arnold Highfield (eds.), *Theoretical Orientations in Creole Studies* (New York: Academic Press), 389–423.

—— (1983), *Essays in the History of Linguistic Anthropology* (Amsterdam: John Benjamins).

—— (1990), 'Thomas Paul's "Sametl": Verse Analysis of a (Saanich) Chinook Jargon Text,' *Journal of Pidgin and Creole Languages*, 5: 71–106.

—— and HYMES, VIRGINIA (1972), 'Chinook Jargon as "Mother's Tongue",' *International Journal of American Linguistics*, 38: 207.

—— and ZENK, HENRY (1987), 'Narrative Structure in Chinook Jargon,' in Glenn G. Gilbert (ed.), *Pidgin and Creole Languages: Essays in Memory of John E. Reinecke* (Honolulu: University of Hawaii Press), 445–65.

JACOB, BETTY, NICKLAS, DALE, and SPENCER, BETTY LOU (1977), *Introduction to Choctaw* (Durant, Okla.: Choctaw Bilingual Education Program, Southeastern Oklahoma State University).

JACOBS, MELVILLE (1932), 'Notes on the Structure of Chinook Jargon,' *Language*, 8: 27–50.

—— (1936), 'Text in Chinook Jargon,' *University of Washington Publications in Anthropology*, 7: 1–27.

JEFFERYS, THOMAS (1760), *The Natural and Civil History of the French Dominions in North and South America* (2 parts; London).

JOHNSON, KATHRYN S., and LEEDS, PAUL (1964), *Patteran: The Life and Works of Paul Leeds* (San Antonio: Naylor).

JOHNSON, SAMUEL V. (1975 MS), 'Chinook Jargon Variation: Toward the Compleat Chinookee,' paper presented at the International Conference on Pidgins and Creoles, Honolulu.

—— (1978), 'Chinook Jargon: A Computer-Assisted Analysis of Variation in an American Indian Pidgin' (Ph.D. diss., University of Kansas).

JONES, GEORGE FENWICK (1966) (ed.), *Henry Newman's Salzburger Letterbooks* (Athens, Ga.: University of Georgia Press).

KAUFMAN, TERRENCE S. (1971), 'A Report on Chinook Jargon,' in Dell Hymes (ed.), *Pidginization and Creolization of Languages* (Cambridge: Cambridge University Press), 275–8.

KAWASHIMA, YASUHIDE (1989), 'Forest Dipolmats: The Role of Interpreters in Indian–White Relations on the Early American Frontier,' *American Indian Quarterly*, 13: 1–14.

KAY, PAUL, and SANKOFF, GILLIAN (1974), 'A Language-Universals Approach to Pidgins and Creoles,' in David DeCamp and Ian F. Hancock (eds.), *Pidgins and Creoles: Current Trends and Prospects* (Washington: Georgetown University Press), 61–72.

KENDALL, MARTHA (1977), 'Forget the Masked Man: Who was his Indian Companion?,' *Smithsonian*, 8 (6): 113–20.

KERSEY, Jr., HARRY A. (1975), *Pelts, Plumes, and Hides: White Traders among the Seminole Indians, 1870–1930* (Gainesville, Fla.: University Presses of Florida).

KILPATRICK, JACK FREDERICK, and KILPATRICK, ANN GRITTS (1967), 'Muskogean Charm Songs among the Oklahoma Cherokee,' *Smithsonian Contributions to Anthropology*, 2: 29–40.

KIMBALL, GEOFFREY D. (1987), 'A Grammatical Sketch of Apalachee,' *International Journal of American Linguistics*, 53: 136–74.

——(1988), 'An Apalachee Vocabulary,' *International Journal of American Linguistics*, 54: 387–98.

KNIFFEN, FRED B., GREGORY, HIRAM F., and STOKES, GEORGE A. (1987), *The Historic Indian Tribes of Louisiana. From 1542 to the Present* (Baton Rouge, La.: Louisiana State University Press).

KNIGHT, Jr., VERNON JAMES (1990), 'Social Organization and the Evolution of Hierarchy in Southeastern Chiefdoms,' *Journal of Anthropological Research*, 46: 1–23.

—— and ADAMS, SHERÉE (1981), 'A Voyage to the Mobile and Tomeh in 1700, with Notes on the Interior of Alabama,' *Ethnohistory*, 28: 179–94.

LA BARRE, WESTON (1971), 'Materials for a History of Studies of Crisis Cults: A Bibliographic Essay,' *Current Anthropology*, 12: 3–44.

LANDAR, HERBERT (1965), *Language and Culture* (New York: Oxford University Press).

LANG, GEORGE (1991), 'Voyageur Discourse and the Absence of Fur Trade Pidgin,' *Canadian Literature*, 131: 51–63.

LATORRE, FELIPE A., and LATORRE, DELORES L. (1976), *The Mexican Kickapoo Indians* (Austin, Tex.: University of Texas Press).

LAWSON, JOHN (1967 [1709]), *A New Voyage to Carolina*, ed. with an introduction and notes by Hugh Talmage Lefler (Chapel Hill, NC: University of North Carolina Press).

LE JAU, FRANCIS (1956), *The Carolina Chronicle of Dr. Francis Le Jau, 1706–1717*, ed. with an introduction and notes by Frank J. Klingberg, University of California Publications in History, 53 (Berkeley and Los Angeles: University of California Press).

LE PAGE DU PRATZ, ANTOINE SIMON (1758), *Historie de la Louisiane, contenant la découverte de ce vaste pays; sa description géographique; un voyage dans les terres;*

l'historie naturelle; les mœurs, coûtumes & religion des naturels, avec leurs origines; deux voyages dans le nord du nouveau Mexique, dont un jus-qu'à la mer de Sud (3 vols.; Paris: De Bure).

—— (1975 [1774]), *The History of Louisiana, or of the Western Parts of Virginia and Carolina . . .*, facsimile of the 1774 edition (Baton Rouge; La.: Louisiana State University Press).

LEAP, WILLIAM L. (1977) (ed.), 'The Study of American Indian English: An Introduction to the Issues,' in William L. Leap (ed.), *Studies in Southwestern Indian English* (San Antonio: Trinity University Press), 3–20.

—— (1982), 'The Study of Indian English in the U.S. Southwest: Retrospect and Prospect,' in Florence Barkin, Elizabeth Brandt, and Jacob Ornstein-Galicia (eds.), *Bilingualism and Language Contact: Spanish, English, and Native American Languages* (New York: Teachers College Press), 101–19.

—— (1993), *American Indian English* (Salt Lake City; University of Utah Press).

LEBRETON, D. R. (1947), *Chahta-Ima: The Life of Adrien-Emmanuel Rouquette* (Baton Rouge, La.: Louisiana State University Press).

LEECHMAN, DOUGLAS, and HALL, ROBERT A. (1995), 'American Indian Pidgin English: Attestations and Grammatical Peculiarities,' *American Speech*, 30: 163–71.

LEVINE, VICTORIA LINDSAY (1991), 'Arzelie Langley and a Lost Pantribal Tradition,' in Stephen Blum, Philip V. Bohlman, and Daniel M. Neuman (eds.), *Ethnomusicology and Modern Music History* (Urbana, Ill.: University of Illinois Press), 190–206.

LOUGHRIDGE, R. M., and HODGE, DAVID M. (1964 [1890]), *English and Muskogee Dictionary* and *Dictionary of the Muskogee or Creek Language in Creek and English* (Okmulgee, Okla.: B. Frank Belvin, Baptist Home Mission Board).

LOUNSBURY, FLOYD G. (1968), 'One Hundred Years of Anthropological Linguistics,' in J. O. Brew (ed.), *One Hundred Years of Anthropology* (Cambridge, Mass.: Harvard University Press), 151–264.

McLOUGHLIN, WILLIAM G. (1974), 'Red Indians, Black Slavery and White Racism: America's Slaveholding Indians,' *American Quarterly*, 26: 367–85.

MADDEN, JOHN (1928), 'Mobilian Tongue Trade Language among the Gulf Tribes,' *The American Indian*, 2(6): 8.

MALANCON, RICHARD, and MALANCON, MARY JO (1977), 'Indian English at Haskell Institute, 1915,' in William L. Leap (ed.), *Studies in Southwestern Indian English* (San Antonio: Trinity University Press), 141–53.

MALINOWSKI, BRONISLAW (1936), 'The Problem of Meaning in Primitive Languages,' in C. K. Ogden and I. A. Richards, *The Meaning of Meaning: A Study of the Influence of Language upon Thought and of the Science of Symbolism*, (4th edn., London: Kegan Paul, Trench, Trubner and Co.).

MALKIEL, YAKOV (1981), 'Drift, Slope, and Slant: Background of, and Variation upon, a Sapirian Theme,' *Language*, 57: 535–70.

MARGRY, PIERRE (1876–86) (ed.), *Découvertes et établissements des français dans l'ouest et dans le sud de l'Amérique septentrionale (1614–1754): Mémoires et documents originaux* (6 vols.; Paris: D. Jouaust).

MARSH, RALPH HENRY (1974), 'The History of Polk County, Texas, Indians,' in David Agee Horr (ed.), *Alabama-Coushatta (Creek) Indians* (American Indian Ethnohistory: Southern and Southeast Indians; New York: Garland Publishing), 257–361.

MARTIN, JACK (1994), 'Modeling Language Contact in the Prehistory of the Southeastern United States,' in Patricia Kwachka (ed.), *Perspectives on the Southeast: Linguistics, Archaeology, and Ethnohistory* (Southern Anthropological Society Proceedings, No. 27; Athens, Ga.: University of Georgia Press).

MARTIN, JOEL W. (1991), *Sacred Revolt: The Muskogees' Struggle for a New World* (Boston: Beacon Press).

MASTHAY, CARL (1991) (ed.), *Schmick's Mahican Dictionary: With a Mahican Historical Phonology* (Philadelphia: American Philosophical Society).

MATISOFF, JAMES A. (1990), 'On Megalocomparison,' *Language*, 66: 106–20.

MATTHEWS, G. HUBERT, and RED THUNDER CLOUD (1967), 'Catawba Texts,' *International Journal of American Linguistics*, 23: 7–24.

MERENESS, NEWTON D. (1916) (ed.), *Travels in the American Colonies* (New York: Macmillan).

MILFORT, [LOUIS] (1802), *Mémoire ou coup-d'œil rapide sur mes différens voyages et mon séjour dans la nation Crëck* (Paris: De Giguet et Michaud).

MILLER, MARY RITA (1967),' Attestations of American Indian Pidgin English in Fiction and Nonfiction,' *American Speech*, 42: 142–7.

—— (1986 MS), 'Tidewater Pidgin' (MS).

MILLER, WICK R. (1978), 'Multilingualism in its Social Context in Aboriginal North America,' *Proceedings of the Fourth Annual Meeting of the Berkeley Linguistic Society*, 4: 610–16.

MITHUN, MARIANNE (1983). 'The Genius of Polygenesis,' *Papers in Anthropology*, 24 (2): 221–42.

—— (1990a), 'Language Obsolescence and Grammatical Description,' *International Journal of American Linguistics*, 56: 1–26.

—— (1990b), 'Studies of North American Indian Languages,' *Annual Review of Anthropology*, 19: 309–30.

MOCHON, MARION JOHNSON (1972), 'Language, History and Prehistory: Mississippian Lexico-Reconstruction,' *American Antiquity*, 37: 478–503.

MOONEY, JAMES (1900), *Myths of the Cherokee* (19th Annual Report of the Bureau of American Ethnology, 1897–1898, i; Washington: Government Printing Office).

—— (1932), *The Swimmer Manuscript: Cherokee Sacred Formulas and Medicinal Prescriptions*, ed. Frans M. Olbrechts (Bureau of American Ethnology Bulletin 99; Washington: Government Printing Office).

MÜHLHÄUSLER, PETER (1986), *Pidgin and Creole Linguistics* (Oxford: Basil Blackwell).

MUNRO, PAMELA (1984), 'On the Western Muskogean Source for Mobilian,' *International Journal of American Linguistics*, 50: 438–50.

—— (1987a), 'Introduction: Muskogean Studies at UCLA,' in Pamela Munro (ed.), *Muskogean Linguistics* (UCLA Occasional Papers in Linguistics, 6; Los Angeles: Department of Linguistics, University of California, Los Angeles), 1–6.

—— (1987*b*), 'Some Morphological Differences between Chickasaw and Choctaw,' in Pamela Munro (ed.), *Muskogean Linguistics* (UCLA Occasional Papers in Linguistics, 6; Los Angeles: Department of Linguistics, University of California, Los Angeles), 119–33.

—— (1993), 'The Muskogean II Prefixes and their Significance for Classification,' *International Journal of American Linguistics*, 59: 374–404.

—— (forthcoming), *Muskogean Cognate Sets.*

—— and GORDON, LYNN (1982), 'Syntactic Relations in Western Muskogean: A Typological Perspective,' *Language*, 58: 81–115.

MURRAY, DAVID (1991), *Forked Tongues: Speech, Writing, and Representation in North American Indian Texts* (Bloomington, Ind.: Indiana University Press).

MURRAY, STEPHEN O. (1983), *Group Formation in Social Science* (Edmonton, Alberta: Linguistic Research, Inc.).

NICHOLS, JOHANNA (1992), *Linguistic Diversity in Space and Time* (Chicago: University of Chicago Press).

NICKLAS T. DALE (1979), 'Siouan and Muskogean,' in Ralph E. Cooley, Mervin R. Barnes, and John A. Dunn (eds.), *Papers of the 1978 Mid-America Linguistics Conference* (Norman, Okla: Department of Speech, University of Oklahoma), 44–58.

—— (1991), 'The Pronominal Inflection of the Biloxi Verb,' in Frances Ingemann (ed.), *Papers of the 1990 Mid-America Linguistics Conference* (Lawrence, Kan.: Department of Linguistics, University of Kansas), 534–50.

—— (1994), 'Linguistic Provinces of the Southeast at the Time of Columbus,' in Patricia Kwachka (ed.), *Perspectives on the Southeast: Linguistics, Archaeology, and Ethnohistory* (Southern Anthropological Society Proceedings, No. 27; Athens, Ga.: University of Georgia Press), 1–13.

NUNEZ, Jr., THERON A. (1958), 'Creek Nativism and the Creek War of 1813–1814,' *Ethnohistory*, 5: 1–47, 131–75, 292–301.

NUTTALL, THOMAS (1905 [1821]), 'Nuttall's Journal of Travels into the Arkansa Territory, October 2, 1818–February 18, 1820,' in Reuben Gold Thwaites (ed.), *Early Western Travels 1748–1846*, iii (Cleveland: Arthur H. Clark Co.).

PAPEN, ROBERT A. (1984), 'Quelques remarques sur un parler français méconnu de l'ouest canadien: le métis,' *Revue québécoise de linguistique*, 14: 113–39.

PAREDES, J. ANTHONY (1992) (ed.) *Indians of the Southeastern United States in the Late 20th Century* (Tuscaloosa, Ala.: University of Alabama Press).

PAYNE, DORIS L. (1980), 'Switch-Reference in Chickasaw,' in Pamela Munro (ed.), *Studies of Switch-Reference* (UCLA Papers in Syntax, 8; Berkeley and Los Angeles: University of California Press), 89–118.

—— (1982), 'Chickasaw Agreement Morphology: A Functional Explanation,' in Paul J. Hopper and Sandra A. Thompson (eds.), *Syntax and Semantics*, xv. *Studies in Transitivity* (New York: Academic Press).

PEARCE, GEORGE F. (1980), *The U.S. Navy in Pensacola: From Sailing Ships to Naval Aviation (1825–1930)* (Pensacola, Fla.: University Presses of Florida).

PEARSON, BRUCE L. (1987), 'Savannah and Shawnee: The End of a Minicontroversy,' *International Journal of American Linguistics*, 53: 183–93.

PEASE, THEODORE CALVIN, and JENISON, ERNESTINE (1940) (eds.), *Illinois on the Eve of the Seven Years' War 1747–1755* (Collections of the Illinois State Historical Library, 29; French Series, Springfield Ill.: Illinois State Historical Library).

PERDUE, THEDA (1988), 'Indians in Southern History,' in Frederick E. Hexie (ed.), *Indians in American History: An Introduction* (Arlington Heights, Ill.: Harlan Davidson), 137–57.

PORTER, KENNETH W. (1971), *The American Negro on the Frontier* (New York: Arno Press and *New York Times*).

POWELL, J. V. (1990), 'Chinook Jargon Vocabulary and the Lexicographers,' *International Journal of American Linguistics*, 56: 134–51.

PRINCE, J. DYNELEY (1912), 'An Ancient New Jersey Indian Jargon,' *American Anthropologist*, 14 NS: 508–24.

PULLUM, GEOFFREY K. (1977), 'Word Order Universals and Grammatical Relations,' in Peter Cole and Jerrold M. Saddock (eds.), *Syntax and Semantics*, viii. *Grammatical Relations* (New York: Academic Press), 249–77.

—— (1981), 'Languages with Object before Subject: A Comment and a Catalogue,' *Linguistics*, 19: 147–55.

RANKIN, ROBERT L. (1977), 'From Verb to Auxiliary to Noun Classifier and Definite Article: Grammaticalization of the Siouan Verbs "Sit," "Stand," "Lie" ' in R. L. Bown, K. Houlihan, L. Hutchinson, and A. MacLeish (eds.), *Proceedings of the 1976 Mid-America Linguistics Conference* (Minneapolis: Department of Linguistics, University of Minnesota), 273–83.

—— (1980), [Abstract of] 'Some Unpublicized Areal Features of the Southeast,' *International Journal of American Linguistics*, 46: 44–5.

—— (1986), [Review of] ' "A Grammar of Biloxi" by Paula Ferris Einaudi,' *International Journal of American Linguistics*, 52: 77–85.

—— (1988), 'Quapaw: Genetic and Areal Affiliations,' in William Shipley (ed.), *In Honor of Mary Haas: From the Haas Festival Conference on Native American Linguistics* (Berlin: Mouton de Gruyter), 629–50.

READ, WILLIAM A. (1940), 'Notes on an Opelousas Manuscript of 1862,' *American Anthropologist*, 42 NS.: 546–8.

—— (1963 [1931]), Louisiana-French (rev. edn., Baton Rouge, La.: Louisana State University Press).

REINECKE, JOHN E. (1937), 'Marginal Languages: A Sociological Survey of the Creole Languages and Trade Jargons' (Ph.D. diss., Yale University).

—— (1938), 'Trade Jargons and Creole Dialects as Marginal Languages,' *Social Forces*, 17: 107–18 [repr. in Hymes (1964)].

—— (1969), *Language and Dialect in Hawaii: A Sociolinguistic History to 1935*, ed. Stanley M. Tsuzaki (Honolulu: University of Hawaii Press).

——, TSUZAKI, STANLEY M., DECAMP, DAVID, HANCOCK, IAN F. and WOOD, RICHARD E. (compilers) (1975), *A Bibliography of Pidgin and Creole Languages* (Oceanic Linguistics Special Publication, No. 14; Honolulu: University Press of Hawaii).

RENFREW, COLIN, and CHERRY, JOHN F. (1986) (eds.) *Peer Polity Interaction and Socio-Political Change* (Cambridge: Cambridge University Press).

RHODES, RICHARD (1977), 'French Cree—a Case of Borrowing,' in William Cowan (ed.), *Actes du huitième congrès des algonquinistes* (Ottawa: Carleton University), 6–25.

—— (1982), 'Algonquian Trade Languages,' in William Cowan (ed.), *Papers of the Thirteenth Algonquian Conference* (Ottawa: Carleton University), 1–10.

—— (1986), 'Métchif—A Second Look,' in William Cowan (ed.), *Actes du dix-septième congrès des algonquinistes* (Ottawa: Carleton University), 287–96.

RIDAUGHT, HORACE (1957), *Hell's Branch Office* (Citra, Fla.: published independently).

ROBERTS, JULIAN M. (1995), 'Pidgin Hawaiian: A Sociohistorical Study,' *Journal of Pidgin and Creole Languages*. 10: 1–56.

ROBIN, C[LAUDE] C. (1807), *Voyages dans l'intérieur de la Louisiane, de la Floride occidentale, et dans les isles de la Martinique et de Saint-Domingue, pendant les années 1802, 1803, 1804, 1805 et 1806*, vols. i–iii (Paris: Chez F. Buisson).

ROMAINE, SUZANNE (1988), *Pidgin and Creole Languages* (London: Longman Group).

ROMANS, BERNARD (1962 [1775]), *A Concise Natural History of East and West Florida: A Facsimile Reproduction of the 1775 Edition with an Introduction by Rembert W. Patrick* (Gainesville, Fla.: University of Florida Press).

ROTHE, ALINE (1963), *Kalita's People: A History of the Alabama–Coushatta Indians of Texas* (Waco, Tex.: Texian Press).

ROUQUETTE, DOMINIQUE (1839), *Meschacébéennes: Poésies* (Paris: Librairie de Sauvaignat).

—— (1937–8 MS) 'The Choctaws: With Data on the Chickasaw Tribe and Other Sketches,' trans. Olivia Blanchard (MS, Survey of Federal Archives in Louisiana, Louisiana and Lower Mississippi Valley Collections, LSU Libraries, Louisiana State University, Baton Rouge).

ROWLAND, DUNBAR, and SANDERS, A. G. (1927), (ed.), *Mississippi Provincial Archives 1729–1740, French Dominion: French–English–Indian Relations, Wars with the Natchez and Chickasaw Indians* (3 vols.; Jackson, Miss.: Press of the Mississippi Department of Archives and History).

RYDJORD, JOHN (1968), *Indian Place-Names: Their Origin, Evolution, and Meanings, Collected in Kansas from the Siouan, Algonquian, Shoshonean, Caddoan, Iroquoian, and Other Tongues* (Norman, Okla.: University of Oklahoma Press).

SALISBURY, NEAL (1974), 'Red Puritans: The "Praying Indians" of Massachusetts Bay and John Eliot,' *William and Mary Quarterly*, 31: 27–54.

SAMARIN, WILLIAM J. (1986), 'Chinook Jargon and Pidgin Historiography,' *Canadian Journal of Anthropology/Revue canadienne d'anthropologie*, 5: 23–34.

—— (1987), 'Demythologizing Plains Indian Sign Language History,' *International Journal of American Linguistics*, 53: 65–73.

—— (1988), 'Jargonization before Chinook Jargon,' *Northwest Anthropological Research Notes*, 22: 219–38.

SANKOFF, GILLIAN (1980), 'Variation, Pidgins and Creoles,' in Albert Valdman and Arnold Highfield (eds.), *Theoretical Orientations in Creole Studies* (New York: Academic Press), 139–64.

SAPIR, EDWARD (1949), *Selected Writings of Edward Sapir in Language, Culture and Personality*, ed. D. G. Mandelbaum (Berkeley and Los Angeles: University of California Press).

SAVILLE-TROIKE, MURIEL (1982), *The Ethnography of Communication: An Introduction* (Baltimore: University Park Press).

SCHERMERHORN, JOHN F. (1814), 'Report Respecting the Indians, Inhabiting the Western Parts of the United States,' *Collections of the Massachusetts Historical Society*, 2nd ser. 2: 1–45.

SCHMIDT, JOHANNES (1872), *Die Verwandtschaftsverhältnisse der indogermanischen Sprachen* (Weimar: Hermann Böhlan).

SCHOOLCRAFT, HENRY R. (1852), *Information Respecting the History Condition and Prospects of the Indian Tribes of the United States. Collected and prepared under the direction of the Bureau of Indian Affairs per act of Congress of March 3rd 1847* (Philadelphia: Lippincott, Grambo and Co).

SCHUCHARDT, HUGO (1889), 'Beiträge zur Kenntnis des englischen Kreolisch I,' *Englische Studien*, 12: 470–4 [English translation in Schuchardt (1980)].

—— (1979), *The Ethnography of Variation: Selected Writings on Pidgins and Creoles*, ed. and trans. T. L. Markey (Ann Arbor: Karoma).

—— (1980), *Pidgin and Creole Languages: Selected Essays by Hugo Schuchardt*, ed. and trans. Glenn Gilbert (Cambridge: Cambridge University Press).

SCHUHMACHER, W. W. (1977), 'Eskimo Trade Jargon: Of Danish or German Origin?' *International Journal of American Linguistics*, 43: 226–7.

SCHWERIN, KARL H. (1976), 'The Future of Ethnohistory,' *Ethnohistory*, 23: 323–41.

SCOLLON, RONALD, and SCOLLON, SUZANNE B. K. (1979), *Linguistic Convergence: An Ethnography of Speaking at Fort Chipewyan, Alberta* (New York: Academic Press).

SEBEOK, THOMAS A. (1973), (ed.), *Current Trends in Linguistics*, x. *Linguistics in North America*, parts I–IV (The Hague: Mouton).

SHERWOOD, DAVID F. (1983), [review of] 'Languages and Lore of the Long Island Indians,' ed. Gaynell Stone Levine and Nancy Bonvillain, *International Journal of American Linguistics*, 49: 438–44.

SHERZER, JOEL (1976), *An Areal-Typological Study of American Indian Languages North of Mexico* (Amsterdam: North Holland).

—— and BAUMAN, RICHARD (1972), 'Areal Studies and Culture History: Language as a Key to the Historical Study of Culture Contact,' *Southwestern Journal of Anthropology*, 28: 131–52.

SIBLEY, JOHN (1807), 'Historical Sketches of the Several Indian Tribes in Louisiana, South of the Arkansa River, and between the Mississippi and River Grand,' in [Meriwether] Lewis, [William] Clark, [John] Sibley, and [William] Dunbar, *Travels in the Interior Parts of America, Communicating Discoveries Made in Exploring the Missouri, Red River, and Washita* (London: Richard Phillips), 40–53.

SIEBERT, Jr., FRANK T. (1975), 'Resurrecting Virginia Algonquian from the Dead: The Reconstituted and Historical Phonology of Powhatan,' in James M. Crawford (ed.), *Studies in Southeastern Indian Languages* (Athens, Ga.: University of Georgia Press), 285–453.

Silverstein, Michael (1972), 'Chinook Jargon: Language Contact and the Problem of Multi-Level Generative Systems. Part I and II,' *Language*, 48; 378–406, 597–625.

—— (1973 MS), 'Dynamics of Recent Linguistic Contact,' in Ives Goddard (ed.), *Handbook of North American Indians*, xvi. *Languages* (Washington: Smithsonian Institution, in preparation).

—— (1974), 'Dialectal Developments in Chinookan Tense-Aspect Systems: An Areal-Historical Analysis,' *International Journal of American Linguistics Memoir*, 29.

—— (1978), [review of] 'An Areal-Typological Study of American Indian Languages North of Mexico' by Joel Sherzer, *Language*, 54: 737–41.

Simms, W. Gilmore (1856), *The Wigwam and the Cabin*, (rev. edn., New York: W. J. Widdleton).

Skinner, Alanson (1913), 'Notes on the Florida Seminole,' *American Anthropologist*, 15: ns 63–77.

Smith, Bruce D. (1978), (ed.) *Mississippian Settlement Patterns* (New York: Academic Press).

—— (1984), 'Mississippian Expansion: Tracing the Historical Development of an Explanatory Model,' *Southeastern Archaeology*, 3: 13–32.

—— (1985), 'Mississippian Patterns of Subsistence and Settlement,' in R. Reid Badger and Lawrence A. Clayton (eds.), *Alabama and the Borderlands: From Prehistory to Statehood* (University, Ala.: University of Alabama Press), 64–79.

—— (1990) (ed.), *The Mississippian Emergence* (Washington: Smithsonian Institution Press).

—— (1992) (ed.), *Rivers of Change: Essays on Early Agriculture in Eastern North America* (Washington: Smithsonian Institution Press).

Smith, Marvin T., and Hally, David J. (1992), 'Chiefly Behavior: Evidence from Sixteenth Century Spanish Accounts,' in Alex W. Barker and Timothy R. Pauketat (eds.), *Lords of the Southeast: Social Inequality and the Native Elites of Southeastern North America* (Archaeological Papers of the American Anthropo-logical Association, No. 3; Washington: American Anthropological Association), 99–109.

Speck, Frank G. (1934), *Catawba Texts* (Columbia University Contributions to Anthropology, 24; (New York: Columbia University Press).

Sprague, John T. (1964 [1848]), *The Origin, Progress, and Conclusion of the Florida War*, facsimile reproduction of the 1848 edition (Gainesville, Fla.: University of Florida Press).

Stefánsson, V[ilhjálmur] (1909), 'The Eskimo Trade Jargon of Herschel Island,' *American Anthropologist*, 11 ns: 217–32.

Stewart, George R. (1970), *American Place-Names: A Concise and Selective Dictionary for the Continental United States of America* (New York: Oxford University Press).

Stiggins, George (1873–4 MS), 'Letters to L. C. Draper,' in *Georgia, Alabama, and South Carolina Papers* (MS, Draper Collection V: Manuscripts. Archives of the State Historical Society of Wisconsin, Madison).

STIGGINS, GEORGE (*cont.*) (n.d. MS), 'A Historical Narration of the Genealogy Traditions and Downfall of the Ispocoga or Creek Tribe of Indians, Written by One of the Tribe,' in *Georgia, Alabama, and South Carolina Papers* (MS, Draper Collection V: Manuscripts. Archives of the State Historical Society of Wisconsin, Madison) (printed in Nunez (1958)).

STILES, EZRA (1794 MS), 'Itineraries VI,' (MS, Beinecke Rare Book and Manuscript Library, Yale University, New Haven).

—— (1980 [1794]), 'Wordlist of Mohegan-Pequot, collected by Ezra Stiles at Guilford, Connecticut, dated May 20, 1793,' in Gaynell Stone Levine and Nancy Bonvillain (eds.), *Languages and Lore of the Long Island Indians* (Readings in Long Island Archaeology and Ethnohistory, 4; Lexington, Mass.: Ginn Custom Publishing), 51.

STOCKING, Jr., GEORGE W. (1968), *Race, Culture, and Evolution: Essays in the History of Anthropology* (New York: Free Press).

—— (1974), 'The Boas Plan for the Study of American Indian Languages,' in Dell Hymes (ed.), *Studies in the History of Linguistics: Traditions and Paradigms* (Bloomington, Ind.: Indiana University Press), 454–84.

STRACHEY, WILLIAM (1849 [1612]), *The Historie of Travaile in Virginia Britania . . .*, ed. R. H. Major (London: Hakluyt Society).

STURTEVANT, WILLIAM C. (1962), 'Spanish–Indian Relations in Southeastern North America,' *Ethnohistory*, 9: 41–94.

—— (1971), 'Creek into Seminole,' in Eleanor Burke Leacock and Nancy Oestreich Lurie (eds.), *North American Indians in Historical Perspective* (New York: Random House), 92–128.

—— (1994), 'The Misconnection of Guale and Yamasee with Muskogean,' *International Journal of American Linguistics*, 60: 139–48.

SWADESH, MORRIS (1951), 'Diffusional Cumulation and Archaic Residue as Historical Explanations,' *Southwestern Journal of Anthropology*, 7: 1–21.

—— (1959), 'The Mesh Principle in Comparative Linguistics,' *Anthropological Linguistics*, 1: 7–14.

—— (1971), *The Origin and Diversification of Language*, ed. Joel F. Sherzer (Chicago: Aldine Atherton).

SWANTON, JOHN R. (1911), *Indian Tribes of the Lower Mississippi Valley and Adjacent Coast of the Gulf of Mexico* (Bureau of American Ethnology Bulletin 43; Washington: Government Printing Office).

—— (1992), *Early History of the Creek Indians and their Neighbors* (Bureau of American Ethnology Bulletin 73; Washington: Government Printing Office).

—— (1931), *Source Material for the Social and Ceremonial Life of the Choctaw Indians* (Bureau of American Ethnology Bulletin 103; Washington: Government Printing Office).

—— (1946), *The Indians of the Southeastern United States* (Bureau of American Ethnology Bulletin 137; Washington: Government Printing Office).

SYLESTINE, CORA, HARDY, HEATHER K., and MONTLER, TIMOTHY (1993), *Dictionary of the Alabama Language* (Austin, Tex.: University of Texas Press).

TANNER, HELEN NORBECK (1989), 'The Land and Water Communication Systems of the Southeastern Indians,' in Peter H. Wood, Gregory A. Waselkov, and M.

Thomas Hatley (eds.), *Powhatan's Mantle: Indians in the Colonial Southeast* (Lincoln, Nev.: University of Nevada Press), 6–20.

TAYLOR, ALLAN ROSS (1975), 'Nonverbal Communication Systems in Native North America,' *Semiotica*, 13: 329–74.

—— (1976), 'Words for *Buffalo*,' *International Journal of American Linguistics*, 42: 165–6.

—— (1981), 'Indian lingua francas,' in Charles A. Ferguson and Shirley Brice Heath (eds.), *Language in the USA* (Cambridge: Cambridge University Press), 175–95.

TAYLOR, DOUGLAS (1977), *Languages of the West Indians* (Baltimore: Johns Hopkins University Press).

THOMASON, SARAH GREY (1980), 'On Interpreting "The Indian Interpreter," ' *Language in Society*, 9: 167–93.

—— (1981), 'Chinook Jargon in Areal and Historical Context,' in A. Manttina and T. Montler (eds.), *The Working Papers of the 16th International Conference on Salishan Languages* (Occasional Papers in Linguistics, No. 2; Missoula, Mont.: Department of Anthropology, University of Montana).

—— (1983), 'Chinook Jargon in Areal and Historic Context,' *Language*, 59: 820–70.

—— and KAUFMAN, TERRENCE (1988), *Language Contact, Creolization, and Genetic Linguistics* (Berkeley and Los Angeles: University of California Press).

THORNTON, RUSSELL (1990), *The Cherokees: A Population History* (Lincoln, Nev.: University of Nebraska Press).

TIXIER, VICTOR (1844), *Voyage aux prairies osages, Louisiane et Missouri, 1839–1840* (Paris: Clermont-Ferrand).

—— (1940), *Tixier's Travels on the Osage Prairies*, ed. John Francis McDermott (Norman, Okla.: University of Oklahoma Press).

TRUMBULL, J. HAMMOND (1872), 'Words Derived from Indian Languages of North America,' *Transactions of the American Philological Association*, 3: 19–32.

—— (1873), 'Notes on Forty Algonkin Versions of the Lord's Prayer,' *Transactions of the American Philosophical Association*, 3: 113–218.

TUGGLE, W. O. (1973), *Shem, Ham, & Japheth: The Papers of W. O. Tuggle Comprising His Indian Diary, Sketches & Observations, Myths & Washington Journal in the Territory & at the Capital, 1879–1882*, ed. Eugene Current-Garcia with Dorothy B. Hatfield (Athens, Ga.: University of Georgia Press).

The United States Dictionary of Places (1988), (1st edn., New York: Somerset Publishers).

URLSPERGER, SAMUEL (1735) (ed.) *Ausführliche Nachricht von den Salzburgischen Emigranten, die sich in America niedergelassen haben* (Halle: In Verlegung des Waysenhauses).

—— (1738), *Erste Continuation der ausführlichen Nachricht von denen Salzburgischen Emigranten, die sich in America niedergelassen haben* (Halle: In Verlegung des Waysenhauses).

—— (1968), *Detailed Reports on the Salzburger Emigrants Who Settled in America . . .* , i. 1733–1734, ed. George Fenwick Jones and trans. Hermann J. Lacher (Athens, Ga.: University of Georgia Press).

URLSPERGER, SAMUEL (*cont.*) (1969), *Detailed Reports on the Salzburger Emigrants Who Settled in America* . . . , ii. *1734–1735*, ed. George Fenwick Jones and trans. Hermann J. Lacher (Athens, Ga.: University of Georgia Press).

USNER, Jr. DANIEL H. (1988), 'Economic Relations in the Southeast until 1783,' in Wilcomb E. Washburn (ed.), *Handbook of North American Indians*, iv. *History of Indian–White Relations* (Washington: Smithsonian Institution), 391–5.

—— (1992), *Indians, Settlers, and Slaves in a Frontier Exchange Economy: The Lower Mississippi Valley before 1783* (Chapel Hill, NC: University of North Carolina Press).

VALENTINE, J. RANDOLPH, and COWAN, WILLIAM (1993), 'Algonquianists Claim Kemosabe,' *SSILA Newsletter*, 11 (4): 3.

VAN RHEENEN, MARY (1987), 'Place as an Indicator of Ethnicity for the Hispanic-Indian People of Sabine Parish, Louisiana,' *Southern Anthropologist*, 15 (1): 5–14.

VAN TUYL, CHARLES D. (1980), *The Natchez: Annotated Translations from Antoine Simon le Page du Pratz's "Histoire de la Louisiane" and A Short English–Natchez Dictionary*, with Ethnographic Footnotes, Natchez Transcription, Sound System, Kinship Terminology, and Kinship System by Willard Walker (Oklahoma Historical Society, Series in Anthropology, No. 4; Oklahoma City: Oklahoma Historical Society).

VOEGELIN, C. F. (1937–40), 'Shawnee Stems and the Jacob P. Dunn Miami Dictionary,' *Prehistory Research Series, Indiana Historical Society*, 1: 61–108, 131–67, 287–341, 343–89 407–78.

—— (1945), 'Influence of Area on American Indian Linguistics,' *Word*, 1: 54–8.

—— (1959), 'An Expanding Language, Hopi,' *Plateau*, 32: 33–9.

—— (1961), 'Culture Area: Parallel with Typological Homogeneity and Heterogeneity in Respect on North American Language Families,' *Kroeber Anthropological Society Papers*, 25: 163–80.

VOORHIS, PAUL H. (1988), *Kickapoo Vocabulary* (Algonquian and Iroquoian Linguistics, Memoir 6; Winnipeg, Manitoba).

WASELKOV, GREGORY A. (1989), 'Indian Maps of the Colonial Southeast,' in Peter H. Wood, Gregory A. Waselkov, and M. Thomas Hatley (eds.), *Powhatan's Mantle: Indians in the Colonial Southeast* (Lincoln, Nev.: University of Nevada Press), 292–343.

WATKINS,LAUREL J. (1976), 'Position in Grammar: Sit, Stand, Lie,' in Walt Hull *et al.* (eds.), *University of Kansas Working Papers in Linguistics and Anthropology* i (Lawrence, Kan.: Department of Linguistics, University of Kansas), 16–41.

WEINREICH, URIEL (1953), *Languages in Contact: Findings and Problems* (The Hague: Mouton).

—— LABOV, WILLIAM, and HERZOG, MARVIN (1968), 'Empirical Foundations for a Theory of Language Change,' in W. P. Lehmann and Yakov Malkiel (eds.), *Directions for Historical Linguistics: A Symposium* (Austin, Tex.: University of Texas Press), 95–195.

WENKE, ROBERT J. (1984), *Patterns in Prehistory: Humankind's First Three Million Years* (2nd edn.; New York: Oxford University Press).

WERNER, OSWALD (1963), 'A Typological Comparison of Four Trader Navaho Speakers' (Ph.D. diss., Indiana University, Bloomington).

WHINNOM, KEITH (1971), 'Linguistic Hybridization and the "Special Case" of Pidgins and Creoles,' in Dell Hymes (ed.), *Pidginization and Creolization of Languages* (Cambridge: Cambridge University Press), 91–115.

WILLIAMS, WALTER L. (1979) (ed.), *Southeastern Indians since the Removal Era* (Athens, Ga.: University of Georgia Press).

WILLIS, Jr., WILLIAM S. (1971 [1963]), 'Divide and Rule: Red, White and Black in the Southeast,' in Charles M. Hudson (ed.), *Red, White, and Black*, Symposium on Indians in the Old South (Southern Anthropological Society Proceedings, No. 5; Athens, Ga.: University of Georgia Press), 99–115.

—— (1980), 'Fusion and Separation: Archaeology and Ethnohistory in Southeastern North America,' in Stanley Diamond (ed.), *Theory and Practice: Essays Presented to Gene Weltfish* (The Hague: Mouton), 97–123.

WOOD, PETER H., WASELKOV, GREGORY A., and HATLEY, M. THOMAS (1989), (eds.), *Powhatan's Mantle: Indians in the Colonial Southeast* (Lincoln, Nev.: University of Nevada Press).

WOODWARD, THOMAS S. (1939 [1859]), *Woodward's Reminiscences of the Creek, or Muscogee Indians, Contained in Letters to Friends in Georgia and Alabama* (Tuscaloosa Ala.: Weatherford Printing Company).

WURTZBURG, S., and CAMPBELL, L. (1995), 'North American Indian Sign Language: Evidence of its Existence before European Contact,' *International Journal of American Linguistics*, 61: 153–67.

YORK, KENNETH H. (1982), 'Mobilian: The Indian Lingua Franca of Colonial Louisiana,' in Patricia K. Galloway (ed.), *La Salle and his Legacy: Frenchmen and Indians in the Lower Mississippi Valley* (Jackson, Miss.: University Press of Mississippi), 139–45.

ZENK, HENRY B. (1984), 'Chinook Jargon and Native Cultural Persistence in the Grand Ronde Indian Community, 1856–1907: A Special Case of Creolization' (Ph. D. diss., University of Oregon, Eugene).

—— (1988), 'Chinook Jargon in the Speech Economy of Grand Ronde Reservation, Oregon: An Ethnography-of-Speaking Approach to an Historical Case of Creolization in Process,' *International Journal of the Sociology of Language*, 71: 107–24.

Index